KA 0030065 9

REELING

Books by Pauline Kael

I LOST IT AT THE MOVIES
KISS KISS BANG BANG
GOING STEADY
THE CITIZEN KANE BOOK
DEEPER INTO MOVIES
REELING

Pauline Kael

REELING

Marion Boyars
London

A MARION BOYARS BOOK
distributed by
Calder & Boyars Ltd
18 Brewer Street
London W1R 4AS

Originally published in the United States in 1976
by Little, Brown and Company

First published in Great Britain in 1977
by Marion Boyars Publishers Ltd
18 Brewer Street
London W1R 4AS

All the material in this book appeared originally in *The New Yorker*, with the exception of "A Rip-off with Genius" which appeared in *The New York Times Book Review*. © 1973 by the New York Times Company. Reprinted by permission.

ISBN 0 7145 2581 2 Cased edition
ISBN 0 7145 2582 0 Paper edition

Printed and bound in Great Britain by
REDWOOD BURN LIMITED
Trowbridge & Esher

Contents

PART TWO

Foreword

Movies — which arouse special, private, hidden feelings — have always had an erotic potential that was stronger than that of the live theater. Enlarged so that they seem totally ours, movie actors are more purely objects of contemplation than people who are physically present. Since they're not actually there on the stage, speaking, rushing off to change a costume, we can fantasize about them with impunity; by etherealizing the actors, film removes the contraints on our imaginations. This was obviously a factor in the early disapproval of movies, even if it wasn't consciously formulated. Probably movies weren't culturally respectable for a long time because they are so sheerly enjoyable; in a country with a Puritan background, the sensuality of movies was bound to be suspect. Even now, it's common for older educated people to insist on the superiority of live theater. This may mean that they prefer the feeling of control which they can generally maintain at a play.

Movies can overwhelm us, as no other art form, except, perhaps, opera does — although folk and rock music can do it, too. For some people being carried away by a movie is very frightening: not everyone wants to have many senses affected at once. Some people feel that they're on the receiving end, being attacked. The appeal of movies seems to go against the grain of everything they've been told during the processes of education — how they should learn to discriminate, learn to think for themselves, learn not to be led blindly.

No doubt movies attract us from earliest childhood because they excite us and work on us, and perhaps movies came to the fore in the sixties because, unlike books but like rock music, movies could be experienced tribally, yet they also provide aesthetic experiences of a sensual complexity that it's merely priggish to deny. People bred on TV and weaned on movies often feel sensually starved at a play — and they experience that starvation as boredom. When they are used to movies, live theater no longer works for them on a fantasy level. There aren't enough elements going for them in a play; they miss the constant flow of imagery, the quick shifts of place, the sudden rush of feeling. They miss all the compensatory elements which can sustain them during even a bad movie.

There's a reason for that "Wow!" which often seems all that a person can say after coming out of a movie house. So many images, sounds, and awakened memories may contribute to the film's effect on us that often we can't quite sort out what we think about the way we've been moved. We're not even sure sometimes if we liked it, but we certainly *felt* it. I think many people experience a sense of danger as part of the attraction of movies — they're going to be swept up in they know not what. Unstable people, people with a record of nervous disorders, leap to see a hyped-up Gothic, such as *The Exorcist,* knowing they may flip out on it. That, maybe, is the extreme of what we all sometimes want from the movies — sensations we can't control, an excitement that is a great high. Preferably a high without a sullen hangover, but sometimes moviegoers, particularly the generations of the counter-culture and after, want sensations so much that they don't really mind the downers. Those who go to the documentary *Janis* may alternate between an exploding high and a nervous discomfort, yet that masochistic element can be what they want, too. It makes them feel closer to the subject of the film: it makes them feel that Janis Joplin went through what they're going through, just as the young audiences of earlier generations did when they watched James Dean in *Rebel Without a Cause* or the heroes of *Easy Rider.* However, *Janis,* with the raw erotic charge of the musical numbers one after another, affects them far more overpoweringly than those earlier films. And some, of course, go to it stoned to intensify the sensations of losing control. That's what Janis Joplin, losing triumphantly, in a spirit of comic defiance, celebrates.

It says something about the nature of movies that people don't say they like them, they say they love them — yet even those who love movies may feel that they can't always handle the emotions that a film heats up. They need to talk to friends, to read critics, in order to understand why they're reacting as they are, and whether it's an aberration or others feel the same way. People didn't have this same need when the movies they went to were on the order of *Going My Way, The Greatest Show on Earth,* or *My Fair Lady.*

The greater sensory impact of films in recent years — the acceleration in violence and in shock-editing — makes a critic's job tougher than before. Moviegoers have very different thresholds of response and of gullibility; some are almost unbelievably susceptible to suspense devices. And large numbers of them — educated and uneducated alike — react to the incineration of characters in *The Towering Inferno* as marvelous entertainment. That indicates one of the problems of movies: they can be effective on shameless levels. Who isn't terrified of burning to death? You don't have to be an artist to frighten audiences by fire. Yet when a movie has startled people, like *The Towering Inferno,* or enlisted their sympathies and made them weep, like *Walking Tall,* or made them feel vindictive and sadistic, like the Charles Bronson film *Death Wish,* the hardest thing for a critic to do is to convince them that it isn't necessarily a great picture. It's almost impossible to persuade people that a shallow, primitive work can give them a terrific kick.

Movies operate in a maze of borderlines; criticism is a balancing act, trying to suggest perspectives on the emotions viewers feel, trying to increase their enjoyment of movies without insulting their susceptibilities to simple, crude pop. I know that I've failed in some of these reviews — dismissing big, bludgeoning movies without realizing how much they might mean to people, rejecting humid sentiment and imagining that no one could be affected by it. I still can't quite get it through my head that tricks that I laugh at are being played on some moviegoers for the first time — and may trigger strong, anxious responses.

But if dealing with some of the thickset films has been a chore (and my crowbar writing shows it), there were also the opportunities that a reviewer dreams of. Film artists have the capacity to give us more than they consciously know, more than they could commit to paper. They can reach out beyond themselves; that is what the greatest film masters — highrollers, all of them — have tried to do. The artists who seem natural filmmakers — D. W. Griffith, Jean Renoir, Satyajit Ray, Bernardo Bertolucci — accept the simple pleasures of moviegoing and extend them. They use everything at hand, and yet imbue their films with their own emotion. That is what is beginning to happen once again among American directors: they're trying to go all the way with movies. Expansionist personalities such as Robert Altman, Francis Ford Coppola, and Martin Scorsese allow for the surprises an actor may come up with; they seize whatever delights them and put it to fresh uses. They don't simplify for a mass audience. They work in movies for the same reason we go to movies: because movies can give us almost anything, almost everything. There are moments in recent films when we get the mind-swaying sensation of experiencing several arts — at their highest — combined. We come out reeling.

When you think back on the movies of the past, or when you watch them on television, they're like samples — swatches of cloth — of the period in which they were made: *In The Heat of the Night* belongs to the Lyndon Johnson age as clearly as *Dirty Harry* belongs to the heyday of the Nixon era. This book covers the end of that era — 1972–1975. Pictures such as *Mean Streets, The Godfather, Part II,* and *Nashville* don't supply reassuring smiles or self-righteous messages, but they have something in common (and it's something they share with films from abroad such as *Last Tango in Paris* and Jan Troell's *The Emigrants* and *The New Land*) — a new openminded interest in examining American experience. This interest is at once skeptical, disenchanted, despairing, and lyrical. Our filmmakers seem to be on a quest — looking to understand what has been shaping our lives. A few decades hence, these years may appear to be the closest our movies have come to the tangled, bitter flowering of American letters in the early 1850s.

There are so many good pictures written about in this book that when I look at the table of contents, it seems like a binge. I may not have rendered justice to the best, but I've done my damnedest. Once again, I owe gratitude to William Shawn of *The New Yorker*, William Abrahams of the Atlantic Monthly Press, and my exacting daughter, Gina James, who keeps pushing that damnedest further.

Part One

Soul Food

IT'S EASY to say why you think a movie is bad, but elements of embarrassment sneak into praise, and, besides, in American studio-financed movies, in which the director must often squeeze blood from stones, there is an element of the mysterious, plus fantastic luck, when the infinity of things that could go wrong go right, or when what goes right overwhelms the disasters. And of the movies that have gone superlatively right *Sounder* must be one of the most difficult to explain. At the beginning, the actors playing black sharecroppers in the Depression years looked rigid and inexpressive, and I expected one of those priggish, worthwhile stinkers that the movie industry can cite as proof that people don't go to the clean-minded family pictures they say they want. But the picture grows startlingly better. Who would have believed that an inspirational movie about black strength and pride — and one based on a prize-winning children's book, by a white author, that takes its name from a symbolic coon hound — could transcend its cautious, mealy genre to become the first movie about black experiences in America which can stir people of all colors? In theme — the child of the sharecroppers finds a path to the larger world — it resembles the Welsh boy's story that Emlyn Williams told in *The Corn Is Green,* but it is an infinitely superior movie, and with a far greater emotional range. The director, Martin Ritt, working from a scrupulous, unsentimental script by Lonne Elder III, based on the William H. Armstrong novel, avoids charging up the scenes; Ritt never pushes a moment too hard or too far — the movie earns every emotion we feel. And I think it will move audiences — move them truly, that is — as few films ever have.

It does this even though we don't quite believe in any of it. The performers are wonderful — Cicely Tyson as the gaunt mother, Paul Winfield as the father, Kevin Hooks as the oldest of their three children, Taj Mahal as their singing friend Ike, and Janet MacLachlan as the teacher. But in some part of the brain we are always conscious that these are trained, educated, modern city folks playing poor country folks. When we look at Cicely Tyson, we know that those are high-fashion bones passing for starving gaunt; we know that that is Taj Mahal, the superb musician, play-acting in worn overalls on the back-country road; the volumes on Crispus Attucks that the teacher gives the boy to read are a very tony selection. This movie about the poor and uneducated is the opposite of artless; yet it isn't corrupted by the sophistication — it's the sophistication that makes it possible for us to accept it. I doubt whether a movie could be successfully simple and artless on any black subject now. Our nerves are raw, our sensitivities exacerbated. We need a modern consciousness on the screen even though the year in the movie is 1933, because the conventional movie trust-in-the-Lord black mother would be intolerable to us, a superstitious black mother a scandal. Rebecca, the illiterate woman Cicely Tyson plays, is unconned and intelligent, and we can see the workings of her mind, although the white people she deals with don't see through her guardedness — the protective mask of anonymity she turns to them. In too many melodramas, the sympathetic characters among the blacks and half-breeds and Asians have been as children, naïve and helplessly dependent on the decency and generosity of the stalwart white heroes. This movie shows the Deep Southern whites playing their custodian-of-the-childish-blacks role as it is seen from the other side — by black people who are not fooled. That shifts the audience's identification completely around. The film's view is that deprivation, suffering, and being cheated have destroyed the sharecroppers' illusions and sharpened their wits: they are people who can't afford illusions and hence do not have them. This may be a slight idealization, but it's closer to the truth; it has the force of justice, and it's what we now want to believe. And Ritt validates this view in the film. He endows his actors with the dignity that accuses us when we look at photographs by Walker Evans or Dorothea Lange or Helen Levitt, or when we read Robert Coles or *Let Us Now Praise Famous Men. Sounder* is authentic to the spirit of that documentary art — the art of photographers, mainly, but of novelists and other writers, too — which has helped create a general awareness of injustice and brought many whites to share the sorrow of it.

Simplifying their performances to essentials, the actors achieve the desperate dignity of the very poor, their faces purged of all but the primary human anxieties. They never ask for sympathy, and the reserve in the performers enables us to respond: we don't have to believe in this specific story, or in the actors as the characters they're playing, to be moved. The movie opens us up emotionally, not to them but to everything they evoke — to what they're standing in for. When the actors' faces and gestures echo the people caught by the Depression artist-photographers, we think of all those trashed lives. The characters on the screen are coexistent with the memory of the black people in the recent civil-rights demonstrations who put on their Sunday clothes to be beaten up in. Memories like this distance us, painfully, and we need an element of formality in the performances so that we don't allow ourselves the release of easy forms of identification. This movie enables us to feel without feeling for *ourselves,* and that's what the artists among the photographers did for us, too. In addition, the movie taps one of the enigmas of this century: that the people in old photographs (and not just rural black people or poor people but even middle-class and rich white people) have an inexplicable nobility. We look into the photographs of people now dead and we feel a twinge that we don't feel when we look at paintings of them; it's an acute sense of mortality and loss. *Sounder,* with its links to photojournalism, affects us in this same way: the people are puzzlingly, achingly beautiful.

Cicely Tyson has the singular good fortune to play the first great black heroine on the screen. Long overdue; but Miss Tyson makes us feel that her Rebecca was worth waiting for. She is visually extraordinary — every movement true to the archetype in our heads — and her voice is so precisely controlled that her soft words can pierce one's defenses. Her cry as she runs down the road toward her husband, returning from prison, is a phenomenon — something even the most fabled actresses might not have dared. This scene will live, along with descriptive images of the terrified poor which Agee gave us, along with the Dorothea Lange faces. To audiences now, this homecoming scene could mean as much as that other great homecoming scene — the little colonel's return from the war in *The Birth of a Nation* — did to early movie audiences. If so, it may help to right the balance, because this story of resilience and triumph is the birth of black consciousness on the screen. *Shaft* and its ilk are merely in blackface. *Sounder* distills — and in the most delicate, unstressed way — the prodigious, deep-down gaiety of black people. Taj Mahal helps, with the earthy-hip score he provided, and Paul Winfield, in the critical role of the volatile father, with his quick smile. One could do an iconography of smiles from this movie; often it is a smile that ends a scene, and it always seems the perfect end, just what was needed — an emblem of the spirit of a people, proof that they have not been destroyed.

Ritt uses the Louisiana locations unostentatiously; he gets the tone he needs, and the gracefully measured pace. Each shot lasts long enough for us to perceive what's in it, and feel at ease, before we move on; the rhythm is unusually satisfying. Still, the look of the film is not quite right: *Sounder* was shot in Panavision — a process I like for its ultra-sharp focus, and yet a process that gives this subject too much visual weight. The scale of the Panavision imagery produces a slight aesthetic discomfort: it's a little grandiloquent for a sharecropper's family. Maybe because this is an American-made film that starts from an inspirational story and is somewhat overproduced, it doesn't completely cross the barrier that separates the fine commercial craftsmen from the poets like Renoir and De Sica and Satyajit Ray, who at their best make a movie seem easy and natural, just the most direct and simple way to express yourself. (The Europeans who have worked here have never been able to express themselves in the same natural way, either.) In feeling, though, *Sounder* does cross over; it works directly on our feelings the way film poets do. Ritt shows situations in their complexity through the simplest of means, as in the Christmas scene in Claude Jutra's *My Uncle Antoine* when the mineowner rides through town in his carriage tossing trinkets at the children of the mineworkers, and the parents are torn, not wanting to deprive their children of the toys yet humiliated to see them pick up this miserly beneficence. We watch the hesitant, eager children and the parents divided against themselves, and we, too, are divided — between the beauty of perception that brings us such moments and the anguish of having, from this time on, to live with this perception. *Sounder* has performances that do this to us, and sequences, too. You wake up the morning after you've seen the picture and you hear the father's voice as he tells his son that he doesn't have to stay at home, that wherever he is, the father will love him, and you can't bear it.

I said that what goes right in *Sounder* is difficult to explain: I can't think of any other movie that is questionable as a work of film art that is so emotionally rich that it stays with you this way. Like certain great political pamphlets and muckraking novels, it is informed with a moral indignation that raises it to a plane above its genre. Perhaps *Sounder,* with its vestigial dog story and do-gooding plot line, was somehow transformed into this root black myth of the strong mother and the loving, rash father fighting for his manhood by a director who was fighting for his manhood as a director. I've tried to avoid describing the action of *Sounder* too specifically, because I should like others to have the pleasures of discovery that I had.

LIKE "SOUNDER," "THE EMIGRANTS" HAS REVERBERATIONS. Some recent very well-made films don't — *Fat City,* for example, which is beautifully directed around the edges but mechanical, and hollow at the center. I watched all those losers losing and I didn't know why they were losing or why I was watching them; their losing wasn't even a metaphor, it was just a plot necessity for the sake of a faded idea of classic structure. Even *Deliverance,* powerful and remarkable as it is — and it's the most impressive American movie I saw this past summer — is sterile in its conception. There isn't enough life in the characters to connect with, and so it's a self-contained experience. You're held by the director's control, and the picture has a wallop, but you don't take anything away. When you come out, the movie is really *over,* because there's no counterpoint, nothing else going on in it. These are cool, soulless exercises — directors' demonstrations of what they can do with the given material. But you know why you're watching *Sounder* and *The Emigrants.*

Jan Troell's broad-backed nature epic on the mid-nineteenth-century Swedish emigration to this country, which was shot in Sweden and here, tells the story of why and how Swedes became Americans. It covers the grim farm life, under a hierarchy of masters, that drove a group to emigrate, the brutal sea voyage, and then the landing of the survivors and their trip by train, by Mississippi paddle boat, and on foot until they staked out a claim in Minnesota. (A sequel, *The Settlers,* which Warners promises to import in the near future, deals with their fates in the new land.) Hollywood movies have often touched on the subject, but only touched — they imposed the ploys of popular melodrama, and made the migration incidental. Even *America America* inflated the gigantic theme with a ragbag collection of Christ and Judas figures. *The Emigrants* goes at the subject directly — bluntly, unseductively — finding its drama in that unprecedented migration.

Initially, for a long stretch, the film gave me some trouble: those crabbed, morose Swedes. They seemed to be living in the Dark Ages. They were so monotonously stolid they didn't even talk to each other; the closeups of sealed faces made me impatient, and I began to think the Swedes should leave Sweden just to get away from the other Swedes (though, of course, when they got here, they stuck pretty close together). The contrast between the Swedish response to adversity and the tenderness and humor of the family life in *Sounder* could not be more extreme. The Swedish family life is cheerless, and the thick, doomy Protestantism austere. I once had a conversation, with a man I know, about whether there really were people we might be uneasy to see our children marry — were there cultures that felt so alien to us that we could never quite be in tune with a person from them? I said maybe someone from India, and he said a Swede. After due reflection on *The Emigrants,* I think I agree with him. It was the experience of flight to a dreamland the characters took part in that began to catch me up, and it wasn't until they were packed together on the ship, a degraded, frightened bunch of people trying to hang on to some trace of their identities, that they began to matter as individuals and I wanted to know what was going to happen to them. However, as the picture develops we can forget how temperamentally alien they are to us because of something else that's alien, something that Swedish artists often have: earth spirit, earth poetry.

Troell's massive visual exuberance shows him to be the least blasé of the new directors; he's a nature poet telling stories. He photographs his own movies, in addition to directing and editing them and collaborating on the writing; in the whole history of the screen there have been only a handful of directors who actually shot their own movies, and no other cinematographer-director has ever undertaken a work of this sweep. As the first major cinematographer-director, he brings a new visual and thematic unity to fiction films. He seems to owe very little to traditional moviemaking and (unlike Bergman) almost nothing to the theater. One gets the feeling that he didn't even have to break away, that — and this may be possible because of how films are produced in Sweden — he developed in his own way, out of photography. Although the leading characters are played by Liv Ullmann and Max von Sydow, it's almost impossible to discuss their performances; there don't seem to be any performances. Ullmann and von Sydow move in and out of frame, courting, marrying, having children. They belong to the region and the life there, and after a while you forget that this is the same Liv Ullmann you've seen in the Bergman films. (It's maybe a little harder to forget you've seen von Sydow; that long-jawed face is so familiarly mulish, and, besides, he's stuck with lines that are translated for us as "It bodes ill for the crops.") Troell's celebration of air and trees and water includes the people with the land, and, despite the initial human gloom, the sensual passion of his imagery incorporates those people. American directors who love the outdoors usually love vast spaces: their characters move through them; nature is used for beautiful backgrounds. Troell loves nature for itself — nature, weather, changes of light. The film provides what those great descriptive passages in novels used to provide — a sense of what the natural environment did to the characters. The shipboard ordeals are devastating because, suddenly, we see those people cut off from everything that has formed them, trapped and sick, turned into fools — greenhorns — and we begin to feel the whack and terror of that culture shock experienced by first-generation Americans. The picture, adapted from a group of recent novels by Vilhelm Moberg, has a heavyset sensibility. That may sound awful — I must admit that I'm somewhat repelled by the sound of it myself — but movies are usually so piddling that *The Emigrants* fills a need. I came to respect the heavy cut of Troell's mind, and, after an hour, to find the sheer bulk of the film awesome.

Troell composes every shot as if it were to be his last, but at the same time he expands our notions of what screen lyricism is, because he's solemn and yet lyrical, disciplined yet rapturous. He will not be hurried. He gives the shimmer of the sun on sails equal weight with the lice and scurvy belowdecks, the redness of a paddle wheel equal weight with a misplaced child; he pauses to frame a magic image of the lighted riverboat at night. The imagery is intense, naturally lighted but frequently soaked in bright, deep color. Troell has a ravening appetite; it almost seems as if he loved nature so much he wanted to plunder it all. You wonder what can be left for him after this picture and its sequel — over six hours altogether. Warners apparently decided that we wouldn't have the time for his unhurried view, however, and he had to cut *The Emigrants,* which ran a hundred and ninety minutes in Sweden, to a hundred and fifty minutes. Perhaps that explains our slight confusion about what route the group takes; we're not always sure how they're getting to Minnesota. (There are also a few minor eccentricities, probably due to unfamiliarity with certain aspects of American life: the slaves the Swedish arrivals see are surprisingly light-skinned, and the Americans talk in the modern American idiom, though the Swedes are still — in subtitles, at least — saying "toil" for work.) Even reduced in length, it's a bursting, resonant film, and the great American cliff-hanger. We want to go on into the second film, *The Settlers.** That ocean voyage is in the background of most of us. We want to know: Did those people find what they hoped for?

[September 30, 1972]

Sex in the Head

ERIC ROHMER'S *Chloe in the Afternoon,* which opened the New York Film Festival, will probably be called a perfect film, and in a way I suppose it is, but it had evaporated a half hour after I saw it. It's about as forgettable as a movie can be. The French title of the sixth (and last) of Rohmer's "moral tales" is *L'Amour, l'Après-Midi.* This time, the setting is Paris, and the hero, Frédéric (Bernard Verley), is a proper, thirtyish, married bourgeois who, out of boredom in the afternoons and vague feelings of anxiety and temptation, becomes involved with a bohemian drifter, Chloe (Zouzou), whom he fundamentally disapproves of. Roh-

*It arrived in 1973, under the title *The New Land.*

mer's distinctive quality here, as in *Claire's Knee*, is a jokiness that we can't quite tell how to interpret, but the theme of the series (a man in love with one woman is drawn to another, whom he finally rejects) comes dangerously close to self-parody this time, as we watch Chloe cast her nets and Frédéric squirm out of them. Maybe Rohmer, who has become a specialist in the eroticism of non-sexual affairs, has diddled over a small idea too long; perhaps intentionally (but who can be sure?), this is a *reductio ad absurdum*. The will-he-or-won't-he game (an intellectualized version of the plight of Broadway virgins) goes on so long that the squeamish hero must be meant to be an ass. When, finally, Chloe gets him to dry her after her shower and lies in bed waiting — as inviting as a Modigliani nude — his flight to his wife is comic. Too comic for us to know how to accept the scene that follows — an expression of the love his wife and he feel for each other. We sense, however, the supreme value Rohmer places on marriage, just as we sense his condescension toward women who are available. In Rohmer's world, people have immutable characters, and they act out what they are; *Chloe in the Afternoon* is a demonstration of what you see when you first look at Frédéric, still boyishly handsome but already puffy-faced, repressed, sullen from rectitude. There are no surprises in him; he will do everything up to *that*. Chloe is a danger that he runs from.

The film is trivial because the ambiguities derive not from complexity in the people or the situation but from the fact that so much information is deliberately withheld. Rohmer supplies only enough to tease — nothing that might jar the amused, cultivated tone. The movie centers on Frédéric's reasons for not going to bed with Chloe, and this is just what Rohmer doesn't let us in on. When Frédéric wanders the city, glaring — half sick with longing — at beautiful women while telling us it is his love of his wife that makes him love them all, is he a self-deceiving fraud? We don't know whether his belief in marriage is meant to be a bourgeois love of safety (as Rohmer hints) or a mark of a Catholic sense of honor and of true love and respect for his wife (as Rohmer also hints).

While most artists set up situations selected for their power to reveal, Rohmer, refusing to reveal, sets up arbitrary situations in which he can control everything and not have to bother with the psychology or the messy texture of common experience. In *Claire's Knee*, there was the pretext of a novelist's setting a novel in motion, and the reduction of sexual passion to the delicate impulse to caress a knee; yet the conceits were so charmingly conceited that they were all but irresistible. But what are we to make of this trumped-up condition of anxiety in the afternoons, as if men's desires for a variety of women were created only by afternoon idleness? Chloe is not lusted after. She happens to come along — less attractive to Frédéric than the gorgeous women he sees on the streets and fantasizes about — and out of his lassitude he lets her draw him into her life. It may or may not be conscious, but Rohmer systematically downgrades and minimizes threats to monogamy. It is priggishly implicit in this movie that Chloe's attraction is only sensual, not spiritual. A shopworn woman like Chloe, with her big mouth and her Left Bank bangs, is an accident in Frédéric's life, while his wife represents the ideal attained, the other half of oneself found. Though the wife reveals nothing to us — and her tears are just water — we are, I think, meant to believe in the mystery and beauty she has for Frédéric. The enclosed situation, the foregone conclusion are part of Rohmer's method. He specializes in taking the energy and drive out of sex; with the passion removed, the old love triangle is turned into urbane chamber music.

The picture's only achievement is that it goes on so long it gets funny. The prolongation of Frédéric's miserable indecisiveness makes the audience laugh at him in impatience. Infidelity in the head — unconsummated infidelity — makes a man seem queasy, unmanly. We are meant to laugh. There's nothing else to do, because Rohmer's cool game excludes any issues more earthshaking than how long Frédéric can go on stewing before a decision is forced on him. There are, however, small gambits to keep us perplexed: Frédéric tells Chloe he hasn't talked with anyone so much in years; does he actually have this rapport with her (we don't see it), or, even if he only thinks he does, does this mean that he feels something has been missing from his life? Is he suffering from a little bourgeois angst? We have no way of answering such teasers. Rohmer plays the role of observer, but his neutral objectivity is totally superficial — an affectation. He's created a situation with nothing under it.

Eric Rohmer works on a literate, small scale, and, maybe because his work is so different in both scope and appeal from movies made for a mass audience, and especially from our movies, he has been acclaimed here as a much greater artist than I think he is. He's a superb lapidary craftsman but, I think, a very minor master. *Chloe in the Afternoon* is impeccably shot (by Nestor Almendros), and everything in it seems precise, fastidious — exactly what Rohmer sought. The words and images are expertly matched, and they're so prettily rhythmed they seem cadenced. It is a movie of the highest gloss. It is not, however, a movie of deep insight — or generosity of spirit, either. It is, rather, a movie of poetic complacency, a movie for mild chuckles. As for such judgments as the first sentence in a recent article on Rohmer in the *Times* — "In the four decades since the motion picture found its voice, few filmmakers have used it as intelligently" — I think the truth is that few filmmakers have used it as limitedly, and that perhaps Rohmer's unruffled assurance and his commitment to the surface of sexual attraction are being confused with intelligence. What is frequently described as rigor and austerity may be no more than polished aridity, polished *pettiness.* He's a clever traditionalist in a medium in which bourgeois worldliness can pass for much more.

IN "BAD COMPANY," A HIP-PICARESQUE COMEDY set in the Civil War period, a traveling gang of young con-artist orphans and runaways head West and bump up against a mangy assortment of robbers and killers. The movie was made from an original scenario by Robert Benton and David Newman, the magazine-writer collaborators who wrote *Bonnie and Clyde* and *There Was a Crooked Man. . . .* Benton also directed this picture, and without the intervention of another mind it becomes easier to get a fix on Benton's and Newman's talents. They're terribly bright and almost insistently amoral; that is to say, they lack the gift of conviction. (It is a gift, I think—a form of grace—which often deserts smart, inventive screenwriters, while the stupid come by it all too easily.) Benton and Newman will shape the material in *any* way in order to get an audience reaction. And the absence of conviction wrecks them here. What might have been a glorious comedy fails on one level because of tepid, almost nonexistent direction and on the conceptual level because there is nothing for the audience to become involved in, except admiration for Benton's and Newman's bits of flash and filigree. To put it plainly, they outsmart themselves.

There may be some justice in this, but the waste is maddening: talent is not in such long supply in comedy writing, and Benton and Newman have a style and a spark of inspiration. Their humor is often a syncopated version of Western saloon stories—those gruesomely funny anecdotes about incompetent gunmen and ornery kids and insane, implausible accidents. The authors find their comic horrors in this yokel Americana we share, and their spiked pathos in American cultural anomalies—Bonnie Parker admiring the teeny fingers on a figurine, these mongrel boys who have never known a home listening to a reading of *Jane Eyre* and trying to decide what a drawing room is. The writers' slapstick tragicomic tone is peculiarly their own, but unless this tone carries conviction, unless it takes off and becomes magical, it sinks into throwaway gags, or worse. Arthur Penn's direction supplied the emotional depth that made us care about *Bonnie and Clyde,* while Joseph L. Mankiewicz's heavy cynicism in *There Was a Crooked Man . . .* compounded and soured the flip amoralism, and the movie was offensive

— deeply ugly. This movie gets off to a poor, slow start and it never takes shape, yet it has qualities that plague one — emotions underdeveloped or stepped on, poignancies squashed for the sake of a casual tone.

The script of *Bad Company* probably reads like a box-office dream. But you can practically read the script in the movie. Without a director's art to hide them, the tricks are all visible. You sit in front of the tiresome yellow-brown autumnal West (Gordon Willis doing in Kansas a reprise of the brownish color and overhead lighting of *The Godfather*) listening for the zingers and noticing how the plot elements are meant to intersect. You can perceive the dazzle in the script, but what's on the screen is pictorial and lifeless. If Benton's direction were up to the dialogue and the incidents, *Bad Company* might nevertheless fail commercially, because of an excess of cleverness, but it could have made it into the *Beat the Devil* fluke-classic category, where the vacuousness would have become a nutty virtue. When *Bad Company* toys with the disgusting — when a rabbit is skinned and cleaned just below our line of vision while we listen to the obscene sounds of entrails being pulled out — we know that the movie is putting us on, just for fun, but most of the time Benton's direction has a bland, surprisingly dulcet tone, and the jokes simply keep coming instead of being sprung on us. They still manage to be funny (the quick editing on the gun battles helps), but you're aware that they're not funny the way they should be. The serious moments aren't sprung right, either, and they go flat. When a ten-year-old boy stealing a pie is blasted by a shotgun and his body lies in a chicken yard, we can see all the elements for an emotional response; it has what the moments of tragicomic horror in *Bonnie and Clyde* have, but we don't feel it.

The bumpkin Fagin of the scrounging boys is played by Jeff Bridges, who, deservedly, has been getting almost as many difficult roles this past year *(The Last Picture Show, Fat City)* as his talented brother Beau Bridges did before that *(Gaily, Gaily, The Landlord)*. In *Fat City*, the role of a nice, dumb young fighter didn't give Jeff Bridges much chance for characterization, but his body supplied some. The way he moved was so unobtrusively natural and right that you felt you knew the kid and understood him. Unusual among young actors, Bridges seems to live in a role easily, physically (the way his father, Lloyd Bridges, used to, in roles like the fighter in *The Goddess*). This physicality creates immediate empathy for the cheerful vandal he plays in this movie, even though he rattles off his lines without much variation, in that indifferent, fast way that is becoming a new movie cliché. Barry Brown plays a contrasting role — a handsome, courtly boy of "breeding" who joins up with the young toughs in order to travel West with them. Brown is shot in admiring closeups too often, like a juvenile prima donna, and sounds eerily like James Stewart, but the two boys make a good team — the ignorant low-lifer and the sleek, educated moralist — though the contrast is thrown away for a sappy finish.

Benton's sweetness of touch as a director — which suggests an innate gentleness — comes across best in the quiet sequence in which the ten-year-old's account of his life is mingled with the well-bred boy's reading of *Jane Eyre* to the group. But the writers don't trust feeling. As in *There Was a Crooked Man* . . . they just can't leave you with anything, and so the movie doesn't go anywhere; it self-destructs. The tall-tale writing produces one triumph, however. The most fatally funny of the boys' encounters is with a gang of seedy, moronic outlaws led by Big Joe (David Huddleston), a roaring, disgusted egomaniac, Fieldsian in size. He is the most successful satirical character in the movie, and, as anyone who has ever seen Joe Mankiewicz on TV can perceive, a stunning caricature — maybe the funniest portrait we've had — of a big-time movie director. Somehow, movie directors are never funny when they're meant to be movie directors; maybe Benton and Newman had the right idea in making this one a robber chief. The florid self-esteem of a brigand or a buccaneer may go to the heart of what makes a Hollywood winner. When Big Joe hears praise of a younger outlaw's tricks, he demonstrates how he taught those tricks to the youngster, and crows, "I'm the oldest whore on the block." There is some danger that Benton and Newman may be trainees. I don't know who it is that their super-amoralism is for — for some imaginary audience of the frightfully knowing? Is it possible that these extraordinarily gifted men are dumping on everything that could matter most in their work in order to satisfy illusions about swinger-nihilism which they themselves, in their magazine careers, helped to create? How is one to react to the talents of those who don't value their own talents highly enough? It's not a question that comes up often in the movie business.

[October 7, 1972]

Dusty Pink

WHEN A FILM is scaled to be a monument, it may seem a bit depraved to say that it's silly in a good-natured, enjoyable way, with some very agreeable adventure scenes. But when you consider how monumentally sluggish such films as *Waterloo* and *Cromwell* and *Nicholas and Alexandra* have been, this is really saying quite a lot for *Young Winston.* Although Carl Foreman, the writer and producer, and Richard Attenborough, the director, may have hoped high honors would be heaped upon them, I don't think my judgment is really at cross-purposes with their approach to the subject. They covered themselves against total failure. The production is English, but the movie is full of the old Hollywood Yankee know-how. "What's to become of you?" Winston Churchill's despairing pappy asks the boy, and though it may be impossible to react to Foreman's ten-ton ironies as he means us to, his tricks aren't boring. A few parts popular psychiatry, a few parts adventure, a few parts politics, and a dash of family scandal: that's a basic pop mixture, and at least the movie is benign — it isn't a downer.

The child who impersonates the seven-year-old Winston is a cuddly, chubby dead ringer (not a difficult piece of casting, I imagine, since every second English child looks like the latter-day Churchill). As the young man, Simon Ward is beautiful to look at — fine-boned, perhaps a bit too alabaster, but a face that holds the camera and draws us. His Churchill doesn't feel remote. Ward seems to be a strong, clear-headed performer; his intelligent impersonation fills in some of the script's deficiencies, though others are basic. Foreman's point of view is that the young Winston, crushed by his father's disappointment in him and his mother's neglect, poured all his energies into trying to win love through achievement. (This doesn't explain why he did so poorly in his studies and didn't show his intellectual gifts until he was liberated from his twelve years of rote schooling.) Foreman, hoping to "grab" the audience, chooses the poor-unfortunate-child theory of fame, like those newsmagazine cover stories on movie stars which try to make us feel sorry for the stars by explaining that they *had* to become rich and successful and glamorous because of their miserable childhoods and adolescent insecurities. (Yes, we may say, but why didn't all the other deprived kids become famous, too?) The picture not only fails in its naïve attempt to account for the emergence of a prodigy but fails to prepare us for that emergence: when we hear that our hero has published a book, we don't know where it came from. One moment he is a crushed, unhappy thirteen-year-old, a few moments later a cunning poseur. His sudden bright intelligence and egotism and flair might have been plucked from a cabbage patch. The scriptwriter has not merely a popularizing mind but a popularized one, coarsened by conventional plotting, yet bouncingly full of high spirits and remembered twists. Foreman is an indefatigably bold master of doggerel, and one grows fond of the fertility of the bad ideas. His commercialism seems, finally, no more corrupt than that of, say, Ed Wynn or Milton Berle; he has an entertainer's soul.

Foreman shows some class, however, as well as expertise, in the handling of the action scenes. The fighting — in the Sudan, in India, in the Boer War — is smoothly engineered so that we can see it the way the very young Churchill saw it, as an opportunity for courage and advancement, without the movie's accepting his enthusiasm for the glory of proving yourself in battle or justifying the colonial issues at stake. It's a neat balancing act. The movie makes its point — that the glory of battle belongs to the thinking of another age — without laboring it, and this simultaneous avoidance of jingoism and avoidance of superiority toward jingoism is no small accomplishment. Attenborough's direction of these action scenes is smoothly entertaining; the one high-voltage sequence, the ambush of an armored train during Churchill's days as a war correspondent, has a neat mixture of adventure and suspense and bravado. (So neat that one doesn't worry about whether Churchill, in his book *My Early Life,* on which the movie is based, fabricated these exploits or merely embellished them, since they feel apocryphal anyway.) But Attenborough, though an actor himself, fails in the biographical and political scenes: Foreman's dialogue is unduly declamatory, and Attenborough allows the actors to read the lines as if they were written in stone. As Winston's American mother, Anne Bancroft is far from the diamond-studded panther of description. Regal and eye-popping haughty, as if she'd learned about great ladies from watching Joan Crawford, she looks embalmed, that slightly open-mouthed, tremulously puzzled smile set for eternity. The worried bewilderment that was fluid in the days of *The Pumpkin Eater* has broken down into a series of classifiable expressions; no characterization draws them together — she tries on one and then the next, and we already know them all. Granted that as written Jennie Jerome is a stale charmer, at best — still, this is an appalling performance from a reputable actress. Her predictable pauses and stresses are the stuff of parody; we keep waiting for the other shoe to drop. "Don't you think that was a little . . . excessive?" she asks her husband, Lord Randolph (Robert Shaw), after he has stormed at the child. Lord Randolph is almost an archetypal Robert Shaw role — the proud, irritable, high-strung father going mad from syphilis — though Shaw manages to play it fairly straight, even in the obligatory scene that is maybe no longer obligatory and might at least have been trimmed, when Lord Randolph loses his grip while speaking in the House of Commons. There are the usual august names in the supporting cast (doesn't John Mills ever take a sabbatical?); I was happiest to see again the broad face of Pat Heywood (the nurse in Zeffirelli's *Romeo and Juliet*), as Winston's nanny, and, as Brockie, Maurice Roeves (the Stephen Dedalus of *Ulysses*), who looks tougher now, and racy, like a young Sean Connery.

Whether for some sort of visual pun or for a visual style that would assimilate the rotogravure photos and the interpolated newsreel footage, the whole picture is in faded pinks, as if it had been shot through rose-colored glasses. The mauve-grays and pale pinkish browns are so lulling that once when I saw some blue I was actually startled, like a child hearing that bang in the "Surprise" Symphony. It's an amusingly tasteful style of rose-sepia cinematography that suggests how far in the past Churchill's early life appears to us, but it also makes the interpolated footage of Churchill during and after the Second World War seem aeons away. Part of what is compelling in Churchill's story is seeing how a man's long life may begin in a Victorian society that seems to have nothing to do with ours until we recognize that he will bring that far-off age into modern decision-making. Tinting the actual Second World War footage pink is a visual anachronism; it kills any possibility of urgency in the movie, turns it all into distant, comfortable memories.

And, on the other hand, Foreman tries for a deliberately anachronistic modernism by a series of TV-style interviews: on several occasions a disembodied voice asks the principals, who face the camera, questions about themselves. The style of the movie can't accommodate this misconceived daring; a TV interviewer's intrusiveness into personal lives is unsuitable here, because these characters did not have to deal with intrusiveness of this particular kind, and so their answers are out of character and are not in key with their own period or with our TV period, either. Besides, the interviews are a cheat: the embarrassing questions asked and parried provide an illusion of penetration but are really no more than gossipy impertinences. The technique seems to have been inserted as another audience-grabber, and in order to protect the movie from the charge of sycophancy, without actually tapping any deeper springs of character or of political behavior.

It's not easy to explain, even to one's own satisfaction, why *Young Winston* is enjoyable. Its secret is the secret of Hollywood's long-time domination of the world film market, and sometimes that "magic" — i.e., that vulgarizing energy — still works even while we're conscious of its antique obviousness. *Young Winston* represents the triumph of mediocrity. In wit or audacity, in visual beauty or imagination, this picture doesn't compare to a movie such as Tony Richardson's *The Charge of the Light Brigade,* and in some ways I'm hard pressed to explain how I could take so little pleasure in the brilliance of *Light Brigade* and yet find these tinny theatricals about Winnie's adventurous life inoffensively relaxing. Perhaps it's because of a difference in attitudes. Heaven seems to have sent English moviemakers the upper class so they would have something to justify their malice. Richardson and his scenarist, Charles Wood, caricatured imbecilic snobs, who were shown callously sacrificing lives, and it's simply too sophomorically easy to blame stupidity. If intelligent, suffering men were — as they often are — responsible for oppressive policies and rash mistakes and bloodshed, would the horror not be as great? But then we could not feel such easy contempt for the men at the top. The small-mindedness of *Light Brigade* shrank the epic subject. Foreman, an American, isn't obsessed with attacking the class system. True, *Young Winston* has no teeth, but it has no fangs, either. The movie's very conventionality— its middle-of-the-roadness — leaves matters relatively open. It's neither stuffy and reverential nor satirical, and, considering how complicatedly mixed a subject Winston Churchill is — undoubtedly a great man, even if we're not altogether sure what kind — this box-office-inspired golden mean isn't repugnant. To adore Winston Churchill or to demolish him might equally stick in our craws. *Young Winston,* which doesn't raise any issues, can be enjoyed on its own junk terms.

TRUFFAUT HAS WRITTEN, "Once a picture is finished, I realize it is sadder than I meant it to be," but with *Two English Girls* he must have had the realization while he was shooting the picture, because he keeps trying to cover up the sadness with pat bits of gentleness and charm — his stock-in-trade. Yet what is intended to be light lacks the requisite gaiety; everything is muted, almost repressed. And Truffaut is too personal a director, too close to us — inside us, even — for us not to be aware that something is wrong in this adaptation of *Les Deux Anglaises et le Continent,*

which is the only other novel by Henri-Pierre Roché, the author of *Jules and Jim.* Roché was seventy-three when, out of his memories of his youth, he published *Jules and Jim,* a story of the friendship of two men who love the same woman. At seventy-seven, he published this inverted version (said to be what actually happened), about two English sisters who throughout their lives love the same man, a Frenchman — the "Continent" of the title.

The movie of *Jules and Jim* was about wrecked lives, too, but wildly wrecked and so intensely full of life that the movie had an intoxication all its own. Here, despite the links to that earlier film and occasional references to it, the exhilarating spirit has flickered out, and we can't be sure how much of the change is intentional, how much uncontrollable. The movie meanders, following the characters' endless arrivals and departures and changes of mind. They seem to waste away, pointlessly. When the older sister is dying of consumption and, seeing herself as Emily Brontë's heroine, says she has earth in her mouth, she might be describing the taste of the movie itself. What makes us feel so uneasy about it is not that it's morbid but that it's shallowly morbid, as if Truffaut couldn't enter all the way into the emotions of the characters. The turn-of-the-century period is made so very far past that it is distanced beyond our recall or empathy. The color is faded here, too, but reddish-brown, darker sepia. The atmosphere surrounding the hopelessly messed-up lives has been perfumed, but the people are never discovered. We barely see them, they're so dim. Partly, this must be because of casting.

"It was from Jean Renoir that I learned that actors are always more important than the characters they portray, or, to put it in a different way, that one should always sacrifice the abstract for the concrete," Truffaut says. But that's just what he hasn't done. At the apex of the *Jules and Jim* triangle, Jeanne Moreau's Catherine, in her charismatic capriciousness, spilled out all over the movie; the whole audience could feel what Jules and Jim were responding to, and the men physically embodied their characters, so we knew them immediately. The three principals in the new movie make pallid attempts to represent their characters. The hero, Claude, is Jean-Pierre Léaud — standing in for Truffaut once again, we must assume, since Truffaut has said, "He's part of me, I'm part of him. I see myself in him when I was his age." To us, it may seem that Truffaut sees himself falsely now in Léaud — that Léaud does not project Truffaut's mind or emotional complexity. He lacks the sustained animation to tie his quick-shifting moods together. In this pivotal role, he's quiet and pleasant but docile and fatally lacking in radiance; it's as if mad Catherine in *Jules and Jim* were played by Susan Clark of *Tell Them Willie Boy Is Here,* and it seems almost masochistic to use him. (Such masochism isn't new in Truffaut's work: in the portrait of himself as an older man, in *The Soft Skin,* he saw only his own weaknesses.) The fact that Truffaut thrusts his autobiographical figure, Léaud, into this adaptation of the Roché novel may get to the heart of the problem. Truffaut says of *Two English Girls,* "The reasons for which a filmmaker chooses one subject rather than another are often shrouded in mystery even to himself." Perhaps it's a private film, in ways he can't deal with. For those of us to whom Truffaut's films have become a part of our lives, it may be very difficult to watch this film without seeing the images of those two beautiful sisters — Françoise Dorleac and Catherine Deneuve, the older, Dorleac, now dead — who alternately starred in his movies. Truffaut may be out of his depth because he didn't know what depths he would get into — that he would be caught between Roché's reminiscences and his own. Perhaps this is why the film seems so uncomfortable, and, when it's over, unresolved yet emotionally affecting.

Truffaut's most engaging quality — his tender, easy acceptance of life — defeats him here. The Roché story is about cross-cultural misunderstandings: the Frenchman's attitudes toward love are different from those of the English sisters — the older, Anne, an emerging independent bohemian, and the younger, Muriel, a rigidly high-principled puritan. Truffaut knows how to make French innocence witty, but he draws a blank on English innocence. The sisters are not mysterious, as his French heroines often are; they're merely incomprehensible. They emerge as dull rather than as English; one suspects that Truffaut may not see that there is a difference. Inhibited, languishing maidens are not his style; he endows them with strength only at the moments when they make direct, decisive sexual overtures. Anne (Kika Markham) finally comes alive when she is having affairs with two men, like Catherine, but, just when she has begun to capture our interest, she dies, and Muriel (Stacey Tendeter), the exhaustingly strong-minded virgin who, after seven years of on-and-off courtship, finally gives herself to Claude, whom she loves, but only for one night (because he has slept with her sister), seems a neurotic gorgon. Truffaut has always filled out his movies with odd, idiosyncratic examples of human behavior, but Muriel's oddness is way beyond charming quirkiness and he obviously doesn't dig her — so we don't, either. At times, such as during Muriel's pathetically prudish confession of her masturbatory habit, we desperately need a tone that would clue us in. The atmosphere isn't dreamlike, but it's unreal; the passions that drive the girls seem no bigger than pimples. It isn't apparent what Claude's appeal is to the girls or what the girls mean to him, or why, fifteen years after his night with Muriel, he is still thinking of her; as he wanders among the embracing statues in the gardens of the Musée Rodin, he hears an English child being called Muriel and asks himself if she is his Muriel's daughter. We're conscious that the moment is meant to be Proustian, but "meant to be" is all it is. In *Jules and Jim,* each moment was seized (and we felt its essence); here the moments slide by, out of Truffaut's grasp and beyond ours. Only once does the director seem in true high spirits — in the sweetly funny moment when Anne and Claude leave the island of their lovemaking, their rowboats heading in different directions. Truffaut has a characteristic way of using old tricks so lightly and uninsistently that he alters their tonalities and almost, though not quite, turns them into allusions to old tricks. But I wish he had not fitted out *Two English Girls* with a fortune-teller whose prophecy is fulfilled. When he ends the movie on that fortune-teller's face, resorting to fate as if in apology for his own failure, we are left trying to sort out the feelings that he couldn't. It's an incredibly sad movie — bewilderingly sad.

[October 14, 1972]

The Irish Inheritance

IT'S QUITE POSSIBLE that the struggle in Northern Ireland isn't fully accessible to us. That is, we can't go about our own tasks and keep up with the *other* trouble spots and still bear in mind the origins and history of the Irish mess. It goes back too far and it has become too complicated; even listening to Bernadette Devlin when she was on American TV, we could easily have got confused at certain points and given up. In his new documentary movie, *A Sense of Loss,* Marcel Ophuls (who made *The Sorrow and the Pity*) attempts to uncover what is going on in that terrible struggle. Not the history — that, I think, we must, if we wish it, get from books in any case — but a sense of how that long history of injustice is at work in the lives of the people: how they carry it in them, and how it flames up. He uses news clips, and interviews with leaders, ordinary citizens, and — generally in their own homes, among their families — victims of official cruelty and of rebel terrorism. We never lose contact with the raw fact that this bloodshed is going on *now.* In a clincher that's almost a cartoon of the insane difficulty of Ophuls' undertaking, a TV reporter standing in front of a chaotic street scene and talking to us in the formal, faintly pompous tone we're used to on TV is suddenly blasted by the force of an explosion behind him. Since the picture attempts a cross-section of a society at war while all the issues are still unresolved, it has an immediacy that puts an unusual emotional strain on the viewer. The chaos is in front of us, and there is no position from which to distance it, and so we become involved in the faces and voices and the specific incidents. We become sensitized to the particulars of suffering. Ophuls presents not a brief or an overview, exactly, but, rather, an inner view.

He gets into what the Irish troubles are about in a far deeper sense than an account of the factions or the recent political moves would. There's no taint of propaganda: he's never ahead of us, leading us on. He's in there — an undeceived, intelligent observer, asking questions that we, too, might ask, and we try to make some sense of the answers. We observe the living roots of the hatred, in family folklore, in the schools, on the streets; we can see how it is passed from generation to generation, how it feeds upon violence and repression, how it has become part of the souls of the people. It is present in the language they speak — in the slang and the curses, in lullabies the mothers sing, in stories the fathers tell. We begin to feel how the economic and political inequities are concealed under layers of fear and prejudice, just as they are in societies polarized by racial differences. The Protestants who refer to the Catholics as scum and filth see the Catholic slums not as evidence of poverty and discrimination but as demonstrations that the Catholics are animals — because people couldn't live that way. The Catholics are reared in dirt, Protestants tell us, not because they're poor but because they're pigs.

It's no consolation to Americans to hear this parody-reprise of white Americans' debasement of black Americans. But if we used to believe that people could think like that only when there was a difference in skin color, here is proof that people can convince themselves that their twins are subhuman, if their twins threaten their slightly higher status. The Protestants and the Catholics don't live together and don't go to the same schools. Unlike white and black Americans, they don't even go in for the same sports.

Conor Cruise O'Brien tells Ophuls that the sides have got farther apart, and we can see that the violence and the reprisals on both sides must result in even worse polarization. The baby whose father was killed before he was born, the children whose homes have been destroyed or whose fathers have been beaten or interned, the children orphaned by terrorists' explosions are fiercely committed to their hereditary side. "All the children in Ireland are political now," says a left-wing Catholic, surrounded by his children. His young wife, shot in the pelvis by British soldiers, must be carried up and down the stairs. We sense his pride in that politicization of the children; he is not shocked by it — he really sees it as politicization. But we see the children's rabid, mindless loyalty to their parents' side, and the faces pinched and tight with anger. A little carrot-top girl whose older sister has been accidentally killed by soldiers looks crushed, shrunk, her face so closed that we can't imagine what could ever open it. The children of this struggle seem shattered not just by fear and clamor but by the burden of premature adult hatred. They look chilled. No political solution now could heal them. Whatever the compromises eventually arrived at, whatever the repressions or revolutionary victories, this rankling hatred runs deeper than any solutions and will surely be passed on.

The politicization of children means that they are politically formed, on faith, before politics can mean anything but a set of organic reflexes. The little *macho* micks throwing stones at the soldiers have been conditioned. For the Catholics, heroism means only one thing: fighting the traditional enemies and, of course, dying. Grief and pride have become fused: the fighting Irish are very tall when they march in funeral processions. It seems just possible that the Catholic parents *use* their children — that they exploit their children's love and naïveté to turn them into baby applauders and avengers. It may be the most damaging heritage parents can pass on, yet who could deny that it is charged with love, and is most passionately received by the children?

To those for whom objectivity has come to mean the way TV documentaries often strike a balance between two positions, it may easily seem that Ophuls has loaded the picture on the side of the Catholics, because as people they come off so much better. But objectivity is not the same as neutrality. Those of us who have seen *The Sorrow and the Pity* know what qualities Marcel Ophuls takes into the situation with him: curiosity; receptiveness to information, and a habit of poking under it; a capacity for eliciting unexpected points of view; irony; and a diffidence that is a form of decency. We may or may not be convinced that what he finds is what we would find (that may depend on our temperaments and our politics), but we can see how he works and that he is trustworthy. It is a journalist-filmmaker's job to show us where his investigation leads him, not to emerge with a meaningless neutrality the only purpose of which is to protect him. The Catholics are the underdogs here, and the hereditary rebels, and so it's difficult not to prefer them to those trying to keep them down. If the Protestants, trying to justify their historical advantages and their hostility, indict themselves, unknowingly, by their own words, while the Catholics, despite their heavier dependence on terrorism, seem to have more tolerance and humanity, this isn't necessarily what the filmmaker looked for. It could be what he discovered. The two groups are not quite twins, of course, since the Northern Irish did not divide into Catholics and Protestants; the Protestants, who are of Scottish extraction, began migrating to Ireland in the early seventeenth century, with the encouragement of the English, and have long identified with them rather than the Irish.

When Ophuls asks the revolutionary Catholic leaders the crucial question — how can they encourage people to die for long-range goals, for a freedom that is so far away? — their answers are glib and ideological, though Bernadette Devlin's face is bleak, as anguished as a child's. However, Ophuls doesn't ask them a question that may nag at the viewer — how do those who justify terrorism as a necessary, valid resource for the legally oppressed actually feel about the innocent victims? How do they live with themselves? He interviews a thin-lipped Protestant publisher who prints scurrilous songs about the joys of killing Catholics; without a visible pang, this man defends his songs, while standing in his office, flanked by huge official portraits of Her Majesty the Queen. Still, when this repellent man tells how terrorists set fire to his shop while he was away and burned his mother alive, you *need* to know: Did the terrorists realize his mother was inside, and if they did, how do they feel about it? What would they say? And would we feel better or worse if their temperaments and their style were more appealing to us than the publisher's? I would willingly have sacrificed some of the political speeches in the film for a closer understanding of the psychology of the terrorists. I don't underestimate the difficulty of interviewing them, but since some factions claim credit for their bombings, they might be willing to talk, and perhaps their supporters would. We already know the bureaucratic self-righteousness of military authorities and how they depersonalize the pain they inflict; we know their trained ability to see their victims as the enemy. So the English don't surprise us. What we don't know, in the documentary-film sense — what we haven't seen, that is — is how in the name of freedom rebels can bomb a department store and mutilate poor young working girls out looking for a bargain, or kill a baby, or burn an old woman to death. And we don't know how the leaders feel about it, either. Would their answers be fluent here, too?

Humanly, Ophuls is hard to fault; in terms of feeling and sensitivity, there is a *rightness* about what he asks, and about the way he knows how to pull back before tears or misery would plunge us into private sorrows. I think he has succeeded at the very highest and most important level. We can feel that he cares for the people. There is true affection in the way he lingers with a soft, smiling Catholic woman whose unemployed husband has been interned. She sits with her children lined up on the couch and chairs, like beads on a string stretching around the room — children past counting — and she explains that she could never practice birth control, and, with utter, sweet ingenuity, that if the Protestants are worried about being numerically swamped, why, they should just have more babies. Few men with as subtle an intelligence as Ophuls are so open to many kinds of people and so generous in their responsiveness. But structurally and aesthetically *A Sense of Loss* is less successful. We have been spoiled, of course, by the pictures of war-torn countries that TV brings us; it may not give us the insight into the differences between Catholic and Protestant that Ophuls provides, but it gives us superlative images of devastation and death. Ophuls works on a humbler scale: the photography is just barely functional (with changes from color to black-and-white determined, I assume, by the amount of light and other external considerations). A more serious flaw is that the film is not lucidly structured: the early scenes are so powerful that we are too exhausted to take in the material introduced later on. A half hour before the end, we await it. He crams the movie full, and there is far too much hurtling back and forth, with returns to places and people we feel done with, and repetitions of lines of dialogue we don't need to hear again. Ophuls appears to have a restless, ruminative spirit; he doesn't seem to know when it's time to go on — he keeps going back. After a while, the short scenes and the staccato editing jar against our own reflections on what we've been seeing. If he had devised a clearheaded, smoother structure, the film would be far more effective. For the gifts of feeling he offers, however, a little discomfort is a small price. Few films have contributed as much to our understanding of the psychology of political conflict. *A Sense of Loss* is perhaps the first film to demonstrate how the original crimes against a people go on festering, blighting the lives of those yet unborn. It's the tragedy of every trouble spot.

URBAN CHAOS IS USED as spectacle in *Fellini's Roma,* an ambivalent celebration of decay. The opulent rotting city of the film is indeed his own, with extras painted up as voracious citizens, and mock excavations, and a high-camp ecclesiastical fashion show that is also meant to be some sort of glittering, satirical comment on the old aristocracy, though it's hard to know exactly what the point is. *Roma* is an imperial gesture at documentary — a document about the city of Fellini's imagination, an autobiographical fantasy in which he plays ringmaster to the Roman circus. Technically, *The Clowns* (made for TV) was modest, though one might wonder why Fellini simulated the documentary form when it was so obvious that the crew he showed was not shooting the movie and that the people acting surprised at being caught at home or at work were made up and ready, in rooms lighted for the color cameras. The heaviness of the conceit weighed on one: a tribute to clowns that failed to show us great clowning and recorded, instead, Fellini's childhood infatuation and the sad "realities" of aged, retired clowns. The picture celebrated the grandeur of his illusions. Now Fellini has combined that fake-documentary style with the full peacockery of *La Dolce Vita* — and in magnificent color. Designed by Danilo Donati, who is a magician, and shot by the great Giuseppe Rotunno, the film is like a funeral ode to an imaginary city under purplish, poisoned skies. The usual critical encomium "No one but Fellini could have made this movie" is certainly appropriate. Who else could have raised the money? Over three million dollars, for a sketchbook-movie. And who but Fellini would construct in a studio parts of the motorway circling Rome, in order to stage a traffic jam that would be a miracle of lashing rains and stalled cars under darkly beautiful skies? And in the middle of it there is another false movie crew, pretending to be shooting what we see — the camera high above the congestion, with silky white plastic flapping around it, as if protecting a mikado. The conceits are becoming so ornate they're getting spooky.

Fellini's love-hate dream-nightmare city is more familiar to us by now than Rome itself. We've all been tourists before in Fellini's big-top city, so once again we look and say, "Isn't it fantastic?" And we look at the people and say, "Aren't they incredible? So gross, so ugly, so lewd, etc." He stages familiar scenes from his youth, and we know we're supposed to smack our lips at the gorgeousness. It is all food, sex, and vanity, and in the Fellini style of exaggeration — a rooming house packed with preening grotesques, a summer dinner on the street with people gorging, processions of strutting, wiggling whores in a cheap brothel and a fancy brothel. What are we expected to feel toward the people stuffing themselves or the old whores ogling the young soldiers? Ah, yes, Rome is a series of crumbling façades, and life is a circus. But what more? We can repeat, "Incredible — such flirtatious freaks, so profane. That wicked Fellini!" And there's nothing more to say. His plump pleasure in decay is the constant in his movies.

This ringmaster feels no need to relate to the circus people. Fellini is an unparalleled extrovert, even for a profession rich in extroversion; he is so extroverted he has abandoned interest in characters and is interested only in his own projections. He is at the center of the movie, played as a young man fresh from the provinces by a toothsome, lusciously handsome actor (dimply Peter Gonzales, from Texas), and then by himself, speaking in English — most of it dubbed — in this version. He interacts with no one; he is the only star, our guide, and, like many another guide, he often miscalculates our reactions, especially to his arch, mirthless anticlerical jokes. The ambience is least oppressive when he stages a forties vaudeville show — a return to the world of his early movies. Here his nostalgic caricatures aren't so cruelly limiting, and the performers briefly take over. Emotionally, Fellini obviously lives in the past; the modern scenes have no emotional tone and no precise observation — not even any new caricatures. One modern sequence — a sci-fi treatment of subway digs and the uncovering of a Roman villa, with frescoes that disappear as soon as the air from outside hits them — is so clumsily staged that we may become embarrassed for the Maestro, and particularly by the Sears, Roebuck quality of the frescoes. The tragedy of their disappearance is a blessing. The new elements in this film are the psychedelic use of sound — din, actually — to empty our heads and intensify our sensory impressions, and the semi-abstraction of several of the modern sequences: the torrents of rain falling on the movie company caught in traffic, the wind in the subway excavations, a horde of black-leather-jacketed, death-symbolizing motorcyclists speeding to an unknown destination, and so on. Some of these images are magisterial and marvelous, like a series of stormy Turners. If one could turn off the assaulting noise — a lethal mix of car horns and motors and gothic storms — these passages might be mysteriously exciting, though they go on too long. But whenever there's dialogue, or *thought,* the movie is fatuous. In the choking modern city, Fellini goes celebrity-chasing; the picture reaches its nadir when Gore Vidal informs us that Rome is as good a place as any to wait for the end of the world. Fellini appears to see himself as official greeter for the apocalypse; his uxorious welcoming smile is an emblem of emptiness.

[October 21, 1972]

Tango

BERNARDO BERTOLUCCI'S *Last Tango in Paris* was presented for the first time on the closing night of the New York Film Festival, October 14, 1972; that date should become a landmark in movie history comparable to May 29, 1913 — the night *Le Sacre du Printemps* was first performed — in music history. There was no riot, and no one threw anything at the screen, but I think it's fair to say that the audience was in a state of shock, because *Last Tango in Paris* has the same kind of hypnotic excitement as the *Sacre,* the same primitive force, and the same thrusting, jabbing eroticism. The movie breakthrough has finally come. Exploitation films have been supplying mechanized sex — sex as physical stimulant but without any passion or emotional violence. The sex in *Last Tango in Paris* expresses the characters' drives. Marlon Brando, as Paul, is working out his aggression on Jeanne (Maria Schneider), and the physical menace of sexuality that is emotionally charged is such a departure from everything we've come to expect at the movies that there was something almost like fear in the atmosphere of the party in the lobby that followed the screening. Carried along by the sustained excitement of the movie, the audience had given Bertolucci an ovation, but afterward, as individuals, they were quiet. This must be the most powerfully erotic movie ever made, and it may turn out to be the most liberating movie ever made, and so it's probably only natural that an audience, anticipating a voluptuous feast from the man who made *The Conformist,* and confronted with this unexpected sexuality and the new realism it requires of the actors, should go into shock. Bertolucci and Brando have altered the face of an art form. Who was prepared for that?

Many of us had expected eroticism to come to the movies, and some of us had even guessed that it might come from Bertolucci, because he seemed to have the elegance and the richness and the sensuality to make lushly erotic movies. But I think those of us who had speculated about erotic movies had tended to think of them in terms of Terry Southern's deliriously comic novel on the subject, *Blue Movie;* we had expected *artistic* blue movies, talented directors taking over from the *Shlockmeisters* and making sophisticated voyeuristic fantasies that would be gorgeous fun — a real turn-on. What nobody had talked about was a sex film that would churn up everybody's emotions. Bertolucci shows his masterly elegance in *Last Tango in Paris,* but he also reveals a master's substance.

The script (which Bertolucci wrote with Franco Arcalli) is in French and English; it centers on a man's attempt to separate sex from everything else. When his wife commits suicide, Paul, an American living in Paris, tries to get away from his life. He goes to look at an empty flat and meets Jeanne, who is also looking at it. They have sex in an empty room, without knowing anything about each other — not even first names. He rents the flat, and for three days they meet there. She wants to know who he is, but he insists that sex is all that matters. We see both of them (as they don't see each other) in their normal lives — Paul back at the flophouse-hotel his wife owned, Jeanne with her mother, the widow of a colonel, and with her adoring fiancé (Jean-Pierre Léaud), a

TV director, who is relentlessly shooting a sixteen-millimeter film about her, a film that is to end in a week with their wedding. Mostly, we see Paul and Jeanne together in the flat as they act out his fantasy of ignorant armies clashing by night, and it *is* warfare — sexual aggression and retreat and battles joined.

The necessity for isolation from the world is, of course, his, not hers. But his life floods in. He brings into this isolation chamber his sexual anger, his glorying in his prowess, and his need to debase her and himself. He demands total subservience to his sexual wishes; this enslavement is for him the sexual truth, the real thing, sex without phoniness. And she is so erotically sensitized by the rounds of lovemaking that she believes him. He goads her and tests her until when he asks if she's ready to eat vomit as a proof of love, she is, and gratefully. He plays out the American male tough-guy sex role — insisting on his power in bed, because that is all the "truth" he knows.

What they go through together in their pressure cooker is an intensified, speeded-up history of the sex relationships of the dominating men and the adoring women who have provided the key sex model of the past few decades — the model that is collapsing. They don't know each other, but their sex isn't "primitive" or "pure"; Paul is the same old Paul, and Jeanne, we gradually see, is also Jeanne, the colonel's daughter. They bring their cultural hangups into sex, so it's the same poisoned sex Strindberg wrote about: a battle of unequally matched partners, asserting whatever dominance they can, seizing any advantage. Inside the flat, his male physical strength and the mythology he has built on it are the primary facts. He pushes his morose, romantic insanity to its limits; he burns through the sickness that his wife's suicide has brought on — the self-doubts, the need to prove himself and torment himself. After three days, his wife is laid out for burial, and he is ready to resume his identity. He gives up the flat: he wants to live normally again, and he wants to love Jeanne as a *person.* But Paul is forty-five, Jeanne is twenty. She lends herself to an orgiastic madness, shares it, and then tries to shake it off — as many another woman has, after a night or a twenty years' night. When they meet in the outside world, Jeanne sees Paul as a washed-up middle-aged man — a man who runs a flophouse.

Much of the movie is American in spirit. Brando's Paul (a former actor and journalist who has been living off his French wife) is like a drunk with a literary turn of mind. He bellows his contempt for hypocrisies and orthodoxies; he keeps trying to shove them all back down other people's throats. His profane humor and self-loathing self-centeredness and street "wisdom" are in the style of the American hardboiled fiction aimed at the masculine-fantasy market, sometimes by writers (often good ones, too) who believe in more than a little of it. Bertolucci has a remarkably unbiased intelligence. Part of the convulsive effect of *Last Tango in Paris* is that we are drawn to Paul's view of society and yet we can't help seeing him as a self-dramatizing, self-pitying clown. Paul believes that his animal noises are more honest than words, and that his obscene vision of things is the way things really are; he's often convincing. After Paul and Jeanne have left the flat, he chases her and persuades her to have a drink at a ballroom holding a tango contest. When we see him drunkenly sprawling on the floor among the bitch-chic mannequin-dancers and then baring his bottom to the woman official who asks him to leave, our mixed emotions may be like those some of us experienced when we watched Norman Mailer put himself in an indefensible position against Gore Vidal on the Dick Cavett show, justifying all the people who were fed up with him. Brando's Paul carries a yoke of masculine pride and aggression across his broad back; he's weighed down by it and hung on it. When Paul is on all fours barking like a crazy man-dog to scare off a Bible salesman who has come to the flat,* he may — to the few who saw Mailer's *Wild 90* — be highly reminiscent of Mailer on his hands and knees barking at a German shepherd to provoke it. But Brando's barking extends the terms of his character and the movie, while we are disgusted with Mailer for needing to prove himself by teasing an unwilling accomplice, and his barking throws us outside the terms of his movie.

Realism with the terror of actual experience still alive on the screen — that's what Bertolucci and Brando achieve. It's what Mailer has been trying to get at in his disastrous, ruinously expensive films. He was right about what was needed but hopelessly wrong in how he went about getting it. He tried to pull a new realism out of himself onto film, without a script, depending wholly on improvisation, and he sought to bypass the self-consciousness and fakery of a man acting himself by improvising within a fictional construct — as a gangster in *Wild 90,* as an Irish cop in *Beyond the Law* (the best of them), and as a famous director who is also a possible Presidential candidate in *Maidstone.* In movies, Mailer tried to will a work of art into existence without going through the steps of making it, and his theory of film, a rationale for this willing, sounds plausible until you see the movies, which are like Mailer's shambling bouts of public misbehavior, such as that Cavett show. His movies trusted to inspiration and were stranded when it didn't come. Bertolucci builds a structure that supports improvisation. Everything is prepared, but everything is subject to change, and the whole film is alive with a sense of discovery. Bertolucci builds the characters "on what the actors

*This scene was deleted by the director after the New York Film Festival showing.

are in themselves. I never ask them to interpret something preëxistent, except for dialogue — and even that changes a lot." For Bertolucci, the actors "make the characters." And Brando knows how to improvise: it isn't just Brando improvising, it's Brando improvising as Paul. This is certainly similar to what Mailer was trying to do as the gangster and the cop and the movie director, but when Mailer improvises, he expresses only a bit of himself. When Brando improvises within Bertolucci's structure, his full art is realized. His performance is not like Mailer's acting but like Mailer's best writing: intuitive, rapt, princely. On the screen, Brando is our genius as Mailer is our genius in literature. Paul is Rojack's expatriate-failure brother, and Brando goes all the way with him.

We all know that movie actors often merge with their roles in a way that stage actors don't, quite, but Brando did it even on the stage. I was in New York when he played his famous small role in *Truckline Café* in 1946; arriving late at a performance, and seated in the center of the second row, I looked up and saw what I thought was an actor having a seizure onstage. Embarrassed for him, I lowered my eyes, and it wasn't until the young man who'd brought me grabbed my arm and said "Watch this guy!" that I realized he was *acting*. I think a lot of people will make my old mistake when they see Brando's performance as Paul; I think some may prefer to make this mistake, so they won't have to recognize how deep down he goes and what he dredges up. Expressing a character's sexuality makes new demands on an actor, and Brando has no trick accent to play with this time, and no putty on his face. It's perfectly apparent that the role was conceived for Brando, using elements of his past as integral parts of the character. Bertolucci wasn't surprised by what Brando did; he was ready to use what Brando brought to the role. And when Brando is a full creative presence on the screen, the realism transcends the simulated actuality of any known style of *cinéma vérité*, because his surface accuracy expresses what's going on underneath. He's an actor: when he shows you something, he lets you know what it means. The torture of seeing Brando — at his worst — in *A Countess from Hong Kong* was that it was a *reductio ad absurdum* of the wastefulness and emasculation (for both sexes) of Hollywood acting; Chaplin, the director, obviously allowed no participation, and Brando was like a miserably obedient soldier going through drill. When you're nothing but an inductee, you have no choice. The excitement of Brando's performance here is in the revelation of how creative screen acting can be. At the simplest level, Brando, by his inflections and rhythms, the right American obscenities, and perhaps an improvised monologue, makes the dialogue his own and makes Paul an authentic American abroad, in a way that an Italian writer-director simply couldn't do without the actor's help. At a more complex level, he helps Bertolucci discover the movie in the process of shooting it, and that's what makes moviemaking an art. What Mailer never understood was that his *macho* thing prevented flexibility and that in terms of his own personality he *couldn't* improvise — he was consciously acting. And he couldn't allow others to improvise, because he was always challenging them to come up with something. Using the tactics he himself compared to "a commando raid on the nature of reality," he was putting a gun to their heads. Lacking the background of a director, he reduced the art of film to the one element of acting, and in his confusion of "existential" acting with improvisation he expected "danger" to be a spur. But acting involves the joy of self-discovery, and to improvise, as actors mean it, is the most instinctive, creative part of acting — to bring out and give form to what you didn't know you had in you; it's the surprise, the "magic" in acting. A director has to be supportive for an actor to feel both secure enough and free enough to reach into himself. Brando here, always listening to an inner voice, must have a direct pipeline to the mystery of character.

Bertolucci has an extravagant gift for sequences that are like arias, and he has given Brando some scenes that really sing. In one, Paul visits his dead wife's lover (Massimo Girotti), who also lives in the run-down hotel, and the two men, in identical bathrobes (gifts from the dead woman), sit side by side and talk. The scene is miraculously basic — a primal scene that has just been discovered. In another, Brando rages at his dead wife, laid out in a bed of flowers, and then, in an excess of tenderness, tries to wipe away the cosmetic mask that defaces her. He has become the least fussy actor. There is nothing extra, no flourishes in these scenes. He purifies the characterization beyond all that: he brings the character a unity of soul. Paul feels so "real" and the character is brought so close that a new dimension in screen acting has been reached. I think that if the actor were anyone but Brando many of us would lower our eyes in confusion.

His first sex act has a boldness that had the audience gasping, and the gasp was caused — in part — by our awareness that this was Marlon Brando doing it, not an unknown actor. In the flat, he wears the white T-shirt of Stanley Kowalski, and he still has the big shoulders and thick-muscled arms. Photographed looking down, he is still tender and poetic; photographed looking up, he is ravaged, like the man in the Francis Bacon painting under the film's opening titles. We are watching *Brando* throughout this movie, with all the feedback that that implies, and his willingness to run the full course with a study of the aggression in masculine sexuality and how the physical strength of men lends credence to the insanity that grows out of it gives the film a larger, tragic dignity. If Brando knows this hell, why should we pretend we don't?

The colors in this movie are late-afternoon orange-beige-browns and pink — the pink of flesh drained of blood, corpse pink. They are so delicately modulated (Vittorio Storaro was the cinematographer, as he was on *The Conformist*) that romance and rot are one; the lyric extravagance of the music (by Gato Barbieri) heightens this effect. Outside the flat, the gray buildings and the noise are certainly modern Paris, and yet the city seems muted. Bertolucci uses a feedback of his own — the feedback of old movies to enrich the imagery and associations. In substance, this is his most American film, yet the shadow of Michel Simon seems to hover over Brando, and the ambience is a tribute to the early crime-of-passion films of Jean Renoir, especially *La Chienne* and *La Bête Humaine.* Léaud, as Tom, the young director, is used as an affectionate takeoff on Godard, and the movie that Tom is shooting about Jeanne, his runaway bride, echoes Jean Vigo's *L'Atalante.* Bertolucci's soft focus recalls the thirties films, with their lyrically kind eye for every variety of passion; Marcel Carné comes to mind, as well as the masters who influenced Bertolucci's technique — von Sternberg (the controlled lighting) and Max Ophuls (the tracking camera). The film is utterly beautiful to look at. The virtuosity of Bertolucci's gliding camera style is such that he can show you the hype of the tango-contest scene (with its own echo of *The Conformist*) by stylizing it (the automaton-dancers do wildly fake head turns) and still make it work. He uses the other actors for their associations, too — Girotti, of course, the star of so many Italian films, including *Senso* and *Ossessione,* Visconti's version of *The Postman Always Rings Twice,* and, as Paul's mother-in-law, Maria Michi, the young girl who betrays her lover in *Open City.* As a maid in the hotel (part of a weak, diversionary subplot that is soon dispensed with), Catherine Allegret, with her heart-shaped mouth in a full, childishly beautiful face, is an aching, sweet reminder of her mother, Simone Signoret, in her *Casque d'Or* days. Bertolucci draws upon the movie background of this movie because movies are as active in him as direct experience — perhaps more active, since they may color everything else. Movies are a past we share, and, whether we recognize them or not, the copious associations are at work in the film and we feel them. As Jeanne, Maria Schneider, who has never had a major role before, is like a bouquet of Renoir's screen heroines and his father's models. She carries the whole history of movie passion in her long legs and baby face.

Maria Schneider's freshness — Jeanne's ingenuous corrupt innocence — gives the film a special radiance. When she lifts her wedding dress to her waist, smiling coquettishly as she exposes her pubic hair, she's in a great film tradition of irresistibly naughty girls. She has a movie face — open to the camera, and yet no more concerned about it than a plant or a kitten. When she speaks in English, she sounds like

Leslie Caron in *An American in Paris,* and she often looks like a plump-cheeked Jane Fonda in her *Barbarella* days. The role is said to have been conceived for Dominique Sanda, who couldn't play it, because she was pregnant, but surely it has been reconceived. With Sanda, a tigress, this sexual battle might have ended in a draw. But the pliable, softly unprincipled Jeanne of Maria Schneider must be the winner: it is the soft ones who defeat men and walk away, consciencelessly. A Strindberg heroine would still be in that flat, battling, or in another flat, battling. But Jeanne is like the adorably sensual bitch-heroines of French films of the twenties and thirties — both shallow and wise. These girls know how to take care of themselves; they know who No. 1 is. Brando's Paul, the essentially naïve outsider, the romantic, is no match for a French bourgeois girl.

Because of legal technicalities, the film must open in Italy before it opens in this country, and so *Last Tango in Paris* is not scheduled to play here until January. There are certain to be detractors, for this movie represents too much of a change for people to accept it easily or gracefully. They'll grab at aesthetic flaws — a florid speech or an oddball scene — in order to dismiss it. Though Americans seem to have lost the capacity for being scandalized, and the Festival audience has probably lost the cultural confidence to admit to being scandalized, it might have been easier on some if they could have thrown things. I've tried to describe the impact of a film that has made the strongest impression on me in almost twenty years of reviewing. This is a movie people will be arguing about, I think, for as long as there are movies. They'll argue about how it is intended, as they argue again now about *The Dance of Death.* It is a movie you can't get out of your system, and I think it will make some people very angry and disgust others. I don't believe that there's *anyone* whose feelings can be totally resolved about the sex scenes and the social attitudes in this film. For the very young, it could be as antipathetic as *L'Avventura* was at first — more so, because it's closer, more realistic, and more emotionally violent. It could embarrass them, and even frighten them. For adults, it's like seeing pieces of your life, and so, of course, you can't resolve your feelings about it — our feelings about life are never resolved. Besides, the biology that is the basis of the "tango" remains.

[October 28, 1972]

Pop versus Jazz

"LADY SINGS THE BLUES" fails to do justice to the musical life of which Billie Holiday was a part, and it never shows what made her a star, much less what made her an artist. The sad truth is that there is no indication that those who made the picture understand that jazz is any different from pop corruptions of jazz. And yet when the movie was over I wrote "I love it" on my pad of paper and closed it and stuffed it back in my pocket. In certain kinds of movies, the chemistry of pop vulgarization is all-powerful. You don't want to resist the pull of it, because it has a celebrity-star temperament you don't get from anything else; this kitsch has its own kind of authenticity. It's a compliment to the brand of tarnished-lady realism Motown has produced that one thinks of Warners and such Bette Davis vehicles as *Dark Victory* and *Dangerous* rather than of M-G-M. This movie isn't heavy and glazed. Factually it's a fraud, but emotionally it delivers. It has what makes movies work for a mass audience: easy pleasure, tawdry electricity, personality — great quantities of personality. Pop music provides immediate emotional gratifications that the subtler and deeper and more lasting pleasures of jazz can't prevail against. Pop drives jazz back underground. And that's what this pop movie does to the career of a great jazz singer.

How can you trash an artist's life and come up with a movie as effective as *Lady Sings the Blues*? Well, at one level Billie Holiday trashed her own life, and so her morbid legend works for the picture. Movie-trade reporters say that movies with "lose" or "loser" in the title always make money; a movie about Billie Holiday hardly needs the word in the title. Who could be a more natural subject for a flamboyant downer than Billie Holiday, whose singing can send the cheeriest extroverts into a funk? Good Morning, Heartache. Billie Holiday expressed herself in her bantering with lachrymose lyrics, making them ironic and biting, or else exploiting them for their full measure of misery, giving in so deeply to cheap emotions that she wrung a truth of her own out of them. Maybe not quite a truth but an essence. How many masochists have sated themselves on her "Gloomy Sunday"? And the defiance of her "Ain't

Nobody's Business If I Do" was always borderline self-pity: the subtext was "I don't need any of you, I'm so miserable." We've all got a lot of slop in us, and she glorified it, so she was irresistible. She lived so close to those self-destructive suffering-star myths epitomized by the term "a Susan Hayward picture" that only by suggesting the Billie Holiday who was an intuitive innovator and played her oboe voice like a jazz instrument, the artist who was fully happy only when she was singing, could the movie have transcended the old gallant-victim-paying-the-price-of-fame routine. Instead, it stays snugly within commercial confines, relying on the variation of the black sufferer to make it new. This bio-melodrama wasn't made with love for Billie Holiday, exactly (except perhaps from Diana Ross, who plays the role), but *I'll Cry Tomorrow* and *Love Me or Leave Me* (which we think of as "forties" but which were actually mid-fifties — not very far in the past) didn't show much love, either, and they were made with much less energy and spirit.

Still, it's shocking to see a great black artist's experience poured into the same Hollywood mold, and to see that it works — and works far better than it did on the white singers' lives. There's an obvious, external cause for the torments Billie Holiday goes through, and black experience is still new and exotic on the screen — a fresh setting with a new cast of characters, a new vernacular, and a different kind of interplay. And since you can show almost anything in movies now, you don't have to find euphemisms and substitutions. A whore is no longer a "hostess." But this freedom in language and atmosphere isn't to be confused with freedom from commercialism. The movie prefers invented horrors to the known (and much worse) horrors of Billie Holiday's actual life. Her promiscuity has been jettisoned; the lovers and domestic messes and quick affairs all disappear, and her third husband, Louis McKay (Billy Dee Williams), becomes the only man she loves and wants. It's when they're separated (because of her career) that she's so lonely and unhappy she tries drugs; and she falls back on them again later on when he must be away for a few months. Billie Holiday's music certainly doesn't send us messages about a good man who's always there when she needs him; her torch blues express the disorder and dissatisfaction of her human relations. How could anybody listen to her high-wire singing and write this monogamous script? Well, that's not what the troop of writers were listening to.

When this Billie Holiday announces that she is giving up singing to marry Louis and spend her time in the kitchen, audiences cheer. The way they have been conditioned by movies and TV, how else can they react? In terms of the movie, they're reacting *appropriately*; the movie itself can't deal with why Billie wants to go on singing after she has married her fairy-tale prince. The picture is solidly aimed at a mass audience that knows a junkie is damned lucky to get a fine, substantial husband to take care of her, and Louis McKay has been made such a deep-voiced, sexy Mr. Right that the audience's sympathies tend to go to him rather than to her. At times, the movie seems deliberately shaped to make Billy Dee Williams a star. One can almost feel the calculation that swooning teenagers will say to themselves, "*I* wouldn't take dope if I had a man like that waiting for me." McKay is black, but he's an early-model Clark Gable dreamboat. This ridculously suave, couth man (who is involved in some unspecified business that permits him to be a hot-shot big spender) belongs in another sort of movie altogether. Since he doesn't save her, what's he here for? For black popular romance, of course, and maybe it's only a commercial dividend that he embodies the stability against which Billie Holiday is then judged.

The assumption is that the basic audience will be black, and so the movie plays a few get-Whitey games: you never see Billie with any of her *white* lovers, or in her quarrels with blacks (including her own mother), and she's turned onto dope by a smiling white dude (platinum-blond Paul Hampton, who overdoes the white sliminess). Operating on a scrambled calendar of events, the movie avoids the complexity of the race issues in her life, making her strictly a victim. Her tour with Artie Shaw's band has been turned into the road to ruin for a little black girl who should have stayed with her own people. And with this approach Billie Holiday seems so weak a person that we can't see how she ever made it to the peak of her profession. For reasons that are obscure — possibly in order to sustain the victim image — her records, by which the whole world came to know her, are omitted. One would never suspect that she began to record at the age of eighteen and that by her early twenties she was an important figure in the world of jazz. How shrewd it is, consciously or unconsciously, to show us not the woman who had made over a hundred recordings by the time she was twenty-five, not the embattled woman who broke down racial barriers while creating a new musical style, but a junkie girl who makes it to the top — the stage of Carnegie Hall — yet at too great a price. A loser. A movie that dealt with Billie Holiday's *achievements* wouldn't be hip; what's hip is the zingy romanticism of failure. *Lady Sings the Blues* is about a junkie who has it made but keeps pulling herself down.

Diana Ross, a tall, skinny goblin of a girl, intensely likable, always in motion, seemed an irrational choice for the sultry, still Billie Holiday, yet she's like a beautiful bonfire: there's nothing to question — you just react with everything you've got. You react in kind, because she has given herself to the role with an all-out physicality, not holding anything back. At times, she reminded me a little of the way Carole Lombard used to throw herself into a role; Lombard wasn't a great comedienne, but she had such zest and vitality that you liked her better than mere comediennes. She was striking and special — an original. So is Diana Ross, and with gifts that can't be defined yet. She couldn't have won us over so fast if the director hadn't shaped and built our interest in her from the childhood scenes. She's knockabout, tomboy angular as an adolescent, and a little later she has a harlequin beauty: huge eyes and a pointed chin and an impishly pretty smile. When she wears ruby lipstick, it's so absolutely right it looks like part of her. She's made up to look uncannily like Billie Holiday in flashes in the latter part of the film, but she's most appealing in the early scenes, when she's least like Billie. The elements of camp and self-parody in Diana Ross's performances with the Supremes and in her TV solo appearances are gone, but, in her whore's orange dress with ruffles at the shoulders and a snug fit over her wriggly, teasing little bottom, she still has her impudence. She's scat-fast with a funny line, she's inventive when she delivers her dialogue like lyrics, and she has a sneaky face for the times when Billie is trying to put something over on Louis. The drugs act like a dimmer: the lights in her voice go down. She differentiates the stoned singing from the "clean" singing by a slight slippery uncertainty (though there's a kitchen scene when she's clean but depressed and she sings — inappropriately, I thought — in this desultory way).

In the established Hollywood tradition, Billie Holiday doesn't have to become Billie Holiday, musically speaking; the first time she sings in public, she has the full Holiday style. But, of course, Diana Ross doesn't pierce us the way Holiday does. She's strong in everything but her singing; as a singer, she's caught in the trap of this bio-melodrama form. *Funny Girl* was a stylized musical comedy, and so no one expected Streisand to sing like Fanny Brice; besides, Fanny Brice isn't on many jukeboxes. But the star of *Lady Sings the Blues* is expected to sound like Billie Holiday. And the key problem for me with the movie is that Diana Ross's singing is *too* close. Her voice is similar — small and thin and reedy, and suspended in air, like a little girl's — and when she sings the songs that Holiday's phrasing fixed in our minds and imitates that phrasing, our memories are blurred. I felt as if I were losing something. I could hear Billie Holiday in my head perfectly clearly as Ross sang each number, but by the time she had finished it, I could no longer be certain of the exact Holiday sounds. What's involved here isn't quite like the vandalism that Stokowski and Disney committed in *Fantasia,* with cupids and winged horses cavorting to the "Pastoral" and volcanoes erupting to Stravinsky — wrecking music for us by forcing us to hear it forever after with incongruous images welded to it — or like the way Kubrick played droog to Beethoven, and even to "Singin' in the Rain." But something similar is at work: Kubrick left Moog-synthesized versions of classics echoing in our skulls, and I think *Lady Sings the Blues,* by its pop versions of Billie Holiday's numbers, will deprive people of the originals. Yes, of course, they still exist, just as the originals of the Benny Goodman and Duke Ellington records that Time-Life has had imitated by modern bands still exist, but new generations are effectively deprived of them just the same. Movies never use the original records in these bios, because the contemporary sound always sells better, and so movies use art as grist.

With Holiday, it was as if everything extra — the padding, all the resonances — had been pared away by troubles: just this thin, wounded sound was left. She made her limited voice yield pure emotion — what jazz horn players sought to do. And her plaintiveness made even her vivacious numbers hurt. There's no pain in Diana Ross's voice, and none of that lazy, sullen sexiness that was a form of effrontery and a turn-on. In song after song in *Lady Sings the Blues,* the phrasing has been split off from its emotional meaning. Diana Ross's "Them There Eyes" comes at the happiest moment in the movie and she's charming on it, but it works on a simple, pop level. She sings the showpiece number, "Strange Fruit," very well, and it's pretty, but it lacks Holiday's chilling tautness that keeps you silent until the final word, "crop," flicks you like a whip. Holiday's acrid edge is missing, and her authority. Ross gives you the phrasing without the intensity that makes it dramatic and memorable, and fresh each time you hear it.

What one always knew, with Billie Holiday, was that there was one thing her voice could never do: heal, the way a rich, full voice can — as Bessie Smith could and Aretha Franklin can. Maybe Billie Holiday willed that effect of being a lone, small voice in the wilderness — isolation rooted in the sound — because that was the only way she could make a great instrument out of her limited voice, and because she meant to wound, not to heal. She wasn't hiding anything: her voice was a direct line from her to us, hurting us (exquisitely, of course) because she'd been hurt (and not exquisitely at all). She was a jazz singer; Ross is a pop singer singing in the Holiday manner. It's imitation soul. That was the letdown of Billie Holiday's later singing — her creativity gave out and she was imitating her own style. Diana Ross's imitation may be an act of homage as much as a requirement of the role, but what she had with the Supremes — which was freaky and as commercial as hell — was recognizably hers. Singing in the style of someone else kills her spark, though she has it here as an actress. Perhaps the decision to spare us the dregs of Billie Holiday's life — the club appearances when her voice was shot and she could barely be heard and the scattering of audience was mostly narcotics agents anyway — was based on a recognition that it wouldn't jibe with Diana Ross's lively, quick spirit. She doesn't have the punishing personality of Billie Holiday; she wants to give pure, crazy, hip pleasure.

So, in his own way, does the director, Sidney J. Furie, the young Canadian with a mottled career of hits and flops *(The Leather Boys, The Ipcress File, The Appaloosa, The Naked Runner, The Lawyer, Little Fauss and Big Halsy).* Furie is wily and talented in small ways that count, but sometimes in his pictures it's *only* the small ways that count — the marginal details and minor characters. He hammers out the heavy stuff, such as the hokey-powerful opening scene, under the titles, with Holiday being hauled into jail and tied in a straitjacket while Michel Legrand's hyperactive crime-suspense music cues us in to the overwrought genre, but he also disposes of a lot of second-rate dialogue by fast throwaway delivery and overlaps, and his best sequences are unusually loose. In one, a scene of gruesome comic confusion, Billie and Richard Pryor, as her accompanist, Piano Man, are backstage at a club, with her connection waiting to give her a shot, when she learns of her mother's death; they're in no shape to deal with the situation, and the talk dribbles on in a painfully lifelike way. Pryor, a West Coast coffeehouse comic, has such audience rapport that a shot of him in Los Angeles in fancy clothes and a beret is enough to bring down the house. Billie and Piano Man have a sequence that feels improvised, on a California beach, when she asks him to get her some dope, and then a long unstructured "high" scene together, when they're like two innocently obscene junkie babies. Elsewhere, Furie's direction is often crude (as with the Smilin' Jack villain, and Black Beauty Billy Dee Williams), but he has a sense of pace and a knack for letting the audience know that he wants us to have a good time. The bad side of his hardboiled expertise — the insistence on being modern and tough by not showing too much compassion — is that though Diana Ross wins you and holds you, your feelings about Billie Holiday become uncertain and muddy as the film progresses. The keys to her life are in her art, and that's not in the movie. (It almost never is in movies, because how do you re-create the processes of artistic creation?) *Lady Sings the Blues* is as good as one can expect from the genre — better, at times — and I enjoyed it hugely, yet I don't want Billie Holiday's hard, melancholic sound buried under this avalanche of pop. When you get home, you have to retrieve her at the phonograph; you have to do restoration work on your own past.

[November 4, 1972]

Anarchist's Laughter

"THE DISCREET CHARM OF THE BOURGEOISIE" is a cosmic vaudeville show — an Old Master's mischief. Now seventy-two, Luis Buñuel is no longer savage about the hypocrisy and the inanity of the privileged classes. They don't change, and since they have become a persistent bad joke to him, he has grown almost fond of their follies — the way one can grow fond of the snarls and the silliness of vicious pets. He looks at them now and they're such perfectly amoral little beasts they amuse him; he enjoys their skin-deep proprieties, their faith in appearances, their sublime confidence. At the same time, this Spanish exile-expatriate may have come to a point in life when the hell he has gone through to make movies is receding into the past, like an old obscene story; he is so relaxed about his medium now that he enjoys pinching its nose, pulling its tail. He has become a majestic light prankster — not a bad way for a man full of disgust and pity to age. The movie is slight, but it has a special enchantment: it's a development — more like an emanation — of Buñuel's movies which couldn't have been expected but which seems *right*; that is, the best thing that could have happened. Buñuel's cruelty and mockery were often startlingly funny, but they were also sadistic; that was the power of his work and part of what made his films scandalous. He was diabolically antibourgeois, and he wasn't just anticlerical — he was hilariously, murderously anticlerical. Here his old rages have become buoyant jokes. (Might Swift without his disease have ended up like this?) The movie comes close to serenity, and it's a deep pleasure to see that the unregenerate anarchist-atheist has found his own path to grace. Buñuel has never given in, never embraced the enemy, and maybe that's why the tone of this spontaneous chamber music is so happy.

In *The Exterminating Angel,* which was about guests who came to a dinner and couldn't leave, the jest grew heavy and allegorical. We were stuck there waiting to leave, too. He has turned that situation upside down here. A group of six friends — three men and three women — have trouble getting together for dinner, but they're not trapped: the series of interrupted dinners spans an indefinite period while food, that ritual center of bourgeois well-being, keeps eluding them. And Buñuel has left himself free: this is his most frivolously witty movie, and it's open in time and place. It's a divertimento on themes from his past movies — the incidental pleasures of twists and dream logic for their own sake. It's all for fun — the fun of observing how elegantly these civilized monsters disport themselves in preposterous situations. This offhand, trickster approach to the medium is very like that of the comedy *Assassins et Voleurs* (called *Lovers and Thieves* here), which Sacha Guitry wrote and directed, also at the age of seventy-two. That film, too, looked unbelievably easy, the technique imperceptible. It's as if they both just sat on a sunny balcony with a bottle of good wine and waved a hand to direct the company. (Actually, Guitry worked from a wheelchair.) But there's a different atmosphere in the Buñuel film — there's a strong sense of timelessness, stronger than in his genial but antiquarian and rather innocuous *The Milky Way*, in which the characters travel through many eras. Here it is achieved in modern clothes and modern settings; one is simply aware of having lost a sense of time, and that this timelessness, which is tonic, is somehow linked to Buñuel's ironic detachment. The characters hit the road of life here, too; we don't know where they're heading, but they're such energetic travellers they seem to be going to a picnic. Their heads are stuffed with clichés, and they're indifferent to anything except their own self-interest, but they were there when Buñuel began making movies, and they'll survive him. Why not be playful, when all your rage and cruelty have hardly dented their armor?

The three men — Fernando Rey, as the bachelor Ambassador to France from Miranda (in South America), and his respectable married friends Jean-Pierre Cassel and Paul Frankeur — are secret business associates with a thriving trade in dope, brought in via diplomatic pouch. (Fernando Rey also played the suave gentleman with the silver-handled umbrella who sold the cache of heroin in *The French Connection* — the man who got away.) His friends' wives are Stéphane Audran and Delphine Seyrig (with whom he is dallying); the sixth member of the group is Delphine Seyrig's sister, played by Bulle Ogier. The other principals are representatives of the Church (Julien Bertheau as a bishop) and of the Army (Claude Piéplu), and Michel Piccoli does a small turn as a government minister. There is not, however, as much acting as this list of eminent names may suggest. Bertheau plays with supreme finesse, but most of the others don't really act characters; they represent something more like "humors." Buñuel works fast; he obviously prefers casual performances (and even the awkward performances he gets from the minor players) to sentimentality. He uses the actors matter-of-factly to make his points, and this unemotional approach results in such a clean, thin-textured style that the merest anecdote begins to resemble a fable. In comedy, underdirected acting often dampens the jokes; here it becomes part of the exhilarating ease of the film, and of its simplicity. The principals — especially Stéphane Audran — embody their roles with professional awareness: they have that discreet charm, and they do nicely judged turns in a polished drawing-room style, as if they were doing charades at a party.

American novelists sometimes parody the processes of artistic creation too early in their own lives, when their parody means little to us except a demonstration of cleverness, but when Buñuel parodies the methods by which a movie director can lead you into story structures, and into dreams, and dreams within dreams, and tales of the supernatural, the joke is how easy it has become for him. The charm of the film is that the old magician can show off his skills and make fun of them at the same time. He can say, "Look, there's nothing to it. Just take the rabbit out of the hat." (The first shot in the movie looks like a black cat's face, yellow eyes glowing, but turns out to be a car coming toward us with its headlights on.) There is nothing else in the movie — just the surprises, and the pleasures of his dexterity as he springs them. You have no idea what's coming from minute to minute; he keeps leading you down garden paths that disappear. (Only once, I found his dream logic faulty: when the bishop gives a dying man — the murderer of the bishop's parents — absolution and then shoots him, the idea is perhaps too cutely paradoxical to go with the ugliness of the act. The gunshot — definite and resonant, like nothing else in the film — violates the light, unpremeditated style.) The movie proceeds by interruptions: just as you have been gulled into getting interested in a situation he pulls the rug out from under you, and goes on to something else. And, in the same way that he parodies bourgeois instincts and manners in the day-to-day episodes, he parodies bourgeois fears and superstitions in the supernatural-fantasy episodes. He hokes up these scary death jokes with fancy lighting and cutting that he disdains in the rest of the movie, demonstrating how easy it is to draw an audience into childish ghost stories, demonstrating how primitive audience responses are. He says, "If you want cheap mysteries, this is how simple it is." Then each time the interruption comes one can almost hear the director laughing. The old anarchist has planted his bombs under bourgeois moviemaking.

❖

THE ULTIMATE PRINCESS FANTASY is to be so glamorously sensitive and beautiful that you have to be taken care of; you are simply too sensitive for this world — you see the truth, and so you suffer more than ordinary people, and can't function. *Play It As It Lays* is set in the *Red Desert* region of Hollywood, which means it's about empty lives, acute anguish, Hollywood and Hell. The beautiful and damned heroine —Maria Wyeth, a onetime model and sometime screen star, played by Tuesday Weld — walks the tree-lined paths of a sanatorium and tells the story of her disintegration. Needless to say, it is the world that is having the breakdown, not Maria. I know I have a lower tolerance for this sort of thing than many people; but should it be tolerated? I found the Joan Didion novel ridiculously swank, and I read it between bouts of disbelieving giggles. I whooped at the first line:

> What makes Iago evil? some people ask. I never ask.

I whooped at the ending:

> One thing in my defense, not that it matters: I know something Carter never knew, or Helene, or maybe you. I know what "nothing" means, and keep on playing.
>
> Why, BZ would say.
>
> Why not, I say.

I even whooped when I saw an article about Joan Didion and read the epigraph:

> I am haunted by the cannibalism of the Donner Party.
>
> —*Joan Didion in conversation.*

Certainly I recognize that Miss Didion can write: the smoke of creation rises from those dry-ice sentences. You know at once that you're in the fast company of *Butterfield 8* and *Miss Lonelyhearts* and *The Day of the Locust* and Fitzgerald and Zelda herself. But you also know that this is what movies have done to the novel. What's missing from these books is the morally tough common sense that has been called the strongest tradition in English letters. As a novel, *Play It As It Lays* is a creature of the movies, celebrating the glamour abyss, transferring Fitzgerald's spoiled-rotten rich to the movie-colony locale — a perfect mass-culture home for them, their spiritual home all along.

The book itself was already show business — a writer's performance, with every word screwed tight, and a designer's feat, the sparse words placed in the spiritual emptiness of white pages. Reading the book was, in fact, like going to the movies. And it drew upon many films — especially, I thought, upon Bergman's *Through a Glass Darkly,* in which the racked, misunderstood heroine who sees God as a spider is also hauled away. But the waif sensibility in a Hollywood novel — that was an inspiration. The novel was a touchstone of a sort, and I imagine the movie will be, too. Joan Didion wanted Frank Perry to direct — possibly because he had already glorified the suffering little-girl-woman in *Diary of a Mad Housewife* — and he has been extremely faithful to her book. She and her husband, John Gregory Dunne, did the adaptation,* and her brother-in-law Dominick Dunne co-produced with Perry. The adaptation is a novelist's wish fulfillment: narration that retains the most "eloquent" passages in the book, dialogue virtually intact, and a transfer to the screen of the shattered-sensibility style by means of quick scenes that form a mosaic. Even the coiled rattler that decorated the book jacket turns up signalling evil throughout the movie (and perhaps inspiring those dissidents, like me, who hissed when the picture was over). For what it is, the movie is well done: posh, narcissistic, flashy. Image by image, it's handsome. Perry hasn't found a "visual equivalent" for the famished prose, but maybe this high-class-whorehouse style of moviemaking is the *true* equivalent.

The movie doesn't have that glittering austerity that made me giggle, but the emotional content is basically the same. It's all there: the romance of suicidal despair and the gloriously bleak lives of the lucky people. Maria, throwing herself away on men she doesn't like, is different from the crowd of decadent, calculating studs and stars and witches who surround her. (Tammy Grimes, Adam Roarke, Ruth Ford, Richard Anderson, and Paul Lambert are among them.) She's superior because she can't adjust to the "sick arrangements" they accept, even though — and here is the real cheat of this genre — in the movie there is no other way to live. This soulless high life represents the moral corruption of our time, and the apocalypse. Maria, separated and then divorced, comes equipped with a brain-damaged child she can't communicate with, and in the course of the movie she has an abortion; the fetus in the garbage is — like the snake — a recurrent motif. Maria herself has lost interest in communicating, and her success-satisfied movie-director husband accuses her of playing at catatonia, but his producer — a homosexual, BZ (Tony Perkins) — understands her all right. Because BZ, too, has discovered the nothingness of life. "Tell me what matters," he says to her, but she has no answer, and he commits suicide while she cradles him in her arms. The cotton-candy misery of all this might have been dreamed up by a Catholic schoolgirl who loses her God and thinks that if she doesn't find something to put in His place the world will come to an end. If you use Hollywood as the test tissue for mankind, what

*Their *first* choice for director was Sam Peckinpah, who wanted to do it but wasn't acceptable to the studios, except on "men's pictures."

could the prognosis be? Brimstone, of course, brought on by the fornication and bitchery that audiences enjoy.

The movie feels like a remake of the book. But it has lost the book's accumulating sense of dread — possibly because the splintered opening doesn't help you get your bearings the way the splintering in the book did. And what Frank Perry misses out on is that Maria is meant not just to be numb but to be numb because she hurts. That never comes across in Tuesday Weld's limited, mannered performance. She doesn't use her body anymore; as in last year's *A Safe Place,* she does everything with her face, mainly with her mouth — there are a lot of puckers. With her Alice in Wonderland forehead and her calm, wide eyes, she's like a great pumpkin-headed doll, and she doesn't express pain — just a beautiful blobby numbness that suggests childlike abstraction as much as suffering. Tony Perkins uses his contrasting skinny tightness, in his supporting role, very well; when his lines are dry, he's the best thing in the picture. But who could deliver lines like, "We've been out there where nothing is"? Tuesday Weld is onscreen steadily. Maria drives the freeways in search of the reasons that they're there; she shoots at highway signs; and she broods. "Maybe I was holding all the aces, but what was the game?" she says to us — a line that echoes the Mickey Spillane parody in *The Band Wagon.* But Maria is the twin sister of the Jack Nicholson character in *Five Easy Pieces,* and this is classy — plastic L.A. and the freeways, sin and loss. Poor Maria keeps asking the meaning of it all, and because she's thinking this heavy question she can't do anything for herself or anyone else. And the movie cuddles her and cuddles her *Cosmopolitan*-girl questions.

[November 11, 1972]

Hyperbole and Narcissus

IT WOULD BE CONVENIENT to be able to say that Ken Russell's *Savage Messiah* is bad strictly on formal and technical grounds, but that would, I think, be fundamentally a lie. It *is* very poor technically, but that's not all that makes it bad. I want to be specific about my grounds, because so many people — and reviewers especially — have been falling back on narrow or simply trumped-up-for-the-occasion notions of form whenever the content of a movie presents problems. This was obvious last summer in relation to *The Candidate*: those who were bothered by its smug, shallow cynicism and by what it says — that political life in the United States is *all* manipulation — generally said that it was badly done, and maybe even boring, while those who got onto the same wavelength as the movie (which is easy to do since it's shrewd and hip and lively) tended to find it marvelous fun, accepting, or not really caring much about, what it says. It's impossible to judge how much of the content of *The Candidate* or any other movie actually seeps into a viewer's consciousness; that depends on the individual viewer, and for some, perhaps for all of us, there may be a considerable cumulative seepage. It's just a dodge to say that if a film is exciting, it's good, and that's all there is to it — unless there's something in it that bugs one, in which case one decides that it's badly made. This can result in such bad jokes as the way the press of two continents lavished praise on the rancid, mechanical *Frenzy* — a movie so obviously engineered that the reviewers couldn't help seeing its "form."

Is there any other movie director with the flair and imagination and, yes, the force of Ken Russell who has so little actual command of what is generally considered "film technique"? *Savage Messiah* starts by lunging into the middle of a situation and then just keeps throwing things at you. It's more hurried than his other films, and not so visually lush. You feel as if it were rushing through the projector at the wrong speed and with the sound turned up to panic level. Russell edits with a cleaver, and the frenetic intercutting is choppy and rhythmless. Nothing is prepared for, and the disjointed scenes are played as if they all had the same value; he charges from one to the next, and his inventiveness gets buried under the avalanche. Yet all this could be considered a new approach, a way of breaking conventional molds. Maybe the shouting and the shock cuts and the emphasis on knockout episodes instead of on the over-all structure are simply an extension of his highly successful TV methods. There's no expansiveness in his vision here; he reduces the big screen to the TV screen. But this constant battery of sensations may be perfectly acceptable to those who have grown up with TV; in fact, preferable.

Ken Russell's admirers say they experience sensual intoxication from his highly theatrical, whirling lives of celebrated, scandalous artists. And those who are intoxicated are willing to accept his passionate, compulsively ambivalent romanticism — in which tumult and rapture are carried to madhouse pitch and everything is a joke, nothing is a joke. They find the extremities exciting; they get stoned on his excesses. But what if his visions of artists' lives — it's Henri Gaudier-Brzeska's turn this time — that are sometimes acclaimed as too shocking for Philistines are camp fantasies derived from Hollywood's wildest kitsch? What does it then mean if you're swept up by it? It doesn't necessarily mean that the picture that does it is art; it could just mean you've been softened. As a picture of bohemian life in Paris and London, *Savage Messiah* is about as convincing as *The Subterraneans* was about the Beats in San Francisco; but you understood the commercial pressures that shaped that, while with *Savage Messiah* the pressures are from Russell's insides. He's a one-man marketplace, a compulsive Hollywoodizer, and his images of the artist's suffering are frantic versions of Hollywood's. This movie is like a continuation of *The Music Lovers*, but now it's all random buffoonery. Russell seems almost cursed by his subjects; he seems to want something from them, but each time he gets close to them he dances away. His movies are charged with sex, but it's androgynous sex, and sterile. There's a giddy violence to the sensations of dislocation that this new film produces. The abrupt contrasts score points against the characters. Russell celebrates the pandemonium and senselessness of art and life. Yet in the middle of this lurid debauchery the virginal hero seems to be saving himself for something: he's like Alice Faye singing "No Love, No Nothin'."

The actual Henri Gaudier, a gifted sculptor, born near Orléans in 1891, had been helped by scholarships as a boy, but he was proud and frail and starving in Paris, and, worst of all, desperately lonely, when he met Sophie Brzeska, a Polish woman, even more lonely than he — she'd been lonely all her life. Weakened by years of near-starvation, she was studying languages and trying to become a writer. He was eighteen and she was thirty-eight. For the next five years — until he died in battle in 1915, at twenty-three — they were platonic lovers, joining their names into Gaudier-Brzeska and living as brother and sister. Had he survived, Henri Gaudier-Brzeska might have become a major sculptor, but he is known to us as a minor artist and, of course, a legend. Considering the age difference between him and Sophie, and Sophie's background, her fear and reluctance to change the terms of their relationship from intellectual and artistic comradeship to the full, consummated, and legal marriage that he eventually wanted is perhaps not so strange; but their relationship — more mother and son than sister and brother — was painful and stormy. Sophie was a woman of passionate ideals who had had a bitter life; of middle-class background, she had been deserted by her suitors because she had no dowry, and her determination to be independent had gone sour in a series of jobs as a governess, including a long stint in the United States, where she had been stranded. Failure and deprivation had left her a high-strung, near-mad woman, and an angry woman. When Henri's work began to sell and he began to make friends — Roger Fry, Frank Harris, Enid Bagnold, Wyndham Lewis, Katherine Mansfield and Middleton Murry, Ezra Pound (who was a friend until Henri's death, and who wrote a small book about him) — her assertiveness often drove them away. Many people tried to help them, though they concealed their extreme poverty. Gaudier-Brzeska is known not only through his sculpture and drawings but also through his letters, which form a large part of the book that H. S. Ede put together in 1931 under the dubious but selling title *Savage Messiah.*

The title seems so appropriate to Ken Russell, however, that some people have thought the film — written by Christopher Logue, from Ede's book — to be autobiographical. And in a sense it is, because Russell has wrested Gaudier-Brzeska's story from its place in art history and made it one more of his unstable satires on romanticism. Gentle, delicate-looking Gaudier, who was so embarrassed not to be sleeping with Sophie that he used to lie to people and say he was, and who once went to a prostitute but fled in disgust, becomes Russell's strutting, phallic artist assaulting society. His whole life builds up to the final Hollywood-style irony: he is taken up after death by the fashionable world, for its amusement. In a musical-comedy finale, Russell concocts a parade of rich and vapid young people with pink parasols who attend a posthumous exhibition of Gaudier-Brzeska's work and flirt and politely smile their approval. Russell seems drawn to the old movie story of the unappreciated "immortal" artist recognized after his death. But Gaudier-Brzeska never did become a major figure — he's hardly a household word now — and to suggest that his art was immediately taken up by smart young society people is to miss out on the meaning of his dedication to the avant-garde movement of his time, which was what kept him poor.

In Hollywood bios, the consummation of the artist's life was, of course, the romanticizing movie itself; Russell seems to be tormented by this convention — he keeps jabbing at it, angrily demonstrating that artists are not the ethereal dreamers those silly movies said they were, yet accepting the Hollywood myths of genius and "inspiration." This movie doesn't have the deliberate shocks and horrors of *The Music Lovers* or *The Devils* — the sores and the burning, bubbling flesh, and the Rube Goldberg machines inserted into women. This time, Russell's full energy — a kind of mad zip — goes into parodies that burst out where they don't belong. The most inventive sequence is a freakily decadent erotic entertainment in a Vorticist night club in London, with red lips protruding through the mouth hole of a painted nude, and singing. The canvas is then slashed by a suffragette; she proceeds to strip and do a number about votes for women. To anyone who knows anything about the Vorticist movement or the Bloomsbury group — or, for that matter, the suffragettes — Russell's jokes don't work, because they're so maniacally off target. The points aren't satirically valid; they're simply for kicks (though I imagine that Russell himself would defend them as valid, and would *also* say it's all meant to be a joke on us). Russell has his actors declaiming in a way that makes everything unbelievable, and we can't always judge whether this is intentional (he seems to have a very bad ear for speech); but he sometimes deliberately uses Christopher Logue's stylish, overwritten dialogue as rant, flinging literary epigrams at the audience. His hyperbolic method — going from climax to climax — is itself a form of ridicule, and it's orgiastic. And I think this is a large part of his fascination: some people can't resist his movies, because they can hardly wait to see what mad thing he'll do next. His films are preceded by puffery about the biographical research and the authentic incidents. But he removes those incidents from their human context: the attraction for him and for the audience is the porn of fame. That's why artists' lives appeal to him; he's getting back at them for their glamour. His stars-of-the-arts subjects are taking-off places for his *Hollywood Babylon* extravagances. He's not trying to deal with the age any of his artist subjects lived in, or the appetites and satisfactions of that age, or the vision of a particular artist, but is always turning something from the artists' lives into something else — a whopping irony, a phallic joke, a plushy big scene.

A famous anecdote about how Gaudier-Brzeska boasted to Epstein that he had worked directly in stone, and then, when Epstein said he would come visit his studio the next day, stayed up all night and produced three small pieces of sculpture, which were casually lying about when Epstein arrived, is turned here into a promise to visit by a malicious, epicene art dealer named Shaw (played by John Justin, in 1940 the Thief of Bagdad), who fails to show up, enraging the young sculptor, who hurls the statue he has worked on all night through Shaw's gallery window. Russell is as crazed in his hatred of art lovers as some reactionary fantasists are about liberals. The world of the movie is made up of repulsive desiccated poseurs like Shaw (and Mme. von Meck in *The Music Lovers*), who are mocked for the sensuality in their love of art. To Russell, love of art is an affection: these ghoulish art lovers really want the artist's flesh. Shaw has a wrinkled face and a rotting smile, and is covered with jewelry. Russell seems to share with Hollywood the view that a supercilious manner and an aristocratic style and homosexuality equal decadence. For him, decadence is glitzy camp — which at one level he must love, because he compulsively turns everything into it. He garbles until there is no base of truth left in a situation; his volatile mixture of bombast and venom and parody isn't an exaggeration of anything we can recognize; we no longer know what world we're in.

That's why, at a certain point in a Ken Russell movie, I always say to myself, "The man is mad." But it's why those who adore his movies say, "He's a genius." Genius is, of course, his subject — genius and possession. His possessed artists burn with an intensity that is so exhausting they seek death. But he can't help making them fools, too. He turns pop into highbrow pop. This is "art" for people who don't want to get close to human relationships, for those who feel safer with bravura splashiness.

While his heroes posture and suffer, the emotional tensions are in the female performances. Dorothy Tutin's Sophie Brzeska is the only reason to consider going to this movie, even though her Sophie exists only in bits. Perhaps Dorothy Tutin *had* to play the role so bracingly in order to survive, yet without the very special psychosexual dynamics that are at work for her here — as they were at work for Glenda Jackson's Gudrun in *Women in Love* and for some parts of Glenda Jackson's Nina in *The Music Lovers* — she wouldn't have this ambivalent force. Opposite her, Scott Antony is like a young, *less* talented Rock Hudson or Stewart Granger; he doesn't appear to be an actor at all — he acts young by jumping around — and his husky, almost buxom Gaudier is merely an embarrassment. But Dorothy Tutin makes something theatrical yet original and witty and psychologically stupefying out of the distraught Sophie's rant. Her long monologues and songs are witchlike, but Shakespearean-witchlike in their ferocious lilt. (Women have rarely delivered complex monologues from the screen, and, whether we think of that or not, probably her feat here startles us more than an actor's monologues would.) Sophie talks to herself and harangues everyone; her rhythmic tirades on the horrors of her past life and the treatment she has had as a woman are delivered at a mad speed and at a constant, loud, high pitch — and, for once in the film, the speed and the pitch are justified. Russell's fevered style doesn't allow her great scenes to grow out of anything; he even cuts away from her most extraordinary diatribe (while she's chopping half-rotten vegetables) to show us vacuous reaction shots of Scott Antony listening. Yet Russell's antipathy for and fascination with strong, hard-edged women makes her intermittent triumphs possible. When, in an idyll at the sea, she and Antony celebrate being together, dancing symbolically separate dances, she on the sand, he on the cliffs high above, her little jigging mazurka is so compelling that she wipes poor Antony off the screen.

There is a link between Russell's two authentic, flawed creations: Gudrun and Sophie. Katherine Mansfield (on whom D. H. Lawrence based his Gudrun) not only knew Sophie Brzeska but was so repelled by her that she had to break off her friendship with Henri Gaudier. In *Women in Love,* Glenda Jackson was photographed and made up to look extraordinarily like Katherine Mansfield (the photograph of Mansfield in the new Quentin Bell biography of Virginia Woolf could be a study for the movie), and Dorothy Tutin exactly fits Ede's description of Sophie: "She was small, flat-chested, with a pointed chin, thin lips, tilted nose, sensitive nostrils, and high cheekbones, which rose up to meet the large eyelids sheltering strange tired eyes, eyes that often stared big and vacant, and then of a sudden melted into roguish intimacy. Her movements were rapid, abrupt, and angular." Gudrun and Sophie are alike, of course, and on the screen they're both shrews, comic, high-powered, and erotically nasty — Gudrun a strident, castrating female who drives Gerald Crich to suicide, and Sophie, who by her neurotic hatred of sex drives Gaudier to death in battle. (Russell seems to have no interest in the fact that Gudrun was an artist herself, and Sophie a failed artist.) Both are without a core and without any soft spots at all, yet both are glittering portraits. But what are we to make of them? Russell doesn't tell us, doesn't show us. You never get to see what brought Henri Gaudier and Sophie Brzeska together, and you never get to understand why he needed the woman who called him her little son. There's one quiet moment in a shelter on the beach when Henri and Sophie talk together and you actually begin to feel something; but Russell doesn't trust it, and he throws it away. He's in his full show-off glory with Scott Antony leaping on the huge stone blocks above the sea, trying to act like a genius.

What is the sum total of his vision but a sham superiority to simple human needs, a camp put-down of everything? Like a *Yellow Book* diabolist of the eighteen-nineties, Russell lusts for a purity he doesn't believe in. He turns Gaudier-Brzeska into the virgin-artist raped in life by his dilettante admirers and raped in death by the fashionable world. One can't just dismiss Russell's movies, because they have an influence. They cheapen everything they touch — not consciously, I think, but instinctively.

[November 18, 1972]

Foundering Fathers

WHAT COULD BE MORE soul-curdling than a Broadway folk operetta featuring the founding fathers, and double-entendres, and national tragedy? The movie version. The opening of *1776* is perfectly timed for post-election regression, and Thanksgiving and Christmas at the Music Hall, and maybe Easter, too. Even before the titles, we're treated to a little cornball joke about whether the Rhode Island militia should have matching uniforms; this cues you in to the finicky silliness of the American Revolution. *1776* is shameless: first it exploits the founders of this country as cute, clodhopping fools, and then it turns pious and reverential, asking us to see that their compromise on the issue of slavery may look like a sellout but was the only way to win the unity needed to break away from England — that what they did we would have done, too. So it sends us home better, more mature Americans, presumably. "Ah, yes," we are meant to think, "it was the only way, but . . ." Yocks and uplift — that's the formula. And, of course, a thick padding of mediocrity. Put it all together and you may have a hit, a musical *Airport.*

The actors who impersonate the men gathered at the Second Continental Congress snicker and guffaw and josh each other, and the director Peter H. Hunt's idea of camera movement is to follow them as they scamper about. His camera is as busy as a nervous puppy chasing its master. The dialogue features current slang, for sure cackles, and frisky anachronisms, for belly laughs. The actors are like kids dressed up as lovable old codgers. John Adams, the sparkplug of this Revolution, is the sarcastic schoolboy who shows off his smartiness and makes himself unpopular (the prim William Daniels), and his snoozing sidekick is Benjamin Franklin (that blue-ribbon coy attention-getter and overactor Howard Da Silva). Thomas Jefferson (Ken Howard) moons for his bride, Martha (Blythe Danner), and can't write the Declaration of Independence until that pandering cupid Ben Franklin sends for her; Franklin and Adams, eager for their Declaration, wait outside, chortling, while the couple go to bed. This movie says, Behind every great man, and underneath him, too. Afterward, Franklin and Adams dance with the bride while Jefferson writes the paper. Everything is trivialized: the Congress rocks with laughter at sex jokes and toilet jokes. The show doesn't even have enough spirit to be campy; it's just arch — about a quarter of the way to camp. It might be possible to take the beginning as some sort of low-burlesque *opéra bouffe* if it had style or buoyancy, or any good jokes, but when you realize that this is priming you to accept the switcheroo to pseudo-seriousness, when that paper becomes a life-and-death issue, how is it possible not to be offended? The show is nothing if not "relevant": the melodramatic peak comes when the Southerner Edward Rutledge (John Cullum) sings the rousing "Molasses to Rum" — demonstrating that New Englanders are involved in the slave trade — so the show can prove it's not afraid of the tough issues. Slavery and its consequences are treated in the most impassioned musical-comedy style before being laid to a reassuring rest. After the show degrades the men into yokel jokers, it asks us to see their dignity and stature; when the sneering villain, John Dickinson (Donald Madden), reveals his hidden streak of patriotism and gallantry, it's one cheap piece of melodrama upon another. Our history is turned into a mincing, childish romp, and then further exploited to fill us with surges of national pride.

Peter Stone wrote the original show and adapted it for the screen, and Sherman Edwards conceived it (what a pregnancy was there!) and did the music and lyrics; they touch every Broadway base they can — they even throw in an anti-war song ("Momma Look Sharp") that is about as appropriate as the double-entendre number Martha Jefferson sings about her husband's "fiddle" after she gets out of bed. There's the obvious Broadway "showstopper" — a comic number about "The Lees of Old Virginia," delivered by Richard Henry Lee (Ron Holgate) as if he were a hillbilly eunuch at the Grand Ole Opry. Most of the other songs are just glorified recitative. The single most unbelievable (and revolting) sequence is a soul-searching dialogue held in the bell loft of the Liberty Bell between John Adams and a vision of his wife, Abigail (Virginia Vestoff); he sings, if you will forgive me for saying so, a song called "Commitment." The demagogic self-conceit of this sequence is so vast and so apparently unconscious that the dialogue and the lyrics deserve to be immortalized in the cement in front of Grauman's Chinese.

1776 is a hymn to self-righteous commerce. Stone and Edwards have the kind of commitment you can take to the bank. This show had to be made into a movie; where but in Hollywood do they put crests and monograms on hair shirts? *1776* probably can't fail, because it has those gulping, throat-clogging emotions for the suckers. I guess this is a movie for people like the Sally Kellerman nurse in *M*A*S*H* before she snapped out of it — for the Regular Army clowns and their liberal-clown cousins. Why else are the two women turned into lyrical, hair-flowing Jeanette MacDonalds, so soft-focus, ultra-wonderful feminine that you feel Sigmund Romberg will rise and write "One Alone" all over again? W. C. Fields would have eaten them both for breakfast. Blythe Danner is pretty, and Ken Howard is a little more restrained than most of the others, but what does it matter? The dumb, crusty jocularity had me shrinking in my seat. The whole damned thing has the emasculated, giggly tone that passes for clean family entertainment; it may go on to reap millions and collect awards. Can this show really please multitudes of Americans? Have we lost the capacity for knowing when we're insulted?

❖

"THE FRED ASTAIRE & GINGER ROGERS BOOK," by Arlene Croce, has verve and wit, like the series of musicals it covers. Movie criticism suffered a loss when, in the mid-sixties, Miss Croce abandoned the field and gave most of her energies to dance criticism; now she has joined her two major talents. No one has ever described dance in movies the way she does: she's a slangy, elegant writer; her compressed descriptions are evocative and analytic at the same time, and so precise and fresh that while bringing the pleasure of the dances back she adds to it. There is a sense of pressure in her style that has something like the tension and pull of the dances themselves. Her descriptions are original and imperially brusque in a way that keeps the reader alert; one responds to her writing kinesthetically, as if it were dance. This small book, published this week by Outerbridge & Lazard, and about half text, half photographs (with two flip-page dances, of which one is effective, the other badly cropped), is a history of the team and an assessment of its place in dance and movie history, and also an acute examination of how movies were made in the factory-system days. We learn who did what on those musicals and how they "happened," and yet, just as Astaire never lets you see the hard work, so that his dances appear to be spontaneous, Miss Croce doesn't present the history as history; she lets it come in casually, jauntily, as she covers the series of films, fitting the background material to the illustrated section on each movie. There are times when one may want her to expand on a point or explain, but the reward of her brevity is the same achieved nonchalance that she prizes in these movies; it comes out of her controlled ecstatic response to the dances. Here is a sentence of Miss Croce's on Astaire in the "I Won't Dance" number from *Roberta:*

Two big Cossacks have to carry him protesting onto the dance floor, and there he does his longest and most absorbing solo of the series so far, full of stork-legged steps on toe, wheeling pirouettes in which he seems to be winding one leg around the other, and those ratcheting tap clusters that fall like loose change from his pockets.

And here a fragment on Astaire's singles:

With him, a dance impulse and a dramatic motive seem to be indivisible and spontaneous, so that we get that little kick of imaginative sympathy every time he changes the rhythm or the speed or the pressure of a step. And though we don't perceive the dance as "drama," the undertone of motivation continually sharpens and refreshes our interest in what we do see.

And, on the pair in "Let's Face the Music and Dance," from *Follow the Fleet:*

The mood is awesomely grave. The dance is one of their simplest and most daring, the steps mostly walking steps done with a slight retard. The withheld impetus makes the dance look dragged by destiny, all the quick little circling steps pulled as if on a single thread.

Every few sentences, you're stopped by the audacity of a description or by some new piece of information; we learn what that mysterious name Van Nest Polglase in the credits actually meant, and of the writing contribution of Laurette Taylor's son, Dwight Taylor, and we get such footnotes to social history as this, from the section on *Top Hat:*

The most quoted line in the film is the motto of the House of Beddini, delivered with supreme flourish by Erik Rhodes: "For the women the kiss, for the men the sword." This was originally written, "For the men the sword, for the women the whip," and was changed when the Hays office objected.

I doubt if anyone else will ever love Astaire the dancer and creator as fully as this author: the book is a homage to him and the simplicity and mastery he represents. Miss Croce documents how he choreographed the dances — improvising them with Hermes Pan, with Pan doing Rogers' steps and later training her to do them. ("With Fred I'd be Ginger," Pan says, "and with Ginger I'd be Fred." After the dances were photographed, Hermes Pan usually dubbed in the taps for her as well.) It was Astaire himself who controlled the shooting, and he insisted that each dance be recorded in a single shot, without fakery, and without the usual cuts to the reactions of onlookers. But sometimes the ideal of "perfection within a single shot" — the dance just as it would be done for a live audience, so that moviegoers would see it as if from the best seats in a theater — wasn't attained. There is a cut toward the close of the "Never Gonna Dance" number, in *Swing Time*; Miss Croce explains that it "may have been one of the few Astaire-Rogers dances that couldn't be filmed entirely in one continuous shot, for its climax, a spine-chilling series of pirouettes by Rogers, took forty takes to accomplish, and in the middle of shooting Rogers' feet began to bleed."

For Miss Croce, in the best Astaire-and-Rogers films *(The Gay Divorcée, Roberta, Top Hat, Follow the Fleet, Swing Time)* something happened that "never happened in movies again" — "dancing was transformed into a vehicle of serious emotion between a man and a woman." And from this, I think, flow my disagreements with her. We have had many happy arguments about dance and movies; I suspect that they hinge on temperament. Miss Croce (she is the editor of *Ballet Review*) is a perfectionist — a romantic perfectionist. I, too, find Astaire and Rogers rapturous together, but Miss Croce's romanticism about the two leads her to ascribe a *dance* perfection to them. I think that Astaire's dry buoyancy comes through best in his solos, which are more exciting dances than the romantic ballroom numbers with Rogers. Miss Croce says Rogers' "technique became exactly what she needed in order to dance with Fred Astaire, and, as no other woman in movies ever did, she created the feeling that stirs us so deeply when we see them together: Fred need not be alone." Well, that's maybe a bit much. Of Rogers in a rare tap solo (on "Let Yourself Go," in *Follow the Fleet*), she writes, "It's easy to underrate Rogers' dancing because she never appeared to be working hard. . . . She avoided any suggestion of toil or inadequacy. She was physically incapable of ugliness." But she was certainly capable of *clumsiness* when she danced with Astaire, and you can see that she *is* working hard. She doesn't always look comfortable doing the steps — her arms are out of kilter, or she's off balance. And, from Miss Croce's own account of how the dances were devised, you can see why: If Astaire had improvised the choreography with Rogers instead of with Hermes Pan, Rogers would probably have worked out things that came more easily and naturally to her, and you wouldn't have the sense you often get — that it's too difficult for her and she's doing her damnedest just to get the steps right. Rogers, of course, who was making three pictures to each one of Astaire's, was too valuable a property of R.K.O.'s to be spared for these sessions (even if the men had wanted her, which is doubtful). A ballet dancer, whose technique is set in training, can accept the choreography of others far more easily than a pop dancer. In the case of this team, Astaire, with his winged body, his weightless, essentially bodiless style, devised his own personal balletistic jazz form of dance, and then Ginger Rogers had to try to fit into it. But her clumsiness is rather ingratiating; it isn't *bad,* and the choreography and the whole feeling of their dances is so romantically appealing that you don't *mind* Ginger's dancing. We don't care if Ginger Rogers isn't a *superb* dancer. (The team might be boringly ethereal if she were.) It's part of Ginger's personality that she's a tiny bit klutzy. Yes, she has that beautiful figure, which Miss Croce rightly admires, but there is also the slight grossness of her face and her uncultivated voice. What makes Ginger Rogers so unsettling, so *alive,* on the screen is the element of insensitivity and the happy, wide streak of commonness in a person of so much talent. Maybe it's her greatest asset that she always seems to have a wad of gum in her mouth. I don't mean to suggest that Miss Croce is unaware of this side of Ginger Rogers (she's at her satirical best on Rogers as an actress, and there really isn't much that Arlene Croce is unaware of) — only that she and I view it differently. Miss Croce sees it as what was *overcome* in the dance — "Astaire would turn her into a goddess"; she believes Rogers was transformed, that she "turned from brass to gold under his touch." Sure, she was Cinderella at the ball, but we still thought of her as the spunky, funny, slightly pie-faced chorus girl trying to keep up with him. Rogers seems most fully herself to me in the comic hoofing showing-off numbers, and that's when I love her dancing best; in the more decorous simulated passion of the dramatic dances with Astaire, she's not that different from other fancy ballroom dancers — she's not quite Ginger.

Miss Croce takes their dancing perhaps a bit too seriously, seeing it not just as heavenly romance or — as perhaps many of us did — as a dream of a date but as something more: "Astaire in his flying tails, the pliant Rogers in one of her less-is-more gowns, were an erotic vision that audiences beheld in the electric silence of the dance. Everyone knew what was happening in these dances." But how could Fred Astaire be erotic? Fred Astaire has no flesh, and I think the only conceivable "eroticism" in their dances is a sort of transfigured view of courtship and romance, a fantasy of being swept off one's feet.

I suspect it is this *Camelot* view that leads Miss Croce to be rather unfair to Gene Kelly. She says, "The major difference between Astaire and Kelly is a difference, not of talent or technique, but of levels of sophistication." I should say the difference starts with their bodies. If you compare Kelly to Astaire, accepting Astaire's debonaire style as perfection, then, of course, Kelly looks bad. But in popular dance forms, in which movement is not rigidly codified, as it is in ballet, perfection is a romantic myth or a figure of speech, nothing more. Kelly isn't a winged dancer; he's a hoofer, and more earthbound. But he has warmth and range as an actor. Kelly's "natural," unaffected line readings, in a gentle, unactorish voice, probably come from the same basic sense of timing that leads Astaire to the clocked, tapped-out readings. Kelly's inflections are subtle and delicate, while his acting is slightly larger than life. He leaps into a simple scene, always "on" (as "on" as Cagney), distinctively eager and with a chesty, athletic, overdramatic exuberance that makes audiences feel good. Though there was something moist and too exposed in the young Judy Garland, Kelly and Garland, both emotional performers, had a special rapport based on tenderness. They could bring conviction to banal love scenes (as in *Summer Stock*) and make them naïvely fresh. They balanced each other's talents: she joined her odd and undervalued cakewalker's prance to his large-spirited hoofing, and he joined his odd, light, high voice to her sweet, good, deep one. Their duets (such as "You Wonderful You," in *Summer Stock,* and the title song in *For Me and My Gal*) have a plaintive richness unlike anything in the Astaire-Rogers pictures. They could really sing together; Astaire and Rogers couldn't, despite Astaire's skill and charm when he sang alone. Astaire's grasshopper lightness was his limitation as an actor — confining him to perennial gosh-oh-gee adolescence; he was always and only a light comedian and could function only in fairy-tale vehicles. Miss Croce, for whom ballet is the highest form of dance, sees the highest, subtlest emotional resonances in the most stylized forms. I don't think she's wrong in her basic valuation of Astaire and Rogers, but she's too exclusive about it: she has set up an ideal based on Astaire which denies the value of whatever he didn't have.

What it comes down to is that Miss Croce, as in her discussion of Astaire and Rogers in *Swing Time,* sees "the dance as love, the lovers as dancers"; in a funny way, Astaire and Rogers are both too likable for that, and it's the wrong kind of glorification of their frivolous mixture of romance and comedy — a fan's deification. Astaire and Rogers were fortunate: they embodied the swing-music, white-telephone, streamlined era before the Second World War, when frivolousness wasn't decadent and when adolescents dreamed that "going out" was dressing up and becoming part of a beautiful world of top hats and silver lamé. It was a lovely dream, and perhaps Miss Croce still dreams it. A possible indication of the degenerative effects of movies on our good sense is that a writer with a first-class mind can say of Astaire, after the partnership ended, "He never ceased to dance wonderfully and he has had some good dancing partners. But it is a world of sun without a moon." However, it is also because of such swoony romanticism that this writer has brought her full resources to bear on the kind of subject that generally attracts pinheads. I think it's perfectly safe to say that this is the best book that will ever be written about Astaire and Rogers.

[November 25, 1972]

Notes on Black Movies

PEGGY PETTITT, the young heroine of the new film *Black Girl,* doesn't have a white girl's conformation; she's attractive in a different way. That may not seem so special, but after you've seen a lot of black movies, you know how special it is. The action thrillers feature heroes and heroines who are dark-tanned Anglo-Saxons, so to speak — and not to lure whites (who don't go anyway) but to lure blacks whose ideas of beauty are based on white stereotypes. If there is one area in which the cumulative effect of Hollywood films is obvious, it is in what is now considered "pretty" or "handsome" or "cute" *globally;* the mannequins in shopwindows the world over have pert, piggy little faces.

In the mock-documentary *Farewell Uncle Tom,* the Italian moviemakers aren't content with simulating the historically recorded horrors of slavery; they invent *outré* ones, including a slave-breeding farm, so they can mix prurience with their piety about how white Americans are the scum of the universe. On this farm, white Southerners call the black babies "pups," and a slender, sensitive young black girl is mated with a huge, shackled Wild Man of Borneo stud while the white owners watch. In order to make us aware of the outrage, the film selects for the terrified girl a black *jeune fille* who resembles Audrey Hepburn. Presumably, if she had larger features we might think the drooling, snarling stud just right for her.

"BLACK GIRL" is too touching to be considered bad. It is derivative, and its crude techniques seem almost deliberately naïve in the sophisticated medium of modern sound-and-color films, but there is something here struggling to be heard. The film is trying to express a young girl's need to free herself from the patterns of ghetto apathy; it's trying to express black experiences while encased in an inappropriate, TV-shopworn, domestic-drama form (J. E. Franklin's own adaptation of her Off Broadway play). The struggle seems anachronistic. Not just because the cumbrous structure that is falsifying the experiences is the well-made second-rate serious play of thirty years ago, the sort of play that has never got by on the screen (though it still occasionally turns up: *The Subject Was Roses, I Never Sang for My Father*), but because the whole attempt represents the birth pangs of honest and idealistic black moviemaking—which is like witnessing the birth of something that has already died. *Black Girl* arrives when, after just two years, black movies have reached the same stage of corruption as white punch-'em-and-stick-'em-and-shoot-'em action movies. It isn't in the class of *Sounder;* it's faltering and clumsy, yet the black audience enjoyed it, and, in a way, I did, too — I liked watching the people on the screen. They embody different backgrounds and different strategies for survival, and the phenomenal strength of the older actresses in the cast said more than the script itself. However, in casting the older roles and in breaking with the white conventions of beauty by giving Peggy Pettitt the leading role, Ossie Davis, who directed, may not have realized what he was doing to Leslie Uggams, who is also in the picture. Her role requires her to be a model of strength, but Miss Uggams, a TV cutie and a stereotype of the prettiness accepted in the media, seems shrivelled and trivialized by that prettiness. A movie that tries to deal with matriarchal black family life, and that features the rich talent of Louise Stubbs as well as that powerhouse Claudia McNeil, can't accommodate media models.

Ossie Davis also directed the first black hit, *Cotton Comes to Harlem,* in 1970 — an ingenuous detective comedy that was like a folkloric version of an early-thirties movie. When a sexy black siren outsmarted a white cop by stealing his pants, it was a silly, naïve joke — the tables being turned, and a white man being ridiculed the way black men onscreen used to be. The racial humor might have been considered vilely insulting from a white director, but the picture began to suggest the freshness that black performers could bring to movies—just as Ossie Davis himself, when he acted in such movies as *The Hill* and *The Scalphunters,* brought a stronger presence to his roles than white actors did, and a deeper joy. What a face for the camera! He was a natural king, as Louise Stubbs is a natural queen. There seemed to be a good chance that black talent on the screen, on TV, in literature, and in the theater would infuse new life into the whole culture, the way jazz entered American music and changed the beat of American life.

But then the white businessmen saw the buying power of blacks and how easy it would be to do black versions of what was already being done. And they took over, along with the black businessmen-artists, and so we have separate cultures — black-*macho* movies and white-*macho* movies, equally impoverished, equally debased. But movies of this kind are not the only ones that deal with white experience, while for blacks they are virtually all there is. Right now, there are more than fifty in the planning stages or in production, of which about half will probably be completed.

This has happened at the same time that black performers on TV and in movies have got close to us, just as white performers in the past got close to blacks. Despite racial fears, whites obviously accept black performers as part of American life, and respond to them in a new way. (I am told that big-city white families with several kids often have a black child; that is, a kid who wants so badly to be black that he or she talks as if he were, so that if you overhear him you assume he *is* black.)

IF THE FREEDOM OF BLACKS has always involved a sexual threat to white men — who fear that their wives and daughters would prefer blacks, and imagine that for blacks freedom means primarily sleeping with white women, and turning them into whores — the black-*macho* movies have exploited retaliatory black fantasies. The heroes sleep with gorgeous white girls, treating them with casual contempt. They can have any white women they want, but they have no attachment to them; they have steady gorgeous black girls to count on in time of trouble. They act out the white men's worst fears: fully armed and sexually as indomitable as James Bond, they take the white men's women and cast them off.

The black superstud has very different overtones for the black audience from what Bond or Matt Helm had for mixed audiences, because the black movies are implicitly saying to the black audience, "See, we really *are* what the whites are afraid of; they have reason to be afraid of our virility." One would have to be a little foolish to take offense at this when it so obviously serves an ego need, and there's a good deal of humor (and justice) in acting out the white man's fears. (That movie ad showing creamy Raquel Welch's embrace of Jim Brown's beautiful black chest was a great erotic joke.) But there are times when the black hero's condescension to the white women who are eager for his favors becomes mean and confused — when the white women are so downgraded that it seems as if only a stupid, shallow white tramp could want a black man. Whose fantasy is this? The contempt for white women can be really foul. In *Sweet Sweetback's Baadasssss Song*, the police break into a room where a black man and a white woman are in bed together; the police beat the man while the woman watches and smiles with pleasure. The scene is racist at fairly low levels, since it assumes that the white woman has no feelings (except sadistic ones) about the man she has been making love to — because he's black. But this movie, like the others, posits a black-stud virility, which should insure *some* feeling. Probably the author-director, Melvin Van Peebles, couldn't resist the chance to score an ideological racist point, and what he's saying is that black men shouldn't waste themselves on white women, who are nothing but vicious little beasts, using them.

ALL WEAPONRY HAD BECOME PHALLIC in the James Bond pictures, and in the ads for *The Silencers* Dean Martin rode his trusty automatic while girls crowded around him; the black movies feature not only the sexual prowess and the big guns of their black heroes but also an implicit "Anything you can do we can do better." The weapons in the black-*macho* movie ads are a big phallic put-on, but they're also real avengers; they announce to blacks that now we've really got our own. (They're probably also a very effective deterrent to attendance by white males, and the action genre has never attracted many white women. It's not surprising that so few whites go to black-*macho* movies: they know the show isn't meant for them, and it's very uncomfortable to be there.) The heroes are sex-and-power symbols for an audience that has been looking at white symbols, and so the heroes are revenge figures as well. Sex means you can get anybody you want, and power is what comes out of a gun, and money is the key to everything. You can even buy your way out of your life, change your way of living, if you've got enough money — as in the fantasy of *Super Fly.* These movies say that the white man had his turn to play God and now it's ours. But the movies are controlled by white men, and a big gun is a *macho* kid's idea of power.

THESE FILMS SAY that the smart black man gets what the white man has: the luxury goods of a consumer society, including luscious broads. The hero of *Super Fly* is told that his "eight-track stereo and color TV in every room" are "the American dream." These films say that there is nothing but consumerism, so grab what you can; what's good enough for the white man is good enough for you. The message is the exact opposite of the Martin Luther King message; he said, in essence, that you must not let the white man degrade you to his level. King wanted something better for blacks than the consumer-media society. Since his death, if black people have been dreaming of something better the media have blotted it from sight. That dream has been Shafted, Hammered, Slaughtered.

WARTIME PROPAGANDA FILMS did to the Germans and the Japanese what is done to whites in these films — turned them into every available stereotype of evil. Whites are made treacherous, cowardly, hypocritical, and often sexually perverse; the subsidiary black villains are often sexually kinky, too. And these movies are often garishly anti-homosexual; homosexuality seems to stand for weakness and crookedness — "corruption." They have already developed some classic clichés: they feature blacks beating up white men with excessive zeal, and very likely the white villain will rasp "Nigger!" just before the black hero finishes him off (something many a black has probably dreamed of doing when he was called "nigger"). Except when we were at war, there has never been such racism in American films. There have been numberless varieties of condescension and insult, but nothing like this — not since D. W. Griffith made the one terrible mistake of his life in *The Birth of a Nation*, when he showed a black man attempting to rape a young Southern girl, a mistake that shocked the country into awareness of the dangerous power of the emerging art. Only in wartime (and immediately after, in dealing with war themes) have Hollywood movies used this primitive power to encourage hatred of a race or a national group.

The obvious conclusion would seem to be that black people are using the screen to incite race war, but if one examines how the films are made it's apparent that the white companies are making the films for profit, and that the blacks involved are mostly boastful yet defensive about the content. The archetypal black superhero Shaft was, admittedly, lifted out of Dashiell Hammett by Ernest Tidyman, the white writer who got an Academy Award for his screenplay for *The French Connection*; he had tried to latch on to an earlier movement with his book *Flower Power*. These movies use black resentment to turn blacks on to the excitement of getting back at whites; the racism is a slant, a shtick. *Super Fly*, in which the cocaine-hustler hero puts down two weakling black civil-rights representatives who are trying to raise money by telling them that he won't be interested until they buy guns to shoot the whites — a speech calculated to crush the finky, cowardly pair and to get cheers from the audience (and it did when I saw the film) — was produced by a white man (Sig Shore) and is distributed by Warner Brothers, a company headed by a white liberal (Ted Ashley), who probably contributes to civil-rights organizations. With only a few exceptions (*Sweetback* is one), the black films are packaged, financed, and sold by whites, who let the black actors or directors serve as spokesmen for the therapeutic function these films are said to have for the black community — by creating black heroes. Do people actually make movies for therapeutic purposes? Only if wealth can be considered a form of therapy. When their arguments are challenged by CORE and other black groups, the spokesmen generally say that these films are at least providing jobs and training for black actors and technicians, who will then be able to do something better. But when a movie is made that isn't pure exploitation, they can't resist sniping at it and pointing to their own huge grosses as proof that they're giving blacks the right entertainment. This is what big-money success does to people; they want honors, too. The black artists who want to do something worth doing find themselves up against what white artists in films are up against, and with less training and less to bargain with.

If there's anything to learn from the history of movies, it's that corruption leads to further corruption, not to innocence. And that each uncorrupted work must fight against the accumulated effects of the pop appeal of corruption. How is it going to be possible to reach black audiences after they have been so pummelled with cynical consumerism that any other set of values seems hypocritical and phony — a con?

EXPLOITING BLACK RAGE is a dangerous game, but the stakes are high for men like Jim Aubrey (president of M-G-M) and Ted Ashley and their competitors. The movies are made on the cheap, on B-picture budgets, and the profits are enormous. *Shaft,* which cost just over a million dollars, is credited with "saving" M-G-M, though the slick black shoot-'em-ups *(Cool Breeze, Melinda)* and the white action films *(Skyjacked)* that Aubrey is picking up or producing are far removed from what probably comes to mind when one thinks of the salvation of M-G-M. (Aubrey's triumph as head of the C.B.S. television network was *The Beverly Hillbillies.*) Warner Brothers bought and released *Super Fly,* which cost well under a half million dollars and has grossed over twelve million, and Warners is now producing its sequel.

Black films are not recapitulating film history; they went immediately from the cradle to this slick exploitation level. For the movie companies, blackness is a funky new twist — an inexpensive way to satisfy the audience that has taken over the big downtown theatres now deserted by the white middle classes. Jokers are now calling Broadway "The Great Black Way."

AMONG THE QUEASIEST RACIST RATIONALES for a black hero yet is the plot device in *Super Fly* that allows the cocaine hustler (and user, who is also a pimp) to be a black hero: the cocaine he sells goes to whites. This is not only a strange rationale (particularly for a movie produced by a white man and distributed by Warner Brothers) but a highly specious one. The nonfiction book *Dealer,* Richard Woodley's "portrait of a cocaine merchant," reads almost like the script of *Super Fly,* except that the dealer, who is black, is selling to blacks, because, he explains, a black man dealing downtown would be dangerously conspicuous. In this book, as in the movie, the dealer dreams of getting enough loot to get out of the grind, but in the book it's perfectly clear that he can't — that there's no way. It's easy to see why a fantasy movie made for entertainment and profit should turn him into a winner who fulfills his dreams, and certainly the black audience enjoys his triumph over the white homosexual Mr. Big. And, yes, it's easy to see why the movie made him a man of "principle," who is selling to whites, not blacks, even though it's pretty funny to think that dope hustlers are principled about black people. But the self-righteousness of the men getting rich on this movie is unclean.

THE MOST SPECIFIC and rabid incitement to race war comes in *Farewell Uncle Tom,* a product of the sordid imaginations of Gualtiero Jacopetti and Franco Prosperi, whose previous films include *Mondo Cane, Women of the World,* and *Africa Addio.* Bought for this country by the Cannon Releasing Corporation (*Joe* and soft-core exploitation porn), it had to be toned down, because theater operators were afraid to show a movie featuring a fictional re-creation of slavery, from slave ship to plantation life, and concluding with modern blacks butchering middle-class whites in their homes. The movie, set in the United States but shot mostly in Haiti, was trimmed, and some new scenes were added, so that what was expected to be "the ultimate exploitation vehicle" could be released without violence and damage within the theaters themselves. The limited partnership formed by Cannon's young chairman and president, Dennis Friedland, to acquire the film includes Evan R. Collins, Jr., Richard Heinlein, Victor Ferencko, Marvin Friedlander, Thomas Israel, Michael Graham, Arthur Lipper, James Rubin, and Steve Wichek; I doubt if any of them are black. There must have been considerable fear of a public outcry about the film, because when they finally opened it a few weeks ago they did so with a minimum of publicity.

The film, which purports to be a "documentary" of exactly what America was like in the days of slavery, includes, in addition to the slave-breeding farm, Southern white women rolling in the hay with their young slaves, a group rape with children watching, and a bizarrely fanciful sequence in which blacks in cages are used for mad scientific experiments, and all this is thrown together with scenes on board a slave ship which can't help affecting you. One's outrage at the voyeuristic hypocrisy of the movie gets all tangled up with one's emotions about the suffering people on the ship. No one has ever before attempted a full-scale treatment of slave-ship misery; how degrading to us all that by default it has fallen into the hands of perhaps the most devious and irresponsible filmmakers who have ever lived. They use their porno fantasies as part of the case they make for the slaughter of the whites, who are shown as pasty-face cartoons, then and now. It becomes the blacks' duty to kill whites. "He was a white and so he had to die," Nat Turner says as he kills a man who has been good to him, and then the film cites Eldridge Cleaver and the Black Panthers and cuts to a modern black on a beach staring at disgusting whites. Unlike the black hits, the film lacks a central figure for the audience to identify with, but the black audience in the theater was highly responsive to Jacopetti's and Prosperi's fraudulent ironies, and in the ads are quotes from black papers saying, "An all time great gut-busting flick," and "Don't miss *Farewell Uncle Tom,* it is must viewing. Eyeball-to-eyeball confrontation with stark reality and chilling candor." Since the anticipated outcry did not develop, and the film, chopped up and sneaked in as it was, didn't do the expected business, it has been withdrawn, to be brought back in the new year with a new publicity campaign.

THE MOVIE HUSTLERS — big-studio and little — are about as principled as cocaine hustlers. There is a message implicit in *Super Fly* — everyone is a crook, and we all just want what's best (most profiable) for us — and when the hero pulls off his half-million-dollar haul of cocaine the audience cheers. That's the practicing ethic of the movie business; that's what it lives by, and it gets its cheers from stockholders and the media whenever it pulls off a big box-office haul like *Super Fly.* By now, if a black film isn't racist, the white press joins in the chorus of the exploitation filmmakers who claim it's a film not for black people but for white liberals. That's how fast racism can become respectable when it's lucrative.

ARE THE BLACKS who participate in these movies naïve enough to believe that they are directing rage only against whites? Since what is being peddled is a consumer value system and a total contempt for ethics or principles, why should the young blacks in the audience make the nice discrimination of the hero of *Super Fly*? Cheat and rob and kill only whites? Surely, when you glorify pragmatic cynicism blacks in the audience can take the next step; they already know there's less risk in stealing from other blacks and in terrorizing the poor.

When a popular culture is as saturated in violent cynicism as ours, and any values held up to oppressed people are treated with derision as the white man's con, or an Uncle Tom's con, the cynicism can't fail to have its effect on us all. What M-G-M and Warner Brothers and all the rest are now selling is nothing less than soul murder, and body murder, too.

[December 2, 1972]

New Thresholds, New Anatomies

NOTHING IS AS RARE in American movies now as comedy with a director's style and personality. Elaine May finds her comic tone in *The Heartbreak Kid,* and she scores a first, besides: No American woman director has ever before directed her daughter in a leading role. As Lila, Jeannie Berlin not only is her mother's surrogate but plays the Elaine May addled nymph probably better than Elaine May could on the screen. As a performer, Elaine May is slightly withdrawn; the faint distraught hesitancy in her delivery is part of her out-of-it persona. Jeannie Berlin, an actress playing an out-of-it character, can go much further. Lila is a middle-class Jewish peasant, her ripe lusciousness a cartoon of sensuality. You can read her life story in her face and her gypsy-red dresses; she is too open to hide anything, too dumb to know she has anything to hide. *The Heartbreak Kid* starts from a good comic idea: a man on his honeymoon falls in love with another girl. Lila is the eager, bulging bride; Charles Grodin's Lenny is the bridegroom. At Miami Beach, three days after the wedding, he sees Kelly, a golden girl from Minneapolis — Cybill Shepherd, the cool American dream. She plays Daisy to his Gatsby, or, to be more exact, the Wasp princess to his Jewish go-getter.

Lenny turns out to be more complicated, more guileful — and nuttier — than we first suspect. That's what makes the story more than a skit — that, and Miss May's direction. The script, by Neil Simon, is a good one; I swallow deeply as I say it, because I despise most of the movies made from his plays. I find it nightmarish to sit in a movie house and listen to Neil Simon's one-liners being shot back and forth; at the movies, *who* says a line is very important, but with Neil Simon's vaudeville snappers what matters is that they come on schedule. The actors are stand-up comics grimacing and gesticulating in a vacuum. (At the movie of *The Odd Couple,* I became fixated on the greenish walls of the apartment the two men lived in; I don't remember the bad jokes — just the sense of suffocation.) But Neil Simon also has some talent; there were unobjectionably funny scenes in the screenplay he did in the mid-sixties for the patchy De Sica-Peter Sellers *After the Fox,* and this new script, from the Bruce Jay Friedman story "A Change of Plan," has, as it is directed here, almost none of his Broadway whiplash.

Elaine May has the rarest kind of comic gift: the ability to create a world seen comically. Her satirist's malice isn't cutting; something in the befuddled atmosphere she creates keeps it mild — yet mild in a thoroughly demented way, mild as if impervious to sanity. It may be a trait of some witty women to be apologetic about the cruelty that is inherent in their wit; Miss May, all apologies, has a knack for defusing the pain without killing the joke. The dialogue sounds natural and unforced. The humor sneaks up on you, and it's surprisingly even-handed and democratic; everybody in the picture is a little cockeyed. Your laughter isn't harsh, since you can see that poor Lila, the bride of five days, sitting in a seafood restaurant and clutching Lenny to keep from collapsing while he tells her it's all over, is perhaps less mad than Lenny, who is so carried away by his new dreams of Wasp glory that he won't even let her go throw up. He almost seems to expect her to share his excitement. You knew she was empty-headed, and you were identifying with him; now you begin to see what's in his head.

Elaine May's tone often verges on the poignant (and is best when it does), but there are unkillable demons in her characters, and you never know what you'll discover next. Working almost entirely through the actors, she lets those demons come to the surface in a scene before she moves on. The characters don't seem to be middle-class survivors (though they are) — they seem to be crazy people in leaking boats, like other people. She supplies a precarious element of innocence that removes them from Simon's pandering, hard-core humor. Simon himself may be far more innocent than seems possible for a man who admits to earning a million and a half a year, but it's in a different way. The innocence in her comic world is a form of ambivalent affection for the characters, while Simon's innocence is in his belief in pleasing the audience — his innocence is what is corrupting his work. She's a satirist; he is the audience's fool.

Official jester to the middle-class mass audience, Simon degrades it, on its own sufferance. In his plays, the characters are often greedy and crude, but Simon isn't satirizing them; he's milking them for laughs. Millions of people accept his view, but some of us can't — we're appalled by this comfy vision of an acquisitive, never satisfied society. People who enjoy Neil Simon's work say that we snobbishly reject anything that gives people a good time. But what we reject is that people can be given a good time by *this*: lechery and greed and impotence domesticated by wisecracks. It is the audience's readiness to see itself mirrored in Neil Simon's plays that freezes even the dumb laughs his jokes could pull out of us. Like a fully assimilated Jewish comic (which is essentially what he is), he's now at one with his target; he sends the audience home reconciled to a depersonalized bourgeois meanness. Elaine May keeps the best of Neil Simon but takes the laugh-and-accept-your-coarseness out of it. She reveals without complacency, and so the congratulatory slickness of Neil Simon is gone. Lila and Lenny and Kelly have inadequate dreams; they're on their way to missing out because of these tinkly little dreams. In this sense, they're younger editions of the middle-aged failures Simon has been writing about in his latest plays. Cybill Shepherd's Kelly, the magazine-cover ideal, is a daddy's girl and an efficient tease; Lenny, pursuing one decrepit dream after another, is a classic American climber. But Elaine May humanizes them, and she doesn't send you home reconciled to their self-love. *The Heartbreak Kid* is anarchically skeptical about the ways in which people bamboozle themselves; it gets at the unexpected perversity in that self-love.

Charles Grodin and Jeannie Berlin are like a new, fresh Nichols and May, but a Nichols and May with the range of actors. Grodin is a master of revue-style moods, and Lenny, the warped hero, is alternately bashful and brash, while Miss Berlin uses revue skills to burst through to a wilder, more vivid comic range. She looks so much like Elaine May that it's as if we were seeing the Elaine May comic mask but with real blood coursing through her — revue acting with temperament, revue brought to voluptuously giddy life. As the contrasting siren, Cybill Shepherd embodies her role but isn't given much to act; she is certainly not a deadbeat actress, like Candice Bergen or Ali MacGraw, but the movie doesn't bring anything new out in her. We never really see why (or when) Kelly is drawn to Lenny, and most of the Wasps in the film don't have the dimensions of the New York Jewish characters. Eddie Albert, as Kelly's father, works hard at pigheadedness, and it's an amusing idea to have Kelly's mother (Audra Lindley) sweetly suggestible — so docile in her openness to ideas that she's practically an idiot — but there isn't enough dissonance in these people. It may have seemed enough for the conception for Cybill Shepherd to be as gorgeously narcissistic as in her

TV-commercial appearances, and with that sexy suggestion of surliness in the Bacall curly lips, but the movie would be richer if we got to know how Kelly might suffer; there's no contrast to her vacuousness. However, the only actual flaw is that the picture just sort of expires, with an undersized "thought-provoking" ending when we're expecting something outrageous that would clarify the hero's new quandary. What's worse, we can sense that the moviemakers didn't know how to end it. But this indecisive ending isn't as disastrous as it would be in a Simon play, in which everything is explicit. Elaine May's work has a note of uncertainty about people and their fates — things may change at any minute, you feel — and so an ambiguous ending isn't jarring, just a little disappointing.

It's always difficult to try to seduce people into going to see a comedy without giving away some of its humor, and in this case I risk damaging the pleasures of *The Heartbreak Kid* by overpraise. It is a *slight* film but a charming one. I guess what I like best about it is that although Miss May's touch is very sure (and although the picture is, technically, in a different league from her wobbly first movie, *A New Leaf;* I mean it isn't shot in murko-color, and the framing of the action — the whole look of it — is professional), sureness in her doesn't mean that mechanical, overemphatic style which is the bane of recent American comedy and is Broadway's worst legacy to the movies. That crackling, whacking style is always telling you that things are funnier than you see them to be. Elaine May underplays her hand. The element of uncertainty that results in a shambles when she isn't on top of the situation as a director can, as in this case, where she's functioning well, result in a special, distracted comic tone, which implies that you can't always tell what's funny. It is uncertainty as a comic attitude — a punchiness that comes from seeing life as a series of booby traps.

"THE POSEIDON ADVENTURE" is about an ocean liner that turns turtle. The suspense is in the method of escape and the narrowing number of survivors; you watch as fate ticks them off in photogenically horrible ways — engulfing water, flames, scalding liquids, falling chandeliers. In order to lend a movie cataclysm some spiritual importance, it is customary to clue us in on who will perish and who will survive by making the former cowardly, life-denying types and the latter courageous and life-enhancing, and so the hero, Gene Hackman, is a robust, forward-looking radical clergyman. This hallowed, wheezing formula can be hilariously inappropriate, but here it's just a drag, since it makes the picture lofty when we want it to get right to the vulgar bravado inherent in its

Grand Hotel approach to the romance of catastrophe. The movie is advertised in terms of Oscars ("In the cast and staff there is a total of fifteen of these precious golden statuettes"), but it's a lackluster bunch we see. The picture would be more fun if we cared about who got killed and who survived; there's a lot of Red Buttons (one Oscar, but not my candidate for survival). The only loss I regretted for an instant was Roddy McDowall; on the other hand, it was a wise decision to dump Arthur O'Connell early. We could certainly do with less of the antique feminine hysteria that slows down the action, especially since we can see perfectly well that the girls (Stella Stevens, Carol Lynley, and Pamela Sue Martin) are there for the splendor of their rear ends as the camera follows them climbing ladders toward safety. Shelley Winters (two Oscars) yearns to see her grandson in Israel and makes endless jokes about her bloated appearance. (She's so enormously fat she goes way beyond the intention to create a warm, sympathetic Jewish character. It's like having a whale tell you you should love her because she's Jewish.) The script is the true cataclysm. The writers, Stirling Silliphant and Wendell Mayes, don't do anything for the actors, and they don't provide a speck of originality. Their attempt to turn Stella Stevens, as a former prostitute, and Ernest Borgnine, as her police-lieutenant husband, into the Jean Harlow-Wallace Beery pair of *Dinner at Eight* merely exposes how mangy their writing is. Only once do they achieve true camp: just before the ship capsizes, a crewman says to the captain (Leslie Nielson), "I never saw anything like it — an enormous wall of water coming toward us." Ronald Neame directs about the same way Leslie Nielson acts — stalwart, dull — and the special effects, literal and mostly full-scale, have none of the eerie beauty of early-movie catastrophes designed in miniature and employing illusions (as they were by the Ufa technicians). There's no beauty anywhere in this movie, but as a dumb, square adventure story — expensive pop primitivism manufactured for the *Airport* market — it is honestly what it is, and the logistics of getting out of an upside-down ship are fairly entertaining. That enormous wall of water hits while the characters are celebrating New Year's Eve. Ah, movie men and their exquisite calculations! How much does it add to the TV sale if a picture can be shown on holidays from here unto eternity?

MAKING HIS DÉBUT as a motion-picture producer with *Child's Play,* David Merrick does not exactly arrive in style; in fact, it's hard to believe he traveled first class. The Robert Marasco play is a stylish bit of artifice — evil on the loose in a Catholic boarding school for boys. The trouble with this kind of Victorian gothic job is that there's never any way to resolve the situation satisfactorily (the explanations are always a letdown), and so you really have to enjoy the style and atmosphere of the game — the tonalities and the deftness and the neat little gambits. The movie version of *Child's Play* needed a polished surface and suave craftsmanship. Instead, it has been turned into a horror melodrama — to cash in, one assumes, on the young movie audience's new interest in diabolism. A changed ending reduces the "metaphysical" malevolence to conscious manipulation, and the movie gets its shocks in the easiest ways (a bloody mutilation at the outset made my head hurt). The music is obtrusive, with rattlesnake rattles for lurking depravity, and the film is very ugly visually, with straitjacket framing. The director, Sidney Lumet, must have decided that James Mason, as the harried pedant Malley, was going to get awards (the way Fritz Weaver, who played the role on the stage, did), and, in order to hand them to him, destroyed his performance. Just about every time he says a line, he is presented in an abrupt, badly cropped closeup, so instead of observing his performance in rhythm with the rest of the picture (and, indeed, he's quite good) you have it thrust on you in visual isolation. The movie tries to be a Black Mass, and Robert Preston, as the popular, hearty teacher Dobbs, is lighted to suggest Satan. Once a fine screen actor, Preston is now ageless and painfully (probably unconsciously) actorish; on the stage his energy is joyful, but in movies he seems to project all over the place, even when he isn't doing anything. He feels wrong in every shot here, but it doesn't really matter, because the film is crudely effective on its own tense but unpleasant horror-thriller level. You can't help being frightened at times, especially when Beau Bridges, as the young gym teacher, is surrounded by malignant boys, but the mutilation of children for our enjoyment is not to my taste. The picture seems to me fairly disgusting, and might have even if it had been elegantly contrived, without blood and without noisy vipers on the track.

JACQUES TATI IS PRAISED so extravagantly by others that maybe I will be forgiven if I say that he lost me on *Mon Oncle* and that his new film, *Traffic,* could be a whole lot funnier. Tati had a nice spare buoyancy in *Jour de Fête* and was poignantly quick and eccentric in *Mr. Hulot's Holiday,* but he really isn't much of a performer, and by the time of *Mon Oncle* his spontaneity had vanished. At best, his films just seem to happen, but when he tries for careful charm, as he does in *Traffic,* and it doesn't come, the bumbling begins to seem rather precious and fatuous. Hulot is now a car designer on his maundering way to an international automobile exposition in Amsterdam. He has his familiar fidgety, gawky lope, with his arms sailing in front or behind, and he's as impersonal as ever. He has less to do this time, but those who surround him are just as impersonal. The dubbing into English adds to the non-involvement, and so does Tati's predilection for long shots. The actors are kept at a distance — an oddly depersonalizing style for a movie that is commenting on modern depersonalization. The color and the design of the film are pretty, and Tati is in his purest form — evocative and bittersweet — when two garage mechanics simulate walking on the moon. But most of the confusions and the disjointed bits are fuzzy and only vaguely comic. There's sprightly music to let you know when the sequences are meant to be droll, and the perky whimsey of it all is damn near overpowering.

[December 16, 1972]

Round Up the Usual Suspects

PAUL NEWMAN has learned an immense amount about making movies since his directing début, with *Rachel, Rachel,* in which the camera loitered while the actors acted and acted. In *The Effect of Gamma Rays on Man-in-the-Moon Marigolds* he has blended Paul Zindel's play into a naturalistic setting, and he has shaped the film sensitively. Newman has done as well with this type of material as anyone has ever managed to do on the screen, and Robert Brustein, a critic not normally given to leniency, referred in the *Times* of December 10th to "Paul Newman's superior movie version which manages to disguise, through sensitive performances, all the inadequacies of Zindel's play." I wish that that were possible, but you can't disguise the inadequacies of the play, because they're absolutely central. Alvin Sargent's adaptation skillfully expands and peoples Zindel's sketchy theater piece (the original has only five characters), but does so in a way that is true to Zindel's vision. There's no other way to retain what makes the material effective; you can't scrape the crud away or disguise it — or there's nothing there. The play works on its crud, and so does the movie.

Paul Zindel writes what are essentially camp versions of the matriarchal mood-memory plays of Tennessee Williams and William Inge; his specialty is sentimentality made piercing by cruelty. The major characters are gutsy, wisecracking broads — for actresses, the female equivalent of swashbuckling roles. Beatrice (Joanne Woodward), also known as Betty the Loon, is a rampaging jokester-mother who is lost and doesn't know how to find a way out of frustration and poverty. Zindel wrings laughs out of her sour sarcasm and wrings pathos out of the misery she suffers and then inflicts on her two high-school-age daughters — Ruth, who is epileptic and destroyed (Roberta Wallach, the Eli Wallachs' daughter), and Matilda, who is intelligent and shyly, stubbornly unscathed (Nell Potts, the Newmans' daughter). Ruth's fits bring out Beatrice's maternal tenderness, but Matilda's need to learn fills her mother with jealous resentment. This bitchy comic Gorgon — mother as a drag queen — is exploited for a series of vaudeville turns. She's Auntie Mame as a failure — a sick Mame. Beatrice humiliates her daughters while raucously cracking jokes; she even (God help the American theater, and the Pulitzer Prize committee) threatens to kill Matilda's rabbit and, inevitably, carries out the threat on the night the child wins a prize at school — for the science experiment that gives the play its metaphoric title. Yes, the material gets to you: how could you help being affected when children are heartlessly shamed by their own mother in front of their teachers and classmates? And the movie fills out what's implicit in the play. Stella Dallas herself didn't lay on the makeup and the crazy-lady clothes any heavier than bellowing Beatrice. The scene of her showing up at the school for the award ceremony is the gaudiest of its kind since James Mason slapped Judy Garland when she was on the stage getting her Academy Award in *A Star Is Born.* The final mood is of horror and hope, a sort of upbeat resignation: Beatrice and the blighted Ruth will sink lower, but Matilda, the young scientist, will bloom. This muted optimism is the neatest Broadway heart-clutcher imaginable. Manipulative realism — that's what the mood-memory play has come to.

Full of echoes of old plays and movies as Zindel's devices are, they have some theatrical vitality; he has talent, I suppose. But his plays are worthlessly "moving" — lyricized sudsers with stand-up-comic numbers, and synthetic to the core. I've watched Julie Harris and Maureen Stapleton trying to go the full distance with his showcase roles, and all I could see up there was the actress working to get laughs. In a theater that's starved, *Marigolds* (the best of his works) can get by, because it "plays," but Beatrice, the good-bad witch, terrible when you're under her spell, funny and pathetic when you escape and can look back on her, is a mawkish travesty of Amanda in *The Glass Menagerie.* She is mother the destroyer, the twisted belle — the ogress in the psychosexual fantasy that pervades theatrical Americana.

There's a likable "trouper" quality about Joanne Woodward. She's a briny actress, with her feet on the ground, and with great audience rapport: she has a wide streak of humor about herself that you sense and respond to. Unlike the fabled goddess-stars, she's very "real" in her presence, and she makes far more direct contact with the audience. And she's Southern, which gives her the right quality for a role that is fifties-TV out of Southern gothic — the slatternly mother in her faded cotton bathrobe trying to sell dance lessons on the phone while dreaming (of her father, of course). *Splendor in the Grass* comes to mind; Beatrice is like one of those Inge fifties people who were washed up as soon as they got out of high school — victims of baroque circumstance. Joanne Woodward had the right forlorn gallantry for *The Stripper* (from Inge's *A Loss of Roses*), and she gives this Zindel role the sashaying toughness it requires, but it's a strident, unconvincing performance. Her solidity — just what we respond to — works against her here. There are said to be actresses who can carry off this tender-tough stunt in the theater by bringing a "magic" of their own to it, but I've never seen it done. (It may depend on your threshold level for slobbiness.) I did not see Sada Thompson in the role, but Woodward achieves what the other actresses who play Zindel's women on the stage achieve: you admire her for what she can do, but you don't believe a minute of it. To bring conviction to Beatrice's vengeful meanness and all that self-hate and the stomping on frightened kids and the rabbit slaughter, she'd have to be the kind of actress (fortunately, there are fewer of them now) who goes in for knee-jerk heartbreak — and I doubt if anybody could get by with running this old gamut on the contemporary screen.

Paul Newman can't turn camp Americana into naturalistic Americana, but he gives it some sensibility — a tasteful version of fifties-TV "depth." He's an unobtrusive director, keeping the camera on what you'd look for in the theater; his work is serene, sane, and balanced. The movie is touchingly well made — touchingly because the treatment the material gets is much better than it deserves.

AT FIRST, THE ELATION OF SEEING Laurence Olivier in a starring role, after the merely tantalizing glimpses of him in recent films, is sufficient to give *Sleuth* — Joseph L. Mankiewicz's transcription of the Anthony Shaffer play — a high spirit. Olivier seems to be having a ripsnorting high old time in this show-off confection about an eccentric author of detective novels and his prey (Michael Caine), and he calls up memories of the giggly, boyish Olivier with the pencil mustache who used to dodge pursuing ladies in the thirties. But when the cleverness of Shaffer's excessive literacy wears down and the stupid tricks the two men play on each other keep grinding on, with each in turn being humiliated, and Olivier is sweating anxiously while hunting for clues, one begins to feel very uncomfortable that the greatest actor of our day — the man who must surely be the wittiest actor who has ever lived — is chasing around in the kind of third-rate material he outgrew more than thirty years ago. A friend in the theater muttered, "It's Laurence Olivier playing a role that would have been perfect for George Sanders."

The waste wouldn't be so apparent if Shaffer's situations and dialogue were genuinely clever. But he's far from a master of triviality. He tries to give the detective games additional weight by making the Olivier character an upper-class snob, sneakily prejudiced, and suffering the punishment that the triumvirate of God and Freud and Marx mete out to snobs: impotence. This little edge of righteousness to a movie that doesn't succeed on its own arch and frivolous terms may have deceived Shaffer and Mankiewicz into believing that our interest could be maintained for over two and a quarter hours. The ornateness of the conceits becomes heavy, and *Sleuth* stops being fun at the end of the first round, long before the end; it stops being fun when Michael Caine stops walking around in his clown shoes. And the fact is Olivier *has* outgrown this and he's not really right for it; he tries to give it too much — his intensity and bravura are too frantic for this pseudo-civilized little nothing of a play. We may think that we could watch Olivier in anything and be ecstatically happy, but when the director is filling the void with repeated shots of mechanical toys grinning ominously we have plenty of time to experience the shame of being part of a culture that can finance Laurence Olivier only in a gentleman-bitch George Sanders role.

ONE OF THE PEOPLE who didn't see *Man of La Mancha* on the stage even once (those lyrics, which sounded as if they were translated from Esperanto, weren't much of a come-on; besides, I like Cervantes), I went to the movie, directed by Arthur Hiller, with some curiosity about the nature of the work's appeal. The first hour, with Cervantes (Peter O'Toole) being arrested by the Inquisition and staging *Don Quixote* in a dungeon with his fellow-prisoners as the supporting cast, didn't tell me, but then — maybe I had simply got used to the unvarying rhythm of the storytelling and to the tears flowing around me in the theater, the way they did at *The Song of Bernadette* — I think I began to understand it. The picture improved during Don Quixote's victorious battle at the inn, and the whole thing began to make a little sense. At the beginning, O'Toole spits out his lines rhythmically, garbling the meanings, but then he starts to get his effects physically. His face quirky, he is like an elongated Alec Guinness, and he is brittle-boned and horsy enough to play Rosinante, too. He has the staring, unseeing eyes of a harmless madman, and a facial tic — a rattled shake of disbelief. His woefulness is so deeply silly that he turns into a holy fool, and, with the barber's basin on his head, a Christ figure — yet funny. *Don Quixote* has become a primitive Christian myth in this version: Aldonza/Dulcinea is Don Quixote's one true achievement — Mary Magdalene redeemed. Once this emotion began to take hold, and it was clear that "The Impossible Dream" meant purity in the carnal sense, the movie became more compelling. This happens mostly because Sophia Loren, with her great sorrowing green-brown eyes, is magnificently sensual and spiritual. She is always on the verge of being gang-raped, or recovering, but the men tearing at her tattered bodice are just flies tormenting her. Loren is in herself the soul of Italian opera, and that's what she brings to this scrambled, bastardized version of the novel, which comes to us via Dale Wasserman's TV play, Broadway show, and movie script. Loren does not get to use her comedy talents, but there has never been a woman on the screen more beautiful in her full maturity than Loren is now, and she brings *Man of La Mancha* a substance of her own. She seems to incarnate the sinful, suffering humanity that Peter O'Toole, the cardboard dreamer, loves without being flesh enough to understand it.

Comedy seems to bring out something weak and helpless and unmanly in O'Toole, yet he is able to use this weakness as part of the Knight's ridiculous, infirm courage. O'Toole is a dotty, saintly scarecrow, wafer-thin and stylized; Loren is full-bodied and realistic. And, at some primitive emotional level, the contrast works. Nothing else in the movie is worth mention, except, perhaps, that Gino Conforti, giving a straightforward Broadway-style performance as the comic barber, is effective, while James Coco's Buster Brown-style Sancho Panza, though not as dreadful as one might fear, is a blob, of no clear purpose, Aldonza having displaced him.

❖

SAM PECKINPAH is such a gifted moviemaker that he gives even a sausage like *The Getaway* the benefit of expert craftsmanship. Lucien Ballard's near-abstract cinematography is so clean and muscular it deserves a subject — not just Steve McQueen looking trim in his whites in a Texas jail. There's no reason for this picture — *another* bank heist — to have been made, and there's no energy in the tossed-together script. McQueen and Ali MacGraw are given the cute names Doc and Carol

McCoy; when McCoy is released after four years in prison, he waits outside for his loving and devoted wife to pick him up. After a considerable interval, Miss MacGraw arrives and casually explains that she was having her hair done "and the girl was slow." What this cracked scene is doing in the movie I guess we'll never know.

This is the most completely commercial film Peckinpah has made, and his self-parasitism gives one forebodings of emptiness. When a director repeats his successful effects, it can mean that he is getting locked in and has stopped responding to new experience. (Hitchcock is the most glaring example.) *The Getaway* is long and dull and has no reverberations except of other movies, mostly by Peckinpah. And there's something else that's a bad omen: the most effective sequence — spareribs being thrown back and forth in an erotic eating scene in a car, involving a gangster (Al Lettieri) and a couple he has kidnapped (Sally Struthers and Jack Dodson) — is so vicious, and the whole relationship between the gangster and the woman, involving lewd pleasure in sex play with him while her husband watches helplessly, is gross. It's frightening to see how this viciousness can be used to embellish a mechanical job like *The Getaway*; it just may have been the director's only chance for self-expression in this film — and this type of artistic frustration only feeds misanthropy.

The picture meticulously avoids nudity, and gets its reward: a PG rating from the M.P.A.A. Its real cunning, however, is in the way it allows its robber hero and heroine to kill practically everybody in the movie and get clean away with their loot and remain America's sweethearts: those they kill are always shown to be sons of bitches first; they earn their deaths, so to speak. With the utmost caution, the killing couple manage to avoid shooting any cops. There is no code anymore (or yet) that requires this sort of fastidiousness about whom you kill, but movies are already preparing for the new morality and the new Supreme Court. The picture's bewildering con is that it makes the pair such lovely, decent gangsters that they can stroll off into the sunset with their satchel stuffed with money as if they'd just met over a malted at the corner drugstore. As for McQueen and MacGraw, they strike no sparks on the screen. (They don't even look right together; her head is bigger than his.) His low-key professionalism is turning into minimal acting and is indistinguishable from the blahs, while she is certainly the primmest, smuggest gangster's moll of all time. The audience, which had a good time hooting at her, loved it when he smacked her face — her haughty nostrils and schoolgirl smirk seemed to ask for it. Miss MacGraw communicates thought by frowning and opening her mouth, and, having exhausted her meager vocal resources in two pictures, she reads each line as an echo of Brenda or Jennifer. Last time I saw Candice Bergen, I thought she was a worse actress than MacGraw; now I think that I slandered Bergen. It must be that whichever you're seeing is worse.

❖

ROBERT ALTMAN IS ALMOST FRIGHTENINGLY NONREPETITIVE. He goes out in a new direction each time, and he scores an astonishing fifty per cent — one on, one off. *M*A*S*H* was followed by *Brewster McCloud,* and *McCabe & Mrs. Miller* has now been followed by *Images.* I can hardly wait for his next movie.

Images, made in Ireland, is a modern variant of the old *The Cabinet of Dr. Caligari* ploy — the world as seen through a mad person's eyes. A classy schizo (Susannah York) duplicates herself, confuses the living with the dead, and can't tell her husband (René Auberjonois) from her lovers (Marcel Bozzuffi, Hugh Millais). Miss York's madness has no roots, no nourishment; it is a matter of tinkling wind chimes, slivers of glass, windows, lenses, mirrors — "images." To be effective, the movie needs to draw us in to identify with Susannah York's hallucinations, but the cold shine of the surfaces doesn't do it. The imagery itself fails to stir the imagination, though Vilmos Zsigmond shot some unusual landscapes, inhumanly clear and visible at a great distance, and there are a few ravishing pastoral scenes (with sheep and miniature horses) that seem *about* to tell us something. This is a psychological thriller with no psychological content, so there's no suspense and the climax has no power. We know from the heroine's dashingly casual clothes and the exquisitries of the super-modern décor that this film is concerned not with why she is going mad but with the coquetry of madness; that is, with suggestive objects (eyeglasses, camera, binoculars), with fragmentation, and with the bizarre situations a rich, sexy schizo can get into. A young girl (Cathryn Harrison) who looks like Susannah York at an earlier age enters into the situation, and the idea of seeing yourself as the adolescent you once were is so resonant (mightn't she hate this child she once was?) that we wait, though in vain, for the potentialities to be explored; it's just another fragment. But Altman is a fantastic technician; the rhythms of the cutting are seductive, and there are inventive moments (the creepy use of the telephone in the early scenes; Millais caught by death while he is pulling his sweater over his head; later, the blood thickly oozing from his chest onto the carpet). Altman could probably turn, say, a Daphne du Maurier novel into stylish screen terror, but he himself doesn't seem to have the gothic sensibility to make the scare effects matter. You stop being frightened as soon as you know that he takes it all seriously, and that it will be a hollow puzzle, a moviemaker's show-business view of schizophrenia, a prismatic *Repulsion.*

When he has a dramatic framework, Altman can do so much to affect us emotionally by his virtuosity with visual images that he may at times think that words don't matter, that images do it all, and *Images* seems to have been made in that conviction. But this movie (from an original screenplay by Altman, plus improvisations) is not conceived to work without words; rather, it is indifferent to them. It is full of words, and they're runty words or they're the stupefyingly high-flown literary language we hear in Miss York's narration of the story for children, *In Search of Unicorns,* that her character is composing (and that Miss York has actually written). In this ornamental visual setting, with so much care given to twirling glassy baubles, the occasional flat improvised lines are like peanut shells stuck in jewelry. The movie appears to represent something Altman had wanted to do for a long time — perhaps for too long. He said in interviews at the 1972 Cannes Festival, at which Miss York won the Best Actress Award, that he'd written the script five years before and hadn't changed a word until the day he started shooting. The actors seem cut adrift. Susannah York doesn't have the histrionic presence of a star; she's satiny smooth in her small-scale proficiency, especially in comedy. (Even miscast, as in *Happy Birthday, Wanda June,* she had more style than anybody else in the picture.) This role, however, is serious and emotional, yet it supplies her with no character, leaving her to rely on just what she shouldn't — her pallid, wearying luminosity. You don't feast on Susannah York the way you can on some stars, even when their material is thin, because she's thin, and lacking in a strong sexual presence. A little too contained, and not an empathic actress, she doesn't provide a true focus of attention; you don't care enough about her.

The style of this film is different from anything of Altman's I've seen before, and it's not like any other director's. It's an empty, trashy chic film, but, scene by scene, Altman doesn't do anything ordinary; *Images* is not remotely an example of hack work — it's an example of a conceptual failure. Altman often trusts a very bad instinct, the kind of instinct that some people may expect an artist of his stature to have outgrown. But artists, particularly in show business, often retain gaping areas of naïveté and of flossiness, and though sometimes they pull something out of those areas that seems miraculously right, other times we may wish to avert our eyes. It's possible that this formidably complicated man has as many facets as this gadgety movie's tiresome prisms, and that in reaching out instinctively and restlessly he's learning techniques that he hasn't yet found a use for. My bet is that he *will*; when he's bad he's very bad, but when he's good he's extraordinary.

[December 23, 1972]

Star Mutations

"UP THE SANDBOX" is a joyful mess — a picture, full of sass and enthusiasm and comic strokes, that doesn't seem to have discovered what it's meant to be about. It's marginalia in search of a movie, but it's as full of life as its pregnant heroine. Barbra Streisand has never seemed so mysteriously, sensually fresh, so multi-radiant. As Margaret, wife of a Columbia instructor and mother of two, she's a complete reason for going to a movie, as Garbo was. The Anne Richardson Roiphe novel is a celebration of the heroine's deep pleasure in marriage and maternity; in the novel, Margaret fantasizes — spinoffs from her life, daydreams in which she sees herself as the heroine of garish, improbable exploits. She is not, however, a female Walter Mitty or a woman trying to find her identity. It is clear that she loves her own life — that it is what she has chosen because it satisfies the deepest needs of her character. This doesn't give a movie much to work with, but the attempt here to open the material into a speculative fantasy-essay on women's conflicting desires (though elating in its own way) plays havoc with Margaret's character and situation. At a realistic level, Margaret's physical contentment with her children and her seductive, happy abandon with her husband (David Selby) feel so true that the actual problems that come up (such as her needing someone to take care of the baby so she can keep a doctor's appointment) seem minor. Margaret isn't crushed or exploited; all she needs to do is speak up and tell her husband that sometimes she needs help for a few hours. The small indignities she experiences aren't in scale with the major confrontations that the film gets into. Trying to turn her into a revolutionary woman who must leave the family and decide for herself what she wants to do violates her character. There are, no doubt, women who need to consider walking out and slamming the door, but Margaret isn't one of them.

However, despite Margaret's blissful acceptance of husband and children, her daydream life is apparently similar to the daydream life of incensed and angry women, because many women appear to read the book as a statement of the need for liberation. That is, they read it in terms of their own needs, and so there is some warrant for the movie's using Margaret's fantasy world as a taking-off place for speculations. And Mrs. Roiphe provided a conveniently loaded basis for discussion, since Margaret's husband is doing the kind of exciting intellectual work that can so easily be contrasted with women's supposed dreary existence with their kids (though it isn't dreary for Margaret). The women's-lib material gives the film pungency; it deals in imponderables, but for the most part wittily and never abstractly. Margaret's life is used to raise questions about how a woman might try to juggle the claims of her husband, her children, her implacable, wheedling mother, and her own fitful, half-forgotten aspirations. In a sequence of rude, snorting satire — the clamorous celebration of her parents' anniversary — she makes it plain that the devouring mother isn't going to get a nibble off her. That much is settled, but the other claims aren't. These questions have never before been dealt with on the screen so eagerly and openly; there's never been anything like this hip, sharp, free-association-style treatment of a modern theme. You can't tell where the movie is going until you realize that it's simply going to take off, and that it's trying not just to deal with Margaret but to use her as a stand-in. It may be tempting for those who are put off by the subject, or the flighty style and lack of dramatic tension, to get fixed on specific defects, such as the African trip, which doesn't have much point, and the abortion fantasy, which is rather ineffectual. But *Up the Sandbox* is full of knockabout urban humor, and full of beauty — which one rarely finds in the context of battered feelings and slumps in self-esteem. It's a comic, dissonant cantata on loving and being tugged in different directions.

The movie feels as if it should go on longer — one wants more. Though a random harvest, it's deft and exhilarating all the way. The director, Irvin Kershner, may be caught in a conceptual muddle, and the film doesn't have the fine structure of his *Loving,* but it has a sparkle beyond anything in his previous work and a new volatile, unconstrained atmosphere. His domestic scenes are more spontaneous and more tender than those of any other current American director; he has a poet's feeling for the sensuous richness in ordinary life, and the sexy domestic scuffles are pure comedy-romance. The film is technically as beautiful as Eric Rohmer's work, though in a much faster tempo, with cheering, constantly surprising editing rhythms. The cinematographer Gordon Willis's New York City vistas have the intoxication that is integral to Mrs. Roiphe's vision (only the playground scenes lapse into conventional lyricism). *Up the Sandbox* can't figure out what its terms are (it's too bad Mrs. Roiphe didn't adapt it, instead of Paul Zindel), but there's the incidental amusement of watching male moviemakers try to inject women's-lib points — try to fit their guilt-ridden notions of women's consciousness-raising — into a story in which they don't quite belong.

And there's Streisand. No one else has ever been so appealingly wry, or so funny when self-deprecating, or so ardently and completely *hopeful.* That's why even the thought of Margaret's walking out on her children is such an impossibly wrong, male-conceived device. The picture might seem a cop-out if nothing was changed at the end, but Streisand's Margaret, like Mrs. Roiphe's, enjoys her kids and is too healthily intelligent to sacrifice them to some confusion in her head. As Streisand's pictures multiply, it becomes apparent that she is not about to master an actress's craft but, rather, is discovering a craft of her own, out of the timing and emotionality that make her a phenomenon as a singer. You admire her not for her acting — or singing — but for herself, which is what you feel she gives you in both. She has the class to be herself, and the impudent music of her speaking voice is proof that she knows it. The audacity of her self-creation is something we've had time to adjust to; we already know her mettle, and the dramatic urgency she can bring to roles. In *Up the Sandbox,* she shows a much deeper and warmer presence and a freely yielding quality. And a skittering good humor — as if, at last, she had come to accept her triumph, to believe in it. That faint weasellike look of apprehensiveness is gone — and that was what made her seem a little frightening. She is a great undeveloped actress — undeveloped in the sense that you feel the natural richness in her but can see that she's idiosyncratic and that she hasn't the training to play the classical roles that still define how an actress's greatness is expressed. But in movies new ways may be found. If there is such a thing as total empathy, she has it, and (to steal a phrase Stark Young once employed to describe a character in a Goldoni play) she has a "blunt purity" that makes her the greatest camera subject on the contemporary American screen.

CAROL BURNETT, WHO IS PROBABLY THE MOST GIFTED comedienne this country has ever produced, does a plain acting role in *Pete 'n' Tillie*; it's as if the Admiral of the Fleet had turned ordinary seaman. She comes before us as a lot less than she is. (We never even get to see her beautiful Edna May Oliver smile.) She plays it close-in, tame, as if acting meant putting a straitjacket on her talent. She is one of the least self-infatuated of the inspired comics, and her professional modesty is the extra blessing that makes you feel good when you watch her television show. The sketches are the most sophisticated satire on the air (and with the wittiest costuming television has known), and Carol Burnett can get away with it because she isn't self-congratulatory and because she manages to behave like a levelheaded, nice woman.

But "nice" is a double-edged word. *Pete 'n' Tillie,* which is adapted from Peter De Vries' short novel *Witch's Milk* and co-stars Walter Matthau, is a nice picture, a modern-day equivalent of the solid, semi-forgettable, semi-memorable pictures about decent people trying to live their lives somewhat rationally which the studios used to put out — the sort of picture that starred Irene Dunne and Cary Grant. Millions of people will probably enjoy this movie, and I wasn't bored by it, but it wasn't my kind of picture the first time around (under titles like *Penny Serenade*), and it isn't now, either, though I wanted it to be, because I love Carol Burnett. On TV, her niceness is part of what gives her show its balance and keeps it from getting frantic; her easy relationship with the regulars, and with the guests, is a relief from the edgy, hostile over-familiarity on most shows — it's like the niceness that is part of Mary Tyler Moore's appeal. But in *Pete 'n' Tillie* an inhibited version of this niceness is all she uses. Her dry delivery of her lines is often skillful, and her slow, deliberate movements suggest a contemplative sort of woman, but I don't understand why, in the cause of realism, her spirit is so withered.

The movie is the story of Tillie's romance with Pete, a jokester who works in motivational research, and their marriage. In the book, Tillie is a bit of a calculating bitch (and Carol Burnett has the knack of being underhanded — she's a genius at it), but the producer-adapter, Julius J. Epstein, makes Tillie innocuously pleasant and the most straightforward of heroines. And I can't believe in this dutiful, milk-drinking wifey-woman who accepts her role in life with quiet strength. (I couldn't believe in it when Irene Dunne did it, either; I always wanted to slam her one.) Carol Burnett plays this feminine version of "grace under pressure" in an almost grimly controlled way. The romance is inexplicable, because Pete is a charming, waggish reprobate and you expect her to respond to his aberrant humor; you keep hoping for some rapport to develop. But she's stony-faced when she should be breaking up. Tillie is apparently meant to be likable, but the absence of spontaneity in her, and of flirtatiousness, too, is stolidly inhuman. How can a jokester fall in love with a deadpan moo-cow woman who never relaxes or cracks a smile? (Pete's commendatory "Good girl!" to a particularly plainspoken example of her common sense is a clue to Epstein's view of what attracts Pete.) It's understandable that Miss Burnett doesn't want to resort to slapstick, and she has never been a laugh-jerking or applause-jerking performer. It's understandable that she should play straight woman to Matthau. But this is an unnecessarily confined and schoolmarmish performance.

Pete's and Tillie's life together is all so aseptically the middle-class ideal it looks like death. They are romanticized versions of "ordinary" middle-class people — not romanticized in the old Hollywood way, which resulted from casting glamorous stars in the roles, but romanticized by their highly articulate, epigrammatic conversations and their low-key self-control and stiff-upper-lip civility. Now that the couple's economic level has been raised and they have been elevated to comfortable suburban Doris Dayville, the story seems more complacent than when you read it. It's a depressing expensive house they live in, and this picture's whole notion of the good life is pretty damned depressing. What's the purpose of Tillie's dispensing with bra and girdle, at Pete's suggestion, if she's going to wear those immaculate suburban outfits Edith Head sticks on her? (They look as if they'd fumigate anyone who came within a range of five feet.) Tillie may act like Pete's bad luck, but the picture says she's an ideal wife. If there is such a thing as a consciousness-lowering movie, this is certainly it.

The discreet sentimentality of old movies, with their idealized, unimperilled middle-class values, seemed smug and narrow and fake even then, and now the celebration of those values seems to come out of a time warp. Perhaps at the behest of Epstein, a veteran scriptwriter, who worked on dozens of the romantic comedies of the past, Martin Ritt has directed prudently, letting each line gather its full effect, which is to say, the director seems to be in a period of amiable dotage. There's a particularly stiff composition in which a nurse hovers over Tillie as if she were waiting to swoop down with a butterfly net. The only relief is a lively, fiendish fight between Carol Burnett and Geraldine Page, who plays Tillie's bitch-gossip friend (but with the way Epstein has cleaned up Tillie's character, her friend's sudden fury at her comes out of nowhere). When, near the end, the couple, who have split after losing their son, are talking in a garden, and a boy, running away from his mother, comes between them, and they both begin to cry, it is apparent that Epstein carries the secrets of forties movies' heartbreak in his pockets; he ought to rip a few holes in those pockets. *Pete 'n' Tillie* is a buttoned-up movie, and I'd trade it in for the stripping act Carol Burnett did nine years ago in *Who's Been Sleeping in My Bed?* Matthau, with his ramshackle slouch and the incongruity of his courtly manner and mashed-potato face, saves the picture from being cloying; the best moment comes when Tillie, in bed, asks him to exhibit what sex manuals call afterglow, and for a fleeting instant he has the balmy, sweet smile of Ferdinand the Bull. The two of them could be great together if she'd let herself go. For

Carol Burnett to be so staid on the screen is a form of deprivation for the audience, like Barbra Streisand's not singing in recent movies.

A YEAR OR SO AGO, I turned on the television set in the middle of a Rod Serling *Night Gallery* presentation of a play called *A Fear of Spiders;* Patrick O'Neal was telling Kim Stanley that he'd seen a spider as big as a dog, and then he explained, "Perhaps it's a mutation. There's a lot of that going around." Maybe so. Doesn't it seem a little soon for Robert Redford to be presiding over his own mutation into a legend? I was still waiting for him to become a new kind of hip and casually smart screen actor, and he's already jumped into the mythic-man roles in which tired, aging stars can vegetate profitably. Even before the titles of *Jeremiah Johnson,* he is photographed in a shamelessly glamorous style that evokes the young Gary Cooper, while a ballad informs us that he's a "mountain man," a loner, and — by implication — a dropout from dirty civilization. It's a new-style Hollywood-factory epic poem, constructed by grafting together Vardis Fisher's novel *Mountain Man* and the story "The Crow Killer," by Raymond W. Thorp and Robert Bunker. The strong, silent man is now self-consciously cool, and aware as hell of the larger social ironies of his situation. This is Hollywood youth-grabbing alienation, set circa 1825. All that Jeremiah wants is to live his own life in the wilderness, as a trapper, but when the wife he has acquired and the mute child he has adopted are slaughtered by Crows (in reprisal because American soldiers have made him violate the Indians' sacred burial ground), he goes on a revenge rampage, killing Crows for the rest of the movie. Maybe Redford and Sydney Pollack, the director, really believe they're doing something different from the conventional new, brutally "realistic" Westerns, because *Jeremiah Johnson* crawls through the wilderness at a snail's pace and is stretched out with ponderous lore.

Isn't it late in the history of movies for Redford's tall-in-the-saddle star games — the stern, blank face and the quick grin like rain in the desert? Redford must want to be an old-timey hero. His underplaying has begun to seem lazy and cautious and self-protective; he never opens himself up, as a major actor must. He's playing the star games of an earlier era, and they don't mean the same things now. His model is Coop (he used the name itself in *Tell Them Willie Boy Is Here*), and he manages that dumb look; what's missing is what Coop, the Westerner, conveyed — a quiet, unshakable belief in a code and a way of life. The Westerner stood for a basic idealism, and when he used his guns it wasn't for revenge, it was for justice. Probably young audiences can no longer relate to what the Westerner stood for, but are they supposed to like

Redford because he's so sheepish and silent and straight? Hell, so was Lassie. The cool silence of the Coop archetype implied depths. There are no depths in Redford that he's willing to reveal; his cool is just modern, existential chic, and it's beginning to look sullen and stubborn rather than heroic. When Redford is in a competitive buddy-buddy co-star relationship, the cool can be a put-on, but in this fake-authentic Western setting it's cool gone dank and narcissistic. The screwed-up script, by John Milius and Edward Anhalt, is empty; it exploits the appeal of the disillusioned romantic loner trying to escape the corruption of civilization, but when Jeremiah becomes corrupt himself and starts killing Indians, he's even more romantic. In the guise of gritty realism, action films have become far more primitive, celebrating tooth-and-claw revenge in a manner that would have been unthinkable in early Westerns, or even ten years ago.

This movie banks on action and brutality, but it aims for allegorical big game, squeezing whatever resonance it can out of having the hero addressed as "Pilgrim," and piling on the kind of legend talk that gives me a bellyache. When the Crows are chasing our hero and he's advised to escape by going down to a town, he says, "I been to a town." Grizzled, cantankerous types give him sage advice: "Keep your nose to the wind and your eye to the skyline." This movie was made with its nose to the wind; that's what's the matter with it. First, it demonstrates that you can't escape corruption — that Jeremiah is forced to become a murderer — and then it uses this demonstration to give its hero a license to kill. When the Crows, recognizing Jeremiah's courage, end their war against him, and the chief gives him a peace sign, Jeremiah signals him back, giving him the finger. In that gesture, the moviemakers load him with guilt for what the white Americans have done to the Indians, and, at the same time, ask us to laugh at the gesture, identifying with his realism. How many different kinds of consciousness can a movie diddle with? *Jeremiah Johnson* seems to have been written by vultures.*

[December 30, 1972]

*When I saw the film it seemed implicit that Jeremiah was going to go on killing Indians, and the audience laughed cynically at his salute. This laughter may have influenced my interpretation of his movement: although the script had had him continue with the killing, the director says that he finished on the gesture so the end would be ambiguous.

Flesh

"CRIES AND WHISPERS" is set in a manor house at the turn of the century where Agnes (Harriet Andersson), a spinster in her late thirties, is dying of cancer. Her two married sisters have come to attend her in her final agony — the older, the severe, tense Karin (Ingrid Thulin), and the shallow, ripe, adulterous Maria (Liv Ullmann) — and they watch and wait, along with the peasant servant Anna (Kari Sylwan). We see their interrelations, and the visions triggered by their being together waiting for death and, when it comes, by death itself. But the gliding memories, the slow rhythm of the women's movements, the hands that search and touch, the large faces that fill the screen have the hypnotic style of a single dream. It is all one enveloping death fantasy; the invisible protagonist, Ingmar Bergman, is the presence we feel throughout, and he is the narrator. He is dreaming these fleshly images of women that loom in front of us, and dreaming of their dreams and memories.

Bergman is not a playful dreamer, as we already know from nightmarish films like *The Silence,* which seems to take place in a trance. He apparently thinks in images and links them together to make a film. Sometimes we may feel that we intuit the eroticism or the fears that lie behind the overwhelming moments in a Bergman movie, but he makes no effort to clarify. In a considerable portion of his work, the imagery derives its power from unconscious or not fully understood associations; that's why, when he is asked to explain a scene, he may reply, "It's just my poetry." Bergman doesn't always find ways to integrate this intense poetry with his themes. Even when he attempts to solve the problem by using the theme of a mental breakdown or a spiritual or artistic crisis, his intensity of feeling may explode the story elements, leaving the audience moved but bewildered. In a rare film such as *Shame,* the wartime setting provides roots for the anguish of the characters, and his ordering intelligence is in full control; more often the intensity appears to have a life of its own, apart from the situations, which don't account for it and can't fully express it. We come out of the theater wondering about Bergman himself and what he was trying to do.

Like Bergman, his countryman Strindberg lacked a sovereign sense of reality, and he experimented with a technique that would allow him to abandon the forms that he, too, kept exploding. In his author's note to the Expressionist *A Dream Play* (which Ingmar Bergman staged with great success in 1970), Strindberg wrote:

> The author has sought to reproduce the disconnected but apparently logical form of a dream. Anything can happen; everything is possible and probable. Time and space do not exist; on a slight groundwork of reality, imagination spins and weaves new patterns made up of memories, experiences, unfettered fancies, absurdities, and improvisations.
>
> The characters are split, double, and multiply; they evaporate, crystallize, scatter, and converge. But a single consciousness holds sway over them all — that of the dreamer. For him there are no secrets, no incongruities, no scruples, and no law.

That is Bergman's method here. *Cries and Whispers* has oracular power, and many people feel that when something grips them strongly it must be realistic; they may not want to recognize that being led into a dreamworld can move them so much. But I think it's the stylized-dream-play atmosphere of *Cries and Whispers* that has made it possible for Bergman to achieve such strength. The detached imaginary world of the manor house becomes a heightened form of reality — more literal and solid, closer than the actual world. The film is emotionally saturated in female flesh — flesh as temptation and mystery. In almost every scene you're aware of bodies and parts of bodies, of the quality of Liv Ullmann's skin and the miniature worlds in the dying woman's brilliant eyes. The almost empty rooms are stylized, and these female bodies inhabit them overpoweringly. The effect — a culmination of the visual emphasis on women's faces in recent Bergman films — is intimate and hypnotic. We are put in the position of the little boy at the beginning of *Persona,* staring up at the giant women's faces on the screen.

In the opening shots, the house is located in a series of autumnal landscapes of a formal park with twisted, writhing trees, and the entire film has a supernal quality. The incomparable cinematographer Sven Nykvist achieves the look of the paintings of the Norwegian Edvard Munch, as if the neurotic and the unconscious had become real enough to be photographed. But, unhappily, the freedom of the dream has sent Bergman back to Expressionism, which he had a heavy fling with in several of his very early films and in *The Naked Night,* some twenty years ago, and he returns to imagery drawn from the *fin de siècle,* when passion and decadence were one.

Bergman has often said that he likes to use women as his chief characters because women are more expressive. They have more talent for acting, he explained on the Dick Cavett show; they're not ashamed of looking in the mirror, as men are, he said, and the camera is a kind of mirror. It would be easy to pass over this simplistic separation of the sexes as just TV-interview chitchat if Bergman were still dealing with modern women as characters (as in *Törst, Summer Interlude, Monika*), but the four women of *Cries and Whispers* are used as obsessive male visions of women. They are women as the Other, women as the mysterious, sensual goddesses of male fantasy. Each sister represents a different aspect of woman, as in Munch's "The Dance of Life," in which a man dances with a woman in red (passion) while a woman in white (innocence) and a woman in black (corruption, death) look on. Bergman divides woman into three and dresses the three sisters for their schematic roles: Harriet Andersson's Agnes is the pure-white sister with innocent thoughts; Liv Ullmann's Maria, with her red-gold hair, wears soft, alluring colors and scarlet-woman dresses with tantalizing plunging necklines; and Ingrid Thulin's death-seeking Karin is in dark colors or black. The film itself is predominantly in black and white and red — red draperies, red wine, red carpets and walls, and frequent dissolves into a blank red screen, just as Munch frequently returned to red for his backgrounds, or even to cover a house (as in his famous "Red Virginia Creeper"). The young actress who plays Agnes as a child resembles Munch's wasted, sick young girls, and the film draws upon the positioning and look of Munch's figures, especially in Munch's sickroom scenes and in his studies of the laying out of a corpse. *Cries and Whispers* seems to be part of the art from the age of syphilis, when the erotic was charged with peril — when pleasure was represented by an enticing woman who turned into a grinning figure of death. "All our interiors are red, of various shades," Bergman wrote in the story (published in *The New Yorker*) that was also the working script. "Don't ask me why it must be so, because I don't know," he went on. "Ever since my childhood I have pictured the inside of the soul as a moist membrane in shades of red."

The movie is built out of a series of emotionally charged images that express psychic impulses, and Bergman handles them with the fluidity of a master. Yet these images are not discoveries, as they were for Munch, but a vocabulary of shock and panic to draw upon. Munch convinces us that he has captured the inner stress; Bergman doesn't quite convince, though we're impressed and we're held by the smoothness of the dreamy progression of events. The film moves with such eerie slow grace that it almost smothers its own faults and absurdities. I had the divided awareness that almost nothing in it quite works and, at the same time, that the fleshiness of those big bodies up there and the pull of the dream were strong and, in a sense, did make everything work — even the hopeless musical interludes (a Chopin mazurka, and a Bach suite for unaccompanied cello played romantically) and the robotized performances of all but Harriet Andersson. Still, there's a dullness at the heart of the movie, and the allegorical scheme leads to scenes that recall the conventions of silent films and the clichés of second-rate movie acting. The dying Agnes is devout as well as innocent. Liv Ullmann's Maria seduces a visiting doctor with the telegraphic leering of a Warner Brothers dance-hall hostess. Her conversation with him is a variant of the old "You're dirt, but so am I; we deserve each other," and the picture supports the doctor's view of her — that her physical desires and flirtatiousness are signs of laziness and vacuity. And that peasant Anna — the selfless, almost mute servant, close to nature, happy to do anything for the three sisters — has the proud-slave cast of mind that is honored in barrelfuls of old fiction. When Anna bares her breast to make a soft pillow for the dying Agnes, and, later, when she gets into bed, with her thighs up, supporting the dead Agnes in a sculptural pose that suggests both a "Pietà" and "The Rape of Europa," these are Bergman's visions of the inner life of a peasant mindlessly in harmony with the earth. The latter pose is altogether extraordinary, yet the very concept of Anna as a massive mound of comforting flesh takes one back (beyond childhood) to an earlier era. *Cries and Whispers* feels like a nineteenth-century European masterwork in a twentieth-century art form.

The words, which are often enigmatic, are unsuccessful attempts to support the effects achieved by the images. Most of Ingrid Thulin's acting as Karin belongs in a frieze of melodrama, alongside such other practitioners of the stately-stony dragon lady in torment as Gale Sondergaard and Cornelia Otis Skinner. Karin shuts her eyes to blot out her own despair and expresses herself in such dialogue as "I can't breathe anymore because of the guilt" and "Don't touch me!" and "It's all a tissue of lies." Most of her lines can be reduced to "Oh, the torment of it all!" — which actually isn't much of a reduction. That's how she talks when she isn't prowling the halls suffering. The suicidal, hate-filled Karin represents Bergman's worst failure in the movie. She escapes from the stereotype only twice — in a moment of manic humor when she complains of her disobedient big hands while wiggling them, and when she acts out a startling Expressionist fantasy of self-mutilation (followed by more lip-licking pleasure than the fantasy can quite accommodate). It is the advantage of the dream-play form that these two scenes appear to belong here, and people don't have to puzzle about them afterward, as they did with comparable passages in, say, *The Silence.* If Bergman can't make us accept the all-purpose complaints about guilt and suffering that are scattered through his films, his greatest single feat as a movie craftsman is that he can prepare an atmosphere that leads us to accept episodes brimming with hysteria in almost any makeshift context. Here, as Strindberg formulated, the dream context itself makes everything probable; the dreamer leads, the viewer follows. In *Cries and Whispers* Bergman is a wizard at building up a scene to a memorable image and then quickly dissolving into the red that acts as a fixative. The movie is structured as a series of red-outs. We know as we see these images disintegrate before our eyes that we will be taking them home with us. But Bergman doesn't have Strindberg's deviltry and dash; he uses a dreamlike atmosphere but not the language of dreams. He stays with his obsessional images, and his repressed, grave temperament infects even his technical surrender to the dream. (Strindberg, by contrast, was making twentieth-century masterworks in a nineteenth-century art form.)

Who knows how we would react if someone came back from the dead? But here, as in an old Hollywood movie, everyone reacts as scheduled. When Agnes's decaying corpse speaks, pleading for Karin to comfort her, Karin says she won't, because she doesn't love her; Agnes calls next for Maria, who also fails the test, fleeing in horror when the dead woman tries to kiss her. It is, of course, as we knew it would be, the peasant-lump Anna who is not afraid of holding the dead woman. This gothic-fairy-tale test of love is shown as Anna's dream, but it is also integral to the vision of the film, which is about the sick souls of the landed-gentry bourgeoisie. I think it is *because* Bergman lacks the gift for bringing order out of his experiences that he falls back on this schematism. It would be ludicrous if he similarly divided "man." The men in the movie are a shade small — so narrowly realistic they're less than life-size — while the women are more than a shade too splendidly large and strange: allegorical goddesses to be kept in the realm of mystery; never women, always facets of "woman."

Death dreams that come equipped with ticking clocks and uncanny silences and the racked wheezes of the dying are not really very classy, and Bergman's earnest use of gothic effects seems particularly questionable now, arriving just after Buñuel, in *The Discreet Charm of the Bourgeoisie,* has turned them on and off, switching to the spooky nocturnal as a movie joke. But even when Bergman employs sophisticated versions of primitive gothic-horror devices, he is so serious that his dream play is cued to be some sort of morality play as well. Other chaotic artists (Lorca, for example, in his dream play *If Five Years Pass*) haven't been respected in the same way as Bergman, because their temperaments weren't moralistic. But Bergman has a winning combination here: moral + gothic = medieval. And when medieval devices are used in the atmosphere of bourgeois decadence, adults may become as vulnerable as superstitious children.

Bergman is unusual among film artists in that he is an artist in precisely those terms drawn from the other arts which some of us have been trying to free movie aesthetics from. He is the movie director that those who are not generally interested in movies can recognize as an artist, because of the persistent gloom and weight of his work. It is his lack of an entertaining common touch — a lack that is extremely unusual among theatrical artists and movie artists — that has put him on a particular pinnacle. His didact's temperament has obtained this position for him, and although he is a major film artist, it's an absurd position, since he is a didact of the inscrutable. He *programs* mystery. *Cries and Whispers* features long scenes in which the camera scans the faces of Liv Ullmann and Ingrid Thulin as they talk and touch and kiss (scenes similar to the ones that led some people to assume that the sisters in *The Silence* were meant to be Lesbians); the camera itself may be part of the inspiration for these scenes, and perhaps some male fantasy of Sisterhood Is Powerful. The eroticism of this vision of sisterly love is unmistakable, yet the vision also seems to represent what Bergman takes to be natural to women. The dreamer, fascinated, is excluded from what he observes, like the staring, obsessed boy in *Persona.* This film is practically a ballet of touching, with hands, like the hands of the blind, always reaching for faces, feeling the flesh and bones. Maria's husband touches her face after she has committed adultery, and feels her guilt. Touching becomes a ritual of soul-searching, and Karin, whose soul has been rotted away, is, of course, the one who fears contact, and the one who violates the graceful ballet by — unforgivably — slapping Anna. Even the dead Agnes's hands reach up to touch and to hold. Didacticism and erotic mystery are mingled — this is Bergman as a northern Fellini. Strindberg's dream plays do not have the great tensions of the plays in which he struggled to express his ferocity, and this movie, compellingly beautiful as it is, comes too easily to Bergman. The viewer can sink back and bask in flesh, but to keep scanning woman as the Other doesn't get any of us anywhere.

[January 6, 1973]

Unfair

THE GENTEEL QUOTES in the ads for *César and Rosalie* ("A movie to see with someone you love," "An enchanting story of what love is all about," etc.) are somewhat misleading. It's not all that bad. The movie looks like those mistily expensive love potions the French have been exporting, and it's certainly loaded with the appurtenances of the pleasurable whirl of the beautiful rich, but it's really a jazzier version of a Marcel Pagnol film, with Yves Montand in the Raimu role. César (Montand) is a tycoon in scrap metal, a self-made man who enjoys being No. 1 in work and in play, and he adores Rosalie (Romy Schneider) and loves to amuse her child by a marriage now dissolved. There are no obstacles to their happiness and their eventual marriage; they have everything — yet almost inexplicably, before our eyes, it evaporates. Nobody's fault — just bad luck. An old love of Rosalie's — David, an eminent cartoonist (Sami Frey) — returns to France after an absence of five years, and when Rosalie sees him again, her feelings about César change. She still loves him, but she begins to look at him differently, and the love goes flat. It's as if César were cuckolded by a moonbeam.

The action skitters back and forth as Rosalie leaves César, then returns to him, and as César tries to help her get over her attraction to David, and that fails, and so on, but whenever you think the relationships are going to be stabilized into formulas, the picture wiggles free. And just when you think the picture is on the skids, the director, Claude Sautet, picks everything up for the end, and it becomes apparent that the irresolute behavior was a way of demonstrating an unresolvable unstable situation. It's a silly movie — a fluky, wry ode on the imperfect, haphazard nature of romantic love. What sustains it is that it never takes its three subjects too solemnly — never makes too big a deal out of their happiness or unhappiness. The movie's essential frivolousness makes its melancholy tone acceptable: we can laugh at the characters' self-centered sorrows.

Romy Schneider, a ripe *Fräulein* now, her kittenish face larger but also more luscious, so that she occasionally suggests the sensual beauty of Simone Signoret in the postwar films, is perfectly convincing as the one woman César wants. The contrasting character sketches of the men are, however, what give the film its wit: as the loud, blatantly materialistic, what-makes-Sammy-run tycoon, Montand provides the confident super-male energy that draws us into the situation (and it's César's whipping around in fast cars that sets the film in motion). He's playing a likable maniac, the kind of part an actor can sink his teeth in, and Montand chomps on everything in sight, overdoing the character in a jovial parodistic style. César's sudden violent squalls are in the earthy, whole-souled Raimu tradition, and when he bluffs his way through something or tries to ingratiate himself, his thinking processes are so childlike and easy to read we might be seeing them above his head in comic-strip balloons. (It's the sort of role Anthony Quinn thinks he can play.) Sautet has a very delicate sense of tone: we get to know César so well that when he comes up against the challenge he can't fight — Rosalie's changed feelings — we recognize that his collapse isn't pathetic, it's funny. And Sami Frey's wan elegance is just right for the man who hoodoos César's and Rosalie's happiness, since Frey's romantic appeal comes from what he is; he has what you can't get if you don't have it — the right blend of nuances. It's impossible to dislike César after you've heard him performing Bach without the aid of an instrument; you enjoy him so much that you're implicated in his foolishness. But you can also see that he looks like a hyperactive clown when Rosalie watches him while she is talking to the exquisitely modulated David, and the energy of clowns isn't very sexy. Rosalie begins to feel protective toward him, which is fatal to romance (though it may sometimes be the substance of marriage). It can't be held against César that he has the tiresomeness of the self-made man who can't just relax and take things for granted, the way the unobtrusively tasteful David can. And it can't really be held against David that he doesn't make much of an effort to hang on to Rosalie, and that losing her adds only the teeniest bit to his permanent air of despondency. The piquancy of the movie is that it reveals the two men's deadlocked characters without the usual pretense that a man's love turns him into just what a woman wants. The movie isn't quite as satisfying once César begins to unravel — it loses some of its charge — but the disconsolate confusion that sets in is integral to the theme. The film is a situation comedy about a love triangle, but it's also a *chanson*, saying ever so softly (why make a big noise about it?) that life is unfair. It's a movie not to be taken any more seriously than a tune one hums for a season — a little tedious, faintly absurd, but really quite pleasant.

"TRAVELS WITH MY AUNT" seems to run down before it gets started. Maybe the material couldn't have made it anyway (who knows what private joke Graham Greene was working out in the novel?), but for it to have a fighting chance the director should have a ravishing style and the actress who plays Aunt Augusta needs a charismatic presence; both are impossible to fake, and in this movie George Cukor and Maggie Smith don't have them — though they try exhaustingly hard. Cukor practically lusts for movement and a light touch, but the camera seems to go off on its own; he fails to keep us inside the situation, and things become so diffuse we don't remember why we're supposed to be watching the people on the screen. Maggie Smith gives a desperate, flustered performance, full of busywork with the hands and so many body tilts and high-piping vocal effects that after a while you just want her to stop vibrating and lie down and rest. Her great-lady, scintillating bit seems to mimic Edith Evans and Estelle Winwood and Cyril Ritchard, but where is Maggie Smith? When everything in a character is italicized this way, you never get a chance to feel the glamour or the aura; you never get a minute to surrender in (though the slurpy romantic score keeps telling you to).

Augusta, the disreputable Englishwoman in her seventies, induces her stuffy, plodding middle-aged nephew Henry (Alec McCowen) to accompany her on her travels, and brings him to a new something or other. Freedom? Gaiety? Anyway, an end to the humdrum. It's another of those "live, live, live" movies that feature tight-knit epigrams and proselytize for the loose, carefree life. The idea may sound like a good movie idea, but it never seems to work as a theme; maybe it needs to slip in from the side instead of coming at us foursquare. *Travels with My Aunt* isn't stale and squawking, like the Rosalind Russell version of *Auntie Mame,* but all the intangibles of casting and spirit and touch seem to have dried up, despite everybody's best intentions. Even the dynamics of the plot go wrong, when Augusta is pointlessly humiliated. Watching Maggie Smith, I remembered Constance Collier as the battered old acting coach in *Stage Door* who was tutoring the icy young Katharine Hepburn for her début; in a last surge of hope for her own long-abandoned career, she asked the producer, "Could you see an older woman in the part?" The answer here is yes. Augusta has no real zing, and Henry is so stodgy a cipher (as he was in the book) that your mind wanders from McCowen, who is perfectly good and totally uninteresting, to wonder if Alec Guinness might have been able to do more with Henry — give him, perhaps, a furtive spark for Augusta to fan. When you begin to speculate about who should have played a role, it means that the person on the screen doesn't touch your imagination and isn't going to leave much trace on your memory. And though this movie isn't painfully bad, just about everyone in it, from the bottom up, seems miscast.

❖

PROBABLY MANY OTHERS FEEL about Paul Newman as I do: I like him so much I always want his pictures to be good, for his sake as well as for my enjoyment. Newman is throwing away a lot of beautiful goodwill because of his bad judgment. The people who go to see *The Life and Times of Judge Roy Bean* go because they like him, and it's a logy, thick-skinned movie that seems to spend most of its time trying to tone down the moral ugliness of its premises. Basically, it's another of the spinoffs from *Butch Cassidy and the Sundance Kid,* this one, too, featuring nihilism plus sentimentality, which comes in the form of building up emotion for the star. Newman crinkles up so pretty when he smiles that he looks darling killing people, so even the large-scale carnage is cute. In *Roy Bean,* as in the also current *Jeremiah Johnson,* the writer, John Milius, provides a brutal, absurdist landscape while he is working up sympathy for his alienated modern version of a rugged individualist. Milius, a former University of Southern California film student, still in his twenties, received three hundred thousand dollars for his original screenplay for *Roy Bean,* but other film students may know what's coming in just about every scene, because they, too, have seen the movies (John Ford, Kurosawa, Jodorowsky) that have fed Milius's imagination.

It used to be that the studios cannibalized their own properties; now film students cannibalize their own favorites — a dubious tribute — and the sour joke is compounded here, because John Huston, whose finest work broke with the clichés that Milius feeds upon, is the director. After the explanatory data about Texas "near the turn of the last century," we're given the lead-in to the action — "Maybe this isn't the way it was. It's the way it should have been" — and I thought, I haven't read that title in decades. And then we get the opening shots of the stranger, Roy Bean, an outlaw, coming into town and into a saloon where a whole troupe of amoral monsters — a fat woman being bathed, freakily taciturn men, silent whores — set upon him, without provocation (in fact, just as he is buying them drinks), and rob and beat him and put a rope around his neck, to strangle him while he is being dragged through the desert by his horse. The snapping of the rope saves him. Even before the young Mexican angel came to give him water, I knew I'd seen this stuff fairly recently — in *El Topo,* of course. And, just like El Topo, Roy Bean comes back in righteous wrath to clean up that town full of besotted monsters, and, singlehanded, blasts them down.

The big scenes don't grow out of anything, and there are no characters —just mannerisms. In the published version of the script, that "It's the way it should have been" is followed by "and furthermore the author does not give a plug damn." This spirit seems to have carried through the whole production, which is full of the kind of inside jokes that do so little for an audience they suggest schoolboy pranks. Newman, his voice lowered to a gruff, nonmusical level, sounds like John Huston. Hiding in a beard throughout, he also goes in for a lot of beer-drinking. What with the actor's and the director's former associates turning up to do "cameos," the movie often resembles a log-rolling politicians' picnic. Stacy Keach appears in a camp vignette as a wild albino — he has his only moment of screen comedy so far, as his hands quiver at his sides, eager to draw. It's a funny bit, but it belongs in a revue parody of *El Topo,* not in this mock epic that keeps turning serious. The movie is made of scrap parts: the whores-who-become-respectable shtick; the Lily Langtry shtick, from the 1940 *The Westerner,* with Ava Gardner now doing the walk-on, etc. But the old story of Roy Bean becomes a new-style myth. Roy Bean sets himself up as a judge, and builds his own town by confiscating the property of the men he hunts down and hangs. We are expected to laugh at the dangling, twitching men he strings up, because he's a cool rogue and a charmer, but when his beer-guzzling pet bear is killed and his angel — now his adoring, loyal "woman" — dies after childbirth, both tragedies are milked while our hero suffers. Stoically, of course, and showing his pain only in manly, violent acts. Roy Bean, the biggest killer, is a law unto himself, and a legend, like Jeremiah Johnson. He goes into the desert for twenty years, and when he returns, white-bearded, to purge the town again — of its new "generation of vipers" — he's asked who he is, and he replies, "Justice."

Milius, who wears a gun and adds to his gun collection by getting a new one as part of each movie contract, is having a flamboyant success in fantasyland. A hunting enthusiast, he had it written into his contract with Warners for *Jeremiah Johnson* that he would get to shoot the numerous animals that his script (later modified) required be slaughtered. He has already directed his first feature, from his own script, on Dillinger; if it's a hit, he can probably get a contract to shoot the actors in his next one. It wouldn't be fair to John Huston to call *Roy Bean* a Huston picture; it's his only in the sense that he consented to direct it, and lent it a few touches. He couldn't transform the enthusiasm for mayhem; he merely diluted it. The result doesn't work on any terms, and you can make out the script pattern underneath, particularly if you've just seen *Jeremiah Johnson.* (Milius will probably go all the way with his specialty in his own movie.)

We're meant to laugh at Roy Bean's burlesque of frontier justice and see the "truth" in it. Milius is another of the boys in the *Naked Ape* movie colony; he's saying that belief in law is square and hypocritical. In his vision, the cool, smart thieves and killers *are* the only heroes. It's the sort of hipster's social theory you could develop if you grew up at action movies, or maybe if you lived your life around the film indust. y. Some of the primitivism that is being celebrated in movies now may be a reflection of the dealings behind the scenes in the movie business itself; writers and directors may have begun to see the world and the American past in terms of the cool-killer psychology of the barracudas and the smiling cobras who have taken over the studios (and who are financing principally action pictures). The ethos of ruthless, double-dealing winners is used as a model of the way things are — not to attack it but to become a winner. And the Vietnam war (which is in the background of the modern consciousness of practically all our action films now) is being exploited as a rationale — as a proof of rottenness that *justifies* brutality. Milius, a product of action movies, perpetuates what he got out of them: he piles on the slaughter, and is careful to twang the old-movie heartstrings and to keep the glamorous star center-stage. What I don't understand is: don't such stars as Redford and Newman — men who take an active interest in the environment and other good causes — realize what these films are saying? At some level, they must know, or the directors wouldn't be trying to garble the issues. Essentially, *Roy Bean* goes. way beyond being a *Dirty Harry* on the range, because there is no rational order to keep in Roy Bean's world; we're supposed to laugh in agreement when he takes a lawbook and tears out the page that doesn't suit his purposes (another old-movie shtick). He is the law, and there is no other, except for fools and weaklings who are "taken in." Newman's twittering and Huston's small jokes with the famous performers making cameo appearances are just stardust they're throwing in their own eyes — maybe so they won't have to see the ugly right-wing fantasy they've trapped themselves in. Their only achievement is in blunting the impact of the material: the audience, trying desperately just to have a good time, takes its cues from the tacky genial tone and reacts as if it were watching a more violent version of a spoofy James Garner TV show, until the snarled point of view locks the audience out altogether. It might have been better if Huston and Newman hadn't softened the viciousness; then they'd have had to face the disgrace of what they were working on. Of course, if they hadn't tampered with it, it might have been a hit, and then maybe they wouldn't have been ashamed at all.

[January 13, 1973]

Poetry and Politics

THE MOVIE OF Alexander Solzhenitsyn's *The First Circle* goes against the grain of all those old movies in which the heroes struggled to complete an invention or to perform a feat while inwardly, in our childish souls, we cheered, sharing the heroes' victories as they won fame and fortune. For the prisoners — or *zeks* — in this movie, heroism means destroying their inventions and refusing to carry out the tasks that might win them freedom and honors. Unlike Solzhenitsyn's *One Day in the Life of Ivan Denisovich,* which deals with an Everyman, a mere dot, in the slave-labor camps, *The First Circle* is a view of the top echelon of the slave-labor world — the mathematicians, scientists, engineers, and professors working in a technical institute near Moscow. They have spent years in the labor camps — they have survived the bottom — and now they are, as the novelist puts it, in "the highest, the best, the first circle of Hell." The tasks assigned them are to solve "security" problems: the government wants a device for putting a hidden camera in a door so that everyone who opens the door is automatically photographed; the government wants a scientific method of identifying people by their voice patterns so that incoming calls on monitored phones can be traced; and other such projects. These prisoners can improve their own situations only by helping to entrap others, and they succeed — as human beings — by deliberately failing. They know what the consequences will be, and the movie brings us to an awed admiration of their heroism; though we can't quite cheer, we draw in our breath, feeling, now, like adults.

The movie isn't drab — which is what one may fear. It's tense and inspiriting: not a great film but good enough to dramatize Solzhenitsyn's themes and to leave us facing the issues the novel raises — the moral and intellectual choices left open to the prisoners. It isn't often that a movie tries to engage us in one of the central political experiences of our own time, and it's far from simple to re-create modern Russia — the novel is set in 1949 — without Russians. Alexander Ford, the well-known veteran Polish director, who was for many years head of the

Polish film industry, left Poland in 1968, because of the anti-Semitic persecutions, and he made this film in Denmark as a Danish-German co-production. The film is in English, and I can't see how one can rationally object. The performers are Scandinavian (mostly Danish), Polish, and German; they spoke their lines in English — accented, of course — and then, under the director's supervision, non-accented voices were dubbed in. Under the circumstances, it's an almost impeccable solution, because the somewhat uncharacterized, impersonal voices make the argument of the film very easy to follow. The camerawork, the subdued color, the editing are all craftsmanlike; Ford must be a very modest man, deeply engaged with the material, because he doesn't intrude between Solzhenitsyn and us.

The high intelligence of this movie is that it does not try to replace the novel. The book has that density of episodes and individual stories and interconnected lives which makes for a great "read." The picture of the new Soviet bourgeoisie and the discussions within the prison about supporting the regime have the richness of high journalism, and the sudden, majestic big scenes — such as the arrest of Volodin, the young state counselor in the Ministry of Foreign Affairs — stay in your memory. In the movie, you lose that spacious, beautifully controlled outpouring of incident; you lose the orchestration of the themes, and what some might call the Russianness. Ford eliminates characters and telescopes others, and he doesn't try for the contradictions within them, or the depth. Some of the big scenes are in the movie, and they're not great scenes now, but, if their sublimity is lost, you can still get their import. I think Ford's approach is sound: what makes most movie adaptations of novels of the first or second rank so embarrassing is that the director tries to rival the author. The movie becomes a pop vulgarization, which is then advertised as if the movie itself were a classic. The acceptance of pop has become a self-putdown for many of us; when we see a movie in which people behave like adults, we come out feeling clean, for a change. There is no pop distortion here, nothing tinny. By concentrating on the themes — on precisely what is most controversial — the movie performs an inestimable service. In the book, Solzhenitsyn's great gift of specificity and the other pleasures of his narrative crowd out one's niggling doubts about what he's saying. The movie, stripping away those pleasures, brings us to confront the material *politically.*

Structurally, Ford is very faithful. The action begins with the phone call that Volodin (Peter Steen) makes to warn an eminent professor — who as a doctor had saved Volodin's mother's life — that he may be arrested. Then the action moves to the life within the prison-institute during the three days in which experiments conducted there lead to

Volodin's arrest. Volodin enters the prison just as a group of obstructionists, including the hero, the mathematician Nerzhin (Gunther Malzacher), are being sent back to the lower rungs of Hell, where they may expect to rot and perish. The movie is faithful even to a defect in the novel: as we become involved with the prisoners, we lose track of the imminent danger to Volodin, and it isn't until we hear the tape of his phone conversation being studied in the institute that we are brought back to the story line. It may be a defect in both novel and film that there is no real suspense — that it is only a matter of time before Volodin is arrested. That is, in Solzhenitsyn's vision the police apparatus is like a doomsday machine, so incredibly, fatally efficient that nobody can get by with anything. This isn't necessarily based on actual observation. For the author's purposes, the superficialities of chance are unimportant, and it doesn't really matter if Volodin escapes detection this time; sooner or later the impulse that led him to warn the professor will land him in prison. And what Solzhenitsyn is concerned with is how an individual in the extremity of suffering finds his humanity. I think this is why the spring of the trap as Volodin is caught doesn't have the effects of suspense that it would in an ordinary melodrama, in which we would have been sweating it out with him and hoping for his escape.

In the movie, Nerzhin, a man much like the author (who is also a mathematician), is given some of the action that the designer Sologdin is assigned in the book, and also bits of Gerasimovich, the physicist (both these characters have been eliminated), but Nerzhin takes on the additional burdens with ease, since all three characters appear to speak for the author. Malzacher, a lean actor with an intelligent manner (a little like Richard Basehart), is successful in suggesting that Nerzhin is satirical and amused about his own adamant gadfly nature — that his irony includes his own loftiness. What Malzacher doesn't suggest is that look of a man from an earlier century which we begin to see in the photographs of the bearded Solzhenitsyn — the severe look of an Amish elder. This Solzhenitsyn is the greatest poet of freedom, and his integrity gives him an intimidating moral authority, but his aura of intellectual clarity can be deceptive. It is too easy for us to blur the distinction between two ideas: one, that in an oppressive system if you try to act like a human being you risk martyrdom, and that martyrdom may be your only way not to lose your self-respect; and, two, that this martyrdom will bring down the system. The first is not difficult to believe, though Solzhenitsyn himself carries it further than we may assent to; in the novel, he has Gerasimovich thinking that "those who were free lacked the immortal soul the *zeks* had earned in their endless prison terms." The second idea, however, is slippery. *The First Circle* is the story of a moral victory — of Nerzhin, primarily, but of others also

— but in the terms of the novel and the movie this moral victory defeats the oppressors. Harrison Salisbury, who is quoted on the cover of the book, said in the *Times Book Review,* "It is not in the end the prisoners who are destroyed, even though they may lose their lives. It is the jailers. . . . It is the oppressors who are doomed." For Solzhenitsyn the oppressors may be spiritually doomed, but that shouldn't be confused with actual political doom. We must, of course, believe in moral courage, but as an end in itself — as the realization of what man can be. It would be immaculate justice if moral incorruptibility destroyed the corrupt, but that goes back to the high-minded naïveté we had as children, when we overestimated the power of words and believed that virtue would conquer all, without a fight, just in the nature of things.

Because Solzhenitsyn, in his beautiful, stiff-necked intransigence, clearly makes a difference in the world, we are in danger, I think, of accepting his Christian mysticism as if it were a political solution. His heroes become stronger in themselves when, at the end, they are "filled with the fearlessness of those who have lost *everything,* the fearlessness which is not easy to come by but which endures." They are resigned but not broken. It is, of course, a great triumph, but it's a peculiarly insulating personal triumph. And although the assumption that the spiritual strength of men who have lost everything will defeat the oppressors may be a psychological necessity for the heroes, it is, when viewed from the outside, heavenly rhetoric. When you get to the point of believing that the *acceptance* of powerlessness is true power, you're no longer talking about the visible world.

Deep in the author's writing — and even in his face — one can feel the belief that man was put on this earth to suffer. And this has somehow got mixed with the idea of defeating your enemies by the purity of your suffering. But your gestures may do more for you than to them. It is not really surprising that this great Christian novelist should spring from the Soviet Union: totalitarianism drives one to the last outpost — fighting to save your soul (which, psychologically, may not be so very different from American blacks fighting for their manhood). But it's easy for us to overvalue our own suffering, romantically. An individual here may immolate himself assuming that his suffering will change the world, that the people who don't care about the deaths of thousands — of millions — will be transformed by his. (Does he perhaps think that one white charred body will do what all the brown corpses can't?) The truth of political life is even more horrible than Solzhenitsyn's truth. We can certainly believe that in the Soviet Union the heroes are in the camps, if by "the heroes" we mean the irritable or defiant people who express their revulsion at the social order, even though only inadvertently. But are they *fortunate* to be there, as (in some strict, recondite area of his mind) Solzhenitsyn sometimes seems to think — earning their immortal souls? Nerzhin-Solzhenitsyn, shoving his contempt down the oppressors' throats, is a strong, robust hero, a dissenter with the humor of his rectitude. And Solzhenitsyn himself, as the survivor of everything "they" dished out, is the greatest symbolic artist-hero in the modern world. But politically, despite the intelligence of his descriptive passages, he looks toward some special mystical endowment of the Russian people. And that famous Russian soul doesn't seem to come through in political life — it comes through only in novels. Probably what comes through in political life in the Soviet Union is what comes through in political life here now — hopelessness, apathy, suspicion, fear, cynicism, violence.

What gives the movie its impact is how close the whole situation feels to us, and Solzhenitsyn is inspiring because many of us feel that we, too, need moral leadership. But I was bothered in the novel by Volodin's saying, "After all, the writer is a teacher of the people. . . . A greater writer is, so to speak, a second government." And I was bothered, too, by the words of Solzhenitsyn's undelivered speech accepting the Nobel Prize for Literature in 1970: "One word of truth shall outweigh the whole world." (If it did, the Vietnam war would have ended — would never have started. If it did, editorial writers wouldn't have to go on saying the same things over and over.) When Solzhenitsyn speaks those words, he takes risks, and the words have political consequences, but people who believe that one word of truth will really outweigh the whole world are mistaking poetic power for political power. Yet I think that at times we all play this game with ourselves. Solzhenitsyn's own depth of feeling is not in question. He sets a peerless example that lifts our spirits, but our exaltation may allow us to feel that evil can be dealt with by poetry alone. We react the way we react to a stargazing valedictorian: we can see that he believes what he's saying, and we find his belief inspiring because we want to believe. We respond to the beauty of the message. But we know that when more people actually believed that the poetic truths would conquer, it didn't improve their social conditions; it merely helped them to bear their suffering. There's a soaring upbeat element in *The First Circle* — an old-fashioned Christian Russianness — that may have helped to make the book popular. At the end of the novel, when the group, including Nerzhin, is being transported to Siberia, Solzhenitsyn writes:

> Yes, the taiga and the tundra awaited them, the record cold of Oymyakon and the copper excavations of Dzhezkazgan; pick and barrow; starvation rations of soggy bread; the hospital; death. The very worst.
>
> But there was peace in their hearts.

The challenge of the movie — coming to us at this time — is that even though we're not living in a totalitarian state, and we know that the hopelessness Americans now feel isn't fully justified, we fear increasingly that the only self-respecting choices that are left us may lead to martyrdom. That "peace in their hearts" is maddening, because we haven't got peace in our hearts, even in its simpler forms. But in Solzhenitsyn's form it's spiritual solace when everything else is gone.

[January 20, 1973]

Out of Tragedy, Suds

INCREDULITY IS THE FIRST REACTION to *Limbo,* a movie about the wives of Americans missing or imprisoned in Vietnam. It's set on an Air Force base in Florida in 1972, though its spiritual setting is a deterged *Peyton Place* — a movie that, like *Limbo,* was directed by Mark Robson, a director of no distinction and no visible style. (A week after seeing his last film, *Happy Birthday, Wanda June,* I couldn't remember who had made it.) Yet Robson's impersonality is perfect for *Limbo*; because of his plodding, egalitarian attention to each detail, the movie can take up a "dangerous" — that is, war-related — subject in absolute safety. The look of the movie tells us it's not about the effects of the Vietnam war on the wives and children of those absent men; it's not even set in the America that the war has torn apart. It's about the perennial plight of women trying to cope, and it's set in a calibrated, canned dreamworld in which we know exactly how to read each nuance of feeling, how to interpret every inflection. It all fits together: this world is so Pop-ugly — like old Coca-Cola billboards — that the stale, sweet emotions are right at home.

Yet what are we to make of this vision? The film is a representation of a form of actual suffering, but everything in it seems synthetic. And the synthetic begins to seem *true.* The words spoken are pitifully simp-ordinary: "nice," "a lot of," "You're a wonderful woman," "You have wonderful kids." The scriptwriters might have worked for the astronauts. *Limbo* has a frightening superficial realism — it's the same kind of fright we feel when we walk into a suburban supermarket and see customers who look just like the people who polish and spray in TV commercials. These sanitized war wives, immaculately coiffed, taking care of their storybook children, writing daily letters to their husbands, are coexistent with Billy Graham and the President's Inaugural Balls. It's apparent that the mediocrity of their lives — the rooms devoid of reading matter, the absence of any sign of taste or thought — is meant to guarantee the audience's sympathetic identification with them. Even to be "too involved" with the war might make them seem "unbalanced human beings" — not "real people." So they don't listen to the news on the radio or watch it on TV; they don't even read a newspaper. If they knew anything, they might be controversial and off-putting. Their impeccable feminine ignorance makes them acceptable mass-market heroines. They take you back: they might be a collection of Miss Rheingolds. Their innocence, the cinematography that looks like enlargements of Kodacolor snapshots of a family vacation, the sound of "You Belong to Me" on the radio all contrive to turn the Vietnam war into the Second World War. The film might have come out of a time capsule buried in 1943 — the *So Proudly We Hail* period of the sacrificing women on "the home front" — except that it's not as gaudy. There are no vivid personalities now — no boozing broad, no nympho, no psycho, no bitch — and no wisecracks. It's not meant to be fun; that's what's new about it — it's unrelieved.

There's not a single false note of originality. The clichés come at you full face: the bright-eyed cheerleader-ingénue (Kate Jackson) married only two weeks before her husband went overseas and disappeared; the devout-Catholic redhead (Kathleen Nolan) with her four kids and a husband who has been a prisoner for five years; the rich Southerner (Katherine Justice) who refuses to accept the fact of her husband's death; the standby suitors, decent and honorable. Most of the wives we see are educating themselves or doing professional work, but they're career women as *superior* housewives. Their ordinariness is perfect, a form of intellectual virginity; they live, metaphorically, in a supermarket. The movie is almost uncannily condescending in its touches — the orchid corsage given to the wife who goes to greet her returning husband, the crummy look of Christmas decorations in a house in Florida, the forties sound of the music that comments on the action. It's pure Pop, but lugubrious and ultimately baffling. This must have been the image of America that Antonioni was trying to get at in *Zabriskie Point;* Mark Robson, trying for poignance and mass-market "sensitivity," blunders into it. Robson has a knack for it, like Norman Rockwell; *Peyton Place* was probably his most assured piece of direction, and *Limbo* equates obsolete trash with ideal Americanism in a way a satirist can't. This Pop aspect of American life is its own satire. Immersion in the media produces people who appear to be as "unreal" as the models they soak their imaginations in. Media zombies are spreading throughout the land. That's why we stare incredulously at the shallow universe of *Limbo* — because after a while its exactly detailed pseudo-realism begins to seem like a truer realism than we know what to make of.

This is one of the few films that attempt to touch on the war directly, but it comes out of a morally exhausted popular culture: the moviemakers can find no drama in their subject, no characters, and nothing to reveal. The movie never really gets into the hell of not knowing whether your husband is alive or dead, and though it's about love and loneliness more than anything else, it never gets into the predicament of wives who don't know if they're married or kidding themselves — or what they're married to, after five or seven years. The movie doesn't get into anything; it mentions things, but no thought is developed. It's about driving, and car trips in shiny new cars; even when a group of the women go to Paris to talk to the North Vietnamese, we see them in a taxi while the sound track gives us perky Paris music. It's about makeup; the creamy-beige and peach-bloom masks dominate the action, and they tell us that there's nothing underneath. Everything there is is on the masks. The precision of the actresses' features is a testimonial to American know-how: Kate Jackson (who comes to us via TV's *Dark Shadows*) goes from crisis to crisis, but she never obscures the shining white of her eyes by so much as a blink, and her winged eyebrows are tweezed to a laser edge; her nostrils are never wet, her lips never dry, her hair never oily. These mask women all have skins that are triumphs of depilation. And they know how to dress properly — nothing sexy or sloppy that might diminish the respect we are meant to feel for them. They carry their self-image in every single article of apparel: they know their place in the middle class.

Limbo has a fascination as evidence of a decline in national style — a photograph album of a goody-goody nation in a depressed condition. Every detail says "regression" — even the way the movie yanks tears is regressive. When the Catholic who has waited five years learns of her husband's death by disease, Kathleen Nolan's exhibition of suffering perplexes us, because she turns on the spigot so efficiently, with such certainty, and yet we can't deny that by now, after generations of women have read slick housewives' magazines and watched television, her changes in makeup, posture, dress — her professional (veteran of over eight hundred TV shows) abandonment to grief — could be exactly how a woman might react to the death of her husband. Mightn't an Air Force wife have learned from TV how to express her emotions, and maybe what to feel? Pain itself is domesticated when it is made so explicit. Throughout the movie, there is a suggestion of baby talk in the women's articulation, and in the men's, too; nothing could be hidden under the sound of these childish voices. In the 1956 movie *Invasion of the Body Snatchers,* our bodies were taken over during sleep by vegetable pods, and we kept on going through the motions of life, but soullessly, as vegetables. This movie represents a society taken over by the media: awake (or maybe only half-awake), we turn into the masks of a consumer society. The people on the screen live by the formulas of daytime television. Everything is revealed; they cast no shadows. There is no mystery in human behavior: that is the message of the shadowless style.

The black actresses, prettily integrated, also wear their tidy outfits and their glossy masks. There is no differentiation between black and white, not because the movie (which starts from the middle-class subject of Air Force wives) is democratic — condescension isn't democratic — but because it levels everything. No one in the movie wants for anything but love; as far as the material things are concerned, prosperity and sanity seem to be identical. If you plan for the future — and retool if necessary — everything goes as scheduled. It's a limbo in a fuller sense than was intended, but an orderly one. Nobody would guess from this movie that there had ever been public protests against the Vietnam war; *Limbo* allows itself only the merest hints of malfunctioning in the democratic system. The women don't bitch about the way they're treated; they don't resent the military men's bureaucratic paternalism. The Catholic redhead protests the inadequacy of the day of prayer a congressman proposes, but her protest might be something that came to her in a dream. "The war is an unworthy cause," she says, and "We have made a mistake. Why don't we admit it?" Even children have been saying these things for years; that's why it's safe for her to say it. She's not tainted with radicalism; we can see that she and the others have no contact with the outside world. And the ingénue isn't tainted with brains: she is getting her teaching credentials, but when her new suitor tells her about his hope of doing some more space research because of the knowledge to be gained, she touches her head in bewilderment and says that that's too much for her to follow.

Are we back to this, and in a movie produced by a woman (Linda Gottlieb, Phi Beta Kappa, Wellesley, 1960, and a Woodrow Wilson Fellow at Columbia) and co-scripted by another woman (Joan Silver — Sarah Lawrence, 1956 — in collaboration with James Bridges)? Can Linda Gottlieb and Joan Silver (who wrote the book on which the movie is based) get by in the movie business only by showing us a society more patriarchal than ours actually is? When educated women come up with a heroine who can't follow her space-dreamer's manly aspirations through two sentences before her poor little head begins to hurt, something is rotten somewhere. And something is rotten when it's considered expedient for the scientist (Russell Wiggins) to appear first as a filling-station attendant and to be so rustic and boyishly sincere he might be auditioning to play the young Tom Edison. This "women's picture" is so exploitative it's some sort of classic — a salute to banality. It's regressive even in its cue-card music. According to the publicity, Anita Kerr is "the first woman in the history of Hollywood to write the original music and conduct the score for a major motion picture"; she may be a pioneer, but she's something less than a heroine. The score makes it practically unnecessary to watch the screen: the music tells you how to react.

The release of *Limbo* is a masterpiece of timing; the returning prisoners of war are sure to be on the front pages. The film has already been highly praised by *Variety:*

> The Universal release avoids polarized politics, keeps its focus on real problems and people, and will evoke tears among audiences of all ages and philosophies.

Tears, and maybe stupefaction.

[February 3, 1973]

Lady Zelda

WHEN PEOPLE OF TALENT get involved in the movie business, they rarely play their talent straight; they bend it to what they think of as the "demands" of the medium — that is, to what movies have always done. And so they bring to movies not the best of themselves but the worst. Robert Bolt appears to think that the shopworn conceits of old trash become "filmic" gestures when they're staged big enough — and with a full orchestra sighing, throbbing, and moping. After adapting his play *A Man for All Seasons,* and working on three screenplays for David Lean, Bolt has now directed his own screenplay of *Lady Caroline Lamb.* The movie tries for the same colossal lyricism as *Ryan's Daughter,* his last collaboration with Lean; this, too, is Panavision pulp — five-and-dime romantic passions made gothic by the magnitude of the back-drops. The movie opens with Caroline (Sarah Miles) galloping furiously across vast landscapes to arrive, finally, at a huge palace, where she makes her way through a corps of servants and dashes upstairs through acres of corridors to locate her mother (Pamela Brown) and announce breathlessly, "Mama, he has proposed!" After such an amusingly overblown introduction, we look forward gaily to more romantic camp — especially since Sarah Miles barely attempts to sustain the period illusion, and wears androgynous adaptations of Regency clothes, and cropped hair. But Bolt can't reach this visual hyperbole again, and he studied with a dull master — the movie is in the calendar-art school of late David Lean. Bolt is less "tasteful" than Lean but equally lacking in energy. He actually pulls out the old wheeze of having the heedless, impetuous Caroline toss her diamond bracelet into a crowd of Italian beggars and then stand paralyzed with horror while the one who retrieves it is killed by the others. (Bolt seems as thoughtless as his nincompoop heroine, since he tries to make poetry out of the arc of the diamonds flying through the air.) And at the end when Caroline, in her nightie, wanders chilled and forlorn to fall dead of a broken heart in a moonlit gazebo, Bolt cuts to her husband, far away, who wakes from his sleep at the moment she hits the deck. This telepathic bit was corny in 1922, in *Nosferatu,* but there's nothing, apparently, that Bolt is ashamed to throw in. Some movie directors can make this sort of garbage pay off, but not Bolt. It's easy to perceive that he admires lush extravagance, and wants to take the old M-G-M style and do it to the hilt. And though that might not be worth doing, it would be fun. However, he can't: he has neither the technique nor the flair. What you see is careful preparation for excess — which then fizzles out. Intellectually, he's shameless; but he's inhibited. He's a square Ken Russell. Russell overheats everything; Bolt can't get anything warmed up.

The Caroline Lamb of this movie, unlike purring Joan Greenwood, with her naughty sweet-shepherdess smiles, in *The Bad Lord Byron,* in 1948, is a bewildered, neurotic, mistreated woman. However, this new movie is about the *romance* of mistreated women, the romance of self-destruction. Sarah Miles looks impish — more changeling than great lady — but she goes through a revamped version of the agonies of the big women stars of the past. She fights to live to the utmost, openly and fearlessly, but she is frail and becomes confused by the hypocritical standards of a society that cares more for discretion than for honesty; she suffers and she sacrifices herself. In other words, Bolt has absorbed some women's-lib attitudes into his gush, so that Caroline Lamb can seem an early free spirit wrecked by sexist double standards. She is misunderstood by everyone; considered irrational for wanting to be open; humiliated; and driven into melancholia. Her fineness of spirit is never truly appreciated. (Remember Susan Hayward in *I Want to Live!*)

In order to present her in this light, Bolt has distorted history in countless ways, and has knocked off his heroine before she could do what she's probably best known for: write the scandalous novel *Glenarvon*, in which she paid Byron back for wearying of her and attacked her estranged husband, William Lamb, who later became Prime Minister under Victoria (he is played here by Jon Finch). Bolt has, in fact, through most of the movie made her brainless and resourceless — a victim of society rather than an engaged member of it. (The woman who had the buttons on her page boys' uniforms inscribed with the words "Don't trust Byron" was certainly more flamboyantly bitch-foolish than Bolt's pitiable creature.) In the movie, she ruins herself for the sake of her husband after he has helped her recover from her infatuation with Byron — Richard Chamberlain, trying to be demonic in beetle brows that give him a permanent scowl. This Byron is presented as a hulking, arrogant boor and a phony. (As a piece of miscasting, Chamberlain's Byron rivals Gregory Peck's Ahab.) Maybe for the sake of her being a total victim, and the only victim, this Byron doesn't even have a limp. Bolt plays it both ways — Caroline is a symbolic confused modern woman trying to liberate herself, and she is also the hapless heroine of traditional fiction, giving her all for love. She's a loser who limps enough for everybody.

The movie thrashes about from one style and point of view to another. There's that Ken Russell side: kinky Caroline in jewels and black paint entering a ball as Byron's blackamoor slave; Caroline, cast off by Byron, dressed like a coach boy and running alongside his carriage, carrying a torch; Caroline hysterically stabbing herself at a formal dinner party and the camera spinning so the blood can splatter a roomful of shocked ladies. There's the arch British historical movie, with snooty epigrams for Margaret Leighton, as Lady Melbourne (William Lamb's mother), to deliver, and show-off bits for Laurence Olivier, as the Duke of Wellington, and Ralph Richardson, as the King. And there's the sad-sack women's-lib kitsch. If we can tell where Bolt's heart is from his writing style, his sympathies are with the worldly-wise cynics. When Caroline's housekeeper says, "A broken heart, that's what she died of," Bolt gives the jaded Lady Melbourne the best line of the movie: "My God, wouldn't she!" He seems to be divided between thinking Caroline a fool and wanting to exploit her as a female rebel-without-a-cause. But you can't tell anything from his style as a director. The film has no sweep; the scenes are like beads on a string. Though the movie was photographed by the normally fluent Oswald Morris, it looks almost as stiff as the movies Freddie Young shoots for David Lean. Like Lean, Bolt doesn't know where to place actors or how to move crowds; the groupies who cluster about Byron in military formations are a flagrant example of ineptitude. Nevertheless, the subject sounds like fun even if the movie isn't, and it's just possible that by providing so many cheap fantasies, along with an aura of deep sympathy for women, Bolt may have a commercial success. If *Ryan's Daughter* could get by, it may be that, in this expensive-slop genre, anything's possible.

And that brings us back to Sarah Miles: I have half a hunch that her deficiencies may work to the film's commercial advantage. On talk shows, Miss Miles, who is Mrs. Bolt, is a mad camp almost in the league of Viva, but as an actress she's minimal. As Ryan's daughter, she was trying seriously hard; as Caroline, she bashes her tantrumy head on one big emotion after another. This Caroline isn't much of a temptress; when we see her on her honeymoon, surrounded by courtiers and trying to be rash and alluring, she's just silly. But we can't tell when it's Sarah Miles who isn't up to the grand style she's affecting and when it's Caroline. (Bolt's direction doesn't clue us in. Even when it's clearly Caroline, we don't always understand what has gone wrong. There's no explanation, for example, of why she fails to carry off her blackamoor number and just embarrasses herself.) Sarah Miles can't get by with big romantic scenes, because the most a man would be likely to say of her was that she was a delicious little thing. She has no largeness of spirit; she lacks the presence of a star and the emotional resources of a major actress. She's such a gimcrack personage that susceptible viewers can fill in the psychological void with their own romantic-masochistic distress. She really *is* a flop up there, so her pathos (which comes mostly from her inadequacy as an actress and Bolt's as a director) may invite identification — not with triumphs and pleasures, as most romantic works do, but with weakness and misery. Her Caroline integrates neurotic modern self-pity with an old form of pseudo-aristocratic pulp carried farther than before: Sarah Miles acts like a dizzy shopgirl dreaming of being a great lady and falling flat even in her dreams. This movie answers the prayers of those who want to be "understood" — that is, not just forgiven for their lapses of judgment and the scenes they make but admired for them.

❖

CON-GAME COMEDIES are fun to watch on the screen because we're not put in the position of the mark, and because the marks we see generally illustrate Fields' theorem (which is patently untrue) that "you can't cheat an honest man." It wouldn't be fun to watch con men hustle poor people out of their savings, but it *is* fun to watch smart crooks dupe dumb crooks, or, better still, to watch them fleece rich hypocrites; the more pious the victims, the more we can enjoy the hip justice of it. For as long as *Trick Baby,* based on the book by Iceberg Slim (Robert Beck, the black pimp turned writer, and a better writer than his pseudonym might suggest), plays by the old rules of the genre, it's an agreeable time-killer. The cast is mostly black, and the Philadelphia ghetto provides a grimy counterpoint to the fairy-tale pleasures of the various cons. But when the good guys are trapped, they ought to pull a real boss hustle and get off the hook. Instead, the character we've been rooting for (Blue) is squashed by the mobsters and their cops — which spoils the audience's good time. The audience, quite rightly, isn't taking things seriously and doesn't want to, and it's just damn foolishness on the scriptwriters' part to destroy that happy suspension of belief.

Still, the film is neat up to the halfway point, and in Mel Stewart's Blue it has a tall-tale swindler who seems to have stepped out of urban black folklore. Blue is the con man as the artist of the lie; shearing the sheep is a craft to him, and Stewart gives the role the black equivalent of old-world grace. Blue's partner, played by Kiel Martin, is the son of a black whore and her white trick. His black friends call him White Folks; his enemies call him Trick Baby. For the black audience, he is meant to provide a special satisfaction, since although he can pass as a white he *chooses* to be black. And both blacks and whites should be able to enjoy the joke when a rich white woman, taking him for white, is astounded by his sexual prowess. But, for the racial-switch-hitter premise of the picture to be effective, White Folks needs to have some recognizable "soul," which we in the audience can perceive, even if the whites in the movie are blind to it, and Kiel Martin, with his dimply, spoiled-baby face, doesn't have it. (The very young Tyrone Power, with his black-Irish look, might have been right for the role.) The director, Larry Yust, brings off some smooth new bits, such as a contrast of white dress-up "society" and black dress-up "society," and he has a good documentary feel for street life; he's weak, however, in his handling of the actresses, both black and white, who are unnecessarily degraded. You can sense what this movie should be — it strikes some fresh sparks, even if most of the best ideas remain potentialities.

THE MOVIE OF "UNDER MILK WOOD" offers a beautiful reading of the Dylan Thomas material, with illustrations, and fundamentally it doesn't try to be anything else, but the work was already complete in its original form, as a radio play — a play for voices. Though the movie doesn't really add to it, I enjoyed sitting back and listening. If the sound track has a life of its own, it *should* have, in this case. The special quality of the work is that the teeming words rub against each other in your head; the sounds and meanings pile up, with feelings leaping in every direction. Dylan Thomas transcends his own excesses; he redeems emotionally charged language for people who had grown suspicious of it. But you couldn't handle the sensations this language produces and take in rich visual imagery, too. (The only strong visual images in the movie — some superb dark shots of seals — may, on one level, extend the poetry, but they also add something foreign, because they, too, have a life of their own.)

The film is narrated by characters who slide in and out of the dialogue sequences. The method of the adapter-director, Andrew Sinclair, is like Joseph Strick's method in the film of Joyce's *Ulysses*: Sinclair clarifies the action for us, locates the characters in an area, makes their relationships apparent, gives them faces and bodies — all of which helps us to distinguish the voices and keep them straight. The faces and bodies are rather well-known ones: Richard Burton, who was in the original radio production, is the principal linking voice (he also participates in the action by returning — as if he were the author — to his hometown, and he plays a role lifted from Thomas's short story "Just like Little Dogs"); Peter O'Toole is the blind Captain Cat, and he takes over some of the narration, the Captain's blindness providing a convenient excuse for descriptive passages; Elizabeth Taylor plays the Captain's lost love, Rosie Probert. And in the cast of about seventy there are also Victor Spinetti, Glynis Johns (for a moment she provides a reprise of her mermaid in *Miranda*), Vivien Merchant, Sian Phillips, and Ann Beach mourning "Little Willy Wee." Sinclair isn't unctuously faithful, and his imagery generally avoids the obvious forms of redundancy — he's intelligently faithful. But this still leaves him with a wild effusion on the track while a modest, sometimes undernourished set of visual images passes before us. However, Sinclair brings the material emotionally close. In a sense, *Under Milk Wood* is a people's poem — a celebration of the originality and eccentricity in "ordinary" life — and the movie is a very warm experience. You feel the affection of the cast and you share in it — which I don't think was the case with *Ulysses*. Joyce's work was too great and too big to be comprehended by the movie: we seemed to be looking at a diagram, and, of course, we were hearing only bits. With *Under Milk Wood,* the movie is a satisfying way to hear the language. Since the images don't take over, they don't conflict with the words, yet our seeing the people seems to set the experience in our minds.

What one may lose is the unkempt luxuriance of Thomas's vision: Sinclair has pinned it down, contracted it. The characters have acquired exact contours, and we've seen where they live, and how. And one may lose something else — the freedom not to visualize the work. For some of us, it took place nowhere but in the poet's unruly head, and the disembodiment played a part in its glorious windiness. I never thought of those voices in terms of characters, never thought of them as real people at all; that was the big difference between *Under Milk Wood* and the work that it superficially resembles, *Our Town.* It was Dylan Thomas's moonstruck voice I heard in all the voices, and I loved the work as a roaring piece of exhibitionism; he was the high-flier poet keeping all those swarming words aloft.

[February 10, 1973]

The Businessman-Pimp as Hero

As HARRY, the fiftyish Los Angeles garment manufacturer of *Save the Tiger,* Jack Lemmon has to do a lot of suffering, and he can't stop jabbering while suffering. Harry lives in a well-staffed Beverly Hills mansion, but he is desperate for money, and he is carrying such a wad of anxiety that he's on the verge of a breakdown. He keeps a whore (Lara Parker) on a retainer, and he pimps for his customers so that they'll give him their orders, and now he's planning to set fire to his warehouse so that the insurance money will finance filling those orders. The movie is desperate, too; though it begins promisingly, it is so overwritten and overplotted that it becomes inflamed and puffed up. Its heart is in rationalizing seventies corruption, but its techniques are from the fervent, socially conscious thirties. When Harry recalls going ashore at Anzio, or when he chants old baseball scores or plays his tapes of Benny Goodman, he dreams of what might have been, like the old man in *Awake and Sing!* listening to Caruso's "O Paradiso!" Harry's threnody about his plight and the plight of America ("They're making jockstraps out of the flag. . . . There are no more rules") is a lurid derivative of Arthur Miller. You keep wondering why John G. Avildsen, who directed, didn't throw out some of this blat or overlap it or tell the actors to mumble; maybe he just hasn't much taste (a plausible supposition about the director who made *Joe, Guess What We Learned in School Today?,* and *Cry Uncle*), but more likely he couldn't get rid of the crippling barrage of language because the author of the screenplay, Steve Shagan, is also the producer of the film. Shagan is obviously out to create a tragic hero for us — to make Howl of a Businessman the follow-up to *Death of a Salesman. Save the Tiger* has a special quality of brag and presumption that one associates with other writer-produced films based on original screenplays, such as the recent *T. R. Baskin*; Shagan is determined to pack in all his bristling wit and wisdom. After an hour, the words overpower the images, and great gobbets of sardonic philosophy seem to be hanging from one's eyelids.

A displaced admirer of Clifford Odets, Shagan wants us to feel the poetry and vitality in upper-middle-class life; this movie is about the anguish of people who are in danger of losing their swimming pools. Their anguish may not affect all of us the way Shagan means it to. A manufacturer who can sell his goods only by providing girls for his customers and who can raise money only by committing arson is obviously incompetent. But Shagan never raises the question of whether Harry (and others like Harry) *should* be in business. Instead, Shagan attempts to justify Harry by showing us what a human fellow he is — lovable and warm-blooded, protective of his partner (Jack Gilford), decent to his "ethnic" employees, and an admirer of traditions of craft. We're even supposed to see that the pathetic buyer (Norman Burton) he's pimping for *needs* that session with the prostitute. And it won't wash. If that poor bastard of a buyer needs a girl, that doesn't justify Harry's lining her up for him in order to make a sale. Harry's pity for him is one thing; Shagan's manipulation of that pity into a rationalization for pimping as part of a business deal is another. Shagan can't make it come clean, because his whole case for Harry is based on the notion that in this country at this time corruption is compulsory, and it isn't — no matter how many cases like Harry come to mind (as, of course, they do). Shagan's use of Harry's good deeds and sweet nature and concern for his employees to justify his business practices is like saying that a man isn't guilty of murder if he sends his mother a check every month, or that murder isn't murder if the profits from it go to a worthy cause.

Save the Tiger asks us to weep for Harry — for what he wanted to be versus what he has become. O.K. — if you weep easily; Arthur Miller asked the same of us. But Shagan goes on and asks us to accept Harry's own justification for what he does — that American materialism has turned him into what he is. And this is a moral hustle that must have enchanted the movie executives who financed this picture. There's nothing you can't justify that way: the production of frozen scrambled eggs or frozen French toast; the economies that cause river pollution; the paperback publishers who say they are bringing out schlock so they can pay for the books they care about, and are then so geared to volume sales they can't handle "quality" books; the movie companies that produce only action movies. Business becomes its own justification, and when staying in business becomes the only goal, everything can be explained in terms of needing to make money to keep other people employed. Why, the Harrys are working so hard to enable other people to have swimming pools that they hardly have time to use their own.

Harry is often so floridly self-righteous that he sounds like the Harry Cohn movie-mogul character in Odets' *The Big Knife*, but whereas that character made movie executives squirm, this one will make them think they're thinking. Shagan's inflation falsifies what we knew when we came into the theater, and even what we see on the screen. Harry sits in a bar with the whore, who has overstimulated his customer into a heart attack, and he talks to her about how they're both in the same business — they both "sell imagination." This from a garment manufacturer whose dresses are copies of big-time designers' clothes to a hooker who provides mechanical pleasure and whose big specialty seems to involve spreading strawberry jam on her clients' chests. Shagan demonstrates that he's in the same business himself when he throws in a girl hippie to represent a new, free way of life — and perhaps so that the movie won't be too middle-aged in its appeal. His notion of "freedom" is taken from the "youth" movies of a few years back, and Laurie Heineman, who plays the girl (and who has a slight resemblance to Susan Sontag), is clearly too intelligent and well organized to be spending her days hitching rides back and forth on Sunset Strip. The movie is so pushy that none of its characters can appear free; everything is schematic. At Malibu with the girl, Harry becomes hysterical while muttering names remembered from the past, and in one hokey and unconscionably prolonged scene he almost cracks up while addressing potential customers at his annual fashion show. Lemmon — always best in comedy moments when he can act slightly touched in the head — does some fresh bits at the beginning and then plods through in a workmanlike way, and Avildsen, though too single-minded and emphatic, has energy as a director and tries to give the verbal delirium some matching visual glare. But their efforts become one with the strident ambitiousness of this film. In a movie that seeks credit as a blast at materialism while saying that the hero is a victim and not to be blamed, it seems just about perfect that the Benny Goodman tapes Harry listens to aren't authentic; the movie, produced by that idealist Shagan, uses a new, "enhanced" version of Goodman's music.

There's a subject that comes up in the movie that isn't dealt with and yet — psychologically — seems central. Harry peremptorily rejects his partner's suggestion that they cut down on their "overhead"; that is, that Harry cut down on his high living. Harry will not even consider it. The movie seems to say that the mansion, the cars, the Mexican cook, the pool man, the tree surgeon, the gardener, the Swiss school for his only child, the expensive dinner parties, and the twenty-year-old Scotch are all part of "the system"; Harry, obviously, would rather risk prison for insurance fraud than live differently. But if Harry's style of life is draining the business and if — as we can see — he doesn't even particularly enjoy it, what does it mean to him? The movie ducks around the issue, making that elaborate case for Harry's being a better man than most. Yet it must be this lavish living, above his legitimate profits, that is driving Harry to fraud. When Harry talks to the old cutter, Meyer, once in flight from pogroms, later a refugee from the Nazis (though played by William Hansen with a mysterious Scandinavian accent), Meyer's happiness with his wife and his work and his "simple" life is set up as a contrast to Harry's drive and discontent, but all we can gather is that something to do with his lost goals and the American poison must be keeping Harry from this simple happiness and from living within his means. If Shagan dealt with the psychology of the big spender — the ersatz aristocrat who must pretend he's a bigger businessman than he is, the man who accepts grossness and cupidity as his values — *Save the Tiger* would not, of course, be pleasing to the movie executives and to the viewers who accept those values. It's by passing the blame on to "the society" and "our whole way of life" that Shagan gets Harry off the hook. That's how you make a tragic hero out of a high-living, show-off moral butterball. And that's how you flatter greedy people, who can think the movie is saying something profound.

"STEELYARD BLUES" MIGHT HAVE PROVIDED material for a couple of "The Monkees" shows of some seasons back; it's about a band of thieves and hookers — meant to be adorably nutty — who, persecuted by the squares of this world, repair a plane by skill and theft, and plan to fly off to a better one. It's infantile anarchism, and if the tone were different it might seem both sly and innocent, yet I found it offensive — a smug game for rich stars to play and for kids trying to be hip to laugh at. Donald Sutherland tries to make the hero, Veldini, a modern François Villon, a free spirit, and the prophet of a new religion; the actor's satisfaction with the role is damned near unwholesome. When he delivers Veldini's big speech about his dream of a demolition derby in which he can smash school buses and campers and, finally (dream of dreams), mobile homes, he has the beatific smile of an actor who is sure he's sneaking into our hearts. Doesn't he know that it's the poor people in this society who save for years to buy a mobile home, because what else can they afford? It's a show-business vice that the stupidly romantic artists who banded together to make this movie should have so little sense of reality and of their own privileged status that the pickpockets and other petty miscreants are considered nonconformists and friendly "outlaws," while the people who work for a living — the straights — are a piggy, vindictive, stupid lot.

This polarization can be very appealing to adolescents, and a director with a light touch, like the playful young Godard or the skilled young Richard Lester, might have made a fresh fantasy out of the gags in David S. Ward's script. Maybe at this late date it would still have been possible to get a *Goon Show* feeling into the tuba playing and the pickpocket routines and the rounding up of an army of dropouts and ex-cons to steal the parts necessary for the plane, but you can't really ask an audience to enjoy the precarious fiction of defecting from reason while you're trying to rack up ideological points. With Alan Myerson's amateurish, erratic direction, the film never gets a rhythm going and doesn't draw us in. It's awkwardly stitched together; comedy doesn't play very well when the shots don't match — unless the mismatching is deliberate (and Myerson isn't in the league for that kind of aberrant style). Frequently, the picture cuts from a person talking to the face of the listener, who is obviously not listening, and the slight wrongness of position produces definite discomfort. Jane Fonda plays a happy hooker, but she's just doing a long walk-through. She has charm — even without a character to play — but her and Sutherland's roguish complacency at being hip outlaws in a straight society isn't the charming nonsense they mean it to be. Their little digs and grimaces about the meanness of the straights are almost a parody of their offscreen characters, and it's embarrassing to watch them, because they've turned blithe exuberance into cant. Peter Boyle, whose role is no more than a collection of skits and costume changes, comes off somewhat better. However, now that he has gone all the way and made a vaudeville turn out of the Brando imitation he regularly does in his heavy-breathing moments — this time putting on a blond *The Young Lions* wig and rigging himself in *The Wild One* black leather — he's really finished it.

WHY DOES ONE FILM REACH AN AUDIENCE when another film — like the first one, only better — fails to? Is it a tide in the affairs of men, or clever promotion, or both? There is no tide and no promotion for the Czechoslovakian film *If I Had a Gun,* which strikes me as considerably more skillful than such successes in this country as *Loves of a Blonde* and *Closely Watched Trains.* It's true that the subject — the Nazi Occupation as seen through the eyes of a Slovakian boy of perhaps thirteen — is not exactly calculated to create panic at the box office, but it's also true that the small fashion for Czechoslovakian films has passed and that there were no public-relations people working for this one. There's some minor irony involved, because the man who directed *If I Had a Gun,* Stefan Uher, though he is only forty-two now, was the first New Wave director in Czechoslovakia and the man who — with *The Sun in the Net,* in 1962 — broke new ground. When that film was banned in the director's native Slovakia, it was taken up by the young film enthusiasts in Prague, and it influenced the Prague directors whose work we saw — the group that since the fall of Dubček has been demoralized and disbanded. Uher, however, who went on working in Slovakia, experimented with *cinéma vérité* and with poetic dream styles, and revived the prewar Slovakian Surrealism, and, in 1971, made *If I Had a Gun,* from Milan Ferko's volume of wartime reminiscences. Ferko, too, is Slovakian — a culture that movie audiences here have had practically no acquaintance with. Because of a shift in internal politics which I can't pretend to understand, filmmakers seem able to do in Slovakia what can't be done now in Prague.

The major surprise of *If I Had a Gun* is the contrast between the sophistication of Uher's style and the mixture of folk witchcraft and Christianity in his peasant characters. The villagers suggest the mad Polish peasants that Jerzy Kosinski described in *The Painted Bird,* but Kosinski was writing from the perspective of a terrified child, an outsider wandering alone from one nightmare encounter to the next; the boy of *If I Had a Gun* lives with his family in relative security, despite the Nazi Occupation, and though the village life is semi-surrealist, the petty cruelty and the superstition bounce off him and are mixed with discoveries and pranks. An old woman's refusal to give up the money she has hidden for her funeral, though it might save the life of her granddaughter, touches that macabre peasant spirit of Kosinski's account, but *The Painted Bird* is out of Hieronymus Bosch, and this is closer to Brueghel. There's a pagan, healthy quick-wittedness about this boy's perspective — life as seen by a resourceful young human animal. The behavior and events in the village have the lunacy of a put-on, yet it's all part of his growing up: seeing where a black-marketeering uncle's loot is stashed, and watching a Jewish woman being hauled off; serving as an altar boy, and watching his grandmother prepare a witch's brew; peeking at girls bathing, and eavesdropping on the Nazis. The principal effect of the war is on his fantasy life; he lives in a maze of self-glorifying revenge dreams in which he destroys the Nazis and becomes the village hero. Few movies have dealt so effectively with the way historical events affect our fantasy lives; at the climax of the film, when the boy actually does get a crack at the Nazis, we see how his dreams change.

The movie is episodic, but it doesn't feel that way; there are so many jokes and incidents that they run together, and they trip by so fast that they're always just a little ahead of the viewer. The abrupt, sprinting film rhythms make the life of the villagers seem spontaneous. Nothing is loitered over (with the possibly unavoidable exception of a too ingratiating Russian soldier hiding in the town), and nothing looks programmed (except, at the end, after the Nazis leave, a celebration that includes the arrival of the Russians). The film, which is in black-and-white, has a large cast, expertly deployed, especially in the fantasies. Uher is a superb technician; this is probably the most precise and stylized of the Czechoslovakian films to open here. There may be no way for *If I Had a Gun* to reach much of an audience in this country (it has already closed at the theater in which I saw it), but it's a small classic. It shares with the Czechoslovakian films that succeeded here the sense of recording a modest chapter of the human comedy, yet it has a knobbiness — an eccentric spring and speed — all its own. And it's "dry" — it doesn't make us feel how alike we all are but how different. Maybe Slovaks are a little crazier than Czechs, and craziness is what those other films lacked.

[February 17, 1973]

The Riddles of Pop

RIP TORN, with his smirking satyr grin, will probably never have a role that suits him better than Maury Dann, the country singer of *Payday.* Torn projects the magnetism of unstable personalities. He is so volatile and charged he really does have the pop charisma the role demands; you don't necessarily think Torn is a good actor, but you don't look away from the screen when he's up there. He can do split-second seizures of rage and pain, and he can flip in an instant from his usual nakedly appraising look to a fiend-pixie smile that is so broad it's hardly human. He is one of the few actors who are convincingly goaty; nobody else does rancidly unromantic sex scenes with the dippy arrogance — the near-madness — he brings to them. Always a little meaner and more self-sufficient than his roles seem to require, he is also freakishly, slyly funny. Torn has life to him, no matter what, and here his terrifying, sneaky smartness *fits.* Maury Dann has been touring in the Deep South for months, doing one-night stands. In the back of his Cadillac, between two girls, he's a sweating rajah, drinking Coke and beer and bourbon, smoking pot and popping pills. In the thirty-six hours that the film spans, just about everything goes wrong for him, and, already tense and exhausted, he is wound up so tight he's ready to explode.

The people who made *Payday* knew what they were doing. From the opening shots of a couple going in to a country-music concert through to Maury Dann's ultimate explosion, the film lays open his scrambling, chiseling life. An exceptionally functional script, by the novelist Don Carpenter (the first he has had produced), makes it possible for the film to cover the grimy pop scene of a small-time recording "star" — the barnstorming life of deals and motels and restaurants, of groupies, quarrels, blackmailing disc jockeys, and payoffs. Maury, a third-rate Johnny Cash, travels in a two-car caravan with his entourage: his manager, McGinty (Michael C. Gwynne); his driver, cook, and "chief bottle washer," the fat, loyal Chicago (Cliff Emmich); and his musicians and girls. They are rootless refugees from poverty, out of nowhere and rushing to a more affluent nowhere. A teen-age groupie with the slow smile of a Southern belle (Elayne Heilveil) works in a dime store and doesn't know what an omelet is; all her life she's eaten at counters and at McDonald's — "maybe three thousand hamburgers," she says. Being taken along by Maury is like being drawn into orbit. The people in the small towns idolize Maury, because he's somebody; he may be the only kind of somebody they feel is theirs.

Payday was made by an independent company, with Ralph J. Gleason, the veteran writer on jazz, who is vice-president of Fantasy Records, as executive producer. Financed by Fantasy Records and completed last year, it was brought in for under seven hundred and eighty thousand dollars. Universal, Warner Brothers, Twentieth Century-Fox, and Columbia all turned it down for distribution — though it's doubtful if they could bring in a film that looked this professional for three times that amount. To direct, Gleason and Carpenter picked Daryl Duke, who worked for the National Film Board of Canada before moving into Canadian and American television; he had not directed a theatrical feature before, but he knew the music scene. He's maybe too professional a director — too businesslike and slick — but he never lets your attention falter. *Payday* was shot entirely on location in Alabama, and with a cast partly of professionals and partly of local people, who play the drifters and the small-town characters without any false notes that I could detect. *Payday* isn't designed to be conventionally gripping or to have the usual melodramatic suspense; even halfway through, we're not quite conscious of where it's heading. Everything that happens is prepared for, yet in such an unforced way that we don't feel shoved. The editing (by Richard Halsey) seems to carry us along on the undercurrents; when from time to time the plot surfaces, we receive small hair-trigger shocks.

We get to know Maury Dann in different relationships, and we see what he came out of. On the way to a date in Birmingham, he visits his wreck of a mother, who bore him at sixteen, and now, fifty-one and a pill head, looks eighty; he goes out on a quail shoot, has a fight about his hunting dog, stops in on his ex-wife but doesn't stick around to see his three kids. After each contact with the past, his frustrations need release, and when his blond mistress (Ahna Capri, doing an Ann-Margret role, and very well) goads him at the wrong moment, he throws her out of the car. Carpenter's writing is skillful; each person is given his due — no one is put down or treated condescendingly. Yet this very awareness, this intelligence that informs and controls every detail, shuts us out. The conception precludes Hollywood "heart," as it precludes "poetry" — yet, perhaps irrationally, we want more than accuracy and slice-of-life understanding. We want an illumination, a sense of discovery — *something.*

Rip Torn seems perfect in the role, but there is a disadvantage to him: who could have empathy with Rip Torn? He's always on his own malevolent wavelength. And the movie keeps its distance at all times; we observe what the characters feel, but we are never invited to feel with them. When we stay on the outside like this, there's no mystery. We don't sense other possibilities in the people; we never intuit what else they might have been, never feel anything larger in them than the life they're caught in. It's part of the picture's realistic integrity to show them for what they are, without sentimentality; yet to view stunted lives is not altogether satisfactory — as I think *Fat City* also demonstrated. This picture is much tougher-minded, and it's up-to-date — it has none of the blurring, softening (and antiquing) effect of a tragic tone. I don't know *how* it would be possible to present this life as acridly and faithfully as *Payday* does and infuse into it the beauty of some redeeming illumination without falsifying and destroying it. But this realism is close to the realism of hardboiled fiction; the astuteness is self-protective, and it prevents *Payday* from rising above craft.

When you hear people in the pop-music business swapping stories, you may think that someone should make a movie and show how it really is, and that's what these moviemakers have done. But to lay out what you know is a limited approach to realism. We grasp exactly what we are meant to think and feel about each detail of these dissolute, messy lives.

And it frustrates the imagination when a world is so clearly defined — more clearly than is possible, I think, for an artist.

A clue to what's missing may be found by making a comparison with, say, Francesco Rosi's extraordinary 1965 film *The Moment of Truth* — socially a comparable story, dealing with a poor Spanish boy's road out of rural poverty and his barnstorming life as a matador. It, too, is about poverty, dislocation, and corruption, and the movie's method is also apparently objective and impersonal. The difference is that *The Moment of Truth* raises emotions that neither its moviemaking team nor we can fully comprehend, and so the material draws us in and stays with us. It does so, I think, because Rosi's style expresses a larger vision of life than that of his characters — his art is in itself a cry of rage about what the poor are deprived of. The largeness of his vision is proof of the human possibilities that his hero, living in a circle of corruption, is cut off from. *Payday* doesn't have an expressive style that says there's something more than Maury Dann's corruption. There's no rage in the film, and no sensibility that goes beyond awareness, except in a few flashes. There are brief memorable moments: the blowsy blonde's face when she wakes from a nap in the car to see her lover making out with the little groupie belle right next to her; the driver Chicago's mixture of emotions when he hands the car keys over to Maury Dann before being hauled off by the police. And they're memorable just because something larger and not easy to define is going on in them — because they transcend programmed realism. They have what a work of film art has in its *approach* — a sense of wonder.

In *Payday* we see only the crudiness of the pop scene; the music itself is largely neglected. But country music has links to the past, and if we could feel that there was love for this music in Maury Dann himself, and in his followers and audiences, the movie might have that transforming quality we miss. Because when a people's folk art is corrupted — and they're still trying to find some joy in it, since it's still the only art that's theirs — there is deprivation, all right, and rage isn't far away. To show corruption as it is is the honest reporter's way, and although it's a great deal for a movie to do, it's not enough. (It may even imply assent — though I don't think that happens here.) To show corruption as it is and by your style to reveal why it shouldn't be — that's the honest artist-reporter's way.

JIMMY CLIFF, the reggae singer who stars in *The Harder They Come* — made in Jamaica, and the first feature made there that deals with Jamaican life — has radiance and the verve of an instinctive actor. The film itself is a mess, but the music is redeeming, and Jimmy Cliff's joy in music, along with the whole culture's, stays with you. (The title song goes on playing in your head.) The director, Perry Henzell (who was also the producer, and the co-author with Trevor D. Rhone), begins to tell a basic hero myth, like that of the poor Spanish boy who dreams of becoming a matador, or the poor American boy who dreams of becoming a prize-fighter, or the early life of a Maury Dann. And as long as he stays within the bounds of this story — which is probably very close to that of Jimmy Cliff himself — the film is satisfying, because the Jamaican ferment and spontaneity are new to the screen, and how can we not be interested in the home ground of the people who keep that lilt even in the New York noise? In Jamaica, the rhythmic swing of the voices is hypnotic even without the reggae, which is a further development of the cadenced speech. Reggae — a mixture of calypso and rock and the blues — is the pop pulse of the country. The music seems organic; a church choir syncopating the hymns makes them as lush as the island itself.

The film has been shot in vivid, opaque color; you get an immediate impression of glow and warmth. And of the people's passion for pop, which is maybe just another term for Americanization. The soft drinks and the billboards go right along with the transistor radios on the bicycles which pour out the reggae rhythms. A movie the hero, Ivan, goes to in Kingston — a spaghetti Western — is bastard pop, bloody and primitive, and more vital to the giggling, gleeful audience than the American Westerns it's based on. There must be a natural affinity between pop and heat; it seems perfectly at home in beach cultures — part of the corruption and tourism. (Hawaii *is* pop.) In this Jamaican setting, the blatant immediacy of pop becomes a new form of exoticism. The early, best passages of the movie are crude but sensual, and almost magical in their effect on us.

As Ivan, Jimmy Cliff is such a thin-skinned, excitable innocent and his lyrics are so naïvely upbeat that it would be bad enough if his life turned into a smudged dream, and at the outset we expect that the movie will be a folk fairy tale set in decadence — a modern hero's education in the rot of the record industry. (It would be instructive to know why Jimmy Cliff left Jamaica and now lives in London.) But Henzell tries to combine a singer's life with the life of Jamaica's first criminal hero — Rhygin, an actual outlaw of the fifties. Ivan makes a record, but the head of the record combine perceives that he's a troublemaker, so the record isn't pushed; rash and angry, Ivan gets involved in the drug trade, kills three policemen, and shoots a woman, and only then, because of his celebrity as a murderer, does his record become famous. The movie turns into a feverish social-protest fantasy, and infectious charm and social convulsions mix badly. (The Elia Kazan-Budd Schulberg film *A Face in the Crowd,* which tried to turn a pop idol into a Fascist political figure, ran into comparable problems of rabid inflation and hysteria.) The continuity is hurried and haphazard. By the time Ivan is writing slogans on walls, going from "I Was Here" to "I Am Everywhere," he has turned into a symbol of revolt, and because of him the businessmen try to starve the people into submission. The episodes aren't dramatically intact, and they're not rounded off enough to explain the hero's change from country boy to defiant, publicity-loving outlaw. The movie itself becomes an example of pop sensationalism when Ivan is on the Most Wanted posters and at the top of the hit-record charts. There are so many ironies and cross-currents in the culture that we can't handle this ironic martyrdom, too. We're left without help to account for the irony that is central: the people's true and deep enjoyment of pop synthetic, which they transmute into folk art.

[February 24, 1973]

A Generation's Clown

STILL BOUNDING ONSTAGE at talk shows, telling jokes at seventy, seventy-five, and eighty, the old comedians have become boring immortals — members of a raffish Academy that sits in Las Vegas. The exception — the one who barely seems a performer at all now — is that mere infant Sid Caesar. The Sid Caesar who appears on TV is scarcely recognizable as the funnyman who appeared on *Your Show of Shows* during the early fifties. The mighty Caesar was a popular favorite then, especially of bright kids and educated people — rather like Woody Allen in recent years. Now, at fifty, he doesn't seem to be a professional funnyman, or a funny person, either; he's like a civilian who was once in the Army — it all rubbed off him. In the new film *Ten from Your Show of Shows,* Sid Caesar appears in ten sketches selected from the kinescopes of the live weekly show — live in the sense of being done in front of an audience (at the beginning in a theater that seated eight hundred and then in a theater that seated thirty-five hundred) and of being seen at the same time in most of the country. *Your Show of Shows* lasted from 1950 to 1954; there were a hundred and sixty ninety-minute shows, all produced and directed by Max Liebman. (When the ratings declined and the show ended, Caesar's co-star, Imogene Coca, got her own series; Liebman went on to produce spectaculars — the ancestor of specials — and Caesar, for three years, appeared on *Caesar's Hour,* which he produced himself.) Liebman and Caesar made this selection of clips, from their own copies of *Your Show of Shows,* N.B.C. having admittedly junked its collection as a matter of routine, since it owned rights for one airing only and would have had to pay for any additional use. There had been no reruns: no station or network ever put the shows back on as a series, despite their legendary status and the clips that turn up on those salutes to TV (which are generally put together by morticians, like the Ed Sullivan graveyard special last week).

Still in his twenties when *Your Show of Shows* started, handsome and over six feet tall, Caesar put on weight rapidly. By the end of the series, people had forgotten what he looked like at the beginning. Although the audience didn't associate him with one comic character — in the way that Fields became the lovable misanthrope or Groucho the cynic — and he played many types, everything he did in these sketches has extra dimensions because of his size. This round-faced Big Sid is an overgrown boy who can't quite handle what he has turned into; he has the pomposity and the chagrin of heavyweights. You're often aware of the delicate movements of other large comics; with Sid Caesar, you're aware of the mugging and the deep boom-rumble of his voice and the sheer bullying weight of him. His weight isn't jolly, like Jonathan Winters' flab; he's adept at comic voices and silly noises, but he isn't lighthearted or light anything else. Even his reasonable, put-upon average men are likely to be beefy, compulsive characters who have over-scale emotions. In the first sketch here, "Breaking the News," in which Imogene Coca, as his guilt-stricken wife, confesses that she has wrecked their car, he's a morbidly defeatist husband whose distress builds to manic pain. In the sketch "Sunday Salon," he unintentionally destroys a singer's performance by the uncontrollable noises his big bones make. Caesar is a domineering misfit, who, often in spite of himself, can't be soft and gentle. Chaplin had the towering Mack Swain to intimidate him, Keaton had Ernest Torrence and other huge, overbearing foils; with Caesar, the roles are reversed, and gaunt-faced, cheekless little Howard Morris — selected because Caesar could pick him up by his lapels — is intimidated by Caesar.

In this compilation movie, the teamwork revolves around the big boy in the center. The only skit that doesn't, the pantomime "The Clock" (which also appears under the credits), is stolen by Carl Reiner, whose movements are trickier and more inventive. Most of the time, Reiner, officially the second banana, plays straight man to Caesar, feeding him lines. Tall and eager-looking, in a conventional sappy-stage-juvenile way, Reiner didn't have a defined comic presence in this period. Howard Morris gets some of the best physical bits: clinging to Caesar's leg in the parody of *This Is Your Life;* and in the classic skit "Slicking Up," in which Caesar does a supremely imperious garbled German dialect, Morris is a valet who runs around his master in terrified circles while dressing him in his uniform and medals. Imogene Coca appears in most of these sketches, and in some she's much funnier than Caesar. She has that fool's spark — the skittish light-headedness — that he lacks, and she has more variety. Playing pixie terrier to his elephant, Imogene Coca is perky, with a traditional clown's small, lean face and big, bright mouth — as classic a rubber face as Joe E. Brown's. Her little head makes Caesar's seem stupendously round; the chemistry is right — Laurel and Hardy, and with the extra fillip of the difference in sex as well as temperament. She's best, here, in the sketch "The Sewing Machine Girl," one of their silent-movie parodies, which comes midway in the film. They sit side by side in a sweatshop; when the boss, Carl Reiner, forces them to work faster, she does a spastic jig before she collapses, and the first time I laughed out loud at Caesar was when he did a reprise of her movements. He's more imaginative in the skits with her. He pushes one joke to its limits in the sketch "Big Business," in which she doesn't appear (and which lags); and his faker-professor dialect role in "Airport Interview," with just Reiner and him, depends too much on the crazy accent. With Coca, in the life-situation comedies, his characters exist on more than one plane — he's a man who is trying to be moderate but is driven to immoderate emotions; still, it's just as well that this film doesn't include more of these skits, because they have since been attenuated into a staple of sitcoms. (That comic-strip angel Edith Bunker regularly bears the brunt of Archie's male exasperation.)

A series show depends on our growing familiarity with the performers and their range of comic characters; *Ten from Your Show of Shows* is no more than a sampling — teasers, really. Those who ask what of television will last are still going on the assumption that the future sorts things out, as "the future" has done in the high arts, and even in crafts. But popular culture operates on different principles: now whatever is considered to have the possibility of future revenue survives. It does not have to have ever been good to have such a possibility; movies that were a total washout artistically and financially turn up on TV, and TV doesn't select even its summer reruns on the basis of quality. Worth as assessed by critical judgment and popular taste may determine what lasts in the high arts; when it comes to movies or TV shows having a new life on television, the survival of something good is as accidental as the survival of rubbish. *Your Show of Shows* was in black and white, so the most we can hope for is reruns in the daytime (which would be stupid) or late at night (which wouldn't be). Whether they'd be watchable, I truly can't say. The film *is*, but it's far from exciting. On the big screen, the kinescopes blown up to 35-mm. don't look like much — the performers play directly to us and it's rather like watching a Punch-and-Judy show on a furry, polluted day — but I don't think anybody expects high visual quality. It's Caesar that is the attraction.

In his great days, Sid Caesar was a special kind of comic actor, with a gift for expansion. He could swell himself and become living slapstick, but his style was blunt. Milton Berle's comedy wasn't sophisticated or satiric, as the comedy on *Your Show of Shows* often was, but Berle could do the same mugging bits as Caesar and ring many more changes on them. What Berle couldn't do was convey power like Caesar's. Caesar looked stronger physically than any other American comic. ("He could kill a Buick with his bare hands — punch it in the grille and kill it," Mel Brooks once said.) Red Skelton is large (which limits him, too, I think) but not powerful, not remotely a yeller or boomer. Milt Kamen is large but gentle-spirited; he defuses his satire with a shrug and a dreamy smile. Harvey Korman, though huge, is amiably silly and uses his size mostly as a joke — as in his cringing matadors or outsize Jewish mothers. The power that comes from size isn't of the essence of their comedy, as it was of Caesar's. In his German-dialect bits, he sometimes suggested the actor Herman Bing, who also did the ballooning face, the eye-popping, and the sputtering puffed-out baby mouth, though Bing was fat rather than powerful.

Sid Caesar has never been a special hero of mine, though he is of most of my friends; I laugh at him, and I guess I could be considered a fan, but there is a deeper level at which I don't respond. In terms of *Your Show of Shows* he probably was, as he was generally considered, the finest comedian in TV history, but I never felt that he personally was funny — that his *core* was funny. I didn't feel myself smiling whenever I thought of him — the way I've always done when I thought of Harry Ritz or Ben Blue or Phil Silvers, or the way I do now when I think of Anne Meara, who's a female Phil Silvers. Or the way I've done even about people who, technically, haven't been clowns — Louis Armstrong, for example, or Laurence Olivier, who has a core of wit that draws one to him in anything, or Fred Astaire, Ray Bolger, Gene Kelly, Donald O'Connor, and the young Buddy Ebsen, who at their best had a gift for silliness that could turn dancing into high foolishness. Probably much more than the other celebrated comedians, Caesar was dependent on a team and a format. He didn't have the years of seasoning that most comics have had. He was a saxophonist, playing in the Borscht Belt, who had worked up some material of his own — impressions and comic characters — as a side thing; he was only twenty-one, and in the Coast Guard during the Second World War, when Max Liebman, who had previously developed Danny Kaye, went to direct the Coast Guard show *Tars and Spars,* met him, and began to work with him. Caesar never mastered the skills of the veterans who grew up in the business, dancing, singing, and clowning, working in vaudeville, the Borscht Belt, night clubs — anywhere. (I first saw Bob Hope perform in the men's gym at Berkeley.) When he went into television after only a few years' experience, he was backed by a small strategic force, and he was inspired to become a general. His writing troops on *Your Show of Shows* were Mel Tolkin, Lucille Kallen, Mel Brooks, Tony Webster, Caesar and Liebman themselves, and, for a brief period, Neil and Danny Simon; and later, on *Caesar's Hour,* Carl Reiner began to do some of the writing, and Woody Allen and Larry Gelbart joined up. My guess is that the room where the team gathered and built up the numbers was where Caesar was tuned in, and that's what kept him keyed up. He probably drew upon Liebman and Imogene Coca and that team of writers not just for ideas but for excitement, the way other comics draw upon the audience.

Caesar rose to stardom faster than any other comedian who comes to mind, and he was flung into the pressure-cooker existence of live TV. Without underestimating the burning-out effect of eight seasons of live TV (ten if one includes the *Admiral Broadway Revue* series, done in 1949, and the final series, *Sid Caesar Invites You,* in 1958, in which he and Reiner reunited with Imogene Coca, but which ran only a half season), I think that he might have come back — been restored, after a period of rest, the way Jonathan Winters bounces back, punchy but game — if he were a madman at heart, maybe with or without the early experience, though possibly only with. The training of a lifetime shows. Even if you couldn't take Milton Berle years ago, when you see him on TV now you're staggered by his knowledge of the mechanics of his craft, and the spark in him seems to have taken over the whole man. George Burns can do his dotty but charming patter songs with the ease of a master. Groucho, barely audible, still sings and engages in repartee. They are all simply older versions of themselves. The shock of seeing Sid Caesar when he first appeared on TV looking thinner, in the sixties, was that his funnyman's fat moon face was burned away. The comic drive seemed to be gone, too; the thinner Sid Caesar was no longer the mighty Caesar. His energy had made his size seem unlimited; now the energy was apparently gone, along with the exaggerated grief of the heavyset man, which was often his dominant expression — as it was with Herman Bing, too. Can one imagine a thin Herman Bing or, say, a frail Sig Rumann? Their entire personality and style grew out of their size, just as, at the opposite end, Keaton's and Chaplin's did. Sid Caesar is an ordinary man now, and it's strangely upsetting. It's as if what his ten years on TV did to him were symbolized by his loss of flesh. When he does funny faces, they're not funny; the abnormality has gone out of them. Sid Caesar isn't Sid Caesar.

Your Show of Shows allowed us to be ridiculous and smart at the same time — which is the blessing Woody Allen confers. It's something Milton Berle couldn't do; he allowed us only to be ridiculous. Berle was a true popular comedian. He drew upon the traditional sources of comedy; he used everything he'd learned since his appearances as a tiny kid in early Chaplin comedies, and he used it to create mass-medium comedy. Sid Caesar was for a smaller audience — those who responded to satire and caught allusions. The reason people cling to the memory of Caesar rather than of Coca is that although she may have been the more skilled, she was a traditional comic and that wasn't what they watched the show for. Sid Caesar drew upon a large body of tradition — particularly, I think, from the style of the Ritz Brothers (Woody Allen says, "When I was one of the writers on *Caesar's Hour,* sometimes when Sid was nervous about facing the audience, he would straighten up and say, 'Tonight I'm Harry Ritz' — and go on"), but he and his team adapted the vaudeville traditions to the topical needs of the fifties. His comedy appealed to highbrows, but it was never genteel; it had the frenzy of great sophomoric humor, of the *Mad* comics. That's what we wanted of him. If you saw him when you were young enough, maybe he'll always be the greatest clown for you. Yet the spirit of comedy wasn't in him, and, without a fuller range of show-business experience, he had nowhere to go when that topical vein was used up.

Possibly Caesar was never a funnyman unless the situations were prepared. For a period they were, and if performers are used up after a brief time on TV (talk-show hosts and politicians are the most glaring examples), there is the fact that it is a great medium for comics in their prime — Sid Caesar and Ernie Kovacs in the fifties, Bill Cosby right now. Like our best pop singers, they can reach a vast audience when they're young and at their fullest vitality, in a way that performers before TV could not. They no longer have to barnstorm until they're half-dead, and then, when they're recognized, become imitators of themselves. The mistake we make is looking for the young Sid Caesar in the tall, quietly unobtrusive, distinguished-looking man he is now. He's a clown who has grown up; maybe when he stops fighting that, he'll emerge as an actor.

[March 3, 1973]

Crooks

A N ORDINARY JOGGER coming up behind you might give you a split second of fear if unseen people had been shooting at you and following you and you didn't know why. When the jogger had gone past, however, your relief might make both him and your fear seem funny. James Caan lives in this precarious state of seriocomic anxiety in *Slither,* and we see the world as he does — as a nut-bin mixture of the sinister and the ordinary. It can't be sorted out, because crooks and killers can be as square as anybody else — and this movie is in love with square crooks, especially roly-poly ones. *Slither* is a suspense comedy that keeps promising to be a knockout entertainment; it never delivers, and it finally fizzles out, because the story idea isn't as good as the curlicues. But it has a pleasant slapstick temperament — a sort of fractured hipsterism. The director, Howard Zieff, the advertising ace who did the "You Don't Have To Be Jewish" series for Levy's bread and the Alka-Seltzer and Benson & Hedges commercials, has never made a feature film before; the original screenplay, by the talented twenty-six-year-old W. D. Richter, is his first to be produced. The offbeat rhythm of their sneaky gags keeps taking the audience by surprise. The best aren't big gags — they're a matter of a look, a turn of phrase, a character trait — and they don't advance the plot, or even bear on it; they're happily inconsequential. Caan, a high-school football hero turned car thief, who has just been released from two years in prison, is thick-witted and decent; he is thrown into situations that require him to act hip when he's most befuddled, and his permanent expression is a double take. His brain seems to be clogged; he can't quite get the import of the remarks strangers address to him. When he hitches a ride with an amphetamine freak (Sally Kellerman), the velocity of her compulsive talk leaves him openmouthed. The movie's flea-hopping humor depends on the permutations in these encounters; Caan is never quite sure whether the strangers are innocent bystanders or enemies, crazy-square or crazy-hip.

The hero's quest for a fortune promised him by an embezzler he met in prison (Richard B. Shull) takes him through a series of northern-California towns and then south to Pismo Beach. The quest itself is a tired gimmick; it's too bad that the hero's nomadic movement doesn't center on something less mercenary — it wouldn't matter if the goal were even more implausible, but this one just seems dutiful, perfunctory. And it has become a little insulting to the audience that we're always expected to care about whether the hero — our surrogate — can grab some loot. However, Zieff knows the value of funny people, and he plants some of his former associates in those towns. The crazies are often as entertaining as when we first spotted them in commercials. Shull, who sings "Happy Days Are Here Again" in the train that is taking Caan and him away from prison, is eliminated during the pre-credits sequence, but he helps to make it the best come-on a movie has had in years. (If the end were as good as this dadaist shoot-'em-up beginning, the picture would be a sensation.) Allen Garfield, the slob of the porno spoofs, plays an investment counselor, and Peter Boyle and Louise Lasser are Caan's companions in the rambling chase for the money. Their spooky married love is the closest thing to romance in the movie; Boyle's obsessive concern to shield his wife from obscene language is like a reversal of the obsessions in the pornies. Sally Kellerman doesn't have the innate funniness of these people, or of some of the bit players, like Virginia Sale as the bingo caller. The others underplay for humor; Kellerman, who has the laugh lines, gets her effects by overplaying. She's becoming a little like Betty Hutton: her desperate energy is lively and appealing, but it also throws her scenes a little out of whack. Caan, who plays stooge to everybody, and the rest of the cast are goofy, friendly caricatures; we can grasp the contours of their personalities — and that's part of what's distinctive about the film. The people don't act like anybody else.

I'd like to think that Zieff is a put-on artist and is parodying the TV commercials' idea of realism, but there's a strong possibility that this waggish style is his idea of realism. And it may turn out that he has only this one facility: the ability to bring people out, to let funny people do their funny things, as in his commercials, and to get the timing blissfully right. He's not adept at handling a more complex sequence in a bingo hall, and he doesn't quite succeed with the neat idea of the bright-red car with its camper trailer (which holds Caan and Boyle in front and Lasser in back) versus the sinister big-bug black van with invisible occupants that follows them — the black-knight-in-armor villain, a Basil Rathbone tank. Zieff doesn't locate the action for us in the effortless, taken-for-granted way of a skilled director; despite the movement in Laszlo Kovacs' warm outdoor cinematography, we don't always have our bearings — where does the crowd in that bingo hall come from? But

Zieff does know his people; he introduces some of them by their voices before we quite see them, and when we hear Louise Lasser, we laugh before she appears. Her performance is an extension of what made her funny in commercials, and it's her best work on the big screen; her amiable, toothy carrot-top is an American authentic, a woman who treasures and protects her own quirks — and why not? Boyle, with his dreams of avarice, has a glint of the indefatigable greed of Casper Gutman of *The Maltese Falcon*, but he seems to be the happiest, luckiest husband since Nick Charles. The movie has a fatuous, prickly humor; it doesn't get anywhere, but it stays prickly; it never goes straight.

WE DON'T ASK FOR LASTING VALUE from an escapist fantasy about a nonchalant gentleman-jewel-thief, but it should give us the giddy sensation of daydreams fulfilled, and the irresponsible fun of an hour and a half with witty, glamorous people who live by make-believe rules. It should give us the transient pleasures, which are often all we want of movies. That's not a lot to ask, but it's far above what Bud Yorkin, the producer and director of *The Thief Who Came to Dinner*, and Walter Hill, who wrote the screenplay (from a novel by Terrence Lore Smith), provide. This is a new factory version of old factory movies — to our dwindling delight. It has the same formula as *The Getaway*, which Hill also wrote: everybody in it is crooked, and we're supposed to root for the young attractive pair who outsmart them all — in *The Getaway*, Steve McQueen and Ali MacGraw (the McCoys), and in this one, Ryan O'Neal (McGee) and Jacqueline Bisset (his sexy socialite friend). Hill worked as assistant director on *The Thomas Crown Affair*, and there are strong reminiscences. And the insurance investigator (Warren Oates) who is doggedly tracking O'Neal carries more than a hint of the Edward G. Robinson role in *Double Indemnity*. But in this synthesis no one bothered to devise characters for the actors to play, so the actions (the setting is the posh parts of Houston) don't grow out of anything — they're just mechanical, with a pulse supplied by Henry Mancini. It isn't merely that the picture has no style but that it has no soul; it's a romance without romance. The audience becomes inordinately grateful for the bits of humor supplied by Jill Clayburgh (who resembles Jennifer Jones), as O'Neal's ex-wife, and the tormented sissy of Austin Pendleton, as a chess columnist. Ryan O'Neal, playing a debonair, swinging Steve McQueen, is meant to be totally sympathetic. We're supposed to be charmed by his cute corruption (though O'Neal can convey weakness without too much effort, and that might have given the character some depth). Jacqueline Bisset is so velvety a projection of masculine fantasies that she doesn't have enough rough edges to be alive. She isn't just richly made up; she's anointed. She's a walking ad for soft, sleek curves and luscious passivity. As for Warren Oates, he has so little character to play that his personality seems to scurry away from the camera. We don't know what his foxy-eyed tenacity is based on. In *Double Indemnity,* Robinson had principles, and that's what separated him from the crooks; here Oates simply seems nebulously backward. And it's dismaying when a sausage movie like this one, which should be tied up, is open-ended. The picture isn't terrible; it's faintly diverting while you're watching, largely because of O'Neal's processed charm, but the vacuity and even that charm become oppressive.

Ryan O'Neal has such an easy presence that he can get by with almost no material, supplying personality and pace out of himself; he's a relaxed smoothie — a confident winner, like Dean Martin — and it's unbecoming in one so young. No other star has ever been so *professional* a likable all-American personality at the start of his career. O'Neal is so assured — so exploitative of his own cuteness — that our responses curdle. When he does the old bare-chested-romantic-male-star stuff here, it doesn't work, because there's no shyness in this man — just flesh and muscle. It all adds up to something callous and spoiled in his attitude toward acting. However, there's one hopeful sign in his performance: he shows an instinctive physical rejection of the fraudulent serious lines. He may be a corrupt actor, but he's not a hypocrite.

What O'Neal balks at is the defensive moralizing that Yorkin and Hill pour over themselves and the movie. The hero, a computer engineer, turns thief at the beginning of the picture and tells his co-workers why. It's because people cheat on their income taxes and pad their expense accounts — because "everybody steals from everybody and we program the whole mess." O'Neal says, "In a world of thieves, I wanted to be an honest thief." This is the usual modern movie-colony cynicism; when moviemakers say "Everybody cheats," it means merely "People like us cheat," since, of course, most working people can't cheat on their income taxes and don't have expense accounts. The dishonesty of Yorkin and Hill is that they must posture about a world of thieves to justify doing what they were going to do anyway — try to make a movie about a modern Raffles, because romantic action movies are the easiest to finance and the easiest to market. Yorkin, the co-producer of *All in the Family, Sanford and Son,* and *Maude,* has become a leading exponent of self-righteous entertainment. An escapist fantasy doesn't need justification, but it needs quality. O'Neal's cute, bare-chested thief and Bisset's gorgeous curvy number are inadequate as fantasy figures. There's nothing in this movie to kindle an audience's spirit. It's a cold-hearted movie. People may buy tickets, but they'll come out sour and hungry. O'Neal gives the honest insurance investigator a copy of *Don Quixote,* explaining that it's about a man who refuses to accept reality. Yorkin and Hill could use a few dreams.

[March 10, 1973]

Lost and Found

TO LAMBASTE a Ross Hunter production is like flogging a sponge. At first, with his remakes of *Magnificent Obsession, Imitation of Life,* and *Madame X,* he was involved in camp parasitism. Since the phenomenal success of *Airport,* he has become America's most sanctimonious apostle of old-movie-queen glamour and the kitsch of our ancestors. Now he brings us his *Lost Horizon.* In a sense, all his movies are lost horizons; they're for people nostalgic for a simpler pop culture. He is to movies what Liberace is to music, and once, on a television talk show, I saw them both — Hunter castigating "dirty entertainment," and Liberace leaning over, his jacket twinkling, to say how much he agreed — and the two unctuous smiles came together. Mr. Bland and Mr. Bland.

James Hilton's *Lost Horizon,* with its inspired gimmick — longevity — was published in 1933 and took off immediately; the name Shangri-La was already in widespread use in this country as both a dream and a joke before the first movie version, in 1937. Ross Hunter's version, directed by Charles Jarrott, is in color and is padded out with a wan operetta score by Burt Bacharach and Hal David. Hunter has retained Hilton's invincibly banal ideas — *virgo intacta,* so to speak — though the screenwriter, Larry Kramer, has made some cosmetic changes in the minor characters, the most amusing of which is the transformation of the hysterical prostitute into a hysterical, world-weary woman photographer from *Newsweek* — she, too, is redeemed. Set in uncharted territory high in the Himalayas, Shangri-La is a middle-class geriatric utopia — an idealized retirement village, where, if you're sensible and do everything in moderation, you can live indefinitely, lounging and puttering about for hundreds of years. The "harmony" and the air in this magical valley will cure your diseases and mend your aching broken bones. It's a prospectus conceived by a super con artist. The valley is ruled by a benevolent despot — the High Lama — and his male factotums, and the "harmony" must be protected by discreet restrictive covenants, since the Orientals are kept in their places, and no blacks, or even the brown-skinned people of nearby India, are among the residents. There's probably no way to rethink this material without throwing it all away. Shangri-La is the embodiment of an aging, frightened white man's dream — a persistent one, even though the cheery-goody haven, with its innocent pleasures, that Ross Hunter concocts is so vapid that the inhabitants might be driven to slide down the mountains to the nearest Sin City. Hunter has carried his campaign for moral cleanliness on the screen to unprecedented chastity. The actresses are as covered up as if they were in purdah. There are no love songs, and there isn't a chemical trace of sexual attraction in the pairs of "lovers" — Liv Ullmann and Peter Finch (as Conway), Sally Kellerman (as the hysteric from *Newsweek*) and George Kennedy, Olivia Hussey and Michael York. Two of the songs involve happy, frolicking children, and the big production number is a peasant celebration of the family called "Living Together, Growing Together." (The biggest laugh in the theater greeted the arrival of the young men of the village — Broadway-style and mostly Caucasian men dancers, whose progeny in the film are Oriental.)

The leads are pitilessly miscast. As Conway in the old version, Ronald Colman had a fatuous charm; he spoke his lines rhythmically, and they glided by and could be taken with faintly pleased derision. But Finch, a firm, unobtrusive actor who creates characters, has no personality-star resources to fall back on. His shrouded performance consists of a series of sickly, noble little smiles, as if to reassure himself and his fellow-actors that this role, too, will pass. He's sympathetic in a stolid way that makes one wince for him when he's called upon to speak — or, worse, to soliloquize in song. Liv Ullmann, cast in what was a hopeless dear-sweet role even in the first version, manages to keep her dignity, though dignity on the screen is practically a negative quality. It's easy to forget that she's in the picture — which, all things considered, is probably the best thing that could happen to her; Finch is too painfully aware of his predicament to be forgotten. Nor can we forget the ingénue (played by the pregnant Olivia Hussey) twirling heavily and being told by the adoring Michael York that in the outside world people would fight to see her dance. The altitude seems to have got to everybody. From the tone of the lyrics that Hal David gave the performers, he must have enlisted in Moral Re-Armament. At his most vigorous, poor Finch expresses himself in these words:

> Will I find
> There is really such a thing

As peace of mind?
And what I thought was living
Was truly just confusion,
The chance to live forever
Is really no illusion
And this all can be mine.
Why can't I make myself believe it?
Can I accept what I see around me?
Have I found Shangri-La or has it found me?

To which his Tibetan little chickadee, Liv Ullmann, rejoins:

Where knowledge ends — faith begins
And it shines like a star
Till your heart fills with hope and with love.
I have looked in your heart,
I have faith in you.

This flatulent salvationary spirit is to be Shangri-La's gift to the world. It is the belief of the High Lama (Charles Boyer) that Shangri-La is an oasis of culture, and that when "the strong have devoured each other" this valley of brotherly love, with Finch as its ruler, will guide the meek survivors out of chaos. Shangri-La is *nice* people's idea of a cultural oasis. There is no discussion of ideas in the valley, no printing, no creative life, virtually no arts, or even crafts; everything is brought in from outside. And the government is invisible. Shangri-La hasn't solved any of the problems that drive nations to war; the story simply omits them. (Asked what would happen if two men wanted the same woman, the chief factotum, Chang — John Gielgud — replies that then the man who wanted her less would courteously yield to the other. Is it assumed that a woman necessarily wants the man who loves her most?) The have-nots are cheerful and obedient, and the haves enjoy their position. (The source of wealth is unspecified, but the valley is rich in gold, and, from the looks of the chintzy furnishings, it has been used "in moderation.") The culture consists of a collection of books, handsomely bound in leather, in a wood-paneled library. We don't have to be told that it's not for the use of the Asian peasants and servants; it's definitely not a lending library. In this place that's going to guide the world, knowledge is for storage only. No one has apparently ever thought of consulting those books to learn how to build a dam, so the peasant women wouldn't have to carry water, bucket by bucket, from a stream. It's a dead culture they're preserving in their mausoleum, like a rich college's rare-book collection.

A daydream world of peace and health is best left to the imagination; constructed, it turns into a sanitarium, or worse. After directing

Anne of the Thousand Days and *Mary, Queen of Scots,* Charles Jarrott could have been selected for another spectacle only by a producer who wanted a man with no style and no personality—just a traffic manager. With their talents pooled, Hunter and Jarrott turn the valley of eternal life into the valley of eternal rest — a Himalayan Forest Lawn. It's not as if they had destroyed anything of value. Ross Hunter never starts with anything that one need have anxiety for. The 1937 movie was part popular adventure and part senile sentimentality, but Frank Capra, who directed, made the initial trip through the icy wastes lively, gave the think-tank vision a little cracker-barrel enthusiasm, and kept some pace even in the midst of all that serenity. Jarrott's version lacks visual contrasts, the narrative has no energy, and the pauses for the pedagogic songs are so awkward you may feel that the director's wheelchair needs oiling. It's entirely possible that to the nostalgic viewers Ross Hunter is aiming at, this torpor will be soothing. They may like to doze from time to time without fear of missing anything.

"IT ADDS YEARS TO YOUR LIFE," the young men from Calcutta in Satyajit Ray's *Days and Nights in the Forest* say of the country quiet, and it's easy to believe. Ray's images are so emotionally saturated that they become suspended in time and, in some cases, fixed forever. Satyajit Ray's films can give rise to a more complex feeling of happiness in me than the work of any other director. I think it must be because our involvement with his characters is so direct that we are caught up in a blend of the fully accessible and the inexplicable, the redolent, the mysterious. We accept the resolutions he effects not merely as resolutions of the stories but as truths of human experience. Yet it isn't only a matter of thinking, Yes, this is the way it is. What we assent to is only a component of the pattern of associations in his films; to tell the stories does not begin to suggest what the films call to mind or why they're so moving. There is always a residue of feeling that isn't resolved. Two young men sprawled on a porch after a hot journey, a drunken group doing the Twist in the dark on a country road, Sharmila Tagore's face lit by a cigarette lighter, her undulating walk in a sari — the images are suffused with feeling and become overwhelmingly, sometimes unbearably beautiful. The emotions that are imminent may never develop, but we're left with the sense of a limitless yet perhaps harmonious natural drama that the characters are part of. There are always larger, deeper associations impending; we recognize the presence of the mythic in the ordinary. And it's the mythic we're left with after the ordinary has been (temporarily) resolved.

When *Days and Nights in the Forest,* which was made in 1969, was shown at the New York Film Festival in 1970, it received a standing ovation, and it seemed so obvious that a film of this quality — and one more immediate in its appeal than many of Ray's works — would be snapped up by a distributor that I waited to review it upon its theater opening. But distributors are often lazy men who don't bother much with festivals, least of all with films that are shown at the dinner hour (it went on at six-thirty); they wait for the *Times.* The review was condescendingly kindly and brief — a mere five and a half inches, and not by the first-string critic — and *Days and Nights in the Forest,* which is a major film by a major artist, is finally opening, two and a half years later, for a week's run at a small theater. On the surface, it is a lyrical romantic comedy about four educated young men from Calcutta driving together for a few days in the country, their interrelations, and what happens to them in the forest, which is both actual and metaphorical. As the men rag each other and bicker, we quickly sort them out. Ashim is a rising executive and the natural leader of the group. Lordly and disdainful to underlings, he is the worst-behaved; the most intelligent, he is also the most dissatisfied with his life and himself — he feels degraded. He and Sanjoy, who is more polite and reticent, used to slave on a literary magazine they edited, but they have settled down. Ashim is much like what Apu might have turned into if he had been corrupted, and he is played by Soumitra Chatterji, who was Apu in *The World of Apu.* On this holiday in the forest, Ashim meets Aparna, played by the incomparably graceful Sharmila Tagore (who ten years before, when she was fourteen, played Aparna, Apu's exquisite bride). In his fine book on the Apu Trilogy, Robin Wood wrote that the physical and spiritual beauty of Soumitra Chatterjee and Sharmila Tagore seems "the ideal incarnation of Ray's belief in human potentialities." And I think they represent that to Ray, and inspire him to some of his finest work (he used them also in *Devi*) because they are modern figures with overtones of ancient deities. Unlike the other characters in *Days and Nights in the Forest,* they bridge the past and the future and — to some degree — India and the West. As Ray uses them, they embody more than we can consciously grasp. But we feel it: when Sharmila Tagore in her sunglasses and white slacks stands still for a second, she's a creature of fable — the image carries eternity. Even her melodious voice seems old and pure, as if it had come through fire.

Ashim has been strangling in the business bureaucracy of Calcutta; frustrated, he has become an egotist, and confidently condescending to women. Aparna, a city girl vacationing at her father's house in the forest along with her widowed sister-in-law, is not impressed by his big-city line. Her irony and good sense cut through his arrogance, and, made to feel foolish, he rediscovers his humanity. Underneath their love story, and the stories of Ashim's companions, there's the melancholy and corruption of their class and country. In a quiet way, the subtext is perhaps the subtlest, most plangent study of the cultural tragedy of imperialism the screen has ever had. It is the tragedy of the bright young generation who have internalized the master race (like many of the refugees from Hitler who came to America); their status identity is so British that they treat all non-Anglicized Indians as non-persons. The caste system and the British attitudes seem to have conspired to turn them into self-parodies — clowns who ape the worst snobberies of the British. The highest compliment the quartet can bestow on Aparna's father's cottage is to say, "The place looks absolutely English." We don't laugh at them, though, because they're achingly conscious of being anachronistic and slightly ridiculous. When we see them playing tennis in the forest, the image is so ambiguous that our responses come in waves.

Ray not only directed but did the screenplay (from a novel by Sunil Ganguly), drew the credit titles, and wrote the music. His means as a director are among the most intuitively right in all moviemaking: he knows when to shift the camera from one face to another to reveal the utmost, and he knows how to group figures in a frame more expressively than anyone else. He doesn't butt into a scene; he seems to let it play itself out. His understatement makes most of what is thought of as film technique seem unnecessary, and even decadent, because he does more without it. (No Western director has been able to imitate him.) The story is told with great precision at the same time that the meanings and associations multiply. Ray seems to add something specifically Eastern to the "natural" style of Jean Renoir. Renoir, too, put us in unquestioning and total — yet discreet — contact with his people, and everything seemed fluid and easy, and open in form. But Renoir's time sense is different. What is distinctive in Ray's work (and it may be linked to Bengali traditions in the arts, and perhaps to Sanskrit) is that sense of imminence — the suspension of the images in a larger context. The rhythm of his films seems not slow but, rather, meditative, as if the viewer could see the present as part of the past and could already reflect on what is going on. There is a rapt, contemplative quality in the beautiful intelligence of his ideal lovers. We're not at all surprised in this film that both Ashim and Aparna have phenomenal memories; we knew that from looking at them.

Ray takes a risk when he contrasts his poetic sense of time against the hasty Western melodramatic tradition. One of the four young men is a figure in the sporting world — Hari, who is quick-tempered and rash. He has just been jilted by a dazzler of a girl for his insensitivity. (He answered a six-page letter from her in a single curt sentence.) Hari picks up a local "tribal" girl in the forest for some fast sex, and he is also attacked and almost killed by a servant he has wrongly accused of stealing. The scenes relating to Hari (especially those dealing with the equally thoughtless local girl) feel very thin and unconvincing, because they are conventional. They have no mystery, no resonance, and though this is surely deliberate, the contrast doesn't succeed; the scenes seem more contrived than they would in an American movie. In a scene by a river, Sharmila Tagore's glance brings Hari back into the film's harmony, but he goes out again. The fourth young man, Sekhar, has no subplot; he's a plump buffoon, a fawning hanger-on, who drops pidgin-English phrases into his conversation as if they were golden wit. Like Joyce Cary's Mr. Johnson in Africa, he's a joke the British left behind. Nothing happens to him; spinelessly affable, he behaves in the country as he does in the city.

It is the shy Sanjoy who has the worst experience. Aparna's sister-in-law, the young, heavily sensual widow, makes a physical overture to him. She has been flirting with him for days, and we have observed the ordinariness of her middle-class character, listened to the coyness in her slightly disagreeable voice; we know that he is flattered by her attention and oblivious of the import of her broad smiles and provocative, teasing manner. When she lures him in at night with an offer of real coffee and puts her hand on his chest, we see his stricken face, and we are torn in half. She hadn't seen in him what we had, or he in her. Ray, without our full awareness, has prepared us, and now we are brought closer to them both than we had ever anticipated. This desperately lonely woman might be too much for most men, and this man is less secure than most. The moment of his petrified indecision about how to retreat and her realization of the rejection is a fully tragic experience. Ray is a master psychologist: the pain for us is the deeper because Ray had made her so coarse-grained that we hadn't cared for her; now her humiliation illuminates what was going on in her while we were dismissing her for her middle-classness and the tension in her voice. No artist has done more than Satyajit Ray to make us reëvaluate the commonplace. And only one or two other film artists of his generation — he's just past fifty — can make a masterpiece that is so lucid and so inexhaustibly rich. At one point, the four young blades and the two women sit in a circle on picnic blankets and play a memory game that might be called Let Us Now Praise Famous Men; it's a pity that James Agee didn't live to see the films of Satyajit Ray, which fulfill Agee's dreams.

[March 17, 1973]

Kings

LUDWIG II OF BAVARIA, the supreme childish fantasist among kings — and one of the most harmless of all kings — is such an obviously magical, gaudy subject for the movies that many people may look forward with glee to Visconti's *Ludwig.* But it's well to bear in mind that though Ludwig is remembered because of the pleasures his candied-rococo follies give us, Visconti's follies are grimly humorless. Of the major filmmakers, Luchino Visconti is certainly the most estranged from the audience. Sometimes, in his films, the vital connection between the material on the screen and us disappears, and Visconti doesn't seem to notice or to care — he just goes on without us, heavily treading water. This happens for almost the entire duration of *Ludwig,* which is two hours and fifty-three minutes long. The subject is so juicy and frivolous that bravura pageantry on its own, without much drama, might be enough, but, incredibly, this movie about the king's obsession with a mock-heroic fairy-tale mode of life has no *style.*

The translated, partly dubbed dialogue is neither formal and elegant nor colloquial; it's like an earnest translation of a dowdy libretto, and it makes the actors sound like the talking dead. The early portions of the film are shot in badly lighted compositions resembling those wide-canvas nineteenth-century academic Russian paintings of a convocation of stiff, important people. The continuity is a splatter of choppy, confused scenes; there are constant amputations, so we don't find out why we have been watching a sequence but simply move on to something else, and the arbitrary compositions and abrupt closeups destroy the sense of what's going on. Visconti has been able to photograph Ludwig's actual castles and to reproduce interiors he couldn't shoot in, and yet we don't have a chance just to rove around and luxuriate in them. We always seem to be driving up to the carriage entrance; then we're stuck in a room without finding out how we got there. The film gets better-looking, and every now and then there's a great shot, which goes by infuriatingly fast. The rhythmless, disruptive cutting does the movie in, even more than Visconti's usual failing — his lack of dramatic drive.

Typically, his allegorical melodramas, such as *Rocco and His Brothers* and *The Damned,* are pushed to such heights that they turn into epics — witless but passionate and strangely self-absorbed. There can be a grandeur in their hollow heaviness and languid monotony; they have generally had style, even when we couldn't be sure of anything else about them. Visconti's first epic, the lyrical yet austere and socially conscious *La Terra Trema,* is beautifully proportioned; I think it's one of the best boring movies ever made. Although you may have had to get up to stretch a few times, you didn't want to leave. But sometimes it has seemed necessary to repress one's instinctive responses in order to sit through Visconti's movies: Alain Delon, as the saintly Rocco, photographed as though he were the young Hedy Lamarr and meant to be a prizefighter? *Rocco* suggested an operatic spectacle with a libretto by Dostoevski based on the Warner Brothers social-protest films of the thirties; Visconti gave us not characters but highly theatrical, reminiscent images — Annie Girardot's scrawny, glamorous prostitute was like a young Bankhead, her murder out of *Wozzeck. The Damned* was a mixture of Wagner and Thomas Mann and the classical Greek crazies. Elements got slammed together that didn't quite make sense together, but they made thunder, and a flowing style can connect a lot. When the Visconti style collapses, you look for the links; they're still buried in the director's mind — in his Jacobean nostalgia.

Granted that it's not easy to make a movie about a very *private,* highly neurotic man whose fantasy world took over his life, it still should have been possible to show how Ludwig's deepest longings were expressed, first in his patronage and adoration of Wagner — that is, in living in the romantic-heroic world of Wagner's operas — and then, when Wagner was exiled and lost to him, in the actual construction of the mythological domains of those operas. Madly fanatic about these projects, Ludwig probably wasn't really insane. What distinguished him from the run of royal builders was that they built boring public monuments to themselves, while he built make-believe, storybook castles. A lover of sweets and Versailles, Ludwig, with his schlocky lavish taste that half a million people a year still pay to revel in, was a premature pop movie director, and perhaps no more bizarre than a Disney or De Mille.

In the film, Helmut Berger looks like the young Ludwig, but he stalks around, a tense, prissy-mouthed, miserable mess; he's such a gloomy cuckoo he doesn't enjoy his toys. Ludwig, whose family dynasty had ruled Bavaria for seven hundred years — plenty of time to intermarry and become highstrung — ascended the throne at eighteen, in

1864, and stayed on it until 1886. At seventeen, according to historical record (but not in the movie), he was so transported during a performance of *Tannhäuser* that he became convulsed — and the excitement wasn't the music, for Ludwig was not particularly musical. Visconti seems almost not to want us to respond to Ludwig's rapturous dedication to the dreams of his adolescence; the film uses Wagner's music oppressively, as a weight. It isn't until the beginning of the third hour, when Ludwig is in his grotto based on *Tannhäuser* — living in a stage set and gliding among the swans in his gold cockleshell boat — and then when he has his crush on the actor Kainz and expects Kainz to speak privately in the declamatory mode of his roles, that the picture begins to be fitfully amusing. Berger, who looks like a perverted mannequin during the first hour, is more fun when he loses his front teeth and gets crabbed and morose, but he never really has the authentic gleam of the private fantasist that you see in pictures of the later Ludwig. Berger isn't magnetic, the way Ludwig is in those photographs, with those bright, elated eyes in that pudgy and secretive face. Ludwig looks *smart* (and apparently he was); Berger doesn't suggest the workings of Ludwig's mind — how it closed in on itself. Franz Josef's wife, the Empress Elisabeth (Ludwig's cousin), is played by Romy Schneider, and it's Visconti's whim that Ludwig loves her passionately; when she spurns him it appears to be her fault that he shows no further interest in women. (Eve gets it again.) Romy Schneider doesn't take all this nonsense very seriously. She goes through her scenes serenely, with a light good humor; her big, flat face makes her look like a jolly Buddha, and she has a piquant way with those thudding lines, giving them an occasional lilt. It seems characteristic of the private nature of Visconti's fantasies that the only sequence in the film that has any kind of visual integrity is, at the end, the torchlight search for Ludwig's body, when a lake is dragged at night. Visconti is more carried away by the possibilities of operatic splendor in Ludwig's death than by the *opéra bouffe* of his life. Ludwig's talented aunt Princess Alexandra had her existence blighted by her conviction that she had swallowed a grand piano made of glass. Ludwig's grandfather Ludwig I had ruined himself over Lola Montez. How could Visconti resist the Alpine-Byzantine sick joke of this family, and be so solemn, so dour? Maybe he just couldn't bring himself to treat Ludwig's romanticism as a comedy; maybe he couldn't risk seeing the humor in it. I think Visconti dislikes Ludwig's bad taste so much that he refuses to identify with his subject, refuses even to show Ludwig a little affection. Yet though Visconti may well have superior taste in home furnishings and the decorative arts, his taste for lurid theatrics isn't the highest. He makes very classy horror movies.

A disaster on the scale of *Ludwig* is a prodigy. I long to see the outtakes; and I'd love to know if there was any greater visual or dramatic logic in what Visconti shot than in what he wound up with. By ordinary dramatic standards, Visconti isn't a writer; his scripts (written in collaboration) seem to be blueprints for the big scenes he visualizes — obsessive scenes with overtones of other theatrical works — which are just loosely strung together. Since he uses international casts (Trevor Howard is Wagner, while Silvana Mangano is Cosima), he may assume that the audience will adjust to the mélange of inflections as we adjust to the language problems in opera. (Why he has never gone ahead and made an opera on film — which would appear to be the logical extension of his talents — I don't understand; it seems a tragedy that he hasn't.) He appears remarkably insensitive to national and ethnic differences: when he casts an English actor like Dirk Bogarde as Aschenbach, the whole concept of *Death in Venice* is diminished — there's no real horror in the painted face. But Visconti aims for florid effects as if they were independent of the psychology of the characters. Rocco was Myshkin without any of the psychological depths that explained Myshkin's sacrificial behavior. Visconti's sense of length — that is, of the running time of his movies — may also relate to opera; like the popular arias in dull operas, his overwrought, garish scenes (and a few funny scenes here) rouse us from apathy. My guess about why the continuity is so jumpy is that he rather magisterially goes on shooting scenes that fascinate him, and later finds he has no place for them. The credits list Adriana Asti in the role of an actress who was actually rather important in Ludwig's life, since his people at first took her for his mistress and were overjoyed at this indication — false, as it turned out — of heterosexual inclinations. Miss Asti does not appear in the film now; no doubt she's on the cutting-room floor. Visconti uses a flashforward near the beginning and then most of the movie is in flashback, and many of the key relationships are never made clear.

It wasn't until I sat down and read Wilfrid Blunt's exquisitely lucid (and entertaining) *The Dream King* that I could figure out what was meant to be going on. Blunt, who is far more sympathetic to the king than Visconti is, explains Ludwig's brother-sister "soul unions" with women, his relations with his subjects, how he paid for his castles, and all the other questions that plague you while you're staring at the movie — and reading the book takes less time. (I think you even get better views of Ludwig's castles and furnishings in the book's illustrations than you do in the movie.)

The contrast of the compact lucidity of Blunt's book with this unyieldingly private, sprawling, cranky movie suggests what may happen to a moviemaker like Visconti. There is a grandiosity inherent in moviemaking, and particularly in making certain types of movies, such as the spectacle and the epic. Experimental films may attract sensitive, even shrinking artists, and middle-sized productions are often made by unassuming directors, but the big, famous moviemakers are men with an imperial cast of mind, and they very often get carried away — shoot far more than they can possibly integrate into a film, and then cut on the assumption that the gaps don't matter. Big movie directors are the modern mad kings, and the truth is that, as with Ludwig, there is a rationale for their follies. Which are harmless, too. If they sometimes throw away a few million dollars, why should they feel there's anything wrong in that, since they have either made many millions for the businessmen or have conferred such majesty and excitement on the businessmen's lives that they have, so to speak, paid their way. The only director with a string of authentic titles, Visconti — not a gypsy Von but the real thing, whose lineage goes back to Charlemagne's father-in-law — must confer something special on the businessmen. So if he squanders and they moan, surely the moan has a few trills in it. The damage the directors do is to their own visions. You have to be a monomaniac to make a big movie that is artistically yours — that isn't just a mechanized production. But a sort of crazed omnipotence sets in. Fighting for money to finance their dreams, sure that the dreams are clearer than they actually are, the big moviemakers scatter their energies and wreck their biggest projects. They push on to ever bigger ones until that happens. And sometimes they are powerful enough to keep the process going, moving from one giant failure to the next.

There was speculation that *The Damned* (called *Götterdämmerung* in Europe) would be Visconti's last film. But perhaps the German-decadent spirit of that film got to him (he has said, "I'm very German. I like German culture — German music, German philosophy — and also the origin of the Visconti family is in Germany"). He went on to *Death in Venice,* which looked as if he couldn't bear to end it; Tadzio, the boy with the revolving head, kept reappearing in the piazza, and that poor scarecrow Aschenbach kept clutching himself. And then he went on to *Ludwig,* and laid plans for what sounded like the biggest dream castle of them all, *Remembrance of Things Past.* However, he had a stroke before *Ludwig* was completed (he supervised the editing, but his illness may help to explain the botched assemblage of the scenes), and the Proust project has passed into Joseph Losey's hands. Now Visconti says that he's contemplating doing *The Magic Mountain,* if he has the strength. However, if *Ludwig* proves to be Visconti's last film — his swan song — this visual gibberish will appear to be the chaos he was always heading toward. Maybe the subject of Ludwig the dream king is just too close for a big moviemaker-dreamer to handle. When Fritz Lang tried to do the Wagnerian legends in his two-parter, *Siegfried* and *Kriemhild's Re-*

venge, he got ponderously lost. Could Griffith have tackled Ludwig, or could von Sternberg or von Stroheim or Gance or Welles or Fellini, without wallowing, and sinking in the wallow? An enigma like Ludwig, a king who disappears inside his fantasies of greater kings, might be a safe subject for a director of modest gifts, but it could be the ultimate dangerous subject for a movie king.

❖

"TWO PEOPLE," starring Peter Fonda and a new-to-movies actress, Lindsay Wagner, is meant to be a sensitive modern love story. There is nothing grossly wrong with it; the script, an original by Richard De Roy, is painstakingly tooled, and the direction, by Robert Wise, is tasteful and accomplished. The trouble is this kind of moviemaking is obsolete. *Two People* isn't offensive; it merely has no interest whatsoever. Twenty years ago, this sort of boy-meets-girl movie would have opened on a double bill; it would have been made more carelessly, and it might have had a little zip. But paralyzing insecurity about what the new audience wants has killed the chances for a confident, entertaining quality, and now it has nothing.

Fairly suddenly, a few generations of competent old-style directors — Robert Wise isn't yet sixty, but he's one of them — have been stranded. Wise — unpretentious but also unimaginative, a dependable, efficient director — is particularly unlucky, because his brand of academic pop, in Hollywood terms "prestigious" only a few years ago because it wasn't crude and sleazy, has less personality than much sleazier work. The impersonality and inexpressiveness of this type of moviemaking is stifling now; it was part of a factory system that television absorbed, and the material and techniques have been reproduced so often that there is no conviction left in them. When we go to the movies now, we expect something different, and watching *Two People* seems like watching part of a TV series. The movie begins in Marrakesh, where Fonda and the girl meet, and when they take the train to Casablanca there are ravishing views of the Moroccan countryside; the action moves on to Paris and, finally, to New York. However, to adapt a vulgarism, you can take a director out of the studio, but you can't take the studio out of a director. Not this director, anyway. Wise tries to simulate spontaneity and improvisation and a documentary surface, but the spirit isn't there; nothing has really been left to chance. Competent directors like Wise can't start over, and yet they're in the position of blacksmiths after Henry Ford came along — only it's the other way around. Wise, who has directed such films as *The Body Snatcher* (1945), *The Set-Up* (1949), *Executive Suite* (1954), *Somebody up There Likes Me* (1956), *I Want to Live!* (1958), *West Side Story* (1961), *Two for the Seesaw* (1962), *The Haunting* (1963), *The Sound of Music* (1965), *The Sand Pebbles* (1966), *Star!* (1968), and *The Andromeda Strain* (1971), is still working mechanically when we have come to expect some sort of organic expression of personality on the screen.

The travelogue material in *Two People* (the great Henri Decae was the cinematographer) is very handsome — it looks like the sumptuous photographs in *Réalités* — but it's shot and edited impersonally, so it is only background, and the hero and heroine seem to be tourists. Peter Fonda is playing an American who deserted in Vietnam and has finally decided to go home and serve his prison sentence. "I'm tired of running," he says. "I want my life back." It's after he has made the arrangements to return that he meets Lindsay Wagner, a highly successful American model. This is a decent-hearted film, and, by Hollywood standards, daring in its generous treatment of the hero and his reasons for deserting. If we could believe in the lovers, the picture might have some of that droopy, romantically-doomed ambience that people used to enjoy at the movies. But Wise is not a romantic director; there are touches — such as the lights going on in Paris — and he tries hard in the lyrical, sexy-sweet Paris bedroom scenes, with the music pouring on syrup, but the game is already lost. The picture is dead smooth. Lindsay Wagner, a tall, large-featured girl with a big mouth, who has been "groomed" by Universal on TV and is making her movie début here, speaks her lines with TV proficiency, but she's not very likable, and she doesn't give off the torrid rays she's meant to; and although Peter Fonda, who has a righteous set to his mouth and jaw, is well cast and probably does his best-controlled acting, he doesn't have a core of tension. Something in him is still asleep, and perhaps always will be; he could be the Richard Carlson or David Manners of the seventies. The two leads are well used, but they are only used; maybe we've come to expect a little participatory democracy in movie acting. There's no freedom for them here, or for us.

[March 24, 1973]

A Rip-off with Genius

"Marilyn," A Biography by Norman Mailer

IT'S THE GLOSSIEST of glossy books — the sexy waif-goddess spread out in over 100 photographs by two dozen photographers plus the Mailer text and all on shiny coated paper. It's a rich and creamy book, an offensive physical object, perhaps even a little sordid. On the jacket, her moist lips parted, in a color photograph by Bert Stern taken just before her death in 1962, Marilyn Monroe has that blurry, slugged look of her later years; fleshy but pasty. A sacrificial woman — *Marilyn* to put beside *Zelda.* This glassy-eyed goddess is not the funny bunny the public wanted, it's Lolita become Medusa. The book was "produced" by the same Lawrence Schiller who packaged the 1962 Hedda Hopper story congratulating 20th Century-Fox for firing Monroe from her last picture; now there are new ways to take her. The cover-girl face on *Marilyn* is disintegrating; and the astuteness of the entrepreneurs in exploiting even her disintegration, using it as a Pop icon, gets to one. Who knows what to think about Marilyn Monroe or about those who turn her sickness to metaphor? I wish they'd let her die.

In his opening, Mailer describes Marilyn Monroe as "one of the last of cinema's aristocrats" and recalls that the sixties, which "began with Hemingway as the monarch of American arts, ended with Andy Warhol as its regent." Surely he's got it all wrong? He can't even believe it; it's just a conceit. Hemingway wasn't the monarch of American arts but our official literary celebrity — our big writer — and by the end of the sixties, after *An American Dream* and *Cannibals and Christians* and *The Armies of the Night* and *Miami and the Siege of Chicago,* the title had passed to Mailer. And Marilyn Monroe wasn't a cinema aristocrat (whatever nostalgic reverie of the "old stars" is implied); a good case could be made for her as the first of the Warhol superstars (funky caricatures of sexpot glamour, impersonators of stars). Jean Harlow with that voice of tin may have beat her to it, but it was Monroe who used her lack of an actress's skills to amuse the public. She had the wit or crassness or desperation to turn cheesecake into acting — and vice versa; she did what others had the "good taste" not to do, like Mailer, who puts in what other writers have been educated to leave out. She would bat her Bambi eyelashes, lick her messy suggestive open mouth, wiggle that pert and tempting bottom, and use her hushed voice to caress us with dizzying innuendos. Her extravagantly ripe body bulging and spilling out of her clothes, she threw herself at us with the off-color innocence of a baby whore. She wasn't the girl men dreamed of or wanted to know but the girl they wanted to go to bed with. She was Betty Grable without the coy modesty, the starlet *in flagrante delicto* forever because that's where everybody thought she belonged.

Her mixture of wide-eyed wonder and cuddly drugged sexiness seemed to get to just about every male; she turned on even homosexual men. And women couldn't take her seriously enough to be indignant; she was funny and impulsive in a way that made people feel protective. She was a little knocked out; her face looked as if, when nobody was paying attention to her, it would go utterly slack — as if she died between wolf calls.

She seemed to have become a camp siren out of confusion and ineptitude; her comedy was self-satire, and apologetic — conscious parody that had begun unconsciously. She was not the first sex goddess with a trace of somnambulism; Garbo was often a little out-of-it, Dietrich was numb most of the time, and Hedy Lamarr was fairly zonked. But they were exotic and had accents, so maybe audiences didn't wonder why they were in a daze; Monroe's slow reaction time made her seem daffy, and she tricked it up into a comedy style. The mystique of Monroe — which accounts for the book *Marilyn* — is that she became spiritual as she fell apart. But as an actress she had no way of expressing what was deeper in her except in moodiness and weakness. When she was "sensitive" she was drab.

Norman Mailer inflates her career to cosmic proportions. She becomes "a proud, inviolate artist," and he suggests that "one might literally have to invent the idea of a soul in order to approach her." He pumps so much wind into his subject that the reader may suspect that he's trying to make Marilyn Monroe worthy of him, a subject to compare with the Pentagon and the moon. Laying his career calibrations before us, he speculates that "a great biography might be constructed some day" upon the foundation of Fred Lawrence Guiles's *Norma Jean* and proceeds to think upon himself as the candidate for the job: "By the logic of transcendence, it was exactly in the secret scheme of things that a man should be able to write about a beautiful woman, or a woman to write about a great novelist — that would be transcendence, indeed!"

Has he somehow forgotten that even on the sternest reckonings the "great" novelists include Jane Austen and George Eliot?

But no he decides that he cannot give the years needed for the task; he will write, instead, a "novel biography." "Set a thief to catch a thief and put an artist on an artist," he hums, and seeing the work already in terms to give Capote shivers, he describes it as "a *species* of novel ready to play by the rules of biography." The man is intolerable; he works out the flourishes of the feat he's going to bring off before allowing his heroine to be born. After all this capework and the strain of the expanding chest on the buttons of his vest, the reader has every right to expect this blowhard to take a belly flop, and every reason to want him to. But though it's easy — in fact, natural — to speak of Mailer as crazy (and only half in admiration) nobody says dumb. *Marilyn* is a rip-off all right but a rip-off with genius.

Up to now we've had mostly contradictory views of Monroe. Those who have taken a hard line on her (most recently Walter Bernstein in the July *Esquire*) never accounted for the childlike tenderness, and those who have seen her as shy and loving (like the Strasbergs or Diana Trilling or Norman Rosten) didn't account for the shrill sluttiness. Arthur Miller had split her into *The Misfits* and the scandalous *After the Fall,* and since each was only a side of her, neither was believable. With his fox's ingenuity, Mailer puts her together and shows how she might have been torn apart, from the inside by her inheritance and her childhood, by the outside pressures of the movie business. But it's all conjecture and sometimes pretty wild conjecture; he's a long way from readiness "to play by the rules of biography" since his principal technique — how could the project interest him otherwise? — is to jump inside everyone's head and read thoughts.

He acknowledges his dependence for the putative facts on the standard biographies — principally Guiles's *Norma Jean,* and also Maurice Zolotow's *Marilyn Monroe* — but deciding to interpret the data researched and already presented by others is a whopping putdown of them; their work thus becomes grist for his literary-star mill. Some of his milling is not so stellar. He quotes trashy passages (with a half-smile) and uses them for their same trashy charge. And his psychoanalytic detective work is fairly mawkish; we don't need Norman Mailer to tell us about Marilyn Monroe's search for parent figures — even fan magazines have become adept at this two-bit stuff about her claiming to her schoolmates that Clark Gable was her father and then winding up in Gable's arms in *The Misfits.*

Mailer explains her insomnia and her supposed attraction to death by her own account of someone's attempt to suffocate her when she was thirteen months old. But since there's no evidence for her account (except hindwise, in her insomnia) and since she apparently didn't start telling the story until the mid-fifties, when she was embroidering that raped and abused Little Nell legend that *Time* sent out to the world in a cover story, isn't it possible that before building a house of cards on the murderous incident one should consider if it wasn't linked to her having played (in *Don't Bother to Knock* in 1952) a psychopathic babysitter who blandly attacks a little girl? (The faintly anesthetized vagueness of her babysitter prefigured the ethereal vacuity of the face in the last photos.)

When the author says that it was his "prejudice that a study of Marilyn's movies might offer more penetration into her early working years in film than a series of interviews. . . ." one may guess that his model is Freud's book on Leonardo da Vinci, which is also an ecstasy of hypothesis. But surprisingly, Mailer makes only perfunctory use of her movies. He can't be much interested: he doesn't even bother to discuss the tawdriness of *Niagara* (made in 1953, just before she won Hollywood over with *Gentlemen Prefer Blondes*), in which her amoral destructive tramp — carnal as hell — must surely have represented Hollywood's lowest estimate of her.

Nor is he very astute about her career possibilities: He accepts the pious view that she should have worked with Chaplin and he says, complaining of Twentieth Century-Fox's lack of comprehension of her film art, that she could "have done *Nana, The Brothers Karamazov, Anna Christie* or *Rain* to much profit, but they gave her *Let's Make Love.*" Who would quarrel with his judgment of *Let's Make Love,* but do the other titles represent his idea of what she should have done? (To *her* profit, he must mean, surely not the studio's.) Yes, probably she could have played a Grushenka (though not a Russian one), but does Mailer want to look at a Hollywood *Karamazov* or new versions of those other clumping war-horses? (Not a single one of those girls is American, and how could Monroe play anything else?)

Monroe might have "grown" as an actress but she would have died as a star. (Isn't the vision of the Reverend Davidson kneeling to her Sadie Thompson the purest camp?) The pity is that she didn't get more of the entertaining roles that were in her range; she hardly had the stability to play a mother or even a secretary and she was a shade too whorey for Daisy Miller or her descendants, but she was the heroine of every porny-spoof like *Candy* come to life, and she might have been right for *Sweet Charity* or for *Lord Love a Duck* or *Born Yesterday* or a remake of the Harlow comedy *Bombshell* or another *Red Dust.* She might have had a triumph in *Breakfast at Tiffany's* and she probably could have toned down for Tennessee Williams's *Period of Adjustment* and maybe even *Bonnie and Clyde.* Plain awful when she suffered, she was best at demi-whores who enjoyed the tease, and she was too obviously a product of the movie age to appear in a period picture.

It isn't enough for Mailer that people enjoyed her; he cranks her up as great and an "angel of sex" and, yes, "Napoleonic was her capture of the attention of the world." Monroe the movie star with sexual clout overpowers Norman Mailer. But most of her late pictures (such as *The Prince and the Showgirl, Let's Make Love* and *The Misfits*) didn't capture the public. Audiences didn't want the nervous, soulful Monroe — never so dim as when she was being "luminous"; they wanted her to be a mock-dumb snuggly blonde and to have some snap. When Mailer writes about her "artist's intelligence" and "superb taste" and about the sort of work she did in *The Misfits* as "the fulfillment of her art," he just seems to be getting carried away by the importance of his subject. Back in 1962, he wrote that "she was bad in *The Misfits,* she was finally too vague, and when emotion showed, it was unattractive and small," and he was right. It was already the Marilyn legend in that role — the baffled, vulnerable child-woman; she didn't have the double-edged defenselessness of her comedy hits, she looked unawakened yet sick — anguished.

But Mailer understands how Hollywood uses its starlets and how Marilyn Monroe the star might have reacted to that usage, and that is the key understanding that most commentators on her have lacked (though Clifford Odets's obit of her had it, also the story Ezra Goodman wrote for *Time* in 1956, which *Time* didn't print but which appears in his *The Fifty Year Decline and Fall of Hollywood*). And who but Norman Mailer could have provided the analysis (that starts on page 35, the real beginning of the book) of the effect on Monroe of the torpor of her twenty-one months in an orphanage and why it probably confirmed her into a liar and reinforced "everything in her character that was secretive"? And who else, writing about a Pop figure, would even have thought about the relation of narcissism to institutional care? His strength — when he gets rolling — isn't in Freudian guesses but in his fusing his knowledge of how people behave with his worst suspicions of where they really live.

His best stuff derives from his having been on the scene, or close enough to smell it out. When it comes to reporting the way American rituals and institutions operate, Mailer's low cunning is maybe the best tool anyone ever had. He grasps the psychological and sexual rewards the studio system offered executives. He can describe why Zanuck, who had Monroe under contract, didn't like her; how she became "a protagonist in the great American soap opera" when her nude calendar was "discovered" — i.e., leaked to the press by Jerry Wald to publicize *Clash by Night*; and what it may have meant to her to date DiMaggio, "an American king — her first. The others have been merely Hollywood kings." He's elegantly cogent on the Method and his paragraphs on Lee Strasberg as a critic of acting are a classic.

About half of *Marilyn* is great as only a great writer, using his brains and feelers could make it. Just when you get fed up with his flab and slop, he'll come through with a runaway string of perceptions and you have to recognize that, though it's a bumpy ride, the book still goes like a streak. His writing is close to the pleasures of movies; his immediacy makes him more accessible to those brought up with the media than, say, Bellow. You read him with a heightened consciousness because his performance has zing. It's the star system in literature; you can feel him bucking for the big time, and when he starts flying it's so exhilarating you want to applaud. But it's a good-bad book. When Mailer tries to elevate his intuitions into theories, the result is usually verbiage. (His theory that men impart their substance and qualities into women along with their semen is a typical macho Mailerism; he sees it as a one-way process, of course. Has no woman slipped a little something onto his privates?) There are countless bits of literary diddling: " — she had been alive for twenty years but not yet named! — "; the exclamation points are like sprinkles. Mailer the soothsayer with his rheumy metaphysics and huckster's magick is a carny quack, and this Hollywood milieu seems to bring out his fondness for the slacker reaches of the occult — reincarnation and sob-sister omens ("a bowl of tomato sauce dropped on her groom's white jacket the day of her first wedding"). We know his act already and those words (dread, existential, ontology, the imperatives) that he pours on like wella balsam to tone up the prose. And there's his familiar invocation of God, i.e., mystery. But it's less mysterious now because it has become a weapon: the club he holds over the villain of the book — respectable, agnostic Arthur Miller, a writer of Mailer's own generation (and closer than that) who won Marilyn Monroe. Set a thief to catch a thief, an artist on an artist, and one nice Jewish boy from Brooklyn on another.

It's not just a book about Monroe, it's Mailer's show. "Feedback has become the condition of our lives," he said in an interview in 1972. "It's the movies. We've passed the point in civilization where we can ever look at anything as an art work. There is always our knowledge of it and of the making of it." Whether true or false, this applies to Mailer, and he has made us more aware than we may want to be of his titles and campaigns, his aspiration to be more than a writer, to conquer the media and be monarch of American arts — a straight Jean Cocteau who'd meet anybody at high noon. Something has been withheld from Norman Mailer: his crown lacks a few jewels, a star. He has never triumphed in the theater, never been looked up to as a Jewish Lincoln, and never been married to a famous movie queen — a sex symbol. (He's also not a funny writer; to be funny you have to be totally unfettered, and he's too ambitious.) Mailer's waddle and crouch may look like a put-on, but he means it when he butts heads. *Marilyn* is his whammy to Arthur Miller.

In 1967, in an article written to promote the off-Broadway version of *The Deer Park,* Mailer said of himself, "There were too many years when he dreamed of *The Deer Park* on Broadway and the greatest first night of the decade, too many hours of rage when he declaimed to himself that his play was as good as *Death of a Salesman,* or even, and here he gulped hard, *A Streetcar Named Desire.*" The sly sonuvabitch coveted Miller's success and cut him down in the same sentence. *(The Deer Park* wasn't Mailer's *Salesman;* based on Mailer's own second marriage and dealing with integrity and the McCarthy period and sex and love, it was more like Mailer's *After the Fall.)* In his warm-up in *Marilyn* Mailer points out that though he'd never met Marilyn Monroe, she had for a time lived with Miller in Connecticut "not five miles away from the younger author, who [was] not yet aware of what his final relation to Marilyn Monroe would be. . . ." It appears to be destiny's decree that he should take her over. Mailer isn't the protagonist of this book; Marilyn is. But Mailer and God are waiting in the wings.

How can we readers limit ourselves to the subject when he offers us this name-play: "it was fair to engraved coincidence that the letters in Marilyn Monroe (if the 'a' were used twice and 'o' but once) would spell his own name leaving only the 'y' for excess, a trifling discrepancy, no more calculated to upset the heavens than the most miniscule diffraction of the red shift"? (What would happen to any other serious writer trying to foist his giddy acrostics on us?) He fails to record that both Miller and Mailer probably derive from Mähler. Siblings. He had said in *The Armies of the Night* that he dreaded winding up "the nice Jewish boy from Brooklyn," that that was the one personality he considered "absolutely insupportable," but it was clearly a love-hate game — or why dread it? Actually he's in no danger. He's cut off from respectability, like our country; the greatest American writer is a bum, and a bum who's starting not to mind it. The time to begin worrying is when both he and the U. S. start finding virtues in this condition; we could all wind up like drunks doing a music-hall turn.

He can't get Arthur Miller's long bones, but he's busy trying to take off his skin; he wouldn't do it to Robert Lowell. But Miller and Mailer try for the same things: he's catching Miller's hand in the gentile cookie jar. Mailer doesn't get into confessional self-analysis on Miller as he did with Lowell; he writes as if with lordly objectivity — but the reader can feel what's going on. He says of Miller's possible fear of the marriage's failing, "a man who has lost confidence in his creative power sees ridicule as the broom that can sweep him to extinction" and then proceeds to make every kind of fool of him, attributing to him the impulses and motives that Mailer considers most contemptible. Ultimately what he's saying is that Miller wasn't smart enough to get any more out of Monroe than *After the Fall.* With Mailer, if you're going to use, use big. The second half of the book is supremely cruel to Miller — and it infects and destroys one's pleasure in the good parts. The "novel biography" becomes Mailer's way to perform character assassination with the freedom of a novelist who has created fictional characters. He's so cold-blooded in imputing motives to others that he can say of Yves Montand, for example, that Marilyn Monroe was "his best ticket to notoriety." Is this how Mailer maneuvers — is Marilyn Monroe Norman Mailer's surefire subject after a few box-office flops? Is that why he shoots the works in his final orgies of gossipy conjecture and turns her death into another Chappaquiddick — safe in the knowledge no one is left to call him a liar?

He uses his gifts meanly this time — and that's not what we expect of Mailer, who is always billed as generous. This brilliant book gives off bad vibes — and vibes are what Mailer is supposed to be the master of. *Marilyn* is a feat all right: matchstick by matchstick, he's built a whole damned armada inside a bottle. (Surely he's getting ready to do *Norman*? Why leave it to someone who may care less?) But can we honor him for this book when it doesn't sit well on the stomach? It's a metaphysical cocktail-table book, and probably not many will be able to resist looking for the vicious digs and the wrap-up on the accumulated apocrypha of many years, many parties. To be king of the bums isn't really much. What are we actually getting out of *Marilyn*? Good as the best parts of it are, there's also malevolence that needs to be recognized. Is the great reporter's arrogance so limitless that he now feels free to report on matters to which he's never been exposed? Neither the world nor Marilyn Monroe's life should be seen in Norman Mailer's image.

[July 22, 1973]

Part Two

After Innocence

THE WATERGATE HEARINGS have overshadowed the movies this summer, yet the corruption that Watergate has come to stand for can be seen as the culmination of what American movies have been saying for almost a decade. The movies of the thirties said that things would get better. The post-Second World War movies said that villainy would be punished and goodness would triumph; the decencies would be respected. But movies don't say that anymore; the Vietnamization of American movies is nearly complete. Today, movies say that the system is corrupt, that the whole thing stinks, and they've been saying this steadily since the mid-sixties. The Vietnam war has barely been mentioned on the screen, but you could feel it in *Bonnie and Clyde* and *Bullitt* and *Joe*, in *Easy Rider* and *Midnight Cowboy* and *The Last Picture Show*, in *They Shoot Horses, Don't They?* and *The Candidate* and *Carnal Knowledge* and *The French Connection* and *The Godfather*. It was in good movies and bad, flops and hits, especially hits — in the convictionless atmosphere, the absence of shared values, the brutalities taken for granted, the glorification of loser-heroes. It was in the harshness of the attitudes, the abrasiveness that made you wince — until, after years of it, maybe you stopped wincing. It had become normal.

In earlier action and adventure films, strength — what the strapping American hero was physically and what he embodied as the representative of the most powerful nation on earth — had to triumph. The American in those movies was the natural leader of men; he had to show the natives of any other country how to defend themselves. Even little Alan Ladd used to show them how to fight. Of course, it was a fantasy world, but this set of fantasies must have satisfied something deep down in the audience; it didn't come out of nowhere. Now the American man of action has become the enemy of all men — a man out for his own good only, and, very likely, a psychotic racist. In recent films, if a character spoke of principles or ideals the odds were he would turn out to be a ruthless killer, or at least a con artist; the heroes didn't believe in anything and didn't pretend they did. American history was raked over and the myths of the Old West were turned upside down; massacre scenes, indicting our past as well as our present, left us with nothing. Just jokes and horror. Whatever the period — in *Little Big Man* or *Butch Cassidy and the Sundance Kid* or *The Wild Bunch* — you could be sure nobody was going to amount to much. The air wasn't right for achievement.

In action pictures, there was no virtuous side to identify with and nobody you really felt very good about cheering for. Both sides were unprincipled; only their styles were different, and it was a matter of preferring the less gross and despicable characters to the total monsters. In cops-and-robbers movies, the cops were likely to be no better than the crooks; sometimes they'd be worse crooks. The freshest, most contemporary element in the current movie *Cops and Robbers* is that the cops commit a robbery to get away from the hell and hopelessness of trying to keep law and order. There was a cycle of movies about drugs, and, of all those addicts sinking down and down, was there one who got himself together? In some of the most popular films, the heroes were helpless losers, self-destructive, or drifters, mysteriously defeated. Defeated just in the nature of things. Sometimes, as in *Five Easy Pieces,* the hero was so defeated he was morally superior. There were few happy endings; when a comedy such as *The Owl and the Pussycat* or *Made for Each Other* wound up with a matched pair, the characters were so knocked out that if they didn't want each other who would? It wasn't exactly as if they'd taken first place in a contest; it was more like the last stand of bedraggled survivors. And it was emotionally satisfying just because it wasn't the sort of upbeat finish that you'd have to put down as a Hollywood ending.

Though it was exhilarating to see the old mock innocence cleared away, a depressive uncertainty has settled over the movies. They're seldom enjoyable at a simple level, and that may be one of the reasons older people no longer go; they watch TV shows, which are mostly reprocessed versions of old movies — the same old plots, characters, and techniques, endlessly recombined. The enjoyment has been squeezed out, but not the reassuring simplicity. Almost three-fourths (73 percent) of the movie audience is under twenty-nine; it's an audience of people who grew up with TV and began going out to theaters when they became restless and started dating. Chances are that when they have children of their own they'll be back with the box. But while they're going out to the movies they want something different, and this demand — in the decade of Vietnam — has created a fertile chaos, an opportunity for artists as well as for the bums who pile on the meat-cleaver brawls, and for those proud of not giving a damn. Maybe the effects of the years of guilt can be seen in the press's inability to be disgusted by the witless, desiccated *The Last of Sheila,* with its pinched little dregs of chic, its yearning for Weimar. Often even the fairy-tale films are indecisive and not quite satisfying, as if the writers and directors were afraid of showing any feeling. If *Paper Moon* had been made in an earlier decade, the con man (Ryan O'Neal) would have embraced the child (Tatum O'Neal) at the end and maybe he'd have told her he was her father (whether he was or not), and the audience would have had some emotional release. The way Peter Bogdanovich did it, it's pleasant while you're watching, but you're waiting for something that never comes; it's finally a little flat and unfulfilled. But if the story had been carried to the classic tearful father-daughter embrace, mightn't the audience — or, at least, part of it — have been turned off by the unabashed sweetness? By the hope for a better future? (In movies now, people don't talk about the future; they don't make plans; they don't expect much.) Possibly the very flatness makes it easier for audiences to accept the movie.

American movies didn't "grow up"; they did a flipover from their prolonged age of innocence to this age of corruption. When Vietnam finished off the American hero as righter of wrongs, the movie industry embraced corruption greedily; formula movies could be energized by infusions of brutality, cynicism, and Naked Apism, which could all be explained by Vietnam and called realism. Moviemakers could celebrate violence and pretend, even to themselves, that they were doing the public a service. Even though some writers and directors have probably been conscientious in their attempts to shock the audience by exposing the evils of the past, the effect has not been like that of Costa-Gavras's *State of Siege,* which is literally an SOS, and makes one want to find out what's going on and do something about it. And not like the effects of *I Am a Fugitive from a Chain Gang,* which outraged people, or Fred Wiseman's *Titicut Follies* and *High School,* which shook things up and led to reforms. Outrage isn't the aim of our most violent films; outrage isn't expected. When movie after movie tells audiences that they should be against themselves, it's hardly surprising that people go out of the theaters drained, numbly convinced that, with so much savagery and cruelty everywhere, nothing can be done. The movies have shown us the injustice of American actions throughout our history, and if we have always been rotten, the effect is not to make us feel we have the power to change but, rather, to rub our noses in it and make us accept it. In this climate, Watergate seems the most natural thing that could happen. If one were to believe recent movies, it was never any different in this country: Vietnam and Watergate are not merely where we got to but where we always were. The acceptance of corruption and the sentimentalization of defeat — that's the prevailing atmosphere in American movies, and producers, writers, and directors now make their choices in terms of a set of defeatist conventions.

When Tom Wolfe wrote about stock-car racing in *Esquire* in March, 1965 ("The Last American Hero Is Junior Johnson. *Yes!*"), he tried to evoke the physical sensations of this motor-age sport, with its rural speed-demon kings. Wolfe used the youth culture for excitement just as the movies did. Movies hit us in more ways than we can ever quite add up, and that's the kind of experience that Tom Wolfe tried to convey in prose. He described the sensations without attempting to add them up or theorize about them, and, because he had a remarkable gift for hyperactive, evocative writing, the effect was an impassioned turn-on. And, because in this article and others he didn't make his obeisances to the higherness of the traditional arts, he ran into the sort of disapproval that movies get. It was a compliment, of course — recognition from the enemy, because he had set up a great polemical target: the genteel, condescending press, which had ignored the new sports or treated them marginally. When Wolfe reprinted the racing article, which became the largest section of *The Kandy-Kolored Tangerine-Flake Streamline Baby,* he shortened the title to "The Last American Hero," and that's the name of the film based on it.

As journalism, Wolfe's charged-up pieces had the impact of an explorer's excited report on new terrain. But the youth culture that he brought into star journalism was already in the movies (just as the movies were in it). That culture was partly created by the movies, and his surfers and rockers and racers had been the lifeblood of the Grade B pop-genre films of the fifties. The car and the movie came along together, and chases, usually involving cars, have been surefire for so long that there was a time when the chase used to be called "pure movie"; there's barely a male star who hasn't served his days as a racer. The first demolition derby wasn't held until 1961, but moviemakers had always known about people's loving to see cars bashed. Demolition scenes were the primeval laugh-getters of silent pictures, and smashed cars and planes still get the biggest laughs in a new primeval picture like *Live and Let Die.* (Geoffrey Holder's leering wickedness as the impresario of the revels in the picture is kiddie camp.)

In the introduction to his book, Wolfe recorded the discovery that a builder of baroque custom cars he talked with "had been living like the *complete artist* for years," and went on, "He had starved, suffered — the whole thing — so he could sit inside a garage and create these cars which more than 99 percent of the American people would consider ridiculous, vulgar and lower-class-awful beyond comment almost." That's a strange overestimate of the number of people with good taste arrayed against the car builder; racing pictures were made for audiences to whom such a man had been an artist all along. So when you make a movie out of Tom Wolfe's reports on the world outside the class biases of Eastern-establishment prudery, you're taking the material back where it came from, and there's no occasion for whoops of revelation. The movie of "The Last American Hero" isn't startling, the way Wolfe's pieces were; but, with a script that uses Wolfe as the source for most of the story elements, Lamont Johnson, who directed, has done the Southern racing scene and the character of the people caught up in it better, perhaps, than they've ever been done before. The movie has everything *but* originality.

The title (which is a tired one anyway) no longer means what it did for Tom Wolfe. The Junior Johnson that Wolfe wrote about beat the system and won on his own terms; that was what made him a hero and a legend. Driving whatever he could stick together, he won out over the cars sponsored and specially built by the motor industry. He won even when his own car couldn't go as fast, by tricks such as catching free rides — by tailgating and being sucked along by the vacuum of the faster cars. A Southern country boy who became a hot-rod genius by running his father's moonshine whiskey in the middle of the night, he beat the big pros by ingenuity, skill, and blind impudence, and he beat them over and over — seven times, even though he was out for a couple of seasons when he was sent to federal prison for helping his daddy with some of the heavy labor at the still. (The agents were gunning for him, because he'd made them look ridiculous on the back roads years before.) That's the stuff of legend, all right. By the time Junior Johnson made his peace with Detroit and started to drive the factory-built racing cars, he was too much of a hero to be judged a sellout. He had already proved himself and then some, so it was all right for him to settle down, like a man of sense.

But between the publication of the Wolfe article and the making of the movie there was Vietnam. The hero of the movie — called Junior Jackson — starts out by cheating to win a demolition derby, and when he moves on to racing he can't make it with his own car. He wins his first big race *after* he starts driving as a hired hand for a big-money man, Colt (Ed Lauter). Even the steady girl the real Junior had gone with since high school, and later married, is replaced by a track follower (Valerie Perrine), who floats along with the winners. So there's sex without romance, sex without a future. The movie also avoids the easy possibilities for sympathy; it doesn't make Junior's path as hard as it was. He doesn't go to prison in the movie — it's his father who is busted as a result of Junior's bravado at the wheel. Colt, rather like George C. Scott in *The Hustler,* suggests a personification of the power of money, rather than just a representative of Detroit. Colt is almost lascivious about winning, and his winning is evil (but we never learn what winning gets him, or what it did for the diabolical Scott character). In *The Last American Hero,* corruption seems to be inescapable: if you want to win, you learn to take orders even from people whose idea of winning you don't understand. And at the end Junior Jackson is growing up — which is to say, learning the price of success in the real world. He is forced to sacrifice his friendships and his principles. The film says that to win you give up everything you care about except winning. It tells the story not of a man who fights for his independence but of a man who is smart enough not to sell himself too cheap.

Who would believe the actual story of Junior Johnson now — how hard it really was for him, and that he made it? This version will seem far more honest to movie audiences, because the new conventions are that you can't win and that everybody's a sellout. Even the absence of romance makes the movie more convincing — tougher, cool. And since Junior, played by Jeff Bridges, has a visible capacity for tenderness, the absence of romance is cruelly felt by the audience. By turning Junior Johnson's story around, the director, Lamont Johnson (and his writer, William Roberts, with a sizable, though uncredited, assist from William Kerby, who wrote the best scenes), has been able to make a hip, modern movie. It is, ironically, the most honest and gifted and tough-minded people in Hollywood who are fighting for defeat. The picture has total fidelity to its own scrupulous, hard-edged vision: the hero pays a price. It costs Junior Jackson something to win races; you can see that in Jeff Bridges' face.

Lamont Johnson doesn't exploit the backwoods people for the folksy touches that can make urban audiences laugh; he perceives the values in Junior Jackson's family life — in his affection for his mother (Geraldine Fitzgerald) and his vacuously grinning brother (Gary Busey), and, especially, in his bond to his father (Art Lund, in a towering performance). The picture was shot in Virginia and the Carolinas, using footage from actual races and derbies, and the crowds and details, the excited Southern faces at the stock-car tracks — everything feels right. Lamont Johnson has the feel for the South that John Boorman (who is English) couldn't get in *Deliverance.* Boorman is such an aestheticizing director — alienated, inhuman, yet the more gripping for the distance he keeps — that *Deliverance* held audiences by its mannered, ghastly-lovely cumulative power. It had the formality of a nightmare. (There was a hush in the theater when it was over.) *Deliverance* demonstrated that a movie can be effective even if you are always aware of the actors' acting and don't really believe in a single character, down to the bit players (except maybe James Dickey as the sheriff). But there is a special elation about a movie when the casting and the acting and the milieu seem effortlessly, inexplicably right. Paul Mazursky can get Los Angeles *(Alex in Wonderland, Blume in Love)* but can't get Venice *(Blume in Love).* Lamont Johnson's feeling for the milieu here amounts to an unusual sensibility: a gift for bringing all the elements of film together so that the people breathe right for where they live. He isn't an original — not in the way that, say, Mazursky, manic poet of middle-class quirk, is. (Has there ever been another self-satirist like Mazursky — humanly understanding and utterly freaked out?) But Lamont Johnson's work is attentive and satisfying. He's a far better movie man than many of the more original talents, and this film, if one sees the version he made, has everything going for it. (Twentieth Century-Fox tampered with the film, cutting a couple of the best scenes and then opening it in the South as an action racing picture. Since it isn't, it bombed out. And then the Fox executives decided it was a dog that wouldn't go in the big cities, because they knew that sophisticated people don't go to racing pictures. It opened in New York for a week in the summer as a "Showcase" presentation — that is to say, it got a second run without a first run — and its failure was the movie company's self-fulfilling prophecy. Though the reviews were excellent, they came out too late to attract an audience; Fox hadn't bothered with advance press screenings for a racing picture. But this movie transcends its genre; *The Last American Hero,* which is coming back next week, isn't just about stock-car racing, any more than *The Hustler* was only about shooting pool, and in terms of presenting the background of a sports hero it goes far beyond anything in *Downhill Racer.* If *The Last American Hero* finds a fraction of its rightful audience now, perhaps someone in the head office at Fox could do the sane, decent thing and restore the cuts?)

Sometimes, just on his own, Jeff Bridges is enough to make a picture worth seeing, and he's never before been used so fully, or in a way so integral to a film's conception. Only twenty-two when this picture was shot, he may be the most natural and least self-conscious screen actor who ever lived; physically, it's as if he had spent his life in the occupation of each character. He's the most American — the loosest — of all the young actors, unencumbered by stage diction and the stiff, emasculated poses of most juveniles. If he has a profile, we're not aware of it. He probably can't do the outrageous explosive scenes that Robert De Niro brings off in *Mean Streets* or the giddy-charming romantic clowning that De Niro did in the otherwise forgettable *The Gang That Couldn't Shoot Straight,* but De Niro — a real winner — is best when he's coming on and showing off. Jeff Bridges just moves into a role and lives in it — so deep in it that the little things seem to come straight from the character's soul. His brother Beau shares this infallible instinct, but Beau's effects don't seem to come from as far down; Beau Bridges has a lighter presence, an easier smile. Jeff Bridges' Junior Jackson is a cocky Huck Finn in the age of Detroit: impulsive, dogged, and self-sufficient; sure enough of himself to show his rank, shrewd enough to know where he's outranked. In a monologue scene (possibly suggested by Godard's *Masculine Feminine*), Junior, away from home for a race and feeling sentimental, uses a make-your-own-record machine to tell his family he's thinking of them and loves them; then, realizing he's beyond this kind of kid stuff, he throws the record away. The quality of Bridges' acting in this scene enlarges the meaning of the movie, yet he doesn't seem to be using anything more than a few shrugs and half-smothered words.

"THE LAST AMERICAN HERO" never goes soft, and maybe that's why the picture felt so realistic to me; it wasn't until I reread the Wolfe piece that I realized what a turnaround it was. But we believe the worst now — maybe *only* the worst. When we see a picture from the age of happy endings, the conventions may stick out as antiquated and ludicrous (and often they did when the picture was new), but the conventions that flow from the acceptance of corruption are insidiously believable, because they seem smart, while the older ones seem dumb. We will never know the extent of the damage movies are doing to us, but movie art, it appears, thrives on moral chaos. When the country is paralyzed, the popular culture may tell us why. After innocence, winners become losers. Movies are probably inuring us to corruption; the sellout is the hero-survivor for our times.

[October 1, 1973]

Everyday Inferno

MARTIN SCORSESE'S *Mean Streets* is a true original of our period, a triumph of personal filmmaking. It has its own hallucinatory look; the characters live in the darkness of bars, with lighting and color just this side of lurid. It has its own unsettling, episodic rhythm and a high-charged emotional range that is dizzyingly sensual. At the beginning, there's a long, fluid sequence as the central character, Charlie, comes into a bar and greets his friends; there's the laying on of hands, and we know that he is doing what he always does. And when the camera glides along with him as he's drawn toward the topless dancers on the barroom stage, we share his trance. At the end of the scene, when he's up on the stage, entering into the dance, he's not some guy who's taken leave of his senses but a man going through his nightly ritual. Movies generally work you up to expect the sensual intensities, but here you may be pulled into high without warning. Violence erupts crazily, too, the way it does in life — so unexpectedly fast that you can't believe it, and over before you've been able to take it in. The whole movie has this effect; it psychs you up to accept everything it shows you. And since the story deepens as it goes along, by the end you're likely to be open-mouthed, trying to rethink what you've seen. Though the street language and the operatic style may be too much for those with conventional tastes, if this picture isn't a runaway success the reason could be that it's so original that some people will be dumbfounded — too struck to respond. It's about American life here and now, and it doesn't look like an American movie, or feel like one. If it were subtitled, we could hail a new European or South American talent — a new Buñuel steeped in Verdi, perhaps — and go home easier at heart. Because what Scorsese, who is thirty, has done with the experience of growing up in New York's Little Italy has a thicker-textured rot and violence than we have ever had in an American movie, and a riper sense of evil.

The zinger in the movie — and it's this, I think, that begins to come together in one's head when the picture is over — is the way it gets at the psychological connections between Italian Catholicism and crime, between sin and crime. Some editorial writers like to pretend this is all a matter of prejudice; they try to tell us that there is no basis for the popular ethnic stereotypes — as if crime among Italians didn't have a different tone from crime among Irish or Jews or blacks. Editorial writers think they're serving the interests of democracy when they ask us to deny the evidence of our senses. But all crime is not alike, and different ethnic groups have different styles of lawlessness. These Mafiosi loafers hang around differently from loafing blacks; in some ways, the small-time hoods of *Mean Streets* (good Catholics who live at home with their parents) have more in common with the provincial wolf pack of Fellini's *I Vitelloni* (cadging, indulged sons of middle-class families) than with the other ethnic groups in New York City. And these hoods live in such an insulated world that anyone outside it — the stray Jew or black they encounter — is as foreign and funny to them as a little man from Mars.

Many people interpreted the success of *The Godfather* to mean that the film glorified the gangsters' lives. During the Second World War, a documentary showing the noise and congestion of New York City was cheered by nostalgic American soldiers overseas; if audiences were indeed attracted to the life of the Corleone family (and I think some probably were), the reaction may be just as aberrant to the intentions of *The Godfather,* the best gangster film ever made in this country. It's likely that Italian, or Sicilian, Catholicism has a special, somewhat romantic appeal to Americans at this time. Italians appear to others to accept the fact that they're doomed; they learn to be comfortable with it — it's what gives them that warm, almost tactile glow. Their voluptuous, vacant-eyed smiles tell us that they want to get the best out of this life: they know they're going to burn in eternity, so why should they think about things that are depressing? It's as if they were totally carnal: everything is for their pleasure. Maybe it is this relaxed attitude that gave the Mafiosi of *The Godfather* their charm for the American audience. Was the audience envying them their close family ties and the vitality of their lawlessness? Was it envying their having got used to a sense of sin? It's almost as if the non-Catholic part of America wanted to say that *mea culpa* is *nostra culpa.*

Before *Mean Streets* is over, that glow gets very hot and any glamour is sweated off. The clearest fact about Charlie (Harvey Keitel), junior member of a Mafia family — and, in a non-literal sense, the autobiographical central figure — is that whatever he does in his life, he's a sinner. Behind the titles you see him smiling his edgy, jocular smile and shaking hands with a priest, as if sealing a pact, while the words appear: "Directed by Martin Scorsese." Charlie, you can see in his tense ferret's face, feels he was born to be punished. Like his friends, round-faced, jovial Tony the barkeep (David Proval) and pompous Michael (Richard Romanus), a chiseling dude, he basks in the life. Running numbers, gambling, two-bit swindles: they grew up in this squalor and it's all they've ever known or wanted. To them, this is living it up. But Charlie isn't a relaxed sinner; he torments himself, like a fanatic seminarian. He's so frightened of burning he's burning already. Afraid of everything, he's everybody's friend, always trying to keep the peace. He's a dutiful toady to his Uncle Giovanni (Cesare Danova), the big man in the Mafia, and he fails those he really cares about: his girl, Teresa (Amy Robinson), and his friend Johnny Boy (Robert De Niro), a compulsive gambler — more than compulsive, irrational, a gambler with no sense of money. Charlie is too vain and sycophantic not to give in to social pressure. Teresa isn't rated high enough by his uncle; and his uncle, his king, the source of the restaurant he hopes to get, has told him not to be involved with Johnny Boy. Johnny Boy was named after Giovanni, but the family protects you only if you truckle to the elder statesmen and behave yourself — if you're a good timeserver.

Johnny Boy isn't; he flouts all the rules, he just won't "behave." He's fearless, gleefully self-destructive, cracked — moonstruck but not really crazy. His madness isn't explained (fortunately, since explaining madness is the most limiting and generally least convincing thing a movie can do). When you're growing up, if you know someone crazy-daring and half-admirable (and maybe most of us do), you don't wonder how the beautiful nut got that way; he seems to spring up full-blown and whirling, and you watch the fireworks and feel crummily cautious in your sanity. That's how it is here. Charlie digs Johnny Boy's recklessness. De Niro's Johnny Boy is the only one of the group of grifters and scummy racketeers who is his own man; he is the true hero, while Charlie, through whose mind we see the action, is the director's worst vision of himself.

The story emerges from the incidents without dominating them; it's more like a thread running through. The audience isn't propelled by suspense devices, nor is the cataclysmic finish really an end — it's only a stop. Johnny Boy needs help. He owes Michael, the dude, a lot of money, and it hurts Michael's self-esteem that he can't collect; nagging and spiteful, he threatens violence. But Charlie doesn't save Johnny Boy by going to his big-shot uncle for help, because he just can't risk taking a problem to his uncle. A good Mafia boy is not only subservient; unless something important is happening to him, he maintains his visibility as near to invisibility as possible. Uncle Giovanni, a dignified, dull, dull man, doesn't really see Charlie — doesn't register his existence — and that's what keeps Charlie in his good graces. But if Charlie asks for help for a crazy friend in trouble, he loses his low visibility. So Charlie talks a lot to Johnny Boy about friendship and does nothing. He's Judas the betrayer because of his careful angling to move up the next rung of the ladder. How can a man show his soul to be pettier than that? Charlie, the surrogate for the director, is nobody's friend, and — as the movie itself proves — least of all his own. Charlie knows from the beginning that he pays for everything. Scorsese isn't asking for expiation of Charlie's sins in the movie; sins aren't expiated in this movie. (The director has cast himself in the bit part of Michael's helper; when Johnny Boy makes Michael look so bad that Michael decides to get satisfaction, it is Scorsese who, as the gunman, pulls the trigger.)

It's twenty years since Fellini's *I Vitelloni* planted the autobiographical hero on the screen. Fellini did it in a fairly conventional way: his Moraldo (Franco Interlenghi) was the sensitive, handsome observer who looked at the limitations of small-town life and, at the end, said goodbye to all that. In *La Dolce Vita,* the Fellini figure was the seduced, disillusioned journalist (Marcello Mastroianni) to whom everything happened, and in *8 1/2* Mastroianni, again standing in for Fellini, was the movie director at the center of a multi-ring circus, the man sought after by everyone. In *Roma,* Fellini threw in new versions of several of his earlier representatives, and himself to boot. No other movie director, except among the "underground" filmmakers, has been so explicitly autobiographical. But in *I Vitelloni* we never caught a glimpse of the actual Fellini who emerged later; we never saw the fantasist as a young man, or the energy and will that drove him on. Movie directors have not yet learned the novelists' trick of throwing themselves into the third person, into the action, as Norman Mailer does even in his reporting; directors tend to make their own representatives passive, reflective figures, with things happening to them and around them, like Curt (Richard Dreyfuss) in George Lucas's nice (though overrated) little picture *American Graffiti.* Scorsese does something far more complex, because Charlie's wormy, guilt-ridden consciousness is made abhorrent to us at the same time that we're seeing life through it. Charlie is so agitated because he is aware of his smallness.

Scorsese's method is more like that of the Montreal filmmaker Claude Jutra, who, playing himself in *À Tout Prendre,* masochistically made himself weak, like those chinless self-portraits with traumatic stares which painters put at the edges of their canvases. Jutra left out the mind and energies that made him a movie director, and apparently put on the screen everything in himself he loathed, and this is what Scorsese does, but Scorsese also puts in the tensions of a man in conflict, and a harlequin externalization of those tensions. He's got that dervish Johnny Boy dancing around Charlie's fears, needling Charlie and exposing him to danger despite all his conciliatory nice-guyism. Johnny Boy's careless, contemptuous explosions seem a direct response to Charlie's trying to keep the lid on everything — it's as if Charlie's id were throwing bombs and laughing at him. When Johnny Boy has finally loused everything up, he can say to Charlie, "You got what you wanted."

While an actor like Jeff Bridges in *The Last American Hero* hits the true note, De Niro here hits the far-out, flamboyant one and makes his own truth. He's a bravura actor, and those who have registered him only as the grinning, tobacco-chewing dolt of that hunk of inept whimsey *Bang the Drum Slowly* will be unprepared for his volatile performance. De Niro does something like what Dustin Hoffman was doing in *Midnight Cowboy,* but wilder; this kid doesn't just act — he takes off into the vapors. De Niro is so intensely appealing that it might be easy to overlook Harvey Keitel's work as Charlie. But Keitel makes De Niro's triumph possible; Johnny Boy can bounce off Charlie's anxious, furious admiration. Keitel, cramped in his stiff clothes (these Mafiosi dress respectable — in the long, dark overcoats of businessmen of an earlier era), looks like a more compact Richard Conte or Dane Clark, and speaks in the rhythms of a lighter-voiced John Garfield, Charlie's idol; it's his control that holds the story together. The whole world of the movie — Catholicism as it's actually practiced among these people, what it means on the street — is in Charlie's mingy-minded face.

The picture is stylized without seeming in any way artificial; it is the only movie I've ever seen that achieves the effects of Expressionism without the use of distortion. *Mean Streets* never loses touch with the ordinary look of things or with common experience; rather, it puts us in closer touch with the ordinary, the common, by turning a different light on them. The ethnic material is comparable to James T. Farrell's Studs Lonigan trilogy and to what minor novelists like Louis Golding did in the street-and-tenement novels of the thirties, but when this material is written on the screen the result is infinitely more powerful. (In a film review in 1935, Graham Greene — a Catholic — said that "the camera . . . can note with more exactitude and vividness than the prose of most living playwrights the atmosphere of mean streets and cheap lodgings.") And though *Mean Streets* has links to all those Richard Conte Italian-family movies, like *House of Strangers,* and to the urban-feudal life of *The Godfather,* the incidents and details are far more personal. Scorsese, who did the writing with Mardik Martin, knows the scene and knows how it all fits together; it's his, and he has the ability to put his feelings about it on the screen. All this is what the Boston Irish world of *The Friends of Eddie Coyle* lacked; the picture was shallow and tedious, because although we could see how the gangsters victimized each other, the police and the gangsters had no roots — and intertwined roots were what it was meant to be about. It was a milieu picture without milieu. In *Mean Streets,* every character, every sound is rooted in those streets. The back-and-forth talk of Charlie and Johnny Boy isn't little-people empty-funny (as it was in *Marty*); it's a tangle of jeering and joshing, of mutual goading and nerves getting frayed. These boys understand each other too well. Charlie's love for Johnny Boy is his hate for himself, and Johnny Boy knows Charlie's flaw. No other American gangster-milieu film has had this element of personal obsession; there has never before been a gangster film in which you felt that the director himself was saying, "This is my story." Not that we come away thinking that Martin Scorsese is or ever was a gangster, but we're so affected because we know in our bones that he has walked these streets and has felt what his characters feel. He knows how natural crime is to them.

There is something of the Carol Reed film *The Third Man* in the way the atmosphere imposes itself, and, like Reed, Scorsese was best known as an editor (on *Woodstock, Medicine Ball Caravan, Elvis on Tour,* C.B.S. documentaries, etc.) before he became a director *(Who's That Knocking at My Door?, Boxcar Bertha).* Graham Greene, the screenwriter of *The Third Man,* wrote a prescription for movies that fits this one almost perfectly. "The cinema," Greene said, "has always developed by means of a certain low cunning. . . . We are driven back to the 'blood,' the thriller. . . . We have to . . . dive below the polite level, to something nearer to the common life. . . . And when we have attained to a more popular drama, even if it is in the simplest terms of blood on a garage floor ('There lay Duncan laced in his golden blood'), the scream of cars in flight, all the old excitements at their simplest and most sure-fire, then we can begin — secretly, with low cunning — to develop our poetic drama." And, again, "If you excite your audience first, you can put over what you will of horror, suffering, truth." However, Scorsese's atmosphere is without the baroque glamour of evil that makes *The Third Man* so ambiguous in its appeal. There's nothing hokey here; it is a low, malign world Scorsese sees. But it's seen to the beat of an exuberant, satiric score. Scorsese has an operatic visual style (the swarthy, imaginative cinematography is by Kent Wakeford), and, with Jonathan T. Taplin, the twenty-six-year-old rock-record impresario, as producer, he has used a mixture of records to more duplicit effect than anyone since Kenneth Anger in *Scorpio Rising.* It's similar to Bertolucci's use of a motley score in *Before the Revolution* and *The Conformist* and to the score in parts of *The Godfather,* but here the music is a more active participant. The score is the background music of the characters' lives — and not only the background, because it enters in. It's as if these characters were just naturally part of an opera with pop themes. The music is the electricity in the air of this movie; the music is like an engine that the characters move to. Johnny Boy, the most susceptible, half dances through the movie, and when he's trying to escape from Michael he does a jerky frug before hopping into the getaway car. He *enjoys* being out of control — he revels in it — and we can feel the music turning him on. But *Mean Streets* doesn't use music, as *Easy Rider* sometimes did, to do the movie's work for it. (In *American Graffiti,* the old-rock nostalgia catches the audience up before the movie even gets going.) The music here isn't our music, meant to put us in the mood of the movie, but the characters' music. And bits of old movies become part of the opera, too, because what the characters know of passion and death, and even of big-time gangsterism, comes from the movies. In Scorsese's vision, music and the movies work within us and set the terms in which we perceive ourselves. Music and the movies and the Church. A witches' brew.

Scorsese could make poetic drama, rather than melodrama laced with decadence, out of the schlock of shabby experience because he didn't have to "dive below the polite level, to something nearer to the common life" but had to do something much tougher — descend into himself and bring up what neither he nor anyone else could have known was there. Though he must have suspected. This is a blood thriller in the truest sense.

[October 8, 1973]

Three

"THE WAY WE WERE" is a fluke — a torpedoed ship full of gaping holes which comes snugly into port. There is just about every reason for this film to be a disaster: the cinematography is ugly; several scenes serve no purpose, and the big dramatic sequences come butting in, like production numbers, out of nowhere; the decisive change in the characters' lives which the story hinges on takes place suddenly and hardly makes sense; a whining title-tune ballad embarrasses the picture in advance, and it has the excruciating score of a bad forties movie. Yet the damned thing is enjoyable. It stays afloat because of the chemistry of Barbra Streisand and Robert Redford. The movie is about two people who are wrong for each other, and Streisand and Redford are an ideal match to play this mismatch: Katie Morosky, always in a rush, a frizzy-haired Jewish girl from New York with a chip on her shoulder; and Hubbell Gardiner, a Wasp jock from Virginia with straw hair and the grin of a well-fed conquistador. She's a hyper-emotional Communist who's always sure she's right; he is incapable of any kind of commitment. The movie, directed by Sydney Pollack — from Arthur Laurents' novel, which reads like a screenplay — deals with their collision course. Theirs isn't a Bridget-loves-Bernie type of marriage. He tells her she pushes too hard, and she answers that she'll push him to be what he should be — which she thinks is a great writer. A hideous basis for a marriage — and she can't stand his friends. We can see what draws them to each other: she's attracted to the fairy-tale prince in him, and he can't tear himself away from her emotionality, from her wistfulness and drive. And we can certainly see what creates the tension between them; Katie and Hubbell have been breaking up since they got together.

The picture opens in New York in 1944, goes back to their college days (Class of 1937), and then returns to 1944 and goes on to their married life in Hollywood, where he becomes a screenwriter and she a reader for a studio; it continues through the onset of the blacklisting troubles, breaking off in 1948, with a coda in New York in the early fifties. I offer this chronology as a libretto, because the movie has the sweat stains of interfering hands and is so bewildering about the passage of time that you can't tell how long Katie and Hubbell have been married before she gets pregnant, and, once she is, she seems to stay that way for years. The climactic Hollywood section, which should have been played for high irony, is so botched and overwrought that the picture becomes more hysterical than Katie. The changes she goes through are, however, psychologically accurate: the quicksilver gaucheness as an undergraduate in the thirties; the wavy long bob and the carefully groomed attempt to emulate a woman of the world in the forties; the more relaxed Los Angeles style; and then the recovery of the earlier look, but accepted by her now, in the fifties. Her changes are attempts to get closer to Hubbell's style, whereas he stays much the same — very much the same, since Redford doesn't pass for college-student age as easily as Streisand does.

The movie doesn't overtly take sides in the characters' political arguments, but its simplifications put the past in a phony perspective. This is worth noting, I think, because movies seep through the consciousness of audiences. We laugh now at the old story about Clark Gable's destroying the undershirt industry when the whole country discovered he wasn't wearing one in *It Happened One Night,* but applications for admission to Radcliffe skyrocketed after the movie of *Love Story* came out. And a lot of people get their knowledge of history from movies. (In some schools, history is now being taught with the aid of movies set in the past.) Because of the sordid injustices to the blacklisted, and their suffering, it's easy for new generations to get the idea that what they stood for politically was an intelligent and moral position. This movie doesn't actually say that, but it's the impression that the audience may come away with, because there appears to be nothing between Communist commitment and smug indifference. Hubbell makes valid points against Katie's blind faith in Stalin's policies, but since he represents polite cynicism and defeatism, her allegiance to those policies seems to be the only form of activism. (Implicitly, the movie accepts the line the Communist Party took — that it was the only group doing anything, so if you cared about peace or social injustice you had to join up.) Hubbell is reasonable when he tries to calm Katie down so they can have an evening together without her screaming at his Beekman Place spoiled rich friends, but in a movie a person who stands back and does nothing is likely to come out even worse than he should, in contrast to someone who is full of fervor and does something, however misguided and ineffective. Katie, who has no common sense, cares so much about everything, and cares so much for Hubbell, that our feelings go out to her, even when her outbursts are offensive — perhaps most when they're offensive, because we can see that she's destroying Hubbell's tolerance of both her and her politics.

There's another factor that puts the audience on Katie's side: Streisand. She has caught the spirit of the hysterical Stalinist workhorses of the thirties and forties — both the ghastly desperation of their self-righteousness and the warmth of their enthusiasm. Katie hangs on to her man as monomaniacally as she hangs on to the Party's shifting positions, but she's a painfully vulnerable woman, a woman of great sweetness, and Hubbell drowns in that sweetness. Redford's role is necessarily less colorful, but that doesn't do him a disservice. It's good to see Redford with a woman again after all that flirting with Paul Newman, and he has the glamour that is needed for the young Hubbell, and the opacity, the reserve. He gives a good performance whenever he can (in the college-classroom scene in which Hubbell's story is read aloud, and in the scene when Hubbell tells Katie that he's sold a story), though he's betrayed toward the end by the film editor, who allows him to be caught staring at her wonderingly a few too many times. (When Redford hasn't anything special to register, his blankly anguished look can get very stony.) At the end, Katie is a believer still, and still radiant, while Hubbell, a man with so many doubts he had nothing to sell out, remains tentative and tormented, but he's older, and drained. Streisand has her miraculous audience empathy, while Redford loses touch with us, but this is just as much what his personality and appeal are all about as that self-deprecating empathy of Streisand's is what her appeal is all about. The roles and the temperaments of the stars are inseparable here. That's what makes the movie so effective a throwback (with a political difference) to the romantic star vehicles of an earlier era. But when Redford's glamour is overdone and his white teeth glitter, the movie seems to share Katie's infatuation, and you have to laugh at yourself for what you're enjoying.

We've had time now to get used to Streisand. (A friend of mine who "couldn't stand her" in *Funny Girl* confessed that she had capitulated totally when she saw the film again, on television.) The tricky thing about the role of Katie Morosky is that Streisand must emphasize just that element in her own persona which repelled some people initially: her fast sass is defensive and aggressive in the same breath. But it's part of her gradual conquest of the movie public that this won't put people off now. Even the unflattering photography and the forties makeup (the bright-red lipstick is hideous on her large, expressive mouth — her finest, most sensitive feature) don't damage her.

At the moment, there are so few women stars in American movies: Streisand, Minnelli, Fonda, that charming, ultrafeminine survivor-waif Mia Farrow — anybody else? Shirley MacLaine hasn't been crinkling and twinkling lately; it's too soon to know if Liv Ullmann or Blythe Danner will get good enough parts; and that waxed blonde Faye Dunaway won't stir much interest unless somebody renovates her. A movie with a woman star or co-star has become a rarity, and the male-female story of *The Way We Were* gives it a vital connection to people's lives that the spoofy male-dominated odd-couple movies have often lacked; besides, the humor doesn't have to be so coy. It's hit entertainment, and maybe even memorable entertainment; it's a terrible movie because of that ugly glossy superstructure and the crushed midsection, but it's got Streisand and Redford, and some very well-written (Alvin Sargent was among the uncredited writers) and well-directed moments. I'm not sure it's going to be possible for people who know Sydney Pollack to look him in the eye after they watch Streisand and Redford making love in front of a sexy fire while the plaintive schlock music rises up in the general direction of paradise, but at least there are no sexy storms.

FRANCOIS TRUFFAUT has immense quantities of goodwill built up with his audience — more than any other director. That goodwill probably didn't extend to *Such a Gorgeous Kid Like Me,* because it was shrill, and dumb even when it was funny. But it can extend to his new film, *Day for Night,* which is a return to form, though it's a return only to form. It has the Truffaut proportion and grace, and it can please those who have grown up with Truffaut's films — especially those for whom Jean-Pierre Léaud as Antoine Doinel has become part of their own autobiographies, with Antoine's compromises and modest successes paralleling their own. The gentle tone is similar to that of the later Doinel films, and the casting of Léaud as a film-nut actor and everybody's pet is incestuously close. *Day for Night* has none of the strange, touching uncertainty and downright fumbling of *Two English Girls*; everything in it appears to be what Truffaut wanted. It has a pretty touch. But when it was over, I found myself thinking, Can this be all there is to it? The picture has no center and not much spirit. It's a backstage story about the making of an American-financed movie, "Meet Pamela," set on the Riviera, in which Jacqueline Bisset, married to Jean-Pierre Léaud, falls in love with his father, Jean-Pierre Aumont. Truffaut brings it all off, but he sings small. He appears to have nothing more on his mind than does Ferrand, the efficient, colorless director of "Meet Pamela," whom he himself plays.

Is it enough just to want to make movies, and to be in love with the process? For those who can say yes, *Day for Night* may be a full enough experience. Truffaut dedicates the film to Lillian and Dorothy Gish, shown in a still from Griffith's *An Unseen Enemy,* of 1912. (The Gish girls, the first of the great sister acts in films, suggest the sisters Françoise Dorléac and Catherine Deneuve, who alternately starred in Truffaut's movies.) He opens the film with a voice declaiming to music (in the style of Cocteau, whose name in a tapestry he lingers on later), and Ferrand has a nightmare in which he's a child stealing stills from *Citizen Kane.* The film is full of homage to movie immortals. How, then, can this conventional salute to conventional filmmaking satisfy Truffaut? Does it? A picture that lacks freshness, and with wonderful-spoiled-children characters who are no more than anecdotal? Among the actors, Valentina Cortese is the liveliest, in her juicy, if familiar, theatrical turn as a drunken has-been star, and Léaud's elfin piques are amusing enough, but the large cast is very ordinary, with Jacqueline Bisset, as usual, looking warm and beautiful and acting monotonously. *Day for Night* is tender but too fan-magazinish in approach, too tenderly shallow for its own good. Yet at some level it may truly satisfy Truffaut. He has turned out a great many movies in a very few years — thirteen features since 1959. It's possible that his world has closed in, that it has become the world of filmmaking.

Day for Night is very childlike — filled with a deeply innocent love of the magic of moviemaking. I think this film helps to explain Truffaut: his (excessive, to me) admiration of Hitchcock (the master of a piddling domain, a *petit maître* if ever there was one), and the way Truffaut can go from the high intelligence of one film to the diminutive virtues or outright silliness of another. In his version of Ray Bradbury's *Fahrenheit 451* Truffaut made the point that booklovers don't love only great books; he treated books as magical objects, valuable in themselves, apart from their quality, and I think he extends this feeling to movies, and attaches a special feeling even to the making of a mediocrity like "Meet Pamela." In *Day for Night,* his tribute to the old way of making movies, he's saying that he doesn't reject the absurdities that once gave him pleasure — that they still do. I admit to having enjoyed more than my portion of drivel, but I don't share Truffaut's fond regard for the kind of moviemaking that "Meet Pamela" represents. I ask for the extraordinary from films, while Truffaut, who finds moviemaking itself extraordinary, is often content to make films for everyday.

Maybe those of us who want the extraordinary are romantics, too, but of a different sort. I think of filmmaking in terms of the tragically wasted master Abel Gance's remark "I see my life as an office of lost dreams." I think of all the projects abandoned for want of money, and of what might have been in place of all the "Meet Pamela"s, and I can't work up much feeling for *Day for Night,* because although it probably doesn't have the rigid approach to following a script that Ferrand's movie has, it doesn't really strike me as so very different. I miss the emotion that goes into the films I care about. When Ferrand says that the way he's been working is finished, that films will be shot in the streets and "there will be no more movies like 'Meet Pamela,' " I wish that were a promise. Or a pledge to be signed, first by men like Herbert Ross, and maybe, eventually, by François Truffaut. Halfway through the shooting of "Meet Pamela," Ferrand says, "It's going well. Cinema is king." At that point, I think, Truffaut is speaking for himself, and I think he's wrong: there's nothing royal in empty moviemaking. Truffaut's soft spot for the sort of movies that formed him and his unwillingness to give them up are part of what makes his work so lovable, but this affection has a negative aspect, too. *Day for Night* is a movie for the movie-struck, the essentially naïve — those who would rather see a movie, any movie (a bad one, a stupid one, or an evanescent, sweet-but-dry little wafer of a movie, like this one), than do anything else. It's for those (one meets them on campuses) who can say, "I love all movies." It's not for someone like me, who can walk out on *A Touch of Class* without a twinge. What encourages one about Truffaut is that at a deeper level he, too, may be dissatisfied with what he's been doing, or why would he have decided to take the next two years off to read and to write? I hope this doesn't mean he's going to read only about movies.

Footnote to movie history: The English insurance man who turns up in a scene near the end of *Day for Night* looks like Graham Greene, but since the role isn't listed in the credits I wasn't sure until I had checked with Truffaut. He said that it was indeed Greene but that he himself hadn't known it until after the scene was shot. He explained that he had rejected the first man offered to him for the role, because the man looked too poetic, and when Greene (who lives in Antibes, near where the movie was made) was brought to him at a party, he thought he looked fine for a businessman — "like a Ray Milland or James Stewart." Greene suffered from stagefright, Truffaut says, and he adds that after the shooting, at dinner with the cast, Greene and he argued about Hitchcock.

SEEING "THE NEW LAND" a year after *The Emigrants* is like picking up a novel you had put down the day before. The story comes flooding back, and what you saw in the first half — the firm, deep-toned preparation— "pays off" in the second half. In *The Emigrants* we saw why a group of Swedes in the mid-nineteenth century left their land, and at the close, in Minnesota, Karl Oskar (Max von Sydow) found the rich earth he had been looking for and rested under a tree in the wilderness. In *The New Land* he brings his wife, Kristina (Liv Ullmann), and family to the spot he selected, and begins to build a house and start a farm. *The Emigrants* had that great push to the new country, but the emigration was a foregone conclusion; *The New Land* is open-ended — full of possibilities. Both halves are wonderful. We meet up again with all the survivors of that ocean trip, and gradually we get the answers to our questions about whether they would find what they hoped for. For Karl Oskar the answer is yes; for Ulrika (Monica Zetterlund), a "fallen woman" in Sweden, yes, also. But for Kristina the answer is a mixed one; she would never have emigrated on her own, and she misses what she left behind more than she dares to admit. And for Karl Oskar's younger brother, the dreamer Robert (Eddie Axberg), whose adolescence had been destroyed by indentured labor, and his friend the burly lummox Arvid (Pierre Lindstedt) the answer is no. If there is anything lacking in this film, it is a sense of what Karl Oskar's and Kristina's children carry over from their parents' past in Sweden. (Could this have been intimated in the footage cut from the American version?) We are told that they forget Swedish, but not told what they remember and pass along. However, we do see the discovery of what will become part of their heritage as Americans: that the land Karl Oskar bought from the United States Government was stolen land.

There is nothing glib and no piousness, no portentousness. Karl Oskar, the practical man, doggedly heroic, isn't romanticized, and Kristina's narrowness of vision isn't used against her; rather, we see the special beauty — the shyness and the awareness of her limitations — that it gives her. Maybe because of the broad sweep of the story, and the way the characters are seen in terms of natural forces, *The New Land* often reminds one of the work of the masters of the silent film. Here, too, everything seems to be on the screen for the first time. Although Jan Troell, the director, cinematographer, editor, is in command of the modern vocabulary of film techniques, he's unencumbered by the vices of commercial films: all those thousands of forms of telegraphic emphasis, most of them inherited from the theater, that commercial films have done to death. Troell shows his debt to movie history in only one section (an effective contrast), when he uses a stylized shorthand form for Robert's fevered recollections of his experiences in the West searching for gold: a horror dream pounding in his ears.

The big events — the saving of a child's life during a freezing storm, a mass hanging of Sioux braves — aren't built up to; they come and go, without the penny-dreadful tricks that cheapen most film epics. Troell takes in the details of work, the quarrels with neighbors, the great, grave head of Karl Oskar's ox in its last moment, Kristina handing some starving Indian women a piece of meat, or cleaning her baby's bottom and apologetically smiling at onlookers while hurriedly wiping her hands on some leaves. He is more open and generous than the other Swedish directors whose work we see — so generous that the small flaws are canceled out. There is nothing prosy in Troell's large, steady embrace; he has a sense of the justice owed to people and the homage owed to nature. Together, *The Emigrants* and *The New Land* offer the pleasures of a big novel with a solid spine. Troell has done what the Americans should have done in *Hawaii* but couldn't, because all our bad Hollywood habits got in the way. Max von Sydow was as remarkable in *Hawaii* as he is here; the difference is that he blends into Troell's film. And Liv Ullmann, pale and fragile, intense and determined, has a delicacy that was never evident in Ingmar Bergman's hot-ice universe. Troell is a film master whose films are overflowing yet calm and balanced; they're rapturously normal.

[October 15, 1973]

Movieland—The Bums' Paradise

EDMUND WILSON summed up Raymond Chandler convincingly in 1945 when he said of *Farewell, My Lovely,* "It is not simply a question here of a puzzle which has been put together but of a malaise conveyed to the reader, the horror of a hidden conspiracy which is continually turning up in the most varied and unlikely forms. . . . It is only when I get to the end that I feel my old crime-story depression descending upon me again — because here again, as is so often the case, the explanation of the mysteries, when it comes, is neither interesting nor plausible enough. It fails to justify the excitement produced by the picturesque and sinister happenings, and I cannot help feeling cheated." Locked in the conventions of pulp writing, Raymond Chandler never found a way of dealing with that malaise. But Robert Altman does, in *The Long Goodbye,* based on Chandler's 1953 Los Angeles-set novel. The movie is set in the same city twenty years later; this isn't just a matter of the private-detective hero's prices going from twenty-five dollars a day to fifty — it's a matter of rethinking the book and the genre. Altman, who probably works closer to his unconscious than any other American director, tells a detective story, all right, but he does it through a spree — a high-flying rap on Chandler and the movies and that Los Angeles sickness. The movie isn't just Altman's private-eye movie — it's his Hollywood movie, set in the mixed-up world of movie-influenced life that is L.A.

In Los Angeles, you can live any way you want (except the urban way); it's the fantasy-brothel, where you can live the fantasy of your choice. You can also live well without being rich, which is the basic and best reason people swarm there. In that city — the pop amusement park of the shifty and the uprooted, the city famed as the place where you go to sell out — Raymond Chandler situated his incorruptible knight Philip Marlowe, the private detective firmly grounded in high principles. Answering a letter in 1951, Chandler wrote, "If being in revolt against a corrupt society constitutes being immature, then Philip Marlowe is extremely immature. If seeing dirt where there is dirt constitutes an inadequate social adjustment, then Philip Marlowe has inadequate social adjustment. Of course Marlowe is a failure, and he knows it. He is a failure because he hasn't any money. . . . A lot of very good men have been failures because their particular talents did not suit their time and place." And he cautioned, "But you must remember that Marlowe is not a real person. He is a creature of fantasy. He is in a false position because I put him there. In real life, a man of his type would no more be a private detective than he would be a university don." Six months later, when his rough draft of *The Long Goodbye* was criticized by his agent, Chandler wrote back, "I didn't care whether the mystery was fairly obvious, but I cared about the people, about this strange corrupt world we live in, and how any man who tried to be honest looks in the end either sentimental or plain foolish."

Chandler's sentimental foolishness is the taking-off place for Altman's film. Marlowe (Elliott Gould) is a wryly forlorn knight, just slogging along. Chauffeur, punching bag, errand boy, he's used, lied to, double-crossed. He's the gallant fool in a corrupt world — the innocent eye. He isn't stupid and he's immensely likable, but the pulp pretense that his chivalrous code was armor has collapsed, and the romantic machismo of Bogart's Marlowe in *The Big Sleep* has evaporated. The one-lone-idealist-in-the-city-crawling-with-rats becomes a schlemiel who thinks he's tough and wise. (He's still driving a 1948 Lincoln Continental and trying to behave like Bogart.) He doesn't know the facts of life that everybody else knows; even the police know more about the case he's involved in than he does. Yet he's the only one who *cares.* That's his true innocence, and it's his slack-jawed crazy sweetness that keeps the movie from being harsh or scabrous.

Altman's goodbye to the private-eye hero is comic and melancholy and full of regrets. It's like cleaning house and throwing out things that you know you're going to miss — there comes a time when junk dreams get in your way. *The Long Goodbye* reaches a satirical dead end that kisses off the private-eye form as gracefully as *Beat the Devil* finished off the cycle of the international-intrigue thriller. Altman does variations on Chandler's theme the way the John Williams score does variations on the title song, which is a tender ballad in one scene, a funeral dirge in another. Williams' music is a parody of the movies' frequent overuse of a theme, and a demonstration of how adaptable a theme can be. This picture, less accidental than *Beat the Devil,* is just about as funny, though quicker-witted, and dreamier, in soft, mellow color and volatile images — a reverie on the lies of old movies. It's a knockout of a movie that has taken eight months to arrive in New York because after opening in Los Angeles last March and being badly received (perfect irony) it folded out of town. It's probably the best American movie ever made that almost didn't open in New York. Audiences may have felt they'd already had it with Elliott Gould; the young men who looked like him in 1971 have got cleaned up and barbered and turned into Mark Spitz. But it actually adds poignancy to the film that Gould himself is already an anachronism.

Thinner and more lithe than in his brief fling as a superstar (his success in *Bob & Carol & Ted & Alice* and *M*A*S*H* led to such speedy exploitation of his box-office value that he appeared in seven films between 1969 and 1971), Gould comes back with his best performance yet. It's his movie. The rubber-legged slouch, the sheepish, bony-faced angularity have their grace; drooping-eyed, squinting, with more blue stubble on his face than any other hero on record, he's a loose and woolly, jazzy Job. There's a skip and bounce in his shamble. Chandler's arch, spiky dialogue — so hardboiled it can make a reader's teeth grate— gives way to this Marlowe's muttered, befuddled throwaways, his self-sendups. Gould's Marlowe is a man who is had by everybody — a male pushover, reminiscent of Fred MacMurray in *Double Indemnity.* He's Marlowe as Miss Lonely-hearts. Yet this softhearted honest loser is so logical a modernization, so "right," that when you think about Marlowe afterward you can't imagine any other way of playing him now that wouldn't be just fatuous. (Think of Mark Spitz as Marlowe if you want fatuity pure.) The good-guys-finish-last conception was implicit in Chandler's L.A. all along, and Marlowe was only one step from being a clown, but Chandler pulped his own surrogate and made Marlowe, the Victorian relic, a winner. Chandler has a basic phoniness that it would have been a cinch to exploit. He wears his conscience right up front; the con trick is that it's not a writer's conscience. Offered the chance to break free of the straitjacket of the detective novel, Chandler declined. He clung to the limiting stereotypes of pop writing and blamed "an age whose dominant note is an efficient vulgarity, an unscrupulous scramble for the dollar." Style, he said, "can exist in a savage and dirty age, but it cannot exist in the Coca-Cola age . . . the Book of the Month, and the Hearst Press." It was Marlowe, the independent man, dedicated to autonomy — his needs never rising above that twenty-five dollars a day— who actually lived like an artist. Change Marlowe's few possessions, "a coat, a hat, and a gun," to "a coat, a hat, and a typewriter," and the cracks in Chandler's myth of the hero become a hopeless split.

Robert Altman is all of a piece, but he's complicated. You can't predict what's coming next in the movie; his plenitude comes from somewhere beyond reason. An Altman picture doesn't have to be great to be richly pleasurable. He tosses in more than we can keep track of, maybe more than *he* bothers to keep track of; he nips us in surprising ways. In *The Long Goodbye,* as in *M*A*S*H,* there are climaxes, but you don't have the sense of waiting for them, because what's in between is so satisfying. He underplays the plot and concentrates on the people, so it's almost all of equal interest, and you feel as if it could go on indefinitely and you'd be absorbed in it. Altman may have the most glancing touch since Lubitsch, and his ear for comedy is better than anybody else's. In this period of movies, it isn't necessary (or shouldn't be) to punch the nuances home; he just glides over them casually, in the freest possible way. Gould doesn't propel the action as Bogart did; the story unravels around the private eye — the corrupt milieu wins. Maybe the reason some people have difficulty getting onto Altman's wavelength is that he's just about incapable of overdramatizing. He's not a pusher. Even in this film, he doesn't push decadence. He doesn't heat up angst the way it was heated in *Midnight Cowboy* and *They Shoot Horses, Don't They?*

POP CULTURE takes some nourishment from the "high" arts, but it feeds mainly on itself. *The Long Goodbye* had not been filmed before, because the book came out too late, after the private-eye-movie cycle had peaked. Marlowe had already become Bogart, and you could see him in it when you read the book. You weren't likely to have kept the other Marlowes of the forties (Dick Powell, Robert Montgomery, George Montgomery) in your mind, and you had to see somebody in it. The novel reads almost like a parody of pungent writing — like a semi-literate's idea of great writing. The detective-novel genre always verged on self-parody, because it gave you nothing under the surface. Hemingway didn't need to state what his characters felt, because his external descriptions implied all that, but the pulp writers who imitated Hemingway followed the hardboiled-detective pattern that Hammett had invented; they externalized everything and implied nothing. Their gaudy terseness demonstrates how the novel and the comic strip can merge. They described actions and behavior from the outside, as if they were writing a script that would be given some inner life by the actors and the director; the most famous practitioners of the genre were, in fact, moonlighting screenwriters. *The Long Goodbye* may have good descriptions of a jail or a police lineup, but the prose is alternately taut and lumpy with lessons in corruption, and most of the great observations you're supposed to get from it are just existentialism with oil slick. With its classy dames, a Marlowe influenced by Marlowe, the obligatory tension between Marlowe and the cops, and the sentimental bar scenes, *The Long Goodbye* was a product of the private-eye films of the decade before. Chandler's corrupt milieu — what Auden called "The Great Wrong Place" — was the new-style capital of sin, the city that made the movies and was made by them.

In Chandler's period (he died in 1959), movies and novels interacted; they still do, but now the key interaction may be between movies and movies — and between movies and us. We can no longer view ourselves — the way Nathanael West did — as different from the Middle Westerners in L.A. lost in their movie-fed daydreams, and the L.A. world founded on pop is no longer the world *out there,* as it was for Edmund Wilson. Altman's *The Long Goodbye* (like Paul Mazursky's *Blume in Love*) is about people who live in L.A. because they like the style of life, which comes from the movies. It's not about people who work in movies but about people whose lives have been shaped by them; it's set in the modern L.A. of the stoned sensibility, where people have given in to the beauty that always looks unreal. The inhabitants are an updated gallery of California freaks, with one character who links this world to Nathanael West's — the Malibu Colony gatekeeper (Ken Sansom), who does ludicrous, pitiful impressions of Barbara Stanwyck in *Double Indemnity* (which was Chandler's first screenwriting job), and of James Stewart, Walter Brennan, and Cary Grant (the actor Chandler said he had in mind for Marlowe). In a sense, Altman here has already made *Day of the Locust.* (To do it as West intended it, and to have it make contemporary sense, it would now have to be set in Las Vegas.) Altman's references to movies don't stick out — they're just part of the texture, as they are in L.A. — but there are enough so that a movie pedant could do his own weirdo version of *A Skeleton Key to Finnegans Wake.*

The one startlingly violent action in the movie is performed by a syndicate boss who is as rapt in the glory of his success as a movie mogul. Prefigured in Chandler's description of movie producers in his famous essay "Writers in Hollywood," Marty Augustine (Mark Rydell) is the next step up in paranoid self-congratulation from the Harry Cohn-like figure that Rod Steiger played in *The Big Knife*; he's freaked out on success, L.A.-Las Vegas style. His big brown eyes with their big brown bags preside over the decaying pretty-boy face of an Eddie Fisher, and when he flashes his ingenuous Paul Anka smile he's so appalling he's comic. His violent act is outrageously gratuitous (he smashes a Coke bottle in the fresh young face of his unoffending mistress), yet his very next line of dialogue is so comic-tough that we can't help laughing while we're still gasping, horrified — much as we did when Cagney shoved that half grapefruit in Mae Clarke's nagging kisser. This little Jewish gangster-boss is a mod imp — offspring of the movies, as much a creature of show business as Joel Grey's m.c. in *Cabaret.* Marty Augustine's bumbling goon squad (ethnically balanced) are the illegitimate sons of Warner Brothers. In the Chandler milieu, what could be better casting than the aristocratic Nina van Pallandt as the rich dish — the duplicitous blonde, Mrs. Wade? And, as her husband, the blocked famous writer Roger Wade, Sterling Hayden, bearded like Neptune, and as full of the old mach as the progenitor of tough-guy writing himself. The most movieish bit of dialogue is from the book: when the police come to question Marlowe about his friend Terry Lennox, Marlowe says, "This is where I say, 'What's this all about?' and you say, 'We ask the questions.' " But the resolution of Marlowe's friendship with Terry isn't from Chandler, and its logic is probably too brutally sound for Bogart-lovers to stomach. Terry Lennox (smiling Jim Bouton, the baseball player turned broadcaster) becomes the Harry Lime in Marlowe's life, and the final sequence is a variation on *The Third Man,* with the very last shot a riff on the leave-taking scenes of the movies' most famous clown.

The movie achieves a self-mocking fairy-tale poetry. The slippery shifts within the frames of Vilmos Zsigmond's imagery are part of it, and so are the offbeat casting (Henry Gibson as the sinister quack Dr. Verringer; Jack Riley, of the Bob Newhart show, as the piano player) and the dialogue. (The script is officially credited to the venerable pulp author Leigh Brackett; she also worked on *The Big Sleep* and many other good movies, but when you hear the improvised dialogue you can't take this credit literally.) There are some conceits that are fairly precarious (the invisible-man stunt in the hospital sequence) and others that are waywardly funny (Marlowe trying to lie to his cat) or suggestive and beautiful (the Wades' Doberman coming out of the Pacific with his dead master's cane in his teeth). When Nina van Pallandt thrashes in the ocean at night, her pale-orange butterfly sleeves rising above the surf, the movie becomes a rhapsody on romance and death. What separates Altman from other directors is that time after time he can attain crowning visual effects like this and they're so elusive they're never precious. They're like ribbons tying up the whole history of movies. It seems unbelievable that people who looked at this picture could have given it the reviews they did.

THE OUT-OF-TOWN FAILURE of *The Long Goodbye* and the anger of many of the reviewers, who reacted as if Robert Altman were a destroyer, suggest that the picture may be on to something bigger than is at first apparent. Some speculations may be in order. Marlowe was always a bit of a joke, but did people take him that way? His cynical exterior may have made it possible for them to accept him in Chandler's romantic terms, and really — below the joke level — believe in him. We've all read Chandler on his hero: "But down these mean streets a man must go who is not himself mean, who is neither tarnished nor afraid." He goes, apparently, in our stead. And as long as he's there — the walking conscience of the world — we're safe. We could easily reject sticky saviors, but a cynical saviour satisfies the Holden Caulfield in us. It's an adolescent's dream of heroism — someone to look after you, a protector like Billy Jack. And people cleave to the fantasies they form while watching movies.

After reading *The Maltese Falcon,* Edmund Wilson said of Dashiell Hammett that he "lacked the ability to bring the story to imaginative life." Wilson was right, of course, but this may be the basis of Hammett's appeal; when Wilson said of the detective story that "as a department of imaginative writing, it looks to me completely dead," he was (probably intentionally) putting it in the wrong department. It's precisely the fact that the detective novel is engrossing but does not impinge on its readers' lives or thoughts that enables it to give a pleasure to some which is distinct from the pleasures of literature. It has no afterlife when they have closed the covers; it's completely digested, like a game of casino. It's a structured time killer that gives you the illusion of being speedy; *The Long Goodbye* isn't a fast read, like Hammett, but when I finished it I had no idea whether I'd read it before. Essentially, we've all read it before.

But when these same stories were transferred to the screen, the mechanisms of suspense could strike fear in the viewer, and the tensions could grow almost unbearable. The detective story on the screen became a thriller in a much fuller sense than it had been on the page, and the ending of the movie wasn't like shutting a book. The physical sensations that were stirred up weren't settled; even if we felt cheated, we were still turned on. We left the theater in a state of mixed exhilaration and excitement, and the fear and guilt went with us. In our dreams, we were menaced, and perhaps became furtive murderers. It is said that in periods of rampant horrors readers and moviegoers like to experience imaginary horrors, which can be resolved and neatly put away. I think it's more likely that in the current craze for horror films like *Night of the Living Dead* and *Sisters* the audience wants an intensive dose of the fear sickness — not to confront fear and have it conquered but to feel that crazy, inexplicable delight that children get out of terrifying stories that give them bad dreams. A flesh-crawler that affects as many senses as a horror movie can doesn't end with the neat fake solution. We are always aware that the solution will not really explain the terror we've felt; the forces of madness are never laid to rest.

Suppose that through the medium of the movies pulp, with its five-and-dime myths, can take a stronger hold on people's imaginations than art, because it doesn't affect the conscious imagination, the way a great novel does, but the private, hidden imagination, the primitive fantasy life — and with an immediacy that leaves no room for thought. I have had more mail from adolescents (and post-adolescents) who were badly upset because of a passing derogatory remark I made about *Rosemary's Baby* than I would ever get if I mocked Tolstoy. Those adolescents think *Rosemary's Baby* is great because it upsets them. And I suspect that people are reluctant to say goodbye to the old sweet bull of the Bogart Marlowe because it satisfies a deep need. They've been accepting the I-look-out-for-No. 1 tough guys of recent films, but maybe they're scared to laugh at Gould's out-of-it Marlowe because that would lose them their Bogart icon. At the moment, the shared pop culture of the audience may be all that people feel they have left. The negative reviews kept insisting that Altman's movie had nothing to do with Chandler's novel and that Elliott Gould wasn't Marlowe. People still want to believe that Galahad is alive and well in Los Angeles — biding his time, perhaps, until movies are once again "like they used to be."

THE JACKED-UP ROMANTICISM of movies like those featuring Shaft, the black Marlowe, may be so exciting it makes what we've always considered the imaginative artists seem dull and boring. Yet there is another process at work, too: the executive producers and their hacks are still trying to find ways to make the old formulas work, but the gifted filmmakers are driven to go beyond pulp and to bring into movies the qualities of imagination that have gone into the other arts. Sometimes, like Robert Altman, they do it even when they're working on pulp material. Altman's isn't a pulp sensibility. Chandler's, for all his talent, was.

[October 22, 1973]

Un-People

JOHN HOUSEMAN once remarked, "Nobody can really like an actor" — a comment one can easily imagine issuing from the star faculty member of the Harvard Law School, Professor Kingsfield, played by Houseman, in *The Paper Chase.* The movie, written and directed by James Bridges, from a novel by John Jay Osborn, Jr., is a job of manufacture — a modern commercial version of a problem play-*cum*-Socratic dialogue — but at its center Houseman, who carries the weight of his years and the stiff elegance of his personal authority, brings the picture his own authenticity. He has an indefinable air of eminence. I am not sure what it comes from — having as a child (when I was more sensitive than I am now) vomited after seeing a play he directed — but it certainly doesn't come from the context that Bridges supplies him. Houseman shines because he's the only one in the movie who suggests that he was formed by experience.

Timothy Bottoms, miscast, I suspect, and meticulously tousled for the camera, is Hart, an eager first-year law student; he's a zealot about the legal profession, and he idolizes Kingsfield, but after meeting Kingsfield's daughter Susan (Lindsay Wagner), who is negative and derisive about almost everything, he becomes uncertain whether the grueling discipline of law school is worth it. (And it's really hysterically grueling in this movie; cracking a book seems to be like walking into enemy gunfire.) Hart discovers that he doesn't know what his zeal is about or "who he is" — to use the cant phrase that the movie implies. Since the picture never defines Hart's goal, we are left to identify it with the showy tyrannical processing that Kingsfield imposes on his students. Kingsfield challenges his intimidated students, jousts with them, and demonstrates his arrogant superiority; these fancy contests in the lecture hall appear to be here for "drama," but the director equates his own dramatic device with the study of the law. It's as if he were to whip up a kindergarten situation in which a splendid ogre of a self-dramatizing teacher cowed the admiring but terrified little kids, and then went on to use this entertaining example of theatrical know-how as a serious demonstration that education was corrupt and dehumanizing. The movie never indicates that there might be ways of learning law which don't involve being humiliated — which don't even involve all this competitive combat — and the study of law is presented not in terms of what the law means in this society but only in terms of the martinet Kingsfield. Hart's alternatives are to be shaped into a pseudo-Kingsfield and become part of the establishment or to throw it all over. Is it possible for a complex technological society to function democratically — at any level — without a complex legal system? If it isn't possible, then there are sound reasons for studying law. But the movie never indicates the existence of the lawyers who have served as draft counselors, or worked with the poor or for civil liberties or with Ralph Nader, or who function as a judicial check on the other branches of government; it lumps the study of law with the establishment, so that Hart's confusion about what it's all for flatters the young movie audience.

It isn't that *The Paper Chase* is deliberately dishonest but that it's basically mindless. Bridges isn't a revolutionary making an assault on the American legal system. He's just trying to turn out a movie that will "say something" and entertain audiences, too, and he has nothing to say. He doesn't seem any more aware of what he's got into here than he did in his last "Meet Pamela," *The Baby Maker.* James Bridges isn't really a movie director in the sense that many of the new young directors are; he's a theatrical telegrapher, whose only means of expression is by signal. Every shot makes a point, even though the target is fuzzy. How are we to interpret Hart's obsession with Kingsfield, or his penchant for breaking into campus buildings? Is he meant to be unstable, or is his erratic behavior just for cuteness — to add a little color to the academic setting? With Timothy Bottoms trying to be the brainy, charismatic Hart, the viewer can't tell what's going on. Bottoms is essentially a vague, wondering actor; there's a blur at his center, and when he tosses his thick, unruly mane he looks like a romantic anarchist who's lost his bombs. Bridges tries to do something more thoughtful and "provocative" than the usual industry product, and he has some skill, but movies have already gone far beyond the way he works. Bottoms somehow eludes him (Bottoms eludes us, too), but Bridges turns the other actors who appear as law students into clockwork performers. You can tick off the nuances.

The Paper Chase isn't a terrible movie, but its preconceptions are all wrong: it's about an un-situation and un-people. Look at Susan, the patrician professor's daughter. Lindsay Wagner is well matched physically to Houseman; she has the requisite stature, and even the faint sneer, and you can't decide whether she's hateful-looking or beautiful or both simultaneously. But why is that old contrivance the professor's daughter turning up in this movie? Susan isn't really a character. We have no idea what she does with her life, besides pick up her father's law students and castrate them of their ambitions and ideals. We don't know whether her contempt for the law is meant to be resentment of her father (and, if so, why) or whether it's supposed to be part of a realistic appraisal of the society. She exists only because the movie needs someone to undermine Hart's beliefs and precipitate his crisis, and because the movie needs sex. Hart isn't a character, either, but at least he has the dignity of being the protagonist. Susan is modern and neurotic-looking, but that's only a cosmetic difference: like generations of movie women before her, she's waiting and worrying on the sidelines. Essentially, Susan is no different from the ingénue in an old adventure film who just happened to be around because she was the daughter of the scientist on the expedition, or the daughter of the missionary stranded in a remote outpost, or (daring) the widow of someone lost on safari, or the murdered rancher's niece. Those women never got anywhere under their own steam, and that's true of Kingsfield's daughter. In movies, the kooks and prosties and pushovers seem to be the only ones who do get out on their own.

USING WOMEN (and not only women) as plot functions may be a clue to the shallowness of many movies, even of much better movies — *American Graffiti*, for example. The audience at *American Graffiti* appears to be ecstatically happy condescending toward its own past — how cute we were at seventeen, how funny, how lost — but for women the end of the picture is a cold slap. Set in 1962, *American Graffiti* compresses into one night the events from high-school graduation to the opening of college in the fall. At the close, it jumps to the present and wraps up the fates of the four principal male characters — as if lives were set ten years after high school! — and it ignores the women characters. This is one of those bizarre omissions that tell you what really goes on in men filmmakers' heads and what women — who are now, for the first time in movie history, half the moviegoing audience — bitterly (or unconsciously) swallow. Cindy Williams plays that hard little number Laurie the cheerleader with such tight intensity that she almost camouflages the fact that Laurie's I-can't-wait routine is there just to keep the plot contrasts functioning by holding the equally contrived Steve (Ronny Howard) in town. He's like the all-American-soda-jerk hero of the forties, but we're meant to believe in him and care about his future, while she is dropped into limbo. And it turns out that the baby daredevil Carol (twelve-year-old Mackenzie Phillips), the most entertaining character in the movie, is there for the jokes, like the precocious-brat younger sisters that Diana Lynn used to play, while the stock adolescent creep Terry the Toad (whose experiences are the cheapest and worst-staged in the movie) is actually meant to be taken seriously — we are informed that he was reported missing in Vietnam.

Because of the energy of the performers, Laurie and Carol stay in the memory more vividly than the boys, but that chilling omission at the end is indicative of the limited male imagination of the picture. I don't think the director, George Lucas, who also worked on the script, ever wondered whether Laurie, who wants her boy-man Steve so fiercely and wants nothing else, could sustain the giving over of herself or whether her intensity would sour into neurosis. Was Steve really enough for her, and could he stand being her everything? These questions arise because of the shrill vibes in Cindy Williams' performance, not because of the context; the garish, overdrawn blond swinger Debbie (Candy Clark), who comes out of the comic strips, is probably meant to be as believable as Laurie. The facile wrap-up of the men's lives (so like the brisk, neat finishes of old movies — everything in place) is consistent with the naïve seriousness of the film which audiences find so appealing. I like the look of *American Graffiti,* and the feel of it. Lucas has a sensual understanding of film which James Bridges doesn't have; Lucas is a real filmmaker. But *American Graffiti* fails to be anything more than a warm, nice, draggy comedy, because there's nothing to back up the style. The images aren't as visually striking as they would be if only there were a mind at work behind them; the movie has no resonance except from the jukebox sound and the eerie, nocturnal jukebox look. And I don't like the pop narcissism of it — the way it invites the audience to share in a fond, jokey view of its own adolescence. Mel's Drive-In has replaced the old soda fountain, and a good rock score has been added, but *American Graffiti* isn't much more than an updating of Booth Tarkington's *Seventeen* and those high-school comedy-romances with Donald O'Connor, Peggy Ryan, and June Preisser — and, yes, of the Mickey Rooney pictures, too.

The audiences allow the fifties jukebox tunes on the track to define their early lives for them. I think they can laugh so easily because the shared recognitions are all external; it's the giggle you get from looking at a false image of yourself. Though done with style, this is fake folk art, and the kids are stock characters. Andy Hardy had all these boys' troubles: he was the runt (the buck-toothed, bespectacled Toad), the popular freckle-face (Steve), the rash driver (John), and the introspective protagonist (Curt). Scared innocence (male division) is standard stuff, and there's no reason Andy Hardy shouldn't be divvied up and set to rock, but has pop gone so far in dominating the experience of growing up that people in the audience who are now heading for thirty are justified in taking these ancient adolescent tribal rites for the sum of their experience? Every few years, there seems to be a new movie that young audiences say is the story of their lives; they said it of *Rebel Without a Cause* and again of *Easy Rider,* and, even without awarding those pictures any laurels, one could see why. One can also see why they're saying it of *American Graffiti.* But they're demeaning their own lives when they do; they're responding to a national trivia show for youth. It's the peer-group view of life, and audiences still respond as a peer group when they laugh at the picture and then say, "That's just what it was like." *American Graffiti* makes it possible for them to enjoy the pop culture of their past while feeling how banal and limited it was, yet the movie never gets at the part of them that knew it then. It sticks to stereotypes — to adolescents who exist to be laughed at. The picture throws in everything: forty platters and a thousand old-movie shticks, including a car race and that sure-fire old laugh-getter, smashing up a police car. For whom was it "just like that," I wonder. Not for women, not for blacks or Orientals or Puerto Ricans, not for homosexuals, not for the poor. Only for white middle-class boys whose memories have turned into pop.

The protagonists of *The Paper Chase* and *American Graffiti* (both titles seem to be wearing elevator shoes) don't know what they want; they're searching. The girls in both movies want nothing but men. I raise this point not to make a feminist issue of it (though that's implicit) but to make an aesthetic one: mechanical people, including searching young men, are a blight on the movies — evidence that the filmmakers aren't thinking freshly, that they're resorting to the stockpile.

❖

"SISTERS," A LOW-BUDGET HORROR movie about a psychotic ex-Siamese twin, is a long way from being the brilliant thriller the ads say it is, but its limp technique doesn't seem to matter to the people who want their gratuitous gore. The movie supplies it, but why is there so much gratuitous dumbness, too? The director, Brian De Palma (who made *Greetings*), can do flaked-out humor, as in the TV-game-show parody at the beginning, and he can do high-pitched demented knife-slashings (if that's your idea of a good time). But he can't get two people talking in order to make a simple expository point without its sounding like the drabbest Republic picture of 1938. *Sisters* is enough like old movies to pass for a send-up, but in many scenes ineptitude and send-up mingle. The director's control is so desultory that I couldn't tell whether the girl detective-reporter (Jennifer Salt) was intended to be a complete goosey dum-dum or whether that was partly the result of the actress's logy girlishness and her lack of skill. Enough imbecility was written into the role, however, to raise this question: why is it that the siren, with her delish crazed grin (Margot Kidder, who has a demon-slut's curly lips and knows how to turn on the sexiness with a witch's precision), is smart and appealing in a new-style way, while the girl reporter is the nitwit meddler as before? She's so dumb she makes Priscilla Lane seem like Mary McCarthy, and the picture would be better — both as horror film and as comedy — if she were at least as smart as James Stewart in *Rear Window*. The facetious dialogue is a wet blanket, and De Palma's technique isn't up to his apparent intention, which is to provide cheap thrills that are also a parody of old corn. But he manages the thrills, and the audiences seem to be so turned on to the trashiness and so freaked out by Bernard Herrmann's music, with its old radio-play throb and zing, that they're happily crazy-scared. The crudeness of this movie — it's zero on atmosphere — obviously works for some people, but you probably have to be highly impressionable, with a very active, very gaudy fantasy life, to fall for it.

[October 29, 1973]

Moments of Truth

"THE ICEMAN COMETH" is a great, heavy, simplistic, mechanical, beautiful play. It is not the Eugene O'Neill masterpiece that *Long Day's Journey Into Night,* the finest work of the American theater, is, but it is masterpiece enough — perhaps the greatest thesis play of the American theater — and it has been given a straightforward, faithful production in handsome dark-toned color in the subscription series called the American Film Theatre. A filmed play like this doesn't offer the sensual excitement that movies *can* offer, but you don't go to it for that. You go to it for O'Neill's crude, prosaic virtuosity, which is also pure American poetry, and, as with most filmed dramas, if you miss the "presence" of the actors, you gain from seeing it performed by the sort of cast that rarely gathers in a theater. John Frankenheimer directed fluently and unobtrusively, without destroying the conventions of the play. The dialogue is like a ball being passed from one actor to the next; whenever possible (when the speakers are not too far apart), the camera pans smoothly from one to another. We lose some of the ensemble work we'd get from a live performance, but we gain a closeup view that allows us to see and grasp each detail. The play here is less broad than it would be on the stage, and Frankenheimer wisely doesn't aim for laughs at the characters' expense (even those that O'Neill may have intended), because the people are so close to us. The actors become close to us in another way. Actors who have been starved for a good part get a chance to stretch and renew themselves. In some cases, we've been seeing them for years doing the little thing that passes for acting on TV and in bad movies, and their performances here are a revelation; in a sense, the actors who go straight for the occasion give the lie to the play's demonstration that bums who live on guilt for what they don't do can't go back and do it.

Set in 1912 in a waterfront saloon, much like the one in which O'Neill had attempted suicide that year, the play was written in the late thirties and was first produced in 1946, on Broadway, under his supervision, but it achieved its present eminence from the Circle in the Square revival in 1956, starring Jason Robards, who then appeared in the celebrated television version of 1960, directed by Sidney Lumet. The characters are drunken bums and whores who have found sanctuary in Harry Hope's flophouse saloon; each has a "pipe dream" that sustains him until Hickey the salesman, the "iceman," who attempts to free them all by stripping them of their lies and guilt, takes the life out of them. It is both a pre-Freudian play and a post-Freudian one, and that may be the source of the trouble people have "placing" it; you can't call this play dated, and you can't quite call it modern, either. The thesis is implicitly anti-Freudian: the play says that the truth destroys people — that it wipes them out. Like most thesis plays, this one rigs the situation to make its points. There are no planned surprises in O'Neill's world — no freak characters who go out and make good. The people forced by Hickey to rid themselves of illusions are such ruins that they can live only on false hopes; without illusions they have nothing. O'Neill has rather cruelly — and comically (which is the most cruel, I think, though others may say the most human) — designed the play to demonstrate that they're better off as lying, cadging bums. With his stageproof craft, O'Neill sets in motion a giant game of ten little Indians. Each of the many characters has his lie, and each in turn has it removed and must face his truth, and we look to see who's next. It's as if illusion were a veil, and under it lay truth. This simplistic view of illusion and reality is the limiting thesis device of the play, and O'Neill's demonstration that mankind is too weak to live without the protective veil is — well, maudlin. But O'Neill was too powerful and too instinctual a dramatist to stay locked within the thesis structure. Not quite all of mankind is reconciled to wearing the veil that protects the weak, and that's where the ambiguities burst through the mechanics of *The Iceman Cometh.*

The play is essentially an argument between Larry, an aging anarchist (Robert Ryan), and Hickey (Lee Marvin); they speak to each other as equals, and everything else is orchestrated around them. Larry speaks for pity and the necessity of illusions, Hickey for the curative power of truth. They're the two poles of consciousness that O'Neill himself is split between. Larry, a self-hating alcoholic, is a weak man and a windbag, but Robert Ryan brings so much understanding to Larry's weakness that the play achieves new dimensions. In the most difficult role he ever played on the screen, Ryan is superb. Larry's dirty "truth" is hidden under a pile of philosophizing, and the actor is stuck with delivering that philosophizing, which rings like the fakery it's meant to be but which we know O'Neill half believes. Ryan becomes O'Neill for us, I think. George Jean Nathan said that O'Neill carefully selected the photographs of himself that were to be published, and "always made sure that the photographs were not lacking in that impressive look of tragic handsomeness which was his." Ryan has that tragic handsomeness here and O'Neill's broken-man jowls, too, and at the end, when Larry is permanently "iced" — that is, stripped of illusion — we can see that this is the author's fantasy of himself: he alone is above the illusions that the others fall back on; he is tragic, while the others, with their restored illusions, have become comic. Yes, it's sophomoric to see yourself as the one who is doomed to live without illusions, but then so is the idea of the play sophomoric, and yet what O'Neill does with that sophomoric idea is masterly. And Ryan gets right to the boozy, gnarled soul of it. According to his associates, Ryan did not know he was dying until after the picture was finished, but he brought to this role the craft that he had perfected in his fifty-nine years and that he certainly knew he might never be able to exercise to its fullest again. The man who had tested himself against such uncompromisingly difficult roles on the stage as Coriolanus and the father in *Long Day's Journey* and on the screen as the depraved Claggart of *Billy Budd* got a last chance to show his stature, and he was ready. Ryan is so subtle he seems to have penetrated to the mystery of O'Neill's gaunt grandeur — to the artist's egotism and that Catholic Cassandra's pride in tragedy which goes along with the fond pity for the foolish clowns lapping up their booze.

Lee Marvin's Hickey is another matter. The characters have been waiting for Hickey, as for Godot, and his entrance is preceded by a whore who acts as herald; it's an unparalleled opportunity for an actor, as Jason Robards demonstrated so memorably in the TV version. I remember that during his long, scarily self-lacerating monologue I felt as if I couldn't breathe until it was finished. Suddenly, you knew that Hickey had been punishing the others for what he had been trying to live with, and that he was totally indifferent to them as people, and the play rose to heights you hadn't anticipated. But Hickey, with his edgy, untrustworthy affability, is a part for a certain kind of actor, and Lee Marvin isn't it. Marvin has a jokester's flair for vocal tricks and flip gestures; he can project the tough guy's impassive strength that is needed for the films he's generally in, and I don't think I've ever seen him give a bad performance in an action film. Here it's a matter not just of his not being up to it but of his being all wrong for it. We need to see the man under the salesman's exterior, and instead we realize how little interior life Marvin's action-film characters have had and how few expressive resources he has had besides a gleam in the eye. With his snub nose and long upper lip, he has a great camera face, but he's been acting for a long time now on star presence, and though that may be what you attract backers with, it's not what you play O'Neill with. What Marvin does is all on one level. At first, he's like a pudgy, complacent actor having a go at Mr. Scratch in *The Devil and Daniel Webster,* and then he just seems to coast. Hickey needs an element of irony and an awareness of horror; Marvin's Hickey exudes hostile, stupid arrogance — the impatience of the prosperous, well-fed, insensitive man with the sick. Marvin is so poorly equipped for the kind of acting required for Hickey that as the monologue approached I began to dread it. As it turns out, the monologue goes by without really being experienced by the viewer. Marvin's best recourse is to shout, because when he doesn't shout there's nothing going on. We don't seem to see this Hickey's eyes; Marvin offers us a blank face. He's thick, somehow, and irrelevantly vigorous. Marvin doesn't appear to have found anything in himself to draw on for the role. The film isn't destroyed by this performance, but it's certainly marred; yet who knows whether we will ever get a definitive version on film? We're lucky to get as much as we get here, even though the film never rises to the intensity that O'Neill put into the play. Frankenheimer has directed tactfully but not very probingly.

O'Neill is such an orderly madman: he neatly constructs a massive play around a weird conceit — the sexual wordplay on "come" in the title, which refers to Hickey's murderous explosion when he kills his wife. What we don't get, because of Marvin's one-level performance, are the terrifying intimations in this Strindbergian monologue that O'Neill is talking about himself and his wife — that he is giving Hickey the kind of raging emotion that is in *Long Day's Journey Into Night,* the kind that transcended O'Neill's ideas, yet that in this play he used to fuel his thesis. The intensity of the monologue should blow the play sky-high. Maybe O'Neill's conscious plan had become too easy to fulfill, and, as sometimes happened in Ibsen's greatest thesis plays, what was underneath the choice of subject suddenly boiled up. How, one may wonder, did Carlotta O'Neill take it as Hickey talked about the peace he found after he killed his wife? The play has a subtext that fuses with the thesis at this point, and the subtext is the hell and horror of marriage. Every character in the saloon who has talked about marriage has given us a variation on Hickey's murderous solution, and his monologue awakens Harry Hope (Fredric March) to expose his own loathing of the dead wife he's been sentimentalizing about for twenty years. O'Neill twists this male-female hatred in and out of his they-need-their-illusions thesis. It is he as dramatist who furiously, yet icily, tears away the sentimental illusions; that's what gives his kind of playwriting its power. It's not polite entertainment — not a show — but an exploration; he digs down as far as he can go. That he is the worst sentimentalist — the man who needs his illusions the most — is what makes him, like Tennessee Williams, so greatly to be felt for, and respected.

What this play seems to say, in the end, is that O'Neill the man of pity is the illusion, and that the only man he respects is the man without illusions. (I think one could say that it is just the opposite for Williams — that he abandons the man without illusions.) It's Larry, the man too full of self-loathing even to get drunk — Larry the man of pity — who refuses to offer the eighteen-year-old Parritt (Jeff Bridges) any comfort or hope, who judges him pitilessly and sends him to his death. Parritt has come to see Larry, the one person who was ever kind to him, asking to be helped. And Larry, the kindly spokesman for the necessity of illusion, doesn't want to help Parritt lie to himself; he wants him dead. It's a cruel, ambiguous kicker in the neat-looking finish. Larry's compassion, it seems, extends only to those he's not emotionally involved with. O'Neill makes Larry a hard man, finally, and desolate and unyielding, like himself. And though the bums are restored to their illusions, it's a fools' paradise regained; there's a streak of contempt in O'Neill's final view of them. O'Neill gives the lie to his own thesis: the bums need illusions not in order to be fully human (as would be the case in Tennessee Williams) but because they're weak. Those who find life without illusions insupportable are poor slobs — not strong enough to face truth and be broken by it. Hickey deceived himself about why he killed his wife; Larry, the self-hater, the only man Hickey succeeded in stripping of illusions, is, at the end, the iceman. He's stone sober, like the O'Neill of the photographs. How could anyone look at O'Neill's face and believe that he's telling people to be happy with their illusions? Sure, O'Neill is destroyed by "the truth," but he thinks he lives with "truth"; that's the secret in that haunted, sunken-jawed, angry face. And if he didn't linger on the implications of Larry's position at the end, maybe it's because he didn't dare to examine the false glory in it. It's hubris if ever there was hubris in an American play; it's also a common delusion of the mad.

It was only when, in *Long Day's Journey Into Night,* O'Neill abandoned the mechanistic dualisms (such as illusion and truth here) which he used as the underpinnings of his plays — and which make them look dated yet give them structural clarity and easy-to-take-home "serious" themes — that he could see people whole. But though the characters in *Iceman* are devised for a thesis, and we never lose our consciousness of that, they are nevertheless marvellously playable. Fredric March, like Ryan, can let the muscles in his face sag to hell to show a character falling apart. He interprets Harry Hope (who could be a dismal bore) with so much quiet tenderness and skill that when Harry regains his illusions and we see March's muscles tone up we don't know whether to smile for the character or for the actor. March is such an honorable actor; he's had a long and distinguished career. On the stage since 1920, in movies since 1929, and at seventy-six he goes on taking difficult roles; he's not out doing TV commercials or grabbing a series. At a press conference just before the 1946 opening of *The Iceman Cometh*, Eugene O'Neill said that the secret of happiness was contained in one simple sentence: "For what shall it profit a man if he shall gain the whole world and lose his own soul?" I think that once again he was being simplistic (O'Neill didn't sell his own soul, and I seriously doubt he was a happy man), but what he said has a basic truth in terms of the life of theater people. Taking on a role in *The Iceman Cometh* is a moment of truth for an actor. One of the pleasures is the way Bradford Dillman (a hole in the screen in *The Way We Were*) passes the test here. As Willie, singing his Harvard drinking song and shaking from the DTs, Dillman is funny and lively — like a Rip Torn without pent-up aggression. It's a small but flawless performance; you can almost taste the actor's joy in the role — in *working* again. Jeff Bridges has been working all along; he's one of the lucky ones in Hollywood — so fresh and talented that just about every movie director with a good role wants him for it. But he has been cast as a country boy *(The Last Picture Show, Fat City, Bad Company, The Last American Hero)* and used for his "natural" ease on the screen — used, that is, for almost the opposite of what a stage actor needs. What he does here as the kid Parritt (it's the role that Robert Redford played in the TV version) is a complete change from the improvisational style he has developed, and initially it is a thankless role, a pain, really — one of those hideously-obvious-guilty-secret roles that you wish weren't in the play. Every line Parritt utters tells of his guilt. But, of course, O'Neill knew what he was doing; the obviousness turns out to be necessary, and when it pays off in Parritt's big scenes with Larry, Bridges, looking as young as the role requires, and so powerfully built that his misery has physical force, comes through. He is convincing-looking as a boy of that period, and he makes an almost impossibly schematic role believable. Toward the end, there is an instant while he's looking at Larry when his face is childishly soft and vulnerable; it's this instant that reminds us to be grateful for what a camera can add to the experience of a play.

We may think we could do without the irritating repetition of the term "pipe dream," and I know that at times I felt I could do without the three painted whores and maybe without the captain and the general who are still fighting the Boer War (though not without the actors who play them — Martyn Green and George Voskovec). But in O'Neill the laborious and the mysterious are peculiarly inextricable, and, with actors like Sorrell Booke as Hugo (which he played in the 1960 TV version), and Moses Gunn as Joe, and Tom Pedi as Rocky (which he played on Broadway in 1946 and again on TV in 1960), and John McLiam as a lyrically sad Jimmy Tomorrow, the four hours less a minute have a special grace. It was O'Neill's genius to discover what no other dramatist has — that banality in depth can let loose our common demons.

YOU CAN'T TAKE YOUR EYES OFF THE SUBTITLES of the French thriller *The Inheritor* for a moment or you're lost; those talky French rattle on, and the subtitles keep coming. The story isn't all that complicated, but the storytelling technique is. The sheer input of information is exhausting. There's so much going on — flashbacks and crosscutting, plus gadgetry and split-second cityscapes — that you're never allowed any peace. The prop man must have had a breakdown on this one, and the editor may have had to use a computer to keep track of the bits of film. What's it all for? To keep you from being bored. It succeeds in that, but the effect is nerve-jangling. It's a traffic jam of a movie. Philippe Labro, the American-educated journalist-director, made last year's thriller *Without Apparent Motive,* in which he encouraged Jean-Louis Trintignant to bring out his latent resemblance to Bogart; that was more modest trash. In *The Inheritor* he uses Jean-Paul Belmondo so that we're teasingly reminded of his Bogartlike gestures in *Breathless,* and the spoiled cheat out of Chandler is named Lauren (Maureen Kerwin), but the picture aspires to something higher than the thriller category. It throws together the hardware of a Bond film and the sympathies of an anti-Fascist political melodrama, and it's too facilely clever by at least half. One could accept the *Citizen Kane*-style storytelling of *The Mattei Affair* (with Mattei's body as a jigsaw puzzle within the larger jigsaw of the film), because the director, Francesco Rosi, was trying to tell a difficult, open-ended political story, to which he didn't have all the answers. But Labro doesn't even have any questions. *The Inheritor* is just a fast, classy jamboree of journalism and old movies. The hero, American-educated Bart Cordell (Belmondo), returns to France upon the death of his father; the inheritor of steel factories and a weekly newsmagazine, he is the twentieth-richest man in the West. Cordell is a powerful good guy; when he takes over his journalistic empire, he talks the same line about protecting the exploited poor against the powerful interests that Charles Foster Kane did, but it's without ambiguities here. This movie is basically a glamour-star fantasy that Labro takes seriously; he invokes Scott Fitzgerald (by quoting him), but in this neo-swinger's movie the quotation is a form of climbing. Labro has flash and expertise, but the story isn't good enough to justify the tenseness and trickery, and the characters are reincarnated from romantic hardboiled American movies. The movie operates on false energy, and when it's over there's nothing left; you're just tired.

[November 5, 1973]

Bloodless and Bloody

"ENGLAND MADE ME," from the early Graham Greene novel, is far from great, far from original, and it's slight, but it's not a bad film. It has a hushed, becalmed quality that is very pleasing — and peculiar, too, for a film set in Germany during the early thirties. Watching it is rather like seeing the early Nazi period through the paintings of a Manet — the people appearing at their most social, with their prettiest public faces on. You're not quite sure if it's all right to feel this way, but at times you may find yourself thinking, I'd love to be there. The halcyon atmosphere is creepily ambiguous, to say the least. Greene brought out the book in 1935, when he was only thirty-one. It's about a giddy young man, Tony Farrant (Michael York), on the loose in the world of big speculators, to which his beautiful, steadfast sister Kate (Hildegard Neil) has introduced him. Kate, the mistress and business confidante of an international swindler-financier, Krogh (Peter Finch), is ruthlessly worldly, while Tony, with his charming scamp's lies and affectations, is at heart a British schoolboy. The book was set in Sweden; the film (shot in some of the most ravishing parts of Yugoslavia) moves the action to what turned out to be the center of events in that period, and makes the humorless, shady Krogh a German trying to get his money out of the country before Hitler brings everything crashing down.

The change involves the creation of background detail, and the moviemaking team can't bring that up to the level one would expect of Greene (there's an implausible encounter in a night club between Krogh and a Jewish former newspaper owner, and the street with boarded-up Jewish shops looks pictorial-reverential), but the plot and the characters are very close to Greene's original, and the dialogue is nearly verbatim. The lines have almost unerring style, and they're spoken with the snap that good actors bring to good lines, like fish rising to live bait. The most movie-associated of all reputable contemporary writers, Graham Greene has had almost all his novels filmed, has written original scripts, and has adapted his own and other writers' work for the screen. Most of the films he's had a hand in — roughly twenty-five — have had

Greene's emblem: the thrill of evil, the allure of damnation. He must be one of the few writers going for whom squalor still has glamour. But the novel *England Made Me* preceded the Graham Greene we know; at times in the film Tony's character and escapades seem closer to Noël Coward than to Graham Greene, though the character of Minty, an abject, mildewed old newspaperman, anticipates Greene's later characters and evokes smiles of recognition. Michael Hordern gives such a marvellously flamboyant seedy performance as Minty that one wants to applaud him. It's the only flamboyance in this film, which is milder and more rarefied than most Greene films, though it's almost totally dependent on his storytelling gift.

The director, Peter Duffell, hasn't tried to make a harrowing melodrama out of the book (one could); he's kept it a character study of a British arrested adolescent who is upset by what he sees around him yet has no means but a schoolboy's tricks for dealing with it. Tony the innocent — callow, fun-loving, bright-eyed — is perhaps the quiet Englishman, an early cousin to Greene's appallingly callow quiet American. Evil offends Tony — he can't believe people are breaking the rules — but he doesn't even have any way of expressing himself beyond a schoolboy's arch slang. This young Englishman who is so amiable he fits in everywhere doesn't really fit in anywhere — certainly not in Nazi Germany, because events have moved past amiability and unflappable good manners. His end, which is perfectly in character, is a bittersweet irony: he greets his own assassin with an affable exclamation of surprise. Low-key and understated, this film is the most affectionate self-satire to come out of contemporary England. Greene clearly intended Tony to be a winsome male ingénue — an unsubstantial man — and that isn't easy to play, but Michael York brings it off with humor and grace. He manages to make Tony spruce and engaging and airily ineffective. From the evidence here, Duffell is a fine director of actors. As a stolid German, Peter Finch has a stronger presence than he has in most of his movies, and Hildegard Neil (wasted as George Segal's wife in *A Touch of Class*) makes Kate a tantalizing, passionate riddle — a woman at war with herself. But Duffell's method keeps us at a distance. The picture is without the voluptuous vitality that made *Cabaret* so extraordinary, and without star images like Liza Minnelli's Raggedy Ann painted by Kees van Dongen. It doesn't have audacity, and it doesn't have much energy; the decadence is carefully modulated in pastel tones. Since there aren't very many elements to observe in the scenes, you're highly conscious of how color-coördinated Kate's makeup and dresses are with the rooms and the landscapes (and awareness of planning cancels believability) but grateful for how calmly the leisurely sequences are played out. Often, a picture's best qualities work against it even more than its failures do:

how could *Death in Venice* be organized after that long virtuoso opening? After that beginning, there was no way to edit the picture which made sense. Here, you sit watching the languidly lovely scenes in the soft pink light and wondering how the movie can ever gather force. Well, it doesn't — the moviemaking remains rather anemic. Yet the sustained remoteness is seductive, even though it's not fully satisfying. I think there's a definite sense of disappointment about the Peter Finch character's not being developed, because Finch makes Krogh's humorlessness so touching that we want more; and Kate, though well-played, is conceived as a series of images, and they never quite come together to form a person.

With the aid of Ray Parslow's cinematography, Duffell seems to distill the romantic beauty of the past: Michael York's flat, slicked-down hair and flashing naughty-nice-boy smile; Finch's weary-lion head and his mixture of stodginess and imperial splendor as he walks to his immaculate 1934 Chrysler in his broad-brimmed hat, his coat worn like a cape; and Hildegard Neil's feline eyes and ultracivilized cool, and the intensity that sets her off from the little blonde (Tessa Wyatt) that Tony falls for — a girl as appealingly, vacuously English as a Noël Coward musical. The tastefully haunting theme music, by John Scott, has the same weakness and charm as the rest of the movie; it sounds familiar the first time you hear it — "original" movie music often does — yet it's lovely in its pleasures-of-reminiscence, Noël Cowardish way. (The score also includes "Mad About the Boy," sung in a night club, and the way the people listening are seen in zonked-out frozen-faced close-ups, as if in a time capsule, struck me as an almost pure Coward touch.) However, when we leave the theater we're not certain what the mood and the evocativeness were about, really. I think maybe what happens is that the atmosphere soaks up the characters and story, and we're left only with mood. The picture grows so thin it seems to disappear in a mist.

WHY SHOULD PEOPLE GO TO SEE *Charley Varrick*? What are we meant to get out of it? It's about another heist, with another twist: the small-time bank robbers, led by Varrick (Walter Matthau), happen to rob a bank that's holding three-quarters of a million dollars in Mafia money, and are then tracked by both the police and the Mafia. This sort of thing could conceivably be worth seeing if it were done with great technical skill or if the characterizations had some gleam or gaiety. But *Charley Varrick* — from Universal — doesn't even look good; the color is blah and runny, the compositions are squat and no more than functional, and the director, Don Siegel, slogs along from scene to scene. This picture's idea of characterization is to have the Mafia's investigator (Joe Don Baker) a boorish racist who says "nigra," and the bland, smooth, Mafia-connected banker (John Vernon) an anti-Semite. Liberalism rears a bedraggled, feeble-minded head in the implicitly illiberal action-film world of *Charley Varrick*; Don Siegel seems to be trying to kid himself that he's not doing what he's doing. There's an aesthetic pleasure one gets from highly developed technique; certain action sequences make you feel exhilarated just because they're so cleverly done — even if, as in the case of Siegel's *Dirty Harry*, you're disgusted by the picture. *Dirty Harry* had a smooth, exciting suspense style that turned the audience on, and its extreme brutality affected the audience viscerally. The film, which was released late in 1971, drew its special force from its overt extreme-right-wing ideology; it "explained" the law-and-order troubles of the cities by blaming them on the liberals — an explanation that Nixon and Agnew, then at the peak of their popularity, had made credible to their followers. *Charley Varrick* is just brutal and tiresome. Even Lalo Schifrin, who wrote the score, falls down on the job. Maybe he got bored producing the musical trickery that makes directors look better than they are, or maybe his contempt for the assignment got out of hand, because he just throws in noise this time. When Siegel's gruesome sequences need suspense, Schifrin beats your ears.

Charley Varrick is merely a gimmick picture: the movie cannot explain what the decent, sagacious Varrick — brainy and with the wisdom of the heart, too — is doing carrying a gun and robbing banks. There's no correlation between his charming, homely character and his livelihood; we're asked to cheer for a killer because he doesn't behave like the other killers — as if it were their personal style that made us object to them. (If only those other killers would learn to say "black" and not make anti-Semitic remarks, maybe we could cheer for them, too?) The gimmick of putting this Mr. Deeds type into the world of crime isn't even played for parody — that would require writing beyond what Howard Rodman and Dean Riesner, who adapted John Reese's novel *The Looters*, supply. We're asked to take it straight. Varrick is presented as an underdog figure, an old-timey hood David against the Mafia Goliaths; he traps everyone who stands in his way to freedom, and gets everyone killed. Walter Matthau is used for whatever chummy identification the audience has with him by now — he tickles some people, I guess, even when he's just walking through a movie like this looking droll — and the script is played for mayhem.

Don Siegel made his reputation with the clean, efficient shooting of low-budget crime pictures in the forties and fifties; his work had little imagination, but it had precision. It wasn't fancy and dull, like many of the higher-budgeted jobs. But his popular 1968 big-city melodrama

Madigan, though told straightforwardly, was marred by Universal's infamous wide-screen process and by its laboratory work, which turned the cityscapes into a blue soft-focus mess, and the plot was based on an archaic, fake parallel: the adulterous affair of the police commissioner (Henry Fonda) was set up as equivalent to the bribe-taking and corruption of his chief inspector (James Whitmore). This is the sort of phony moralistic bookkeeping that movies went in for thirty-five years ago, and no amount of admiration for a director's skill should hide the phoniness from modern viewers. In *Charley Varrick,* the numerous violent scenes are cloddishly staged; Siegel's victims drool blood while staring at us, and we're supposed to feel happy because Charley never gets hurt. To answer my question: I don't know any reason for going to see *Charley Varrick.* I felt sordid sitting in the theater watching Varrick's last surviving partner — a drunken, cowardly lout (played by Andy Robinson, the hippie rapist of *Dirty Harry*) — slobber while he was being kicked and butchered. And I felt insulted by being asked to get involved with what happens to that foxy Charley Varrick — a good man in bed, in contrast to that Mafia fellow. Racists can't be sexually normal in Hollywood's idiot-liberal bookkeeping — which persists even in corpse-lined heist movies. This line is a holdover from the double-entry forties, when American soldier-heroes could beat up Nazis with an untroubled conscience because the Nazis were shown to be rapists or to be impotent or sexually sadistic, like the Huns before them. This picture turns the Mafia men into Huns in order to justify Varrick's brutality. Sentimentality and violence are a rotten mixture; so are childishness and cynicism.

Don Siegel's making a tribute to "the last of the independents" — as Charley Varrick is called — is a royal Hollywood joke. Siegel is one of the last of the contract directors: a hired hand with his skill for sale. I think that even the best of his crime movies are fundamentally thick-skinned; they're the equivalent of yellow journalism — sensational subjects, tricks that work you up, an appeal to your dumbest impulses. Even when the action and suspense held you, it was always movie pulp. You preferred seeing it to seeing a moldy wholesome movie, because at least it wasn't boring, but you knew enough not to expect much. *Charley Varrick is* boring, because the one real virtue Siegel had — the speed and economy that came from tight planning — isn't in evidence, and the mind at work is the same. It may be no accident that he made his most successful film and, in terms of craftsmanship, probably his best film — *Dirty Harry* — when he did. It's possible that recent American events have stranded him, and left him, like Charley Varrick at the end of the picture, with blue skies, a lot of loot, and no identity.

[November 12, 1973]

Politics and Thrills

GIAN MARIA VOLONTE, a great actor, is a political star the way Germaine Greer, with her Gypsy Rose Lee smile and her Bankhead bravura, is a political star. When Volonte as Vanzetti in *Sacco and Vanzetti* marched to his death, you felt that it would take a lot of juice to kill him. Mastroianni can play a good man but can't play a great man. Volonte can; he isn't smoothly handsome — he's so full of life he's beautiful. As Mattei in *The Mattei Affair,* he had those Laurence Olivier-James Cagney zingy-lion eyes and the foxy intensity that Martin Kosleck patented in his Nazi roles. His Mattei even had a bit of Ralph Nader in the facial contours; in other roles, such as the megalomaniac chief of Rome's homicide squad in *Investigation of a Citizen Above Suspicion,* Volonte often recalls the Paul Muni of *Scarface* and *I Am a Fugitive from a Chain Gang.* The man is a chameleon-star, a fiery Italian Olivier, with the suggestion that he might have Olivier's impudent wit, too. But from a movie like *The French Conspiracy,* how will we ever know? Volonte plays Sadiel, the hero-victim — a character based on the Moroccan revolutionary Ben Barka — and he has the commanding presence for it; he has conscious magnetism, and the ability to project intelligence. (The absence of this ability has often made Hollywood actors grimly pathetic when they impersonated men of historical significance. I don't know anything at all about the late Robert Taylor's intelligence — it may have been enormous — but as an actor he couldn't project brains. Paul Newman has the same incapacity; so has Steve McQueen, and so had Clark Gable.) But in this movie Volonte, with the virile curly white hair of a people's leader, speaks heroic hogwash, while his enemies, smiling their thin, slimy smiles and plotting in their fur-collared overcoats — as if Cecil B. De Mille had coached them in intrigue — are fully aware of the dirtiness of their deeds. They know they're the villains, just as the mustache-twirlers in two-reelers did, and they know that Sadiel is honest and dedicated and incorruptible, and that that's why they have to kill him. This is politics? No, it's show-business politics. *The French Conspiracy* takes the revolutionary political thriller backward about as far as it can go — to the Hollywood historical movies in which the sinister-high-and-powerful (Douglass Dumbrille, in all his evil splendor) schemed against the poor-and-virtuous. The title *The French Conspiracy,* with its echoes of *The French Connection* (Roy Scheider, Popeye's police partner in that, is a C.I.A. agent here), is an attempt to cash in on other movies' success; the original French title is *L'Attentat* — that is, *The Assassination.* The method of this picture could stand as a textbook demonstration of how not to make a political movie.

THE OTHER NEW ASSASSINATION FILM — *Executive Action,* a fictionalization of how President Kennedy *might* have been the victim of a large-scale right-wing plot — is so graceless it's beyond using even as a demonstration of ineptitude. The failures of *The French Conspiracy* are the result of commercialization and so are instructive; the failures of *Executive Action* might be the result of sleeping sickness. In this account, the big, big businessmen who plot Kennedy's death find an Oswald look-alike in order to frame Oswald — for reasons no one will ever understand. The picture, written by Dalton Trumbo from a story by Donald Freed and Mark Lane, and directed by David Miller (the low-budget Richard Fleischer), ends in perhaps the most ludicrous dénouement in thriller history. We are presented with the faces of eighteen "material witnesses" who, we are told, have died, against odds of "one hundred thousand trillion to one." But the movie has failed to introduce those witnesses into the action; we haven't discovered what a single one of them witnessed or how he happened to get involved, so the end is as flat as the beginning and the middle. It's a dodo bird of a movie, the winner of the *Tora! Tora! Tora!* prize — in miniature — for 1973, with matchlessly dull performances from a cast that includes Burt Lancaster (looking very depressed), Robert Ryan, and Will Geer. *Executive Action* could hardly be called a thriller, and it's so worshipful of Kennedy (while treating him insensitively) as to seem to have no politics. David Miller, whose direction is merely halfhearted traffic management, has made a couple of dozen movies (such as *Love Happy, Captain Newman, M.D., Hail, Hero!,* and, with Trumbo, the thickly ironic, overrated *Lonely Are the Brave*), so he doesn't even have the freshness of amateurism. His approach appears to be low-key not by choice but by default; he gives no inkling that he has seen what other directors have been doing lately in the political-thriller form. *The French Conspiracy* is bad, but it isn't stone-dead on the screen; it's bad because it's an ersatz political thriller. One can at least perceive what it aspires to be.

THE FIRST WAVE of revolutionary politics on film came from the newly formed Soviet Union; its masters were Eisenstein, Dovzhenko, and Pudovkin. The second wave broke in 1966, with Gillo Pontecorvo and *The Battle of Algiers,* probably the most emotionally stirring revolutionary epic since Eisenstein's *Potemkin* (1925) and Pudovkin's *Mother* (1926). After him have come Costa-Gavras — with the modern classic political thriller *Z,* in 1969, and then *The Confession,* and *State of Siege,* all three starring Yves Montand — and Pontecorvo again, with *Burn!,* in 1970, and Francesco Rosi, with *The Mattei Affair,* in 1973. Approaching filmmaking as a political act and trying to reach a large audience by putting political material into popular forms, the writers and directors have found themselves sacrificing meaning to thrills, or thrills to meaning. Yet their work has had a potency that ordinary films haven't; their subjects were new to the screen and made restorative contact with the actual world. And even though most of the films weren't imaginatively satisfying, they raised political and aesthetic questions, and showed the intelligence of directors aware of the problems they'd got into.

Like *Potemkin, The Battle of Algiers* is an epic in the form of a "created documentary," with the oppressed, angry masses as the hero. The imperialist enemy and class enemy of the Algerian National Liberation Front — the hyperintelligent French colonel played by Jean Martin — isn't really a character; he represents the cool, inhuman manipulative power of imperialism versus the animal heat of the multitudes rushing toward us as they rise against their oppressors. Pontecorvo and his writer, Franco Solinas, were almost too clever in their use of this device of the colonel — yet it works, and brilliantly. The revolutionaries forming their pyramid of cells didn't need to express revolutionary consciousness, because the French colonel was given such a full counter-revolutionary consciousness that he said it all for them. He even expressed the knowledge that history was on the side of the oppressed colonial peoples, who would win; he himself was merely part of a holding action, preserving imperialism a little longer but bound to fail. To put it satirically but, in terms of the movie, accurately, the Algerian people were spontaneously turned into revolutionaries by historical events, and if they hadn't studied Marx, the counter-revolutionaries had, and knew they were on the wrong side and were doomed by history. In Eisenstein's revolutionary "documentaries," his technique — the formal design of the images, the dynamics of their interaction — had visceral impact, but the films were like giant posters in motion, and the harshly simplified contrasts (the inhumanity of the officers versus the generous camaraderie of the common sailors and soldiers) made one completely aware of the loaded message. In *The Battle of Algiers,* the movie hardly seems to be "saying" anything, yet the historical-determinist message seeps right into your bones. As a propaganda film, it ranks with Leni Riefenstahl's big-game rally, the 1935 *Triumph of the Will,* and it's the one great revolutionary "sell" of modern times.

The Battle of Algiers has a firebrand's fervor; it carries you with it, and doesn't give you time to think. Since the colonel provides the Marxist ideology of the picture, the revolutionaries are spared any taint of ideology (even though you observe how the N.L.F. leadership serves as a spearhead), and the inevitability of the ultimate victory of revolution is established to your — almost ecstatic — emotional relief. You may even accept the movie's implicit message that the N.L.F.'s violent methods are the only way to freedom. Pontecorvo's inflammatory passion works directly on your feelings, saying that both sides kill in a revolution and that it's unavoidable, saying that the bombs set in a city by revolutionaries — resulting in the death of men and women and children — are regrettable but justified, because this movement toward freedom is natural and unstoppable and good. The special genius of Pontecorvo as a Marxist filmmaker is that, though the masses are the hero, he has a feeling for the beauty and primitive terror in faces, and you're made to care for the oppressed people — to think of them not as masses but as people. Pontecorvo — the most dangerous kind of Marxist, a Marxist poet — shows us the raw strength of the oppressed, and the birth pangs of freedom. He gives us a portrait of a revolution that explains it and justifies whatever is done in its name, and serves as the most impassioned, most astute call to revolution ever. (The film, an Italian and Algerian co-production, is said to be the first feature ever made in Algeria; born in Italy, Gillo Pontecorvo is a younger brother of the famous Bruno Pontecorvo, the atomic physicist, part of Fermi's team, who worked in this country and then at Harwell, and disappeared into Russia in 1950, subsequently winning the Lenin Prize.)

No one has carried "immediacy" farther than Pontecorvo — neither Rossellini, from whose post-Second World War films, such as *Open City* (1945) and *Paisan* (1946), he learned so much, nor Francesco Rosi, who had experimented in a similar direction in *Salvatore Giuliano,* a 1962 political "created documentary" that Franco Solinas worked on. *The Battle of Algiers* is probably the only film that has ever made middle-class audiences believe in the necessity of bombing innocent people — perhaps because Pontecorvo made it a *tragic* necessity. In none of the political melodramas that were to follow from his epic is there any sequence that comes near to the complex overtones of the sorrowful acceptance with which each of the three bomb-planting women looks to see who will be killed by her bomb. Pontecorvo produces these mixed emotions in us and *still* is able to carry most of us with him. I think people's senses are so overwhelmed by the surging inevitability of the action that they are prepared to support what in another context — such as newsprint — they would reject. It's practically rape of the doubting intelligence. In *The Battle of Algiers,* music becomes a form of agitation: at times, the strange percussive sound is like an engine that can't quite start; pounding music gives the audience a sense of impending horror at each critical point; the shrill, rhythmic, birdlike cries from the Casbah tell us that all life is trilling and screaming for freedom.

The Battle of Algiers has been the inspiration for other filmmakers — and they have been influenced by its techniques — but it was Costa-Gavras's *Z,* a French and Algerian co-production, set in Salonika but also shot in Algeria, that updated the brutal American thriller of the forties and put it to new — and easily imitable — political use. Jorge Semprun, who adapted *Z,* had written an earlier political film, *La Guerre Est Finie,* with Yves Montand as a Spanish Communist in exile, but that was reflective, elegiac. *Z* is a victimizers-and-victims crime thriller in which the Greek government is the crime ring — and, despite one's queasiness about the thriller techniques, in its own terms *Z* works. Maybe it works so well because we could respond to the high-pressure urgency of the Greek situation which had dictated the daring method, and also because Costa-Gavras, born in Greece, must have felt that the Lambrakis case (on which the film was based) took place on the blood-and-fear-and-bribery level of corrupt politics — that it was the stuff of conspiratorial thrillers.

Costa-Gavras, the suspense storyteller as investigative journalist, uses the form of melodrama to dramatize political injustice as speedily and vividly as possible, in a way that can't be ignored. But a moviemaker who tries to deal with ongoing political situations antagonizes just about everybody in one way or another (and, when he doesn't provide thrills, bores the rest). Probably the more sensitive he is to the problems the more difficulties he faces — and this seems to be what has been happening with Costa-Gavras. Filmmakers who try to combine serious content with a popular form land in trouble. (*Z* only *feels* like an exception.) When Pontecorvo and Solinas carried their French-colonel idea a step farther, in the historical-adventure film *Burn!,* by having Marlon Brando, as a British *agent provocateur,* embody and express the imperialist manipulative role throughout colonial history, they pushed their brilliant ploy over the edge; this cynical oppressor, so conscious of his role that he seemed to have studied Frantz Fanon, became as unconvincing as the villain in an antique swashbuckler. The message was again that revolution was inevitable and that freedom is worth all the suffering it takes — and, in addition, that black men should never trust white men (a message one hopes blacks will extend to the white men who made the movie) — but the didacticism kept sticking out. Pontecorvo was romantic in *The Battle of Algiers* and it worked; here he became obviously romantic. Costa-Gavras is a less gifted artist — his talents appear to be rather shallow — but he's probably a more thoughtful man. He moved away from explosive, morally questionable technique in *The Confession,* and then, moving back — though only part way — in *State of Siege,* with a script by Solinas (Semprun, his collaborator on *Z* and *The Confession,* being busy on *The French Conspiracy*), he was caught in several splits.

At the outset of *State of Siege,* Costa-Gavras worked up so much ingratiating comedy and ominous excitement about the mechanical details of how the Tupamaros (urban guerrillas in Uruguay) kidnapped some officials that those who were turned on felt let down and bored when the film got into its subject — the political meaning of these kidnappings and a demonstration of the why and how of terrorism. For American audiences, the crux of the demonstration was our complicity in the repression that brought on the terrorism. According to the film, Santore, the character Montand plays — which is based on Dan Mitrione, the American A.I.D. official executed by the Tupamaros — was there as a police technician training the native police in torture and counter-revolution. *State of Siege* had a mixed form, and the part of the audience that enjoyed the early action didn't care for the rest, and vice versa. And it had a mixed consciousness, too: the picture succeeds in most of its political intentions — despite those who complained that it was "tiresome" (as one TV reviewer called it), it broke through public indifference to Latin American affairs — but emotionally it doesn't add up right. I think that Solinas is using the unprincipled Santore as he used Jean Martin's colonel and Marlon Brando's *agent provocateur,* to represent imperialism abroad, while Costa-Gavras sees the situation in more specific terms, and perhaps doesn't see the United States' role as so monolithically imperialist throughout Latin America. And Costa-Gavras seems too skeptical to achieve the cumulative power that Solinas is driving toward. Costa-Gavras's theme is justice. He's more tentative than Pontecorvo, perhaps because of his doubts about whether Party-spearheaded movements achieve "freedom." After all, he made *The Confession,* which Solinas has condemned as anti-Communist. Costa-Gavras is full of reservations, and even in the thriller form of *State of Siege,* in which the youthful, idealistic Tupamaros and the old fat-cat government men and businessmen are almost cartoons of good and evil, he presents the political argument on a conscious level. His movies can be as confused as political arguments usually are (and we come out and continue the argument), and so it's easy to pick quarrels with him — and easy to disparage the films because of those quarrels.

Pontecorvo celebrates the proletarian strength of Third World faces; the Algerians and the black slaves in *Burn!* are figures of love and nobility. When he needs to introduce some French troops in *The Battle of Algiers,* the documentary texture falls apart and everything looks set up; the French who man the roadblocks are well handled, but they leave no imprint on one's memory. Pontecorvo's passion vitalizes the scenes of oppressed natives and makes the people seem "real" in a way that the French troops aren't "real." In *Burn!* the treatment of the colonial masters and the mulattoes who side with them is as stilted and visually dead as in a standard swashbuckler. We respond emotionally to the revolutionary message in Pontecorvo's films because even his erotic-aesthetic sense is unified with his revolutionary purpose. Costa-Gavras, not a poet of the masses and hence not an ideal collaborator for Solinas, has a respect for those consciously caught in political dilemmas, even if they're middle-class or professional people, and a respect and sympathy for ineffectual people. It's no accident that Montand, with his sagging, tired face, is Costa-Gavras's hero, and is used even for Santore-Mitrione; that game but already defeated face is the key to the mood. In Costa-Gavras's films, people talk politics. In Pontecorvo's films, people talk history; that is, destiny. Costa-Gavras makes melodramas with thin characters, but he works on the pragmatic short-run political situation as he sees it, and his melodramas are tragic. Pontecorvo works on the visionary's long run and makes heroic epics — triumphant, blinding, incendiary myths.

THE WORLD OF POLITICAL MOVIES has been incestuous — partly, I imagine, because some committed actors have been eager to work on these projects, and partly because the actors could confer their own movie backgrounds on the shorthand storytelling methods of these fast, complicated, information-packed thrillers. The actors have commuted from one revolutionary situation to another, and to other kinds of political films, and to commercial thrillers. *The French Connection* borrowed its villain, Marcel Bozzuffi, from *Z; The Day of the Jackal* took for its right-wing Algerian agent Jean Martin, the French colonel of *The Battle of Algiers; The Inheritor* put Charlès Denner in a role similar to the one he'd played in *Z;* and so on. *The French Conspiracy,* directed by Yves Boisset, raids them all — the borrowers and the originals. It is a colossal job of vandalism. In a sense, it does what Hollywood did in the late forties and early fifties: after the Italian neo-realists had shot their films on the streets, Hollywood "discovered" the documentary look and shot cloak-

and-dagger movies on location. What *The French Conspiracy* does is what that television reviewer who was bored by *State of Siege* really wanted. *Z*, by its success in combining thrills and politics, worked against Costa-Gavras when he attempted the morally more complex *The Confession* and *State of Siege*; some of the audience now regards a political film as a failure if it isn't as thrilling as *Z*. *The French Conspiracy* separates the thrills from the politics. That is, it uses the politics as a stage set for the thrills, and it uses all those other political thrillers as part of the stage set. The Ben Barka kidnapping, which took place in Paris in 1965, also figured in the events dramatized in *The Battle of Algiers*, and Boisset simulates the sense of urgency of *Z*; the score (a muddy hype) is by Ennio Morricone, who did the hypes for *Sacco and Vanzetti* and *Investigation of a Citizen Above Suspicion*; Jorge Semprun is one of the writers (the script is almost worthy of Trumbo); Jean-Louis Trintignant, the investigator of *Z*, is the journalist caught in the plot here; Jean Bouise, from *Z* and *The Confession* and *La Guerre Est Finie*, is the vicious cop; Michel Piccoli, from *La Guerre Est Finie*, is the political villain; François Périer, the public prosecutor from *Z*, is the Paris chief of police. And in the middle of this echo chamber there's the great Left hero-star, Volonte, burning with indignation and revolutionary fervor. The actors bring so many associations that it's almost a satire: Trintignant twists his face to look cowardly, and grimaces at Jean Seberg's glazed, inexpressive, non-actress face, while Michel Bouquet twitches his pursed lips and connives with Philippe Noiret. All the film's energy must have gone into meeting the payroll.

It's got everything and everybody, and it's totally empty — not just because Boisset is a mediocre director, and not just because the concentration of attention on the high-level plotters turns the movie into silly melodrama, but because it has no real political content. One can forgive a political thriller a lack of thrills if the picture has something to say. (By now, many of us may prefer the absence of thrills — the razzle-dazzle beginning of *State of Siege* was a little insulting, a lollipop offered to the audience.) But when politics becomes decorative — when revolutionary heroes are used because they're commercially à la mode — then the filmmaker has to be a damned good director to hack it. If you haven't anything to say, you sure as hell better know how to say it. *The French Conspiracy* hasn't and doesn't.

[November 19, 1973]

Humanoids and Androgynes

What counts in sci-fi movies (and what makes a sci-fi movie a classic) is the gimmicky, eerie metaphor — the disguised form of the thing you fear, or are set off by. The special effects necessary for the working out of the metaphor have often proved to be the most fun, since the actors in sci-fi have almost always been stiffs. (The stories rarely depend on character, so a good actor can be so uncomfortable that he looks worse than an untrained muscle man.) The lavishness and the imaginative skill of the special effects can be innocently, charmingly magical, and the robots (Robby in *Forbidden Planet*, Hal, the computer in *2001*, the drones in *Silent Running*) have come to have more personality than the people. Since the early fifties, however, the dominant metaphor has been a spreading cancer — a "monstrous mutation." Sci-fi of this type could be low-budget; the directors could get by without the technicians they couldn't afford, because the idea was to set the movies in the indefinite near future and to have the green slime or the fifty-foot ants or the moth the size of a 747 in an everyday environment. The film might not look like much, but the suggestive idea could carry it, and if the movie was given a cautionary angle (blaming the heads of state or the scientists for making this expanding horror *possible*), the frugality of the moviemaking could be neatly turned to account. Thrift could pass for realism (though I don't know who was really fooled). In other kinds of sci-fi, thrift can be more crippling.

Michael Crichton's *Westworld* is a moderately entertaining sci-fi film; its major disadvantage is that Crichton's idea is — potentially — too ingenious for what he was able to do with it. This was the first time he'd got a chance to direct his own material, and from the pulped TV-movie look of *Westworld* you can tell it was a shoestring operation. His parody idea (based on Disneyland and its successors) is of an amusement center, called Delos, where vacationing adults go to act out their movie-fed dreams, and this requires a larger scale; it's not that Delos shouldn't be tacky and ordinary — that is certainly part of the satirical point — but that there isn't enough movie. Although you can have a fairly good time at *Westworld* (if you don't expect too much), you can see that everything has been skimped and that the idea hasn't been fully developed. If ever there was a movie that provided opportunities for great Pop Art set designs (such as parodies of the art work of De Mille's spectacles), this is it. But *Westworld* was one of the last films made at M-G-M before James Aubrey, its president, and Kirk Kerkorian, its chief stockholder, shut down most of the shop, having put the company's assets into the completion of a hundred-million-dollar M-G-M Las Vegas Grand Hotel (an almost sinful act, like making guns out of plowshares).

Westworld combines the live-out-your-fantasies vacationland with the robots-that-rebel theme. For a thousand dollars a day, vacationers at Delos can have their choice of Romanworld, Medievalworld, or Westworld — total environments simulating past ages, with computer-programmed humanoids to satisfy the guests' vanity and lust and aggression. Richard Benjamin and James Brolin have a fine time whoring and brawling and shooting up strangers in Westworld — a Western town of the eighteen-eighties — until the humanoids get tired of the victimization and begin to fight back. Yul Brynner, with frosted blue eyes, is the humanoid gunslinger, dressed in black, who has been killed by dudes like Benjamin and Brolin too often and takes his turn to kill. The idea of Brynner as a strutting robot killer is very funny — coming, as it does, after years of his playing just that. Brynner's implacable manly waddle — his muscular chest shifting from side to side in unvarying rhythm, as if to a metronome's beat, while he stalks Benjamin — is both frightening and satiric.

Michael Crichton isn't enough of a director yet to control the nuances, so we can't be sure if he means to say that everyone at Delos is a robot — that the guests, with their canned, movie-spawned, computer-satisfied fantasies, are just as robotized as the humanoids — or if that's the effect we get because of the poor characterization of the guests. And it's a weakness of the movie that we don't see more of how vacationers use the robots, so that we'd get the robots' side. The picture is a little cold, since we don't like either the robots or the people, but Richard Benjamin knows how to involve an audience in his adolescent fantasies (that's always been his specialty), and he's a vast improvement over the usual sci-fi hero. However, the best comic possibilities in Crichton's idea depend on character, and character creation is the defining weakness of science-fiction and other pulp genres. There are little bits of humor and overheards (a computer engineer saying, "I don't know what to do if the stagecoach is late"), and there are neat effects, such as our seeing Benjamin through Brynner's gridlike, infrared vision. But there are too few characters, too few flourishes. Essentially, Delos turns adults back into children by protecting them; the robots' revolt explodes the childishness of this. We want particulars — vacationers killed in specific ways as a reprisal for thinking they could act out their fantasies without danger. For the film's metaphor to move us, we must feel the consumer folly of this vacation plan and the classic, poetic justice of the humanoid revolt, which puts the danger back in — it's a re-establishment of the reality principle. The film is O.K., but it might have been marvelous. The budget for the twenty sets built for the picture was seventy-seven thousand dollars — couldn't Aubrey at least have gone out in glory? He cashed in M-G-M in order to complete that gamblers' Grand Hotel, which is really an extension of Delos based on dreams of avarice.

❖

An isolated Wiltshire farm in the nineteen-forties; an ailing old dog; a lonely woman (Glenda Jackson), the wife of a prisoner of war; and a young conscript (Brian Deacon) who wanders through and — after being given two eggs and a friendly cup of tea — returns to help out around the place. "Sounds like he's got that old tractor going," the woman says cheerily to the wheezing dog, and, sure enough, the soldier beds down with her. Abysmally sprightly music tells us how idyllic their life is, and the soldier goes AWOL and works the farm. Eventually, he takes a shotgun and puts the dog out of its misery, and later, when he is caught and is being horribly beaten, the woman uses the shotgun on him. Everyone is put out of his misery but the audience. *Triple Echo,* adapted from one of H. E. Bates' novels (the script reeks of serious pulp) and directed by Michael Apted, is a gnawing reminder of what the low-budget "different" English film of 1937 went in for. Pastoral tragedy. It's the sort of movie you're supposed to give points to for stark honesty — for the rag-mop realism that nobody enjoys. (Did we need that closeup of the two eggs?) But probably the only thing that keeps anybody in his seat who has anyplace else to go is waiting for the transvestite gimmick (which one has been tipped to) to arrive.

In order to hide her AWOL lover, the farm woman dresses him in women's clothes and pretends he's her sister, and the gimmick is that he begins to dig it. Spiky-thin Glenda Jackson, who speaks as if she were biting on a bullet, is more masculine here than he is even as a man; her androgynous performance gives the movie an extra dimension of sexual ambiguity that is nowhere dealt with. (When you see the shy soldier in frilly clothes and padded breasts, you wonder whom he's imitating.) The bucolic setting and the earnest acting tell you that the boring gentle mood is going to ripen into tragedy, and meanwhile you sit there waiting for the ludicrous situation to get more so. Finally, Oliver Reed, a no-neck bullying brute of a sergeant, turns up and makes his play for Sister. Glenda rages jealously while Sister agrees to be Reed's date for the Christmas ball at the barracks. "I need a bit of fun," Sister announces, lunatically. When Reed tries to deflower his pseudo-virginal date at the big ball, the tragedy winds itself up mercifully fast.

Oliver Reed has an alarming gift for sadistic monsters, as he demonstrated with his Bill Sikes in *Oliver!* He's willing to go all the way with obscene ugliness. His bullfrog face has never been so lewd and hugely plump as in *Triple Echo,* and it *is* funny to watch his salacious sparring with gritty Glenda Jackson, doing her cracker act, though Reed, speaking in an insinuating whisper, is at least half inaudible. Maybe he decided he could do better by the lines if we didn't hear them; his lecherous face is dirtier than his dirty jokes could ever be. Reed here has a little of the surreal aggressive humor of a Don Rickles: gross and hostile, yet funny. He gives the picture its only snap. The brutal beating that the soldier-sister gets from the sergeant and his men may make this film some sort of masochistic gay-liberation classic — if anybody goes to see it — though the soldier's stupidity (after his sexual identity is discovered he runs right back to the farm, where the sergeant will be sure to find him) makes one so impatient with the unconvincing plotting that one's response is no more than a chortle.

Glenda Jackson showed a phenomenal talent when she played the lead in the TV six-part series *Elizabeth R.* The short series — perhaps the only admirable innovation in drama on TV — gives a performer a chance to develop a character over a larger span than the usual play. In this case, it was like a play times six; it was a true test of an actress's range, and she passed it. Why, then, is she so familiarly grating here? She's been in movies only since 1967; it's too soon for us to know her every trick, yet she's as easy to imitate as Bette Davis. Maybe the attempt to give something to a nothing role brings out this unnecessary tension in her voice and body; it could be that she's so determined not to be conventionally smily-sweet that she looks daggers. (In *A Touch of Class,* under a load of glamour-girl makeup and a suspiciously unvarying hairdo, her acrid performance was ridiculous; she was like a mean drag queen.) Glenda Jackson's tough, almost perverse independence is probably what gives her sex appeal; she uses nastiness as an open-eyed come-on. Whatever the role, she's a woman without small talk; she attracts by the sturdiness of her level, appraising gaze — a no-nonsense woman. One imagines that the young Lillian Hellman of *Pentimento* might have been challenging like this. But Glenda Jackson is constricted in *Triple Echo;* she has no ease or expansiveness — she bristles all the time. In *Elizabeth R,* she had a formidable assignment and she trusted to instinct (that is, to everything she knew) and acted, and she was great.

But when she is cast by directors because she will give a nebulous role definition, she thinks it out consciously and we see her thinking — and my guess is that she's always thinking the same things. This may link back to her work with Peter Brook; she seems to program herself to be constantly hyper-conscious. It's this that makes her so clenched and hard on the screen; when she thinks, she overarticulates feeling and she begins to seem like a caricature.

HAROLD PINTER'S MANNERED, floating ominousness has been used to tone up many movies (it was at its most effective in his script for *Accident*), but his own plays — *The Caretaker, The Birthday Party,* and now, in the American Film Theatre's subscription series, *The Homecoming* — transfer to film badly. As a scriptwriter, he tailors his work to the medium, but our having seen so many movies he worked on adds to our awareness of the Pinter manner. (The ugly sex-orgy scene here is like the orgy in *The Servant.*) The true fault in *The Homecoming,* I believe, is in the original material, but when it's presented on the stage the tensions bounce around, and one can respond to the actors' relish in their roles — the roles are actors' dreams (unfortunately, that's all they are) — while on the screen the material is so lethally *set* that Pinter sounds Pinteresque. I'm a little afraid to say it (the specter of philistinism hovers over criticism of Pinter), but, really, this movie comes across as very corny-tricky and cheaply theatrical — with cryptic reversals of attitude, and sudden outbreaks of violence and sex, plus a coronary and some unspecified sort of seizure. And the attitudes are cheap: Michael Jayston, smiling a tiny tight smile, plays the philosophy professor who, accompanied by his wife, Ruth (Vivien Merchant), returns from America to visit his cockney family. The role is none other than that old standby of middlebrow theater — the prissy, unfeeling, vaguely impotent intellectual. Jayston — the pinched-face Czar of *Nicholas and Alexandra* and the dim husband whom Mia Farrow returned to in *The Public Eye* (I rooted for her to go off with Topol) — is so wizened and infantile he's practically a Harry Langdon. I have no idea what Jayston is meant to be doing; in the original Broadway production, directed by Peter Hall — who also did the London version and this film — the conception (Michael Craig played the part) made some kind of psychological sense. Here it's merely bizarre. Stoic Ruth, the one woman in this archetypal-rancorous-family play, is mother-wife-whore and, of course, is sphinx-like — the ultimate, controlling mystery of life. We got rid of "everyman"; are we to drag "everywoman" around forever? Paul Rogers is the domineering father, Cyril Cusack (replacing John Normington, who did it on the stage) the weak uncle, Ian Holm the satanic put-on-artist pimp, and Terence Rigby dumb Joey. The actors in Pinter must always be *on;* this is what makes Pinter so effective in live performance. But in this movie the actors are all playing so high they cancel out each other's performances. The suggestiveness of the play remains, and some of its charge, and Pinter's idiom, with its wit, though in the movie the language sounds crisped — overcalibrated. The cinematographer David Watkin's lighting effects and compositions are often impressive, but *The Homecoming* seems a very sleek, overwrought melodrama. And embalmed. The oblique, like the sinister, dates fast.

IN "THE ALL-AMERICAN BOY," Jon Voight is a prizefighter suffering from a type of working-class alienation that is indistinguishable from bellyache. He mopes through the picture looking puffy, like a rain cloud about to spritz. Charles Eastman wrote and directed this disgracefully condescending view of America as a wasteland populated by grotesques, stupes, and sons-of-bitches; they are incapable of love and have false values, and to prove it Eastman sets Voight to walking the Antonioni walk. This picture is so full of contempt for its own characters that it tells us nothing about them — and far more than we want to know about Eastman. (His sister wrote *Five Easy Pieces*; alienation seems to run in the family.) The one thing I will remember from this movie — because it hits a new high-low in showy intellectuality — is Eastman's scoring a sequence of boxers working out in a California gym to a Gregorian chant. There are some good performers here (such as Carol Androsky), who are made to look so bad that they practically have grounds for suit.

ILLUSION-AND-REALITY GAMES on the screen pall on me faster than just about anything else, and I found *Some Call It Loving* unwatchable, in much the same way that *A Safe Place,* of a couple of years ago, was. *Some Call It Loving* was adapted from a John Collier story, and it shouldn't really be as lifeless as it is, but James B. Harris, who produced and directed, also wrote the blandly dreamy screenplay, and to say that he is not a writer is to put it more gently than he deserves. His dialogue is so plodding that the bubble never gets off the ground. The plot of this enigmatic romantic fantasy in soft-focus photography is something or other about a jazz-musician prince (Zalman King) who buys a sleeping beauty, Jennifer (Tisa Farrow), from a carnival and takes her home to his folly-castle, which is presided over by wicked Scarlett (Carol

White). King smiles to himself ambiguously; whether this is meant to be compassion or distaste, who can say? Tisa Farrow's little-girl thing isn't naughty and appealing, like her sister Mia's, and her baby-girl zombie voice is plain amateurish. Richard Pryor turns up briefly as an amiable, stoned-crazy musician, which is a relief, because at least we know (and he knows) why he's acting high, while the others are mysteriously out of it. Everyone in the picture seems to be sleepwalking, and the director, too. Harris made *The Bedford Incident,* and it was a clean and efficient job of direction, but this drowsy whimsey about enchantment and dreamers has no dream logic, so the fantasies have no resonance; there's nothing to sustain interest. The duration of the film is like an eternity spent with the willfully retarded.

[November 26, 1973]

Strawberry Jam

HAVEN'T WE SUFFERED ENOUGH with Joanne Woodward? Proficient, intensely likable actress though she is, ever since *Rachel, Rachel* she's been turning into the educated people's Lana Turner. Her movies are beginning to overlap, and she keeps the same lump in her throat. While I was seeing *Summer Wishes, Winter Dreams,* I wanted to be somewhere else; I didn't want to be stuck at this level of sensibility — this dun-colored earnestness about what-happened-to-my-life-where-did-I-go-wrong. Grindingly mediocre, *Summer Wishes, Winter Dreams* is about middle-aged self-reproach, about coldness and unfulfillment and regrets. Everything is spelled out; it's *Come Back, Little Sheba* without the lost dog, and I never thought I'd miss that dog so much. William Inge always put in some frail, sad-eyed lyric touch, some homely, misshapen magic; Stewart Stern, who wrote *Summer Wishes, Winter Dreams* for Woodward (he had adapted *Rachel, Rachel* for her), is too smooth and moist for that, and his psychiatrically oriented sensitivity has just the shape you expect. The picture made me feel as if I'd been buttonholed by a bore — an exhibitionistic bore who was whipping up a batch of stale emotions and bogus goodwill for want of anything better to do. It's the same feeling I get when I read Anne Roiphe's pieces in the *Times Maga-*

zine. In an article about the P.B.S. series *An American Family,* Mrs. Roiphe wrote, "The Louds are enough like me and mine to create havoc in my head, and I had to fight a constant strong desire to push away those Louds, dismiss them as unique, empty, shallow, unlike others, and yet on serious reflection, we can all learn from them, perhaps just enough to begin understanding that saddest of mysteries, the American family." Stern has the same nakedly heartfelt tone — compassion by the yard. "That saddest of mysteries, the American family" is the soft-headed subject of this movie, too. *Summer Wishes, Winter Dreams* was made by people who believe in it, I guess, but what is it that they believe in? Probably in the need to say something truthful about ordinary lives — that is, about "real people," as distinguished from the people in Hollywood's escapist entertainment — but what Stern and the director, Gilbert Cates, and, yes, the star, Woodward, take to be "real people" are shriveled versions of people: people reduced to a few traits, and then given a big scene or two so that they can surprise us with their humanity.

Structurally, the movie is a barefaced reworking of *Wild Strawberries,* with an excerpt from the Ingmar Bergman movie used the way a student writing an essay sometimes includes a quote from a published work in order to salve his conscience about paraphrasing it. In Bergman's film, an aged, very eminent physician has a dream in which he is being pulled into his grave, and then, journeying to receive an honorary degree, he revisits his past both in dream and by returning to his old home, and he sees his failures and the damage his cold heart has done. That damage — and the dawning of understanding — is always a popular theme in the movies, the theater, and best-seller fiction. *Wild Strawberries* had the appeal of a secular sermon: it said, "Be warm, love one another." Actually, Victor Sjöström had more feeling in his great, heavy face than anyone around him, and Professor Borg's "coldness" looked a facile, fraudulent issue. The crimes marshaled against him — his failing to reach out to the girl he loved, failing to love the woman he married, failing to give his son affection — seemed no more than conventional setups. But the film was impressive and successful, and, just as *The French Connection* has spawned a batch of movies about cops, *Wild Strawberries* has had its progeny — *Five Easy Pieces* and now this maudlin, semi-serious look at the American woman as snow queen.

Woodward's Rita is given no split between public accomplishments and private failures, but she goes through the same setups as Professor Borg. She's a Manhattan *Hausfrau,* bundled in mink, who walks in a perky dogtrot and — a coy touch — loves strawberry jam. The death of her brassy old harridan mother (Sylvia Sidney) brings out her guilts and regrets, and she breaks down. Visiting the old family farm, she has a vision of the farm boy (now dead) whom she once loved; she dreams about her rejected son (Ron Rickards), who has fled the family; she hallucinates seeing her mother ahead of her on an escalator, beckoning her toward death; and we observe her giving short shrift to her married daughter (Dori Brenner) and repelling the advances of the patient, adoring man she married and has never loved (Martin Balsam). Apparently, after that adolescent romance Rita never met a man who attracted her; she's been in cold storage ever since, and she's spent twenty-four years rejecting her husband's despondent, foolish advances. This is another of the sob stories about middle-aged women which are generated by the needs of middle-aged actresses. Woodward has been precipitate about it, plunging ahead as if she couldn't wait. Sometimes, here, she underplays for a flat-out, put-on humor that is quietly effective, but this is the only distinctive element in a too easily felt performance. Rita is the least vital of Woodward's afflicted women. We observe Rita thinking about what a flop she is, thinking of her cipher's life and the wreckage around her. And Woodward stays in character. God, how she stays in character. All the actors do; they stay cramped in their normal-person corsets the way actors sometimes get locked into historical characters — operating on a narrow preconception and working within a piddlingly small range. It's like the acting in sudsers except that within the narrow limits they're genuinely trying for depth. They try to give us average men and women in depth, but their concept of "average" precludes depth. What they give us instead is actors' sincerity — banality persisted in, under the illusion that banality is the truth of average lives.

"Is Lance the true American son?" Anne Roiphe asked, and though the only answer to this soapy rhetoric is to hoot, this is exactly the kind of psychosexual punditry Stern subscribes to. Unloving Rita is given a homosexual son and a fat daughter. Living clichés. I use the term that Abigail McCarthy applied to the Louds as they were presented to us by the show's producer, Craig Gilbert, whose intentions were probably very close to Stern's. In the most clear-cut writing I've seen on *An American Family*, in *The Atlantic* of July, 1973, Mrs. McCarthy summarized how the Louds came across: "They seem to embody the trite generalizations about the American family grown familiar by repetition in popular psychology and sociology. They are affluent. They are uninvolved. They live beyond their means and for appearances. The parents are in classic middle-aged crisis. The father, Bill Loud (who reminded more than one observer of Willy Loman, in *Death of a Salesman*), faces the downhill path to death, not having made it as he had hoped and neither at ease with nor content with his family. Loud resorts to alcohol and infidelity. The mother, at the peak of her physical maturity, faces an empty nest and empty years, is aware of betrayal and unused potentialities." With a few minor changes (the ophthalmologist husband here is too meek to stray), that might be a summary of *Summer Wishes, Winter Dreams.* Essentially, what Stern has done is to put Pat Loud at the center of *Wild Strawberries.* The triteness in *Summer Wishes, Winter Dreams* is not drawn from life. (It wasn't in *An American Family,* either, as Mrs. McCarthy documented: "Before they were ever found, the members of the family of the series were limited, prejudged, categorized.") The triteness comes out of the same pot that Craig Gilbert and Mrs. Roiphe dip into. The hit TV series *The Waltons* is set in the thirties and features a family of Waspy plaster saints presided over by a mothering bucket of slop; in a recent article, Mrs. Roiphe said that she *aches* with wanting *The Waltons* to be true, and that Mrs. Walton is "the mother we all wish we had . . . the mother we all would like to be." That sounds just like tearful Rita talking.

Rita the failure is made out to be the victim of some sort of American pestilence, and the appeal of Rita's and her husband's crushed, defeated condition to those who did the film and to those who respond to it must be like the appeal of the Louds, who were also made out to be victims. ("I thought," Craig Gilbert said, "that I might find out what was happening between man and woman in this crazy country.") Rita is a mottled, drab character — the heroine of a dirge. Unlike Professor Borg's failures, which were his own, hers are given a generalized, swollen significance. The movie is confused (and possibly less than honest) in its attitude toward her; it plays double games — giving her classically fouled-up children as the consequence of her frigidity, and then shifting to the updated line that the son's homosexuality is O.K. and her problem is that she can't accept it. So she's blamed for feeling guilty about what the film has already indicated she is indeed guilty of. Rita's ferociously tough mother has been put in the film to account for Rita's inability to love, but responsibility stops at an arbitrary point, because Rita's husband, ashen-faced from all that rejection but still a rock of sympathy, assures her that their son's and daughter's troubles aren't her fault. But if they're *not,* what is the picture about? The answer, I fear, is "life." We're meant to think "Life failed her" and "She failed life" — Stern is playing Ping-Pong with mothballs. The picture might have been written by a blackmailing child who says, "I feel sorry for you, Mama, even after what you did to me."

A few years ago, when white middle-class kids started taking drugs, the media gave us movies and TV plays in which the drug takers were shown to have cold, unloving parents. *Summer Wishes, Winter Dreams* is the same sort of problem drama, in a more ambitious yet more vacillating version. It equates the American woman's supposed incapacity for love with the whole American screwup of recent years, but never shows us the connection. *Summer Wishes, Winter Dreams* was originally to be called *Death of a Snow Queen,* and it's like a woman's version of *Death of a Salesman.* With its bewildered, defeated people, its Jewish-family locutions, its big cemetery scene featuring quarrelsome, avaricious relatives, and its generalized accusatory tone, it has many similarities to that masterpiece of loose connections. In *Salesman,* when the wife — speaking in the authentic cadence of the editorial page — said, "Attention must be finally paid," what in Yahweh's name did Arthur Miller mean? What did Willy Loman's life signify?

In this movie's terms, Rita represents the American dream betrayed. That's what Willy Loman was also taken to signify, and that's the way many people took the Loud family, too. These people didn't want to analyze how the method shaped the content of *An American Family*; they wanted to mope over that display of emptiness and be discouraged and upset about it. The famous philistine remark about *Death of a Salesman* — "That New England territory never was any good" — is so funny because by taking the material at a literal level it punctures the emotional balloon. *Summer Wishes* doesn't have the power of *Salesman,* but it's full of gas. Does anyone really believe that if Rita had been madly in love with her superhumanly patient husband and been avid for sex, the spiritual state of this country would be any different? The snow queen is such a tired whipping girl. (Is there even any reason to think that frigid mothers produce more homosexual sons and fat daughters than red-hot mamas do, or is it maybe that some sensitive men writers like to believe that their beautiful mothers never enjoyed going to bed with their plodding fathers?) I wasn't convinced that the movie dealt with the sources of middle-aged crisis — or that it even got near the terror of decay and death. Bergman, in his Gothic, primitive way, did. But this is tame strawberries.

Those who can swallow this gluey jam may also be capable of believing that the Walton family is the ideal to aspire to. What Rita longs for (the farm boy of her youth; the fulfillment of the hopes a teacher once had for her) comes right out of the fake nostalgia of *The Waltons* — fake because it's a nostalgia not for an earlier period of American life but for an earlier period of media schlock. And the film's projected resolution — the melting of the snow queen after she learns to accept her son — says just what *The Waltons* does: that all problems can be solved by warmth and understanding. Television has made many of us dangerously forgiving — but forgiving enough to accept the banalizing of our ideals? Where do these writers get their infantile notions of "the American dream"? What Rita wants to be, and what the picture says she should be — Mother Walton, with arms outstretched and every pore open — is much worse than what she is.

[December 10, 1973]

The Hero as Freak

WHAT COULD BE A MORE APPROPRIATE SUBJECT for a 1973 movie than the ordeal of Frank Serpico, the New York City policeman who became a pariah in the Department because he wouldn't take bribes? Serpico, whose incorruptibility alienates him from his fellow-officers and turns him into a messianic hippie freak, is a perfect modern-movie hero; *Serpico* is a far from perfect movie, but there are probably few who will care about its technical crudities or the frequent slovenliness of the staging. The theme is richly comic: Reacting against the brutality and bribe-taking and hypocrisy of the Police Department, Serpico moved to the Village, let his hair grow, changed his style, and began to costume himself as an outcast. Considered a weirdo because he believed in the oath of office he'd sworn to, he began to act the weirdo; since he could no longer talk with the other officers in any way that made sense to him, he became a put-on artist. The put-on is the paranoid's favorite form of joking: who can say what he believes and what he doesn't, or if he himself knows? Serpico wasn't just playing a nut — he was becoming one. We have no word, as yet, for justifiable paranoia — that is, for the sane person's perception of a world become crazily menacing — and in terms of behavior there may not be much difference between living in terror of actual enemies and living in terror of imaginary enemies, particularly if the actual enemies represent the whole system of authority. When Serpico tried to reach higher-ups within the Department in order to report on the links of crime and vice and the drug traffic with the police, he discovered that the higher-ups were part of the criminal system, and when he went to outside agencies and to the Mayor's office, he couldn't get any action, either. But he became a marked man: brushed off and balked at every turn, he was an informer in the midst of the New York City Police Department. He was *considered* an informer; actually, he couldn't find anyone to inform to — no one would act on his information. He was like Kafka's Joseph K., living in terror in the midst of bureaucratized criminality, where the irrational has become the ordinary. That's the story of Serpico — except, of course, that he and an officer who had a contact at the *Times* and a police inspector willing to give corroborative evidence finally broke the scandal, the Knapp Commission was formed, and police heads rolled, in one of the largest shakeups in American police history. It's a superlative story-legend, combining Judas and Jesus in one small, wiry figure, who sacrificed his career and his health and lost his girl, but who survived and is, despite the bullet fragments he carries in his head, probably a stronger man because of what he went through.

The movie, adapted from the Peter Maas book by Waldo Salt and Norman Wexler, and directed by Sidney Lumet, is a hugely successful entertainment; it's a hit, no question about it — a big, big hit — and I can't imagine anyone, except some thousands of cops, not enjoying it, and it's so energetic and funny it might carry even them to laughter. *Serpico* doesn't have a full, satisfying narrative development, like *The Godfather:* it's more like a Tom and Jerry cartoon of Serpico's career, with the people and issues so simplified they seem exaggerated. When you think it over, you may miss a fuller development, particularly of Serpico's agitated character, but while you're seeing the movie the story itself and the fresh central figure, played by Al Pacino, and the pungent dialogue (never has a cast wrung so many meanings out of one four-letter word, and I don't mean "love") seem just about enough. Yet we never fully empathize with Pacino's Serpico — never imagine what it might be like to live in a snare, constantly apprehensive, and frustrated at every turn — because his situation is played not for the horror in the comedy but, rather, for a put-down of the society. The film keeps us in the position of the knowing; it's the way Mort Sahl might tell the story — making Serpico a poor schnook who didn't know what everybody else knew. Conceivably, greater artists could have put us right inside Serpico's paranoia, trying to cling to our sanity and experiencing the loner's panic as a dizzyingly sly joke. (That's how Kafka affects readers.) What has been done in the film is great fun, but it's a single-note joke, and there's no pain in it. What the film didn't do might have been tragicomic and reverberant — a true howl.

We don't get a clear view of Serpico as a rookie, to see in what ways he was different from the other rookies, and we are never brought to identify with his year-in-year-out doggedness; we merely observe it, and so it's easy to enjoy the humor in his situation when he's hated and isolated and lives fuming in rage. Pacino's poker face and offhand, fast throwaways keep the character remote; this Serpico is spry and laconic, and though we're always on his side, we're as far outside him as we would be if Groucho were playing the part. Groucho comes to mind because Pacino's tilted walk goes even farther down than Groucho's; he's practically at a forty-five-degree angle to the sidewalk, and I'm not sure what keeps him on his feet. Pacino's walk has finally found a character. It's as if Serpico couldn't straighten up, because he was physically locked in his obsession; his crazy pusher-saint look becomes a cartoon of his state of mind. Pacino doesn't seem to have the moral conviction that would make us take the character seriously, but he's charming and brisk as the seething master of the put-on except for one blot on his performance: he is often indistinguishable from Dustin Hoffman. He uses a high, nasal voice and wrangling New York speech, and as he got longer-haired and more bearded, I began to lose track of who it was under the foliage; there were scenes in which I actually thought I was watching Hoffman, and had to remind myself that it was Pacino. (If this shaggy, covered-in-hair look becomes the newest thing, we won't know who anybody is; it will be like living inside the *Duck Soup* mirror routine.) Pacino didn't turn into Hoffman in *The Godfather*, but Coppola, who directed that, probably exercises much more control over his actors than Lumet, whom many actors love to work with because he lets them do what they want. Without much guidance, and with a short shooting schedule and a character who's written to be played on the surface, Pacino must have fallen back on hero-worship of Hoffman.

Once again, Lumet brought a picture in ahead of schedule, although scene after ragged scene cried out for retakes. "He completed the film in ten weeks and one day — incredible, considering the logistics," the publicity boasts, as if making a film were a race and the speedy Lumet the champ. He wins the prize this time, because the cynical, raw, but witty script is right for him and he gives the material the push it needs. But, except for Pacino, almost all the casting seems aberrant, and the actors playing smaller roles — there are around thirty of them — suffer, since they can't direct themselves and work out a conception when they're on for only a scene or two. In some cases, actors with good reputations, such as Lewis J. Stadlen, come off abominably; and Barbara Eda-Young, making her movie début as Laurie, the nurse who loves Serpico but can't stand the pressure of his flare-ups, is given the worst lines in the film and allowed to emote as if she were in a different sort of vehicle altogether — she's chewing the wrong scenery. Visually, the movie is unpleasantly harsh — it might have been lighted for a police lineup. The music — the first score for an American picture by Mikis Theodorakis — is incongruous and is used disastrously; the tunes may be Italian, but the instrumentation sounds Greek, and why this metallic-sounding folksy music is rattling on while Serpico is testifying before the Knapp Commission I can't imagine — unless it's insultingly assumed that no one is interested in what he's saying.

The movie retains Peter Maas's spotty narrative: the episodes are flashbacks from the shooting of Serpico, even though that shooting isn't central to the main theme. Waldo Salt wrote the first script, and his general outline has been followed, but the rowdy spirit and the dry, wacked-out humor come from Norman Wexler, a former advertising man and political speech-writer, best known for *Joe* (and for his arrest for idly remarking on a plane that he was going to shoot Nixon). Wexler and John Avildsen, who directed *Joe* and was to have done *Serpico,* went to Switzerland and lived with Serpico, and, for an intense week high up in the mountains, they all worked on it together. It was to have been a labor of mad love, but Avildsen got into disagreements with the executive producer, Dino De Laurentiis, and was replaced by Lumet, who thus came into the biggest commercial picture of his career. Probably it wouldn't have been very different if Avildsen had made it; the picture has some of the same temperament as *Joe.* Wexler's talent, which is a little like Terry Southern's, dominates the mood. He writes virulent lowlife dialogue with a demented lift, and Lumet sends the comic scenes across. I remember thinking that Joe, the beady-eyed fascist, had so much audience appeal that he could return as the hero of an animated cartoon ("Joe the Hardhat," "Joe Goes Through Changes," "Joe Grows a Beard," "Joe at the Commune"), and *Serpico* has the same cartoon stridency and the same basic view of this society. The flat-out contempt for most of the characters makes the laughs come fast and easy; the laughter isn't deep or lasting, the way it might have been, but it's good and rude, and there's lots of it. The momentum that builds as Serpico gets more irascible and freakier carries you right up to the last fifteen minutes or so, and then you realize that the picture has set you up to expect more than it will deliver. Wexler and Lumet sacrifice Serpico's story to a cynical, downbeat finish — undermining Serpico's accomplishment by closing on his own sense of disgust with the whole scene.

They have worked toward this all along, not necessarily deliberately but in their attitudes — for example, by showing the corrupt police not as self-hating and miserable or as tormented by guilt and fear (why else would they be so down on Serpico for refusing to be like them?) but simply as crude, rotten villains. Yet one is still unprepared for this dim conclusion, which isn't dramatically sound and isn't sound in historical terms or in plain human terms. Suppose that Serpico didn't really change the system very much, suppose that he only pinked it; nevertheless, he survived, and he demonstrated to rookie cops that it was possible to stand up to corruption. The movie leaves out such details from the Maas book as that thirty-five cops wanted to give blood for him the night he was shot; it leaves out the cops who told him they wanted to be straight, like him. The Maas book is a popularizing account of Serpico which practically deifies him, but it also conveys a sense of what his example did for others; it's an account of an authentic hero. Wexler and

Lumet, who enjoy chortling at corruption, are not the kind of men who believe that anything can be done. And so they leave him a broken loner, sitting with his sheepdog — a man who sacrificed everything, and for what? The movie can easily make you feel: for nothing. That's how things are, the ending seems to say, and there's no way to change them; it wasn't even worth trying. The message — as in *Joe* — is that it's all crap. Had Wexler and Lumet been men of greater vision, they might have seen that they could serve Serpico's intransigence and boiling anger — and the dedication and hope for change behind it all — by showing that his survival was in itself a triumph. And, in fact, he did more than survive. Apart from accomplishing what he did (which wasn't everything he hoped for but was something: busting all those high-ranking officers *must* have had repercussions in the behavior of the police force), he learned that busting crooked cops was only a beginning.

Wexler and Lumet have imposed their own careless cynicism on Serpico's life — the last place it belongs. That cynicism goes with the popular new pose about how America is coming apart at the seams and *should* — a pose in which corruption is some sort of retribution for Vietnam and everything else. But if corruption has become a matter of peer pressure and of being part of the team — Peter Maas says that most people who talk to him about Serpico ask, "What was wrong with him?" — that's just what Serpico was fighting. The movie *Serpico,* showing us normal corruption to get a smart laugh of recognition, may be exactly contrary to Serpico's purposes — and not even consciously but because of its exploitative, hip, cynical temperament. Basically, the movie's attitude is like that of the people who think there had to be something the matter with Serpico — who think he had to be crazy to be honest. The wonderful joke of Serpico's life is that he's a winner, and one of the few fighting heroes that the disaffected can accept. The movie is great fun, but — to put it on a moral level — Serpico's crusade becomes Wexler's and Lumet's debauch. They had themselves a ball, and so will the public, but the movie turns this hero into a mere freak, and turns one of the rare hopeful stories of our time into an entertaining downer.

IF ONE LOOKS at a photograph of Frank Serpico, or at the sketch of him on the cover of the Peter Maas book, one sees a much stronger, more worldly face than that of the Christlike Pacino in the movie ads, and Frank Serpico, whom I had coffee with last week, is trim and wily. He's a disgusted man, all right, but he's not a man who has given up, like the character at the end of the movie; he's disgusted because he doesn't feel he's done enough. It's one thing when he says nothing came of his long fight — that's an outraged idealist talking. It's something quite different when the movie says it. What Serpico hoped for was more than a personnel overhaul, and if he is bitter about having accomplished so little, it's because his visceral defiance grew into a fuller understanding and he began to get some perspective on how big the job really is. He's only thirty-seven, and, from his conversation, which is full of ideas and hopes for reorganizing the training of police recruits, it seems very possible that his major effectiveness is yet to come. He said he was sorry that the movie didn't give a sense of the frustration you feel when you're not able to do anything. Although he was referring to most of his eleven years on the police force, it's clear that he still feels frustrated, because he's looking for ways to make changes that go far beyond the scope of the Knapp Commission. He said that in the Police Department "anyone who has anything to say about civil liberties or minorities is considered a weirdo," and that the treatment of minorities is even worse than it is in the brutal episodes shown in the movie. He was angry about one invented bit in the movie — a policeman shoving a black prisoner's face into a toilet bowl. "What was that for?" he asked. I said that it seemed to be the latest thing, since it's done to a white prisoner in another new film, *The Laughing Policeman.* He said, "The truth was so much better. The incident took place in a South Bronx tenement hallway; a couple of policemen were beating a black man, and a little old black lady opened her door a few inches to see what the noise was about. We were in plainclothes, but when she saw us she knew what we were and exactly what was going on — and she closed the door."

Serpico went on, "I'm really down on cops. Whatever the ratio of dishonest to honest, it's the dishonest who rule, because they go all the way up to the top. Pat Murphy couldn't do anything, because he'd been a member of the Department too long; a man like Ramsey Clark could have done it. The police are always saying, 'It's not our fault, it's the public.' This has to be corrected. Cops don't have the right kind of training. The whole system of values has to be overhauled. You ought to be involved in how many people you can keep out of trouble, not how many you can arrest." My impression was that Serpico is desperate to do something, but that perhaps he still harbors that old sad dream of men of goodwill that somebody high up will invite them in and say, "You have the power; do the job." But he's a tough little devil — tough enough to go get that power on his own.

[December 17, 1973]

Labyrinths

NICOLAS ROEG employs fast, almost subliminal imagery in the new English film *Don't Look Now,* and his entire splintering style affects one subliminally. The unnerving cold ominousness that he imparts to the environment says that things are not what they seem, and one may come out of the theater still seeing shock cuts and feeling slightly dissociated. The environment may briefly be fractured; for me ten minutes or so passed before it assembled itself and lost that trace of hostile objectivity. I don't recall having had this sort of residue of visual displacement from a movie before, but it's reasonable if one has been looking at a splintered universe for almost two hours. And one looks at this picture with intense concentration, because here life is treated as a puzzle, and the clues are in visual cross-references that go by in split seconds. Afterward, the environment one moves into holds the danger of discontinuity, as if at any moment something frightening might be intercut. Roeg has an elegant, edgy style that speaks to us of the broken universe and our broken connections, of modern man's inability to order his experience and to find meaning and coherence in it. The style speaks of the lesions in our view of the world; everything on the screen is vaguely incongruous and unnatural. A child outdoors on his bicycle runs over a pane of glass; wherever one turns, there are cracks and spreading stains. But Roeg's modernist style is too good for the use he puts it to.

Taken from a Daphne du Maurier story of the occult, adapted by Alan Scott and Chris Bryant, *Don't Look Now* is about a young English couple (Donald Sutherland and Julie Christie) whose drowned daughter may or may not be sending them messages. The bereaved parents leave their surviving child in school and go to Venice — deserted at the end of the season — where the husband, an art restorer, works at repairing eroded church mosaics. The film, too, is a mosaic, organized on the basis of premonitions. (The present is visually interrupted by glimpses of the future.) The husband is psychic but refuses to admit it; he fails to give credence to the omens that appear to him, and so, misinterpreting them, is destroyed. The material is Daphne du Maurier, but it's treated in the intricate manner of Borges, whose face filled the screen and crowned the murderous climax of *Performance,* the first film Roeg directed (with Donald Cammell as co-director). The atmosphere has too much class for the Gothic paraphernalia: the warnings unheeded, the city plagued by a mass murderer, the worrying bishop (Massimo Serato) with uncanny intuitions, and the ambiguous, dumpy, sub-Hitchcock sisters — one (Hilary Mason) blind and claiming to be psychic, the other (Clelia Matania) a chesty Helen Hokinson woman — who laugh together as if they were swindlers. We've seen all that before — with less style, it's true, but also with more vitality when it wasn't so convoluted and veneered with art. In a less refined picture, one mightn't be so critical of the way Roeg pulls out all the stops in the sisters' creaking, stagy scenes.

When you join the modernist sense of disorder to this canned Gothic mystery, you may satisfy only those who can accept the titillating otherworldly, but you can intrigue the more demanding, too. All that the movie really says to one is that Nicolas Roeg has a modern sensibility without having a modern mind — or, to put it another way, he has the style without the consciousness. And so the lesions are a form of high-fashion chic. It's a great commercial advantage to him not to have a fuller consciousness. Roeg doesn't examine the jaggedness, or ask the why of it, or try to find order within it; he uses this shattered vision to bring a Gothic story up to date. Put them together and you have the new international-celebrity look: the boy or girl looking like Bianca Jagger and talking about psychic phenomena. Unisex and ghosts in one smart, high-style package. And there they are on the screen — the modern couple, Julie Christie and Donald Sutherland, with matching curly hairdos.

The movie has a special ambience: the dislocation is eroticized, and rotting Venice, the labyrinthine city of pleasure, with its crumbling, leering gargoyles, is obscurely, frighteningly sensual. It's a Borgesian setting — the ruins tokens of a mysteriously indifferent universe; Venice might be a reptile-infested Mayan city discovered in a jungle. Roeg, drawn to Borges's tone — the controlled, systematic way in which Borges turns life into a mystical, malevolent nightmare — brings out the sensuality that is hidden in our response to the Borges cool. In *Don't Look Now,* the romanticism isn't of the traditional Gothic variety but a coolly enigmatic sexiness, and though it isn't strong enough to be a turn-on for a large popular audience, it gives the film a reticent, insinuating quality. Nothing in Roeg's style appears to be spontaneous or free-flowing; it's all artifice and technique. And yet the essence of the style is languor. *Don't Look Now* is the newest form of the trip movie. The young couple are at home in this jagged universe; they belong to it, and so does Roeg. He digs it, the way Joseph Losey dug the sunny rot and corruption in *Accident* and *The Go-Between,* but Roeg doesn't feel Losey's need to condemn the decadence that attracts him. *Don't Look Now* particularly recalls Losey's nutty *Secret Ceremony,* but Roeg isn't confused by a sense of shame. He thinks with his eyes, and puffs up what he sees. Roeg has taken Losey's luxuriant, richly ornamental style into a new domain; he may be the genius of chic that, in movies, Warhol and Morrissey only prefigured. Detached and psychedelic, *Don't Look Now* never touches our sympathies, never arouses any feeling for its characters. Roeg's vision is as impersonal and noncommittal as Warhol's, but with the gloss and craftsmanship of Losey. If the elliptical style says that things are not what they seem, it also says that though they're not as simple as people used to think they were, we don't have to worry about it, because they've all gone out of our grasp. We can relax and accept everything. To tie this together with a du Maurier story of the supernatural is to return to a pre-modernist account of why they're not what they seem. How blissfully, commercially acute to join our anxieties to superstition. And not even honest superstition but superstition used to relieve boredom — superstition as a deadpan camp. Believed in only as much as anything else is; that is, not believed in at all. This new Gothic of Roeg's is baby talk joined to dislocation. And isn't that just what Warhol was doing? Only Roeg joins the cool indifference to rich elegance. Maybe it's from the tension between the two that we get that faint, erotic vertigo. Roeg seems to say what Losey never dared to but what the audience for Losey was always responding to: that decay among the rich and beautiful is sexy. Actually, Losey's films and this one of Roeg's tantalize audiences in exactly the way that sad stories of the jazz age do; whatever Losey claimed to be doing, he was giving us the beautiful and damned in a fantasy playground for a daydreaming audience. Roeg, I suspect, knows what he's doing (though I imagine people will cook up the usual elaborate deep meanings for this film, just as they do for Losey's moralizing erotic fantasies).

Julie Christie and Donald Sutherland work together wonderfully here — maybe because their sexual differences are so muted. The other actors are merely exploited for sinister effects, and Roeg is crudely derivative in his handling of them, but his treatment of Christie and Sutherland has a highly original awareness. Psychologically, the film barely exists, but Roeg does so much with the two stars' faces — Sutherland's long and thin, Christie's desperately frail — that they become not characters but an archetype of the new couple: sophisticated, gallant, frightened. Sutherland gives a soft, fine-toned performance, and Christie is lovely — with that delicately rapacious jaw and the poignant eyes.

She has the anxious face of a modern tragic muse. A key sex scene, with the two nude in bed, intercut with flash-forwards to their postcoital mood as they dress to go out together, is almost the reverse of a strip-tease. The images of their getting dressed — their bemused, distant expressions, their isolation from each other, and their movements getting into their perfect clothes — have an erotic glitter that displaces interest from their quiet, playfully tender coupling to its aftermath. (To avoid an X rating for the picture, this sequence has been slightly reëdited, but Roeg himself made the changes — substituting a few frames from the outtakes — and they are said to be so slight that someone seeing the English and American versions might not notice the difference.) The sequence is consistent with the whole premonitory scheme of the film, and it also relates to the way eroticism is displaced throughout; dressing is splintered and sensualized, like fear and death — death most of all, with splashes of red.

Roeg, who used to be a writer and director for British TV besides being a famous cinematographer, did the celebrated second-unit work on *Lawrence of Arabia* and was the cinematographer for *A Funny Thing Happened on the Way to the Forum* as well as for a number of Julie Christie's films — *Fahrenheit 451, Far from the Madding Crowd, Petulia* — which have, I think, a close relationship to his work here. It is the assumption in this film that the juxtaposition of images provides instant meaning. Roeg uses the technique, out of Alain Resnais, more effectively than Richard Lester did in *Petulia*; since Roeg doesn't get into complicated feelings or social attitudes, you don't question what he's saying. Despite the surreal portentousness of the atmosphere, the meanings are very simple, very much on a Hitchcock level, and are often organized with that same mechanical precision. But the deliberate mystification is a problem for Roeg that it wasn't for Hitchcock, because Roeg's systematic trickery doesn't quite jibe with the otherworldly. The discrepancy involved in a tightly planned, interlocking *mystery* made me impatient; the preordained can be experienced as the mechanically delayed. (Borges always keeps it short.) The final kicker is predictable, and strangely flat, because it hasn't been made to matter to us; fear is decorative, and there's nothing to care about in this worldly, artificial movie. Yet at a mystery level the movie can still affect the viewer; even the silliest ghost stories can. It's not that I'm not impressionable; I'm just not as proud of it as some people are. *Don't Look Now* gets fairly moldy when the hero confronts his red-hooded fate (seen rather too clearly). The non-believer hero destroyed by his refusal to trust his second sight (that old, old shtick — the agnostic punished because he refuses to believe in the supernatural) gives one such a strong whiff of Hollywood. But the picture is the fanciest, most carefully assembled gothic enigma yet put on the screen; it's emblazoned in chic, and compared to such gothics as *Seance on a Wet Afternoon* it's a masterwork. It's also trash.

In Borges, mystery and decadence come close together, and at the picture's consummation the perfect, beautiful couple are split by a hideous joke of nature — their own child become a dwarf monstrosity. Using du Maurier as a base, Roeg comes closer to getting Borges on the screen than those who have tried it directly, but there's a distasteful clamminess about the picture — not because Venice is dying (though this sure is a counter-commercial for Venice) but because Roeg's style is in love with disintegration. A little boy can look at his dead sister with no emotion in his face, but terror and decay are made radiant. Julie Christie is the perfect actress for Roeg, because her feelings are so exquisitely modulated and so small; she doesn't project with enough force to disturb the visual surface with rage or pain. Her jagged face — so extraordinarily beautiful yet not adding up right for ordinary beauty — might be the emblem of his style. She gives the picture a soul — but a soul in a body that's trembling on the verge of breakdown. Roeg is a chillingly chic director. *Don't Look Now* is shallow in a way that I think people are looking for right now; I can practically hear someone asking, "What's the matter with shallow?" This could be Warhol's legacy. *Don't Look Now* is going to be a great success, because it represents the new, high-fashion gothic sensibility — what the movie audience is just getting into. But it's like an entertainment for bomb victims: nobody expects any real pleasure from it.

❖

SOLEMNITY IS A CRIPPLING DISEASE that strikes moviemakers when they're on top: a few big hits and they hire Dalton Trumbo and go into their indomitable-spirit-of-man lockstep. *Papillon*, the most expensive movie of the year, is a thirteen-and-a-half-million-dollar monument to the eternal desire of moviemakers to win awards and impress people. How can you play around and try out ideas on a property like the Henri Charrière best-seller, which probably cost a couple of million to start with, and with stars (Steve McQueen and Dustin Hoffman) who definitely cost three and a quarter million between them? It would be like juggling with the Elgin Marbles. What should have been an entertaining escape-from-Devil's Island thriller, with some laughs, some suspense, and some colorful cutthroats and likable thieves, has been treated not as if it were an escape story but as if it were *the* escape story. The story has become practically abstract, and for much of the time the movie can't be bothered telling us where Papillon (Steve McQueen) is escaping from or where he hopes to go. The moviemakers have approached the subject of Papillon (a French safecracker who was sentenced to prison for life for killing a pimp and who, thirty-odd years after he broke out, trumped up his adventures into a best-seller about his many escape attempts) as if they were making an important historical biography — about a pope, at the very least.

The stark ad showing McQueen and Hoffman sweating in their chains seems to be looking for a caption: "What do you mean, what am I doing here? What are you doing here?" It's understandable that, at a cost of two million, Steve McQueen can become an icon to moviemakers, but to put him in a role that requires an intense audience identification with the hero's humanity — the sort of role Jean Gabin played in *La Grande Illusion* and *Pépé le Moko* — is madness. McQueen is an amusing actor of considerable skill but a reserved actor whose expressive resources are very small. That's what's fun about him: when he's placed in tense situations, his tiny, tiny shades of expression become a witty caricature of the American man of action's emotionlessness. If ever there was a wrong actor for a man of great spirit, it's McQueen; as Robert Mitchum once remarked, "Steve doesn't bring too much to the party."

Actually, no actor could have saved this unrelievedly grim picture — not with the Trumbo-Lorenzo Semple, Jr., script, which keeps Papillon shackled and penned up (Trumbo has only one arrow to his bow, and he shot it in *The Fixer*), and not with Franklin J. Schaffner, late of *Nicholas and Alexandra,* directing. Schaffner has a clean, precise camera style for spectacle *(The War Lord, Planet of the Apes, Patton),* but there's no spectacle in *Papillon*; there are a few scenes involving lots of extras but no large-scale action. A director such as John Boorman *(Deliverance),* with his hypnotic talent for charging an atmosphere with fear, might have been able to give even this hollow script some tension, but Schaffner is immaculately literal-minded. Nothing is hidden beneath the methodical progression of the scenes; the film is totally obvious, and there isn't a laugh in its two and a half hours. I was grateful each time Dustin Hoffman turned up, simply because he tries to do something for characterization and he has more life than McQueen. Hoffman usually seems to think he needs a physical gimmick for his characters. He's playing Louis, a smart, rather pedantic convict who was "the best counterfeiter" in France, so the thick lenses make sense (though they're the thickest lenses I've ever seen), but why does he go through the picture with his mouth open, like some adenoidal chinless wonder? Is he trying to be helpful by making himself different from McQueen? (He really doesn't have to worry about that.) This co-starring arrangement between men needs the right chemistry, but McQueen doesn't supply for Hoffman what Voight did in *Midnight Cowboy.* The reverse happens:

McQueen seems to inspire Hoffman to underplay, too. When Papillon prepares for his final escape and Louis says he's not going, he sounds as if he had decided not to shave that day. Theirs is the only emotional bond in the movie, and there's hardly any emotion in it.

All the actors seem too gentlemanly to become characters, and Schaffner too gentlemanly to get anything going in the meticulously constructed sets; authenticity seems to be in everyone's mind, but authenticity of what — of Henri Charrière's self-glorifying adventure romance? I don't really understand Schaffner's concept: after the two principals have been separated for five years, they meet somewhere out on Devil's Island and the cranky, fussy Louis sees Papillon and scuttles away from him — presumably because he doesn't want to become involved in another escape attempt. But the scene is so barren of feeling that we have to interpret the action; the actors supply hardly a clue. Besides, I was confused — and others may be also — because I thought Louis's gangrenous leg had been amputated in an earlier sequence, and now he was hopping about on two perfectly good hoppers. And is McQueen really meant to represent the Henri Charrière who wrote *Papillon*? He doesn't seem to have any words in him. I didn't understand why he wasn't perfectly content when he was on some (unspecified) island with friendly villagers and a loving native girl: true, he didn't speak the language, but most of his earlier communication had been with cockroaches in his cell. I know we're meant to take joy in McQueen's final victory — the proof that he couldn't be broken — but I was glad that he'd finally made it only because I didn't want to have to go back to solitary with him.

Papillon is a strange mixture of grimness and propriety. There are unnecessary brutalities involving characters we hardly know (after an eighteen-year-old convict is killed, we get a close view of his bleeding head; a man is guillotined, and his head rolls toward the audience), and at the same time the movie absolutely refuses the audience any comic relief. (One gets the impression that Schaffner would consider it "levity.") Hoffman's counterfeiter goes through most of the picture subsidizing McQueen's escape attempts with a fortune he carries in a tube in his colon, and as the years pass and he keeps paying and paying, you can't help wondering how much money he can be carrying there. The picture is so sedate it never satisfies our curiosity; is that because when a star costs as much as Dustin Hoffman you don't make jokes about the bankroll he's sitting on?

[December 24, 1973]

Survivor

WOODY ALLEN appears before us as the battered adolescent, scarred forever, a little too nice and much too threatened to allow himself to be aggressive. He has the city-wise effrontery of a shrimp who began by using language to protect himself and then discovered that language has a life of its own. The running war between the tame and the surreal — between Woody Allen the frightened nice guy trying to keep the peace and Woody Allen the wiseacre whose subversive fantasies keep jumping out of his mouth — has been the source of the comedy in his films. Messy, tasteless, and crazily uneven (as the best talking comedies have often been), the last two pictures he directed — *Bananas* and *Everything You Always Wanted to Know About Sex* — had wild highs that suggested an erratic comic genius. The tension between his insecurity and his wit makes us empathize with him; we, too, are scared to show how smart we feel. And he has found a nonaggressive way of dealing with urban pressures. He stays nice; he's not insulting, like most New York comedians, and he delivers his zingers without turning into a cynic. We enjoy his show of defenselessness, and even the I-don't-mean-any-harm ploy, because we see the essential sanity in him. We respect that sanity — it's the base from which he takes flight. At his top, in parts of *Bananas* and *Sex,* the inexplicably funny took over; it might be grotesque, it almost always had the flippant, corny bawdiness of a frustrated sophomore running amok, but it seemed to burst out — as the most inspired comedy does — as if we had all been repressing it. We laughed as if he had let out what we couldn't hold in any longer.

The surreal is itself tamed in Woody Allen's *Sleeper,* the most stable and most sustained of his films. (It also has the best title.) Easily the slapstick comedy of the year — there hasn't been any other — *Sleeper* holds together, as his sharpest earlier films failed to do; it doesn't sputter and blow fuses, like *Bananas* and *Sex.* It's charming — a very even work, with almost no thudding bad lines and with no low stretches. I can't think of anything much the matter with it; it's a small classic. But it doesn't have the loose, manic highs of those other films. You come out smiling and perfectly happy, but not driven crazy, not really turned on, the way his messier movies and some musicals *(Singin' in the Rain, Cabaret)* and some comic movies *(M*A*S*H, The Long Goodbye)* and parts of Paul Mazursky's movies can turn one on. I had a wonderful time at *Sleeper,* and I laughed all the way through, but it wasn't exhilarating. Allen's new sense of control over the medium and over his own material seems to level out the abrasive energy. You can be with it all the way, and yet it doesn't impose itself on your imagination — it dissolves when it's finished. If it sounds like a contradiction to say that *Sleeper* is a small classic and yet not exhilarating — well, I can't completely explain that. Comedy is impossibly mysterious; this is a beautiful little piece of work — it shows a development of skills in our finest comedy-maker — and yet it's mild, and doesn't quite take off.

Woody Allen plays a Rip Van Winkle who wakes up in 2173 — and that's all I'm going to say about the story, because I don't want to squeeze the freshness out of the jokes. His girl is Diane Keaton (who was practically the only good thing in *Play It Again, Sam*), and she has a plucky, almost Jean Arthur quality. She's very appealing, and in *Sleeper* you want to like her; I always felt right on the verge of responding to her (as a broad-faced, Slavic-looking poet of the future), but she isn't quite funny enough. She has good bits (like her Brando parody), but her timing is indefinite, and so is the character she plays. She's really just there to be Woody's girl, and there's nobody else — other than Allen himself — you remember from the movie. *Sleeper* could really use a *cast.* In a Preston Sturges comedy, the various characters' madnesses and obsessions bounced off each other and got all scrambled up; Chaplin and Keaton had their big fellows to contend with; the Marx Brothers had each other, plus Margaret Dumont and Walter Woolf King and Sig Rumann and those blondes wriggling in satin. But Woody Allen has no set characters to respond to. He needs a great stock company, like Carol Burnett's (Who wants to be a crazy alone? That leads to melancholy), but so far in his movies he's the only character, because his conception of himself keeps him alone.

The Woody Allen character suffers, in all his films, from sex in the head which he figures his body can't get for him. It's the comedy of sexual inadequacy; what makes it hip rather than masochistic and awful is that he thinks women want the media macho ideal, and we in the audience are cued to suspect, as he secretly does, that that's the real inadequacy (social even more than sexual). Woody Allen is a closet case of potency; he knows he's potent, but he's afraid to tell the world — and adolescents and post-adolescents can certainly identify with that. His shrimp-hero's worst fear may be that he would be attractive only to women who feel sorry for him (or want to dominate him). The latter is parenthetical because Allen hasn't explored that possibility; the thought of him with, say, Anne Bancroft suggests the sort of gambit he hasn't tried. When we see his films, all our emotions attach to him; his fear and his frailty are what everything revolves around. No one else in his pictures has a vivid presence, or any particular quality except being a threat to him, and even that quality isn't really characterized. Maybe the reason he doesn't invest others with comic character (or even villainous character) is that he's so hung up that he has no interest in other people's hangups; that could be why his stories never really build to the big climactic finish one expects from a comedy. His plots don't tie a gigantic knot and then explode it, because the other characters aren't strong enough to carry the threads. The end of *Sleeper* is just a mild cutoff point — not bad but unexciting. The movie has a more conventional slapstick-comedy structure than *Bananas,* and slapstick isn't something you can do with a pickup cast. The comedy isn't forced, it looks relaxed and easy, but the routines don't gather momentum — they slide off somewhere. Woody Allen loses his supporting players along the way, and one hardly notices. It's likely that he sees his function as being all of us, and since he's all of us, nobody else can be anything.

But, being all of us, he can get too evenly balanced, he can lose his edge. Nobody else could have made *Bananas* or parts of *Sex,* but others could conceivably make a movie like *Sleeper,* just as others are beginning to write in the Woody Allen manner — and one of the most gifted of them, Marshall Brickman, is co-author of the *Sleeper* script. The humor here doesn't tap the mother lode; it's strip-mining. The movie is in the Woody Allen style, but it doesn't have the disruptive inspiration that is the unbalanced soul of Woody Allen. In interviews, Allen has often been quoted as saying that he wants to stay rough in his movie technique; I used to enjoy reading those quotes, because I thought he was right, and in *Bananas* his instinct to let the jokes run shapelessly loose instead of trimming them and making them tidy paid off. The effect was berserk, in an original way. But he tailored his play *Play It Again, Sam* in the smooth George S. Kaufman-Broadway style, and the movie version, which Herbert Ross directed even more smoothly (I hated it), turned out to be Woody Allen's biggest box-office success up to that time, and made him a mass-audience star. How could a man who really trusted the free and messy take up the clarinet, an instrument that appeals to controlled, precise people? You can't really goof around with a clarinet. (The group he plays with, the New Orleans Funeral and Ragtime Orchestra, can be heard on the *Sleeper* track, along with the Preservation Hall Jazz Band.) I think he knows that the free and messy is the right, great direction for his comedy, but he's very well organized, and, like most comedians, he really trusts success. He trusts laughs, and how can a comedian tell when they're not earned? He's a romantic comedian — he goes on believing in love and the simple, good things in life. He's also a very practical-man comedian — he's the harried, bespectacled nice guy who just wants to stay nice and be a success and get the girl. In terms of his aspirations, he's rather like Truffaut's Antoine Doinel — the unpretentious, hopeful joiner of the bourgeoisie — as a jester. In American terms, he's Harold Lloyd with Groucho's tongue.

To have found a clean visual style for a modern slapstick comedy in color is a major victory; Woody Allen learns with the speed of a wizard. *Sleeper* has a real look to it, and simple, elegant design. (The robot servants of the future, in their tuxedos, might be windup dandies by Elie Nadelman.) Physically, Woody Allen is much more graceful in *Sleeper*; he's turning into that rarity, a verbal comedian who also knows how to use his body. And his acting has developed; he can register more emotions now, and his new silly beatific look — the look of a foolish sage — goes with the wonderful infantile jokes that don't make sense. But one might say that *Sleeper* is a sober comedy; it doesn't unhinge us, we never feel that our reason is being shredded. It has a businesslike, nine-to-five look about it, and a faint nine-to-five lethargy. For a comedian, the price of stability may be the loss of inspiration. (Our most inspired comedian, Jonathan Winters, has never found his forms. But then he doesn't have that base of sanity, either.) What's missing is the wild man's indifference to everything but the joke. In Woody Allen's case, this out-of-control edge went way past Groucho's effrontery and W. C. Fields' malice into a metaphysical outrageousness, but the impulse was similar: finally, the pleasure in the joke was all that mattered. That's what put him among the great ones.

Woody Allen has become our folk hero because we felt that if we stuck with him failure could succeed; this was, in a sense, his pact with us to get our loyalty, and it worked. We don't want to have to go through failure; we want to watch him go through it — and come out the other side. I always thought the danger for him was that he wanted to be a universal little fellow — a Chaplin — and that he might linger too long on the depressive, misfit side of his character and let the schleppy pathos take over (as he did in *Take the Money and Run*). And I thought that if he ever convinced us that he was really failing he'd lose us — who wants to watch a wispy schlep? He may not fully know it, but he doesn't need our sympathy; he's got much more than that already. What Woody Allen probably doesn't realize is that when he uses his wit he becomes our D'Artagnan. He isn't a little fellow for college students; he's a *hero.* They want to be funny, like him.

What I had underestimated was another danger. Woody Allen tips the scales toward winning in *Sleeper,* all right, but he overvalues normal-ity; the battered adolescent still thinks that that's the secret of happiness. He hasn't come to terms with what his wit is telling him. He's dumped Chaplin (blessings) and devised a Buster Keaton-style story, but Keaton's refined physical movements were a clown's poetry, while when Allen does physical comedy — even when he's good at it — he's a very ordinary person. His gift is upstairs. It's really lucky that he cares about himself as much as he does, or he might get so balanced out that his jokes would become monotonous, like those of his imitators. If only he can begin to take control for granted, now that he's improving as a physical comedian and gaining infinitely greater skill as a director. Surreal comedy is chaos; to be really funny, you have to be willing to let your unconscious take over. That's what doesn't happen in *Sleeper.*

❖

"THE STING," with Paul Newman and Robert Redford, strings together the chapters of a Saturday-afternoon serial, each with its own cliffhanger, and we're invited to wait around to see what the happy twosome will do next. The happy twosome seem to have something for each other, and for most of the rest of the world, that I don't tune in to. They're fine as actors (on the occasions when they practice their profession), but I don't respond to their arch love games, as in *Butch Cassidy and the Sundance Kid* and this new one, in which they've swapped mustaches — Newman now has the dashing ornament. They were darling desperadoes in their last match; now they're hearty hoods. I would much rather see a picture about two homosexual men in love than see two romantic actors going through a routine whose point is that they're so adorably smiley butch that they can pretend to be in love and it's all innocent. (It was more fun in the forties and fifties, when male couples played these games and we guessed from the way they looked at each other that they really were lovers offscreen.) Newman and Redford are probably the two sexiest male stars in the country, but when they play boyish coquettes the show is cloying. And the absence of women really is felt as a lack in this movie. (The device of giving the heroes unimportant women characters for bedmates just calls attention to where the true box-office feeling is.) But then not only is half of humanity omitted — so is most of what engages the remaining half. *The Sting,* which is about big-time cardsharps and swindlers, is meant to be a roguishly charming entertainment, and I guess that's how most of the audience takes it, but I found it visually claustrophobic, and totally mechanical. It keeps cranking on, section after section, and it doesn't have a good spirit. As for its heroes' vaunted charm, isn't it a little late in life for Robert Redford (who has turned almost alarmingly blond — he's gone past platinum, he must be into plutonium; his hair is coördinated with his teeth) to be playing a raw kid, a novice con artist, and isn't it a little early in life for Paul Newman to be playing an old-pro trickster coming out of retirement for one last score? It's the acting profession that Newman seems to be prematurely retiring from. He looks almost obscenely healthy — as if he never missed his ten hours of sleep a night. And what would be keeping him up? He and Redford let their cute thirties hats do their work for them. The only lines in Paul Newman's face are those exquisitely happy crinkles around his eyes; he's beginning to look *fatuously* happy. The setting is the ragtime thirties — a synthetic period compounded of Scott Joplin's rags (Joplin died in 1917) and thirties gangster films — and the director is once again the implacably impersonal George Roy Hill. The script, by David S. Ward *(Steelyard Blues)*, is a collection of Damon Runyon hand-me-downs with the flavor gone. Robert Shaw plays the sullen, stiff-necked menace with a brogue and some bullying force, but the whole movie is full of crooks as sweeties. *The Sting* is for people — and no doubt there are quantities of them — who *like* crooks as sweeties.

AT A COST OF $8,150,000, *The Day of the Dolphin*, directed by Mike Nichols, is the most expensive Rin Tin Tin picture ever made. Actually, it's somewhat more primitive than the Rin Tin Tin pictures: the dog had a marvelous understanding of English, but he was not required to speak it, like the dolphins here. Trained by their loving master, George C. Scott, Alpha and Beta not only learn to prattle in English but, when they are kidnapped by bad men and a bomb is placed around Beta's head to be delivered to the President of the United States, they foil the assassination attempt. (Just like Rin Tin Tin with those sticks of dynamite.) The movie exploits Watergate and the assassinations for a despairing attitude toward corruption and a resigned anger against the crude villains who care about dolphins only because of their capacity for delivering the explosives. But what of the corruption of this picture, which can think of no way to interest us in dolphins except by dubbing them with plaintive, childish voices and turning them into fishy human babies full of love for Pa (Scott)? His conversations with them are worthy of Tarzan and Jane. (Scott is, however, made out to be a scientific big-daddy superman whose research institute falls apart when he's not there. An analogy with Mike Nichols?) Buck Henry, who wrote the script, from the Robert Merle novel, and the others connected with this movie have a lot to answer for. N.B.C. has already paid two million dollars for the right to show the film on TV in three years. This picture will probably upset more children than any other movie since *Bambi. The Day of the Dolphin* ends with the bawling-baby Alpha protesting love for Pa while Scott tells the pair that he will never see them again and that they must trust no man, and forces the whimpering babies to leave their home forever. It's an ugly-souled, manipulative movie. The moviemakers who put out the Rin Tin Tin pictures didn't take everything away from the kids in the audience and send them out destroyed. What kind of people are they who play games like this? The movie is too archaic for adults, and it can be agonizing, and finally heartbreaking, to children. The drippy message of the picture is (wouldn't you know it?) how terrible people are: if only we could be like the dolphins. The message is that we're unworthy of contact with them — and who wants to argue the point? But, with its cheaply effective anthropomorphic tear-jerking, it makes us even less worthy. If Mike Nichols and Buck Henry don't have anything better to make movies about than involving English-speaking dolphins in assassination attempts, why don't they stop making movies?

A REVERENTIAL, GLOOM-AND-PATHOS NEW MOVIE VERSION of *The Glass Menagerie* was shown on television on Sunday, December 16th. We've probably all had it with this play — thin but funny and touching at the beginning, and now shopworn, so its faults make it seem ludicrous. On television, the play was dead; the English director Anthony Harvey *(The Lion in Winter)* obviously had no grasp of the comedy or the vitality in the Tennessee Williams material. Is it possible that a heavy advertising budget and the highly publicized television début of Katharine Hepburn blinded the press, which praised this truly terrible embarrassment in terms almost as florid as Hepburn's performance? Hepburn is a great actress and has given many fine performances, but she is a preposterously bad actress as Amanda Wingfield. She rattles on in her familiar, girlishly distraught style, and she doesn't make you listen, so you lose the sense of her lines. Amanda is something of a monster, but Hepburn plays her for tender sympathy; Hepburn is so Southern and so actressy, and jabbers on so artificially, that after a while we don't understand a word she says, and don't care that we don't. Sam Waterston has demonstrated his talents elsewhere, but perhaps the director's conception overpowered him here, for he gave us Tom Wingfield's desperation without Tom's resilient, saving humor. Lines that might have been ironic became serious and remote. Michael Moriarty showed no understanding that the "gentleman caller" he was playing was meant to be an earnest, deluded go-getter, and Joanna Miles — physically more solid than the others, and appearing to be more psychologically sound, too

— was blatantly miscast as the frail, lost-in-dreams Laura. Joanna Miles, who has a cold facility, played Laura with a stony face, as if she were an empty shell, utterly devoid of feeling. *The Glass Menagerie* is no great loss; what I found upsetting about the production was that Katharine Hepburn's performance is like a compendium of the remembered mannerisms of her earlier movies. She's beginning to destroy her early performances for us, since gestures that belonged to her earlier characters — gestures that by now belong to us — are turning up promiscuously. The desecration is painful.

[December 31, 1973]

Back to the Ouija Board

SHALLOWNESS THAT ASKS to be taken seriously — shallowness like William Peter Blatty's — is an embarrassment. When you hear him on TV talking about communicating with his dead mother, your heart doesn't bleed for him, your stomach turns for him. Some people have impenetrable defense systems. You can't kid around with a man who says that he wrote *The Exorcist* because "as I went along writing my funny books and screenplays, I felt I wasn't making a contribution to the welfare of the world." He says that he looks upon it "quite frankly as an apostolic work." That the work has made him a millionaire doesn't make him a liar. Blatty is apostle to the *National Enquirer,* and to *Cosmopolitan,* in which the novel was condensed — so those Cosmopolitan Girls could make conversation without looking tired around the eyes. The crushing blunt-wittedness of the movie version, which he produced, tends to bear out Blatty's apostolic claims. Directed by William Friedkin, who won the Academy Award as Best Director of 1971 for *The French Connection,* the film is a faithful adaptation of the Blatty book — and that's not a compliment. Blatty did the intractable screenplay, so Friedkin may have been faithful in spite of himself. The picture isn't a gothic horror comedy, like *Psycho* or *Rosemary's Baby*; it has been made as a heavy, expensive *family* picture. It's faithful not to the way many people read the book — as a fast turn-on entertainment — but to Blatty's claims about what the book was intended to be. It's an obtuse movie, without a trace of playfulness in it. A viewer can become glumly anesthetized by the brackish color and the senseless ugliness of the conception.

Following on the success of *Rosemary's Baby* (Rosemary gave birth to a cloven-hoofed infant, her actor-husband having mated her with Satan in exchange for a Broadway hit), Blatty, a veteran screenwriter, developed an outline for a novel about the demonic possession of a child, and Marc Jaffe, of Bantam Books, subsidized the effort. Harper & Row picked up the hardcover rights, and the movie deal (stipulating that Blatty was to produce) was made even before publication. Blatty, who once hoaxed people by impersonating a Saudi Arabian prince, and whose screen credits include a hand in *Darling Lili, The Great Bank Robbery, What Did You Do in the War, Daddy?, Promise Her Anything, John Goldfarb, Please Come Home,* etc., is not an austere writer. The key personnel in *The Exorcist* are (a) Chris MacNeil (Ellen Burstyn), a beautiful movie-star mother, divorced, agnostic; (b) her twelve-year-old daughter, Regan (Linda Blair), who becomes a foul-mouthed, sex-obsessed, blaspheming, church-desecrating murderess; (c) Father Damien Karras (Jason Miller), a tormented Jesuit psychiatrist who is losing his faith; (d) a jokey, warmhearted Jewish police lieutenant (Lee J. Cobb); (e) a distinguished, ascetic priest, Father Merrin (Max von Sydow), whose archeological work has somehow — it's not made clear how, in either the book or the movie — released the demon that takes over Regan.

The book features a murder victim — a British movie director — whose "head was turned completely around, facing backward"; little Regan rotating her head; little Regan masturbating with a crucifix and grabbing her mother and forcing her mother's face against her bloody vagina; vomit propelled from Regan's mouth into people's faces. And what Blatty didn't manage to have his characters do he had them talk about, so there were fresh atrocities every few hundred words. Like the pulp authors who provide flip-page sex, he provided flip-page torture, infanticide, cannibalism, sexual hysteria, werewolves. The book is a manual of lurid crimes, written in an easy-to-read tough-guy style yet with a grating heightening word here and there, supposedly to tone it up. ("When the Mass was over, he polished the chalice and carefully placed it in his bag. He rushed for the seven-ten train back to Washington, carrying pain in a black valise.") The book turns up on high-school reading lists now, and the Bantam edition carries such quotes as "Deeply religious . . . a parable for our times" and "*The Exorcist* should be read twice; the first time for the passion and horrifying intensity of the story, with a second reading to savor the subtleties of language and phrasing overlooked in the mounting excitement of the first perusal."

For the movie, Blatty had to dispense with a subplot about the butler's daughter, and, of course, he couldn't retain all the gory anecdotes, but the basic story is told, and the movie — religiously literal-minded — shows you a heaping amount of blood and horror. This explicitness must be what William Friedkin has in mind when he talks publicly about the picture's "documentary quality." The movie also has the most ferocious language yet heard in a picture that is rated R, and is thus open to children (to those whose parents are insane enough to take them, or are merely uninformed). *The Exorcist* was budgeted at four million dollars, but, what with swiveling heads, and levitations, and vomit being spewed on target, the cost kept rising, and the picture came in somewhere around ten million. If *The Exorcist* had cost under a million, or had been made abroad, it would almost certainly be an X film, but when a movie is as expensive as this one, the M.P.A.A. rating board doesn't dare to give it an X. Will people complain? I doubt it; the possible complainers have become accessories. Two Jesuits appear in the cast and served, with a third, as "technical advisers," along with a batch of doctors. Besides, the Catholic Church is hardly likely to be upset by the language or actions in a film that says that the Catholic Church is the true faith, feared by the Devil, and that its rituals can exorcise demons. The two heroes of the film are von Sydow and Jason Miller, both playing Jesuits; Georgetown University coöperated with the production, which was shot partly in Georgetown; and one of the Jesuit actor-advisers enriched us, even before the film was finished, with information about its high moral character ("It shows that obscenity is ugly . . . vicious ugly, like the Vietnamese news"). The movie may be in the worst imaginable taste — that is, an utterly unfeeling movie about miracles — but it's also the biggest recruiting poster the Catholic Church has had since the sunnier days of *Going My Way* and *The Bells of St. Mary's.*

Whatever Blatty's claims, if *The Exorcist* scares people that's probably all it has to do, in box-office terms, and basically that's all the whole unpleasant movie is designed to do. "People only go to movies for three reasons, to laugh, cry, or be frightened," Friedkin has said. And "There are only three reasons to make a movie, to make people laugh, to make them cry, or to frighten them." The scaring here is a matter of special effects and sound and editing — the roaring-animal noises from the attic coming at the right instant, Regan's bed shaking just enough, the objects in her room flying about without looking silly, and so on. If the audience ever started giggling at the sounds and tricks, the picture might collapse, because it's entirely mechanical and impersonal. Von Sydow brings some elegance to his role, and the makeup that ages him is one of the most convincing aging jobs I've ever seen, but once you perceive that his Father Merrin is saintly and infirm, that's it. As Father Karras, the most active character, Jason Miller does the gloomy, tormented John Garfield bit — and it's a wheeze by now. All the performances are; there's nothing the actors can do with the juiceless stock roles.

The book's success may relate to its utter shallowness; the reader can go at a fast clip, following the plot and not paying any attention to the characters. But in the movie version the psychology, which is tiresomely moralistic (as in a fifties TV drama), is dead center. There we are with the freethinking mother feeling guilty about her divorce and its effects on Regan; we may not know why the demon picked on Regan, but we're tipped that that broken home — the first step to Hell — gave the Devil his chance. And there we are with the creaking goodness of the Jewish cop, and the jocular bonhomie of the Jesuits. It's all so tired that we can keep going only on fresh atrocities. Apart from the demonic special effects, which are done in staccato quick cuts, the picture is in a slugging, coercive style. It piles up points, like a demonstration. Friedkin, beloved of studio heads for such statements as "I'm not a thinker. . . . If it's a film *by* somebody instead of *for* somebody, I smell art," is not a director given to depth or mystery. Nor is he a man with a light touch — a failing that appears to have been exacerbated by the influence of *El Topo.* He has himself said that Blatty's book took hold of him and made him physically ill. That's the problem with moviemakers who aren't thinkers: they're mentally unprotected. A book like Blatty's makes them sick, and they think this means they should make everybody sick. Probably Friedkin really believes he is communicating an important idea to us. And the only way he knows how to do it is by surface punch; he's a true commercial director — he confuses blatancy with power.

As a movie, *The Exorcist* is too ugly a phenomenon to take lightly. Its gothic seriousness belongs to the class of those old Hearst Sunday-supplement stories about archeologists defiling tombs and the curses that befall them, and it soaks into people's lives. A critic can't fight it, because it functions below the conscious level. How does one exorcise the effects of a movie like this? There is no way. The movie industry is such that men of no taste and no imagination can have an incalculable influence. Blatty and Friedkin can't muster up any feeling, even when Father Karras sacrifices himself — a modern Christ who dies to save mankind. We in the audience don't feel bad when the saintly Father Merrin dies; we don't even feel a pang of sympathy when the words "Help Me" appear on Regan's body. From the mechanical-scare way that the movie works on an audience, there is no indication that Blatty or Friedkin has any feeling for the little girl's helplessness and suffering, or her mother's, any feeling for God or terror of Satan. Surely it is the religious people who should be most offended by this movie. Others can laugh it off as garbage, but are American Catholics willing to see their faith turned into a horror show? Are they willing to accept *anything* just as long as their Church comes out in a good light? Aren't those who accept this picture getting their heads screwed on backward?

Somewhere in the publicity for the film there was an item about William Friedkin's having looked at five hundred little girls before he chose his Regan, and, indeed, Linda Blair is a sparkling, snub-nosed, happy-looking little girl, who matches up perfectly with Ellen Burstyn. I wonder about those four hundred and ninety-nine mothers of the rejected little girls — or about the hundred and ninety-nine, if that's a more reasonable figure. They must have read the novel; they must have known what they were having their beautiful little daughters tested for. When they see *The Exorcist* and watch Linda Blair urinating on the fancy carpet and screaming and jabbing at herself with the crucifix, are they envious? Do they feel, "That might have been my little Susie — famous forever"?

[January 7, 1974]

Killing Time

CLINT EASTWOOD isn't offensive; he isn't an actor, so one could hardly call him a bad actor. He'd have to *do* something before we could consider him bad at it. And acting isn't required of him in *Magnum Force,* which takes its name from the giant's phallus — the long-barreled Magnum 44 — that Eastwood flourishes. Acting might even get in the way of what the movie is about — what a big man and a big gun can do. Eastwood's wooden impassivity makes it possible for the brutality in his pictures to be *ordinary,* a matter of routine. He may try to save a buddy from getting killed, but when the buddy gets hit no time is wasted on grief; Eastwood couldn't express grief any more than he could express tenderness. With a Clint Eastwood, the action film can — indeed, must — drop the pretense that human life has any value. At the same time, Eastwood's lack of reaction makes the whole show of killing seem so unreal that the viewer takes it on a different level from a movie in which the hero responds to suffering. In *Magnum Force,* killing is dissociated from pain; it's even dissociated from life. The killing is totally realistic — hideously, graphically so — yet since it's without emotion it has no impact on us. We feel nothing toward the victims; we have no empathy when they get it, and no memory of them afterward. As soon as one person gets it, we're ready for the next. The scenes of carnage are big blowouts — parties for the audience to gasp at in surprise and pleasure.

At an action film now, it just doesn't make much difference whether it's a good guy or a bad guy who dies, or a radiant young girl or a double-dealing chippie. Although the plots still draw this distinction, the writers and the directors no longer create different emotional tones for the deaths of good and bad characters. The fundamental mechanism of melodrama has broken down, I think: the audience at action pictures reacts to the killing scenes simply as spectacle. A tall, cold cod like Eastwood removes the last pretensions to humane feelings from the action melodrama, making it an impersonal, almost abstract exercise in brutalization. Eastwood isn't very different from many of the traditional inexpressive, stalwart heroes of Westerns and cops-and-robbers films — actors notoriously devoid of personality — but the change in action films can be seen in its purest form in him. He walks right through the mayhem without being affected by it — and we are not cued to be affected, either. The difference is a matter of degree, but it's possible that this difference of degree has changed the nature of the beast — or, to put it more accurately, the beast can now run wild. The audiences used to go mainly for the action but also to hate the ruthless villains, sympathize with the helpless victims, and cheer on the protector-of-the-weak heroes. It was the spaghetti Westerns (which made Clint Eastwood a star) that first eliminated the morality-play dimension and turned the Western into pure violent reverie. Apart from their aesthetic qualities (and they did have some), what made these Italian-produced Westerns popular was that they stripped the Western form of its cultural burden of morality. They discarded its civility along with its hypocrisy. In a sense, they liberated the form: what the Western hero stood for was left out, and what he embodied (strength and gun power) was retained. Abroad, that was probably what he had represented all along. In the figure of Clint Eastwood, the Western morality play and the myth of the Westerner were split. Now American movies treat even the American city the way the Italians treated the Old West; our cops-and-robbers pictures are like urban spaghetti Westerns. With our ethical fabric torn to shreds in this last decade, American action films such as *Magnum Force* and *The Laughing Policeman* are becoming daydream-nightmares of indiscriminate mayhem and slaughter.

The John Wayne figure — the man who stood for the right (in both senses, I fear, and in both senses within the movies themselves) — has been replaced by a man who essentially stands for nothing but violence. Eastwood has to deliver death, because he has no other appeal. He can barely speak a line of dialogue without making an American audience smile in disbelief, but his big gun speaks for him. The concept of the good guy has collapsed simultaneously in our society and in our movies. Eastwood isn't really a good guy; you don't *like* him, the way you liked Wayne. You don't even enjoy him in the way you could enjoy a scoundrel. He's simply *there*, with his Magnum force. For a hero who can't express himself in words or by showing emotion, shooting first and asking questions later has got to be the ultimate salvation. In *Dirty Harry*, Eastwood said to the hippie psychotic, "This is the most powerful handgun in the world, punk. It can blow your head off." The strong, quiet man of the action film has been replaced by the emotionally indifferent man. He's the opposite of Bogart, who knew pain. Perhaps the top box-office star in the movie business, Eastwood is also the first truly stoned hero in the history of movies. There's an odd disparity between his deliberate, rather graceful physical movements and his practically timberless voice. Only his hands seem fully alive. In Italian movies, the character he played was known as the Man with No Name, and he speaks in a small, dead, non-actor's voice that drops off to nowhere at the end of a line and that doesn't tell us a thing about him. While actors who are expressive may have far more appeal to educated people, Eastwood's inexpressiveness travels preposterously well. What he does is unmistakable in any culture. He's utterly unbelievable in his movies — inhumanly tranquil, controlled, and assured — and yet he seems to represent something that isn't so unbelievable. He once said of his first Italian Western, *A Fistful of Dollars*, that it "established the pattern," that it was "the first film in which the protagonist initiated the action — he shot first." Eastwood stands melodrama on its head: in his world nice guys finish last. This is no longer the romantic world in which the hero is, fortunately, the best shot; instead, the best shot is the hero. And that could be what the American audience for action films, grown derisive about the triumph of the good, was waiting for. Eastwood's gun power makes him the hero of a totally nihilistic dream world.

HOLLYWOOD'S FLIRTATION with the ideology of the law-and-order advocates reached its peak two years ago with the release of *Dirty Harry*, a Warner Brothers picture directed by Don Siegel and starring Eastwood as the saintly tough cop Harry Callahan. A right-wing fantasy about the San Francisco police force as a helpless group, emasculated by the liberals, the picture propagandized for para-legal police power and vigilante justice. The only way Harry could protect the city against the mad hippie killer who was terrorizing women and children was by taking the law into his own hands; the laws on the books were the object of his contempt, because he knew what justice was and how to carry it out. The political climate of the country has changed, of course, and, besides, Hollywood is, in its own cheaply Machiavellian way, responsive to criticism. In *Magnum Force,* the sequel to *Dirty Harry,* and also from Warner Brothers, Clint Eastwood, again playing Harry Callahan, is just as contemptuous of the laws on the books, but he believes in enforcing them. John Milius, who had an uncredited paw in *Dirty Harry,* and who gets the screenwriting credit here, along with Michael Cimino, twists the criticism of the earlier film to his own purposes: he takes his plot gimmick from those of us who attacked *Dirty Harry* for its fascist medievalism. The villains now are a Nazi-style élite cadre of clean-cut, dedicated cops who have taken the law into their own hands and are cleaning out the scum of the city — assassinating the labor racketeers, the drug dealers, the gangsters and their groupies. They are explicit versions of what we accused Harry of being; they might be the earlier Harry's disciples, and the new Harry wipes them all out. "I hate the goddam system," he says, "but I'll stick with it until something better comes along." *Magnum Force* disarms political criticism and still delivers the thrills of brutality. Harry doesn't bring anyone to court; the audience understands that Harry *is* the court. The picture is so sure it can get away with its political switch that before it allows Harry to spout his new defender-of-the-system line it actually tweaks the audience (and the movie press) by implying that he is the assassin who's mowing down the gangsters. But the movie — and this is what is distinctively new about it — uses the same tone for the Storm Troopers' assassination orgies that is used for Harry's killing of the Storm Troopers. At no point are we asked to be appalled by homicide. We get the shocks without any fears for the characters' safety or any sadness or horror at their gory deaths. The characters aren't characters in any traditional sense; they're not meant to be cared about.

Studio-machine-made action pictures have the speedy, superficial adaptability of journalism. One can measure some of the past two years' changes in the society by comparing the two films. In *Dirty Harry,* the sniper villain (wearing a peace symbol on his belt) idly picked off an innocent girl in a bikini while she was swimming, and the pool filled with her blood. In *Magnum Force,* one of the young Storm Troopers machine-guns everyone at a gangland swimming-pool party, and you get the impression that the girls prove their corruption and earn their deaths by being bra-less. Generally speaking, the victims now are all guilty of something, even if only of taking drugs, so you're exonerated — you don't have to feel anything. You can walk out and pretend you didn't see what went on. If the élite cadre and their prim Führer (Hal Holbrook) represent what Harry the hero represented the first time around, and if it's now right for Harry the hero to kill them, what of the writers who confect one position and then the next? Do they believe in anything? I think they do. Despite the superficial obeisance to the rule of law, the underlying content of *Magnum Force* — the buildup of excitement and pleasure in brutality — is the same as that of *Dirty Harry,* and the strong man is still the dispenser of justice, which comes out of his gun. Harry says it: "Nothing's wrong with shooting as long as the right people get shot." He's basically Paul Newman's Judge Roy Bean — another Milius concoction — all over again. Although Ted Post's direction of *Magnum Force* is mediocre, the picture isn't as numbing as *The Life and Times of Judge Roy Bean,* because it stays on its own coarse, formula-entertainment level, trying to turn on the audience to the garish killings and sustaining a certain amount of suspense about what's coming next. It sticks to its rationale. In *Magnum Force,* Dirty Harry is still the urban garbage man, cleaning up after us. His implicit justification is "You in the audience don't have the guts to do what I do, so don't criticize me." He says he does our dirty work for us, and so he invokes our guilt, and we in the audience don't raise the question "Who asked you to?" If Milius were a real writer instead of a hero-idolater, he might begin to raise questions about whether Harry unconsciously manipulates himself into these situations because he likes to kill, and about whether he keeps his face stony so as not to reveal this. But *Magnum Force,* the new city Western, has no mind and no class; the moviemakers seem unaware that their hero lives and kills as affectlessly as a psychopathic personality.

"A man's got to know his limitations," Harry keeps saying, and it's a comment not on himself but on his enemies' failure to recognize that he's the better man. Harry is tougher than the élite cadre, just as he was tougher than the mad hippie killer. The Nazis look like a troupe of juveniles in training for stardom in the old studio days, and are suspected by other cops of being homosexual, so Harry's weathered face and stud reputation (which is all hearsay as far as the audience goes) are like additional equipment for destroying them. But Eastwood is not a lover: women flock to him, but he makes no moves toward them. From what we see, they have to do all the work; he accepts one as dispassionately as he declines another. In one sequence, a woman bares her feelings and tells Harry of her desire for him while he just sits there, as unconcerned as ever; he's not going to get involved. Like the Western loner, he's almost surreally proper — lunatically so, considering what he does with his gun and fists. The only real sex scene in *Magnum Force* is a black pimp's murder of a black whore, which is staged for a turn-on erotic effect that I found genuinely shocking and disgusting. But the movie is full of what in a moral landscape would be sickening scenes of death: a huge metal girder smashes right into a man's face, and the audience is meant not to empathize and to hide from the sight but to say "Wow!"

The right-wing ideology functioned in *Dirty Harry;* here the liberalized ideology is just window dressing. What makes Harry the sharpshooter a great cop is that he knows the guilty from the innocent, and in this action world there's only one thing to be done with the guilty — kill them. Alternatives to violence are automatically excluded. If we talk to Harry, if after he dispatches his thirty-fifth or eightieth criminal one of us says "Harry, could you maybe ask the guy's name before you shoot, to make sure you've got the right man?" Harry's answer *has* to be "All criminals are liars anyway," as he pulls the trigger. Because that's what he wants to do: pull the trigger. What keeps the audience watching is one round of killings after another. *Magnum Force* is a far less skillful fantasy than *Dirty Harry,* and so is less involving, and it isn't likely to be as big a hit, yet my hunch is that the audience, after these last couple of years, rather likes its fantasies to be uninvolving.

IT'S THE EMOTIONLESSNESS of so many violent movies that I'm becoming anxious about, not the rare violent movies *(Bonnie and Clyde, The Godfather, Mean Streets)* that make us care about the characters and what happens to them. A violent movie that intensifies our experience of violence is very different from a movie in which acts of violence are perfunctory. I'm only guessing, and maybe this emotionlessness means little, but, if I can trust my instincts at all, there's something deeply wrong about anyone's taking for granted the dissociation that this carnage without emotion represents. Sitting in the theater, you feel you're being drawn into a spreading nervous breakdown. It's as if pain and pleasure, belief and disbelief had got all smudged together, and the movies had become some schizzy form of put-on.

[January 14, 1974]

A New Voice for Hoffman

DUSTIN HOFFMAN mimics a shy young Italian bank clerk in the Italian comedy *Alfredo Alfredo* while a fluent, mellifluous Italian voice speaks for him; in general, dubbing is an abomination, but the stranger's voice does wonders for Hoffman — it brings him out. In American movies, he's the perennial urban weakling-adolescent, doomed to swallow spit forever, but here, rid of the frightened, choked-up voice that constricts his characters, he gives a softer-edged, more relaxed performance. Maybe the director, Pietro Germi, put him at his ease; Alfredo, Hoffman's bank clerk, is warm and friendly and likable. Hoffman's face has never been very expressive (sometimes his rabbit stare makes me think that the great Maureen Stapleton has spawned an emotionally retarded son), but he has always been able to get our empathy. We feel exactly what he wants us to, and in *Alfredo Alfredo* his flickering anxieties are very ingratiating. Perhaps the idea of playing an Italian in an actual Italian movie was like a complete disguise to him, and so he lost that self-conscious worry — "Who am I and what am I meant to be thinking right this minute?" — that makes him so tense an actor. Hoffman's acting along to the sound of someone else's voice makes him seem like a silent comedian doing a routine. I remember thinking, some years back, that in a few scenes the dubbing of the witches added to the humor of the Francesco Rosi fairy-tale fantasy *More Than a Miracle.* (It starred Sophia Loren and Omar Sharif, and had some of the silly sweetness of *The Thief of Bagdad.*) Hoffman has scored a lot of points with his nasality, but the novelty of seeing him without that strangling trademark gives this rather conventional comedy an extra dimension. As it turns out, the picture, which begins promisingly high, sags under a load of uninspired, forced gaiety, and Hoffman himself doesn't have enough comic eccentricity to sustain his stunt. (A Mastroianni might have dipped into himself and come up with more.) Still, the first half hour or so is probably the most pleasing and the least self-conscious screen acting Hoffman has yet done.

Pietro Germi's method pits individuals — heaping collections of foibles — against the rigid Italian legal system, with its irrational laws governing marriage, divorce, and cohabitation. The comic tone is a bit used: almost everything Germi does here he has done before, and better. He overplays his hand this time. He knows how to make comedy move, and knows just the right length for individual scenes, but you get twice too much of everybody, as in the title (which is easy to remember but sounds like a new Italian restaurant). Stefania Sandrelli (the young second wife in Germi's *Divorce — Italian Style,* the seduced young girl in his *Seduced and Abandoned,* and Trintignant's wife in Bertolucci's *The Conformist*) is that rare creature a beautiful, sexy comedienne. She has one of the great walks in movies, a way of moving that doesn't have to be photographed from the rear: this girl comes right at you, and her delicate forward lurch is pure provocation. Her Mariarosa is the beneficiary of the sly trick of nature that gives girls with exquisite features an illusion of mystery; she's an imbecile sphinx, mysterious yet dumb as a cow. Mariarosa is an extravagantly romantic dictator — a maniacal caricature of the dizzy-dame princesses brought up in the fantasy that the man on whom they confer their bodies should live in thrall forever. The early scenes of her imperiousness and her enslavement of the deliriously impressed Alfredo are high slapstick; but perhaps Sandrelli the comedienne should be taken only in short stretches. Since her comedy style here is all based on one gag — that Mariarosa's beauty is empty and her romantic and sexual demands are insatiable — Mariarosa becomes as wearying to us as to her exhausted Alfredo. Once we get the idea, Germi fails to move on to something new, and his attempt to provide a contrast in a modern, independent working woman, played by Carla Gravina (she was the victim with the pained, melancholy eyes in *Without Apparent Motive*), isn't developed comically. He uses Gravina as a straight woman to the possessive, flighty Sandrelli, and so she has nothing to do but be efficient, and undemandingly pleasant to Hoffman, and Hoffman gets nothing to react to.

Sandrelli is the domestic tyrant of the bourgeois past, Gravina the career woman who liberates Hoffman. But the movie misses out by failing to show the dangers in the sexual freedom Gravina represents, and by failing to explore what the liberated Gravina sees in the shy, inexperienced bank clerk. In the conception of the timid, naïvely obliging Alfredo were the moviemakers perhaps saying something about the relation of the sexes? Hoffman is no more aggressive with one woman than with the other, but if Alfredo is the helpless prey of Gravina, as he was of Sandrelli, this isn't something the movie wants to get into. It retreats to old, safe ground. Still, Germi has his moments, especially in the courtship of Alfredo and Mariarosa, and when, on the first night of their honeymoon trip by rail, he finally makes it in, and she pulls the danger cord and stops the train, the joke is worthy of Freud.

⁂

MARK RYDELL'S FILMS ARE NOTHING IF NOT COMMERCIAL, and *Cinderella Liberty* isn't commercial. Rydell has one foot in forties movies and the other in a Gucci; neither is on the ground. In *The Cowboys,* he made a Western about John Wayne and a bunch of kids on a cattle drive — and people who go to Westerns don't want to watch a bunch of runny-nosed kids learning how to become men. In *Cinderella Liberty,* which Darryl Ponicsan adapted from his own novel, Rydell has a Baptist sailor (James Caan) take up with a beat-out whore (Marsha Mason), and mixes their messy affair with a high-minded interracial big-brother story. (Caan can't save Mason, but her little part-black son — Kirk Calloway — stirs his paternal impulses.) And where's the audience for that? It's too sordid for kids and too familiarly "touching" — and insultingly "universal" — for adults. Caan acts and looks like Gene Hackman here, but he does nobly, considering that his sailor is supposed to be simple and decent; he's the sort of fellow who takes a kid fishing and plays basketball with him — just what nobody wants to watch. Rydell shows some taste in handling the performers, but his taste is unrewarding; they don't overact (except for the freakily incorrigible Eli Wallach), but they have no excitement, either. And he doesn't know how to play his emotional ace. He tries to milk too much poignancy from Marsha Mason's big eyes and toothy grin, and our awareness of what we're meant to feel keeps us from feeling anything. Rydell wants to jerk tears, and he follows all the tear-jerking models, and yet he can't get the moisture going. He uses Vilmos Zsigmond as cinematographer and Leon Ericksen as production designer (the movie was shot in Seattle), but their work for him isn't like their work for Robert Altman; it's merely craftsmanship — it isn't infused with a director's spirit. Rydell has nothing new to offer, and in movies the old isn't gone, it's still around, and it has an innocence and a conviction that Rydell can't simulate; it also has superior manipulative skills. If he'd brought *Cinderella Liberty* off, I still wouldn't like it, but maybe I'd have had to fight a lump in the throat. When you aspire as low as Rydell does — all he wants is that universal lump — and fail, you're nowhere. (It's obvious that this movie was directed by a man. The slatternly, boozing whore, who can't bother to feed her son or take him to the dentist, trots off to the hospital to have another baby, and breathes perfectly for a natural childbirth.)

NO ACTOR CAN TRIUMPH over a bad toupee. That's as close to a general proposition as one is likely to arrive at from watching movies. Didn't Walter Matthau learn anything from seeing himself decked out in those terrible wigs in *Plaza Suite*? There isn't much acting honor to be had from *The Laughing Policeman,* but Matthau, playing a black-haired police detective, loses what little there is to Bruce Dern, who plays his partner. In his earlier days, Matthau would have played Dern's role; now he looks like Al Capp and tries to be the young hero. His hair shrivels his stature, the way John Wayne's embarrassing autumnal crop does; I had loved the way Wayne looked in *True Grit* (he was like Finlay Currie in *Great Expectations*), and he had seemed beyond foolish vanity. Matthau used to be a strategic scene-stealer: he used to putter around looking rumpled and sleepy while dropping zingers. This time, he's as square as the squarest of actors; he does the ancient obvious, while Dern's contentious but muffled manner — the way he puts cobwebs on his lines so there's an instant's delay before you quite get the joke — is the latest in fey, ruminative one-upmanship. Dern's performance is the only virgin element in this standard imitation of *Dirty Harry, The French Connection,* and *Bullitt,* adapted from the popular Stockholm-set novel by Maj Sjöwall and Per Wahlöö and moved to San Francisco. Directed by Stuart Rosenberg, the choppy film makes practically no sense (once again the mad mass murderer is some implausible sort of fancy homosexual), but it has been set up to be a ghoul's delight. Cadavers are examined, bloody wounds are inspected. It's best not to take chances with Rosenberg. I wouldn't invite him to a funeral.

EVERY NOW AND THEN, a film turns up that I think is so excruciatingly awful I can't believe anybody is going to open it. Invariably, it not only plays but gets some good reviews. The last of this ilk was *The All-American Boy,* featuring Jon Voight as an alienated boxer; the new one is called *Bone,* and its four principal characters jeer at and taunt each other with what are meant to be hideous truths. Yaphet Kotto is Bone, the symbolic black who cuts through the white man's lies. The picture was written, produced, and directed by Larry Cohen, who has mated the lurid exploitation film with a high-pitched attack on hypocrisy and American values. We can tell from the noise that Cohen thinks he's saying something important. He keeps changing his assaulting camera angles and throwing in big Off Off Broadway scenes, kidding himself that hysteria and hyperbole are Expressionism. He's a fourth-rate Hans Richter, and

Richter strains patience. The setting is L.A.; Yaphet Kotto threatens rich-bitch Joyce Van Patten with rape on a pool table, and weirdo Jeannie Berlin *(Bone* was made before *The Heartbreak Kid)* seduces Van Patten's husband, Andrew Duggan, while she pretends they're at the movies and feeds him popcorn and candy (Black Crows). There's also a variation of the Stuart Rosenberg car masturbation scene from *Cool Hand Luke,* and the antenna rises for a chortle. According to one reviewer quoted in the ads, "Cohen manages to have much fun impaling the fraudulence of sour materialistic Wasps, but his signal achievement is in showing how the stereotypes we have of each other cripple our relationships." Another critic says, "If you are tough enough to laugh at the kind of story that makes you wince *Bone* is your kind of movie. I'm that tough — I did laugh." I didn't laugh, but I winced, repeatedly, at the shrillness, at the overbright color, and at all that stale taunting. Who in the movie audience would still wince at a Wasp cleanly impaled? It's when the arrows are wide of their mark that one winces. It is not enough to be against the status quo; you must have talent.

[January 21, 1974]

Cicely Tyson Goes to the Fountain

AT AMERICAN MOVIES now, black people are just about the only ones looking to find heroes for themselves. Films made for whites are curdled by guilt and confusion; the heroes are corrupted, they fail, they live or die meaninglessly. But the black pictures feature winners, sometimes even non-racist winners — like the heroine of *Cleopatra Jones.* Played by Tamara Dobson, who is six feet two in her stocking feet and looks like a powerful, elongated Eartha Kitt, Cleopatra Jones is a female version of Robin Hood crossed with James Bond. She's protecting her people against the poppy growers and drug pushers, and audiences cheer for her as happily as audiences ever cheered for Robin Hood. Like him, she is guiltlessly heroic, a champion, fighting for the abused and mistreated. In the recent film *Gordon's War,* Gordon, a Green Beret (Paul Winfield), comes back from Vietnam to learn that the dope plague in the cities has taken his wife, and he organizes an army to clean the dope out of Harlem. The picture's celebration of vigilante justice may have been frightening to a white viewer, but the black movie audiences don't need to have it explained that the white-controlled system of authority is imposed on them and is corrupt. For them, Gordon's group represented an attempt by blacks to create their own system of authority. And the audiences could identify with Gordon's army just as at the Second World War movies the audiences identified with the ruthless American heroes — such as Bogart, or Dick Powell in *Cornered,* also avenging his dead wife — who were cleaning out the Nazis. Gordon's dedicated buddies, united by shared ideals, have the camaraderie that white movies used to feature. The shabbily constructed script made it impossible for the director, Ossie Davis, to bring his special gifts to *Gordon's War* — it has none of his feeling for comedy or for joy — and it hasn't been a hit, but it has something that unites the audience, something that one no longer gets out of white movies. Most of the films made for black audiences are exploitation jobs, as cynical and brutal as the current action films made for general audiences (if not more so). But the audiences at black films react more: with more gusto to the killings but also with more disgust to certain kinds of routine phoniness — like weak blacks pleading for their lives, or too much cant from the women characters. The audience seems to want its action, its heroism — even its sex — *pure,* not doctored with cowardice or a lot of bulling around. And if the audience reacts to the victories of Shaft or his progeny with the same pleasure as to the victories of a Cleopatra Jones, this is clearly because the audience enjoys feeling victorious.

To put it bluntly: While white audiences can laugh together at the same things — mainly at evidence of American stupidity and rot — there is nothing positive that they share. (I don't mean to suggest that this is necessarily bad, and I certainly don't mean to suggest that we should have clung to our myths of American heroism, or to that worst myth of all — the self-righteous union of strength and virtue. I'm just trying to pin down a distinction.) The movies for blacks have something that white movies have lost or grown beyond. I point this out because I think it's something that whites miss; it's what they mean when they say that there's nothing to take their children to. It's a lost innocence, a lost paradise of guiltlessness, and some of the black movies have it. A few months ago, when some friends asked me what they could take their kids to that their kids would have a good time at — something like the old Errol Flynn swashbucklers — the only picture I could think of was *Cleopatra Jones.* They told me later that the whole family had enjoyed it. We may have reached such a strange impasse in this country that whites need to go to black movies to relax and partake of guiltlessness.

The ironic miracle of *Sounder* was that whites could respond to its black family far more intensely than they could conceivably now respond to a white family. The blacks of *Sounder* live in hardship circumstances in which their sheer endurance is a victory — their endurance and their ability to sustain their feeling for each other. In the past, American movies celebrated white-pioneer courage and endurance; now the black movies take us back to those satisfying hopeful qualities, but, for whites, with a difference. Implicit in *Sounder* and in the new *The Autobiography of Miss Jane Pittman* is a sense of moral complexity — of a redressing of the balance, of justice at work within the mythology of popular culture. What we can no longer accept about white heroes and heroines we surrender to when the characters are black. I think we absolutely need to; this has nothing to do with the formal aesthetics of a particular piece of popular culture but everything to do with how popular culture works in a society. And we have been lucky. The beautifully made *Sounder* spared us the embarrassments of maudlin emotions; and *The Autobiography of Miss Jane Pittman,* which was produced for television by Tomorrow Entertainment and will be on C.B.S. on Thursday, January 31st (and will run in theaters in other countries), stars Cicely Tyson and was made by John Korty, a self-effacing director who has what might be described as an aesthetics ruled by morality. His past work (such films as *The Crazy Quilt* and *Funnyman,* and the TV film *Go Ask Alice*) shows his principled unwillingness to push for dramatic effect; this makes him the ideal director for *The Autobiography of Miss Jane Pittman.* One shove and we would say, "Oh, here it comes — more guilt piled high on us." But as *Jane Pittman* has been directed, her story, of how a black woman lived and what she went through, with major historical events seen through her eyes, has a far greater meaning than if white viewers were browbeaten into a defensive reaction. The full force of *The Autobiography of Miss Jane Pittman* is that no defense is possible, so none is called for.

Cicely Tyson plays a woman who was born in slavery and lived to take part in a civil-rights demonstration in 1962; the role spans Jane Pittman's life from the age of twenty to the age of a hundred and ten, and Cicely Tyson knows what she's doing every inch of the way. Her Jane Pittman does not have the Biblical strength or the emotional depth of her Rebecca in *Sounder.* Jane isn't a deep woman; childless, uneducated, she's an enjoyer of life. It isn't until extreme old age gives her a privileged status that she loses her fear and becomes — briefly, just before her death — politically active. Old age brings her out in other ways, too; it's as if her life were a series of liberations, so that only at the end is she free enough to speak her mind and to crack a joke and to find herself. When she walks up to a whites-only drinking fountain in front of a Southern courthouse, and drinks from it, all of us in the audience can taste the good water.

Tyson is an extraordinarily controlled actress, and perhaps this control has some relationship to the history of black people in this country. I used to watch her sometimes in the old George C. Scott TV series *East Side, West Side,* and I found her control and her tight reserve slightly antipathetic; she seemed to be holding back from us — not yielding her personality, not relaxing within the minuscule demands of the role. Now I think I can see why. It was a role in which a beautiful pinheaded actress might have been perfectly content, and her contentment might have made her seem delectable. Those secretary roles, black and white, are generally played for comedy or for sex; the black girls are plumped down in an office — to fill the quotas — but they're playing classy maids. What Tyson's strained manner in that series was saying to us was "I can't give myself to this role — I have more than this in me." And, despite her magnetic glamour, she wouldn't give us more than the cold efficiency of the secretary she played — which could only make a viewer slightly uncomfortable. In small, empty roles, this New York-born actress who had sold shopping bags on the streets when she was nine years old seemed aloof. She *felt* aloof from the roles, and she had too much in her to sell herself cheap. She still refuses to sell herself; in her performances as Rebecca and here as Jane, she never bathes us in the ravishing smile of her modeling years or her TV talk-show appearances. She has the haughtiness of the enormously gifted — of those determined to do everything the most difficult way, because they know they can. Her refusal to melt us with her smile is like Streisand's refusal to sing; there's some foolishness in these refusals, but also hard-won pride. In every breath, Cicely Tyson says to us, "I'm not going to make Jane a cute, feisty old darling for you to condescend to. I'm not going to warm the cockles of your heart. And don't treat me kindly as a great black actress; I'm an actress or nothing." She's an actress, all right, and as tough-minded and honorable in her methods as any we've got. You feel you're inside skinny old Jane's head: you get to understand her mixture of shallowness and superstition and pop culture and folk wisdom. And through knowing Jane Pittman you feel closer to a recognition of black experience in this country; at an ironic level Jane's story is the story of how it takes a hundred and ten years to make an activist out of an ordinary black woman. Tyson won't allow her beauty to carry her; she plays Jane with supreme integrity. Jane's charm seems all to belong to Jane; Tyson doesn't shove any of her own onto her. She doesn't yet have the fluidity of an actress who can turn the character into herself, and vice versa; she is still in conscious control. She hasn't made that leap to unconscious control which separates the "divine" legendary actresses from the superlative technicians. I'm comparing Tyson to the highest, because that's the comparison she invites and has earned. She isn't there, but she's on her way. She's great, but she will be even greater when she can relax and smile without feeling she's Uncle Tomming, as Streisand will be a greater artist when she can accept all her gifts and use them together.

The subject of the Ernest J. Gaines novel on which *Jane Pittman* is based is so good that everyone connected with the movie seems to have respected it. There are inevitable losses. The incendiary preaching that, in the novel, leads to one character's murder has been softened, and events sometimes lose their repercussions — no doubt because a novel more sprawling in time than *Gone with the Wind* is being attempted on a TV shooting schedule and budget, to fit a two-hour slot. There are almost eighty speaking parts, and some of the casting and acting — though not blatantly bad — are nondescript. (A Cajun character certainly doesn't help; no Cajun on the screen ever does.) Yet none of this does serious damage. There's one unfortunate change. In the novel, Jane dreads a black stallion that she thinks will kill Joe Pittman (the one man she loves enough to carry his name). For photographic reasons (the sequence was being shot using day for night), an albino was used instead; the eerie white horse, with a ghastly pink look around the eyes, is mystically effective, but the color switch suggests a racial symbolism that doesn't quite fit the situation. The clumsiest addition is the device of using Michael Murphy as a journalist interviewing the ancient Miss Pittman to link the episodes; toward the end, we feel the shift to amateurishness each time he appears. But Cicely Tyson is, I think, all that a reader of the book could ask for, and her performance and the director's tact are more than enough to compensate for these flaws, and for the anachronisms and naïveté in parts of Tracy Keenan Wynn's adaptation.

John Korty tells the story at a satisfyingly leisurely pace, befitting a woman who accumulates a hundred and ten years. Korty is a director who has never quite come into his own; his loose, unlabored style was probably at its best in the charming, neglected 1966 comedy *Funnyman*, starring Peter Bonerz (the dentist of *The Bob Newhart Show*) as a member of The Committee, the improvisational-revue troupe in San Francisco. This hero is wry and self-conscious, and automatically turns human relations into put-ons; he works up whatever situations he's in into routines — his "life situations" have the rhythm of revue acts, and vice versa. Korty didn't make a big thing of his funnyman hero; the movie just skipped along, and in places dawdled along, without solemnity. Probably Korty's movies suffered commercially from his honesty and tentativeness and his refusal to heighten emotions, but those same qualities showed to great advantage in his direction of the TV film about teen-age drug addiction *Go Ask Alice.* The contrast with the usual TV director's hysterically manipulative approach made Korty's work shine. Some of Korty's virtues are dimmed in *The Autobiography of Miss Jane Pittman,* because he's not working as flexibly as he did on his own movies (which he also photographed himself) — the direction here is more stilted — but the movie is still so much cleaner and simpler than just about any other movie made for TV (or any TV series show, either) that the fictional Jane Pittman has the singularity and dignity of a person in a documentary. There never was a Jane Pittman; the character is synthesized from stories that Gaines heard while growing up on a plantation in Louisiana, but, watching the film (which was all shot in Louisiana), one literally forgets (as readers of the novel did) that it is fiction. It seems to be a slightly awkward reënactment of the life of an actual person.

Beauty is almost unknown in movies shot for TV, but Korty has brought his compositional sense and his own unassertive lyricism to this mixture of folk history and agitprop. Visually, the interiors and the closeups of people making polemical speeches are only serviceable, but the exteriors and the closeups of Jane show the sane affection of an artist with no fakery about him. John Korty has no show business in his soul, and sometimes we really need to get away from the show-business hype. *The Autobiography of Miss Jane Pittman* isn't a great movie, though with more directorial freedom and a better script it might have been. But it's quite possibly the finest movie ever made for American television. Would a story about the endurance of an ancient white woman be this effective? There's no way for it to be comparable. There is probably no imaginable way that at this point in American history we could be as deeply moved by a white woman's story — no matter how much truth there was in it — as we are by this black woman's story.

[January 28, 1974]

Love and Coca-Cola

IN "MCCABE & MRS. MILLER," a rangy, buck-toothed young boy discovered undreamed-of pleasures at a snowbound brothel and met a scrawny, scared girl, a widowed bride who had just turned whore. She had teeth and a grin to match his own, and when he left they said goodbye, like the affectionate innocents they were, and he called out that he'd be back the next year. A minute later, still harmlessly affable, he was shot down from a bridge, and his body slowly crushed the ice before disappearing in the water. Robert Altman has reunited the pair, Keith Carradine and Shelley Duvall, in *Thieves Like Us*; he's Bowie, one of three escaped convicts, and she is Keechie, whose drunken father runs the gas station the convicts hide in. Bowie has been in prison for seven years, since he took part in a holdup when he was sixteen; Keechie has never had a boyfriend — not even one to walk her to church. They fall in love; it's two-sided, equal, and perfect — the sort of romantic love that people in movies don't fall into anymore. Keith Carradine takes the screen the way a star does, by talent and by natural right. In his bit role in *McCabe,* he made the audience yield to him so completely that his sequence almost threw the movie out of whack; he makes us yield here for the entire film. He has the rawboned, open-faced look of a young Henry Fonda or Gary Cooper; he's a beautiful camera subject, and the rawness saves him from the too-handsome-juvenile look of earlier stars. There has never been an ingénue like Shelley Duvall, with her matter-of-fact manner and her asymmetrical, rag-doll face; if it weren't for her goofy, self-conscious smile, she could be the child of Grant Wood's "American Gothic" parents. Her Keechie carries candor to the point of eccentricity: she's so natural that she seems bizarrely original. Whatever it was that Altman saw in her when he put the twenty-year-old Houston girl, who had never acted professionally, into *Brewster McCloud* didn't quite come through that time, but it certainly peeped out in her small role in *McCabe,* and here she melts indifference. You're unable to repress your response; you go right to her in delight, saying "I'm yours." She looks like no one else and she acts like no one else. Shelley Duvall may not be an actress, exactly, but she seems able to be herself on the screen in a way that nobody has ever been before. She doesn't appear to project — she's just *there.* Yet you feel as if you read her every thought; she convinces you that she has no veils and nothing hidden. Her charm appears to be totally without affectation. Altman must have sensed in that inexperienced twenty-year-old girl some of the same qualities that separate him from other directors: a gambler's euphoria about playing the game his own way, assurance without a trace of imitativeness.

In other Altman films, there is always something that people can complain about; they ask, "What's that there for?" In *Thieves Like Us,* there's nothing to stumble over. It's a serenely simple film — contained and complete. You feel elated by the chasteness of the technique, and the film engages your senses and stays with you, like a single vision. It's beautiful right from the first, pearly-green long shot. Robert Altman finds a sureness of tone and never loses it; *Thieves Like Us* has the pensive, delicate romanticism of *McCabe,* but it isn't hesitant or precarious. It isn't a heady, whirling sideshow of a movie, like *The Long Goodbye*; it has perfect clarity. I wouldn't say that I respond to it more than to *McCabe* or that I enjoy it more than the loony *The Long Goodbye,* but *Thieves Like Us* seems to achieve beauty without artifice. It's the closest to flawless of Altman's films — a masterpiece.

Altman breaks the pattern of what American directors are commonly supposed to be good at; this picture has the relaxed awareness that we honor Europeans for and that still mystifies Hollywood. Like *Mean Streets,* it didn't cost enough for Hollywood people to understand it. *Thieves Like Us* is based on a neglected, long-out-of-print 1937 novel by Edward Anderson — the novel that Nicholas Ray's 1948 picture *They Live by Night* was derived from. (Edward Anderson won a literary prize with his first novel, *Hungry Men,* in 1935, and then, as far as I can determine, published *Thieves Like Us* and disappeared from the writing world. It is said that he was living in Texas when *They Live by Night* was made, but the novel, according to Avon Books, which is putting out a new edition, is in the public domain, and the publishers have had no contact with the author.*) The Ray film, produced by John Houseman and starring Cathy O'Donnell and Farley Granger as Bonnie-and-Clyde figures, retained Anderson's plot but strayed far from the book's tone; the Altman film stays very close to that tone, while moving the action from Oklahoma and Texas to Mississippi. The picture was shot in se-

*His son and people who worked with him provide the information that he was a screenwriter at M-G-M in 1941, but mostly he supported his family by one crummy newspaper job or another. He died in 1963.

quence in forty-three days, at a cost of $1,250,000. Altman didn't build thirties sets; he found the vegetating old towns that he needed. He took his crew to Mississippi and made the picture in the sort of freedom that Jean Renoir had when, as a young man, he took his family and friends out to make *A Day in the Country.* Before Altman was hired to direct, the producer, Jerry Bick, had commissioned a script by Calder Willingham. Although Willingham gets a screen credit, his script didn't have the approach Altman wanted, and Altman's former script girl, Joan Tewkesbury, then devised another script, in collaboration with the director, which stays on Edward Anderson's narrative line, retaining much of his dialogue. (He was a considerable writer.) The movie has the ambience of a novel; it is the most literary of all Altman's films, yet the most freely intuitive. *Thieves Like Us* is so sensuous and lucid that it is as if William Faulkner and the young Jean Renoir had collaborated.

Robert Altman spoils other directors' films for me; Hollywood's paste-up, slammed-together jobs come off a faulty conveyor belt and are half chewed up in the process. I think I know where just about all the elements come from in most American movies (and in most foreign movies, too), and how the mechanisms work, but I don't understand how Robert Altman gets his effects, any more than I understand how Renoir did (or, for that matter, how Godard did from *Breathless* through *Weekend,* or how Bertolucci does). When an artist works right on the edge of his unconscious, like Altman, not asking himself why he's doing what he's doing but trusting to instinct (which in Altman's case is the same as taste), a movie is a special kind of gamble. If Altman fails, his picture won't have the usual mechanical story elements to carry it, or the impersonal excitement of a standard film. And if he succeeds aesthetically, audiences still may not respond, because the light, prodigal way in which he succeeds is alien to them. Three-quarters of a century of slick movies have conditioned audiences' expectations. But *Thieves Like Us* might win him the audience that was put off by the elliptical poetry of *McCabe & Mrs. Miller* and the offhand pyrotechnics of *The Long Goodbye.* There's no predicting what he'll do next; *Thieves Like Us,* with its soft, unassuming grace, may be the only fully accessible movie he'll ever make. Its vision is just as singular as that of his other films, but the masterly above-board method could put him in touch with a popular audience; Griffith used to reach that audience (less corrupted then, of course) with comparable pastoral romances, such as *True Heart Susie.* *Thieves Like Us* is not just the easiest-to-like picture Altman has ever made — I think one would have to fight hard to resist it.

The scope is small, but *Thieves Like Us* is a native work in the same way that *The Godfather* is; we know the genre (Depression, bank robbers, Bonnie and Clyde), and the characters are as archetypal as one's next-door neighbors. Altman didn't have his usual cinematographer and production designer with him this time; working with Jean Boffety, a French cinematographer who had never done a picture in this country, and with a newcomer, Jackson De Govia, as production designer, he seems to have changed his style of improvisation — to have become calmer, more fluid. Everything in the Anderson book is refined in the movie, instead of what usually happens to novels — the coarsening that results from trying to make things fit a preordained plan, and settling for the approximate. The milky, semi-transparent cinematography makes the story seem newborn. Altman uses the novel as his base, but he finds his story through the actors, and, as Renoir did, through accidents of weather and discoveries along the way. He finds spontaneous comedy; the novel isn't funny, but the movie is. The lovers are far less conventional in the movie than in the book. (With Shelley Duvall, you couldn't be conventional even if you wanted to.) Bowie isn't a psychopath or a crazed dreamer, like his two robber friends; he's still a kid, and his essential healthiness becomes the core of the picture. He wants what Keechie represents, but he's caught, living a life that doesn't make sense to him. When he says to a wandering dog "Do you belong to someone, or are you a thief like me?" we know that for him "thief" means "stray." Identifying with Bowie, we react to each eruption of violence as he does — with a moral chill. Anderson, too, had basically seen him as gentle and straight, but the picture takes its cue from the rapport of Carradine and Duvall, omitting other elements in his character and moving away from the links to *Bonnie and Clyde.*

At first, the two convicts who escape with Bowie — T-Dub and Chicamaw — sit around giggling, high on freedom, but then their characters start to take shape. Bert Remsen, who had given up acting, was working as casting director on *Brewster McCloud* when Altman put him into the picture; he appeared again, memorably, in *McCabe,* and now he's T-Dub, a veteran bank robber. T-Dub is a cheery, likable fool who becomes flushed with success and gets reckless; Remsen plays the role so warmly that T-Dub's careless idiocy is fully believable. John Schuck, who was Painless in *M*A*S*H,* has also turned up in two other Altman films, but there was nothing in his earlier work to prepare one for his major performance here, in the pivotal role of the heavy-drinking, half-mad Chicamaw. Schuck has always had a suggestion of a bulldog in his face, and now, grown corpulent and more powerful-looking, he gives a performance that in some scenes rivals the intensity that Bogart brought to his Fred C. Dobbs in *The Treasure of Sierra Madre.* Schuck's comic, terrifying big scene, when he insists on play-acting a robbery at home with small children and explodes in a murderous rage when they lose interest, and his last scene, in which he's deserted, yelling in torment on a country road, are classic moments. Altman often picks up part of his cast on location, or puts members of the crew to work; the writer Joan Tewkesbury turns up here as the woman in the train-station sequence. Louise Fletcher, who is Mattie, T-Dub's sister-in-law, had been a TV actress in the early sixties and had retired, but she is married to the film's producer and was on location in Mississippi. Altman asked her to play the small part of Mattie, and then, when he saw the presence she brought to it, he enlarged the role. Louise Fletcher has a full, strong body and great rounded arms; her Mattie is a no-nonsense woman who looks as if she had lived through what women in soap operas prattle about. She's a tough-broad earth mother with a coating of banal respectability — an authentic American-woman character.

You can see that Altman doesn't have to prove to anybody that he can re-create the thirties. The movie isn't a work of nostalgia; it's not a glorification of the past. It's localized in an era, and the people can be understood only in terms of that era. They are part of the age of radio, and Altman uses radio programs of the thirties for his score, and Coca-Cola for his motif. Everyone swigs Coca-Cola. Keechie is always reaching for a bottle; the old truck advertising Coca-Cola makes an appearance; and on the prison sign at the Mississippi State Penitentiary, at Parchman, there are Coca-Cola ads. I inquired, to find out if this was on the level, and was told that the crew was denied permission to film at actual prisons, where these ads are indeed on the signs, but that the reproduction is faithful. The prison at Parchman is, of course, a landmark in several Faulkner novels. For the last two years now, friends of mine have been shouting that Altman must do *The Wild Palms* or *As I Lay Dying*; they've been convinced that he is the man to bring Faulkner to the screen. Maybe he knew it all along, and maybe he was smart enough to know that he could do it best by using someone else's material for his text. (Perhaps this is also how someday someone will put Fitzgerald on film.) *Thieves Like Us* comes closer to the vision and sensibility of Faulkner's novels than any of the movie adaptations of them do. Altman didn't start from Faulkner, but he wound up there. If he did a Faulkner novel, he might not be able to achieve what people want him to. But *Thieves Like Us* is *his* Faulkner novel.

[February 4, 1974]

Nicholson's High

JACK NICHOLSON can make his feelings come through his skin, the way Anthony Quinn can make you share the emotion that's making him sweat. Other actors might communicate a thought or an emotion with an economical gesture, but Nicholson does it with his whole body, as if he were electrically prodded, and, watching him, we may not be sure if we're responding to the thought or emotion or to what a terrific turn he can do. Nicholson is puzzling. When he tried to give a quiet performance in *The King of Marvin Gardens,* he was so self-effacingly serious that he was a dead spot on the screen. But when he tears through a role, performing his specialty — a satirical approach to macho — he seems more contemptuous than satirical, and he looks stuck in the act. His actor's instinct seems to lead him to excess; the emotions he expresses don't have enough under them, and often he's like a one-man Pinter play — he expresses nothing but his own dynamism. My usual mixed feelings about him are mostly resolved in his new movie, *The Last Detail.* His performance is a turn, but it doesn't bother me. The turn is inseparable from the role, because the whole movie is a turn — and what else could he have done to make this movie work?

In *The Last Detail,* you can see the kid who hasn't grown up in Nicholson's grin, and that grin has the same tickle it had when he played the giddy, drunken Southern lawyer in *Easy Rider,* but now it belongs to the ravaged face of an aging sailor. The role of Buddusky, the tattooed signalman, first class, is the best full-scale part he's had; the screenwriter Robert Towne has shaped it to Nicholson's gift for extremes. After Buddusky's fourteen years in the Navy, his mind and emotions have been devastated, and he lives on nostalgia, ingrained resentment, a lewd prole's quick anger, and booze. The role has the highs that Nicholson glories in. He plays it like a spaced-out, dissipated James Cagney; his face always has something going on in it, and you feel that you can't get too much of him — though you do. At its best, his performance is so full it suggests a sustained version of Barry Fitzgerald's small but classic portrait of a merchant seaman in *The Long*

Voyage Home; it's easy to imagine Buddusky a few years hence returning to his ship after a binge as Fitzgerald did — a wizened little man with his tail between his legs. The movie is about blasted lives: Buddusky's and those of Mulhall (the black actor Otis Young), a gunner's mate, first class, and Meadows (Randy Quaid), a morose eighteen-year-old seaman who has been sentenced to eight years in a Navy prison for attempting to steal forty dollars from a polio-donation box. Buddusky and Mulhall are dispatched to take Meadows from the brig in Norfolk, Virginia, to the naval prison in Portsmouth, New Hampshire. The movie is the record of their dallying, beer-soaked journey and of their self-discoveries en route.

Nicholson gets a chance to demonstrate his enormous skill, and he keeps the picture going, but he's playing a mawkish role — a sentimentalist with a coward's heart. This time, the emotions he's expressing are, if anything, too clear. *The Last Detail,* based on Darryl Ponicsan's novel, is the newest version of a heart-wrenching genre that used to work with a huge popular audience — and possibly it will this time, too. Essentially, it's the story of doomed people who discover their humanity too late, and nothing in the movie can keep this from being a sell — not Nicholson's and Quaid's imaginative performances, and not Robert Towne's finely tuned script. It's doubtful if there's any way to extract an honest movie from a Ponicsan novel — Ponicsan also wrote the book from which *Cinderella Liberty* was derived — because Ponicsan works on us for a canned response. His material didn't play in *Cinderella Liberty* and it does here, but the same manipulative streak runs through both films, and the same obviousness. Everything in *The Last Detail* tells you how to feel at each point; that's how the downer-tearjerker has always worked. This picture sounds realistically profane and has a dark, grainy surface, and by Hollywood standards it's strong, adult material, but the mechanism is a vise for our emotions — the mechanism is schlock. The downer-tearjerker congratulates you for your sensitivity in seeing the touching hopelessness and misery that are all you've got to look at.

Meadows, the eighteen-year-old, is a petty pilferer, a bawling, uncommunicative kid, too sluggish and demoralized to be angry at the injustice of his harsh sentence. He doesn't know that he has any rights; he has never learned to fight back. As the story is set up, he's a sleeping beauty; on the drunken trip, Buddusky and Mulhall offer him comradeship, and he awakens and discovers his manhood. We perceive the possibilities in him, knowing that prison life will crush him back down to the listless, almost catatonic state he was in. And, in a parallel process, the tough, damaged Buddusky, who has felt warm and paternal while bringing the kid out, can only retreat to his guzzling and brawling. Buddusky couldn't function except in the service; he's quick to identify with the kid, because he's an emotional wreck himself, living in the past, spinning out tired anecdotes. We're programed to recognize that he's a man who is always spoiling for a fight so he can let out his frustrations, and we're programed to respond to each pointedly ironic episode. When the three men go to a Village party, Buddusky comes on with a "line" and he doesn't register that he's bombing out; his peppy cock-of-the-walk act is all he's got — he has no other way to make contact. We see him through the girls' contemptuous eyes; to them he's just a crude blowhard. In contrast, the depressed kid's innocent, solemn dignity is a hit with them. The movie is about the lost possibilities in both Buddusky and Meadows, and about the acceptance of a restricted life by Mulhall. Otis Young's Mulhall has chosen the Navy because it's not a bad deal for him; we can't tell much more about the character. Otis Young has the cheekbones and facial contours of a stronger version of the young Frank Sinatra; his eyes slant upward the same way, and he's marvelous to look at, but the role isn't as flamboyant as Nicholson's or as affecting as Quaid's, and Young's restrained performance doesn't add up to as much as his face suggests. He never quite comes across; he stays as nice-guyish as a black Gregory Peck.

The direction, by Hal Ashby, is not all it might be. I loved much of Ashby's first film, *The Landlord* — a story about a rich white boy (Beau Bridges) who bought a building in a black ghetto and had an affair with a tenant (Diana Sands). It was adapted by William Gunn from Kristin Hunter's novel (both writers are black), and it had a complicated sense of why people behave as they do. It was full of characters; more and more people kept getting into the young landlord's life, and I became interested in every one of them. In several cases, I don't think those performers have been as good since; maybe the writing accounted for the quality as much as the directing did, but I missed Ashby's second film, *Harold and Maude,* and I'd been looking forward to more of his work, hoping for a film full of people whose lives can't be reduced to formulas. The material here, though, is on a single track; we go from city to city, but there's never anything to look at. Visually, the movie is relentlessly lower-depths gloomy; it doesn't allow us to think of anything but the pushy central situation. And though Nicholson does suggest some of the qualities of the characters in *The Landlord,* and Quaid transforms himself before our eyes, they play within a preordained scheme. It's all *required.* The effectiveness of the movie depends on the director's wringing pathos out of the two older men's gruff tenderness toward the kid and their desire to show him a good time before he's locked away; and though Ashby, to his credit, keeps the pathos down, there is still more mugging than necessary. Ashby's weaknesses show — not so much with the three leads as with the minor players and the staging of the large-scale sequences. That's where you can feel the director trying to get a certain emotional effect, and he gets it, all right (an effect I hate anyway), but he's also heavy and clumsy about getting it (which makes me even more aware of how I hate it). There's a fight aboard a train, and the passengers don't react adequately; there's a church scene in which followers of an Eastern religion chant together, and though it may well be authentic, the way it has been shot it doesn't feel authentic; in a Boston brothel scene Carol Kane does her Pre-Raphaelite wasted-beauty number; and so on. And I think I'd be happier without the Johnny Mandel score, with its antic use of military airs, orchestrated in an unfamiliarly thin way to add a musical layer of irony. It all works together, of course, but the overstressed style and the systematized ironies tighten one's responses. Ponicsan has talent, but he degrades his own material; he milks tragedy for pathos. Towne improves on the novel, and his ear for dialogue gives the film some distinction, but there is only one line that seems to be there for its own sweet sake — when Nicholson tells a story about a whore in Wilmington who had a glass eye — and this was the only minute I freely enjoyed.

WHAT IS ONE TO MAKE of the shamelessness of big, old stars? John Wayne must be heading toward seventy, but he's trying to change his image. In *McQ*, he imitates his juniors; he lifts his name from Steve McQueen and his tough-police-officer character from Clint Eastwood's Dirty Harry Callahan. As a member of the Seattle police force, Wayne clutches a little gun in gnarled hands the size of cattle hocks; with his slit eyes and his slit mouth, he looks like a squashed Easter Island statue as he sits hunched over the wheel of his Green Hornet. Directed at a funereal pace by John Sturges, whose better days are beginning to recede into the far-distant past, the picture is a distended version of the other right-wing police thrillers. I think I've read Lawrence Roman's script already, in letters from cranks. A collection of obnoxious hippies are brought into police headquarters, so that one of them can call McQ a "pig" and McQ can deliver a blow that makes the kid crumple up. (Wayne looks triumphant, as if hitting that hippie were going to take ten years off his age.) McQ beats up a drug dealer and boasts of his own brutality. The audience is meant to get vicarious pleasure from the blows Wayne lands and from his sniping at women's lib, and so on, but except for the right-wing piques and the frequent body-splattering shootings *McQ* is like a dull fifties movie. Incompetence like this prostrates one; I got so stoned by the boringness I forgot to get up and go home. The performers look to be in the same condition; they are given no characters to play and they're up there making helpless faces at the audience. (Eddie Albert sputters as if his lines were choking him.) In the most ludicrous single sequence, two huge trucks, specially equipped with murderous battering rams, come at Wayne's Green Hornet, one from the front and one from the back, and they crush the little car like cheese in a grilled sandwich. When they stop, the car has been totaled, but John Wayne gets out unscathed.

The women are all hot for this sexpot McQ, and one of them — Colleen Dewhurst, playing a waitress who works in a bar — coerces him into going to bed with her by promising him the information he wants "in the morning." She looks at that hulk and the granite face and the tousled light-brown bangs and she apologizes for being fat and ugly — Colleen Dewhurst, that giant force of nature, a woman to confer greatness on a man, apologizes for being fat and ugly to John Wayne! We see him assent to the sad truth of what she tells him, and he reveals to us that he's charitable enough to overlook it.

[February 11, 1974]

O Consuella!

"ZARDOZ," a sci-fi fantasy set in the year 2293, wasn't an expensive folly, though it looks like one. Written, produced, and directed by John Boorman, and brought in for one million four hundred thousand dollars, it is clearly a labor of love, dedication, technical-effects craftsmanship, and humorless lunacy. Boorman not only doesn't think like a writer but while directing his own script seems to have forgotten most of what he knows about making movies. It's possible that, gifted as he is, Boorman doesn't have much common sense; the characters speak in an abstract manner, delivering pithy observations about the human condition — and they never talk to each other. Boorman skims ideas off the top of various systems of thought and builds a glittering cultural trash pile. *Zardoz* is probably the most gloriously fatuous movie since *The Oscar,* though the passages between the laughs droop. It's a stately yet cranky vision of a future society dominated by immortal, hyperintelligent women — soulless, heartless, sexless. The men are immortal, too, but, being impotent, they are passive and effete. Together, these Eternals, who protect the science and knowledge of the past, live communally in the Vortex, while in the outlands there are survivors of the old world, slaves called Brutals, who produce grain to supply the Vortex. (For reasons I won't try to fathom, the bread is green.) A privileged group among the Brutals, the Exterminators, worship a giant flying head called Zardoz; Zardoz furnishes these Exterminators with guns to slaughter the excess population of Brutals. The Exterminators are sexually potent; when one of them, an exceptionally well-endowed physical specimen named Zed (Sean Connery), penetrates the Vortex, those bored intellectual ladies go gaga. Zed, a slave who comes to liberate his masters, is clearly meant to be nature's answer to the Vortex, and the Vortex starts to fly apart when the erudite ladies get the itch for this virile savage. May, a geneticist (Sara Kestelman), detects his possibilities before the others do. I had begun giggling early on, but it was when May, with her exquisite British articulation, addressed the most austerely intellectual of the ladies (Charlotte Rampling) as "Consuella" that I collapsed in my chair. When the snooty Consuella fights her passion for Zed — the last man in the world, get it? — my mind slithered back to a laughing fit I'd had as a child when I saw Helen Gahagan as H. Rider Haggard's She. Life in Boorman's Vortex is discothèque H. Rider Haggard.

The place looks like a Victorian health spa, with the bright green of Ireland (where the film was shot) in the background. The women wear the diaphanous gowns of goddesses, the decadent men look like leftovers from an Egypto-Roman epic, and the cinematographer, Geoffrey Unsworth *(2001, Cabaret),* has photographed them in a shimmering, luxuriant style that suggests the paintings buried away in museum basements which are hauled out for Romantic revivals — the style is imitative-pretty-garbage. A prophetess in the middle of a pool might be out of Maxfield Parrish or might be somebody's stoned daughter at a Palm Springs garden party — it's all a flowing blur, both a view of élitist decadence and the richest-looking movie Boorman could get for the money.

Beefy naked, Sean Connery traipses around in a loincloth that looks like a snood; his long, dangling hair is neatly tied, though at times he seems to be wearing a snood on his head, too. What is the actor who rejected the pasha's riches that went with the role of James Bond doing here playing the only potent man at the discothèque? He seems to be asking himself the same question; he acts like a man who agreed to do something before he grasped what it was. He hangs in there stolidly, loyally, his face saying, "I'm wrong, but I'll do it." There are times when his expression — a mixture of irony and incredulousness ("Am I turning into Charlton Heston?") — brings the house down. In the picture's wittiest scene, the hoity-toity ladies perform electronic tests on this lower order of being to find out what stimulates him sexually; their swank blue movies don't have the slightest effect, but when they stop the picture show he looks at Consuella and the chart readings soar. If electronic readings had been taken on audiences over the last few years, Charlotte Rampling would probably be a star by now. She's tantalizingly sexy, but she never seems to be used right. She always shows flashes, but she never delivers, and it's still the same here; she seems like Jeanne Moreau before *The Lovers.* Maybe she has never got the right role, or maybe there isn't any right way to use her: the gimlet eyes and sensual hauteur may be all the personality she's got.

Science-fiction movies always sound faintly silly; people never know how to talk in made-up worlds, and they usually sound abjectly prosaic. Boorman has a vital, humor-filled star and a cool-witch actress, but he gives them unspeakable dialogue and he deadens their impact by post-syncing. Boorman must have a tin ear for what live sound does for a performance. No doubt he gains greater mobility and visual freedom by not worrying about the sound until afterward, but he destroys any possible conviction the actors could supply. Their speech is strained and distant, so you can't tell whether something is deliberately funny or whether it's an unintentional *gaffe.* The actors lose their vividness. It's like watching a dubbed Italian spectacle on TV: it's all tinged with boredom.

And pomposity. Everybody is entitled to a certain amount of craziness, but John Boorman may have exceeded the quota. There has never been anything like the sanctimonious slaughter scene in this movie — a scene based on the obscenely foolish notion that the Eternals are being butchered as a favor to them. Is Boorman actually saying that this static, élitist communal society is where we're heading? And is he really saying that the world needs a male savior, a new Adam to re-establish the masculine principle in a world gone effete? After the destruction of the Vortex, Zed-Adam and his Consuella-Eve begin to replenish the earth; she gives birth to a son and, having accomplished all that's necessary, they ripen, age, and die. Presumably, the next Eve will have to come out of the son's rib all over again — unless he locates a descendant of May or her girl friends (also impregnated by Zed), who rode off on horseback when the other Eternals met their bloody deaths. Boorman wants the world to go back and start on the same course for the second time. He seems to think we've got away from being dominated by fighting, fertile males. What a crotchety — and revealing — cautionary tale. He's worried about the intellectuals' taking over; he thinks we're endangered by feminization and sterile intellectuality and impotence.

Boorman's world view is like a country bumpkin's vision of New York City. He has some other hick attitudes, too. In *Zardoz,* Boorman sees knowledge as a collection of facts that can be poured into a person, thus "educating" him — as if education were the same as preparing for a quiz show. (When the women decide to educate Zed by osmosis and his head gets filled with all the knowledge that has been accumulated, a friend sitting with me moaned, "I can't believe I learned the whole thing.") With Boorman's conception of knowledge, it's no wonder that many of the Eternals become apathetic; there is no intellectual or artistic or scientific creativity, and no growth. He thinks that intellectuals are custodians of dead information and that they're a menace because they're sterile in every sense. Perhaps it's best not to dwell on his amalgam of femininity and decadence.

The film is a mass of inoperative whimsies and conceits; they're inoperative even on the dumbest sci-fi level, because Boorman isn't enough of a writer to make them work together. Many movie directors feel that they are not fully expressing themselves — not functioning as artists — unless they also conceive their projects and write the scripts. For those directors who were writers to start with, or who are able to write, this can sometimes result in unusually personal and expressive films. In Boorman's case, the result lacks the human dimensions that would make us care about the big visual sequences. A gifted creator of a sci-fi world might enable us to perceive things as the inhabitants of that world would. Boorman belongs to the category of sci-fi writers who impose their own hangups on their vision of the future, and if *Zardoz* does little else for us it helps to explain the deficiencies in some of his other films: the ostentatiousness and the absence of vital connections — why the thriller *Point Blank,* for example, was like a mayhem "happening." (We could gorge on faddish tricky effects, but we could never find out what the picture was about.) I remember best a scene of Angie Dickinson wearing herself out trying to hit Lee Marvin, just as from *Zardoz* I remember a shot of Zardoz flying in for a landing. Without a strong writer to supply emotion and a coherent level of meaning, Boorman's movies disintegrate into shots and sequences.

Writers don't become writers overnight, but directors who get in a position to conceive their own projects sometimes feel that getting in that position makes them writers. Boorman has made money for the movie industry; he's earned the right to his follies. (As for the designers and performers and technicians who killed themselves to make a five-million-dollar movie for one million four hundred thousand dollars, probably they had such a good time working on this big, gooey picture that they didn't care what it was all about anyway.) But it's far from a terrible fate for a director as gifted as Boorman to stick to directing and to express himself as a director. His strength is in showing men in conflict; it's not in ideas. On the evidence, he is a greater artist as a director than he will ever be as a writer-director.

◆

THEN THERE'S MEL BROOKS, who isn't a director. When *Zardoz* was being made, Brooks should have been employed to hang around on a cloud, with permission to replace any actor at any point. That, maybe, is the best way he could be employed on any movie. Brooks not only isn't a director — he isn't really a writer, either. He's the cutup in the audience whose manic laughter and unrestrained comments stop the show. Essentially, he *is* the audience; he's the most cynical and the most appreciative of audiences — nobody laughs harder, nobody gets more derisive. He was perfectly cast in the short *The Critic.* His humor is a show-business comment on show business. Mel Brooks is in a special position: his criticism has become a branch of show business — he's a critic from the inside. He isn't expected to be orderly or disciplined; he's the irrepressible critic as clown. His comments aren't censored by the usual caution and sentimentality, but his crazy-man irrepressibility makes him lovable; he can be vicious and get away with it because he's Mel Brooks, who isn't expected to be in control. His unique charm is the surreal freedom of his kibitzer's imagination.

The other side of the coin is that he isn't self-critical. And, as his new picture, *Blazing Saddles,* once again demonstrates, he doesn't have the controlling vision that a director needs. It's easy to imagine him on the set, doubled up laughing at the performers and not paying any attention to what he's supposed to be there for. Mel Brooks doesn't think like a director; he's not a planner. He doesn't even do any formal, disciplined routines; he's a genius at spontaneous repartee — which the movies have never yet been able to handle, though television can, and that's where Brooks is peerless. Out of nowhere, he says things that people talk about for decades. Because of the feeling we've built up about how special he is, we go to *Blazing Saddles* eager to be delighted, gleeful in anticipation of a Mel Brooks film, already having put the disappointment of the last one out of mind. And the first five minutes are what one dreams of. Over the titles, Frankie Laine sings a song with juicy, mock-cliché lyrics that Brooks wrote — a song punctuated with whiplashes — and then a group of black railroad workers in the Old West, goaded to sing by gun-carrying guards who demand a spiritual, break out with "I get no kick from champagne." After that, it's all downhill, though Gene Wilder and Madeline Kahn redeem as much as they can. The story is about a modern black hipster (Cleavon Little) who becomes sheriff in a Western town in the eighteen-sixties — a core idea without much energy in it to start with, a variant of the plot of such movies as *The Paleface,* with Bob Hope. The role is written for a comic, and Cleavon Little is a handsome, ingratiating actor but not a comic. He can't take off and be sneaky-subversive-funny, the way Richard Pryor and Bill Cosby can. Cleavon Little is clean-cut and open-faced, and not at all the raffish con artist he's meant to be; we like him but we don't laugh at him. He seems too nice for what's going on around him in this movie — and that's partly a compliment.

Brooks's humor is intentionally graceless; he seems to fear subtlety as if it were the enemy of all he holds dear — as if it were gentility itself. Brooks *has* to love the comedy of chaos. He wants to offend, and he also wants to be loved for being offensive. We can share his affection for low-comedy crudeness, but not when he pounds us over the head with strident dumb jokes, and not when we begin to feel uncomfortable for the performers — mugging and smirking and working too hard. Brooks's sense of what's funny has sunk to sour, stale faggot jokes, and insults, and to dirtying up mildewed jokes, as if that would make them fresh. I never imagined I'd think back longingly on Brooks's first film, *The Producers* — but it didn't sink to this. His second film, *The Twelve Chairs,* was bland and pokey, but Brooks himself was funny in it. He isn't funny here; there is nothing retrievable in either his moronic Governor Lepetomane or his Yiddish-speaking Indian chief. He's become consciously cuddly and lovable; he acts as if he were the movie's mascot. As the Governor, he does the old ogling-the-luscious-secretary bit. It used to work for Groucho, but it didn't work for Zero Mostel in *The Producers,* and when Brooks does it himself it reaches a point of embarrassment that is almost painful. It's shamefully tired, like his Jewish jokes, which aren't even jokes anymore but just an assertion of Jewishness — as if that were always good for a laugh.

Those performers here whose roles depend on teamwork are stranded. Gene Wilder saves himself by performing in his own dreamer's rhythm, giving his fast-draw artist a relaxed, reflective manner — and is his talent deceiving me, or is Wilder getting more attractive with the years? Madeline Kahn, doing a barroom-songstress Dietrich parody, has some inventive twists of the tongue that work despite the sloppy context, but her role isn't worthy of her — and I didn't enjoy hearing her insulted. The movie is a rehash of *Hellzapoppin* and other slapstick burlesques, and it may appeal to those who enjoyed the rehashed humor of *What's Up, Doc?,* but it doesn't have the wit that made Mel Brooks a hero. He's become like a gag writer with a joke-book memory who cracks up at every terrible joke he recalls. Most of the gags in *Blazing Saddles* never were very funny, and probably Brooks knows that and thinks that what's funny about those rotten old jokes is how unfunny they are. But as a director he doesn't have enough style to make the unfunny funny. In *Blazing Saddles* he makes the unfunny desperate.

[February 18, 1974]

The Street Western

IN THE LANDSCAPE of the traditional Western, the simple, masculine values that the Westerner stood for were ancient and noble. He was the hero of our mass-culture folk art; for the whole world, this mythic hero symbolized American democracy and virtue and justice. If he was part of a reverie, it was a reverie about what was best in this country, and Westerns made us nostalgic for the imagined simplicities of our country's past, and for the naïveté of our own childhood, when we had innocently believed in faultless protector-heroes. Riding to the rescue, the cowboy hero fought fair and punished the guilty. The hero might himself be an outlaw (as in John Ford's *Stagecoach*), but he was a good man. The theme was always good against evil, and the iconography — the horses, the hats, the spurs and leather vests, the sunsets and cactus and cattle — was a reminder of an unspoiled country that the hero was fighting to keep from being destroyed. The villains were spoilers of the American dream. Between the villains and the hero were the farmers or townspeople — ordinary people, who stood up to the villains and lost, or who accommodated to evil because they were defenseless or too scared to fight. They were in the same position as most of us in the audience, but we were not asked to identify with their ineffectiveness, or with their partial victories, either. In the midst of a legend, why consider the actual world? Our hearts rode with the protector. The hero was a natural leader — the American knight. He won because he was physically stronger than the villains; his fists and his gun represented Justice. We didn't worry about his assumption of authority or about his use of force. The story was formal and remote, a ritualized dream of the past that we clung to. It had no direct application; the Westerner's ability to outfight the spoilers was part of our inspirational mythology. The landscape itself — the immensity of deserts and plains that the hero rode through — distanced the Westerns; and horses, with their patrician beauty, were natural carriers of deities.

A few more Westerns may still straggle in, but the Western is dead. Nobody's making even those last-gasp Westerns anymore — the ones about the lonely last cowboy, or the semi-spoofs featuring heavy old movie stars falling off their horses or kinky cowboys going to Mexico or farther south *(Butch Cassidy and the Sundance Kid).* There's been nothing since *Jeremiah Johnson* and *The Life and Times of Judge Roy Bean,* in 1972, and nothing appears to be scheduled. It's the end of a movie era. But the Western cowboy hero hasn't disappeared; he's moved from the mythological purity of the wide-open spaces into the corrupt modern cities and towns *(Dirty Harry),* and on paved streets he's an inflammatory figure. When Buford Pusser (Joe Don Baker), the hero of *Walking Tall,* trims the bark off a stout hickory limb and starts swinging this skull-breaking club against the spoilers who are operating a wide-open Sin City strip near his birthplace in Tennessee, mythology and realism are joined.

Walking Tall is a volcano of a movie — and in full eruption — loosely based on the life of a man who has become a legendary figure through ballads celebrating his exploits. (Johnny Mathis sings an excruciating *Walking Tall* ballad at the close.) From *Bonnie and Clyde* on, our recent powerful, big-box-office hits have mostly questioned the old movie myths, turning them inside out and indicating that the bad guys often win. *Walking Tall* goes right back to *Beowulf* and stays on course. The actual Buford Pusser is a six-foot-six-inch former professional wrestler. As the movie tells it, he returns to Tennessee after several years on the road, and when he complains because a friend of his has been cheated in a dice game at a state-line gambling casino he is beaten, slashed, and left to die. A man of prodigious strength, Pusser recovers, and since the sheriff refuses to prosecute his assailants, he takes a club, goes back to the casino, and fractures the crooked gamblers' arms. On trial, he defends his act of revenge as a man's natural right, tearing off his shirt and showing his knife-scarred chest as evidence. Acquitted, he enters the race for sheriff against the incumbent, Al Thurman (Gene Evans), who had refused to help him, and Thurman, trying to run him off a bridge, is killed — though Pusser tries valiantly to save him and does succeed in rescuing Thurman's deputy. Elected sheriff, Pusser proceeds to clean up the area, though at terrible cost to himself and his family. Buford Pusser's inspirational ordeal is like a small-town version of *Dirty Harry,* but it isn't snide or deliberately right-wing, like *Dirty Harry. Walking Tall* appears to be pre-political, as the traditional Westerns were. It is solemnly, unself-consciously square — a celebration of the same virtues that the Westerns always stood for, but, unlike those

Westerns, not distanced. Those Westerns weren't rabble-rousing; *Walking Tall* is.

Maybe, during all those years of watching Westerns, though we didn't believe in them we wanted to. The child in us wanted to, and maybe the Westerns softened us up for primitivism in the guise of realism. *Walking Tall* appeals to a deep-seated belief in a simple kind of justice — perfect, swift, Biblical justice. It returns us to the moral landscape of the Western, yet the picture is more crude in its appeal than the Westerns, because it works almost totally on the blood-and-guts level of emotionally charged violence. Buford's union of force and righteous wrath has the drive of a crusade against corruption — a crusade for a fundamentalist politics. When Buford began to clobber the bad guys, people in the audience cried out, "Get 'em, get 'em!" — and they weren't kidding. *Walking Tall* has just opened in New York, but it has been playing around the country for the past year, and is said to have already grossed close to thirty-five million dollars. I'm told that in parts of the South it is a ritual that at the end audiences stand in homage and cheer; in New York, audiences scream and shout their assent to each act of vengeance that the towering hero takes upon his enemies. I've heard of people who have already seen it twice and are going back.

Born in 1908, the director, Phil Karlson, has been working in Hollywood since 1932. He made low-budget Westerns and routine pictures until the mid-fifties, when he made the sleeper *Tight Spot* and won recognition for the Alabama-set *The Phenix City Story,* about a crusading candidate for Attorney General and his son who did battle against an earlier Sin City vice operation. Later, Karlson directed the intelligent action melodrama *Hell to Eternity,* and such films as *The Young Doctors, Rampage,* the popular Matt Helm *The Silencers* and *The Wrecking Crew,* and, recently, *Ben.* He has a veteran low-budget action director's skills, and these are what he brings to bear on *Walking Tall*: he doesn't over-prepare a scene; he makes his points and moves on. Karlson pushes and punches, but he's good at it. He can dredge up emotion; he can make the battle of virtuous force against organized evil seem primordial. He has a tawdry streak (there's an exploitation sequence with a nude prostitute being whipped), and he's careless (a scene involving a jewelry salesman is a decrepit mess), but in the onrush of the story the viewer is overwhelmed. *Walking Tall* isn't afraid to pull out all the stops of classical cheapie melodrama, right down to the murder of the Pusser family dog and the weeping face of a bereaved child. One would be tempted to echo Thelma Ritter in *All About Eve* — "Everything but the bloodhounds snappin' at her rear end" — but some of the suffering has a basis in fact. Mrs. Pusser, played by Elizabeth Hartman, was actually ambushed and killed in 1967. The film is a heartbreaker as well as a gut-cruncher. Elizabeth Hartman is a gifted actress who appears too seldom; a delicate-featured redhead with a beautifully modeled brow, she has the appealing quality that the young Janet Gaynor had. You want to reach right out to her; she's huggable. Karlson uses her for as much tearjerking potential as he dares. Brenda Benet (she has lazy, hot eyes, like Gail Russell's) plays a Vietnam widow turned whore, a good-bad temptress who makes overtures to Buford; Rosemary Murphy is a lively dragonlady whore-mistress; and Ed Call, as Lutie, Buford's old high-school chum, practically oozes Southernness — which is right for his role. The cast is frowzily passable; that is, the frowziness passes for authentic (although, as Buford's father, Noah Beery appears to think that he can be Southern by acting Hollywood-cornpone sweet). The pink, freckled faces without makeup carry a message of "truth," the same way the rundown bars do. (The film was shot in Tennessee, partly in McNairy County, where the actual Pusser served three two-year terms as sheriff, from 1964 to 1970.) Even the crummy cinematography gets by, because the picture's very crudeness makes it seem innocently honest. *Walking Tall* doesn't seem a sell, as a movie with a slicker surface might. All of it works to give the audience an exultant sense of the triumph of the heroic common man — his victory over "the system."

In the movie, Pusser as a wrestler is known as Buford the Wild Bull; this name must have been the key for Joe Don Baker's performance. Baker plays Buford as a soft-drawling, peace-loving man who, enraged by injustice, becomes a maddened fighting bull. Astonishingly, even when pummeling an adversary with body blows that are amplified so that they sound as if a tractor were being driven into flesh, he has the dignity of a wounded bull. At six feet two, Baker is a good deal smaller than the actual Pusser, but he looks enormous enough; he comes from Texas via the Actors Studio and TV *(Mongo's Back in Town, That Certain Summer)* and films *(Junior Bonner)*, and he seems Southern redneck — a common man who works outdoors in the sun — to the soul. He has that heavy, flaccid look that Southern white men often get early in life; it goes with a physical relaxation that can fool Northerners like me, who don't always recognize the power hidden in the flab. As Baker plays him, Buford is a nonreflective hero who, when angered, tramples on his enemies uncontrollably. This brute obsessiveness may easily be the result of the moviemakers' desire to show plenty of beatings, but Baker almost makes us believe that Buford fights back because he has to. Baker's Buford has the mighty stature of a classic hero; he seems like a giant from the earth. This Buford is a primitive folk hero worthy of the tales of an earlier era — though actually he's the hero of a modern tall tale.

When Baker, as Buford, says to his little son, "There's nothing wrong with a gun in the right hands," and promises him a rifle when he's nine, the bit of dialogue comes from the same homiletic Hollywood as Clint Eastwood's speeches in *Magnum Force.* Actually, although Mrs. Pusser had two children by a previous marriage, Pusser has only one child — a daughter — but you can see why the fictional son has been added: so that later, when he comes to the hospital to see his injured father, the child can walk down the corridor crying but clutching his rifle. It's the little prince taking up his fallen king's mission, and the audience gasps at the raw power of a device that pre-dates D. W. Griffith. The script, by the producer, Mort Briskin, who first heard of Pusser's heroic ordeal when Roger Mudd did a ten-minute report on him on C.B.S. in 1969, may appear authentic just because it's so shameless and tacky. Briskin's previous credits as a writer are strictly small-time *(A Man Alone, The Magic Face),* but this script didn't require literary talent. Briskin, the producer of such TV series as *Sheriff of Cochise, U.S. Marshal,* and *The Texan,* is also a producer for Bing Crosby Productions,* for whom he has done *Willard, Ben,* and *Walking Tall.* In Buford Pusser, Briskin found a hero whose story embodied the values of the conventional Westerns; Briskin embroidered it, but basically the pattern was already there, shaped by Pusser himself (he had made a deputy sheriff of the man who wrote the first ballad about him), and Karlson knew just how to bring it out. The street Western is a corruption of the Western, an attempt to apply the Western's mythology to actual problems — and since it doesn't apply, the movies (and other forms of pop culture, and politics, too) fabricate situations that are just like those in Westerns so that the mythology *will* apply.

The actual Buford Pusser (not known as Buford the Wild Bull) was beaten up in 1957 in a brawl in a casino over money he himself had lost. Almost three years later, the casino operator was robbed and beaten, and Pusser and two of his friends were charged with armed robbery. At the trial, Pusser didn't defend his right to assault the gambler; he and the two others were acquitted because they had an airtight alibi. Pusser got into police work in 1962, when his father, who was chief of police in Adamsville, retired, having arranged for his son to succeed him. When Pusser ran for sheriff in 1964, the incumbent sheriff *was* killed in an auto crash, but there was no connection between that crash and Pusser, who in fact defeated the dead man, whose name was still on the ballot, by only three hundred votes. Aside from Mrs. Pusser's murder in 1967 — which was what really started the legend of Buford Pusser — and the extraordinary amount of physical punishment that Pusser took and also dished out, there doesn't seem to be a great deal of factual

*Except for the name, the company no longer has any ties to Bing Crosby.

support for the movie. The first new deputy he appointed was not a black buddy, as in the film, but his father. And as for the amazing incident, in the movie, of Buford's magically quick apprehension of the murderers of eight civil-rights workers (only to have the case dismissed on a technicality), I can find no mention of it even in Buford's romantic authorized biography of 1971. As for the powerhouse scenes when Buford rises from his hospital bed, his head swathed in bandages (like the Invisible Man), to attend his wife's funeral and to wreak vengeance once again, and then, Job-like, rests upon his great hickory stick, using it as a cane — pure invention, of course. As sheriff, Pusser had in fact become partial to the less photogenic head cracker the gun. He has boasted that in his first term he "wore out more pistol barrels banging mean drunks over the head than the county would pay for." The movie's basic premise — that Buford Pusser became sheriff so that he could rid the community of vice and corruption — seems shaky. And although he piled up a big number of arrests by busting drunks and raiding moonshiners, the state-line dives operate as usual, and when Pusser ran for sheriff again in 1972 — while the movie was being shot — he was defeated. The man who won explained his victory (in an interview in the *Nashville Tennessean Sunday Magazine*) by saying, "If either man had to arrest your son, which would you prefer? I just don't think the people here cared for killing and beating up on people. They just didn't think that was necessary to enforce the law." The brutalities and killings, including the murder of Mrs. Pusser, seem to have been a chain of reprisals. Pusser, who now does promotional work for supermarkets, Jaycee gatherings, mobile homes, and automobile dealers (he gives away autographed sticks to those who buy cars), has authorized a glorifying industry about himself, as well as this movie (he owns seven per cent). The only complaint he has been known to make about the film is that it isn't violent enough. There is some talk of his running for governor or for Congress. How does one define corruption?

The moral setup in this street Western is a direct carry-over from the myths of the wide-open spaces. No matter how high the odds against him, the virtuous man wins out. And the virtuous man always knows whom to clobber. He can be trusted with his fists, his stick, and his gun because he has absolute knowledge of innocence and guilt. In *Walking Tall,* the forces of corruption are just as easily recognizable as in any early Western; they're basically the same forces — mean crooks. Buford says that he quit wrestling because of the system and he's not going to let the system wreck his town. To put it in the way the audience at *Walking Tall* perceives it: because of the system, the honest small guy doesn't stand a chance, but Buford — the man who cares about what's right — bucks the system. The movie's simplistic outlook is commercial genius: the only serious problems in the community are the problems created by the vice lords — the system is represented by the prostitutes and crooked gamblers and their confederates in the police department and on the bench. The solution is the same as in a Western: kill them or drive them out of town. In *Walking Tall,* as in *Dirty Harry,* the hero could never mistakenly injure an innocent person, or the whole structure of the morality play would collapse. He's a one-man lynch mob, but with the judgment of a god. Buford's sad, sick look in the eyes after he's forced to shoot an evil woman is knightly chivalry modern style.

After a decade of hip but often numbingly cynical movies, the country is on a regression trip — watching the Waltons and the Apples and cheering *Walking Tall.* Breaking a few arms has a basic demagogic appeal; it makes audiences feel that there is a direct, fast way to solve problems. There's a deliberate appeal to the vigilante spirit at the (miserably staged) end: the townspeople make a bonfire of the gamblers' equipment. But vigilantes need to be on horses; vigilantes who arrive in a procession of cars don't jibe with the picture's brute power. It's no accident that the director lingers on those tractor punches that Buford delivers. When the nostalgic dream morality of cowboy movies is imposed on an actual modern town, it becomes a demand for bloodletting. Early on, Karlson showed us the bloody Buford, a red mass of wounds, lying in the road; in the movie's terms, there is only one answer to that. His enemies' blood must flow. And the audience is worked up to believe that bloodletting is necessary, that that is what does the job. In a sense, this is also what *Dirty Harry* said, and the same message is embedded in the new police thrillers that feature cops who are really cowboy heroes. The blood-pounding excitement that most of the street Westerns aim for is simply box-office excitement, but in *Walking Tall* it is integral to the fundamentalist politics that probably all of us carry inside us at some primitive level — even those of us who watch this picture appalled. Buford has a galvanic effect on the audience because he incarnates the blood rage that can so easily be worked up in frustrated people. The visceral impact of this shrewd, humble film makes one know how crowds must feel when they're being swayed by demagogues.

[February 25, 1974]

The Used Madonna

"THE MOTHER AND THE WHORE" is made from inside the state of mind that is thought of as Village or Berkeley-graduate-school or, as in this case, Left Bank. It's about the attitudes of educated people who use their education as a way of making contact with each other rather than with the larger world. Their manner of dress and behavior is a set of signals; they're telling each other that they're illusionless. Their way of life is a group courtship rite, though they court each other not in order to find someone to love but in order to be loved — that is, admired. They live in an atmosphere of apocalyptic narcissism. The characters in *The Mother and the Whore* belong to the café life of St.-Germain-des-Prés, and so does the film, which can be said to represent the dead hopes of a decade and a generation. The Don Juans of this group hardly need to be ambulatory; they cruise from their coffee-house chairs. The hero, Alexandre (Jean-Pierre Léaud), is a thirty-year-old puppy; in his milieu the less you do the cooler you appear. Alexandre has the glib, attitudinizing male-intellectual vanity that is the educated bum's form of machismo. He's a harmless, lightweight liar; he cultivates his whims; he lies for the fun of it. He's an amusing put-on artist, with no visible convictions or depth of feeling. When he sees an old girl friend who's about to be married (Isabelle Weingarten), he makes a declaration of undying passion merely for the pleasure of hearing himself sound passionate. She's smart enough not to take him any more seriously than he takes himself.

Alexandre has no interest in a profession; he's just a professional charmer. He's able to live without working because he has found a "mother" — a mistress who takes care of him. Tough, good-natured Marie (Bernadette Lafont) runs a dress shop, but she's far from being a bourgeoise. She's a coarse, unpretentious working-class woman trying to enjoy herself; she's the solid world that Alexandre returns to from the hours of preening at the café. All his energy goes into his poses and paradoxes, and the strategies of coolness. But when he plots a little campaign to make himself important to Veronika — a new girl he spots

— it's wasted effort. Veronika (Françoise Lebrun), a young, bone-poor nurse, has a tired, stolid madonna face, but she's so whorishly available that, as she says, "it turns a lot of people off." The movie is a fugal series of monologues and dialogues among Alexandre, Marie, and Veronika, almost entirely on the subject of sex. It was shot in grainy black-and-white that's deliberately dark and streaked; there's no musical score — only "natural" sounds and an occasional scratchy record played on a phonograph — and it's three hours and thirty-five minutes long. A viewer's response to this debauch of talk will be determined by whether he can accept the whorish madonna Veronika's monologues as revealing the truth or thinks they're the familiar rant of Catholic women on the sauce. If the former, the film, which was written and directed by Jean Eustache, may seem a depressive-generation masterpiece; if the latter, a sour conceit. I think it's part one and part the other — but the parts are inseparable.

The rough-and-tumble Marie is warmly played. Bernadette Lafont, whose large, generous features make her a natural for working-class women, is open-hearted in the role — crass and likable. The filmmaker goes in for paradoxes, too: Marie, the "mother," resembles the traditional understanding whore of French films (such as Arletty in *Le Jour Se Lève*), and her relationship with Alexandre is an updating of the whore-pimp relationship. Alexandre (and the graduate-school little bohemias of the world are full of Alexandres, though generally they sponge off their parents as well as friends and girl friends) is, in fact, a spoiled-infant pimp, who lives off Marie and doesn't even provide a pimp's protection. He has nothing to offer but his taste, his classy prattle, and some body warmth. He considers that his presence — when he's around — is gift enough. Léaud doesn't just walk through his role (as he sometimes does); he projects the shallow Alexandre's emotional states, and he gives what is probably his most deeply felt performance as an adult. Alexandre is onscreen throughout, reacting to the women, cajoling them, trying on attitudes — so infatuated with his own pranks he hardly cares what effect they have on others. Alexandre likes to perform, and his dry facetiousness is often funny (probably considerably funnier if one knows French well enough to get the slang). Though Jean Eustache has said that he wrote the roles specifically for the performers, Léaud's performance is nevertheless a feat of giving oneself over to a role. He never drops the mask, he never slips away from Alexandre.

However, the picture stands or falls with the character of Veronika (and she's a very creepy, dolorous character), because it's Veronika who carries the burden of Eustache's emotionalism. She looks Slavic (she says she is of Polish origin), and she appears to be Eustache's holy-whory Sonia, an updated version of the heroine of *Crime and Punishment*;

she's there to awaken silly Alexandre's soul, though he's no Raskolnikov. The only thing that keeps Alexandre from being the Léaud specialty — a pet — is that he's forced to listen to Veronika's recital of her ugly, seamy deprivations and her nausea. She's drunken and insistent; once Alexandre has gone to bed with her, he can't get rid of her. She hounds him; she comes to Marie's apartment and climbs into bed with them. Veronika, who wears her hair saint-style, braided around her head, is a sexually abused character; her tiny garret room in the nurses' quarters of a hospital is like a penitential chamber. She volunteers for abuse; she seeks sex and feels humiliated by it. She's the biggest bundle of guilt ever to be hurled on the screen, and once she stops listening to Alexandre and starts talking she never shuts up — except to vomit up all the sex-without-love that she has subjected herself to.

Bernadette Lafont, who made her first screen appearance in the leading role of Truffaut's short *Les Mistons* (1957), and Léaud, whose long scarves here stretch back to his appearance as the twelve-year-old boy in *The 400 Blows* (1959), have been the emblematic New Wave performers; and the characters they play here are further extensions of the characters they've developed over the intervening years. (Even Isabelle Weingarten, who played the lead in Bresson's *Four Nights of a Dreamer,* carries that credential.) But Françoise Lebrun, a graduate student in modern literature who has never acted on the screen before, is completely Eustache's; she gives the picture its sullen, scratched soul. One may guess that her sad, deceptively placid face, with its suggestion of a badly used madonna, inspired Eustache. She has the sort of young-old face that a moviemaker could easily project onto; she's like a beat-out version of the young Dietrich, with her pale-gold braid around her head, as the innocent peasant, soon to be a fallen woman, in *The Song of Songs,* the hokey old Mamoulian-Sudermann film of innocence betrayed. Lebrun's wide-eyed face is blankly opaque — the face of a woman locked in her miseries. She keeps a sullen, suffering deadpan, and as the torrent of obscenities and complaints pours out, we can all project onto that face. *The Mother and the Whore* is a psychodrama that keeps shifting and redefining its terms; those terms are ironic until the last hour, when Veronika is exempted from irony and we are asked to identify with her and to see her as an icon of modern loneliness and suffering and degradation. She's a martyr to callous sex.

Eustache has no distance from Veronika. That's why the movie seems so arbitrary — you may feel that you've been a good sport to sit through it, that it's been an endurance contest — but it's also what gives the film its distinction. Eustache is right in there. His method is rather like that of a French Cassavetes; he's trying to put raw truth on the screen, and this film might be his *Lovers* to set next to Cassavetes'

Husbands. Cassavetes tries to give acted material the look and sound of *cinéma vérité;* Eustache goes even further. He puts in dead stretches and trivia, building in boredom so that the material will seem lifelike; he prolongs the movie after one thinks it's finished — the prolongation seems almost like a director's joke. Eustache's method resembles the static randomness of the Warhol-Morrissey pictures, yet the randomness here is not a matter of indifference but a conscious goal. Chance is the illusion that Eustache seeks. He didn't allow the actors to deviate from the three-hundred-page script, but he keeps the framing a little rough and insecure, as if the cameraman were looking for the action, and it took three months of editing to make this film seem unedited. Eustache wants the look of chance because he's determined not to be ingratiating. It's as if he felt that only by pushing us beyond patience, only by taking us away from the surface pleasures of cinematographic elegance and a full score, only by rubbing our noses in his view of reality, can he make us *feel.* (He may equate us with the infantile, pleasure-seeking Alexandre.)

It's true that films tend to look too rich and that they're often rotten with meaningless "production values" — and sometimes rotten with "beauty." But those who try to strip them down to naked fundamentals usually seem to be puritan aesthetes — and a pain. *The Mother and the Whore* proclaims its honesty and its purity in a way I can't stomach — as if its messiness and its characters' messy lives were holy. The religiously inspired polarity of the title suggests that Eustache sees himself as Alexandre, divided, torn between the mother and the whore. And it's part of the emotional tone of this period to reject the mother and to identify with the whore. Like Veronika, Eustache is saying, "I'm going to show you more of the tormented soul than anybody has ever shown you," and, like Veronika, he confuses rag-chewing and revulsion with holy revelation.

Art and disgust are closely related in the thinking of a number of modern filmmakers of religious background. Paul Morrissey's films seem to be made by a dirty-minded altar boy, and the concept that messy anguish sanctifies is at the very heart of Cassavetes' films. *The Mother and the Whore* is not a negligible film: it's unmistakably a personal expression, and it does achieve moments of intensity. No doubt some people will say more than moments, and some will consider Veronika's ultimate monologue cathartic, though the fact that it signals reprieve for the exhausted viewer may contribute to that feeling. (The three hours and thirty-five minutes feel so long that you want to think you've had something to show for it, and catharsis is big stuff—worth squirming for.) But is Alexandre ultimately moved to ask Veronika to marry him because he's a fool who loves grand gestures, or are we really meant to believe in the authenticity of what she represents? For me, it was as if Alexandre were pressured into confessing a crime he hadn't committed. Veronika rants so much that finally he assumes the guilt for all the men whom this obsessive woman has landed in bed with and then felt lacerated by. He assumes the guilt for the whole world's failure to love. Alexandre may be just trying on his new deep feelings, but she, I'm afraid, is intended to be the real thing. It turns out that Eustache is a sin-ridden bohemian of an earlier school and that the movie is about the penance that must be done for sex-without-love. He has welded together the disaffection of a generation and his own sexual disgust. Isn't that really what Veronika's diatribe is all about? Isn't she really saying "I want to be loved"? I suspect that that's why the movie will appeal to people who feel stranded in a confusion of personal freedom and social hopelessness. Antonioni explored the theme of sex without love, but he placed it among the affluent; in placing this theme among the students and those who go on living like students, Eustache makes direct contact with the movie audience. Antonioni's bleak atmosphere spoke of spiritual emptiness; Eustache's atmosphere is like a spiritual mange, and probably many people in the aging-young movie audience feel mangy and lost and degraded, and have had their share of miserable sex experiences. They may be willing to embrace Veronika's loathing of her life, and perhaps willing to look to the healing power of Christian love. The film is designed to be a religious experience, but the musty answer it offers to the perils of sexual freedom is actually a denial of sexual freedom. In *The Mother and the Whore,* the New Wave meets the Old Wave.

[March 4, 1974]

A Brash Young Man

JON VOIGHT has finally got a chance to loosen up on the screen and play a rude, warm, expansive character. In the title role of *Conrack* he has his best role since Joe Buck in *Midnight Cowboy,* and one that's at the opposite end of the emotional spectrum. His Joe Buck was a limited dreamer, an overgrown adolescent who wanted to market himself as a stud; his fear-filled blue eyes, his ingenuous, stricken face exposed his emotional paralysis. Joe Buck's bravado was a simpleton's bravado, but Voight gave it underpinnings of a simple man's suffering, and it was a beautiful, affecting performance. Voight's subsequent roles restricted him. He had no character to play in *Catch-22* — his rambunctious, grinning, Aryan-cartoon Milo Minderbinder was just a rip-off of Joe Buck. And his puffy face told us that as the alienated prizefighter in the oppressive *The All-American Boy* he was as despondent about the experience as we were. In *Deliverance,* Voight was admirable, but Burt Reynolds, as Lewis, had the juicy part; Voight, aged for his role as Ed — the flash gone from his smile, with a fussy mustache, his blond hair darkened — was subdued and at a disadvantage. Reynolds had almost all the bad lines, and he had to do the heavy dramatics and the freaky-mystic bit, but he brought it off. Reynolds, a swinger Clark Gable, is tuned in to his special audience, and he acts right to it. He reads his lines with a disclaimer attached to them, putting them down. This sleazy cynicism became a sly ploy in *Deliverance*: Reynolds, who kids sex by acting sexy, was able to parody mad Lewis's macho audacity and keep his own. Voight's Ed, the man of conscience who's going to have nightmares about the trip, was pitted not against Lewis, who isn't going to lose any sleep over it, but against Reynolds, who doesn't lose any sleep over acting. When we watch *Deliverance,* we don't know what is on Lewis's mind; we know only what is on Reynolds' mind. He's saying to the other actors, "Why are you getting so worked up about your roles? It's only a movie." If you like Reynolds (and he *is* entertaining — lazy yet garish), you let him get away with his shaggy rogue's cunning; if you don't like him, you think, How cheap! In *Deliverance,* Reynolds the hoodwinker captured the public and, at last, became a star, while Voight, submerged in his dry, tentative character (our representative), seemed awfully mundane and earnest — not as drab as the other characters in the movie but still drab. In *Conrack,* Voight isn't held in; he has a true starring role. He isn't playing a bug's-ear-cute juvenile or a male peach; he plays a loose, imaginative extrovert — a man with a bounding spirit. Voight's features look larger, and the anxious, staring eyes that seemed so close together when he was Joe Buck are bright and confident. He seems to have come strappingly alive, and he has a huge screen presence.

Conrack, directed by Martin Ritt and adapted by the husband-and-wife team of Irving Ravetch and Harriet Frank, Jr., is based on Pat Conroy's *The Water Is Wide,* one of a series of books written in recent years by rebel teachers (Jonathan Kozol, John Holt, Herbert Kohl, James Herndon) looking for new ways to break through centuries of cruelty and neglect. Pat Conroy, an Irish Catholic Southerner, grew up a racist cracker and went to The Citadel, the military college in South Carolina, intending to follow his father into a career in the Marine

Corps. He began to wake up around the time of Martin Luther King's murder, and the following year, 1969, he took a job teaching black children in a two-room school on an island off the South Carolina mainland, near Savannah, Georgia — an island where the people, he wrote, "have changed very little since the Emancipation Proclamation." Treated as members of an inferior race, told that they are "slow," and beaten when they don't pay attention, the children there are ignorant, passive, and resentful. Conroy — the children had trouble pronouncing his name and called him Conrack — discovered that in his class of eighteen students — grades five to eight — not one could tell him what country they lived in, or who the President was, or who the first President was, or that the water that washed up against the island's shore was the Atlantic Ocean. Savannah was the only city any of the children could name. All of them thought that the earth was the center of the universe. Seven couldn't recite the alphabet, three couldn't spell their own names, four couldn't add two and two. As Conroy says to the principal in the movie, "the kids don't know crap." His job is complicated by the fact that this principal, who has intimidated the kids and flogged them for the first four grades, just as she is now flogging their younger brothers and sisters, is a black woman who toadies to whites and despises her own people.

Writing his story, Pat Conroy did not think of himself as a hero, and he dwelt on his failures and his mistakes. But what comes through is the ribald, freewheeling largeness of his nature, his breakneck, roller-coaster temperament, and it's this subtext — Conroy's partly unconscious portrait of himself — that the adapters picked up on. The movie, which was shot on and around St. Simons Island, off the coast of Brunswick, Georgia, using local children, takes most of its dialogue directly from the book, while making Conroy the hero of a modern fable. *Conrack* is the tale of an unrepressed man fighting a slowly dying system of repression. It's about a flippant, nervy poet whose careless defiance of the educational politicians and bureaucrats defeats him. (He gets fired.) Voight's Conroy is a teacher with the soul of an artist; his motto might be "Life is all improvisation." Trying to wake the children up, he throws an impressionistic jumble of information at them: jokes, facts, put-ons, hairy oversimplifications, stories from history, sports, and everywhere. He performs for them, he romances them; he uses anything he can think of to get to them. Inevitably, he runs into a snag with the principal, Mrs. Scott, played by Madge Sinclair with such magnificent physical authority that we know — almost kinetically — what the whipped kids feel. Mrs. Scott has a slave-overseer mentality, yet she's so strong and unyielding that she's like an obstinate natural force. Her straight back is a brick wall Conroy dashes himself against without making a dent. We find ourselves admiring Madge Sinclair (a Jamaican who has been appearing with Joe Papp's Public Theater and in recent movies) not only for her mulish performance but for her stature, for herself. Mrs. Scott's protector, the school superintendent, is played by Hume Cronyn, and, as usual, there's too much of him, resourceful actor though he is. (This virtuoso of the show-them-what-an-actor-you-are school just can't tone down his slimy villainy for the camera. His underplaying is as subtle as the fraternal bonhomie of the Eyewitness News Team.) Ruth Attaway, who looks like a black Martha Graham, plays Edna, the elderly leader of the islanders — who support Conroy — with impish humor; Paul Winfield appears as a local moonshiner; and Antonio Fargas makes a startling impression in the one-scene role of Quickfellow.

The actors and Conroy's students are there to do their bits, and they stand out more than they should; they're visually overbearing, outlined against the skies. They look marooned on the island, because there's no offhand everyday life, no casual background to the action. Martin Ritt and his cinematographer, John Alonzo (they also worked together on *Sounder*), have developed a very clear, elegant, and spacious style for *Conrack,* but this handsome pictorial quality isn't terribly expressive and it's linked with a puzzling emptiness. The problem of adaptation is that a book, if it's any good (and *The Water Is Wide* is), is an organic whole, and what is cut is often missed, while, more often than not, what is added feels tacky. The actual island where Conroy taught had been ruined by waste from a factory on the mainland — it polluted the oyster beds, which had been the islanders' livelihood. To indicate this would make the movie seem a tract. And there was a bigger problem for Ritt and the Ravetches. The young and able-bodied had been leaving — becoming part of the urban ghettos — and the island was inhabited by children and the aged, who lived by hunting and fishing and on welfare. It was a decaying island, full of drunkenness and — with so much hunting weaponry at hand — violence. To have conveyed a picture of this rotting culture might have been inflammatory to white racists and could hardly have been pleasing to black people. And so we get scrubbed faces. But since the movie shows practically no island life, you keep thinking, "Where is everybody?" There's no mess: the marshy, windswept landscapes are almost abstract; the place is like a resort in off season. The movie doesn't show the younger children, in the classroom adjoining Conroy's, so even the school looks deserted. And some of the gaps in information are distracting; it's hard, for example, to understand why the children pronounce "Conroy" as "Conrack," since it isn't explained that their native speech is a patois, a combination of an African dialect and English.

Reading the book after seeing the movie, I discovered (once again) that everything that had bothered me in the movie was the result of a cut or an addition. The Ravetches pare down to the best material, but they can't resist spreading on old Hollywood-liberal jelly: Conroy announces that "something is happening on this island," as if he were part of a revolution that couldn't be stopped; he shouts inspirational hyperbole to the children. There's a perceptible slackening of the director's grip in an episode (added by the Ravetches) that doesn't make sense — Conroy's use of a loudspeaker truck to tell a few straggling old townspeople on the mainland (barren, like the island) that their way of life is moribund. But what comes from the book is fresh, and is told with great gusto. It's a firsthand story, and Ritt and the Ravetches have kept the bloom on it, even with the addition of their secondhand touches. (An invented subplot involving Mary, a thirteen-year-old dropout — played by Tina Andrews — and her possible marriage isn't so vernal.) The film takes its mood from Voight's leapfrogging performance. *Conrack* has the airy, liberated feeling of the teacher's improvising nature, of his impatience and his bursting through restraints.

The movie glorifies its teacher-hero the way movies used to glorify crusading reporters. In the book, although Conroy fights being fired and he passionately — furiously — wants to stay with his class, it isn't really the firing that defeats him. It's the fact that the kids are already so damaged by the time they come to him that, for all his free-form acrobatics, there's little he can do. ("If I'd stood on my head for them for ten years, basically there wasn't much that could have been changed," Pat Conroy recently said, "except maybe for the next generation.") In the movie, it seems as if love could work the miracles that are needed; we come away with the impression that if the bureaucracy hadn't disposed of Conroy the crushed, humiliated children would have become happily educated. It's a fable but a lovely one — a fable with a liberating force. One invention by the Ravetches — the climactic finish — is a facile yet perfect stroke. A touch of pure popular poetry, it elevates the children to a consciousness of their own destruction.

In recent years, there have been few movie heroes with wit and spirit enough to squander their gift of language; Jon Voight's Conroy looms up as just about the lustiest, most joyful presence in current films. But some black people now take the programmatic line that only blacks care enough to want to help blacks, and Voight, freshly shampooed throughout, is a very Nordic type. And there are whites who are so contemptuous of any movie in which a white man cares about something (besides money and violence and sex) that they put it down as sentimental — or, worse, "humanist." It's part of the revision of American history in the films of the last decade to expose white heroes as fools or skunks. The revisionism has gone so far that people may feel they have to resist even a movie that says we've got to stop being fools and skunks. This works to the advantage of the most mercenary filmmakers, and it's tough going for anybody who tries to make a film about a manic, unembarrassed idealist. The hero of *Conrack* is a giant who tries to make a bridge of himself — a bridge that will enable a group of kids to cross over to the outside world without falling. And it's he who falls. The movie isn't great, but it's so lively and touching that that hardly seems to matter.

THE SOUND IS SOMEWHERE BETWEEN a bark, a croak, and a quaver, and it doesn't quite match the movement of the lips. Did Lucille Ball sync her own singing in *Mame,* or did Dick Cavett dub it for her? That voice may be tonelessly flat, but it sure is determined, and it takes determination to plow through the low-camp lyrics of this hippopotamic musical. Why did Lucille Ball do *Mame*? After more than forty years in movies and TV (and five years of chorus work and assorted jobs before that) — after conquering the world — did she discover in herself an unfulfilled ambition to be a flaming drag queen? She doesn't have what it takes — hardly a tragedy. She has a gift for slightly swacked physical comedy and a clown's look of pickled good nature during disasters, but she doesn't have a flair for brittle high fashion or enough acting skill to parody that flair. Decked out in Theadora van Runkle's abominations, she isn't a mirror of style; she's just a smirking, badly overdressed star. She throws up her arms, in their red giant-bat-wing sleeves, crying out "Listen, everybody!", and she really seems to think she's a fun person. But we in the audience are not thinking of fun; we're thinking of age and self-deception. When Mame's best friend, Vera Charles (Beatrice Arthur, television's Maude), asks her "How old do you think I am?" and Mame answers "Somewhere between forty and death," one may feel a shudder in the audience. How can a woman well over sixty say a line like that, with the cameraman using every lying device he knows and still unable to hide the blurred eyes?

Mame isn't boring, like *Lost Horizon*; at its worst it's too terrible to be boring, and it does have a lot of skillful people slamming it forward. Onna White choreographs like mad, with bodies hurtling over and around the near-stationary star, who always looks just about to dance but never really does; and the director, Gene Saks, tries to wring a little humor out of those frayed old skits that serve as the story line. Some of the cast (Jane Connell as a sweetly wan Agnes Gooch, and Robert Preston as a sturdy, relaxed Beauregard) are in there working and doing better than might be expected. But what can be done with this relic of a script? I don't believe that any star could overcome it — not on the screen. Paul Zindel gets a screenwriting credit, but I'd love to know what for. I managed to avoid the *Mame* reincarnations of the sixties, but I still remember how these same lines thumped in the grisly, self-congratulatory Rosalind Russell 1958 movie. Nothing has been done to redeem such ingredients as the mushy loyal house servant Ito, and the unplayable snobbish Upsons — and the complacency with which Mame puts them down. Nothing has been done to revamp the darling colleen that Mame picks out for her adored nephew Patrick. (There hasn't been a darling colleen on the screen in a long time now. Has anyone felt the lack?)

Mame is a female impersonator's dream woman: constantly changing her wigs and her gowns and her décor, basking in jewels and bitchy repartee. Sexy and rich and permissive, Mame has to be played by a smashing, crisp actress who makes it clear why homosexuals find her a turn-on. With Lucille Ball, *Mame* becomes a family musical, and all the numbskull worst in it — the hard-sell uplifting message — takes over. This *Mame* doesn't rise to camp except when Beatrice Arthur is on — and she transcends it. She's monstrously marvelous — like a coquettish tank. When she sings, the low growls that come out of her cathedral chest make Ethel Merman sound like a tinkling virgin. Beatrice Arthur can deliver a single-syllable word with enough resonance to stampede cattle three thousand miles away. Her big number, "The Man in the Moon Is a Miss," takes *Mame* into a different sphere. If she had played Mame, the material could have gone beyond camp into a satire of the whole crazy female-impersonator tradition of modern musical comedy.

Someday, I want to meet Gene Saks; I've got to know whose idea it was to end the picture with a reprise. This reprise is like the sequences in those TV shows that put together a collection of Bette Davis's smoking scenes or Bogart's snarls — only it's the scenes you've just witnessed of Lucille Ball hugging people. It's a hug collage. There is also something unaccountable in the cast; it is listed in the credits as "Kirby Furlong," and it plays little Patrick in the most meticulously irresistible style I have ever witnessed. All twinkles, it delivers lines like "Would you take a kiss on account?" Kirby Furlong makes Tatum O'Neal seem wholesomely amateurish; Shirley Temple in her teeny prime never had this hairbreadth timing. Kirby Furlong is of such inhuman perfection that stamping it out wouldn't be considered murder, would it?

[March 11, 1974]

Sugarland and Badlands

"THE SUGARLAND EXPRESS" is like some of the entertaining studio-factory films of the past (it's as commercial and shallow and impersonal), yet it has so much eagerness and flash and talent that it just about transforms its scrubby ingredients. The director, Steven Spielberg, is twenty-six; I can't tell if he has any mind, or even a strong personality, but then a lot of good moviemakers have got by without being profound. He isn't saying anything special in *The Sugarland Express,* but he has a knack for bringing out young actors, and a sense of composition and movement that almost any director might envy. Composition seems to come naturally to him, as it does to some of the young Italians; Spielberg uses his gift in a very free-and-easy, American way — for humor, and for a physical response to action. He could be that rarity among directors a born entertainer — perhaps a new generation's Howard Hawks. In terms of the pleasure that technical assurance gives an audience, this film is one of the most phenomenal début films in the history of movies. If there is such a thing as a movie sense — and I think there is (I know fruit venders and cabdrivers who have it and some movie critics who don't) — Spielberg really has it. But he may be so full of it that he doesn't have much else. There's no sign of the emergence of a new film artist (such as Martin Scorsese) in *The Sugarland Express,* but it marks the début of a new-style, new-generation Hollywood hand.

The story — based on an occurrence in Texas in 1969 — is about Lou Jean (Goldie Hawn) and her husband, Clovis (William Atherton), petty thieves who lost custody of their infant son while they were in jail, and their attempt to get him back, which involves taking a highway-patrol officer, Slide (Michael Sacks), hostage. The child is with his adoptive parents in the town of Sugarland, and as Lou Jean and Clovis drive there in the patrol car they've commandeered, with a stream of police behind, other cars follow, and crowds gather to wish them well. Spielberg, young as he is, is already a graduate of TV, having caused a stir by his direction of an episode of *Columbo,* and a sensation with a terrifying made-for-TV movie called *Duel,* which was mostly about a truck. *The*

Sugarland Express is mostly about cars; Spielberg is a choreographic virtuoso with cars. He patterns them; he makes them dance and crash and bounce back. He handles enormous configurations of vehicles; sometimes they move so sweetly you think he must be wooing them. These sequences are as unforced and effortless-looking as if the cars themselves — mesmerized — had just waltzed into their idiot formations. It's implicit in the movie's whole scheme that vast numbers of cops are pursuing the kidnapped patrolman, and that people are joining the procession and encouraging the young parents to retrieve their child, because that gives them all an opportunity to get in their cars and whiz across Texas. Photographed by Vilmos Zsigmond, the cars shimmer in the hot sunlight; in the dark, the red lights of the police cars are like eerie night-blooming flowers. The cars have tiffs, wrangle, get confused. And so do the people, who are also erratic and — in certain lights — eerily beautiful. There's a suggestion of a Robert Altman influence in the fast and loose conversations, but they're not really so loose. The flurries of talk aren't casual; these aren't Altman's people, whose talk overlaps, as in life, but rabid people all talking at once — to heat the movie. These huffy characters, riled up and yelling at each other, are in the combustible comedy style of Preston Sturges (of his *Hail the Conquering Hero* and *The Miracle of Morgan's Creek,* especially). This movie enjoys orneriness and collision courses, as the Sturges movies did; it sees the characters' fitful, moody nuttiness as the American's inalienable right to make a fool of himself. It merges Sturges' love of comic confusion with the action world of cars to create a jamboree. We wind up feeling affectionate toward some highly unlikely people — particularly toward the Goldie Hawn character, Lou Jean, who started it all.

Probably everybody knows how talented Goldie Hawn is, and that has made her screen performances the more disappointing. She's done darting, fidgety little bits of business in several roles, but she was stymied; she was thrashing around in tightly blocked pictures. Here you don't see her yanking the director's sleeve and asking "Now?" She just does it. Spielberg's youth and speed release her; she stays in character, and the character grows. Lou Jean has more gumption than brains; she's the American go-getter gone haywire. Right at the opening, Lou Jean gets off a bus and her bouncy, determined walk spells trouble. She could have a sign engraved on her forehead: "I want it now." Whatever it is, Lou Jean can't wait for it. When she goes to the prison farm to visit her husband and starts to scream at him, you know poor Clovis is sunk. In some ways, the world divides into the hysterics — the screamers and scene-makers and weepers — and those who want to keep the peace. Clovis is a pushover for his wife's tantrummy demands; he loves peace, and he loves her, too. He has only four more months to serve, but he'll break out of prison when she tells him to, because he's more scared of her than of the authorities. Lou Jean can't think ahead, and Clovis tries not to. It takes a while before we recognize that, in her own flighty, screwed-up way, she loves him, too, and that she really does want her baby back. Nothing in the movie which involves Lou Jean or Clovis or Slide (or the cars) looks rehearsed or tired. William Atherton (he appeared on the stage in *The House of Blue Leaves, The Basic Training of Pavlo Hummel,* and *Suggs in the City*) has the most difficult role; Clovis knows (intermittently, anyway) what his wife is too easily distracted to grasp — that they're over their heads in trouble. Atherton's performance gives the picture solidity. Without him, it would be a giddy new-style screwball comedy, but he's the sparrow who falls. With the director's help but without a great deal of help from the script, Atherton — he looks like the skinny offspring of Robert Redford and Paul Newman — deepens the picture; we begin to share Clovis's apprehensiveness.

The script, by Hal Barwood and Matthew Robbins, who are also young, is satisfying and full of incident, but it's made up of swipes from other movies; one routine from *Roxie Hart* turns up twice: two crabbed, mean fathers — each decades older than is called for — make dour pronouncements about their own kids. There's a difference in quality between the writing and the direction. You get the feeling that the director grew up with TV and wheels (My Mother the Car?), and that he has a new temperament. Maybe Spielberg loves action and comedy and speed so much that he really doesn't care if a movie has anything else in it. But he doesn't copy old stuff. He isn't deep, but he isn't derivative, either. The scriptwriters are living off the past. I think it's likely that being part of the TV-and-young-moviemaker generation affects a director — changes his perceptions — much more basically than it affects writers. It may turn writers on so that they want to work in movies, but they tend to draw upon old movies for their ideas, and this is particularly true of the film-school and American Film Institute troops (which Barwood and Robbins belong to), whose education has been sitting around and looking at movies, and who are now selling scripts to the major studios. They're not really writers, any more than most of the other Hollywood writers are. They're synthesizers of other people's ideas, even when they write an "original" like *The Sugarland Express.*

Spielberg is a bit leaden with some of the older actors, and can't always redeem the low-comedy effects — the sort of squalls and antic outrage that got laughs in *The Russians Are Coming, The Russians Are Coming.* There are hero-worshipful views of Ben Johnson, who plays the captain who leads the pursuit; the camera regards him as if he were a diva and his face the big aria. The captain's excesses (breaking the weapons of a pair of right-wing nuts, shooting the tires of a TV-crew truck) are in a too cute old-movie style. I'm not a great fan of Ben Johnson's acting in general; he holds positions like a pointer — imparting an air of deliberation and importance to every move he makes. Some of the comic touches that pull down Spielberg's style are probably the result of the editors' leaving a nudging extra beat; their work is mostly split-second right, but they leave a beat on an art effect, too — on the Teddy bear in the road near the end of the picture (the shot featured in the ad campaign). Spielberg can't redeem it all, but he gets away with it; he's one of those wizard directors who can make trash entertaining. That's what *The Sting,* for example, tries to do, and though I may be lonely in this, I think it fails. Spielberg savors film, and you respond to that. *The Sugarland Express* has life to it. Not the kind of life that informs a young film like *Mean Streets* — probably the best American movie of 1973 — but the vitality that a director with great instincts can bring to commercial entertainment.

❖

TERRENCE MALICK, WHO WROTE, produced, directed, and spent a year editing *Badlands,* his first feature, is twenty-nine, the age that Godard was when he made *Breathless.* But Godard liked his outlaw hero and identified with him, while Malick, in his gloss on Godard's theme, shows no feelings. In *Breathless,* Michel (Belmondo) and his Patricia (Jean Seberg) were affectless and disengaged — he about murder, she about betrayal — but we weren't asked to be heartless toward them. If Michel's view of himself was a psychological by-product of the movies — he imitated Bogart, and he treated death as casually as if it were a reversible stunt — his movie cool was part of a romantic temperament, and we could feel warmly toward him, because we in the audience were also caught in movie-fed fantasies. *Breathless* was a romance about the romance of the movies — by no means the first but probably the first to suggest that living in a movie dreamworld might make one guiltless, and the first to suggest that if life can't live up to our movie dreams, this isn't merely comic but tragicomic. This tragicomic attitude fitted into (and also shaped) the attitude of a new generation of moviegoers — romantics spawned by mass culture. It has been a constant of movies ever since — especially of the movies made by young film addicts.

Badlands takes it several steps further, moving from Godard's inside view to an outside view, and using it as a put-down of the society. Set at the end of the fifties, the picture is about a killing spree that starts in South Dakota and is derived from the actual killing spree of Charles Starkweather and Caril Ann Fugate. (*Breathless* was also based on a news item.) Kit (Martin Sheen) and Holly (Sissy Spacek) are emotionless, and the film looks at them emotionlessly. It is an intellectualized movie — shrewd and artful, carefully styled to sustain its low-key view of dissociation. Kit and Holly are kept at a distance, doing things for no explained purpose; it's as if the director had taped gauze over their characters, so that we wouldn't be able to take a reading on them. One may assume that they are meant to be out of touch with their own emotions, but the movie never suggests that they had any to lose touch with. No one in the movie has any more affect than Kit and Holly; no one is surprised by what they do; by implication, everyone wants to do the same. Badlands. Malick's conception is so cold and formal that I felt as if I were watching a polished Ph.D. thesis that couldn't help making the professors exclaim "Brilliant!" The film is a succession of art touches. Malick is a gifted student, and *Badlands* is an art thing, all right, but I didn't admire it, I didn't enjoy it, and I don't like it. It's all rhetoric. Somewhat reminiscent of the work of Monte Hellman, it's an artistically self-conscious counterculture movie like *Five Easy Pieces,* only much more so. It's a counterculture movie in a rather special sense: it isn't on the side of the young characters, but, rather, its condescending tone toward the society makes it easy for people in the audience to feel superior.

Holly narrates, in her corrupted-by-pop, fifteen-year-old baton twirler's notion of a literary attitude. The whole movie is filtered through the callowness of her childish Southwestern voice and her soap-operatic confessional phrasing. "Little did I realize that . . ." An easy laugh for the audience. She's like the girls that Tuesday Weld used to play, but without the spark and sex. She's not corrupt — just blah. We can't fail to observe that she doesn't have a fresh perception and that she never expresses any specific, direct reaction; though she "loves" Kit, she is emotionless about her first sex ("Is that all there is to it?"). She isn't any more upset when her father (Warren Oates) shoots her dog than she is when Kit shoots her father. And we can't fail to observe Malick's tony culture (presumably non-pop) commenting on hers. The photography — empty skies and empty landscapes and Maxfield Parrish storybook color — makes an aesthetic point. (It's as deliberate as staging an abstract play on a bare stage.) Music by Carl Orff and Erik Satie serves as a heightened form of condescension to the culturally dim, frigid lovers. Malick is, of course, telling us that they're empty. Godard's pair were empty, too, but only in a sense, and that sense was part of their attraction. Their not giving much of a damn about anything had a generational chic; it was part of what made them charming. But even the whims of Malick's pair are calculated to be drab.

Our only possible involvement is in admiring Malick's tasteful effects while he demonstrates Kit's and Holly's nothingness. After Kit kills Holly's father, he burns down the house, and we're treated to a fiery little visual poem as the flames encircle such totemic objects as Holly's doll house and her dead father's head. The pair go off to a wilderness and live in a tree house — a phlegmatic idyll. They hole up in a rich man's home furnished in such neutered perfection it could be entered in a museum show of bland gothic; the rich man's deaf housekeeper is a capper to the film's hushed tone. (The director himself appears as the man in a white hat who comes to the door and leaves a note for the captive master of the house.) Each effect is perfectly arbitrary. Kit is said to look like James Dean, but the truth is that Martin Sheen doesn't look like James Dean — he acts like him. And he doesn't act like him the way Kit would but as a trained actor would. But, of course, he's James Dean without the touching vulnerability — so that we won't care about him. Sheen is probably exactly what Malick wanted, because he's a proficient, unexciting actor; he is too finished — he doesn't leave any spaces for us to fill in, and nothing in him spills over. Auburn-haired Sissy Spacek, with her pale eyelashes, has the face of a Memling, but Memlings tell us more. After a half-dozen or so murders, Kit piles up some stones beside a road as a marker, so people will know where he was captured. The troopers who arrest him ask him why he committed the murders, and he says that he always wanted to be a criminal; they smile approvingly. No one shows any anger toward him; the townspeople are quietly eager for the souvenirs of himself he distributes. All this slanting is designed to prove that Kit and Holly are psychologically aberrant and yet that they're just like everybody else — that their moral vacuum is spreading over the flat, dead landscape. The badlands culture isn't hostile — it's just banal. The movie can be summed up: mass-culture banality is killing our souls and making everybody affectless.

Invasion of the Body Snatchers said the same thing without all this draggy art; it managed to be moderately entertaining and very scary. *Breathless* touched on the theme without making it a heavy statement. It's not such a steep perception that we have to suffer all this lethargy to grab hold of it. *Badlands* has no more depth than *The Sugarland Express,* and I found its cold detachment offensive. *The Sugarland Express* shows us the effects of the media on people without putting the people down for their sentimentality or for their pink curlers, or even for Lou Jean's mania for collecting gold stamps at service stations. Lou Jean's and Clovis's scrapping is a sign of life, and the trip to get their baby is a crazy joyride. The joyless flight across the badlands is just a culture trip. Bad taste isn't the worst thing in the world, but in *Badlands,* as sometimes in Antonioni's *Zabriskie Point,* one can easily get the feeling that the director thinks it is. The film is so iced that we react less to Holly's amorality than to her naïveté and pretensions, less to Kit's murders than to his clichés and aspirations to celebrity. Malick may not have recognized what his disengagement device would lead to. It's one thing to look at the rich people in *L'Avventura,* who have everything and are lost and empty; it's quite another to look at ordinary people and be shown that they're ciphers. The attitude becomes ugly, especially since the movie itself is so culturally embellished (though the choice of music is oddly lush; Hindemith would seem to be Malick's composer). And there's a basic flaw in Malick's method: he has *perceived* the movie — he's done our work instead of his. In place of people and action, with metaphor rising out of the story, he gives us a surface that is all conscious metaphor. *Badlands* is so preconceived that there's nothing left to respond to.

[March 18, 1974]

Part Three

On the Future of Movies

SOMETIME DURING THE LAST YEAR, a number of the most devoted moviegoers stopped going to the movies. I say "a number" because I have no idea how many are actually involved, but I keep meeting people — typically, men in their late twenties and early thirties — who say, "You know, I just don't have the impulse to go to a movie anymore," or "There aren't any movies anymore, are there?" The interest in pictures has left these people almost overnight; they turned off as suddenly as they'd turned on, and, since they no longer care to go, they feel that there's nothing to see. It was no accident that the Americans walked off with most of the top awards at Cannes this year. Right now, American movies — not the big hits but many of the movies that Hollywood considers failures — are probably the best in the world. No country rivals us in the diversity of skilled, talented filmmakers, but there are few lines for the sorts of films that young audiences were queuing up for a couple of years ago. They talked fervently then about how they loved movies; now they feel there can't be anything good going on, even at the movies.

Whatever their individual qualities, such films as *Bonnie and Clyde, The Graduate, Easy Rider, Five Easy Pieces, Joe, M*A*S*H, Little Big Man, Midnight Cowboy,* and *They Shoot Horses, Don't They?* all helped to form the counterculture. The young, anti-draft, anti-Vietnam audiences that were "the film generation" might go to some of the same pictures that the older audience did, but not to those only. They were willing to give something fresh a chance, and they went to movies that weren't certified hits. They made modest — sometimes large — successes of pictures that had new, different perceptions. A movie like the tentative, fumbling *Alice's Restaurant* would probably be a flop now, because student audiences are no longer willing to look for feelings, to accept something suggestive and elliptical and go with the mood. Students accept the elliptical on records — the Joni Mitchell "Court and Spark," say, and some of the more offbeat Carly Simon cuts — but not in movies. The subdued, fine-drawn *McCabe & Mrs. Miller,* which came out in 1971, managed to break even, but the soft-colored *Thieves Like Us,* the latest film by the same director, Robert Altman, has been seen by almost nobody. Those who might be expected to identify with Jeff Bridges in *The Last American Hero* are going to see Clint Eastwood in *Magnum Force* instead. They're going to the kind of slam-bang pictures that succeed with illiterate audiences in "underdeveloped" countries who are starved for entertainment. The almost voluptuously obsessive *Mean Streets* — a film that one might have thought would be talked about endlessly — passed through college towns without causing a stir. The new generations of high-school and college students are going to movies that you can't talk about afterward — movies that are completely consumed in the theatre.

There is no way to estimate the full effect of Vietnam and Watergate on popular culture, but earlier films were predicated on an implied system of values which is gone now, except in the corrupt, vigilante form of a *Dirty Harry* or a *Walking Tall.* Almost all the current hits are jokes on the past, and especially on old films — a mixture of nostalgia and parody, laid on with a trowel. The pictures reach back in time, spoofing the past, jabbing at it. Nobody understands what contemporary heroes or heroines should be, or how they should relate to each other, and it's safer not to risk the box-office embarrassment of seriousness.

FOR MANY YEARS, some of us alarmists have been saying things like "Suppose people get used to constant visceral excitement — will they still respond to the work of artists?" Maybe, owing partly to the national self-devaluation and partly to the stepped-up power of advertising, what we feared has come about. It's hardly surprising: how can people who have just been pummeled and deafened by *The French Connection* be expected to respond to a quiet picture? If, still groggy, they should stumble in to see George Segal in Irvin Kershner's *Loving* the next night, they'd think there was nothing going on in it, because it didn't tighten the screws on them. *The Rules of the Game* might seem like a hole in the screen. When *The Getaway* is double-billed with *Mean Streets,* it's no wonder that some people walk out on *Mean Streets.* Audiences like movies that do all the work for them — just as in the old days, and with an arm-twisting rubdown besides. College students don't appear to feel insulted (what's left to insult us?); they don't mind being banged over the head — the louder the better. They seem to enjoy seeing the performers whacked around, too; sloppy knockabout farce is the newest smash, and knockabout horror isn't far behind. People go for the obvious, the broad, the movies that don't ask them to feel anything. If a movie is a hit, that means practically guaranteed sensations — and sensations without feeling.

I often come out of a movie now feeling wiped out, desolate — and often it's a movie that the audience around me has reacted to noisily, as if it were having a high, great time — and I think I feel that way because of the nihilism in the atmosphere. It isn't intentional or philosophical nihilism; it's the kind one sometimes feels at a porn show — the way everything is turned to dung, oneself included. A couple of years ago, I went with another film critic, a young man, to see a hard-core movie in the Broadway area, and there was a live stage show with it. A young black girl — she looked about seventeen but must have been older — did a strip and then danced naked. The theater was small, and the girl's eyes, full of hatred, kept raking the customers' faces. I was the only other woman there, and each time her eyes came toward me, I had to look down; finally, I couldn't look up at all. The young critic and I sat in misery, unable to leave, since that would look like a put-down of her performance. We had to take the contempt with which she hid her sense of being degraded, and we shared in her degradation, too. Hits like *The Exorcist* give most of the audience just what it wants and expects, the way hard-core porn does. The hits have something in common: blatancy. They are films that *deliver.* They're debauches — their subject might almost be mindlessness and futurelessness. People in the audience want to laugh, and at pictures like *Enter the Dragon* and *Andy Warhol's Frankenstein* and *The Three Musketeers* and *Blazing Saddles* they're laughing at pandemonium and accepting it as the comic truth.

The counterculture films made corruption seem inevitable and hence something you learn to live with; the next step was seeing it as slapstick comedy and learning to enjoy it. For the fatalistic, case-hardened audience, absurdism has become the only acceptable point of view — a new complacency. In *The Three Musketeers,* Richard Lester keeps his actors at a distance and scales the characters down to subnormal size; they're letching, carousing buffoons who don't care about anything but blood sport. The film isn't politically or socially abrasive; it's just "for fun." At showings of *Chinatown,* the audience squeals with pleasure when Faye Dunaway reveals her incest. The success of *Chinatown* — with its beautifully structured script and draggy, overdeliberate direction — represents something dialectically new: nostalgia (for the thirties) openly turned to rot, and the *celebration* of rot. Robert Towne's script had ended with the detective (Jack Nicholson) realizing what horrors the Dunaway character had been through, and, after she killed her incestuous father, helping her daughter get to Mexico. But Roman Polanski seals the picture with his gargoyle grin; now evil runs rampant. The picture is compelling, but coldly, suffocatingly compelling. Polanski keeps so much of it in closeup that there's no air, no freedom to breathe; you don't care who is hurt, since everything is blighted. Life is a blood-red maze. Polanski may leave the story muddy and opaque, but he shoves the rot at you, and large numbers of people seem to find it juicy. Audiences now appear to accept as a view of themselves what in the movies of the past six or seven years counterculture audiences jeered at Americans for being — cynical materialists who cared for nothing but their own greed and lust. The nihilistic, coarse-grained movies are telling us that nothing matters to us, that we're all a bad joke.

IT'S BECOMING TOUGH for a movie that isn't a big media-created event to find an audience, no matter how good it is. And if a movie has been turned into an event, it doesn't have to be good; an event — such as *Papillon* — draws an audience simply because it's an event. You don't expect Mount Rushmore to be a work of art, but if you're anywhere near it you have to go; *Papillon* is a movie Mount Rushmore, though it features only two heads. People no longer go to a picture just for itself, and ticket-buyers certainly aren't looking for the movie equivalent of "a good read." They want to be battered, to be knocked out — they want to get wrecked. They want what "everybody's talking about," and even if they don't like the picture — and some people didn't really care for *A Touch of Class,* and some detested *The Three Musketeers,* and many don't like *Blazing Saddles,* either — they don't feel out of it. Increasingly, though, I've noticed that those who don't enjoy a big event-film feel out of it in another way. They wonder if there's something they're not getting — if the fault is theirs.

The public can't really be said to have rejected a film like *Payday,* since the public never heard of it. If you don't know what a movie is and it plays at a theatre near you, you barely register it. *Payday* may not come at all; when the event strategy really works, as it has of late, the hits and the routine action films and horror films are all that get to most towns. And if a film turns up that hasn't had a big campaign, people assume it's a dog; you risk associating yourself with failure if you go to see Jon Voight in *Conrack* or Blythe Danner in the messed-up but still affecting *Lovin' Molly.* When other values are rickety, the fact that something is selling gives it a primacy, and its detractors seem like spoilsports. The person who holds out against an event looks a loser: the minority is a fool. People are cynical about advertising, of course, but their cynicism is so all-inclusive now that they're indifferent, and so they're more susceptible to advertising than ever. If nothing matters anyway, why not just go where the crowd goes? That's a high in itself.

There are a few exceptions, but in general it can be said that the public no longer discovers movies, the public no longer makes a picture a hit. If the advertising for a movie doesn't build up an overwhelming desire to be part of the event, people just don't go. They don't listen to their own instincts, they don't listen to the critics — they listen to the advertising. Or, to put it more precisely, they do listen to their instincts, but their instincts are now controlled by advertising. It seeps through everything — talk shows, game shows, magazine and newspaper stories. Museums organize retrospectives of a movie director's work to coördinate with the opening of his latest film, and publish monographs paid for by the movie companies. College editors travel at a movie company's expense to see its big new film and to meet the director, and directors preview their new pictures at colleges. The public-relations event becomes part of the national consciousness. You don't hear anybody say, "I saw the most wonderful movie you never heard of"; when you hear people talking, it's about the same blasted movie that everybody's going to — the one that's flooding the media. Yet even the worst cynics still like to think that "word of mouth" makes hits. And the executives who set up the machinery of manipulation love to believe that the public — the public that's sitting stone-dead in front of its TV sets — spontaneously discovered their wonderful movie. If it's a winner, they say it's the people's choice. But, in the TV age, when people say they're going to see *Walking Tall* because they've "heard" it's terrific, that rarely means a friend has told them; it means they've picked up signals from the atmosphere. It means *Walking Tall* has been plugged so much that every cell in a person's body tells him he's got to see it. Nobody ever says that it was the advertising that made him vote for a particular candidate, yet there is considerable evidence that in recent decades the presidential candidates who spent the most money always won. They were the people's choice. Advertising is a form of psychological warfare that in popular culture, as in politics, is becoming harder to fight with aboveboard weapons. It's becoming damned near invincible.

The ludicrous *Mame* or the limp, benumbed *The Great Gatsby* may not make as much money as the producing companies hoped for, but these pictures don't fail abjectly, either. They're hits. If Hollywood executives still believe in word of mouth, it's because the words come out of their own mouths.

THE BUSINESSMEN have always been in control of film production; now advertising puts them, finally, on top of public reaction as well. They can transcend the content and the quality of a film by advertising. The new blatancy represents the triumph — for the moment, at least —of the businessmen's taste and the businessmen's ethic. Traditionally, movies were thought linked to dreams and illusions, and to pleasures that went way beyond satisfaction. Now the big ones are stridently illusionless, for a public determined not to be taken in. Audiences have become "realists" in the manner of businessmen who congratulate themselves for being realists: they believe only in what gives immediate gratification. It's got to be right there — tangible, direct, basic, in their laps. The movie executives were shaken for a few years; they didn't understand what made a film a counterculture hit. They're happy to be back on firm ground with *The Sting.* Harmless, inoffensive. Plenty of plot but no meanings. Not even any sex to worry about.

Much — perhaps most — of the students' and educated moviegoers' unresponsiveness to recent fine work can be traced to the decisions of the movie companies about what will sell and what won't. With their overweening campaign budgets for *The Great Gatsby* and *Chinatown,* the Paramount executives didn't even take a full-page ad in the *Times* to announce that *The Conversation* had won the Grand Prize at Cannes. They didn't *plan* on *The Conversation* being a success, and nothing now is going to make them help it become one. *Gatsby* and *Chinatown* were their pictures, but *The Conversation* was Francis Ford Coppola's, and they're incensed at his being in a position (after directing *The Godfather*) to do what he wanted to do; they're *hurt* that he flouts their authority, working out of San Francisco instead of Los Angeles. And they don't really have any respect for *The Conversation,* because it's an idea film. It's the story of a compulsive loner (Gene Hackman), a wizard at electronic surveillance who is so afraid others will spy on him that he empties his life; he's a cipher — a cipher in torment. There's nothing to discover about him, and *still* he's in terror of being bugged. (Hackman is a superlative actor, but his peculiarity, his limitation, like Ralph Richardson's when he was younger, is his quality of anonymity: just what is right for this role.) *The Conversation* is driven by an inner logic. It's a little thin, because the logic is the working out of one character's obsession, but it's a buggy movie that can get to you so that when it's over you really feel you're being bugged. Maybe the reason the promotion people didn't try to exploit the Watergate tie-in was that they suspected the picture might also be saying something about movie companies. If a film isn't promoted, it's often because something about it — the idea itself, or the director's obstinate determination to make it — needles the bosses.

Executives show a gambler's ardor in arranging the financing of a picture. Sometimes they buy into one when it's finished or almost finished, in what appears to be the absolute conviction that it's a winner.

But almost any straw in the wind can make them lose confidence. They'll try out a tricky, subtle movie on a Friday-night preview audience that has come to see *Walking Tall* or John Wayne in *McQ*, and decide that the movie has no public appeal. They pull away from what they fear will be a failure; within the fiefdom of their company they don't want to be associated with a risky venture. They all snuggle deep into the company's hits; a picture like *The Sting* becomes a soft fur collar that they caress themselves with. The company that has *The Sting* doesn't worry about a real sendoff for *The Sugarland Express*: where are the big stars? The company with *The Exorcist* doesn't give much thought to a campaign for *Mean Streets*: some of the executives don't find it "satisfying," so they're sure the public won't. The movie companies used to give all their pictures a chance, but now they'll put two or three million, or even five, into selling something they consider surefire, and a token — a pittance — into the others. And when an unpublicized picture fails they can always cover their tracks by blaming the director. "There was nothing we could do for it," the executives in charge of advertising always say, and once they have doomed a picture, who can prove them wrong?

What isn't generally understood is that the top men don't want to be proved wrong and the lower-echelon executives have a jobholder's interest in proving their bosses right. For all the publicity the companies get from giving a picture "a second chance" — never really having given it a first — I can think of only one or two cases when they honestly did provide a fresh chance, and there's a whole morgueful of movies that were killed despite indications of public response; for example, Gillo Pontecorvo's only picture after *The Battle of Algiers* — *Burn!*, starring Marlon Brando, which came and went so fast that hardly anybody knows it exists.

If the company men don't like a picture, or are nervous about its chances, or just resent the director's wanting to do something he cares about (instead of taking the big assignments they believe in), they do minimal advertising, telling him, "Let's wait for the reviews," or "We'll see how the reviewers like it," and then, even if the reviews are great, they say, "But the picture isn't doing business. Why should we throw away money on it?" And if he mentions the reviews, they say, "Listen, the critics have never meant anything. You know that. Why waste money? If people don't want to go, you can't force them to buy tickets."

THERE'S A NATURAL WAR in Hollywood between the businessmen and the artists. It's based on drives that may go deeper than politics or religion: on the need for status, and warring dreams. The entrepreneur class in the arts is a relatively late social development; there were impresarios earlier, but it was roughly a hundred years ago, when the arts began to be commercialized for a large audience, that the mass-culture middleman was born. He functions as a book publisher, as a theatrical producer, as a concert manager, as a rock promoter, but the middleman in the movie world is probably more filled with hatred for the artists he traffics in than the middleman in any other area. The movie entrepreneur is even more of a self-made man than the others; he came out of nowhere. He has to raise — and risk — more money, and he stands to gain more. In a field with no traditions, he is more of a gambler and less of an aesthete than entrepreneurs in the other arts. He's a street fighter, his specialty low cunning. Even if he's a second- or third-generation movie executive with a college education, or a Harvard-educated lawyer turned agent turned producer, he's learned to be a street fighter if he wasn't born to it, and he has the same hatred of the artist. The artist, with his expressive needs — the artist, who, by definition, cares about something besides money — denigrates the only talent that the entrepreneur has: raising money. Nobody respects the entrepreneur's dream of glory, and nobody respects his singular talent — least of all the artist who needs him, and is often at his mercy.

The entrepreneur has no class, no status; and, whether he was a scrambling junk dealer or a scheming agent or a poor little rich boy who managed to survive his mogul father's ruthless bullying, he knows that. A director or an actor doesn't even have to be an artist — only to identify himself as an artist — to get the cachet, while the moneyman is likely to be treated as a moneygrubbing clown. Some few — Joe Levine, and Sam Goldwyn before him — have been able to make celebrities of themselves by acquiring a comic status, the status of a shrewd, amusing vulgarian. In no other field is the entrepreneur so naked a status-seeker. Underlings are kept busy arranging awards and medals and honorary degrees for the producer, whose name looms so large in the ads that the public — and often the producer himself — comes to think he actually made the pictures. Ross Hunter, Robert Radnitz, even Hal Wallis in recent years hardly have room in their advertising for the writers' and directors' names. The packagers offer themselves as the stars, and in many cases their pictures fail because they insist on employing nonentity directors who don't assert any authority.

The hatred of the moneyman for the ungovernable artist is based on a degradation that isn't far from that stripper's hatred of the audience — furious resentment of the privileged people who, as he sees it, have never had to stoop to do the things he has done. As in Mordecai Richler's exultant novel *The Apprenticeship of Duddy Kravitz* (which really enables one to understand what makes Sammy run), and the teeming, energetic Canadian film based on it, the entrepreneur is, typically, a man who has always been treated like dirt. And even after he's fought his way up, finagling like crazy every step of the way, a profligate director with the world at his feet may not only threaten that solvency but still treat him like dirt, as in Peter Viertel's thinly disguised account, in the novel *White Hunter, Black Heart,* of the relations of John Huston and Sam Spiegel during the making of *The African Queen.* There are few directors who feel such disdain, fewer still who would express it so nakedly, but the moneymen keep looking for signs of it: they tap phones, they turn employees into sneaks and spies — all to get proof of the disloyalty of those ingrate artists. It doesn't help if the artists like the tough bosses personally — if they prize the unconcealed wiliness or the manic, rude drive. In Richler's later novel *St. Urbain's Horseman,* the now rich Duddy Kravitz appears as a minor character. When someone assures Duddy that his blond actress wife loves him, Duddy is exasperated: "What are you talking, she loves me? Who in the hell could love Duddy Kravitz?" Duddy's view of himself doesn't leave much of a basis for friendship, and any affection the artist may feel disintegrates as soon as the businessman uses his power to control the artist's work. The artist's crime is caring less for profits than for what he wants to do; that caring is an insult and a threat. The war of the businessmen against the artists is the war of the powerful against the powerless, based on the hatred of those who can't for those who can, and in return the hatred of those who can for those who won't let them.

The producers' complaint about the hothead director who puts up a fight to try something different is "He's self-destructive. He's irresponsible. You can't do business with him." And they make him suffer for it. The artists in Hollywood are objects of ridicule because they're trying to work as artists. When a gifted director is broke and needs to work, the producers stick him on a project that is compromised from the start, and then the picture is one more failure to be held against him. They frustrate him at every turn because he doesn't respect them, and he is humiliated by men he doesn't even respect. The producers feel secure with the directors and actors who don't have ideas of their own, who will take jobs because they need to work and don't really care what they do. Those are the ones the producers call "artists with discipline."

An actor or a director can become an "artist with discipline" when he has a huge box-office hit, and his reputation for discipline will soar if, like Paul Newman or Robert Redford, he has a string of hits. Actually, to the moneymen discipline means success plus a belief in success. Coppola isn't called disciplined, despite the success of *The Godfather,* because he wants to work on his own projects (such as *The Conversation*), but George Roy Hill *(Butch Cassidy and the Sundance Kid, Slaughterhouse Five, The Sting)* is disciplined, because he believes in big-name, big-star projects. Peter Yates *(Bullitt, John and Mary)* is considered a man you can do business with, despite a flop like *Murphy's War* and the far from successful *The Hot Rock* and *The Friends of Eddie Coyle*; his flops aren't held against him, because he believes in the same kind of projects that the moneymen do and he doesn't try to do anything *special* with those projects. His latest, *For Pete's Sake,* probably won't bring in much of a bundle, but it's a model of Hollywood "discipline."

Peter Yates's lack of distinction, like the veteran Richard Fleischer's, is a proof of trustworthiness. The moneymen want a director who won't surprise them. They're scared of a man like Altman, because they just don't know what he'll do on a picture; they can't trust him to make it resemble the latest big hit. They want solid imitations, pictures that reek of money spent and money to come, pictures that look safe — like those Biblical epics that came rumbling off the assembly lines in the fifties. Twentieth Century-Fox and Warner Brothers are jointly producing a burning-skyscraper picture, *The Towering Inferno,* with Steve McQueen, Paul Newman, William Holden, Jennifer Jones, Robert Wagner, Fred Astaire, Richard Chamberlain, and other assorted big names. It's Grand Hotel in flames at last. Universal, for starters, has signed up Anne Bancroft and George C. Scott for *The Hindenburg,* described as "a multilayered drama with a gallery of international characters." In other words, Grand Hotel in flames in the sky. Every couple of years, the American movie public is said to crave something. Now it's calamity, and already the wave of apocalyptic movies — which aren't even here yet — is being analyzed in terms of our necrophilia. The studio heads are setting up disaster epics like kids reaching hand over hand up a baseball bat — all because of the success of *The Poseidon Adventure,* which probably had about as much to do with a public interest in apocalypse as Agatha Christie's old *Ten Little Indians* had. I doubt whether there's a single one of the directors mounting these disaster specials — becoming commanders-in-chief in an idiot war — who wouldn't infinitely rather be working on something else. By the time the public is gorged with disasters and the epics begin to flop, the studio heads will have fastened on another get-rich-quick gimmick (pirate capers are said to be on the agenda), and the people who work for them will lose a few more years of what might have been their creative lives. The producers gamble on the public's wanting more of whatever is a hit, and since they *all* gamble on that, the public is always quickly surfeited, but the failures of the flaccid would-be hits never anger the producers the way the failures of the films that someone really fought for do. The producers want those films to fail; they often make them fail. A Sam Peckinpah film, an Altman film, a Kershner film — the executives get pleasure out of seeing those films fail. It's a *punishment* of the artist.

Since all the businessmen's energy goes into strategy and manipulation, they can outfox the artists damn near every time; that's really the business they're in. Their right of "final cut" — one of the great symbolic terms in moviemaking — gives them the chance to chop up the film of a director who has angered them by doing it his own way; they'll mutilate the picture trying to remove the complexities he battled to put in. They love to play God with other people's creations. Movie after movie is mangled, usually by executives' last-minute guesses about what the public wants. When they've finished, they frequently can't do anything with the pictures but throw them away. That's their final godlike act — an act easy for them to live with, because they always have the director to blame. To them, the artist is the outsider; he's not a member of the family, to be protected. A few years ago, when word was out in the industry that Brando didn't mean anything at the box office, the producer David Merrick fired him from a picture; I asked an executive connected with the production what Brando had done. "Nothing," he said. "Brando was working hard, and he was cooperative with everyone. But he suggested some ways to improve the script; they were good suggestions — the script was a mess. But legally that was interference, and Merrick could fire Brando and collect on the insurance." "But why?" I persisted. He shrugged at my ignorance. "What could make David Merrick bigger than firing Marlon Brando?" he said.

THE STAR can be defined by what the producer says of him: "If he wants to burn down the studio, I'll hand him the match." That was said, I think, of Jerry Lewis, but it applies to such Hollywood figures as Frank Sinatra and, of course, Clint Eastwood and Robert Redford and Steve McQueen. What it means is very simple: the producers will hand them a match because the producers are banking the money. The producer is saying, "He can degrade me as long as I get mine out of it." And underneath that he's saying, "But wait until he has to come to me for something." The producers hate Brando for refusing to settle down and go for the money; they love-hate McQueen and Redford and Eastwood. They need them; they court them. And, yes, they can make a deal with them, but only on the star's terms, and the producers are never allowed to forget it. If the chance ever comes, they'll make the star pay for that.

The country has never been as star crazy as it is right now; there aren't very many movie stars, but the phenomenon of stardom operates in television, in radio, in literature, in the academic world, in politics, in the women's movement. (The black movement hasn't been getting much publicity recently, because it lacks stars.) Yet can one watch a few TV "roasts" — those ugly-jolly orgies of mock insults and real insults and odious sentimental disclaimers in which celebrities are fêted — without becoming aware of the sense of betrayal that is just under the surface? The best performer at the roast is obviously the one who dares to be the most malicious, and the person honored is forced to be a good sport while others "kid" him, letting out their aggression while he tries to laugh. And then they embrace him and say they didn't mean it. The roast is the show-business form of Shirley Jackson's lottery. It's a public display of the anger and self-hatred of those caught in the system, a ritual gathering of sellouts hitting each other with bladders and pretending it doesn't hurt. And that's how they feel when they're *at the top*. Their contempt for the audience, like the stripper's, is probably what makes it possible for them to keep going. They begin to believe that Las Vegas is all there is. The roast is a metaphor for the truth of the business; that's why it has become impossible for the Academy Awards presentation to have any style or dignity. The members of the Hollywood community can't control their self-destructive impulses any longer; they can't resist humiliating themselves before the whole world. "If that's what people want," the performers say, "I'll give it to them." Essentially, they're all playing to Duddy Kravitz. He's the man backing the international motion-picture roast.

A REVIEWER who pans a producer's picture is just one more person telling him he has no taste. When the reviewers praise movies that are allowed to die, the moneyman's brute instincts are confirmed, and the reviewers' impotence gives him joy. "Why must we sit back and allow the critics to determine if a film is acceptable as a consumer product?" Frank Yablans, the president of Paramount, asked this June. He was speaking to some two hundred people who work in television, explaining to them that word of mouth, which can defeat downbeat reviews, will be Paramount's target. A reviewer speaks out once, or maybe twice. The advertisers are an invisible force pounding at the public day after day. Unfavorable reviews are almost never powerful enough to undo the saturation publicity. Besides, curiosity about an event like *The Exorcist* is a big factor; as the woman quoted in *Variety* said, "I want to see what everybody is throwing up about."

People often make analogies between the world of live theater and the world of movies, and raise the question "Don't movie critics have too much power?" But in movies it's the businessmen who have the power. A reviewer's words can't be heard above the din unless they're amplified in the ads — which usually means reduced to a short, exclamatory quote and repeated incessantly. But that's only if the reviewer provided a quote for a picture that the company "has high hopes for"; if it's a picture that the company has lost interest in, there will be a few halfhearted ads, with apathetically selected quotes. Raves from even the dozen most influential papers and magazines can't make a success of *Mean Streets* if the company doesn't construct a campaign around those raves. The public indifference is a result of something that starts at the top of the movie company and filters down. Five years ago — even two years ago — a handful of reviewers could help persuade people to give a small or unheralded film a chance, but not now. The reviewers spoke to that audience which has lost the impulse to go to movies. The demise of "the film generation" means a sharp break with the past, since there won't be anything like that mass of youth — the Second World War babies reaching maturity — again. Because of its styles of hair and dress and manner, it was an identifiable generation; the members tuned in together for the last time at *American Graffiti* — that pop-comics view of their own adolescence, before they became the counterculture. Now the links are mostly broken and they're the aging young, tuned out.

The younger audience — high-school and college students — grew up with the rating system. As kids, they couldn't escape to the movies, the way their parents did, and so movies weren't an important part of their lives (though television was). When *they* say they love movies, they mean the old movies that they're just discovering, and the new hits. Even the sub-teens want the events; they were born into sixties cynicism and saturation advertising. They've never known anything but the noise and the frantic atmosphere; they think it's a cop-out if a movie cuts away from mayhem and doesn't show them the gore. They loved *Jesus Christ Superstar* (a masochistic revel for eight-year-olds), and they're eager to be part of *The Sting* and *Blazing Saddles.* They're saturated.

The students now who discover movies in college and want to get into film production have a different outlook from the young counterculture filmmakers of the sixties. They're not interested in getting into movie work in order to change movies; they just want to get into movie work. A young film student expressed anger to me about Elia Kazan, who had given a lecture at his university. Kazan had said that the studios wouldn't finance the subjects he was interested in, and offered him projects he couldn't face doing. The student, without a shade of sympathy for those caught in this basic Hollywood trap, said, "How can we listen to him? We would do anything to break in, and he says he's turning down projects!" Students have little interest in why a person refuses to direct the forty-sixth dope-heist picture or a romp about sprightly, beguiling swindlers; they don't care to hear some director say that he turned down *The Exorcist.* A hit makes a director a hero. A critic who speaks at a college now is almost certain to be asked such questions as "How many times do you see a movie before writing your critique?" and "Do you take notes?" The students are really asking, "How do you do it? How did you get to be a film critic?" They sometimes used to ask, "What do you think of Academy Awards?" — a question that was a sure laugh-getter from an audience that anticipated a tart rejoinder. Now they ask, "What [or who] do you think will win the Oscars this year?" And they really want to know the answer. Celebrity and success are so big on campus that the Academy Awards are discussed as if they were a perfectly respectable academic issue.

Stardom is success made manifest, success in human form, and, naturally, the yes-sayers are, in general, the biggest stars. College students are impressed and contemptuous at the same time. Can one imagine any picture so reactionary or vile that it would diminish Clint Eastwood's standing at a university? Even a reputation for corruption — for being willing to do anything for money — increases a star's stature, and the money gained gives him power and standing that are admired in a way the no-sayer's intransigence isn't, especially if his intransigence puts him out of the scene. There is nothing a star can do now that would really disgrace him. "Celebrity" has destroyed the concept of disgrace: scandal creates celebrity, and public misbehavior enhances it. Maybe *The Sting* is such a whopping hit because it's really a celebration of celebrity and stardom; it's not about anything but the golden yes-yes images of Redford and Newman. It doesn't need sex; it's got the true modern sex appeal — success.

In Los Angeles this spring, busloads of high-school students were brought in to listen to a Best-Sellers Panel composed of Helen Gurley Brown, Garson Kanin, Jacqueline Susann, and William Friedkin on the subject of how it feels to sell fifteen million books or to gross a hundred and twenty-five million dollars on a movie. From all accounts, there were no impolite questions, and no one made a rude noise when Kanin *(Tracy and Hepburn)* said, "We have to recognize that the public is smarter than we are. As individuals, one by one, perhaps no. But when that thousand-headed monster sits out there in the auditorium or sits reading your book of fiction, suddenly that mass audience is what the late Moss Hart called 'an idiot genius.' " This conceit of the successful — their absolute conviction that the crap that is sold is magically superior to the work that didn't sell — is the basis for the entrepreneurs' self-righteousness. The public has nothing to gain from believing this (and everything to lose), and yet the public swallows it.

THE BUSINESSMEN'S CONFIDENCE has taken a leap; business is better than it has been in several years, and they've got the artists where they want them. They're sure they're on the right track, because the public likes what they like. It's no longer just a Harry Cohn who could be said to have the world wired to his ass; the world is wired to all their asses. The hits are not uniformly terrible, and in themselves they don't pose any great threat. But if this is all that people want from movies — if even educated people and people of taste and some sensibility settle for the nihilistic brassiness of the hits — there's no audience for new work. In the past ten years, filmmaking has attracted some of the most inspired college students — the aces and prodigies who in previous eras would have headed into poetry or architecture or painting or playwriting. There they are, poised and ready to take off, and there is no place for them to take off to except the same old Hollywood vise — tighter now, perfected. And there are the high-fliers who have been locked out all along — the dozens of artist-filmmakers who work in film not as a collaborative storytelling medium but as a highly individual art form, more closely related to the graphic arts than to Hollywood. Some of them, such as Ed Emshwiller, with his great trip film *Relativity,* and Jordan Belson, who has made flawless abstract visionary shorts, have already reached new peaks of film art; others, such as John Schofill, who works at scarily intense psychosexual imagery, may. Right now, there is no way for their work to reach movie theaters and no way for them to heat up and fertilize feature filmmaking, which needs renewal. Everything is ready for an age of great movies, except the entrepreneurs and the public.

Movies could easily go the way of the theater — and faster, since the moneymen have no aesthetic commitment whatever. And probably there'd be less lamentation for movies than for live theater. Because, of course, there's television. But it's not the same medium. And though if you don't read a book when it comes out you can read it a year later, if you don't see a movie when it comes out, and wait to see it a year later on television, you're not seeing what you could have seen in the theatre. (Nor do you see that movie if you wait to see it in a college, or at a film society in a cheap, grainy 16-mm. reduction.) What's lost on television is the visual beauty, the spatial sense, the fusion of image and sound — everything that makes movies an art form. And movies made directly for television almost never have these qualities; one talks of TV movies in terms of pace and impact and tension, and occasionally — with the prestige ones — subject and performances, but who talks of television movies in terms of beauty? Movies made for TV, or movies made for a big screen and shown on TV, are reduced to just what the businessmen believe in — the bare bones of entertainment. There is something spurious about the very term "a movie made for TV," because what you make for TV is a TV program.

Television as we have it isn't an art form — it's a piece of furniture that is good for a few things. There's a problem of dimensions: no matter what people say, the screen is too small, and that's why the thing TV does best is a closeup of a person being asked a direct question — because both you and that person know that it operates like a lie detector. For perhaps most Americans, TV is an appliance, not to be used selectively but to be turned on — there's always something to watch. If a hundred million people see a movie in two showings on TV, that doesn't mean what it would if a hundred million people saw it in theaters. Sure, forty-two million people saw *The Autobiography of Miss Jane Pittman,* but they saw it sandwiched between two other shows. TV stars with audiences larger than the world has ever before known are eager to appear in a real movie — which, even if a hit, will be seen by only a handful, relatively speaking (until it, too, winds up on TV) — because they know that on TV they're part of the furniture. On TV they're mundane, they're reduced to the routinely, boringly tolerable. There's an aesthetic element in the phrase "larger than life," and the artists working in the movie medium instinctively take that into consideration. What is on the big screen has an aesthetic clarity denied to the box; when you're watching a movie in a theater, you don't need a voice telling you what you have just seen.

There have been some few subjects filmed for TV which nobody would finance for theaters, because it's generally understood that people won't pay to see a film on a subject like that of *I Heard the Owl Call My Name* or *Jane Pittman* or *The Execution of Private Slovik.* But a few TV shows with social themes shouldn't become the occasion for big headlines in the press about how television "has been growing bolder." Bold is just what these shows aren't; even when they're made as well as possible, they're mincingly careful. And they're not a key to new opportunities on TV so much as a key to the constriction of opportunities for moviemakers: moviemakers can't get backing for pictures with social themes — or with any real themes at all. Probably it's true that people wouldn't pay to see the films on social themes which they'll watch on television, but that's because those subjects are treated in the sober, limited TV manner. We have no way of knowing how the public might respond if a hugely talented filmmaker with adequate resources and a campaign to back him took on a large social theme. Nobody has had the chance in decades.

Television represents what happens to a medium when the artists have no power and the businessmen are in full, unquestioned control. People's TV expectations are so low and so routinized that *Brian's Song* can pass for an event, and a pitifully predictable problem play like *Tell Me Where It Hurts,* in which Maureen Stapleton plays a middle-aged housewife who joins a women's-lib group and has her consciousness raised, is received by the press as if it marked a significant advance. And what sort of opportunities does *normal* television offer for the development of talent? Here are the words of Brandon Stoddard, A.B.C.'s vice-president in charge of motion pictures for television:

> I am interested in emotional jeopardy, not physical jeopardy. I want the viewer to really care about the people and to feel something when it is over. . . . I have nothing against exploitative material if it is done right, and the way to do it right is to translate it into human drama rather than gimmicks. I don't want to know about the two Vampires in the casino in Las Vegas. I want to know about the man they are attacking and how it will affect his life. . . . We are looking everywhere for story ideas and even calling colleges to get some new blood into this.

Movies as an art form won't die and go to the heaven of television. If they die, they'll be truly dead. Even if the shift in the audience toward the crude and insensitive is only a temporary derangement, it could be sufficient to destroy movies. The good recent films — all together — can't possibly lose as much money as a single clinker like *Star!* or *Camelot,* but even if each one of them should manage to break even, and some of them to show a small or moderate profit, the businessmen will still see them as failures. The businessmen don't collect medals for moderate profits; they get their medals for box-office killers, and they don't want pictures by people who reject their values. When they tell a director, "Listen, what you call crap is what the public wants," it's not just an objective comment; they want the public to want this crap, and they've made stark sure it will. Since they've cold-decked public opinion, since they promote and sell only what they like, when they say, "That's what the public wants," it's the truth.

NATHANAEL WEST got it upside down. The locusts aren't those poor bastards from Oklahoma who want to touch a movie star and die in the sun; the locusts run the studios, and it's they who, in West's metaphor, will burn Los Angeles — they'll hand *everybody* a match. It's the smart empty people — not the dull-eyed but the beady-eyed — who are whipping up the orgiastic possibilities in irrational violence. We all know in advance that the forthcoming movie version of West's apocalyptic novel won't distance us, as the novel did, so that we recoil from the destructive potential in a numbed, envious crowd, but will, *of course,* seize the opportunity to turn audiences on to the excitement of a mob with murder in its heart.

It's the carnivore locusts at the top who tear the artists apart, but the writers and directors have often (unwittingly) aided them. Writers, who assume an ideal reader when they "do their own writing," accept the moguls' view of the public when they work for the movies. Not that they necessarily write down — probably most scenarists write as well as they can, considering the limitations imposed on them — but that they begin to subscribe to the moguls' attitudes, which are endemic in Hollywood, and so they come to believe in the necessity for those limitations. They don't assume an ideal viewer — they assume a hollow-eyed, empty-souled, know-nothing hick.

And, in some crazy, vindictive way — as if the masses were their enemy — certain writers and directors enjoy satirizing the rootless, uncultured Americans. John Schlesinger in *Midnight Cowboy,* Tony Richardson in *The Loved One,* Antonioni in *Zabriskie Point* — liberals all, but aesthetes first — spin a new baroque out of the grotesqueness of American bad taste. They lose their socially conscious moorings when they treat American culture, just as American liberals and leftists from the East lose them in the West. Nathanael West — and what a misnomer he chose for himself — must have recognized that he was caught in an ideological bind in *The Day of the Locust.* In the middle of his apocalyptic climax, when the hollow-eyed people are gathering, he carefully exempts himself from political criticism by having his hero, Tod, observe, "He could see very few people who looked tough, nor could he see any working men. The crowd was made up of the lower middle classes." That handy, safe target of the left — "the lower middle classes." But, a few lines farther on, Tod describes the people and contradicts himself: "All their lives they had slaved at some kind of dull, heavy labor, behind desks and counters, in the fields and at tedious machines of all sorts, saving their pennies and dreaming of the leisure that would be theirs when they had enough." It's nonsense to think that working people don't get debased, and only the "lower middle classes" are susceptible to the deadening effects of mass culture, but if one makes this false split between the workers and the riffraff it's one hell of a lot easier to take movie money. Generations of screenwriters played the same game that West did, trying to convince themselves that they weren't doing any damage to anyone who really counted. The movie audience became a huge subhuman abstraction to them; it was a faceless joke, and they weren't accountable to it. In modern Hollywood, where most of the writing and directing are for TV, that is now the attitude toward the television audience.

Perhaps no work of art is possible without belief in the audience — the kind of belief that has nothing to do with facts and figures about what people actually buy or enjoy but comes out of the individual artist's absolute conviction that only the best he can do is fit to be offered to others. It's what makes a director insist on a retake even when he knows he's going to be penalized for it; it's what makes young dancers drop from exhaustion; it's what made Caruso burst his throat. You have to believe in the audience, and believe that your peak effort just barely makes you worthy of it. That's implicit when an artist says he does it "because he has to," and even when he says he does it "just for himself." An artist's sense of honor is founded on the honor due others. Honor in the arts — and in show business, too — is giving of one's utmost, even if the audience does not appear to know the difference, even if the audience shows every sign of preferring something easy, cheap, and synthetic. The audience one must believe in is the great audience: the audience one was part of as a child, when one first began to respond to great work — the audience one is still part of. As soon as an artist ceases to see himself as part of the audience — when he begins to believe that what matters is to satisfy the jerk audience out there — he stops being an artist. He becomes a businessman, marketing a commodity — his talent, himself.

PROBABLY THE LAST BIG MOVIE HITS that were also works of genuine talent — that is, of people going the whole length — were *The Godfather* and *Cabaret,* but surely Coppola has already learned from the handling of *The Conversation* that the big boys play the game on their own terms. Even the very biggest hits provide only a feeling of power, an illusion of freedom. You get what you want up to a certain point, and then you're done in. The artists have got to break out of this humiliating, suicidal struggle with the entrepreneurs.

There's only one way: They've got to help each other. It's a matter not of the lunatics' taking over the asylum (how the businessmen love to say that each time an artist tries to wrest control of his work away from them) but of the artists' abandoning the asylum to the lunatics who are the keepers. Before the mass market and the entrepreneurs, people in show business weren't spoiled children — gypsies, yes, but not infants. It is the movie companies that have infantilized them. In the days of the studio system, with its long-term contracts, the stars were encouraged, even pushed, to live like the French dauphins; they showed off the gaudiest, most expensive playthings, and studio publicists worked to create the very image that was used as proof that the artists were indulged. (The vulgar excesses were always attributed to the infantile artists, but the studio heads, those paternal figures who made the decisions for them, lived even higher, and that wasn't taken as a sign of mindless irresponsibility.) Artists in all the arts are made to feel helpless, because they don't know what to do with their gifts, and many believe the image of themselves that businessmen create. They begin to think that they can't do anything unless they sign themselves away, and when offered the opportunity they're scared not to take it. Edward G. Robinson wrote that when he was a young stage actor he made a picture for Irving Thalberg, and Thalberg offered him a three-year, million-dollar contract; he was to work exclusively for M-G-M and be built into a star. Robinson countered with the proposition that he work at M-G-M for six months a year and have the other six months free to work on the stage, but, as he described it, "Thalberg compromised on nothing; he sat there, stern and immovable — the godhead. . . . His eyes showed me that an actor was beneath contempt." Robinson turned the offer down, left the office, and vomited. And Thalberg, the courtly, refined Thalberg, most admired of all the moguls — he was even *thin* — never forgave Robinson for the rejection and never used him in another picture. Yes, they groomed you for stardom, but only if you were theirs — their pet. There's so much bathetic bull about the old days — so many TV hosts have said, "Mr. Capra, why don't you make another one of your wonderful pictures for us?" — that people may actually begin to believe they're being deprived of something great. On TV, people talk about the big old producers as if they really had the magic, knew the secret of how to do it. It's like remembering Captain Kidd as someone who was particularly knowledgeable about the properties of gold and silver. Professional sentimentalists have forgotten — or don't care — that most of the moguls' big "personally supervised" projects were overblown bores. If one looks at the lists of pictures they put their stars in, it's apparent that the stars were buried in garbage up to their necks and only rarely got a chance to climb out and act. The moguls usually fought and despised the people who brought in the hits — the people who didn't want to be owned. Preston Sturges had only four years in his lifetime when he could do the pictures he wanted to; "a comic opera," he called the battle with the producers long after he had been beaten down. When the director Tay Garnett, who had just brought in a big Jean Harlow hit for Thalberg, declined to direct her next picture, because he felt she was miscast, Thalberg simply terminated Garnett's contract. (She *was* miscast, and the picture failed.) Thalberg had fired Erich von Stroheim and Mauritz Stiller and replaced them with functionaries when he was still a boy — a boy wonder.

Now that the studios don't keep stables of indentured stars, they don't even groom young talent; they corrupt and destroy the gifted actors and directors much faster. Performers who are thought to have money in them are sought by all the bosses at the same time; overused and trashed, James Coburn, Sandy Dennis, Tony Randall, Eva Marie Saint are stars one year and gone the next. Yet the agents and entrepreneurs claim that the artists can't think straight and can't do anything without them. The stars are often convinced by the agent or adviser or accountant who says, "You need me. I'll take care of everything for you," though people don't say that unless they get something out of it. Could the artists do *worse* on their own than *For Pete's Sake*?

Pampered children can go rotten; the young Off Broadway actor who was dedicated to his work can in the space of a few years become the star who says that honestly he loves the script a talented young director wants him for, and he would really like to do it, but he can't *afford* to do a small movie, because his price now is a million dollars a picture. The million-dollar-a-picture star can be more corrupt and worse to deal with than any producer, because he usually operates behind the cover of his agent or his manager. The agent represents the truth about this star: the deal has become more important to him than the picture. He has become his own Duddy Kravitz.

THERE'S NO WAY for movies to be saved from premature senility unless the artists finally abandon the whole crooked system of Hollywood bookkeeping, with its kited budgets and trick percentages. Most directors are signed up for only one picture now, but after the deal is made the director gets the full de-luxe ritual: fancy hotels, first-class travel, expense money to maintain cool, silky blond groupies for traveling companions. The directors are like calves being fattened — all on the budget of the picture. The thieving, high-salaried executives and their entourage of whores and underlings are also traveling and living it up on that same budget; that's how a picture that cost $1,200,000 comes in on the books at $3,000,000, and why the director who has a percentage of the profits doesn't get any.

It isn't impossible to raise money outside the industry to make a movie — the studios themselves finance some of their biggest pictures with tax-shelter money (*Gatsby,* in part) — but even those who raise independent financing and make a picture cheaply (*Mean Streets* was brought in for $380,000, plus $200,000 in deferred costs, *Payday* for $767,000) are stuck for a way to distribute it and fall victim to the dream of a big Hollywood win. So they sell their pictures to "the majors" to exhibit, and watch helplessly as the films die or the swindled profits disappear. And they are beggars again. Brian De Palma's *Greetings* was made for $20,000, plus $23,000 in deferred costs in 1968; back in the fifties, Irvin Kershner made *Stakeout on Dope Street* for $30,000, plus $8,000 in deferred costs. If there had been an artists' co-op to distribute the films, the directors might have been able to use the profits to continue working, instead of pouring energy into planning films that they could never finance, and seeing the films they did make get sliced to ribbons.

If the directors started one distribution company, or even several (they could certainly get backing), they might have to spend time on business problems, but, with any luck, much less time on dealmaking sessions: those traumatic meetings at which the businessmen air their grievances while the artists anxiously vulgarize the projects they're submitting, hoping to make them sound commercial enough. If they have a book they want to film or if they try to get development money for a story idea, the lack of enthusiasm is deadly. One director says, "You look at them and you give up. And if, after a year or two years, they finally give you the go-ahead, then they cut you down to a twenty-five-day shooting schedule and *dare* you to make a picture." Right now, all but a handful of Hollywood directors spend most of their time preparing projects that they never get to shoot. They work on scripts with writers, piling up successions of drafts, and if they still can't please the producers and get a deal, the properties are finally abandoned or turned over to other directors, who start the process all over again, with new writers. One could outline a history of modern Hollywood by following the passage of one such project — the French novel *Choice Cuts,* say, which more than a dozen of the best writers and close to a dozen of the best directors have worked on: script after script in insane succession, and the waltz still goes on, each person in turn thinking that he's got a deal and his version will be made. The directors spend their lives not in learning their craft and not in doing anything useful to them as human beings but in fighting a battle they keep losing. The business problems of controlling their own distribution should be minor compared to what they go through now — the abuse from the self-pitying bosses, the indignity, the paralysis. And if the directors had to think out how their movies should be presented to the public — what the basis for the advertising campaign should be — this mightn't be so bad for them. If they had to worry about what a movie was going to mean to people and why anybody should come to see it, they might be saved from too much folly. A fatal difference between the "high" arts and the popular, or mass-culture, arts has been that in one the artist's mistakes are his own, while in the other the mistakes are largely the businessmen's. The artist can grow making his own mistakes; he decays carrying out the businessmen's decisions — working on large, custom-made versions of the soulless entertainment on TV.

Privately, almost every one of the directors whose work I admire tells the same ugly, bitter story, yet they live in such fear of those spiteful, spying bosses that they don't dare even talk to each other. Hollywood is a small, ingrown community where people live in terror that "word will get back." They inhabit a paranoia-inducing company town, and within it they imagine the bosses to have more power in the outside world than they actually do. If such talents as Sam Peckinpah, Paul Mazursky, Martin Scorsese, Coppola, Kershner, Altman, De Palma, Woody Allen, Frederick Wiseman, Lamont Johnson, John Korty, Steven Spielberg, Michael Crichton, and even some of the older directors, such as Kazan and Fred Zinnemann, joined together to distribute their own films, they'd be able to work on the projects they really want to work on, and they'd get most of the writers and performers and craftsmen they want, too. The main obstacles are not in the actual world. It's not impossible to buck the majors and to book movies into theaters, and it's not really hard to publicize movies; the media are almost obscenely eager for movie news, and the businessmen, who know only one way to advertise a film — by heavy bombardment — often kill interest in an unusual picture by halfheartedly trying to sell it as if it were the kind of routine action show they wanted it to be.

There's no way of knowing whether a new audience can be found; it's a matter of picking up the pieces, and it may be too late. But if the directors started talking to each other, they'd realize that they're all in the same rapidly sinking boat, and there'd be a chance for them to reach out and try to connect with a new audience. If they don't, they'll never test themselves as artists and they'll never know whether an audience could have been found for the work they want to do.

The artists have to break out of their own fearful, star-struck heads; the system that's destroying them is able to destroy them only as long as they believe in it and want to win within it — only as long as they're psychologically dependent on it. But the one kind of winning that is still possible in those terms is to be a winner like William Friedkin or George Roy Hill. The system works for those who don't have needs or aspirations that are in conflict with it; but for the others — and they're the ones who are making *movies* — the system doesn't work anymore, and it's not going to.

[August 5, 1974]

Part Four

"Lacombe, Lucien"

INTRODUCING HIMSELF to a delicate, fine-boned Parisienne, the farm-boy hero of Louis Malle's new movie does not give his name as Lucien Lacombe; he gives the bureaucratic designation — Lacombe, Lucien. He presents himself, name inverted, because he is trying to be formal and proper, as he's been trained to be at school and at work, sweeping floors at his local, small-town hospital in southwest France. When he meets the girl, France Horn — and falls in love with her — his new job is hunting down and torturing people for the Gestapo. He likes it a whole lot better than the hospital. The title *Lacombe, Lucien* refers to the case of a boy of seventeen who doesn't achieve a fully human identity, a boy who has an empty space where feelings beyond the purely instinctive are expected to be.

The time is 1944, after the Normandy landings, and the Nazis and their collaborators won't be in power long. Lucien doesn't know that. He had tried to join the Resistance, but the local Resistance leader was his old schoolmaster, who thought him stupid, and Lucien stumbled into a job with the Nazis. Actually, he isn't stupid; he has the kinds of talents that don't show at school — he has a country boy's skills, and he knows how to survive in the wild. The schoolmaster is right, though, in perceiving that Lucien is apolitical and unprincipled — that he just wants some action. Lucien is good to his mother, and in normal circumstances he would work on a farm, taking care of his own and not bothering anybody, and he'd probably be a respected, unconscionably practical member of the community. But in wartime he's a perfect candidate for Nazi bullyboy. Malle's film is a long, close look at the banality of evil; it is — not incidentally — one of the least banal movies ever made. The actions are handled plainly, with restraint — with no attempt to shock anyone, or impress anyone; the actions are what we knew already. There's no special magic involved in the moviemaking technique — it's simple, head-on, unforced. The movie is the boy's face. The magic is in the intense curiosity and intelligence behind the film — in Malle's perception that the answers to our questions about how people with no interest in politics become active participants in brutal torture are to be found in Lucien's plump-cheeked, narrow-eyed face, and that showing us what this boy *doesn't* react to can be the most telling of all.

In *The Sorrow and the Pity* we watched former Nazis and collaborators give their accounts of their behavior, and with some of them we were left staring at big empty spaces. That's the space Malle attempts to define. It can't be done by setting up a character for us to identify with; the whole point of the film is that we have always been unable to identify with these people, and yet we don't know what makes us different from them — if we are. Malle can't think himself into Lucien's shoes; he could think himself into the very soul of the burnt-out, self-pitying hero of *The Fire Within,* but Lucien is outside the normal range of a dramatist's imagination. The screenplay Malle devised (together with the twenty-seven-year-old Patrick Modiano, author of three novels on the Occupation) tries not to dramatize and not to comment. The director sets up his wartime situation and puts in as Lucien a teenage country boy (Pierre Blaise) who has seen few films and has never acted before — a boy, that is, who can respond to events with his own innocence, apathy, animal shrewdness. Malle stages the action, but he uses the camera as an investigative instrument. His technique is to let the story seem to tell itself while he searches and observes. His gamble is that the camera will discover what the artist's imagination can't, and, steadily, startlingly, the gamble pays off.

We look at Pierre Blaise's face in a different way from the way we watch a trained actor. We look *into* it rather than react to an actor's performance. The enigma of a Lucien, whether he is a bullyboy of the right or the left, is the enigma of an open face and a dark, closed mind. Professional actors have the wrong kind of face for this sort of unborn consciousness, and they tend to project thoughts and feelings from the blank area. Pierre Blaise doesn't, and we trust our readings of his silent face almost as if we were watching a documentary. We *examine* it in that way, and we're more engaged than at most fictional films. There's nothing about Lucien that one can take for granted. Even those close to him don't feel close; his own mother (Gilberte Rivet, in a fine performance) isn't sure how to talk to him. His incomprehensibility is a mystery we're caught in, and Malle astutely surrounds Lucien and the girl with unfamiliar faces (actors from the theater, with little exposure in films), so that we won't have past associations to distract us. By the end, the case of *Lacombe, Lucien* has been presented to us. We know the evidence on which he will be judged a traitor, and we've also seen how remote that term is from anything he's ever thought about.

When things are going his way, Lucien is nothing more than a big puppy dog, eager for admiration, and his Gestapo mentor, a seedy, thieving French aristocrat, treats him as a pet, but the wrong tone, the wrong words, or a smile that suggests condescension, and he can be violent. The Parisian girl, France Horn, and her family — Jews who are trying to stay out of sight — have no weapons for dealing with him. They're helpless when Lucien moves out of the Gestapo headquarters at the local hotel and into their attic apartment, sharing France's bed. Mr. Horn (Holger Löwenadler), formerly a tailor to fashionable Paris, is so meticulously cultivated that he seems precious; to Americans it may come almost as a shock that he *has* a daughter — we associate his pursed-lips concern for social proprieties with put-down portraits of homosexuals. But Horn's punctiliousness is a serious — tragic — expression of the dignity he believes in. He cares deeply about the smallest nuances of a class society, yet he finds himself paying extortion money to Lucien's buddy, the son of a count who was part of his own clientele, and he is forced to accept Lucien — an uncouth *child* — at his table and in his daughter's bed. And, worse, he knows that his daughter is not unwilling.

Aurore Clément, who plays France Horn, had not acted before; Malle must have selected her for her fair coloring and tall, slim fragility and her ultra-civilized, poignant little face. She lacks an actress's tension, and so at times she seems a passive camera subject, but she gives us the double nature of France's response to Lucien: her amused derision of his ignorant attempts to play the courtier, and the sensual bond that draws them together. We see, even, that underneath France's fastidiousness and her sharp sensitivity there's a practical animal streak. Aurore Clément's beauty is almost prehensile, like the young Nicole Stéphane's in *Les Enfants Terribles,* and maybe it was this extra quality that attracted Malle. Her old-young face is incapable of surprise yet permanently marked by fear, like a doe's. The French heritage, in all its vaunted refinement, has made her hard in a way that connects with Lucien's pre-civilized obtuseness. She doesn't suffer, as her father does, from the humiliation of their position, and it may be Horn's recognition of this that makes him flail about and bicker with her — berating her as a whore and in the next breath begging her pardon. Lucien, we feel, is the last straw for Horn. After the long period of hiding, behaving prudently, and playing by whatever signals the scummy aristocrat sent out, Horn suddenly can't tolerate the pain of polite self-effacement any longer, and he begins to break. He dresses in his showiest boulevardier's finery and takes a promenade; he decides he must talk things out with Lucien "man-to-man," and when Lucien is too busy to talk at home he strolls over to Gestapo headquarters to wait for him.

Throughout the film, this Gestapo hotel-headquarters recalls the hotel gathering places in thirties French films, yet it has an unaccustomed theatricality about it. The collaborators who work there, live there, torture their victims there, and party there, too, have a wide range of motives. Nothing links them but their willingness to serve the Nazi cause, and that willingness is highly variable, since — not much more political than Lucien — they're primarily serving themselves. There's a former policeman who was discharged from his post; now, a high official, he gets shaved in his office while an adoring spinsterish secretary reads him the latest letters of denunciation from informers. The group also includes a onetime bicycle-racing champion (a nod, perhaps, to the bicycle champ in *The Sorrow and the Pity,* who said he "didn't see any Germans in Clermont-Ferrand") and a movie starlet, the aristocrat's girl friend, waiting for him to gather enough loot so they can take off for Spain. They're much like the ordinary characters in a French film classic, but they're running things now. The hotel is almost like a stage, and, wielding power, they're putting on an act for each other — playing the big time. Nazism itself (and Italian Fascism, too) always had a theatrical flourish, and those drawn into Gestapo work may well have felt that their newfound authority gave them style. The Nazi hotel here represents this troupe's idea of government. Lucien, the country bumpkin, going into the maid's room, at her invitation, or peeking through a doorway to see his old schoolmaster, whom he has drunkenly betrayed, being tortured, may recall the quite different figure in *The Blood of a Poet* wandering in the corridors of l'Hôtel des Folies-Dramatiques. Like Cocteau's poet, Lucien has fallen into a dreamworld. And he and the other collaborators have landed on their feet: they have become criminally powerful and can act out their impulses.

There is nothing admirable in Lucien, yet we find we can't hate him. We begin to understand how his callousness works for him in his new job. He didn't intend to blab about the schoolmaster; he was just surprised and pleased that he knew something the Nazis didn't. But he's indifferent when he witnesses the torture, and he shows no more reaction to killing people himself than to shooting a rabbit for dinner or a bird for fun. After the Maquis have raided the hotel, reprisals are ordered, and Lucien is sent, with an S.S. man, to arrest France and her grandmother (Thérèse Giehse). Lucien has no feelings one way or the other about hauling them in — so little sentiment that he reclaims a gold watch he looted earlier and gave to Mr. Horn in a buttering-up gesture. The German takes it away from him, however, and Lucien, piqued, shoots him. It is perfectly apparent that if the German had not pocketed the watch, which Lucien felt was properly his own, Lucien would have stood by as France was taken away. (He wanted his watch back because he didn't see why it should be wasted.) Yet with the S.S. man dead Lucien needs to get away, and he escapes, with France and her grandmother, to the countryside. When we see him in his natural environment, setting traps, killing game, making love to France, and once even lying flat on the ground and laughing like an innocent, confident boy, we know, with absolute conviction, that he has no sense of guilt whatever. His face is as clear as Lieutenant Calley's.

Malle's hero could have been placed almost anywhere at any time, but it is right for a French artist to place him where Malle did. The director Jean-Pierre Melville, who was himself a member of the Resistance, said in an interview that when he came out of the theater after seeing *The Sorrow and the Pity* he saw Roland Petit and Zizi Jeanmaire in the queue waiting for the next performance, and his first reflex was to pretend that he hadn't seen them — he felt as though he'd been caught coming out from a pornographic film. The pornography of *The Sorrow and the Pity* is in the shameful ordinariness of the people who betray their fellows. The movies, with their roots in stage melodrama, have conditioned us to look for evil in social deviants and the physically aberrant. The pornography that Malle delves into makes us think back to the protests of innocence by torturers and mass murderers — all those normal-looking people leading normal lives who said they were just doing their job. Without ever mentioning the subject of innocence and guilt, *Lacombe, Lucien,* in its calm, leisurely, dispassionate way, addresses it on a deeper level than any other movie I know.

LOUIS MALLE has always been an alert and daring director who didn't repeat himself, but in recent years, since he broke with the smooth professionalism and surface sophistication of his early work and made the series of documentaries that form *Phantom India,* he appears to have begun anew. The picture he made after that experience, the high comedy *Murmur of the Heart,* set in 1954, suggested an artist's autobiographical first work, except that it showed a master's command of the medium. Now he has gone back farther, to the period of his childhood (he was born in 1932), to events he couldn't make sense of. *Lacombe, Lucien* is more of a test even than India: Malle could approach India in terms of his own sensibility, but in *Lacombe, Lucien* he is trying to seek out and create a sensibility utterly different from his own.

In all the most important ways, he succeeds, triumphantly. But in a million small ways he falls flat. Malle's earlier films were very precise, the work of an orderly, classical mind; they were films by a Frenchman who believed in reason, and although the Indian series brought out the humanist in him, he remained the *raisonneur.* This time, he's working on a subject that can't be thought out, and he's going on instinct. His greatest involvement is in the looser material, and when he stays with the gambler-improviser's intuitive method, he wins. In this film, Malle is best at what he's never done before — the almost wordless scenes, especially; he gets perhaps even more than he'd hoped for from Pierre Blaise's Lucien. In these scenes, it's not just that one can't separate Lucien's innocence and his corruption but that they really seem to be the same thing. However, Malle can't give a sense of life to all the situations he puts Lucien in. He seems to have lost interest in the scripted scenes, and there's a fatal hint of the obligatory in some of them. In setting up the atmosphere in the hotel, Malle probably knew that it was tricky to try to suggest that these Nazi collaborators, aping authority, are like bad actors. However, we have to extrapolate his subtle intentions, because the situations are often inert. The two scenes involving Lucien's affair with the hotel maid are glaringly unconvincing, and contradictory besides. In the first, before going to bed with him she gives him a little Resistance talk, telling him that the Americans are winning, and warning him against having any more to do with the Nazis; in the second, after he is involved with France Horn, the maid suddenly comes on like a woman scorned, a provincial Mrs. Robinson full of anti-Semitic fury. We can guess that her outburst is meant to indicate how an angry person can blame the Jews for his frustrations, but this sort of worked-out reason (spite, jealousy) is what we're used to — it's specious, without resonance, like the perfunctory reasons that are given for why the various people in the hotel have become collaborators. No doubt Malle means to tell us that their reasons *are* banal, but his handling of the people is so enervated that we just feel we've seen all these types with their quirks before.

Some artists have a natural feeling for the riches of chaos; when they don't pin things down for us to know exactly what's going on, we understand that they're not giving us that kind of meaning — they're giving us more than that. And Malle achieves that with Lucien, but he isn't skilled yet at merging scripted scenes with found material, and at times we feel that something has been left out. (What is France doing with those piled-up stones? Has her grandmother died?) In the scene of a Resistance doctor's arrest, when the doctor's phlegmatic teen-age son shows Lucien his model ship, it looks as if Malle couldn't control the elements, and chose to retain the scene because of the overtones in the boy's physical resemblance to Lucien, and despite the boy's unconvincing lack of interest in his father's fate. Working with nonprofessionals in the leads and adapting the script to Lucien's emerging character, Malle probably had to cut scenes he needed that didn't pan out, but there are ellipses that aren't easy to account for — principally in Horn's sudden, suicidal carelessness. Some stages in Horn's breakdown seem to be missing, and his later scenes are lamely directed. Holger Löwenadler, a distinguished figure in the Swedish theater for over half a century (he appeared in Bergman's 1947 film *A Ship to India,* and in recent years he has toured Europe in Bergman stage productions, playing leads in Ibsen and Strindberg), prepares Horn's character so carefully in his early scenes that it's puzzling when the later ones are truncated. We miss Horn's shift to recklessness, and not enough is made of the moment when he appears all dressed up, his hat tilted rakishly over one eye. Is he deliberately calling attention to himself? There are brilliant ideas, like that "man-to-man" talk Horn wants with Lucien. (How can a Jew talk man-to-man at Gestapo headquarters, and what could Horn and that thug Lucien possibly talk about?) But Horn's breakdown is too fast, and we can't perceive why he is doing what he's doing; this is the wrong place for Malle to stand back and let the story just seem to happen — he has failed to provide the necessary information.

The picture is a knockout, and the flaws don't diminish its stature, so it may appear silly to discuss imperfections — which could be passed over as ambiguities. But it's because the picture is a major work that it seems necessary to distinguish between the great ambiguities of its theme and the piddling, diversionary gaffes and gaps in its execution. There's another reason for bringing up the crudenesses: they are the price that Malle the aesthete is willing to pay for discovery. Here is a director who achieved sleek technical perfection in his early, limited films and who is now saying that perfection is cheap and easy (which seems to be true for him). He's looking for something that he doesn't have the tools or the temperament to grab hold of, and he's catching it anyway.

Malle's renunciation of conventional drama — or his new indifference to it — cripples him in places where he still needs it. He hasn't fully cast off the hard shell of the brilliant young pro who made *The Lovers* and *Viva Maria!* and *Zazie,* but he's lost his slick. He's in the process of turning himself inside out and reaching into the common experience. Malle isn't used to playing by ear; he keeps looking at the notes and seeing they're wrong, revising them and hoping they're better. Yet somehow, with all the wrong notes he hits, and parts of the bass left out, he gets sounds that nobody's ever heard before.

[September 30, 1974]

Stuck in the Fun

IF THERE IS ANY psychological validity to the basic premise of pornography — that out of violation comes adoration — *The Night Porter* certainly fails to make the case, but by placing this tony cliché in a concentration-camp setting the picture seems to be saying something about the spiritual destruction caused by war. Many of us can't take more than a few hard-core-porno movies, because the absence of any sense of human esteem makes them depressing rather than sexy; *The Night Porter* offers the same de-humanized view and is brazen enough to use the Second World War as an excuse. The picture gives no sign of interest in what actually happened in the Nazi death camps. More likely, it came out of idle speculation: "Gee, I bet there were people sexually enslaved by the Nazis." (You could do a new version of *Drums Along the Mohawk* and turn it into a movie about a girl captured by the Senecas who becomes a cruel, lascivious brave's handmaiden and loves it.) Probably most artists are terrified of confronting the death-camp experience: who feels ready to deal with it? But this picture blunders through without any apparent awareness that it's an insult to the people caught in that holocaust to use them for a creepy, eerie, horror-film ambience. In *The Night Porter,* the emaciated victims of the Nazis are merely variants of zombies — they're used as glassy-eyed witnesses to sodomy and as mute participants in assorted sexual high jinks. They are horror décor, and the death-camp scenes, tinted latrine green, provide the ghoulish backgrounds for a sado-masochistic love story. The film's porno-profundity is humanly and aesthetically offensive. The offense is mitigated by incompetence, however: the picture is simply too crudely trumped up to be a serious insult. *The Night Porter* was directed by a woman, Liliana Cavani — which proves no more than that women can make junk just like men.

This spinoff of *The Damned* doesn't get you hot; the sex is full of self-disgust, and it makes you cold. *The Night Porter* is a porno gothic — it could have been called "Tales from the Nazi Crypt." The film is set in Vienna in 1957. As Max, a former Storm Trooper who now works as a night porter at the Hotel Zur Oper, Dirk Bogarde presides over an s-m Grand Hotel. His role is an extension of all the weak, tormented, vice-ridden roles he's played before. Max goes from room to room ministering to the needs of a clientele of decadents — a hypo in the butt for a homosexual ballet dancer, some surly sex for an aging countess. At the beginning, I thought that this hotel was a place where former prisoners who couldn't escape the sexual patterns of their past hung out, and when there was a flashback to the dancer performing seminude for the Nazis (it's the most effective sequence in the film), I assumed — wrongly — that he was a prisoner at the time. It turns out that Charlotte Rampling, who checks in with her husband (he is to conduct *The Magic Flute* at the Vienna Opera House), is the only former victim. The others were all Nazis, and the place is a hangout for a conspiratorial Nazi encounter group. No, I didn't make that up; Cavani and her co-writers did. The group conducts mock war-crime trials of its members, for therapeutic purposes and also to turn up evidence of camp survivors who might give damaging testimony against them. The survivors are then tracked down and murdered. To judge by the acting, which is wrecked by dubbing, these fanatic Nazis might just as well be businessmen who have lost their Dairy Queen franchise, but the goofy political plot is, in any case, merely a device to set the porno plot in motion.

The film shifts back and forth between the hotel in 1957 and Bogarde's pranks in his Storm Trooper days, when he took pictures of concentration-camp inmates and used them as targets for firing practice, and when, falling in love with the fourteen-year-old Rampling, the imprisoned daughter of a Socialist, he trained her to perform fellatio and brought her such presents as the severed head of a guard who had tormented her. In the 1957 scenes, she wants more of Max's brand of love. But since she's a potential witness against him, his Nazi group wants to kill her, and so the lovers hide out in his apartment, there to reënact their wartime relationship. Like *The Damned, The Night Porter* never deals with its underlying homosexual feeling, and this avoidance probably has a lot to do with the horror-film, ugly-sex atmosphere.

The level of character development is a joke: we can tell that Max is meant to have a conscience because he hides his face in his pillow the night he's killed an old friend. Max's hauteur and his freezing, petty contempt for everyone but "my little girl" just seem like a hangover from Bogarde's past. After such pictures as *Victim, The Servant, Darling, Modesty Blaise, Accident, The Damned, Justine,* and *Death in Venice,* he isn't just overqualified for Max — he's also overexposed. We know his neurasthenic tricks — the semaphore eyebrow, the twitching mouth, the sneaky vindictive gleam, the pinch of suffering. His warmed-over performance here has all the surprise of the César Franck Symphony in D Minor.

The Night Porter is said to be a runaway hit in Italy and France and to have made a big star of Charlotte Rampling, but surely one twinkle doesn't make a star. At our first view of her sullen beauty, the sensual vibrations of her come-hither nastiness promise undreamt-of intensities, but absolutely nothing emerges. As an actress, she has no hidden resources; there's no soul beneath that perverse Mona Lisa face. Maybe that's why she was so effective in *Georgy Girl,* sawing away on her cello, and doing her nails while her baby lay on the bed squalling. Yes, she's reminiscent of Garbo and Moreau, but their sensuality is the sum total of their expressiveness; Rampling is wildly suggestive in a single shot and lifeless in a full performance. Bacall didn't have much more than a look, but her look was a tease, a put-on; Rampling's is an emblem of contamination, and though — both tense and languid — she looks as if she'd be a perfect sex symbol for a dragged-out world, her necrophiliac allure could probably be sustained only if she were confined to fleeting bit parts. She looks all-knowing and weary — exhausted from the weight of her own dirty thoughts — yet she becomes prosaic as soon as she starts to smash things exultantly or drag her chains around or perform sex acts. Nothing lives up to the foul promise.

After all of Bogarde's and Rampling's ominous smiles of complicity, the actual perversions seem awfully tacky. By the time she looks lewdly at a jar of jam and ravenously sticks her fingers in it, and he knocks it out of her hand and then gives her a sweet little love nick with a splinter of jammy glass, the movie has become a Child's Garden of Perversities. I don't mean to suggest that I was looking forward to superexotic forms of bondage, but if the soul-destroying concentration-camp experience is invoked to explain Rampling's behavior, shouldn't she be doing something more than crawling under a table to play pussycat? When the lovers are caged and deteriorating, they're obviously just stuck in the fun. You keep waiting for them to get into their full drag — he in his Storm Trooper uniform and she in her little-girl dress — and finally they really do it. It's crap inevitability.

Since everybody in Vienna seems to be in on the Nazi group's conspiracy, it isn't clear why the lovers are safe in Bogarde's apartment — why the group members don't just come in and kill them. However, those who can accept *The Night Porter* as art probably won't care about this or other oddities. A flashback to the concentration-camp days shows Rampling as a top-hatted, topless singer performing a Lotte Lenya-Dietrich number for the Nazis, who sit around like department-store mannequins. This exhibitionistic number has no follow-up in her character. Presumably, the moviemaker wanted some flash at this point: Rampling's getup for her number is featured in the ads, just as Helmut Berger's transvestite Dietrich getup was featured in the campaign for *The Damned.* Similarly, the theme music — insistently poignant and with an almost Hungarian sweep — tries to create the surge of Gato Barbieri's music for *Last Tango in Paris.* There are scenes that sock in cheap political points with a sledgehammer, such as a meeting of the group at which Bogarde's ironic "*Sieg Heil*" is answered by a solemn round of "*Sieg Heil*"s. But Cavani's slow pacing makes one nervous, anticipating something ugly, and that probably helps to account for the film's success. *The Night Porter* is a doomsday vision of sex. The picture says that human sexuality is loathsome and that every once in a while the beast makes itself heard; its central (though possibly unconscious) mechanism is to use war guilt to account for sex guilt. *The Night Porter* certainly won't do much for the equilibrium of those in group analysis; as a friend of mine put it, "I always knew in those groups that if you ever told them anything you'd get killed."

❖

"THE ABDICATION" TAKES this year's Yevgeny Yevtushenko prize for loftiness. The picture, which is about Queen Christina's stepping down from the Swedish throne in 1654, is embalmed in such reverence for its own cultural elevation that it loses all contact with the audience. During the initial pomposity, we're sustained by the hope that Christina (Liv Ullmann), who makes off for the Vatican and then faces an examination of her motives by a cardinal (Peter Finch), is going to confess to a wildly licentious past and we'll get to see choice bits in flashback. When it turns out she has never "given herself" to a man, we sit in a stupor. Damned if the picture isn't about her high-flown spiritual crisis. Of course, we can see that she's going to get around to propositioning Cardinal Finch, but that's a dry run for sure, since cardinals don't make out in major-studio productions. The movie explains Christina's abdication by what "literate" plays used to call "a queen's dilemma": since she was born to rule, she felt she must not be possessed by a man. And so the desperately frustrated woman — the most important Protestant monarch in Europe, according to the film — becomes a Catholic, looking for sexual release and hoping to find ecstasy in God. I haven't run into such a hokey dilemma since the heroine of *Winterset* asked, "Is it better to tell a lie and live?" Couldn't someone have taken Christina aside and explained that with a little solid experience she would discover that a woman could have lovers without feeling herself any more "possessed" than they did? Surely her advisers could have pointed out many a royal precedent?

Anthony Harvey seems to have directed the picture on his knees. We're never allowed to forget the exalted rank of the characters we're privileged to listen to, and nothing like human speech intrudes upon the relentless dignity of Ruth Wolff's screenplay. Harvey takes pictorial cinematography to be drama, and leaves it to Nino Rota's pseudo-liturgical score to provide the emotional turbulence. There's considerable turbulence but only a few themes — they return as punctually as they did for Max Steiner. Whose idea was it to reunite the lovers of *Lost Horizon*? Peter Finch and Liv Ullmann bring out nothing in each other, and Finch's tempted priest is such a hopeless role that I passed the time imagining Peter Sellers in the part. The trouble with *The Abdication* is not that it's about historical characters but that it's not about historical characters. It's obsequious — for no discernible reason. (Christina was only twenty-seven when she abdicated, and she lived on for thirty-five years. I'd like to know what she did with her life. If she abdicated for the innocent reasons given in this movie, did she discover what a ninny she'd been? There might be a comedy there somewhere.) Anthony Harvey must really have a thing about royalty; Christina may give up her throne, but the whole picture is a throne for Liv Ullmann.

She doesn't belong on it. Garbo bombed out in the role in 1933, but most people don't remember what a stiff the Rouben Mamoulian *Queen Christina* was or how blankly Garbo walked through it; all that stays in the mind is her famous grape-eating scene, and that last glorious closeup, the more glorious for ending the boredom. Liv Ullmann gives a highly competent, emotionally varied performance — a far better performance, I think, than she gave in, say, *Cries and Whispers.* But grand-gesture roles don't suit her; she has no mystery to fill them out and no high style to give them a little camp. She's best in pictures like Bergman's *Shame* and Jan Troell's *The Emigrants* and *The New Land.* She's essentially a too realistic, too practical woman to recite pseudo epigrams, and, though her English is much improved, ironies don't sit naturally on her tongue. You feel that she's play-acting here, working hard at being a great lady, and that's not what we want from her anyway. It's Liv Ullmann's non-actressy quality — her radiant naturalness, her transparency — that's so involving. Her poetry is not in extravagance; she can no more be a haughty, witty queen than Glenda Jackson can play realistic, simple, ordinary women. *The Abdication* probably won't stay around long enough to do Ullmann much damage, but overexposure in other films may already have hurt her — that anxious-eyed look of perplexity is getting to be painfully, sexlessly respectable. Sometimes, even when she performs with great skill, something drab and essentially humorless in her personality begins to defeat the performance. If only she weren't so eager to please. She's too honest an actress; she wants to give fair measure, and every detail of a role is dutifully wrought and properly weighted. She's like a *Hausfrau* who's too conscientious to give good parties.

"JUGGERNAUT" IS FAST, crackerjack entertainment, with the cool, bitchy wit and the outrageously handsome action sequences of some of the best of the Bond pictures. It's surprisingly crisp fun, considering that it was directed by that most misanthropic of talented directors, Richard Lester. Though he eliminates practically every trace of human warmth, he manages to supply the characters with enough blackhearted existential bravado to keep the film sociable. Anybody who makes a picture like this one has to be a bit of a bastard, but Lester demonstrates what a sophisticated director with flair can do on a routine big-action project. Juggernaut is the name assumed by a bomb wizard who has planted seven whoppers on the luxury liner Britannic, carrying twelve hundred passengers on a transatlantic crossing.

Lester lets you know right from the start that if the genre is basically the same as that of *The Poseidon Adventure* the tone certainly won't be. Even before the ship (it's the Maxim Gorky doubling as the Britannic, and the ship's band looks suspiciously Slavic) leaves port, one sees Lesterisms. People who are handed rolls of festive paper streamers to throw drop them limply in disdain. The characters have none of the inviting smiles typical of the genre. Anthony Hopkins, a melancholy-faced police detective, says goodbye to his two children and his wife, dour Caroline Mortimer, who are sailing; she stays in an unexplained funk for the entire trip, from time to time staring abstractedly at her children. Clifton James, the mayor of an American city, has an aging wife, who, when it appears that they'll die, wants assurances that he has always been faithful; Lester undercuts the corn by having the wife, Doris Nolan, done up in a blond wig, like Bette Davis in her hag horror roles. Juggernaut himself, Freddie Jones, might be Anthony Burgess on a reasonably straightforward day. A ship's steward dies while saving a child's life, and absolutely nothing is made of it; it's typical of Lester that he refuses to make the child endearing and refuses to give the rescue an emotional glow. Considering how this child-in-danger situation is generally milked, Lester's cold-bloodedness is nifty. He doesn't go in for scenes of panic or screaming hysteria; instead, he has the ship's social director (Roy Kinnear) constantly rebuffed in his attempts to cheer people up. Where the usual disaster film gives us pathos, Lester gives us slapstick. The movie is a commentary on other directors' groveling for audience response.

Those not used to Richard Lester's neo-Noël Coward mixture of cynicism, angst, and anti-establishment sentimentality (is there anybody more British than an American convert?) may at first be thrown. He's a compulsive gagster, but the jokes are throwaway-fast and tinged with contempt. He uses famous actors, but he uses them like bit players — like props, almost. Omar Sharif, as the ship's captain, can't play in the same quick tempo as the rest of the cast (when he speaks, his words just don't seem to have originated in that head), but he isn't used as Omar Sharif, either. (Lester pulled the same stunt with Charlton Heston in *The Three Musketeers,* scaling him down from his heroic heights.) No doubt Sharif is on board to give the film his romantic box-office attributes, but he's not allowed to smile the famous smile, or even to look soulfully lovesick. He's kept rather grim, as if he were really an actor playing a role. For a sex interest (it isn't love), Sharif is given Shirley Knight as a sharp-witted international playgirl. Shirley Knight, who worked at top form with Lester in *Petulia* (her cookie scene with George C. Scott was the best part of that picture), hits it again here whenever she has tart, brainy lines, though she's burdened with some overly classy remarks about life and death.

The actors who get by with the worst of the lines — and still triumph — are Richard Harris, as the commander of the bomb-dismantling team, and David Hemmings, as his second-in-command. Harris, who delivers a long, drunken oration, might almost be playing Lester's glamorous alter ego; the team commander takes pride in being the best in his profession, though he says he doesn't believe in anything. It's the flossiest bit of rebel-hero nonsense since Humphrey Bogart. Lester likes to turn heroism into a joke, but in *Juggernaut* the derring-do isn't cancelled out, as it was in *The Three Musketeers* — quite the reverse. The cynical, dangling gags that counterpoint the gallantry make it more gallant. The picture has a structural flaw: it reaches its visual climax early, with the arrival of the dismantling team, who parachute down into giant storm waves and then fight their way up rope ladders to board the ship. The subsequent action sequences can't compete with the violent beauty of that arrival, and the actual dismantling of the bombs is too much like the prolonged safecracking scenes of heist pictures, though Lester and his cinematographer, Gerry Fisher, work microscopically close and achieve some almost abstract aesthetic effects. We don't get to see the damage caused by the bombs that explode, but the jaunty superciliousness is more entertaining than the bombs anyway. Lester has discovered a commercial use for his poisonous, flip wit: it provides just what Noël Coward's archness did — a smart, dissonant style to cover the traditional pieties.

[October 7, 1974]

The Actor and the Star

ONCE, as I recall, a TV host showed footage from a film he was involved in and asked Mel Brooks for an opinion, and Brooks said solemnly, "Well, it's the sort of thing that has to be tried over and over again — until it's abandoned." That's how I feel about *The Gambler.* There's dedication in it, and a lot of skill. Karel Reisz directed the picture with a smooth proficiency that doesn't come easy; James Caan's central performance gives it backbone, it's strikingly well edited, and it's dramatically supercharged and compelling. For what it is, it is extremely well done. It's what it is that won't do. The screenplay — an original by James Toback — is a young writer's egocentric conception of what a film should be. There are a lot of characters, but there is really only one, and he is the author's surrogate, the brilliant young Jewish prince, professor of literature to ghetto blacks, potential great novelist, and gambler. The conflicts are in his psyche, and they're spelled out for us in his discussions of will and Dostoevski with his students at City University. The gambler, Axel Freed, is as flamboyantly superior as Norman Mailer's Rojack. Toback (it's his real name) shares Norman Mailer's identification with Dostoevski, and he identifies with Mailer, too. The prevailing tone of *The Gambler* is Mailerian dread, abetted by Jerry Fielding's elegantly oppressive score, which is based on the Symphony No. 1 by Mahler. The script must have looked stunning on paper, because everything is prepared for, structured, explained. The whole movie is explicit: Axel's guilt, his relationship with his intelligent, what-did-I-do-wrong doctor-mother (Jacqueline Brookes), his relationship with his rich merchant-king grandfather (Morris Carnovsky) and with his worshipful girl (Lauren Hutton). The author appears to think that he knows what everything up on the screen means, and that it's his task to tell us.

Axel is as conscious as Toback, and so he explains his compulsion to test himself to the limit and explains the secret of gambling — that gamblers gamble to lose. Superficially, it's devastatingly logical, and it's tied in a neat, airless package — and I don't believe a word of it.

It's like listening to a bad novel: every action has its inflated commentary. A thug (Burt Young) terrorizes a welsher, breaking his arm, and Axel takes the thug's pulse in order to explain to us that it hasn't gone up so much as a notch. Living under threats of violence himself, Axel goes to his grandfather's eightieth-birthday celebration and makes a dazzling speech about the old king; the party becomes Axel's triumph. Toback may think that this movie is about Jewish guilt, but it looks more like Jewish showing off (which he *ought* to feel guilty about). Jean Renoir has often said that when a movie spells everything out, the public "has nothing to add" and there's no "collaboration." The big difference between *The Gambler* and Robert Altman's *California Split* is not just that Altman's allusiveness is vastly entertaining, while *The Gambler* seeks to impress us, but that *California Split* invites us into the world of its characters, while *The Gambler* hands us the wrapped package and closes us out. There is one scene in *California Split* which bothered me — the restaurant meeting between George Segal and his bookie (Joseph Walsh). The scene is very well acted, but it isn't organic, in the way the rest of the movie is; it's literary in structure, and it has a different kind of intensity. *California Split* takes us right into the middle of the action, but that scene belongs to the world of first acts and third acts, with their phony explanations. That scene suggests what all of *The Gambler* is like. This picture is complete without us, and there's nothing for us to do except receive it, feel wiped out, and genuflect. In *Bay of the Angels,* as in *California Split,* we shared in the highs and lows of gambling; for those of us who aren't gamblers it was a heady sensation, like entering a foreign culture. At *The Gambler,* we're trapped at a maniacal lecture on gambling as existential expression.

And, as almost always happens when a movie is predictable and everything is analyzed and labeled, the actions and the explanations aren't convincing. Gambling is too easy a metaphor for life; as metaphor, it belongs to the world of hardboiled fiction. I don't believe, for example, that the secret of gambling is that gamblers are self-destructive people who want to lose. I think gambling is a hell of a lot simpler for most people: they're looking to win. The poor bastard who buys a two-dollar ticket he can't afford is hoping to change his life with the two dollars. How else can he change it? There's no one reason people gamble. Some do it because they enjoy it, and the losses are part of the game; some win fairly consistently, while others win and walk away with their winnings. Probably some are asking whether God loves them, and if they win they feel chosen, while others are driven to lose. This picture's "secret of gambling" is part of its rigid, schematic point of view. Toback is generalizing from his exceptional-man conceit: Axel is such a superman he could win too easily, so his failures are regarded as willful. *The Gambler* is like *Crime and Punishment* written by Raskolnikov at the time he went in to kill the old pawnbroker. He had everything worked out, too.

James Caan sustains the grandiloquent terms set for the two-fisted, Renaissance-man hero — his pride, his prowess, his compulsiveness — and Caan's oversized head and top-heavy frame seem especially right for Axel. The actor has to stay clenched, the bit in his teeth: an uncalculated move and the picture's tension would collapse. It's an impregnable performance; even in the near-ludicrous Harlem scenes at the end, Caan commands the screen by his hammer-and-tongs concentration. (Elliott Gould, in *California Split,* takes it by his relaxation — by playing in his own key, with Altman harmonizing.) Caan is asked to bring off some feverish overreaching. Having lost heavily all night, Axel offers to bet a kid his last twenty dollars on a basketball shot; when the kid says he has only a dime, Axel puts up his twenty anyway, and loses. That's a Toback Mailerism — the gallantry plump with significance. When, in Las Vegas, Axel tells us that he is invulnerable, that he's blessed and can will his victory, the scene has the Mailer self-inflation without the pressure of feeling. Mailer thought out is Mailer diminished, cancelled. Toback is trying for Mailer's craziness, and it conflicts with his own — his perfectly structured, madly irrelevant interpretation of what's going on in this movie. The picture is an expansion of the theme enunciated by the blissfully satisfied German maid in *An American Dream* ("You are absolutely a genius, Mr. Rojack"), but while Mailer instinctively treats it in pop-fantasy terms, Toback is flexed for art: the picture is an art psychosis.

And Caan is stuck with being smarter than everybody else, more ironic, wittier, sexier, handsomer. It must have been a test of stamina to hold on to the character, but Caan gives his most powerful performance — I kept wishing it were in another picture. Caan is a marvelous actor but not quite a star. He's got everything for stardom, but he hasn't yet found — if he ever will — the role that will bring him out. He imparts no extra element of personality to Axel; nothing spills over the edges of his performance — not even as much as Gene Hackman's crinkle smile. Caan and Hackman are very much alike as actors: both can give everything they've got to a role without fusing their own personalities with it. In a way, their acting may be too pure for what — in the past, at least — we've thought of as movie stardom. No one can accuse them of being always the same.

WHEN RAQUEL WELCH WAS KNOCKED DOWN in the mud at the end of *The Three Musketeers,* the director knew perfectly well that a lot of people in the audience would enjoy seeing her get it, and that that enjoyment had nothing to do with the story. When the director of *Chinatown,* Roman Polanski, cast himself in the role of the "midget" hood who takes his knife and slits open the detective's nose, he must have known that many of us would recognize him and that the association with the Los Angeles knifing of his wife would provide an extra dimension of perversity. In the same film, John Huston was used for his rotting charm and the associations he carries with him. Like Orson Welles, Huston drags his legend right into a role, and that is why directors want him. Sterling Hayden carries his own outsize ambience, just as surely as Helen Hayes carries her elfin respectability. Screen actors could never shed their screen pasts, and now, with television exposure added to newspaper and magazine exposure, they can't shed their offscreen lives, either. Frank Sinatra might have been a great screen actor if he'd given the same perfectionist care to acting that he gave to singing, but he knew he didn't need to: he was a movie star because he was Frank Sinatra, and he probably held movies cheap because of that. Jim Brown became a movie star without developing the respect for acting which he'd had for the sport that made him a star, and Dean Martin never stepped out of his own character, relying on his easy presence and his old pro's intuitive timing to sustain him.

But Burt Reynolds, the only actor to have reached stardom via the talk shows, is also the first movie star to make a *style* out of his awareness of the audience's response to him as an off-screen celebrity. Not very long ago, Don Rickles, in his night-club dates, was considered the comics' comic, because he displayed his hostility to the audience; however, television makes "in" attitudes accessible to a wide audience, and now hostility is bursting out all over. Burt Reynolds has become popular by letting the public see his insider's jokey contempt for the whole entertainment business. He had been acting in the theater and on television since the late fifties and had appeared in a dozen movies without creating much of a stir, and when, in 1971, he began to appear on talk shows, other guests laughed nervously at hearing behind-the-scenes smart talk in public. But the TV audience enjoyed the dropping of barriers, and Reynolds was on his way. He showed an amazingly fast, spangly put-down wit, but he also showed something else, which the TV public was probably ready for: he made a joke of his profession. He came on as a man who had no higher values than the buck and the pleasures of the flesh — exactly what many people in the audience had always really believed stardom was about. His message was that stars were just bums, and that he himself was an honest, funny bum — too smart and gamy to give much of a damn about anything except having a good time, and too cocky to lie about it. His message was that he was having a ball being a stud celebrity. The belief is now widespread that the price of success is the loss of privacy, and that the successful person who fights this isn't playing fair. And there's a concurrent belief, almost as widely held, probably, that those rich, lucky people who have become stars — whether of sports, politics, entertainment, or anything else — are out for themselves. Reynolds not only accepted those terms but carried them further. His fun-loving "frankness" seemed the show-business truth, and when he was around, any earnestness looked a solemn fraud. His charm is that of a cheap crook who ingratiates himself by saying, "Look, we're all cheap crooks — why lie about it?"

Reynolds' lines in *The Longest Yard* sound just like his banter on a talk show, because the role of Paul Crewe has been shaped to fit his talk-show personality. The picture is built around that personality: he plays a sellout quarterback turned superstud gigolo, and the story is about how this self-loving, self-hating smarty is redeemed. Crewe rediscovers his manhood through helping a bunch of chain-gang convicts fight for theirs. Reynolds is unmistakably a star, yet what sets him apart from other stars — what's most distinctive about him — is his tinniness, his air of the synthetic. Burt Reynolds must be the only man who can kiss off a fifteen-thousand-dollar Citroën SM more effectively than he can say goodbye to a girl friend. In *The Longest Yard,* his stealing and destroying the car, and then resisting arrest, land him in prison, where the warden (Eddie Albert) coerces him into developing a convicts' team, in order to give the guards' team an easy win that will bolster their confidence. (It's possibly just a bonus for this prison picture that the authoritarian villain Eddie Albert looks so much like Nelson Rockefeller.) Reynolds has become a whiz at his offscreen-onscreen comedy style; he gets the laughs he wants, and he carries the picture by his genial sureness of touch. But there's almost nothing to say about his acting, since it's inseparable from the Reynolds image. His entire style is built around a shrug. His look says "Don't take me — or anything else — too seriously." He's perfect in this brutal comic fantasy about a football game between crazily ruthless convicts and crazily ruthless guards; for all its bone-crunching collisions, the picture is almost irresistibly good-natured and funny.

The Longest Yard is an undisguised attempt by the director, Robert Aldrich, to recoup his fortunes, after a series of box-office failures, by returning to the mode of his smash hit *The Dirty Dozen,* but on a simpler, more buffoonish level. The brutality here is right out of Looney Tunes;

one could say the same of *Death Wish,* except that *Death Wish* makes crude pretensions to realism, while this is almost all unpretentious. It's certainly crudely made, however, with Eddie Albert overplaying by even the broadest standards, and Aldrich cutting to him for reaction shots that have all the visual interest of stones hitting one on the head. The picture's attempts at anti-establishment cuteness are also tossed in like rocks: the tyrant Albert wears a little American flag in his lapel; above the desk of the calmly vicious captain of the guards (Ed Lauter, a good actor, overdue for less sinister parts) one sees John Mitchell's favorite quote from Vince Lombardi ("When the going gets tough . . ."); Reynolds and another convict (Michael Conrad) talk together on the football field while the National Anthem is being played. Even a little joke on *The Defiant Ones* is heavy-handed; Aldrich does better, though, when he kids *The Dirty Dozen* itself, or stages a Laurel and Hardy routine in the prison swamp. The picture's chief comic resources, besides Reynolds, are the assembled giants and plug-uglies. Aldrich uses them primitively, blatantly: they don't merely take part in gags — they themselves, physically, are the gags. He's somewhat less affectionate toward the two women in the cast: the rich bitch that Reynolds dumps on the floor as if to break every bone in her body, and the freak — the warden's secretary (Bernadette Peters), a pale-faced Martian Bride of Frankenstein. With a tall blond beehive that looks like a castle on a hill, the secretary is a weird comic-strip creation, like most of the men. Maybe Burt Reynolds is a comic-strip movie star — the compleat celebrity — and that's why he makes the whole picture work. It's designed for his special, twinkling unauthenticity, and the audience can enjoy his light, fanciful act — which makes a neat contrast with the other actors. His form-fitting chain-gang white togs are a comedy in themselves, and they're topped off by the ostentatious styling of his rug. As soon as he gets out of the mock-*Cool Hand Luke* swamp, the prison begins to resemble a country club, and he sports the emblematic cigarillo of the talk shows. The audience can take it for granted that a woman is hot for him at first sight, because he's a cartoon of a superstud movie star — and *The Longest Yard* is also a cartoon.

The audience roots for the underdog convicts without taking the football game any more seriously than the audiences took the games in pictures like *Pigskin Parade. The Longest Yard* is a brutal bash, but the laughter at the brutality has no meanness in it: everybody knows that the blood isn't real. Though the picture is saying that the wrong people are in jail — that the lawmen are worse than the convicts — it knows its own level (that's what saves it), so even this message is cartooned. Since there are no people in the movie — only comic stereotypes — the mayhem has physical impact but no emotional impact. The public has been losing interest in football; this picture supplies a reason for winning — revenge for injustices — but when Burt Reynolds echoes Ronald Reagan's Gipper speech from *Knute Rockne — All American,* telling the team to win for their fellow-convicts who have been abused or murdered, the speech is half grabber, half burlesque. Aldrich takes macho for a ride even on the sound track, with playfully amplified comic-strip noises for the grinding and cracking of bones.

Burt Reynolds, however, is a good actor who has got himself in a new kind of bind. The personality that he found for himself on the talk shows may have seemed like a liberation, but he plays down to the audience. He plays down the way Johnny Carson does. There doesn't seem to be anything underneath Reynolds' media cheek, and he doesn't ask the audience to respect him. He says, You can envy me, but there's nothing about me to respect. When he goes too shamelessly far with this act, as he did on the Academy Award show, it's horrible — demeaning to him and to everyone else. But even when it works, as it does in *The Longest Yard,* there's a demeaning element in it. Reynolds has an unusual self-dramatizing quality, and he holds the screen like a demon joker. But nothing about him seems his own except that jokiness. At times here, he uses a pained smile, like Walter Matthau. At other times, when he seems to imitate Brando — wearing a droopy Zapata mustache in the early scenes and then, when he's clean-shaven, smiling like a plastic Terry Malloy — is he doing it deliberately or is he a parody of Brando in spite of himself? The trouble with Burt Reynolds is that he sees bravery in exhibiting himself as a sellout swinger; he asks movie audiences and TV audiences alike to admire him for his weakness and love of fame. He is taken on his own terms, so the ads for *The Longest Yard* feature his padded crotch. But there's still a good actor struggling to come out of that media clown. And how is he going to if Reynolds is afraid he can't be a star as anything more?

[October 14, 1974]

The Uprooted Artist

THE CZECH DIRECTORS who have come to this country since 1968 haven't had the internationally useful equipment of such earlier immigrants as Fritz Lang, Max Ophuls, and Robert Siodmak. Hitler's refugees suffered from the transplanting, but they had techniques they could apply to Hollywood genre films, as the Polish expatriate Roman Polanski has, also. But the Czech film movement of the sixties was not based on technique or on innovative style. The films weren't smashingly visual or marked by tour-de-force suspense; they were distinctive precisely because their simple naturalism stood apart from international commercial moviemaking. Their appeal was in their close connection with their subjects — the lives of ordinary people. To Americans, accustomed to more charge and excitement, they seemed very "small" pictures: they were folkloric "human-interest" stories — mild, understated, sad-funny. The movement represented something new — a national cinema that was developing not in terms of the corruptions of an international market, or in terms of the corruptions of a domestic market (as in India), but through the expressive needs of the developing artists. It is the only time in the history of movies that the control of production was in the hands of intellectuals and artists, and the Czechs, who had fought hard for that control, had been showing the whole world what freedom could mean to filmmakers, when the Russian tanks rolled in in August, 1968. The artists who stayed behind have produced almost nothing; the ones who came here — the only country where they stood a chance of making films — are caught in the same circus as American film artists, only worse. The special flavor of the Czech films came from the artists' affectionate, deep-rooted understanding of the people: how does one transplant an art based on unconscious affinities?

While recognizing their qualities, I generally ducked writing about the Czech films, because I wasn't especially drawn to them; their barnyard humor and their air of goodness reminded me of the dialect stories in school readers which used to make me groan. Maybe Hollywood had spoiled me: I wanted a little more corruption. But when I saw Ivan

Passer's new film, *Law and Disorder,* starring Carroll O'Connor and Ernest Borgnine, the disparity between what the picture might have been if it had been made in Czechoslovakia and what it had become here was painful. As the work of an artist — Passer is the most original and gifted of the Czechs whose films I've seen — *Law and Disorder* is a tragedy. It's calamitous evidence of the messed-up lives of uprooted artists, and, in a peculiar way, almost a textbook on what the heartrendingly short Czech renaissance was about. While you're watching it, you can tell how the scenes are meant to play and why they don't; you can see Passer trying to strike a compromise between his feelings and the demands of the American marketing system, and satisfying neither.

Passer's work in his Czech film *Intimate Lighting* depended on unforced comic incidents, and on character vignettes in which we could perceive the embarrassments of people who were unsure of themselves. The special, gentle believability of his comedy came from the resonances of the most ordinary situations: from small incongruities, haphazard jokes, flareups of irritation; from lost opportunities that couldn't be forgotten. In the New York setting of *Law and Disorder,* the comedy is mostly still unforced, but it's also unrealized. In his first American film, *Born to Win,* in 1971, Passer made a startling adaptation to a special, surreal American environment — that of the junkie — and he had the advantages of some sharp writing and a strung-out, high performance by George Segal, which I think is probably still his best. But in *Law and Disorder* Passer has tried to work within his own area; he's aimed at the American equivalent of a humanistic Czech film — a look at the interwoven lives of ordinary people. In other words, he's working right in the area that he doesn't have the unconscious equipment for, and almost everything looks, sounds, feels subtly but jarringly wrong. One doesn't have to be an artist to grasp what he's up against: even those of us Americans who move from one part of the country to another learn what a difference it makes. I will never know New York the way I know San Francisco; at some bottom level, I don't even want to — I don't have room in my feelings for more than one home. But from the evidence of this picture Passer could, I think, adapt to working here, and could bring to American subjects something close to the sensibility he brought to Czech subjects, if the working conditions were anything like the ones he used to have. The wrongness that tears one up in *Law and Disorder* is a compound of his not quite having the feel for his characters and something much more damaging. He didn't follow his instincts. Maybe he didn't trust them, since he was trying to deliver a commercial comedy. In *Law and Disorder,* he attempts to do the sort of thing that gets louder laughs than his own kind of comedy, and he doesn't really know how; it's against his grain.

It is the case of an artist trying to do what clods can do better. The picture is about the frustrations and foulups of a group of white men living in a New York co-op building in a racially mixed, high-crime area who try to protect their families by organizing an auxiliary-police unit. Passer is crippled from the start by a cinematographer (Arthur Ornitz) who doesn't give him a single sensitive frame, and an actor, Ernest Borgnine, who doesn't blend in. A series of gags involving Borgnine's failing beauty-parlor business and his wacked-out beautician (Karen Black) could earn only canned laughter. In the central role of Willie, however, Carroll O'Connor develops the elusive undertones that are the essence of Passer's art. Willie is a cabdriver, but there's no belligerent Archie Bunker in the performance; O'Connor fills in the quiet character of a patient man who doesn't like what has happened to his life and can't find a way to change it. Willie's scenes with his closest friend (Borgnine) are hollow, because Borgnine can't be anybody's friend; he isn't a character at all — he's Borgnine. But Willie has a good scene with his wife, a cocktail waitress (Ann Wedgeworth). He hates hacking and he has found a greasy-spoon luncheonette he wants to buy, but when he shows it to her we can see, by her embarrassed face, that the venture smells of failure, and that she loves her more glamorous job and can't bear to think of working behind the counter in a grubby dump. Willie's hunched, unhostile shoulders tell the story of a man with crackbrained projects but genuine defeats. Most of the scenes, though, are short and don't go anywhere, and the people have empty, blubbery faces that tell us nothing about their lives. There's a quite funny sequence in which Alan Arbus, as a gooney-bird psychologist — an Albert Ellis type, with a tight whine — gives a lecture, under the auspices of the auxiliary unit, on how to prevent rape. In a scene that follows, however, Borgnine's wife (Anita Dangler) uses the psychologist's lecture in reverse to incite her husband to ravish her — an episode that's really wrongheaded here. It doesn't work without the base of innocence that the Czech films had. The wife's ruse might be thought hilarious in a folk comedy, where the people seem anonymous, but there's no ironic reversal when it's Ernest Borgnine leaping upon her — that's what's expected of Borgnine.

Passer's deficient knowledge of American life — his Europeanizing of his New Yorkers — could work as a slightly askew vision, if only it were more consistent in texture. What makes this botched film so plaguing is that it comes off worse than most of the pictures that are just trying to be acceptably commercial. Passer doesn't know how to be gross in the American way, and the American way won't allow him not to be gross. If he were really making a sensitive movie about the effect of urban chaos on family life, he could manage with this loose structure, but since the lumpish families in *Law and Disorder* don't even suggest actual families, the farce scenes would hold together better if there were a simple, dumb plot. And jokes this crude really need to be forced; you can't be a graceful schlockmeister. You can't make mud pies without getting your hands dirty.

❖

THERE MUST BE A SHORTAGE OF MEN who can play the handsome, stalwart Anglo-Saxon adventure hero of old, or why would anybody pick Roger Moore? In *Gold,* as in *Live and Let Die,* he isn't a hero — he's just standing in for the hero, because nobody better could be found. After seven years of his playing The Saint on British TV, his face is so used to the camera that he's unimaginable as anything but an actor. Years of TV-series work give actors a gliding-through style: it's the actors' form of punchiness. Wearing middle-aged juveniles' faces, they look better from a distance. There's nothing recognizably human in their performances; they know how little they have to do to get by, and their acting becomes a repertory of a half-dozen effortless expressions and ritualized line-readings. Dimply suavity is Roger Moore's specialty, and his smoothness seems to have gone to his throat; his refeened, velvety diction makes John Forsythe sound like a Newark truck driver. Resigned, like the cherubim of American TV (David Janssen, Jack Lord, James Garner, Mike Connors, Richard Crenna, and all the rest), Moore confers blasé weightlessness on all his roles impartially. His James Bond in the sloppy, disappointing *Live and Let Die* left no imprint. As Bond, he stood in for Sean Connery; as The Saint he stood in for George Sanders. Moore wasn't born; he was recycled. How can he play the rugged, tough boss of subterranean operations in the vast South African mines of *Gold*? Physically he's large, but his personality is small, pink, and shiny. His mellifluous vowels remove any impact from his lines: he couldn't be *heard* in a gold mine, let alone give orders.

Gold is itself a recycling of the old, straightforward adventure films. An international syndicate based in London and headed by John Gielgud floods a South African mine in order to drive up the price of gold, and Moore and his Zulu buddy Big King (Simon Sabela) try to save the trapped men and the mine itself. Susannah York plays the granddaughter of the mine owner, Ray Milland (working with *nothing,* he gives the liveliest performance); she's married to a vicious schemer (Bradford Dillman), one of Gielgud's partners, but she falls in love with Moore. The plot is musty and the writing dodders, but the picture is mindlessly passable, largely because it was shot on location in and around Johannesburg; in a village called Ellisras, in the Northern Transvaal; and in South African mines. The director, Peter Hunt (not to be confused with

Peter H. Hunt, director of *1776*), worked under the title of editor or second-unit director on the first five Bond pictures, and he was the director of the sixth, *On Her Majesty's Secret Service* — the best of them except for the substitution of George Lazenby for Connery. *Gold* is conceived in far less audacious terms, and Hunt can't do much about such back numbers as the good guys who are earmarked to be patsies or the racist villains, but he deëmphasizes the plot (the waiting for Bradford Dillman to be eliminated, the waiting for Simon Sabela to prove that blacks are loyal and noble by doing the sacrificial bit). Hunt saves the picture from fossilizing by keeping it on an almost impersonal level — by visual tricks in the mine interiors and sumptuous, postcard views of the locale. However, the suspense is unduly prolonged during the climactic pounding-waters sequence near the end, and the end itself is fumbled, since, either through economy or through a whale of a misconception, we never get to see the liberation of the thousand trapped men. (Once Moore gets out of the mine, the crowds waiting above-ground go home, as if that were all there was to it.)

Gold is a tolerable new version of an old-fashioned adventure movie, but it works only at the level of technique; the romantic heroism and melodramatic "heart" were ground out of this sort of material long ago. Hunt is smart enough not to try to squeeze us emotionally on behalf of Roger Moore, but if his solution is a harbinger of how other talented people will try to work within the adventure-picture and disaster-epic prescriptions the entrepreneurs lay down, we're in for a period of formalism. I got a chill from the initial moment of the mine disaster, because I still make an involuntary emotional connection with actual mine disasters. But when the movie didn't bother to give us the elation of seeing the trapped Bantu workers reunited with their families, I felt like a fool for having cared for an instant. This formalism — this visual excitement and suspense in a void — is the result of artists' not getting a chance to work on subjects they believe in, and turning themselves into craftsmen. It's a process of desensitization for the artist which he passes on to the audience.

❖

IF YOU STARTED OUT TO MAKE *The Lavender Hill Mob* without Alec Guinness, and without an intricate joke-plan script, and with a director who didn't know the English scene and whose sense of comedy was a beat off, the results might be *11 Harrowhouse.* It isn't offensive, but it's so negligible that an hour after you've seen it you probably won't remember that you've been to the movies. An awkward, harmless, small-time American (Charles Grodin) — a "fubsy" type, as Guinness called his hero — tries to pull off a twelve-billion-dollar diamond robbery. John Gielgud is the head of the international diamond syndicate this time, and it's called "the system," in a halfhearted effort to suggest that the thieving American hero is bucking the British class system. Grodin *(The Heartbreak Kid)* keeps threatening to be funny, but he rarely makes it. Guinness's deadpan wasn't really dead; his eyes gleamed with larceny, and his straight face sent out tiny, furtive signals. But Grodin's deadpan is just a blank pasty face, and though his lack of vocal inflection is no doubt deliberate, uninflected nasality doesn't do much for a hero. His put-on performance seems designed to be a counterpoint to actions that the director, Aram Avakian, never got going. Dressed by Halston, Candice Bergen (as Grodin's accomplice) outshines the sparklers; she isn't required to act, and she's so consistently gorgeous she looks like a science-fiction creation. The picture has a big-time cast that includes Trevor Howard waving his arms a lot in a helpless attempt to earn his salary, Helen Cherry, and James Mason (as a subordinate of Gielgud's).

Aram Avakian is really rather fubsy at his trade. His last picture, *Cops and Robbers,* also a low-key caper-comedy, but set in New York, had an asset in Joe Bologna, with his bemused quality and his urban everyman's face — as urban in its way for this period as Cagney's was for his. But Avakian never quite found his own comic tone, or got the hang of pacing for suspense. The faults here are similar; Avakian's work is pleasantly lackadaisical, but the comic ideas don't build and erupt. However, *11 Harrowhouse* is much worse, because Avakian is out of his element. *Cops and Robbers* had a feeling for ethnic diversity and a funny, weary New York atmosphere; the burglary itself was the most standard part of it. In the English settings, when Avakian can't get suspense going or lets a chase become hopelessly disorganized there's no comic atmosphere for him to fall back on, and the picture becomes a good-natured but bumbling and stupid romp.

As Gielgud's flunky who joins the thieves, James Mason has the only two good scenes — vacuuming up the diamonds during the robbery, and a final confrontation with Gielgud. Mason doesn't just stay on the surface; he's got a sly, almost dirty sense of farce, as he demonstrated in *Lolita,* and he gives his character an underlying whipped-faithful-dog pathos, so there's a satisfying poetic justice in his screwing up chilly Gielgud. Mason is much more entertaining than Gielgud, because he isn't all dried out and super-perfected; smiling thinly, Gielgud has been playing the precise, satisfied mandarin so long that he's beginning to look Oriental. (He should never have appeared in *Lost Horizon.*) Mason has still got juicy surprises in him.

[October 21, 1974]

Taking a Chance

THE TITLE of the new Luis Buñuel film, *Le Fantôme de la Liberté,* is a variation on Marx's "A spectre is haunting Europe — the spectre of Communism," and that is auspicious: it suggests that the picture will be about freedom, and perhaps about people trying to escape from freedom. That sounds like a great, baited Buñuel theme, and as we wait to see what he's up to this time, the early part seems high-spirited; the spare, matter-of-fact style is so perfectly easy and unforced that one laughs in recognition of his mastery. No one before Buñuel ever made matter-of-factness so funny. The assurance of his images (with their latent pledge of irrationality) is disconcerting; they seem explosively risible, and the surface lucidity of his style is like the greatest joke in the universe — the joke of the universe. But the theme of *Le Fantôme* turns out to be freedom in the sense of "chance," and the Old Master Tease means it quite literally. The picture is a random series of anecdotes and paradoxes, and they miss as often as they connect; it's a piffle, really. The domesticated surrealism of this picture has no sting, no bite, and no aftereffect. At most, it's amusing; at worst, it's tedious. I don't think Buñuel can possibly mean the movie to be more than a whimsical shaggy-dog story. Probably no one could be offended by anything in *Le Fantôme* — it's defanged — so it would be pretty funny if the film were universally acclaimed as a savage masterpiece. The idea of Buñuel's getting this kind of knee-jerk response has more reverberations than anything in the picture.

The gags — even the ones that tickle, such as the dinner party illustrating the relativity of customs (elimination is performed socially; eating is concealed in guilty privacy) — are without resonance of any kind. At first, this unresonant style seems a come-on and a delight, but paradoxes without resonance are dry. The lucidity here doesn't stir the imagination, it inhibits it. I'm not sure I understand why the film has this effect (or if it was meant to); it may be that it's because Buñuel no longer cares to assault us, or even to beckon to us. *Le Fantôme* lacks that dream logic of which he is a master. He just lays out what pleases him, and if it's a dumb little drollery, there it sits. In *The Discreet Charm of the Bourgeoisie,* he kept tweaking us; he would catch us up in an anecdote and then drop it. This time, he doesn't drop it soon enough. I think the tipoff that this movie's mischief is just twinkletoes stuff comes early — in the picture-postcard episode. A little girl playing in a park is given postcards surreptitiously by a leering man. The girl goes home with her nanny and hands them to her parents (Jean-Claude Brialy and Monica Vitti); the parents fire the nanny because of the incident and get hot when they look at the pictures — and then Buñuel shows us the postcards, which are of the Arc de Triomphe, Sacré Coeur, and other monuments. Whether in a Buñuel movie or a TV skit, that is a silly joke on the audience, and not even a new one. Early on, the Brialy character gets a laugh when he announces that he's bored with symmetry, but the film's pat reversals of expectations get to be symmetrical, too. In an anecdote about a sniper (Pierre Lary, Buñuel's assistant), his random killings are set up with immaculate craft, but when he is convicted for his crimes and then, freed, walks out of the courtroom, the kicker has no kick. And a longish episode about a little girl who is said to have disappeared though she's there all the time goes very, very flat. Sequences begin with a flourish and then peter out: could it be that Buñuel loses interest? Maybe it's too roguish an idea to put together a series of episodes linked only by happenstance. *Le Fantôme* has a great tonic style but the sense of humor of a cool sophomore.

CAN UNIVERSAL GET BY with selling TV shows as movies? Is Jennings Lang, one of Universal's "pioneers" in the field of movies made for television, now trying to palm off the same sort of assembly-line productions on theater audiences? He's executive producer of *Airport 1975,* which could only have been designed as a TV movie and then blown up to cheapie-epic proportions. It has a formula plot (a 747 is hit in the nose by a small plane), it has perfunctory dialogue by a TV writer (Don Ingalls), and, like the usual movie made for TV, it offers in place of characters a collection of players — known to old moviegoers and TV-watchers — who can be passed off as stars. When actors work in a TV-movie format that makes it impossible for them to build a characterization, it doesn't much matter whether they're talented or not. They're not cast for their abilities; they're exploited for the public appeal they used to have and the aura that lingers around their names, and they get a stale, used-up look. This depression is endemic to TV movies. Their appeal is part morbid: some people want to see how their old favorites have aged. But no matter what shape the actors are in, they look terrible, because an actor without a role — an unawakened actor — looks half dead.

Gloria Swanson plays herself in *Airport 1975*, while Nancy Olson, who was in *Sunset Boulevard* along with Swanson, turns up as the blond mother of invalid Linda Blair, who's being flown to the West Coast for a kidney transplant. Since William Frye, the producer of *The Trouble with Angels*, is in charge, and nuns did it for him before, Martha Scott and Helen Reddy clamber aboard and play God's little helpers circa 1935. Reddy, all eager, girlish nunniness, sings to little sick Linda while the passengers express amazement that a nun should be able to sing. (Actually, the arrangement is too solemn for her, and she sings sluggishly.) Since Reddy is photographed so unflatteringly that she looks like Beulah Witch from the original *Kukla, Fran, and Ollie* show, and since she makes the mistake of trying to act in a stay-on-the-treadmill-and-collect-your-paycheck TV movie, her film début is a simpering embarrassment. Myrna Loy, playing a tippler, stays aloof and doesn't disgrace herself unduly, but Dana Andrews (who was with Loy in *The Best Years of Our Lives*) is required to have a heart attack, while the camera gloats on his lined face. The film is practically a recognition derby, since there isn't much to do except put names to the faces; some (such as Sid Caesar and Efrem Zimbalist, Jr.) are easy, while others (such as Beverly Garland) are maddeningly tough. Jennings Lang may have decided it would be economical to turn out disaster pictures seriatim: both Charlton Heston and George Kennedy, who do some chores here, appear also in his forthcoming *Earthquake*.

Airport 1975 is processed schlock, and it's really beneath the level at which movie criticism might serve a function; one might almost think it had been conceived as a campy joke — a box of rotten candy for movie junkies and TV dipsos. One can have a fairly good time laughing at it, but it doesn't sit too well as a joke, because the people on the screen are being humiliated. (I didn't really enjoy seeing Helen Reddy make a fool of herself.) It's more than possible that the executives at Universal who hatched this thing and the director, Jack Smight, are so cynical and so untalented that this idiot creation is their idea of popular entertainment. There's considerable evidence that the mammoth new disaster pictures are planned with the thought in mind that if *The Poseidon Adventure* and the original *Airport* hadn't been so clunky they might not have made so much money. In Hollywood, cynicism and incompetence are natural bedfellows — one covering up for the other — but this time they've pulled the covers right over their heads, and they're both laid bare. When the chief stewardess, Karen Black, must take over the controls of the plane, she's so archaically helpless that Heston, on the radio telling her what to do, keeps congratulating her if she manages to keep her hand on a lever without hysterics. She's treated like a puppy who needs to be patted (while women in the theater hiss). But when Charlton Heston comes to the rescue, dropping down from a helicopter into the hole in the cockpit of the 747, Karen Black holds out her arms to pull him in and, openmouthed, in closeup, she jiggles her tongue. If she had winked, too, it might have told us that the director knew what he was doing. But nobody knew what was going on in this one. Even technically, the picture is a shambles. The post-synching is off at the beginning, and the sound is so bad that Karen Black's voice is gratingly metallic. The audience kept breaking up over the hackneyed editing and such howlers as Karen Black's wandering about in the shattered cockpit of the plane going full speed, her hair blowing ever so slightly in the breeze. The tin thinking over at Universal really shines: there's a fagged-out joke about Nixon, and later an angry blast at the media to balance it. Probably everybody will have some reason to hiss this picture — the best one being that it's not about anything except exploitable possibilities. Hissing is more expressive than anything that happens on the screen.

JACK SMIGHT IS A FUMBLER; Joseph Sargent is a pounder. Smight doesn't quite get what he's after; Sargent gets it, all right — his work in *The Taking of Pelham One Two Three* is atrociously on target. Sargent doesn't just make points, he drops weights. John Godey's thriller about how four men of disparate backgrounds hijack a New York subway train and hold the passengers for ransom was no doubt written with a movie in mind, and it provides the one element that carries this picture along — a workmanlike suspense plot. But the movie must have been an editor's nightmare: the scenes are thudders, and the continuity suggests that the whole thing was punched together — with no glue but the basic idea. In the role of the Transit Authority Police detective who negotiates with the hijack chief (Robert Shaw), Walter Matthau plays at half-mast, and that works out much better than his more vigorous performances in *Charley Varrick* and *The Laughing Policeman.* Maybe he instinctively reacted against the noise and squalling. (The film is studded with shots of the terrorized subway passengers yowling in panic, and there's a shameless shot of a shrieking mother clutching her bawling kids — someone loved this so much it's repeated.) Matthau luxuriates in his drooping face; he lets everything hang down. It's an old theatrical trick to play against the prevailing mood of a piece — to become more quiet as everyone else gets more assertive — and it usually works, as it does here. Matthau coasts through the movie without extending himself beyond things he's done a million times, yet he seems an oasis of sanity. Since the Peter Stone script has only a few witty strokes, and features cheap flippancy, a corrupt, infantile New York City mayor to chortle over, and a multitude of "dirty" words for giggly shock effects, Matthau's coasting looks like dignity.

Matthau may be so popular partly because he sets up a secret, direct line of communication with the audience. The quizzical cock of his head and his customary slight abstraction from the other people in a scene put him in collusion with us. Calmly confident, Matthau seems more aware than the others of what's going on, and smarter. He doesn't deliver lines as if he thought they were humorous, he just slips them in. Matthau has the shrewd, sleepy affability of an urban Will Rogers; his raised eyebrows and sagging shoulders — the shoulders of a man used to nothing going right — provide a steady commentary on big-city chaos. He doesn't excite himself unnecessarily. But Matthau's pooped-out appearance is a way of disarming people — and when he uncoils, he moves fast and effectively. So he's both the squinting, spreading-nosed comic and the strapping man of action. When he's good, Matthau gets inside his roles physically, with a sexy clown's grace. The Matthau hero can maneuver in the city the way the Westerner could on the plains; he belongs. He's the New York hero, sour yet self-satisfied.

[October 28, 1974]

Spieler

BRIAN DE PALMA, the writer-director of *Phantom of the Paradise,* thrives on frowzy visual hyperbole. When he tries to set up a simple scene establishing that boy composer loves girl singer, he is a helpless amateur, but when he sets up a highly stylized paranoid fantasy with gyrating figures on a stage and an audience that is having its limbs hacked off, you can practically hear him cackling with happiness, and the scene carries a jolt. De Palma, who can't tell a plain story, does something that a couple of generations of student and underground filmmakers have been trying to do and nobody else has ever brought off. He creates a new Guignol, in a modern idiom, out of the movie Guignol of the past. *Phantom of the Paradise* is a rock horror show about a composer, Winslow (William Finley), who is robbed of his music, busted for drugs, and sent to Sing Sing — all at the instigation of Swan (Paul Williams), the entrepreneur of Death Records, who has made a pact with the Devil for eternal youth. Winslow escapes from prison, is maimed by a record-pressing machine, and haunts Swan's new rock palace, the Paradise, where Phoenix (Jessica Harper), the girl he loves, becomes a star. This mixture of *The Phantom of the Opera* and *Faust* (via *The Devil and Daniel Webster*) isn't enough for De Palma. He heaps on layers of rock satire, and parodies of *The Cabinet of Dr. Caligari, The Hunchback of Notre Dame, Psycho,* and *The Picture of Dorian Gray* — and the impacted plots actually function for him. De Palma is drawn to rabid visual exaggeration and sophisticated, satirical low comedy. This slapstick expressionism is idiosyncratic in the extreme. It's De Palma's flukiness that makes *Phantom* so entertaining.

Though you may anticipate a plot turn, it's impossible to guess what the next scene will *look* like or what its rhythm will be. De Palma's timing is sometimes wantonly unpredictable and dampening, but mostly it has a lift to it. You practically get a kinetic charge from the breakneck wit he put into *Phantom*; it isn't just that the picture has vitality but that one can feel the tremendous kick the director got out of making it. And one can feel the love that went into the visual details of this production — the bird motifs, the shifting patterns of the interiors. De Palma's method is very theatrical, with each scene sharply divided from the next. He may play with crazy-house effects like a hyperactive kid, or he may set up a tricky scene with shrill, hot lighting — a magnesium flare — and have the camera circle some spangly, high-flier performers, providing almost a floating view. You get the feeling he's staring at them, as entranced as we are. His technique is inspired amateurishness; his work resembles what hundreds of student filmmakers have done, but there's a level of personal obsession which makes the material his own. Most student moviemakers are gullible: they harbor a naïve belief in the clichés they parrot. De Palma loves the clichés for their shameless, rotten phoniness. The movies of the past haven't made him their innocent victim; rather, they have wised him up. He doesn't just reproduce grotesque old effects; his driving, redeeming sense of humor cuts through the crap in movies at the same time that it cuts through the crap in the rock world. Few directors work in such a screwily personal way, but that sense of humor of his is like a disinfectant.

De Palma is the only filmmaker to have come up from the underground and gone on for years working the same way with a larger budget. In 1963, I was on the jury at the Midwest Film Festival which gave a prize to *Woton's Wake,* a twenty-eight-minute film he made in 16-mm. when he was still a student. It had many of the same elements as *Phantom* — figures running from skyscrapers, parodies of early horror films. It even had the same William Finley. And it was funny in much the same corny, off-the-wall way. What it didn't have was rock. De Palma has done some bright, giddy work (as in the 1968 *Greetings*) — almost like a revue artist putting together a collection of skits. His intricate sequences are like Rube Goldberg infernal machines — they buzz along and blow up — but in the past he hasn't been able to shape a feature film and keep the whole thing buzzing until it explodes in the viewer's head. However, rock gives *Phantom* a unifying pulse, and De Palma uses the score (by Paul Williams) so that the satirical points, the story climaxes, and the musical numbers all peak together — and sizzle.

Movie directors who break away from the conventional methods of handling material are usually trying to express aspects of experience which haven't been treated in film. But De Palma, like most underground filmmakers, didn't start with conventional methods. And what he's trying to do is to deal with his experience of maniacal movies in terms derived from those movies. From the way his scenes plunge into vacuity whenever he tries to show ordinary human relations it's clear that his energy runs high only when he lets his carny spirit and his movie-fed imagination take over. Back in 1931 — a decade before De Palma was born — a character in a movie listened to a preacher's daughter (Barbara Stanwyck) and said to her, "You've got the hot spiel in your blood." What the evangelical rhetoric had done to her, movies have done to Brian De Palma. He's a movie freak with brains and talent. The faults and virtues are so similar in *Woton's Wake* and *Phantom,* his eighth feature (all but one, *Get to Know Your Rabbit,* made outside the industry), that it's evident that he hasn't learned commercial techniques. I doubt whether he'll ever be able to handle exposition or naturalistic scenes, and his dialogue is unsure and too casual, as if he were still a student filmmaker just playing around.

But this incompetence isn't necessarily crippling: it's in terms of the conventional standards of moviemaking that De Palma is an amateur. Cocteau said that the only movie technique worth having is the technique you invent for yourself. That seems to apply to the highest levels of artistry, but it probably applies to primitives, too, and it may be true for De Palma — not because he's way up there, or a primitive, either, but because he's so totally on his own wavelength. When he sticks to what he can do, he's got a great style, but he can't do the routine scenes that establish character relations and give a movie "heart." He lurched his way through *Sisters* trying to get by with expositional stuff that went flat. In *Phantom,* the scenes in which Winslow shows his affection for

Phoenix seem "obligatory," because they have no satiric edge; we don't care about them, because the director doesn't. A cutaway shot of Phoenix snickering when a male singer scrambles to stand up in his high platform shoes is worse than obligatory: it looks as if the director couldn't decide whether or not he was doing a put-on of klutzy techniques. It can't be simple boredom that blocks De Palma; probably most directors are bored by these scenes, yet they still manage to do what's needed. It must be that something in him (his wit?) fights the material. Maybe the answer isn't that he needs to learn the routine techniques for getting through the normal scenes but, rather, that he needs to let his own attitudes toward those scenes come out. He's being paralyzed by his own unexpressed feelings. *Phantom,* fortunately, has so much spirit that it buckjumps right past the dead spots, but it wouldn't be so blotchy if De Palma weren't a little nervous about the hot spiel in his blood.

What with everything else going on in the country, the noise of rock and the goosiness of it have finally got to me; I can't listen to the new records — they affect me like the drilling in the streets. I've begun to get the feeling that maybe even the people playing rock don't much like it anymore, and that their energy has become false energy. But the rock beat still works for movies, and it works in a special way for De Palma, since he deals with acid-rock decadence and the youth-sell cons of the promoters — which are overripe for parody. Though the elaborately contrived setup that De Palma works best in doesn't always make his actors comfortable, it's dizzyingly right for rock singing, since it provides the same kind of turbulence that light shows do, only more so. The cinematographer Larry Pizer keeps the images full to overflowing, and the gifted young set designer Jack Fisk (he also did *Badlands*) supplies striking takeoffs of the frenzied décor of German silent films. Probably no other music (not even Wagner's) thrives on visual augmentation and grandiose stagecraft the way glitter rock does, and De Palma and Fisk need only push the usual hype staging a few steps further to arrive at satire — provided the singers are also clowns. And they are: the picture's most immediate pleasures come from its singing comedians. As the music parodies successive rock styles from the fifties to the seventies, Harold Oblong, Jeffrey Comanor, and Archie Hahn turn up as three different groups — The Juicy Fruits, The Beach Bums, and, with black-and-white expressionist faces, The Undeads. These three performers and Gerrit Graham, who plays the pill-popper Beef, a rock Gorgeous George, are, by virtue of their gift for stylization, the picture's stars. Graham had some of the best scenes in *Greetings*: he was the dreamily intense tall kid, the assassination aficionado who, in bed with his girl friend, traced bullet trajectories on her naked body. He kept holding up enlarged photographs that he claimed showed figures on the grassy knoll, and announcing, "This will break the Kennedy case wide open," until, finally, he tried to show the pictures to the girl, who rejected them, saying, "I saw *Blow-Up* — I know how this comes out. It's all blurry — you can't tell a thing." That's a typical Brian De Palma ploy — a joke that douses a movie fixation and a political fixation with one pail of water. Graham's grandstanding singer in *Phantom,* like Dick Shawn's in *The Producers,* is a broad satire of theatrical hamminess — collegiate-surreal.

As Swan, Paul Williams, an actual musical potentate, with a childlike smile and a seductive pitchman's manner of speech, acts smart and on top of everything — but then, doesn't he always? Williams, who has composed such pop songs as "We've Only Just Begun" and "Rainy Days and Mondays," played the monstrously precocious child in *The Loved One* when he was twenty-four, and also played a child nasty in *The Chase.* The musical parodies he has composed for *Phantom* aren't wizardly but they're effective. His Caligari-Dorian Gray performance doesn't always get the laughs that seem intended, yet without him the film wouldn't have much resonance. Despite Swan's exaggerated behavior, Williams, who bridges the two worlds of the satire and what is being satirized, remains oddly, limply real. Since Williams looks much the same on talk shows — pushing the same androgynous, soft-bodied creepiness — it is more than a simple put-on; we're not sure exactly how to react to him. There's definitely something going on when Williams is on the screen, but it's all unresolved. Maybe De Palma can't quite get a fix on him: Williams reeks of the seventies mountebanks' transcendence of satire — it's too soon, maybe, to understand what that is all about. De Palma is, understandably, more secure with George Memmoli, who plays Swan's chief thug; Memmoli's comic toughie, with his greasy roots in the fifties, is a classic burlesque type. There's not a lot going on when Finley's Winslow is on the screen. Finley has a nice cloud-borne quality in his opening song, and later he's acceptable (though not particularly scary or touching) as the mad, masked phantom, but he doesn't come across well in the wobbly transitional scenes. Finley's bug-eyed cartoon of a dreamy chump (he's dismantled, like Nathanael West's Lemuel Pitkin) isn't very appealing — maybe there's just too much grimacing in his acting. Tiny Jessica Harper, with a neat barrette in her hair, was a provocative choice for the corruptible Phoenix; she suggests both the demure girl-next-door passivity that would appeal to Winslow, the loser, and the essential amorality that would appeal to Swan. She's got a pixie-ingénue gleam inside an agelessly tired baby face — she looks like a débutante Adrienne Rich. Jessica Harper has a strong voice, and she gives her big audition number the right quality of hard seriousness (to contrast with the parody styles of the other singers), but she's disappointing in the scene near the end which makes her a star. Her white lace granny dress is unflattering, and her singing isn't impressive enough for the crowd's wild enthusiasm to be convincing. The fault is possibly in the music itself, though if De Palma had brought out her depravity in this number — if he had sent up the elements of her singing personality that knock out the audience — it might have been another high point. But he played it soberly straight, and that's where he always sags. The film has real zing, however; De Palma is a genuinely funny director, with a gassy, original comic temperament. Do the rock producers who use horror in their shows have a sense of humor? If they start niggling away at this garish hunk of slapstick with such face-saving, scholarly objections as "It doesn't come to terms with the lingua," the joke of *Phantom of the Paradise* could really bloom.

[November 11, 1974]

When the Saints Come Marching In

"LENNY," the Bob Fosse film starring Dustin Hoffman, is for audiences who want to believe that Lenny Bruce was a saintly gadfly who was martyred for having lived before their time. Julian Barry, who wrote the Tom O'Horgan 1971 stage show, starring Cliff Gorman, has written the screenplay, and the material is conceived for well-meaning innocents who never saw Lenny Bruce and who can listen to Dustin Hoffman delivering bits of Bruce routines and think, People just didn't understand him then — he isn't shocking at all. There was every reason to believe that O'Horgan knew the difference between Lenny Bruce the performer he'd been on the same bill with back in the late fifties and the Lenny Bruce turn-on myth he helped whip up. His *Lenny,* which came between his *Hair* and his *Jesus Christ Superstar,* was part of an effort to create a youth theater; the show dealt with Bruce not as a man but as a sacrificial symbol surrounded by tribal symbols on stilts and decked out in papier-mâché heads and grass skirts. It was James Dean updated — Lenny Bruce as a misunderstood kid, the way *Jesus Christ Superstar* was to be Jesus as a misunderstood kid. Taking over the O'Horgan-Barry material, Bob Fosse has eliminated the totemic haberdashery. His staging goes all the way in the opposite direction: the film is in black and white, in a semi-documentary style. But Julian Barry hasn't rethought Bruce's life or fleshed out the characters, and the closer Fosse gets to them, the more abstract they become. Lenny's wife, the stripper Honey Harlow (Valerie Perrine); his mother, Sally Marr (Jan Miner); a fictitious manager (Stanley Beck); and Lenny himself are still no more than symbolic figures, and they inhabit an abstract, stage-bound world that doesn't seem to relate to a specific period or to the cities where the key events of Bruce's life actually took place.

Fosse has learned a phenomenal amount about film technique in a short time; *Lenny* is only his third movie (after *Sweet Charity* and *Cabaret*), and it's a handsome piece of work. I don't know of any other director who entered moviemaking so late in life and developed such technical proficiency; Fosse is a true prodigy. *Lenny* is far removed in style from *Cabaret*, yet it's controlled and intelligent. But the script is simply too thin for the method Fosse uses. A searching, close-in documentary technique can sometimes provide glimpses of the riches of people's interior lives, but it is rarely effective with actors: their controls are exposed, and we become more conscious of their acting than in a conventionally dramatized work. The idea here seems to be that what the writer has failed to provide, the camera will somehow probe. But since the characters have nothing to yield up, it probes superficiality. Essentially, the method is to cut from episodes recalled by Lenny's family and associates to Lenny performing a sliver of a routine that seems to have developed out of each episode. However, the film never quite achieves a "present": we might almost be watching him perform after the survivors were interviewed. The crosscutting between present and past is smoothly engineered, but it doesn't really do anything for us. I get the impression that, unlike O'Horgan, Fosse thought he was really getting at truth, and that he got so caught up in the complicated structure he didn't see that it surrounded a void. Despite the fluent editing and sophisticated graphics, the picture is the latest version of the one-to-one correlation of an artist's life and his art which we used to get in movies about painters and songwriters. Lenny's life becomes footnotes to his night-club acts — as if the acts needed footnotes! — and often the biographical account has the odd effect of making his stage acts seem like simple rationalizations of what was going on in his life. In the traditional movie, life is transmuted into art; here the hero's routines are so unfunny that no transmutation seems to have taken place.

Fosse may have tried so hard to stretch himself that he lost perspective (and his sense of humor) on this project. Within its serious conception, *Lenny* is very well made. But why does it take itself so insufferably seriously? Why the sociological black-and-white investigatory style for a subject like Lenny Bruce? The style says, Listen, kids, this is going to be about a very important man; be quiet, now — remember you're in church. The movie turns out to be the earnest story of a Jewish prophet who shouldn't have got involved with a shiksa junkie.

There really is no script. There was no play inside O'Horgan's production, either, but there were so many dervishes whirling that most of the audience didn't seem to mind. Gorman delivered large chunks of Bruce's material, and though he lacked the spiv comic's jabbing hostility, he was able to build up a rhythm with the audience. His actor's exertion and the sweetness he brought to the material fitted O'Horgan's sacrificial-lamb concept: the audience could appreciate the humor without feeling the danger that made Bruce's audiences prickle with nervous pleasure. Gorman seemed like such a nice boy up there, harried, and working hard. So does Dustin Hoffman, but he can't even work up a performing rhythm, because in the movie the shticks have been reduced to snippets and high points.

Hoffman makes a serious, honorable try, but he's the wrong kind of actor to play Bruce. Hoffman ingratiates himself with an audience by his shy smile, his gentleness, and his insecurity. He wins people over by his lack of physical confidence; you pull for him because he's so non-threatening — you hope that he isn't actually weak and that he'll prove himself. But that clenched, nasal voice of his is the voice of someone trying to get along in the nervous straight world Bruce fled; his putziness is just what Bruce despised. Hoffman is touchingly childlike (he was at his best on the TV show *Free to Be . . . You and Me,* when he read Herb Gardner's monologue about a child's first crossing a street by himself); there was nothing childlike about Lenny Bruce. He vamped the audience with a debauched, deliberately faggy come-hither that no one quite knew how to interpret; he was uncompromisingly not nice.

Who would be right to play him? Is there an actor with the hooded eyes and sensual come-on of a Persian hipster prince? Lenny Bruce had a treacherous glint under those heavy lids, and his cool pimp's mask of indifference was almost reptilian. He took off on the whole straight world, and that certainly meant the Dustin Hoffmans and it could mean you, because he was more of a hipster than anybody, and it was his vision and his rules (no rules at all) he played by. Hoffman's Lenny Bruce, like Gorman's, is on your side. Lenny Bruce was on nobody's side. The farthest-out hipster, like the farthest-out revolutionary, has an enormous aesthetic advantage over everybody else: he knows how to play his hand to make us all feel chicken. Bruce's hostility and obscenity were shortcuts to audience response; he could get and hold audiences' attention because they didn't know what or whom he was going to attack and degrade next, and they could sense that he wasn't sure himself. He was always open to darts of inspiration, so suspense was built in. He dropped the barrier between the vagrant obscene jokes that club comics, jazz musicians, and assorted con artists might exchange offstage and what was said publicly onstage. Educated left-wingers were probably his natural audience, because his gutter shpritz was often a more extreme and nihilistic form of what they were thinking, and the maggoty vitality of his language was a heady revelation to them. Words whizzed by that you'd never heard before and that may not have existed in any argot but his own, yet their sound was so expressive that the meaning got across. He flew recklessly low, and the audience, awed and delighted, howled at feeling so ridiculously dirty-minded, howled at the joke of how good it felt to be shameless. We hadn't known how many taboos we were living with, and how many humiliations and embarrassments we were hiding, until we heard him pop them one after another, like a string of firecrackers. That's what a Bruce routine did, and why it felt liberating. Bruce's gleeful, surreal, show-biz Yiddish-jive dirtiness was a mind-opener. He was always testing the audience and himself, and for religious people his blasphemy could only be a whack in the face. He wanted to reach audiences and hold them, yet the only way he knew how was to assault them with obscene jokes about everything that could conceivably be sacred to them. For the people sitting there, complacency was impossible. No matter how hip they thought they were, he would find ways to shock them. The prudish were almost forced to walk out.

Bruce's material is practically indelible for many of us who heard him, and his records stay in the mind for a decade, yet some of Bruce's best stuff is in the movie and we don't remember it ten minutes later, because the man who delivers the bits doesn't know why Bruce said them. The scriptwriter of *Lenny* must think that Bruce's material is so good that an actor can say it and that this will be enough. But those routines don't work without Bruce's teasing, seductive aggression and his delirious amorality. If they are presented as the social criticism of a man who's out to cleanse society of hypocrisy, the material goes flat. When Hoffman's Lenny tells the people in a club that he feels like urinating on them, Hoffman's tone is uncertain and his blank face says that he doesn't understand why Bruce felt that way. The screen never ignites: you're listening to Lenny Bruce's shticks and you don't even feel like laughing.

This Lenny, with his flower child's moral precepts, is a drag. When he does the famous Bruce bit about Jacqueline Kennedy trying to climb out of the assassination car, he attaches the moral that it's important to tell the truth about it in order to help other girls who might be in similar situations. When he assaults his night-club audience, singling out individuals as niggers, kikes, and greaseballs, he expounds on how much better the world would be if those words were freely shouted. Apart from the idiocy of the picture's endorsing this dubious theory and trying to wring applause for it, there's the gross misunderstanding of Bruce's methods. If Bruce did in fact stoop that low upon occasion, gathering sanctity around himself, the moviemakers should have had the brains to know that those explanations were false. I certainly don't recall Bruce's smiling at black patrons (as Hoffman does) to take the sting out of having called them niggers, but if he ever did, that wasn't Bruce the comic, it was Bruce the phony. His cruel jokes may have been a release for the audience (I think they were), but that's not why he did them. He didn't ridicule Jackie Kennedy's actions in order to help women, and he didn't use racial slurs in order to cleanse the national air. He did heartlessly cynical bits because there were only two possible audience reactions — to be outraged or to laugh. And either way he was the winner. But when he drove people out, he was the loser, too. He didn't want them to be outraged only: he was a comic, and he wanted them to laugh at what outraged them. Yet some people couldn't laugh at Bruce, because laughter was an admission that the ideas he was shocking you with weren't altogether new to you — or that, if you hadn't entertained them, you knew that you could. There was a good reason for him to become a counterculture hero: his scabrous realism never seemed a matter of choice. However, he went to the farthest lengths he could dream up, not out of missionary motives but out of a performer's zeal.

THERE ARE TWO VIEWS of Bruce competing for public acceptance now, and though a major-studio movie like *Lenny* is bound to set the pattern in which most people will think of Bruce for years to come, this movie suffers in just about every imaginable way by comparison with the Albert Goldman book *Ladies and Gentlemen Lenny Bruce!!* Goldman's greatest value is probably in supplying the show-business milieu that Bruce's humor came from. He provides a sense of how Bruce's act developed, and of who the audiences were, what the clubs were like, and what the other comics were doing. Goldman argues against the saintly view of Bruce, yet in his own way he falls into it — glorifying Bruce the junkie and putting down those who stayed clear of drugs. The book is brilliant, but it made me uneasy, as if Goldman were working off something on Bruce — maybe his own *not* being a junkie. Lenny Bruce got to him — Goldman admires him so much that he feels chicken for his own traces of cautious sanity.

The book has the involvement that is missing from the movie. I felt cold and remote while watching *Lenny,* with its plaster saint; the Goldman book, with its saint junkie, has overheated perils. The book is show business. Goldman gets the hype going and then doesn't go underneath it; the book stays hyped up, and the reader tires. You may begin to feel that Goldman wants the highs of a junkie without really getting hooked, and that he creates the hysterical hero to which his own prose is appropriate. He's so addictively involved that he assumes he's inside Bruce's head, and the interior view he gives is suspect. Goldman doesn't really see Bruce's suffering, because he thinks Lenny Bruce should know he's the great Lenny Bruce. He denies Bruce his pain. In his own way, Goldman competes with Bruce. He isn't just writing a biography; he does what Bruce did — he works the room.

The movie isn't show-biz enough; it's so busy with travail that it never gets any hype going — though Bruce was a hype artist. His view of the world came from the cruddiness and corruption of show business. Bruce spent his youth on the bottom rungs of the sordid club world, guided by his tough, lively mother, Sally Marr, also known as Boots Malloy, who worked as a comic in burlesque joints, managed comedians, and trained strippers. (In *Harry & Tonto,* Sally Marr plays the friendly old broad at the end who suggests to Art Carney that they get together.) And Bruce's seeing the world in show-biz terms was the key to his wit. In his "Religions, Inc." number, the Oral Roberts-type preacher greets Pope John on the phone with "Hey, Johnny, what's shakin', baby?" (This amiable near-obscenity isn't in the movie; if it were, Hoffman's Bruce might explain that it's not good for people to believe in the superstition that the Pope is holier than other men.) Many other comics have lifted Bruce's put-down style of treating the leaders of church and state as cheap hustlers, but when Bruce used show biz as the metaphor for everything squalid and hateful — and lively — in the world, it had a special impact. He was obsessed with bringing everything down to his own terms. Maybe most people who grow up in show business begin to see the world as an extension of it ("Life is a cabaret"), but the traditional performer glosses over the sleaziness with show-biz sentimentality. Even an insult comedian like Don Rickles lays on the sentimental shock absorbers; he titillates the audience by his naughtiness and then asks acceptance as a good boy. Bruce wouldn't play that show-biz game; he despised theatrical sentimentality as the worst form of sleaze (as in his great "Palladium" number). Sentimentality was a rotten, wet show; it disgusted him. Flattering the audience, squeezing for approval, offended his performer's instinct, which was far deeper in him than any social morality and was the base of his satirical outlook. It wasn't until late in his life that he got told that it was a moral base — and after that his instinct began to play him false.

Bob Fosse could have made a sensational movie if he had shown the backstage life that shaped Bruce's awareness, if he had given us a Lenny Bruce who enlarged his satirical perceptions of show biz to include the world — going from imitations of other performers and parodies of movies to parodies of religious show biz and, ultimately, to those labyrinthine, bebop satires of the law in which he was entangled. Maybe for Fosse that approach seems too close to home and too easy. He may devalue the show-biz sensationalism that he's practically a genius at, but the best bit in the movie is Gary Morton's performance as Sherman Hart, a comic based on Milton Berle (who pitched in for Bruce's funeral expenses), and Valerie Perrine's early striptease number has high theatrical dazzle. It's out of character for Honey, because Honey wasn't a top headliner, but if Fosse couldn't resist shooting the works and outblazing Blaze Starr, who will complain? Nothing in Honey's personality ties in with that high-powered strip, but Valerie Perrine gives an affecting, if limited, performance, and her Honey comes closer than Hoffman's Lenny to being a character. Hoffman has his moments; he looks better (and acts less gawky) when he's bearded, and he gets a jazzy performing style going on one piece of tape we hear, but he's respectable, like Paul Muni when he impersonated historical characters. No matter what he does, Hoffman never manages to suggest a hipster.

Lenny Bruce's story is a show-biz story. That's what the Julian Barry script, with its already dated leching-after-youth liberalism, fails to get at. Before his death, in 1966, Bruce himself began the moist process of canonization; it was his amorality that had shocked people, but now he began to claim that it was his morality. This movie swallows the lie that his motivating force was to make the audience well, and, having swallowed that, it can only defuse his humor. The moviemakers are working something off on Bruce, too: they're staking higher claims for themselves, trying to go beyond show business. The black-and-white earnestness of this movie and the youth-culture saintliness laid on Lenny Bruce are the ultimate in modern show-biz sentimentality.

[November 18, 1974]

Shearing the Sheep

DELORES TAYLOR weeps throughout the two hours and fifty minutes of *The Trial of Billy Jack.* She looks so gnarled and exhausted from the leakage that I began to have visions of a machine — an actress's equivalent of a duck press — that was squeezing the moisture out of her. In this sequel to the 1971 *Billy Jack,* she again plays the founder of the Southwestern interracial Freedom School, built on Indian land, which is being harassed by crooked and bigoted townspeople. Both films were made by Miss Taylor and her director-husband, Tom Laughlin, who plays Billy Jack: they do the scripts together; they use their daughter Teresa, now sixteen, in a leading role; and in this two-and-a-half-million-dollar sequel they give the director's credit to their nineteen-year-old son, Frank, who, from the look of *The Trial of Billy Jack,* may actually have done it, though more likely he assisted his father. The 1971 film was, intermittently, a disarmingly innocent fairy tale, a silly-sweet child's greening of America, with idealized, spontaneous long-haired little kids trying to win over the melodramatized villains who represented the hypocritical reactionary forces in American life. It was a jumble, but the loose, good-humored children (they were actually Herbert Kohl's students from the Other Ways school) and the teachers (comedians from San Francisco's cabaret theater The Committee) incarnated the film's hopeful spirit. And there was another factor in the film's success with subteens and teenagers, who went to it over and over again: *Billy Jack* was the only counterculture movie to provide a positive hero. Billy Jack was a counterculture savior, a mystical, selfless Protector who, coming to the aid of children and Indians, personified the good. The 1969 *Easy Rider* had begun to suggest a primitive religious element in the counterculture, and Peter Fonda had exuded traces of sanctity, but the film was a downer. *Billy Jack* tapped an emerging mood — the transition of the flower children into the Jesus people. And now, in *The Trial of Billy Jack,* the Laughlins, *en famille,* have gone all the way into messianic, tent-show moviemaking.

This film probably represents the most extraordinary display of sanctimonious self-aggrandizement the screen has ever known; beside it the George C. Scott of *The Savage Is Loose* is a piker. When Taylor's schoolmistress and Laughlin's Billy Jack meet after a separation, it's a holy rite; the sun's rays glitter behind their embracing figures, and the Grand Canyon itself is hardly large enough to provide the backdrop. Not since David Lean's last film has so much of the cosmos borne witness to the importance of a couple of actors. But, of course, as the aerial views suggest, these actors are playing more than roles; they are the Holy Family in a new, spectacular religious-calendar art for moviegoers, and they are revolutionaries in the same sense in which Jesus is said to have been a revolutionary. A female Ralph Nader and the greatest civil-rights activist of all time, the schoolmistress organizes her students (they're mostly of college age now) into teams of raiders who rip into an assortment of political problems, blasting corrupt officials in the school newspaper and on their own, student-run TV station; she chairs international conferences on subjects as disparate as child abuse and the legal rights of Indians. But she is also the suffering soul of the universe. Her blond hair streaming, her mouth drawn down, she's like those statues of Madonnas which are reported to be dripping, dripping, filling miraculous bucketfuls. Laughlin's Billy Jack, like the hero of TV's *Kung Fu* series (which was very possibly inspired by *Billy Jack*), is a spiritual man of peace spliced with the mythic cowboy who rights wrongs and rescues the innocent. A master of Hapkido (a form of karate), Billy Jack needs no weapons, since his body is a lethal instrument. (His mastery of the physical arts of the Mysterious East is inexplicably linked to his being half American Indian.) His stoic mask never lifts, except for a small, cruel smile — which says, Now let me entertain you — when he lets fly with those avenging feet, but he's into a wad of good causes, too. He doesn't take part in the students' activities that the Madonna calls their "scorching exposés," but his day-to-day life seems to have come out of newspaper headlines. A Vietnam veteran, Billy Jack is the man who blew the lid off My Lai (which is reënacted in a flashback). When the authorities will do nothing about an Indian family lost in a blizzard, he dispatches helicopters and ski patrols from the poshly equipped Freedom School; he's on the scene when the local hospital refuses to treat a critically ill survivor. And periodically he absents himself, returning to his Indian "grandfather," to take part in rites of purification involving peculiarly stolid visions, in which he turns blue and red, walks among serpents, is attacked by bats, and listens to doggerel wisdom supplied by Indian-maiden guides. The movie is abnormally literal-minded: it treats the Carlos Castaneda spinoffs in the same ploddingly unimaginative way it treats the Wounded Knee spinoff and assorted other outrages. The students' TV transmitter is bombed, and the campus is occupied by National Guardsmen. Billy Jack, who has killed a thieving, murderous banker with a kick to the throat, surrenders to the Guards in exchange for their promise to withdraw, but after he's taken away the Guardsmen proceed to a Kent State-style massacre, wounding or killing most of the principal characters. There is also a subplot involving a silent, battered child who has been mutilated by his father and has been brought back to speech (indeed, song) by the loving ministrations of young Teresa Laughlin (who also sings, and has been allowed to perform her own compositions). The pitiful crippled child is cuddling a sweet wittle wabbit when he's mowed down by a National Guardsman.

The Trial of Billy Jack is an orgy of victimization, with the audience put in the same position of helplessness as the Indians and students on the screen. Billy Jack appears to get spiritual strength from his ancestral religion, but the other Indians don't — they're like children waiting for him to lead them. And though the schoolmistress has been running her innovative school for many years and it is a world center of progressive thought, the students are an undisciplined rabble who can't act effectively or defend themselves. The Laughlins, with their spiritual union of suffering Christianity and zonked mysticism, have eternal Mom and Dad status. The Freedom School students are the helpless flock. Billy Jack must always appear magically to smite their enemies; the schoolmistress must inspire them with courage or berate them for their confusions. When, in reprisal for the work of her Nader's Raiders, the school is persecuted by the venal authorities, she becomes fretful and says mournfully to Billy Jack, "I suppose I should have cut back on the exposés," and I heard myself laughing aloud — and alone. Can I really have been the only one in the packed "public-preview" audience to find that funny? It's a Mama-star's view of a free, unstructured school: you turn them on and you turn them off, and whatever you do you're doing on their behalf.

Contradictions — or perhaps one should say conflicting fantasies — don't seem to bother the Laughlins; they are said to have been so dedicated to the education of their own children that they founded and ran the first Montessori school in Los Angeles, but their progressive Freedom School here has a squad of pulchritudinous drum majorettes which would be a credit to a Knights of Columbus convention. The box-office success of *Billy Jack* seems to have expanded the scope of the Laughlins' self-laudation. Gone are the ingenuous counterculture kids of *Billy Jack,* with their four-letter words; and gone, too, are the improvisatory sequences that made that picture likable despite its scrambled thinking. The creative powers of love and youthful innocence are claimed for these college students, but from the way they look, and the look of the production, that claim is about as convincing as in the Doris Day films of the fifties. Everything is expanded: the locations, the cast, the atrocities. When you see the swimming pool at the Freedom School, you half expect the students to plunge into a kaleidoscopic Busby Berkeley ballet. The school is huge, but Delores Taylor appears to be the only faculty member, and though the students are busy foiling the F.B.I. and the C.I.A., and saving the world, you never see one of them crack a book. All learning seems to come from that fount of tears Delores Taylor, whose anxiety about the students' lack of autonomy is expressed in the tiny sobs of a careworn, betrayed mother.

Is this maudlin epic a cynical exploitation of the widespread American sense of hopelessness? It even manages to cash in on the national letdown of the last month with some up-to-the-minute lines of dialogue about Ford's pardon of Nixon. Whether or not the Laughlins believe in what the film says doesn't have much to do with the validity of the message. (Seventh-Day Adventists generally seem honestly convinced of a lot of ideas that aren't any the more sound for being honestly held.) But when a film is a lump of message like this we can't help wanting to know if the moviemakers are on the level, or if it's a bald-faced big con, or if, maybe, they've turned themselves on in order to turn others on. The grandiosity of *The Trial of Billy Jack* suggests that it's a complete con, but it may not be fair to use lack of artistry as evidence of dishonesty. The film's shrewdly sloppy assertions, such as that the order to fire in My Lai came directly from Washington, and that our "two hundred and twenty million people are totally controlled by the votes of four or five men" on congressional committees, indicate that the Laughlins are more interested in the emotional force of their statements than in precision. Actors are notoriously intuitive about what the public will respond to, and the Laughlins may let their antennae do their thinking. The schoolmistress is often quite irrational, ranting at the students, and the movie doesn't seem to recognize how screwed up her thought processes are. Movie stars expect to be listened to, and a big box-office success can make them think that they have something big to say. The shots of Delores Taylor as the world-famous crusading schoolmistress giving interviews from a hospital bed are lighted and composed like sentimental chromos; she's framed like Jesus in the postcards that Americans buy in Mexico to send their hip friends. It's perfectly possible that Miss Taylor really feels she's taking the world's sorrows unto herself, and that Laughlin (he's a tiger at business promotion) feels he's going to save movies by aggressive selling, and at the same time sell peace. The stars may be too self-absorbed to be consciously dishonest, but that doesn't mean that they don't have a tough side.

Laughlin is said to be a charismatic personality — to be so convincing that he can turn people's heads around. The picture can claim to be "true," because almost all the social injustices it chronicles are based on actual events, but if you put together a collection of the sex crimes committed against women in the United States last year and had them all happen to one poor, unprotected girl whom no one would help, would it be an accurate reflection of the life of an American girl? Or would it be a masochistic jamboree that would intensify young girls' feelings of helplessness and might make them feel they needed a savior? In the movie, there is nothing in between the lecherous, greedy, brutal whiteys in power and the Freedom School contingent offering universal love as the only answer to the monolithic corruption of American life. You are asked to join the flock and become part of a holy crusade. When I fled the theater, a sizable part of the audience was still singing along with the movie's pounding rendition of "Give Peace a Chance." Billy Jack was still up there, with his strong arms enveloping the wounded schoolmistress's wheelchair.

The picture is really quite mad, yet the Laughlins may get by with it. They have announced that it's opening in a thousand theaters on the same day; this is probably another case of inflation, but even if there are only seven hundred, that's still a mighty big Pentecostal tub-thumping show. *The Trial of Billy Jack* might be deliberately shaped for the bedraggled remnants of the peace movement, already Jesus-freaked, still grieving and lost, but opportunism and charismatic-star thinking are very difficult to separate. The movies have sometimes told the story of show-business figures who became rabble-rousers, but the movies always placed them on the square, simplistic reactionary right. *The Trial of Billy Jack* is a realization of those cautionary tales except that the Laughlins are on the square, simplistic reactionary left. They've brought the worst of mass culture together with the worst of the counterculture.

COMPARED TO TOM LAUGHLIN, George C. Scott the pitchman is just your ordinary blowhard star. A full-page ad for his picture *The Savage Is Loose* reads:

> AN UNPRECEDENTED OFFER
> FROM GEORGE C. SCOTT:
>
> "I'm putting my picture
> in your hands . . .
> and my money
> on the line!"

One expected a little more tone from Scott. From the way he's been plugging this effort, you'd think he was going to announce special year-end discounts before the '75 models come in. *The Savage* crawls by in slightly under two hours, but they're about as agonizing as any two hours I've spent at the movies. Bad pictures usually have some divertissements — a twerpy bit player, a line or two of dialogue about wombats or spider sperm, a few bars of jazz. This goddam thing is set on a deserted jungle island, and there's nothing to occupy one's time but Scott; his wife, the intensely serious, hard-working Trish Van Devere (who back in *Where's Poppa?* seemed an amusing comedienne — comedienne hell, there isn't an intentional laugh in this whole movie); and their child, played by Lee H. Montgomery when he's little and, as the years stretch on, by John David Carson. Scott is such a powerful actor he didn't really need to load the dice for himself this way.

The family, shipwrecked, is stuck on the island, and so are we. Scott teaches his son meager — and dubious — lessons of survival (e.g., "The strong eat the weak in order to survive"), while Mrs. Scott wants to teach the boy about civilization. They battle over this for years, though there's no imaginable reason that the boy couldn't absorb both sets of lessons. They certainly have plenty of time to teach him, having no pressing social engagements. Eventually, the boy reaches puberty and wants sex with Mommy, and since he is now the Savage his father trained him to be, neither Scott nor Mrs. Scott can sit down and explain to him that boys back home often can't get sex, either, and have to make do. So the boy tries to kill big Daddy, and there are many long, stricken looks before the movie settles down to a repulsive finish, with Mommy deciding to make Sonny happy.

Scott has to take the rap for the crapehanger's direction and for not knowing better than to buy this script, but the scriptwriters, Max Ehrlich and Frank De Felitta, really ought to have their names inscribed in a special hall of infamy. When Sonny the Savage comes into the island shanty, having apparently been poring over Mommy's Bible like a Jesuit seminarian, and demands "Who was Cain's wife? It was Eve, his mother, wasn't it?" the running time of this movie is like a life sentence.

This primordial tale, steeped in the basics, might have been dreamed up by General Patton himself. It would be pleasant to believe that George C. Scott has a somewhat more flexible mind, but he seems to take the film's urgently stated banalities with the utmost seriousness, both onscreen and off. Can anyone who has seen him selling this movie on the talk shows doubt that he thinks the work of his hands is great? As an actor, Scott gives the impression of keen, total awareness: he seems excitingly smart. In this movie, he makes one wonder if that awareness of his adds up to more than angry obsession. In the opening shot of him, his glance fixes the camera, and at the end, with his patriarchal face coated in makeup to signify ruinous burns, he's still eating up the camera. He has done to himself what no other director has ever been able to do to him: he has made his vulture-faced, croaking-voiced magnetism ridiculous — he's a bore.

❖

THERE'S A LITTLE PICTURE KICKING AROUND called *The Groove Tube,* which was also produced and directed by its star, Ken Shapiro, who wrote a lot of it, too. It's mainly a series of innocently scatological skits lampooning TV, but at the end Shapiro does a lovely, flaked-out dance. Looking gracefully berserk in a pin-striped pink suit, he galumphs sidewise through rush-hour crowds along Park Avenue to the tune of "Just You, Just Me," and there's an entrancingly silly purity in his madness. That's what's missing from the big-star madness of *The Trial of Billy Jack* and *The Savage Is Loose.* The Laughlins and Scott come on like philosopher-kings bestowing their grandeur upon us. Their movie roles have gone to their heads and fermented.

[November 25, 1974]

Decadence

THE PEOPLE who reduced Los Angeles to rubble in *Earthquake* must have worked off a lot of self-hatred: you can practically feel their pleasure as the freeways shake, the skyscrapers crumble, and the Hollywood dam cracks. Nothing in L.A. looks as if it were meant to last anyway; it isn't a city you expect will sustain the ravages of time. When you peer up at glass houses perched on the edge of sandy cliffs, you feel that the people who put them there must have been stoned blind and giggling. Los Angeles, a mock paradise, is so perversely beautiful and so fundamentally unsatisfying that maybe just about everybody there secretly longs to see it come rattling down. In an earlier movie era, when a hurricane struck or a volcano erupted the scriptwriters always made it clear that the natural disaster was God's retribution for the sins of the trapped people. But who needs a reason to destroy L.A.? The city stands convicted in everyone's eyes. You go to *Earthquake* to see L.A. get it, and it really does. The picture is swill, but it isn't a cheat, like *Airport 1975*, which was cut-rate swill. *Earthquake* is a marathon of destruction effects, with stock characters spinning through. It isn't fun, exactly; it's ejaculatory, shoot-the-works filmmaking carried to the borderline of satire and stopping just short. Universal Pictures, which produced both, is a microcosm of the old Hollywood picture factories, streamlined for TV-age profits and totally cynical. These pieces of contemptuous entertainment might be the symbolic end point of the studio factory system, and there is something peculiarly gratifying about seeing the smoking ruins of the city that movies like this come from.

Earthquake is Universal's death wish for film art: these destruction orgies are the only way it knows to make money. The people who work on a picture like this are employees, and you can practically hear the executive producer, Jennings Lang, addressing them: There's no room for talent around here; this is belly-busting hard work, and if you want to make movies, this is what you'll do. And maybe the veteran director Mark Robson got into the spirit. He doesn't seem to want to leave any possible calamity effects for other epics to come, and as the bodies keep jumping, falling, or being shot, buried under walls and girders, or drowned, you begin to feel that he'd really like to kill off the whole cast, along with the thousands of extras. Stars like Richard Roundtree (playing a black, second-string Evel Knievel) disappear in the confusion without so much as a sendoff to eternity. Walter Matthau, serenely swacked throughout, may survive, but the picture doesn't care enough to make a point of it. A lot of well-known people are casually left in the debris.

The treatment of the film's two principal stars, Charlton Heston and Ava Gardner, could almost be the in joke of an industry that enjoys the idea of self-destructing. Gardner was one of the last of the women stars to make it on beauty alone. She never looked really happy in her movies; she wasn't quite there, but she never suggested that she was anywhere else, either. She had a dreamy, hurt quality, a generously modeled mouth, and faraway eyes. Maybe what turned people on was that her sensuality was developed but her personality wasn't. She was a rootless, beautiful stray, somehow incomplete but never ordinary, and just about impossible to dislike, since she was utterly without affectation. But to Universal she is just one more old star to beef up a picture's star power, and so she's cast as a tiresome bitch whose husband (Heston) is fed up with her. She looks blowzy and beat-out, and that could be fun if she were allowed to be blowzily good-natured, like the heroine of *Mogambo* twenty years later, but the script here harks back to those old movies in which a husband was justified in leaving his wife only if she was a jealous schemer who made his life hell. Ava Gardner might make a man's life hell out of indolence and spiritual absenteeism, but out of shrill stupidity? *Earthquake,* though, isn't the sort of project in which the moviemakers care whether the role fits the performer. They get what they want. Ava Gardner's name lifts *Earthquake* out of the Universal-action-picture category.

Charlton Heston is the all-time king of prestige epics. However, the repressed acting, granitic physique, and godlike-insurance-salesman manner that made him so inhumanly perfect for fifties spectacles have also destroyed his credibility. He's not a bad actor, but he's humorlessly unresilient. He can't open up: his muscles have his personality in an iron grip. When Universal uses him in its action-disaster pictures, which are all really the same movie, sold by the yard, he underacts grimly and he turns into a stereotype of himself. In *Earthquake* Heston plays a big-time engineer who married the daughter (Ava Gardner) of the boss (Lorne Greene) and has fallen in love with a young screen-starlet widow (Geneviève Bujold), and when the city is all shook up he dashes from one heroic deed to the next, rescuing, rescuing, rescuing. He's a dependably heroic joke. No one is expected to believe in the acts he performs: he's a wind-up hero-machine, and ingenious special effects and trick photography can go on around him. At the end, the movie has the embarrassing problem of what to do with him to avoid the catcalls of a jaded audience, so it cynically trashes him along with Gardner and most of Los Angeles.

Heston's fatigued heroism serves a function: it enables us to retain an amused, disbelieving view. So do the shopworn incidents (the chief seismologist being out of town and his young assistant's warnings not being heeded; the workers on the dam lacking the authority to act in emergencies) and a poorly directed mad-rapist subplot involving Marjoe Gortner as a supermarket manager who lusts after Victoria Principal. The B-picture rituals keep everything unreal, so that, despite the "Sensurround" (rumbling noises on the track which make you feel that the vibrations will bring down the theater plaster), nobody's likely to become involved enough to be upset. And you don't go to this picture for involvement; even those who claim to be scared by it can't mean that in any more than an ooh-scare-me-some-more way. You feel no pang when the various characters get hit: the whole point of a pop disaster epic is for the audience to relish the ingenious ways in which they're brought down. When a drowned man pours out of a flooded elevator, you're meant to gasp at the shock, not lament his passing. I was glad that Gabriel Dell (Roundtree's manager and sidekick) was spared, because his acting had a little snap, but there was really only one person I didn't want picked off—Geneviève Bujold, dressed whimsically, always in pinks — and that was because she had a funny scene at the beginning and I hoped (vainly) that she'd have another. She's a witty comedienne, with a sense of style, and she's able to use her French accent teasingly here (instead of fighting it, as she was forced to do in *Anne of the Thousand Days*). She brings a touch of class to *Earthquake* and lightens the load.

What we really know when we watch this movie is that the destruction orgy on the screen is only a jokey form of the destruction orgy behind the screen, and we begin to take a campy pleasure in seeing the big-name actors and the old plot situations — and the motion-picture capital itself — totaled. L.A. isn't just the city that movies like this come from, it's also the city that movies that mean something to us come from, but Universal's callousness brings out a Roman-circus mentality in the audience, because actually that's the only way to have a good time at this picture. People who wanted to enjoy the degradation of their old favorites used to have to go to the gossip rags, but why should the movie executives let parasites rob them of revenue? Now the movies build that function in. Though you may rather enjoy *Earthquake,* you're not likely to applaud it, because you know that it's decadence you're responding to. Nero was considered crazy, but if he'd sold tickets and made money out of his pyromaniac spectacle, would he be considered smart, like Jennings Lang and the other executives who make profits out of financing bowdlerizations of old movies while refusing to finance new ideas?

They're not unaware; they know what they're doing out there. That's why they're rushing to open these disaster epics before the end of the year, fearing the public's interest won't stretch beyond that. Lew R. Wasserman, the board chairman of M.C.A., Inc., Universal's parent company, who has just completed eight years as the chairman of the Association of Motion Picture and Television Producers, was honored earlier this month by his colleagues. Three hundred and fifty top people in the industry gathered to pay him homage, and Gordon Stulberg, the president of Twentieth Century-Fox, who presented Wasserman with a gift from the association — an 1861 Italian "megalatoscopio," to add to his collection of motion-picture antiques — ventured a high-level sick joke: "We've come a long way to *Earthquake* and *Towering Inferno.*" It is reported that the assembled guests laughed like mad.

❖

ANTOINE DE SAINT EXUPÉRY'S BOOK *The Little Prince* — a reverie about a pilot who crashes in the Sahara and is joined by an imaginative child from another planet — has a small, wan charm, but, translated from French into twenty-eight languages, it has been a worldwide best-seller, and many people have large sentimental attachments to it. The story's not easily definable essence appears to be a quest for purification: the Holy Grail as the holy self. The first of the modern mystic-quest books to become a pop hit, *The Little Prince* inspires the devotion that Tolkien and Hermann Hesse inspire, and that Pirsig's *Zen and the Art of Motorcycle Maintenance* may work up. The author-aviator's envisioning himself as a princely child too pure to go on living is a distillation of melancholy, and maybe this movie musical was doomed for the same reason that so many people are drawn to the book — that the material is so close to self-glorifying, masochistic mush. The ineffable may be effective in print and on records, but it isn't exactly the substance of musicals. Possibly something might have been made of the story if Alan Jay Lerner, who wrote the script, along with the lyrics for Frederick Loewe's music, had a more delicate feeling for poetic yearning, and if, possibly, he'd finessed the pilot's tenderness with cool contrasts. Could the pilot (Richard Kiley) have been made a more blasé man of his time (the book came out in 1943), and given a sense of irony about his infatuation with the innocent child in himself? However one approaches the material, though, there is nothing to link the man or the child (Steven Warner) to the Big Broadway Sound of the Lerner-Loewe score. The songs — Broadway Academic — might just get by, but the orchestration is clinically insane: Kiley can't sing alone in the desert without an instrumental warmup fit for De Mille's Crusaders meeting the entire Northwest Mounted Police. Might the picture have worked better with a light, Parisian-American jazz sound? The alienation is so thin that it needs some counterpoint, and a sense of unanswered questions and hidden layers under what is given. The poignant, forlorn Saint Exupéry tone could be realized on the screen only if the script had a sensuous verbal line. Instead, it blunts the story, and the putdown humor of the lyrics might have been conceived for Ethel Merman to whomp out. The director, Stanley Donen, with his background in dance, may have hoped to capture the story's rhapsodic blend of happiness and grief in choreographic terms, but what he worked from was an intractably graceless script. Worst of all, like most Lerner-Loewe musicals, this one lays on the songs and skimps dance possibilities. As in *Paint Your Wagon* and *On a Clear Day You Can See Forever*, there's no way for a director to bring Lerner's material together, and in this one the director is additionally handicapped by being given too little to work with. The theme of this movie — the loss of imagination — must have paralyzed Lerner.

Donen gets an almost magically bright, glossy look in some of the Sahara scenes — the vast expanses are absolutely clear, as if painted with the purest of pigments — and he has a gentle touch. The desert sequences, which feature the growing affection between the pilot and the boy, set an emotional mood, but this is broken when the Little Prince tells the aviator about his life on his own, cottage-size planet and his visits to other miniature planets, each the domain of one symbolic villain — a king (Joss Ackland), a businessman (Clive Revill), a historian (Victor Spinetti), a general (Graham Crowden). These episodes push dated lessons on the evils of civilization, and Donen's use of fish-eye lenses to bring the villains overpoweringly close doesn't improve matters. A few of the earthly sequences in which the child visits other contacts he has made stand out because their theatricality indicates the direction the movie probably should have gone in. One of the wittiest aspects of *The Wizard of Oz* was the way Bert Lahr's Cowardly Lion seemed to have the burlesque stage right under his paws, and here Bob Fosse, in his dancing role as a snake, suggests a low-down song-and-dance man from the night world of cooch shows. Hooded in a derby, with dark glasses and a cigarillo tongue, Fosse's got wit in his hissing, shifty pimp's menace; his number is a bit extended, but it's the high point of the movie. As a fox who wants to be tamed, reddish Gene Wilder has dewy-eyed thoughts about that old standby the wisdom of the heart, and his dance sequence seems too imitative of passages in *The Wizard of Oz,* but he triumphs over some of his material, and there's a wonderful shot of him, utterly still, staring at us, in a field of tall wheat.

Steven Warner is an English child who looks like Butch Jenkins come back in a tousled bouffant wig — with a wasting disease, however. He holds the screen affectingly and he seems right for the Saint Exupéry conception; he's very pale and puffy-eyed and lost-kitten frail. Fortunately, he has a lovely, slightly harsh voice — half Cockney, half gentleman. After so many movie-musical disappointments with Alan Jay Lerner's name high on the credits, I've begun to wonder if the energy he fails to put into his scripts goes into sheer hypnotism on the sets. His directors do things that they must know they shouldn't. Before seeing this movie, I would have sworn that Stanley Donen, a man of taste, was incapable of the film's final effect — a Heavenly Choir of bell-like laughter to signify that the Little Prince has ascended.

[December 2, 1974]

Dames

THE EAGERNESS OF THE AUDIENCE before the start of *Murder on the Orient Express* suggests that people are hungry for this sort of entertainment and so may take the picture to be what they want it to be. That is, a high-style, slightly camp version of an old-fashioned detective mystery. Nostalgia for old movies is beginning to be used as an element in new ones. With Ingrid Bergman, Lauren Bacall, and Wendy Hiller on hand, along with such comparative newcomers as Vanessa Redgrave, Rachel Roberts, and Jacqueline Bisset, and with the men's roles taken by Albert Finney, Sean Connery, John Gielgud, Richard Widmark, Tony Perkins, Michael York, Jean-Pierre Cassel, Martin Balsam, George Coulouris, Colin Blakely, and Denis Quilley, the cast has the allure of *Grand Hotel* and *Dinner at Eight,* and then some. The atmosphere is gallant and affectionate; the stars aren't asked to play seedy, routine roles. They're unmistakably stars here, and they're allowed to take over and strut. The great ladies of stage and screen gathered together are, perhaps not incidentally, a towering collection. There cannot have been so many tall women stars in one movie ever before; ranging from five feet seven to six feet, and outfitted in plush, costumy versions of thirties swank, they're like a parade of Billy Rose's giant showgirls turned into *grandes dames.* The men don't seem quite so *grand*; most of the male roles don't allow for peacocking. The picture, directed by Sidney Lumet from Paul Dehn's adaptation of an Agatha Christie antiquity — one of her Hercule Poirot series — is utterly inoffensive, and maybe it hardly matters that it isn't very good.

A percussively edited pre-title montage by that wizard of film shorthand Richard Williams covers the crime — a 1930 child-kidnapping on Long Island, much like that of the Lindbergh baby — that is the background for the murder to come, and then the movie (which never lives up to the passionate excitement of the prelude) opens in Istanbul, in 1935, with the arrival of the star-passengers, who board the luxury train. The film proper, shot by Geoffrey Unsworth, of *Cabaret,* reaches its visual peak in the railway station: that majestic, steaming train is so wistfully photogenic, and sighs of yearning and gluttony may be heard in the theater as champagne and oysters, fresh fruits and vegetables are hauled aboard. The picture promises to be a sumptuous spread, and so it is, but not as tasty as one had hoped. Unlike many highly advertised, all-star-cast movies of the past, this one doesn't have the famous people turning up in relays; they're all in the same railway carriage, interacting. Yet the sparks never fly. In the Poirot series, Agatha Christie didn't write characters; that doesn't much matter here, because the passengers are involved in impostures, which give the stars a chance to play some acting games. However, in this unusually static novel she also didn't provide for action, and that's a dampener.

Murder on the Orient Express isn't a jazzy film thriller, like Costa-Gavras's *The Sleeping Car Murder.* In *Orient Express,* a murder is committed at night in the compartment next to that of master detective Hercule Poirot (Albert Finney), and Agatha Christie's plot unravels in his interrogation of the passengers. In the Costa-Gavras film, the hunt for the killer had electricity: it wasn't just a search for the motive but a race to stop the assassin from killing others. In the Agatha Christie plot, there's no suggestion that anyone else is in danger, and after the murder has taken place the rest is deduction. The mystery was planned to be read: the clues by which Poirot trips up the guilty are mostly verbal, and there's nothing much Lumet or Dehn can do to dramatize his erudite fatuity. But perhaps they could have simulated a sense of action if the train had only kept going. When the train stops — it's snowbound throughout Poirot's investigation — the movie loses its impetus, and although the dining accommodations, the compartment furnishings, and the Art Deco woodwork that Tony Walton has designed may make many in the audience ache for splendors they can never know, still we're confined in a stalled train. It's all very handsome, but we're there a long time.

The film isn't directed for suspense (and there isn't any); you don't particularly care who committed the murder. *Orient Express* is strictly an actors' showcase, and some of the performers have such assured technique that you begin to grin each time you see them. Vanessa Redgrave plays a sunny, footloose charmer; it's a dashing, tickled-pink performance, all too brief. The other standouts are Rachel Roberts, witty as a tight-faced Fräulein with a dippy lewd gleam, and Ingrid Bergman, who, unexpectedly, makes one giggle at her portrait of a conscientious, goody-goody missionary. She looks pleased with herself, too, which adds to the amusement; she probably enjoyed the chance to parody her role in *The Inn of the Sixth Happiness.* Gielgud is so polished he shines, but I wish Wendy Hiller weren't buried in old-lady makeup — she's not someone to be hidden. There are only a few obtrusively disappointing performances: Lauren Bacall seems out of her league (when she's acting tiresome, she is tiresome), and Tony Perkins has more tics and neurasthenic smiles than his role (too feyly inbred to start with) can sustain. An editor could cure most of what's wrong with him; one of the side effects of Lumet's generosity toward actors is that he lets their performances run on destructively. The central player, Finney, appears to have decided to be literally faithful to Agatha Christie's Hercule Poirot. His bogus manner reeks of broad impersonation, and he's as unbearably adorable as Poirot is in the novels. At the start, Finney's makeup, and his emphatic (presumably Belgian) accent are off-putting, though he gets quite funny later on (especially in his interrogation of Bergman) and wins the audience over. The film ambles when it should prance, and a key sequence — the events during the night of the murder as Poirot experiences them — is mussy. The picture as a whole lacks that zest for style which one glimpses in some of the performances; the climax — a flashback to the murder itself — has no acting tone, and it's so disheveled it looks like the stateroom sequence in *A Night at the Opera.* Still, no idols are smashed, and there's a lovely farewell scene in which the stars, drinking a toast, seem to be taking their bows.

THE THEORIES OF R. D. LAING, the poet of schizophrenic despair, have such theatrical flash that they must have hit John Cassavetes smack in the eye. His new film, *A Woman Under the Influence,* is the work of a disciple: it's a didactic illustration of Laing's vision of insanity, with Gena Rowlands as Mabel Longhetti, the scapegoat of a repressive society that defines itself as normal. The core of the film is a romanticized conception of insanity, allied with the ancient sentimental mythology of madness centering on the holy fool and with the mythology about why Christ was crucified. The picture is based on the idea that the crazy person is endowed with a clarity of vision that the warped society can't tolerate, and so is persecuted. Laing's approach is a natural for movies at this time, since the view that society is insane has so much to recommend it that people may easily fall for the next reversal that those whom this society judges insane are the truly sane. Possibly it can be a healing step for some people to let themselves go, but Laing — in some ways a super-smooth snake-oil salesman — toys with the rakish notion that going crazy is a sign of health.

Laing has given modern weight to a persistent, emotionally appealing myth, and his books, such as the campus favorite *The Politics of Experience,* tell counterculture readers what they are already disposed to believe. For those who feel blocked or ineffectual, the view that the good are the victims of the family and of society's other authoritarian structures can be wonderfully satisfying. It's the furthest extension of the line taken by William Inge and Elia Kazan in the 1961 *Splendor in the Grass.* In that simplistic Freudian film, the adults, who had lost the ability to love, frustrated their children; the adolescents (Warren Beatty and Natalie Wood) weren't allowed to consummate their passion, and as a result she lost him and went crazy. By the end of the sixties, the division of the world into bullies and victims had become an article of faith for much of the counterculture, with its emblematic figure James Dean, the misunderstood kid.

Whether or not Laing is right in seeing the irrational pressures of family and society as the cause of schizophrenia, his poetic myth that the mad are the pure ones — the ones with true vision — is a piece of seductive nonsense. It's this nonsense that has made Laing a messiah to the drug culture; some acolytes have felt they had to take acid to go fearlessly mad and be worthy of him. In *A Woman Under the Influence* the schizophrenic heroine is the misunderstood kid as the ultimate Friendless One. Mabel Longhetti is basically spontaneous and joyful, but only children respond to her on her own terms. Every impulse she has is denied, and she's stampeded into madness by her violently irascible husband, Nick (Peter Falk). Mabel is as helplessly wronged as a battered baby. This frantic, wilted heroine is a Los Angeles housewife and the mother of three; a big, beautiful blonde in bright, short chemises, she darts about like an anxious speed freak, her manic gestures dissociated and jerky, her face changing rapidly from foolish smiles to uncontrollable punch-drunk agonies. After her husband and his harpy mother (Katherine Cassavetes) have had her locked away for six months of shock therapy, Mabel returns, chastened, a fearful, hurt-animal look on her face, and, in case we missed the point of the process by which society drove her mad, Cassavetes now provides a quick recapitulation by having the key people in her life gather to welcome her home, prepared to do her in all over again.

It's never suggested that there's something wrong with Mabel for not getting herself together. Others reduce her to pulp; she's not a participant in her own destruction. The romantic view of insanity is a perfect subject for Cassavetes to muck around with. Yet even in this season when victimization is the hottest thing in the movie market this scapegoat heroine doesn't do a damn thing for him. He's always on the verge of hitting the big time, but his writing and directing are grueling, and he swathes his popular ideas in so many wet blankets that he is taken seriously — and flops. In *Faces* and *Husbands* Cassavetes might almost have been working his way up to Laing; his people were already desolate, hanging on to marriages that made no sense to them because nothing else did, either. And his last film, *Minnie and Moskowitz,* a screwball comedy about maimed lovers — a loudmouth parking-lot attendant (Seymour Cassel), irrepressibly life-loving, and a bruised, beautiful woman (Gena Rowlands) — could almost have been a garbled sketch for *A Woman Under the Influence.*

Mabel, however, is more (and less) than a character, since she's a totally sympathetic character: she's a symbolic victim, and a marriage victim especially. Cassavetes has hooked Laing on to his own specialty — the miseries of sexual union. The Laingian schizophrenic scapegoat is, typically, one who suffers the irrationality of the mother and father, and this was the pattern in the English film *Family Life* — called *Wednesday's Child* here — which was directed by Kenneth Loach from a screenplay by David Mercer. Its heroine is a passive, weak-willed young girl who can't defend herself against her inhibited, respectability-centered parents and becomes schizophrenic. Sent to a hospital, she is at first treated in a relaxed, informal experimental ward run by a Laingian, and it appears that she needs to learn to stand up to her family — a wondrously simple cure for schizophrenia. But the Laingian is dismissed, and she is given shock treatment and is left, at the end, a vegetable. The Loach film was a far more obvious case of special pleading for Laing than *A Woman Under the Influence* is, but it was also simpler and made better sense. In the Cassavetes film, the husband, Nick, seems to be taking a bum rap, since it's hard to believe that Mabel would be so easy to cut down if she weren't already shattered. (A child can be without recourse, but a wife?) Both pictures suffer from a single-level, one-sided approach: the authoritarians who do the damage are despicable, comic-strip conformists; the good people are liberal, open, natural. It's generation-gap psychology.

Like all Cassavetes' films, *A Woman Under the Influence* is a tribute to the depth of feelings that people can't express. As a filmmaker, he himself has a muffled quality: his scenes are often unshaped and so rudderless that the meanings don't emerge. This time, he abandons his handsome, grainy simulated-*cinéma-vérité* style. The shots are planned to make visual points that bear out the thesis (though there are also arbitrary, ornamental angles, and vistas that make a workingman's cramped house big as a palace). But once again he has made a murky, ragmop movie. Actually, he doesn't know how to dramatize, and one can try to make a virtue of this for only so long. When the actors in his films strike off each other, there are tentative, flickering moods that one doesn't get in other kinds of movies, but these godsends are widely spaced, and it's a desert in between. He still prolongs shots to the point of embarrassment (and beyond). He does it deliberately, all right, but to what purpose? Acute discomfort sets in, and though some in the audience* will once again accept what is going on as raw, anguishing truth, most people will — rightly, I think — take their embarrassment as evidence of Cassavetes' self-righteous ineptitude.

His special talent — it links his work to Pinter's — is for showing intense suffering from nameless causes; Cassavetes and Pinter both give us an actor's view of human misery. It comes out as metaphysical realism: we see the tensions and the power plays but never know the why of anything. Laing provides Cassavetes with an answer. However, his taking over Laing's views has cost him something: he didn't have comic-strip villains — or villains at all — before he swallowed Laing. In his earlier films, he commiserated with those who couldn't make contact except by brutalizing each other. Their drunken hostilities and blighted, repetitious conversations weren't held against them; their insensitivities were proof of the emptiness they felt. He used to love violent characters and outbursts of rage. Now the actors, no longer given their heads, are merely figures in a diagram. When Nick yells, the picture's only concern is the effect on Mabel. Cassavetes has gone so far over to the most literal-minded Laing position that the society he shows us is implausible — a society of boorish people with such limited awareness that they're barely human. Since they are principally blue-collar workers, it looks as if he thought that hardhats were retarded.

Mabel Longhetti is bombed out because she has always wanted to please everyone, so she can be considered one more victim-heroine for "women's liberation" — but only by women's liberationists who are willing to accept textbook spinoffs as art. The Junoesque Gena Rowlands (Mrs. Cassavetes) is a prodigious actress, and she never lets go of the character. Now, at an indeterminate age when her beauty has deepened beyond ingénue roles, Rowlands can look old or young, and shades of expression transform Mabel Longhetti from a radiantly flirtatious beauty into a sad, sagging neighborhood drunk. Rowlands externalizes schizophrenic dissolution. Mabel fragments before our eyes: a three-ring circus might be taking place in her face. Rowlands' performance is enough for half a dozen tours de force, a whole row of Oscars — it's exhausting. Conceivably, she's a great actress, but nothing she does is memorable, because she does so much. It's the most transient big performance I've ever seen.

Mabel tries to slash her wrist, and Nick puts a Band-Aid on the cut: the idiot symbolism may make you want to hoot, but this two-hour-and-thirty-five-minute film leaves you too groggy to do more than moan.

*As it turned out, more of them than I anticipated.

Details that are meant to establish the pathological nature of the people around Mabel, and so show her isolation, become instead limp, false moments. We often can't tell whether the characters are meant to be unconscious of what they're doing or whether it's Cassavetes who's unconscious. Mabel's children keep murmuring that they love her, and there are no clues to how to decipher this refrain. Are the children coddling her — reversing roles and treating her like a child in need of reassurance? Or are they meant to be as unashamedly loving as she is? And what are we to make of Nick the pulper's constant assertions of love? The movie is entirely tendentious; it's all planned, yet it isn't thought out. I get the sense that Cassavetes has incorporated Laing, undigested, into his own morose view of the human condition, and that he somehow thinks that Nick and Mabel really love each other and that *A Woman Under the Influence* is a tragic love story.

[December 9, 1974]

Fathers and Sons

AT THE CLOSE OF *The Godfather*, Michael Corleone has consolidated his power by a series of murders and has earned the crown his dead father, Don Vito, handed him. In the last shot, Michael — his eyes clouded — assures his wife, Kay, that he is not responsible for the murder of his sister's husband. The door closes Kay out while he receives the homage of subordinates, and if she doesn't know that he lied, it can only be because she doesn't want to. *The Godfather, Part II* begins where the first film ended: before the titles there is a view behind that door. The new king stands in the dark, his face lusterless and dispassionate as his hand is being kissed. The familiar *Godfather* waltz theme is heard in an ambiguous, melancholy tone. Is it our imagination, or is Michael's face starting to rot? The dramatic charge of that moment is Shakespearean. The waltz is faintly, chillingly ominous.

By a single image, Francis Ford Coppola has plunged us back into the sensuality and terror of the first film. And, with the relentlessness of a master, he goes farther and farther. The daring of Part II is that it enlarges the scope and deepens the meaning of the first film; *The Godfa-*

ther was the greatest gangster picture ever made, and had metaphorical overtones that took it far beyond the gangster genre. In Part II, the wider themes are no longer merely implied. The second film shows the consequences of the actions in the first; it's all one movie, in two great big pieces, and it comes together in your head while you watch. Coppola might almost have a pact with the audience; we're already so engrossed in the Corleones that now he can go on to give us a more interior view of the characters at the same time that he shows their spreading social influence. The completed work is an epic about the seeds of destruction that the immigrants brought to the new land, with Sicilians, Wasps, and Jews separate socially but joined together in crime and political bribery. This is a bicentennial picture that doesn't insult the intelligence. It's an epic vision of the corruption of America.

After the titles, the action begins in Sicily in 1901, with the funeral procession of Michael's murdered grandfather, and we realize that the plaintive tone that was so unsettling in the opening music is linked to funeral drums and to a line of mourning women. The rot in Michael's face starts here, in his legacy from his father. The silent nine-year-old boy walking behind the coffin with his strong, grief-hardened mother is Vito, who will become the Don, the Godfather (the role played in the first film by Marlon Brando). Shots are heard, the procession breaks up — Vito's older brother has just been killed. And in a few minutes Vito, his mother dead, too, is running for his life. The waltz is heard again, still poignant but with a note of exaltation, as a ship with the wide-eyed child among the hordes in steerage passes the Statue of Liberty. The sallow, skinny boy has an almost frightening look of guarded intelligence; not understanding a word of English, he makes no sound until he's all alone, quarantined with smallpox on Ellis Island. Then, in his hospital cell, he looks out the barred window and, in a thin, childish soprano, sings a Sicilian song. As he sings, we see the superimposed face of another dark-eyed little boy, a shining princeling in white with a pretty flower-face — Michael's son, the little boy who had been playing in the garden with the old Don Vito when he died. It is the rich princeling's First Communion, and there is a lavish celebration at the Corleone estate on the shore of Lake Tahoe. The year is 1958, and the surviving members of the Corleone family, whose base of operations is now in Nevada, are gathered for the occasion.

The first film covered the period from 1945 to the mid-fifties. Part II, contrasting the early manhood of Vito (played by Robert De Niro) with the life of Michael, his inheritor (Al Pacino), spans almost seventy years. We saw only the middle of the story in the first film; now we have the beginning and the end. Structurally, the completed work is nothing less than the rise and decay of an American dynasty of unofficial rulers.

Vito rises and becomes a respected man while his son Michael, the young king, rots before our eyes, and there is something about actually seeing the generations of a family in counterpoint that is emotionally overpowering. It's as if the movie satisfied an impossible yet basic human desire to see what our parents were like before we were born and to see what they did that affected what we became — not to hear about it, or to read about it, as we can in novels, but actually to see it. It really is like the past recaptured. We see the characters at different points in their lives, with every scene sharpening our perception of them; at one moment Michael embraces his young son, at another Vito cradles young Michael in his arms. The whole picture is informed with such a complex sense of the intermingling of good and evil — and of the inability to foresee the effects of our love upon our children — that it may be the most passionately felt epic ever made in this country.

Throughout the three hours and twenty minutes of Part II, there are so many moments of epiphany — mysterious, reverberant images, such as the small Vito singing in his cell — that one scarcely has the emotional resources to deal with the experience of this film. Twice, I almost cried out at acts of violence that De Niro's Vito committed. I didn't look away from the images, as I sometimes do at routine action pictures. I wanted to see the worst; there is a powerful need to see it. You need these moments as you need the terrible climaxes in a Tolstoy novel. A great novelist does not spare our feelings (as the historical romancer does); he intensifies them, and so does Coppola. On the screen, the speed of the climaxes and their vividness make them almost unbearably wounding.

Much of the material about Don Vito's early life which appears in Part II was in the Mario Puzo book and was left out of the first movie, but the real fecundity of Puzo's mind shows in the way this new film can take his characters further along and can expand (and, in a few cases, alter) the implications of the book. Puzo didn't write the novel he probably could have written, but there was a Promethean spark in his trash, and Coppola has written the novel it might have been. However, this second film (the script is again by Coppola and Puzo) doesn't appear to derive from the book as much as from what Coppola learned while he was making the first. In Part II, he has had the opportunity to do what he was prevented from doing before, and he's been able to develop what he didn't know about his characters and themes until after he'd made the first picture. He has also been able to balance the material. Many people who saw *The Godfather* developed a romantic identification with the Corleones; they longed for the feeling of protection that Don Vito conferred on his loving family. Now that the full story has been told, you'd have to have an insensitivity bordering on moral idiocy to think that the Corleones live a wonderful life, which you'd like to be part of.

The violence in this film never doesn't bother us — it's never just a kick. For a movie director, Coppola has an unusual interest in ideas and in the texture of feeling and thought. This wasn't always apparent in the first film, because the melodramatic suspense was so strong that one's motor responses demanded the resolution of tension (as in the restaurant scene, when one's heart almost stopped in the few seconds before Michael pulled out the gun and fired). But this time Coppola controls our emotional responses so that the horror seeps through everything and no action provides a melodramatic release. Within a scene Coppola is controlled and unhurried, yet he has a gift for igniting narrative, and the exploding effects keep accumulating. About midway, I began to feel that the film was expanding in my head like a soft bullet.

The casting is so close to flawless that we can feel the family connections, and there are times when one could swear that Michael's brother Fredo (John Cazale), as he ages, is beginning to look like a weak version of his father, because we see Marlon Brando in the wide forehead and receding hair. Brando is not on the screen this time, but he persists in his sons, Fredo and Michael, and Brando's character is extended by our seeing how it was formed. As Vito, Robert De Niro amply convinces one that he has it in him to become the old man that Brando was. It's not that he looks exactly like Brando but that he has Brando's wary soul, and so we can easily imagine the body changing with the years. It is much like seeing a photograph of one's own dead father when he was a strapping young man; the burning spirit we see in his face spooks us, because of our knowledge of what he was at the end. In De Niro's case, the young man's face is fired by a secret pride. His gesture as he refuses the gift of a box of groceries is beautifully expressive and has the added wonder of suggesting Brando, and not from the outside but from the inside. Even the soft, cracked Brando-like voice seems to come from the inside. When De Niro closes his eyes to blot out something insupportable, the reflex is like a presentiment of the old man's reflexes. There is such a continuity of soul between the child on the ship, De Niro's slight, ironic smile as a cowardly landlord tries to appease him, and Brando, the old man who died happy in the sun, that although Vito is a subsidiary character in terms of actual time on the screen, this second film, like the first, is imbued with his presence.

De Niro is right to be playing the young Brando because he has the physical audacity, the grace, and the instinct to become a great actor — perhaps as great as Brando. In *Mean Streets,* he was a wild, reckless kid who flaunted his being out of control; here he's a man who holds himself in — and he's just as transfixing. Vito came to America to survive. He brought nothing with him but a background of violence, and when he believes the only choice is between knuckling under to the gangsters who terrorize the poor in Little Italy — just as gangsters terrorized his family in Sicily — and using a gun, he chooses the gun. In his terms, it's a simple matter of self-preservation, and he achieves his manhood when he becomes a killer. Vito has a feudal code of honor. To the Italians who treat him with respect he's a folk hero — a Robin Hood you can come to in times of trouble. No matter what he does, he believes he's a man of principle, and he's wrapped in dignity. The child's silence is carried forward in the adult. De Niro's performance is so subtle that when he speaks in the Sicilian dialect he learned for the role he speaks easily, but he is cautious in English and speaks very clearly and precisely. For a man of Vito's character who doesn't know the language well, precision is important — sloppy talk would be unthinkable. Like Brando's Vito, De Niro's has a reserve that can never be breached. Vito is so secure in the knowledge of how dangerous he is that his courtliness is no more or less than noblesse oblige.

The physical contrasts between De Niro's characterization and Pacino's give an almost tactile dimension to the theme. Driving through the streets of Batista's Havana, which he's buying into — buying a piece of the government — Michael sees the children begging, and he knows what he is: he's a predator on human weakness. And that's exactly what he looks like. He wears silvery-gray nubby-silk suits over a soft, amorphous body; he's hidden under the price tag. The burden of power sits on him like a sickness; his expression is sullen and withdrawn. He didn't have to be what he is: he knew there were other possibilities, and he chose to become a killer out of family loyalty. Here in Part II he is a disconsolate man, whose only attachment is to his children; he can never go back to the time before that moment in the restaurant when he shot his father's enemies. In the first film, we saw Don Vito weep when he learned that it was Michael who had done the killing; Michael's act, which preserved the family's power, destroyed his own life. Don Vito had recoiled from the sordid drug traffic, but since crime is the most competitive business of all (the quality of what you're peddling not being a conspicuous factor), Michael, the modernist, recoils from nothing; the empire that he runs from Nevada has few links with his young father's Robin Hood days. It's only inside himself that Michael recoils. His tense, flaccid face hovers over the movie; he's the man in power, trying to control the lives around him and feeling empty and betrayed. He's like a depressed Brando.

There are times when Pacino's moodiness isn't particularly eloquent, and when Michael asks his mother (Morgana King) how his father felt deep down in his heart the question doesn't have enough urgency. However, Pacino does something very difficult: he gives an almost immobile performance. Michael's attempt to be the man his father was has aged him, and he can't conceal the ugliness of the calculations that his father's ceremonial manner masked. His father had a domestic life that was a sanctuary, but Michael has no sanctuary. He cannot maintain the traditional division of home and business, and so the light and dark contrasts are not as sharp as in the first picture. His wife knows he lied to her, just as he lies to a Senate investigating committee, and the darkness of his business dealings has invaded his home. Part II has the same mythic and operatic visual scheme as the first; once again the cinematographer is Gordon Willis. Visually the film is, however, far more complexly beautiful than the first, just as it's thematically richer, more shadowed, more full. Willis's workmanship has developed, like Coppola's; even the sequences in the sunlight have deep tones — elegiac yet lyrical, as in *The Conformist,* and always serving the narrative, as the Nino Rota score also does.

Talia Shire had a very sure touch in her wedding scenes in the first film; her Connie was like a Pier Angeli with a less fragile, bolder nature — a spoiled princess. Now, tight with anger, dependent on her brother Michael, who killed her husband, Connie behaves self-destructively. She once had a dream wedding; now she hooks up with gigolo playboys. (Troy Donahue is her newest husband.) Talia Shire has such beauty and strength that she commands attention. It's possible that she didn't impose herself more strongly in the first film because Coppola, through a kind of reverse nepotism (Miss Shire is his sister), deëmphasized her role and didn't give her many closeups, but this time — pinched, strident, whory — she comes through as a stunningly controlled actress. Kay (Diane Keaton), Michael's New England-born wife, balks at becoming the acquiescent woman he requires, so he shows her what his protection means. It's dependent on absolute fealty. Any challenge or betrayal and you're dead — for men, that is. Women are so subservient they're not considered dangerous enough to kill — that's about the extent of Mafioso chivalry. The male-female relationships are worked out with a Jacobean splendor that goes far beyond one's expectations.

There must be more brilliant strokes of casting here (including the use of a batch of Hollywood notables — Phil Feldman, Roger Corman, and William Bowers — as United States senators), and more first-rate acting in small parts, than in any other American movie. An important new character, Hyman Roth, a Meyer Lansky-like businessman-gangster, as full of cant and fake wisdom as a fund-raising rabbi, is played with smooth conviction by the near-legendary Lee Strasberg. Even his breath control is impeccable: when Roth talks too much and gets more excited than he should, his talk ends with a sound of exertion from his chest. As another new major character, Frankie Pentangeli, an old-timer in the rackets who wants things to be as they were when Don Vito was in his heyday, Michael V. Gazzo (the playwright-actor) gives an intensely likable performance that adds flavor to the picture. His Pentangeli has the capacity for enjoying life, unlike Michael and the anonymous-looking high-echelon hoods who surround him. As the bland, despicably loyal Tom Hagen, more square-faced and sturdy now, Robert Duvall, a powerful recessive actor, is practically a genius at keeping himself in the background; and Richard Bright as Al Neri, one of Michael's henchmen, runs him a close second.

Coppola's approach is openhanded: he doesn't force the situations. He puts the material up there, and we read the screen for ourselves. But in a few places, such as in the double-crossing maneuvers of Michael Corleone and Hyman Roth, his partner in the Cuban venture, it hasn't been made readable enough. There's a slight confusion for the audience in the sequences dealing with Roth's bogus attempt on the life of Pentangeli, and the staging is a little flatfooted in the scenes in which the Corleone assassin first eliminates Roth's bodyguard and then goes to kill Roth. Also, it's a disadvantage that the frame-up of Senator Geary (which is very poorly staged, with more gory views of a murdered girl than are necessary) comes so long after the provocation for it. Everywhere else, the contrapuntal cutting is beautifully right, but the pieces of the Senator Geary story seem too slackly spaced apart. (The casting of G. D. Spradlin in the role is a juicy bit of satire; he looks and acts like a synthesis of several of our worst senators.) These small flaws are not failures of intelligence; they're faults in the storytelling, and there are a few abrupt transitions, indicating unplanned last-minute cuts. There may be too many scenes of plotting heads, and at times one wishes the sequences to be more fully developed. One never wants less of the characters; one always wants more — particularly of Vito in the 1917 period, which is recreated in a way that makes movies once again seem a miraculous medium.

This film wouldn't have been made if the first hadn't been a hit — and the first was made because the Paramount executives expected it to be an ordinary gangster shoot-'em-up. When you see this new picture, you wonder how Coppola won the fights. Maybe the answer is that they knew they couldn't make it without him. After you see it, you feel they can't make *any* picture without him. He directs with supreme confidence. Coppola is the inheritor of the traditions of the novel, the theater, and — especially — opera and movies. The sensibility at work in this film is that of a major artist. We're not used to it: how many screen artists get the chance to work in the epic form, and who has been able to seize the power to compose a modern American epic? And who else, when he got the chance and the power, would have proceeded with the absolute conviction that he'd make the film the way it should be made? In movies, that's the inner voice of the authentic hero.

[December 23, 1974]

A Magnetic Blur

GENE WILDER stares at the world with nearsighted, pale-blue-eyed wonder; he was born with a comic's flyblown wig and the look of a reddish creature from outer space. His features aren't distinct; his personality lacks definition. His whole appearance is so fuzzy and weak he's like mist on the lens. Yet since his first screen appearance, as the mortician in *Bonnie and Clyde,* he's made his presence felt each time. He's a magnetic blur. It's easy to imagine him as a frizzy-haired fiddler-clown in a college production of *A Midsummer Night's Dream,* until he slides over into that hysteria which is his dazzling specialty. As a hysteric, he's funnier even than Peter Sellers. For Sellers, hysteria is just one more weapon in his comic arsenal — his hysteria mocks hysteria — but Wilder's hysteria seems perfectly natural. You never question what's driving him to it; his fits are lucid and total. They take him into a different dimension — he delivers what Harpo promised.

Wilder is clearly an actor who can play serious roles as well as comic ones, and he's a superb technician. Yet he also seems an inspired original, as peculiarly, elusively demented in his own way as the greatest original of them all, Jonathan Winters. You can't tell what makes clowns like this funny. The sources of their humor are split off from the technical effects they produce. (With Chaplin, there's a unity between source and technique — which isn't necessarily preferable.) Like Winters, Wilder taps a private madness. In *Start the Revolution Without Me,* he played a French nobleman who was offering a tidbit to the falcon on his wrist when his wife pointed out that the falcon was dead. With the calm of the utterly insane, he said to her, "Repeat that." Reality is what Wilder's weak stare doesn't take in.

Wilder plays the title role in Mel Brooks's *Young Frankenstein,* and in the first fifteen minutes or so — especially in a medical experiment on skinny, excruciatingly vulnerable Liam Dunn — he hits a new kind of controlled maniacal peak. The movie doesn't take Wilder beyond that early high, but it doesn't need to. It's a silly, zizzy picture — a farce-parody of Hollywood's mad-scientist-trying-to-be-God pictures, with Wilder as the old Baron Frankenstein's grandson, an American professor of neurology, who takes a trip to the family castle in Transylvania. Peter Boyle is the Frankenstein monster, and Madeline Kahn is the professor's plastic-woman fiancée, who becomes the monster's bride. It isn't a dialogue comedy; it's visceral and lower. It's what used to be called a crazy comedy, and there hasn't been this kind of craziness on the screen in years. It's a film to go to when your rhythm is slowed down and you're too tired to think. You can't bring anything to it (Brooks' timing is too obvious for that); you have to let it do everything for you, because that's the only way it works. It has some of the obviousness of *Abbott & Costello Meet Frankenstein,* and if you go expecting too much it could seem like kids' stuff—which, of course, it is, but it's very funny kids' stuff, the kind that made pictures like *Kentucky Moonshine* and *Murder, He Says* into nutbrain classics. You can go to see it when you can barely keep your eyes open, and come out feeling relaxed and recharged.

Wilder wrote the screenplay with Brooks, and he has a healthy respect for his own star abilities. Confidence seems to be making him better-looking with each picture; this time he wears a romantic, droopy mustache, and in full-face, with his eyes outlined and his long chin prominent, he gives a vain, John Barrymore-ish dash to the role. I could have done with less of his pixie hunchback assistant Igor — the English comic, Marty Feldman, who's done up like Barrymore as Richard III. The camera picks up the glints of Wilder's madness; Feldman projects to the gallery. He's too consciously zany; he's funny at times (and he uses a Groucho turn of phrase like a shiv), but he's heavy-spirited and cunning, in the Anthony Newley manner. He emphasizes the picture's worst defect: the director tends to repeat — and exhaust — effects. In the opening sequences, Wilder does a startling spinoff of Sellers' performance as Dr. Strangelove, but then, later on, Kenneth Mars, the Nazi playwright in *The Producers* and the Transylvania police inspector here — equipped with an artificial arm, like Lionel Atwill in the role in the old days — does a full-dress variation on Strangelove. Like Feldman, Mars seems meant to be funnier than he is; his impenetrable accent is one of those Brooks ideas that don't pan out. Sometimes Brooks appears to think he can force something to be a scream if he pounds away at it. Cloris Leachman makes a magnificent entrance as the castle housekeeper, but then, having a one-and-a-half-gag role, she has nothing left to do but make faces. However, Peter Boyle underplays smoothly; he suggests a puckish cutup's spirit inside his monster's bulk, and he comes through with a great sick-joke strangled voice in a musical number that shows what Brooks can do when his instinct is really working. He can make you laugh helplessly.

The picture was made in black-and-white, which holds it visually close to the pictures it takes off from, and Brooks keeps the setups simple. The details are reassuring: there's a little more Transylvanian ground fog than you've ever seen before, the laboratory machines give off enough sparks to let us know that's their only function, and the ingénue (Teri Garr, as Frankenstein's laboratory assistant) is the essence of washed-out B-movie starlet. The style of the picture is controlled excess, and the whole thing is remarkably consistent in tone, considering that it ranges from unfunny hamming (the medical student at the beginning) to a masterly bit contributed by Gene Hackman as a bearded blind man. (Hackman's inflections are so spectacularly assured I thought there was a famous comic hidden under the beard until I recognized his voice.) The movie works because it has the Mary Shelley story to lean on: we know that the monster will be created and will get loose. And Brooks makes a leap up as a director because, although the comedy doesn't build, he carries the story through. Some directors don't need a unifying story, but Brooks has always got lost without one. (He had a story in *The Twelve Chairs,* but he didn't have the jokes.) Staying with the story, Brooks even has a satisfying windup, which makes this just about the only comedy of recent years that doesn't collapse. Best of all, *Young Frankenstein* doesn't try to be boffola, like Brooks' last picture, *Blazing Saddles,* yet it has that picture's prime attractions: Wilder and Madeline Kahn. When she parodied Marlene Dietrich in *Blazing Saddles,* it wasn't the usual Dietrich imitation, because she was also parodying herself. Madeline Kahn has an extra dimension of sexiness; it's almost like what Mae West had — she's flirtatious in a self-knowing way. And everything that's wrong about her is sexy. You look at her and think, What a beautiful translucent skin on such a big jaw; what a statuesque hourglass figure, especially where the sand has slipped. She's so self-knowingly lascivious that she convinces you she really digs the monster. Madeline Kahn is funny and enticing because she's soaked in passion; when you look at her, you see a water bed at just the right temperature.

IN THE NEW DISASTER BLOCKBUSTER *The Towering Inferno,* each scene of a person horribly in flames is presented as a feat for our delectation. The picture practically stops for us to say, "Yummy, that's a good one!" These incendiary deaths, plus the falls from high up in the hundred-and-thirty-eight-floor tallest skyscraper in the world, are, in fact, the film's only feats, the plot and characters being retreads from the producer Irwin Allen's earlier *Poseidon Adventure.* What was left out this time was the hokey fun. When a picture has any kind of entertainment in it, viewers don't much care about credibility, but when it isn't entertaining we do. And when a turkey bores us and insults our intelligence for close to three hours, it shouldn't preen itself on its own morality. *Inferno* knocks off some two hundred people as realistically as it possibly can and then tells us that we must plan future buildings more carefully, with the fire chief (embodied here by Steve McQueen) working in collaboration with the architect (in this case, Paul Newman, who appears to be also the only engineer — in fact, the only person involved in the building's construction or operation above the level of janitor).

The film asks us to believe that until the skyscraper's official opening day the busy Newman never noticed that the contractors and subcontractors had cheated on just about everything. It asks us to believe that this tallest building in the world — a golden glass tower that's a miracle of flimsiness, as it turns out — would have been set down in San Francisco, of all places. It asks us to accept Richard Chamberlain as a rat-fink electrical contractor (one has visions of him negotiating with the electricians' local) and as the city's leading roué (this gives one visions, too). But then this is a movie in which Fred Astaire, as escort to Jennifer Jones, needs a *rented* tuxedo.

The audience's groans and giggles at the bonehead lines of the scriptwriter, Stirling Silliphant, aren't part of a cynically amused response, as they are at *Earthquake;* they're more like symptoms of distress. There's a primitive, frightening power in death by fire. How can we look at scenes of death and listen to this stupid chitchat about love and building codes, interlarded with oohs and ahs for rescued little boy and girl darlings and for a pussycat saved by a kindly black man (O. J. Simpson)? What emotion are we meant to feel for Robert Wagner (as some sort of publicist for the building) and his secretary (Susan Flannery), who have a little fling, get out of bed, and die hideously, the camera lingering on their agonies? Maybe Irwin Allen thinks that *Poseidon* was such a big commercial success because of its plain, square realism. But it was clunky-realistic, and the upside-down-ocean-liner situation was so remote that one could sit back and enjoy it. The realism here is very offensive.

The movie doesn't stick together in one's head; this thing is like some junky fairground show — a chamber of horrors with skeletons that jump up. It hardly seems fair to pin much responsibility on the nominal director, John Guillermin; I can't believe he had a lot of choice in such matters as the meant-to-be-touching fidelity of the mayor of San Francisco (Jack Collins) and his plump wife in pink (Sheila Matthews, the producer's fiancée). I've seen this loving, long-married couple go down with the Titanic so many times that I was outraged that they survived here. Despite the gruesome goings on inside the world's tallest funeral pyre, a few performers still manage to be minimally attractive. Paul Newman has the sense to look embarrassed, which, in addition to his looking remarkably pretty and fit, helps things along. His son Scott Newman, who appears as a nervous young fireman, has his father's handsomeness. William Holden has a thankless role as the builder responsible for most of the chicanery, but he performs with professional force. Best, surprisingly, is Faye Dunaway, as Newman's girl. It's not that she acts much but that she looks so goddessy beautiful, wandering through the chaos in puce see-through chiffon — a creamy, slutty Fragonard in motion. When Dunaway has nothing to do, it's all to the good: she doesn't pull her face together into that tight, Waspy acting mask that she usually puts on. Without it, her porcelain, world-weary face becomes wounded by the fear of falling apart — and she's more beautiful than ever. Perfection going slightly to seed is maybe the most alluring face a screen goddess can have.

Inferno was financed jointly by Twentieth Century-Fox and Warners after the companies discovered that they had both invested in virtually the same novel, and that a rivalry to make the picture could be double suicide; it was not exactly a case of great minds traveling in the same channel. The only disaster picture that has redeemed the genre is Richard Lester's *Juggernaut*, which kidded the threadbare pants off the same clichés that the other pictures still try to make work. Though *Inferno* spares us a prayer scene, it has the gall to try to get us excited by repeated shots of fire engines arriving at the foot of the skyscraper, their sirens piercing our eardrums. And it actually carries a dedication "to the firefighters of the world." *The Towering Inferno* has opened just in time to capture the Dumb Whore Award of 1974.

[December 30, 1974]

Woman on the Road

ALICE (ELLEN BURSTYN) is a thirty-five-year-old blond housewife with a big face and a good-sized behind. She's pretty in a clumsy, ordinary way — the face overblown and a little blubbery but with the kind of smile you can't help smiling back at. Since childhood, Alice has wanted to be a vocalist like Alice Faye, and she did some singing before she got married to a sexy but hardheaded workingman (Billy Green Bush) and wound up in a tract home in New Mexico, trying to keep the peace between a humorless husband and a smart, nervy eleven-year-old son (Alfred Lutter), who takes his cue from his mother's suppressed feelings and openly taunts his father. When Alice's husband is killed in a truck crash, she is left penniless and scared, but she's also freed from the grim boredom of trying to please a dull man; she sells off her possessions in a garage sale, packs her kid in the station wagon, and sets out to make a new life. That's the starting point of *Alice Doesn't Live Here Anymore,* the new Martin Scorsese film, from a script by Robert Getchell — one of the rare films that genuinely deserve to be called controversial. I think people will really fight about it. It's the story of a woman who has a second chance thrust on her; she knows enough not to make the same mistake again, but she isn't sure of much else. Neither is the movie. *Alice* is thoroughly enjoyable: funny, absorbing, intelligent even when you don't believe in what's going on — when the issues it raises get all fouled up.

Alice, like Paul Mazursky's *Blume in Love,* is about the things nobody's got too well sorted out. Mazursky, a satirist as well as a romantic, can't help seeing the pratfall folly of his educated, liberal characters who have consciousness up to their ears but not in their hearts. In *Alice,* the heroine is fighting for consciousness, after a long married sleep. Mazursky's pictures and Scorsese's *Alice* are the closest anybody with talent and brains has come lately to the romantic, marital-mixup comedies of the thirties. How could new marital comedies *not* be controversial? *Blume* was like a hip updating of *The Awful Truth; Alice* is like *It Happened*

One Night played at the wrong speed. But what's the right speed? Now it isn't just a romance in trouble, or an individual marriage in collapse; it's romance itself that's in trouble, and it's the institution of marriage that's in slapstick, role-confusion chaos. Blume's wife, the stiff-jawed Nina, who was trying to find herself, took up the lettuce pickers, nutrition, and yoga but never got to women's liberation. Mazursky didn't raise questions about her rigidity and her frustrations: Nina remained an inscrutably frustrated woman. *Alice* tries to make its heroine scrutable. It's a realistic, new-style version of the wisecracking Depression pictures: the Problem is women trying to figure out a way to be independent, without giving up men.

The comic environment is different now, too. The American road comedy can no longer trot out drawling, innocently canny hicks; the new, media-freak hick is encased in cynicism. He isn't slow on the uptake; he may be faster than the educated, big-city person, who has had more opportunities to break out of cultural traps, and for whom quick comebacks aren't such a big deal. Scorsese is one of the first movie directors to show the hard-edge small-town materialists bred on TV and envy, and he does it without any ostentation or comment. In Mazursky's *Harry & Tonto* — an old-man-on-the-road movie — Harry's three children, in New York, Chicago, and southern California, lived in ways that indicated the tensions of those areas; Scorsese shows Southwestern blue-collar people who accept the sunlit disreputability of their way of life and are pretty cocky about it. These directors don't score easy points by satirizing American oddities; they know that they look pretty funny themselves. Since they don't try to distance themselves and objectify the situations, the type of comedy they produce is peculiarly unstable; you don't always feel like laughing, and even when you do laugh you may have mixed emotions. Mazursky sees the craziness in middle-class attitudes as well as the crazy sadness of those who have the values and can't make it. (He's in love with monomaniacs: he sees them as less tormented than ordinary people.) *Harry & Tonto* is the most difficult kind of comedy to bring off, because it comes directly from the moviemaker's feelings about life; that's why someone in the audience can say, "I don't know why I'm crying — this is such a silly movie." *Alice* doesn't have that transparency; Scorsese doesn't have Mazursky's sweet disposition and he isn't primarily a comedy director. Scorsese doesn't know what his feelings are; they're changing, and he's split and snagged trying to discover what they *should* be. He slips in and out of old-movie conventions, only half-parodying them. *Alice* gives the impression of a picture evolved from a story line that didn't have enough substance to satisfy him or anybody else. The story might have been stuffed and slicked by another director, but Scorsese is young and supercharged — *he's* in love with volatile situations. So he doesn't try to pin Alice down; he wants to understand why she's on the road.

Alice's idea of a new life is to return to what she had hoped to be when she was a girl in Monterey, California. She starts driving back there, stopping at motels along the way, stashing her boy in front of the TV while she looks for work as a singer. The most affecting moments of Ellen Burstyn's performance come when Alice, having shot her last few dollars on a bright-green dress and a curly hairdo, gets her first professional engagement, at a saloon in Phoenix, and starts to sing. She isn't terrible and she isn't good. She's the essence of all the pretty, aging women singers one sees in bars across the country — all those women who never quite made it to the big-time and are now in a losing battle with dry, cracked tonelessness. Alice starts off with the voice of a has-been. When she sings, the sentiment comes in waves from her vulnerable — almost transfigured — flabby face. She's made up to look like a barroom kewpie, but she's more nakedly revealed than at any other time.

However, Ellen Burstyn is interested in a different kind of revelation. Stars, who dominate and control their movies, generally insist on softening their images — refusing to play scenes that show them as selfish or arrogant, claiming that their public doesn't want to see them without their aura. Burstyn, in her first starring picture, does just the opposite: instead of arranging for the cosmetic treatment and lighting that have made her glamorous in the past, she emphasizes a raw, real-person plainness, and Alice is very harsh, with sheared-off emotions and abrupt shifts of mood. She's an impatient woman, quick to yell and given to sudden bursts of tears. Once her oppressively square husband is gone and she's sprung from her tract punishment cell, you might expect that her jokes would bubble up out of sheer joy, but Burstyn doesn't read them for simple laughs. She makes them bitingly funny. Burstyn comes on strong, and at times she's so vehement that we lose the sense of the high spirits that must have formed Alice's joking relationship to her son (and that attract men to her now). Alice has a locked-in resentment — an almost childish, surly refusal to consider anything more than her own needs. Burstyn appears to be so determined not to play a teasing, fake-tender woman that she flings women's-movement anger into her work before she's absorbed it as an actress and discovered what she can use and what she can't. And so instead of seeing Alice we're seeing the collision of Alice with Ellen Burstyn's consciousness as of this moment in history. I think we'd connect more fully with Alice if Burstyn weren't trying to turn the role into a statement. On the other hand, there's a stimulation and excitement in what Burstyn is attempting. I don't really like most of her acting here — her rhythm seems a beat off—yet I'm held by what she's trying to do, and by her need to play against stereotypes. Without her ferocious attack, *Alice* might seem no more than a slight, charming comedy.

Ellen Burstyn stayed within her roles in such films as *Tropic of Cancer* (she played Henry's passionate wife, Mona), Mazursky's *Alex in Wonderland* (she was Alex's obstinate, frustrated wife, an early sketch of Nina in *Blume*), and *The Last Picture Show* (the town bitch's beautiful mother). In each of them, her role was defined by reference to someone else. In *The Exorcist,* as the possessed girl's movie-star mother, she had a slightly strident quality; for the first time on the screen she wasn't quite likable, and it looked deliberate. It wasn't until her brief guest performance as Harry's daughter in *Harry & Tonto,* however, that I got the first suggestion that she was trying to say more than the role could sustain. She seemed almost metallic in her determination not to show warmth toward Harry, and I didn't believe that Harry's daughter would feel like that. She was alone and bitter in ways that impressed themselves on one's memory (I remember the line of her body as she walked with her father), but there wasn't enough under her surface tension to help us understand why she and her father fought. It was a small role, but it was jarring, and it threw me momentarily outside the picture. (Why was she so snappish with the runaway teenager?) Harry's unhappy tough-broad daughter seemed less than a believable person yet more than the role called for. And that, on a much larger scale, is what happens in *Alice*: Burstyn hits so many of those discordant notes that she must think it's a sign of liberation for Alice to be defiantly short-tempered. There is a rationale: nastiness can seem liberating after years of forced charm. But when Alice lays into people her character goes out of whack. You may get the feeling that Burstyn identifies the plight of Alice, who forced herself to be charming and ate off it (often eating crow), with the plight of screen actresses limited to ingratiation and charm.

The trouble with Ellen Burstyn's performance is that she's playing against something instead of playing a character. And she doesn't let you forget that she can act; at times she's almost as busy in the face as Gena Rowlands in *A Woman Under the Influence.* She loses some of the potential comedy in her lines by ripping them out faster than a plausible speed of thought. Diane Ladd, who plays Flo, a brittle-blond, foul-mouthed waitress, has the hash-house rasp, but she's also too fast, and their talks together have a proselytizing sisters-in-consciousness tone. (I could also have done without Flo's sisterly heart of gold.) But better too fast than too slow, and there are bits in Alice's and Flo's conversations that echo in one's head — such as the way Alice says that she felt that her husband took care of her though he didn't. Lelia Goldoni is so vibrant in the small, gentle part of Alice's neighbor Bea, in New Mexico, that one wants to tell the shrill, hyped-up actresses to shut up and observe. But at the same time one knows why they don't. Because where has Lelia Goldoni been in all these years since *Shadows*? Why hasn't she had the big roles she might have played? It's the long history of the waste of actresses like Goldoni and the fact that Burstyn is obviously more than the thirty-five she's meant to be here (how many years has she waited for this starring role?) that have gone into this movie's disorderly energies and jagged, overpacked ambience. Maybe putting down an actress for venting her rage over wasted years would be as opaque as expressing disdain for a black's "irrational" rhetoric. (Ellen Burstyn is said to have used twenty-five different show-business names since she began life as Edna Rae Gillooly.) Sometimes a person's anger and overstatement tell a bigger story than the person knows how to tell. The anger may derive from deprivation of the means to express oneself calmly, "rationally"; people can be too angry to care about balance, while resenting everything that has unbalanced them. *Alice Doesn't Live Here Anymore* is a bigger movie for what's churning around in it.

The heroine isn't a darling; she won't "make nice" for us — and that's going to scrape some nerves. One can think of plenty of movies in which the leading woman was a villainous bitch, as in *Double Indemnity*, but, except for Scarlett O'Hara, where are the heroines who had motives and drives of their own who weren't saints and sweeties, and who weren't put down for their independence? *Alice* is a comedy, but it's also the first angry-young-woman movie, and, as in the angry-young-men British plays of the fifties and the angry-young-men American movies of the late sixties, you can't always be sure what the protagonist is angry about. The anger is resonant precisely because it hasn't a specific cause. The protagonist has gone beyond being "fair"; she wants you to feel her rage. You feel it, all right, and you know that it's expressing something that's in the air. There's no question but that it's harder to accept an angry *woman* stabbing out at everything around her. Before the Movement, most women who went ahead with what they wanted to do probably believed that a woman could think, work, and create without losing her attractiveness, her "femininity." Alice, who assumes her right to be as crude and domineering as a man, represents a new attitude that may offend some women even more than it offends men. What makes the film seem of this moment is the suggestion that Alice has been a victim — it's in Alice's manner more than in anything she says — and that this justifies her truculence. When her husband calls out to her, "You're the cook," her face is like a placard for us to read, and when she goes into a little fit after a sexist insult, she's Alice the standard-bearer.

Alice is a runaway movie. Martin Scorsese seems to have let the characters go loose; the camera is hyperactive, tracking them. Probably Scorsese was ready to question a lot of things he had been taking for granted — even how a movie should be made and how its tone should be set. He took chances on this picture, especially considering that it's a David Susskind Production for Warners. (Susskind, who on his TV show expresses puzzled disbelief that any woman might want something in life besides tidying the nest for his return, must have howled in pain and betrayal when he saw the rushes.) Scorsese's associate producer is Sandra Weintraub, and they are a couple; the production designer is Toby Carr Rafelson, who worked on *Five Easy Pieces* with her director husband, Bob Rafelson; the editor is Marcia Lucas, who worked on *American Graffiti* with hers, George Lucas. Scorsese has brought together some of the most talented young women in Hollywood. You feel that he's listened to them, because he knows that the rumblings and undercurrents he's getting are more urgent — and hotter — than the written conception. And so he frames the movie around what Burstyn is doing.

It would all fall apart if it weren't for the funny malice and good-hearted bitching in the dialogue. Getchell (a California college teacher; this is his first script to be produced) has a talent for scenes that play out differently from what one expects. There's a new comic twist in his domestic situations: Alice and her kid, Tommy, cut each other down lovingly, and sometimes the boy, a little scared, but gutsy and abrasive, like her, tests to see how far he can push her before she'll explode. Their fast-patter twosome may seem like a stunt, but it probably delivers more small shocks of recognition than any other parent-child relationship in films of recent years. (Wiredrawn little Alfred Lutter has crack comedy timing. He doesn't seem studied; he seems to play from impulse, which is practically unheard of in a child actor.) And Getchell has a good sense of where to place action: some of the best scenes are set in a Tucson diner, where Alice works as a waitress. Scorsese uses the floor of the diner like a stage for improvisations, and a dark, scrawny waitress — a complete clumse (Valerie Curtin) — goofs up her orders and skitters about playing musical chairs with the plates. The film has its comic epiphany in the diner when Valerie Curtin links arms with the two other waitresses and they become the three Graces. But Alice doesn't go to enough places. If the script had a valid dramatic logic, we'd see what she made of herself with and without men; we'd see whether she trapped herself trying to be Alice Faye or grew up. Getchell creates a heroine who has the humor and energy to make a new life — to bomb out or get there on her own. But then he (or perhaps those putting up the money?) thinks the answer for a widow must be a new fella — a better kind of guy than the old one. And so the movie contradicts the logic of its own story and, as in the movies of yore, gives Alice a dream prince — Kris Kristofferson as a rancher, but a rancher *who is willing for her to go on with her singing career.* If Ibsen had written *A Doll's House* for the movies, Nora would have taken her children and moved them right into the warm, permissive home of a rich, liberal suitor who was waiting in the wings. Alice gets a double helping of pie in the sky: she gets a warm-and-sexy good provider, and she can pursue her idiot dream of becoming an Alice Faye.

Alice and her suitor work out their compromise in shouts across the crowded diner — a paste-up happy ending from the thirties, and execrably staged. The women involved in the production end of the film may have concurred in this compromise; since they've got their men and their work, they may not have seen how illusory Alice's career is. They — and perhaps Burstyn, too — may have thought that what mattered was for Alice to have the independence to continue with her own career, even if it wouldn't come to anything, and that this was different from just getting the guy, as per old Hollywood. But this ending makes bubble gum of the movie we've been watching — a movie that seemed to be concerned with a woman strong enough to face facts. If the women's movement is about women having the freedom to fantasize, they may just as well go back into the tract house and dream away. The ending is apparently intended as a victory for Alice, yet it's a defense of women's right to be the silly, impractical creatures men have said they were.

The film moves with breakneck vitality, and Scorsese gives it a hotfoot when he puts Harvey Keitel on the screen in the role of Ben. In Scorsese's *Mean Streets,* Keitel was the wormy-souled Sicilian-American protagonist; here he's a young Southwestern stud, with a little-boy grin and a sly, wheedling way with women. He's macho sleaze incarnate; he's the kind of teasing stud a woman can know is rotten and still find irresistible. The movies have rarely shown the sweet-talking sex salesman that women know better than but fall for anyway. There's a very good reason that movies have rarely shown him: he's all too often the hero, and the whole movie is dedicated to keeping everybody in the audience from knowing better than. Keitel has only a few minutes of screen time, but you understand at once that Alice's brains don't enter into the equation where a smiley Ben is concerned, and not because he's a dark, earthy, Lawrencian lover. (Lawrence never dealt with the Bens.) He's a lover to hide; Alice's brains only make her ashamed to have people know she's involved with him. Her son puts her on the spot when he asks her directly if she's sleeping with Ben. Her quiet, lying answer creates more empathy for her than anything else in the movie. Alice the sentimental singer without a voice is a weak woman; Alice the mother who's also a sexual being is a strong woman caught in a bind. She's right to lie to Tommy — she isn't lying for herself (or to herself) when she does. At the turning point where Ben is crossed and becomes violent, Keitel performs with virtuoso intensity; the sequence says as much as any scene on film about the abject terror that women can have of men. The contrast between Keitel, an unconditional, all-out actor, who in this role holds the audience in a macho vise, and Kris Kristofferson, who's barely an actor at all and can only be "natural," is plain funny, because they're both so right for the way they're used.

With Kristofferson as the rancher, the pairing-off ending doesn't seem completely old-style simple. He's so appealingly peaceable that you want to believe in what he offers Alice — the moon. His rancher isn't a pre-city rural; he has been to the city and rejected it. In his first picture, *Cisco Pike,* it was Kristofferson who was on the road — he played a former pop idol who couldn't get off the sixties dream road when the sixties were over. Kristofferson smiles with the knowledge that things aren't really going to get better. He knows there's trouble and accepts it; he's troubled himself, yet tranquil. A soft-spoken, unhurried man who has an immediate intimacy with whomever he's talking to, Kristofferson fuses geniality and sexiness. What other nonthreatening male is so sexy? Who else could placate a stubborn, exasperated woman in as relaxed a way as big, furry-faced Kristofferson? The role might come right out of his affable personality; Kristofferson's motor is always idling. As Elmo the drifter in *Blume in Love,* he was just the right lover for tense Nina: Elmo's stoned contentment was the best protection against her high-mindedness. (Elmo was so likable that even Nina's husband had to like him.) There's an otherworldliness in Kristofferson, with his nice padding and his sensual relaxation — and his angelic, nostalgic spirit. It's the dream tucked away somewhere in him that makes him so sunny; the things going on around him don't get to him much. Alice can grate on him without being afraid, because he has no rough edges to fight back with. His roly-poly fleshiness is a cushion against disaster; he's Big Daddy Santa Claus, he's the greatest goddam pillow in the world. What an ironic hero for a women's-lib movie — a declawed, defanged man who yet offers security and sex.

As in *Mean Streets,* Scorsese uses music as an element in the characters' lives; his choice of barroom songs is convincingly right, but he doesn't use the music as thematically as one might hope. Pop music has shaped Alice's soul, but the split between the slow, soft Alice who gives herself over to sentimental lyrics and the quick, hard Alice who tries to figure out what she's doing in her life is something the movie never really gets into. (There's a terrible dream-red prologue, with Alice as a child and Alice Faye on the track singing "You'll Never Know;" it's staged like an anti-*Wizard of Oz* joke, with Alice as an infant cynic, and it doesn't work even as a cheap gag.) Parts of the picture are very scrappy. The opening scenes are weak, because you feel that Alice's husband is Tommy's stepfather rather than his father. (They don't seem father and son even in their hostility.) After the husband's death, the movie works much better, but it leaves out elements that we could use (such as what Ben means to Alice sexually, and why the rancher is willing to give up his ranch for Alice and her kid when he wouldn't for his ex-wife and his own kids). *Alice* is by no means all that it might be. *Blume* wasn't, either; there were scenes that dawdled on, and in some ways I really liked *Blume* better when I thought back over it than when I was seeing it. (It was funny to think about how Nina's humorlessness had made her seem inhuman, while Blume was redeemed by his romantic foolishness.) Those characters have stayed with me, and I expect that moments from *Alice* will, too. Despite the romantic engineering (which is no more illogical than the endings of the angry-young-men plays and movies), nothing really feels pat. Scorsese's instinct is sharper than the movie's resolution: the last shot he gives us isn't of the happy lovers — it's of Alice and her knobby-minded, maddeningly smart kid. The true relationship in the movie is between these two. Scorsese can't lay a romantic, old-movie benediction on us; he doesn't know how to lie effectively. It's a gift all Hollywood has lost — and if we're lucky it won't be recovered.

[January 13, 1975]

Pure Chrome

CAN THE LOOK and the cutting plan of a movie be so much more absorbing to the director than the subject that he trivializes the characters and the ideas? That seems to be what happened in Alain Resnais's *Stavisky.* The actual life of Serge Alexandre Stavisky, a classic swindler-charmer, had cheap thrills, degradation, and true drama. A middle-class boy of Russian Jewish descent (his family moved to France in 1900, when he was fourteen), he was bored by work; he was first a gigolo, and then climbed up onto the top rungs of organized crime — theft, drugs, extortion. By the late twenties, he was known in France as "the king of crooks," yet he moved on into even larger fields — international-finance shell games. The extent of the corruption centering on him began to be revealed after his death, in January, 1934 (he was found with a bullet hole in his right temple and a gun in his left hand), and there were street riots, shootings, and a general strike; two governments were brought down. *Stavisky* only touches on most of this. Perhaps the film's theme is the relationship of character and history; perhaps Stavisky is meant to be the key to the general political and economic hypocrisy of the era that ended in 1939. But what one sees is a death song for thirties elegance: a silver Hispano-Suiza, an Art Deco diamond necklace, a white plane with a red-circle nose, a white-on-white animal in the snow. Even the buildings and the skies are silvery white, and the slightly acrid neo-Gershwin score, by Stephen Sondheim, enhances the design. Resnais might have directed in white tie and tails. The film seems to be a reverie on façades and contrasts, in which Stavisky (Jean-Paul Belmondo), who hides his origins and his past, who lives as if he had no memories, is paired with his friend Baron Raoul (Charles Boyer), whose character is enriched by his background and memory. Stavisky's adventurism, which weakened France and helped to destroy her in the Second World War, is balanced against the revolutionary hopes of Leon Trotsky, exiled by Stalin, who was living near Fontainebleau.

But all this is so desultory that the characters are no more than emblems. *Stavisky* has been made as if vitality would be a sin against art. The intricate plot provided by the screenwriter, Jorge Semprun, seems purposeless, except that Resnais needs the intricacy for the back-and-forth movement that he wants in the cutting. Resnais is a withholder of pleasure; you can feel it in the way he measures out the information and delays telling you what you need to know. His style here is like that of a melancholy Lubitsch; however, Lubitsch could move the camera through great hotels and richly appointed bedrooms for the sheer romantic delight in high living, while Resnais uses the luxury and beauty iconographically. Each shot, each camera movement, is thought out in design terms. The picture moves with superlative grace, yet it feels inert, because it hasn't been felt, except on a technical level.

Stavisky doesn't show what drove the magnetic con man or how he bribed his way to the top. Instead, we see Stavisky's confederates — despicable, muttering schemers — entering and leaving opulent hotel rooms like conspirators in a stage melodrama. They, too, are contrasts with Stavisky: we appear to be meant to feel that he, being madly profligate, charming, Jewish, and death-obsessed, isn't responsible in the same way as his more stable but less attractive associates (a distinction that his victims, who put their life savings into his forged bonds, probably couldn't appreciate). It shouldn't be really difficult to explain the

Stavisky Affair, if one wanted to. The film prefers the approach that "to understand Alex you have to dream about him." But if we dream after this movie it's of hardware and fashions, and that, I imagine, is what Resnais thinks that dreaming about Stavisky means.

The film's affection for Stavisky's money-squandering gestures is slightly patronizing, and its true hero is Baron Raoul, who stands by his friend even when he learns what Stavisky has done.* The Baron regrets that Stavisky lied to him, but forgives him. It would be one thing if the impoverished Baron, as a member of Stavisky's coterie, liked to fool himself with phony noblesse oblige by condescending to the man he was hanging on to, but the picture appears to endorse the Baron's view and to share his complacency about aristocratic values. I get the feeling that Stavisky's lying is accepted (as the movie also accepts his thievery) because he, being a Jewish outsider, isn't really expected to be a man of honor.

It is not always clear how we are meant to read a movie; neither is it always clear whether the moviemakers are fully conscious of what they're doing. In *The Touch,* for example, when Ingmar Bergman used Elliott Gould as David, a simian American Jewish archeologist excavating near an ancient church in Sweden and destroying the Christian serenity of Bibi Andersson's life, was Bergman expressing feelings of his own about the alien nature of Jews? When Gould shows Andersson the insect larvae that are eating up the centuries-old wooden statue of the Virgin, are the larvae meant to be the Jews? (David, the violently aggressive Jewish outsider, is larval, all right, and he is given an incestuous sister, who runs him a wormy second.) Bergman said that he had based David on the explosive, childish, even boorish side of his own split nature. (How perturbing that this explosive id should be represented as Jewish.) *The Touch* seems to be saying that the woman is brought to life by the suffering that David causes her, and that only by accepting the larvae as just as beautiful as the statue can she be a whole person. But it's a hopelessly inchoate movie. *Stavisky* goes to the opposite extreme: it makes one of the most destructive swindlers in history whimsical and charming. This Stavisky is childlike and irresponsible, though, and perhaps, like Bergman's David, he represents what Christians believe they have repressed or grown beyond. Since the French have different points of pride from the Swedes, this id isn't bestial — it's innocently immoral and uncivilized. If the filmmakers had shown Stavisky's crimes and the poor people he robbed, the film might have been open to charges of

*Possibly Resnais and Semprun intended the adaptable Baron to suggest the aristocratic Frenchmen who were to accommodate the Nazis, but that is not how viewers experience the character; he seems frivolous but generous and decent.

anti-Semitism. Yet their sentimentality about Stavisky turns him into a pet, and perhaps only the French — notoriously given to stroking their language and their culture — would assume a Jew to be without moral traditions.

The streamlining doesn't extend to the dialogue. *Stavisky* is one of those French movies in which the characters are stuffed with philosophical nuggets; as in an Eric Rohmer film, they all think they're La Rochefoucauld. The Baron recites choice bits of wisdom, Mme. Stavisky (Anny Duperey) makes speeches about oaths of fidelity on the golf course at Biarritz, and Stavisky himself goes in for ponderous distinctions between pleasure and happiness. Did Resnais and Semprun give any thought to the episode in which Stavisky courts a bejeweled provincial woman, sweeps her off her feet, and, after seducing her, buys her jewels from her — at a tenth of their value — in order to present them to his (supposedly) smashing wife? It's intended to show not what a low bastard Stavisky is but, rather, what an adorable, sophisticated rascal he is, and we're meant to share his contempt for the provincial woman's passion and for her gaucherie in quoting Baudelaire. And, indeed, people in the audience laugh as if they wouldn't be caught dead doing anything as gross as quoting Baudelaire. People partake of the film's connoisseurship and savoir-faire. So the provincial woman who quotes the wrong poet and doesn't know she's supposed to be discreetly passive is the target.

Resnais surrounds the women in this movie with so many baskets of white hothouse flowers that his ideal feminine position must be rigor mortis. The corpselike Mme. Stavisky is introduced posing for the rotogravures, and she never stops; Anny Duperey is a former mannequin who cannot be said to have changed her profession. When Hollywood told the Stavisky story, back in 1937, in the Michael Curtiz film *Stolen Holiday,* Claude Rains was the swindler and Kay Francis was the clotheshorse. Though she changed her ensembles even more frequently than Duperey does, she wasn't just a shell of a woman. Resnais buries Duperey in feathers and white ermine and deploys her as he did Delphine Seyrig in *Last Year at Marienbad.* But she isn't meant to be a mysterious pawn — she's meant to be an ideal wife, and at the end of the picture this walking death mask is celebrated for the joy she has brought into everyone's life. The only joy Mme. Stavisky could give would be visual, and that at a distance. She's a frame to hang the dresses on. Pure chrome.

The sole character who has any life is Baron Raoul, and that's because Boyer, at seventy-five, understands that the Baron should be a simple, happy man. And Boyer himself seems to be laughing at how easy acting has become for him. He has shown his artistry wherever he could

— in such unlikely roles as the noble Japanese naval commander with a pencil-line mustache in the 1934 *Thunder in the East;* as the sane, smart Napoleon in *Conquest* (he acted circles around Garbo's Marie Walewska); as an authentically shabby, graying Graham Greene hero in *Confidential Agent.* He was a fine actor even in his heart-crusher roles, with the lights trained on his liquid gypsy eyes — as the sensitive, unhappy Archduke Rudolph in *Mayerling,* and as Pépé Le Môko in *Algiers.* Perhaps the only screen role he has ever had that was worthy of him was in the great *The Earrings of Madame de . . . ,* in which he also played a French aristocrat — a very different sort of man, a general who tried to cure his wife of her passion for another man by military discipline. And Boyer has carried over some of the general's character into the role of the Baron — his belief, for example, in style and manners as the civilized protection that class provides. Boyer's performance is so light — a series of reminiscent gestures — that it makes one suffer a little for Belmondo, who works very hard at a role to which he's unsuited. Belmondo is always someone to watch, and he does all he can — there are suggestions of a schizoid rift between Stavisky's smiling mouth and distressed eyes. However, the picture treats Stavisky as victim more than as protagonist, and Belmondo seems rather ineffectual, and uncertain as to what is wanted of him. The audience accepts him, I think, as charming, sexy Belmondo; he goes well with the furniture.

Early in *Stavisky,* in the sequence in the offices of the theater Stavisky owns, I realized that I wasn't paying any attention to the dialogue, because the posters on the wall were more alive than the people talking. Resnais has a beautiful technique, but it's not an expressive technique; I'm not sure what it's good for, and I don't think he's found out yet, either. *Stavisky* is an icy, high-minded white-telephone movie, and it's a waste that this is his first film in six years. Maybe the only way Alain Resnais could ever get to be an artist rather than a master craftsman would be by relaxing and thinking he was doing something commercial. Possibly some instincts could then come into play. There isn't a whole man at work in this movie; if he thought he was whoring, he might warm up enough to be human.

MICHEL DRACH'S *Les Violons du Bal* gets off to a fast start as the bearded, intense-looking Drach tries to persuade a fat-cat producer to back the autobiographical film he wants to make. The moneybags complains that the subject — what happened to Drach's well-to-do French Jewish family under the Occupation — isn't commercial. Determined, Drach gathers his cast — his son David to play him as a child, and his wife,

Marie-José Nat, to play his mother — and then, when the investor gives him the go-ahead if he will get a star to play himself, Drach is replaced by Jean-Louis Trintignant (it's very deft visual sleight of hand) and the story proceeds. But not on the same level. Once Trintignant takes over as the filmmaker, the movie loses its playful movie-within-a-movie spirit, and the technique, which had been a sprinting, jump-cutting shorthand that didn't take itself too seriously, turns glassy smooth. After a while, you think back to the somewhat disingenuous savvy of the opening sequence — to Drach's complaint that it's too bad you need money to tell your own life story and to the moneybags' saying the idea isn't commercial — and you think, What a hoax.

Les Violons du Bal — the title is Drach's private slang for "The others call the tune" — is a romantic memoir about the efforts of Drach's gracious and beautiful mother to save the family from the Nazis. Drach re-creates the Nazi period as he remembers it — in terms of what his vision was when he was a little boy. And his memory seems to burnish everything: everyone in the family is tender, cultivated, and exquisitely groomed. Drach has such a tastefully selective memory that I didn't believe a word of the movie, or any image, either. A man might well remember his mother as supple and sad-eyed, but would everything else be toned up, too? You don't really feel that you're seeing the past through the child's eyes. The incidents — his older brother's sexual fling with a fashionably pale and mysterious refugee woman, his older sister's affair with a wealthy Gentile and her subsequent career as a Paris fashion model, his escape to Switzerland with his mother — have a warmed-over old-Hollywood look. The smartly tailored hat that Marie-José Nat wears for the flight across the border and the fine gloves with which she parts the strands of barbed wire are the height of refugee chic. If this is what the child experienced, he must have had the soul of a couturier.

Was Drach such a precocious, doted-on, and protected child? Why does he want to share this innocuous vision with us? The moneybags refers to the project in terms of Proust, and that must be how Drach intends it. There are analogies in the way the mother and the grandmother function in the household; the apartment atmosphere is more than gently inviting, it's orchidaceous, and the compliant mother suggests the faintly Eastern sensual indulgence of Marcel's mother. (In case we should miss it, Drach puts her in a turban.) I don't know anybody who remembers his family and childhood as lyrically as Michel Drach does. He has managed to make a movie about himself without telling us a damn thing about himself. Drach shifts from black-and-white to color with elegant fluency, but the concept of using black-and-white for the present and pastels for the past may be a key to his romanticization of his childhood. What can this concept tell us but that he finds the present colorless compared to the delicate tones of the past; that is, that he loved his mother so much that, Nazis or no Nazis, he was unscathed by the terrors and dangers his family was exposed to? I find something airless in all this, especially since Drach has cast his own wife as his mother and his own son as the blithe little treasure he imagines he was. (Was he also unscathed by the love he received? Marcel wasn't.)

In the early scenes, Drach, playing himself as filmmaker, has a self-engrossed quality that is consistent with the rest of the movie, but he doesn't create any character for Trintignant to play, and so when Trintignant takes over the role of the director he's a blank. It's easy to forget he's in the movie; he seems separate from it, going through the motions in a void. The child and his mother, and the sister (Nathalie Roussel), who appears to be lifted from every betrayed darling that Natalie Wood ever played, aren't characterized, either, but Drach has drenched them in a sensitivity that he can't quite pour over the dry-eyed Trintignant. *Les Violons du Bal* isn't a child's vision; it's an adult's security blanket of soft illusions.

[January 20, 1975]

Hardboiled Valentine

SHAW'S *Pygmalion* seems to be foolproof — actor-proof and director-proof, that is, and even adapter-proof. And so, possibly, is Ben Hecht's and Charles MacArthur's *The Front Page.* Like *Pygmalion, The Front Page* is really *built.* The high-potency melodrama and the cynical farce are joined so unerringly that the play comes across no matter what you do to it. Bulging with the embellishments added by the director, Billy Wilder, and his co-scenarist, I. A. L. Diamond, the structure still stands up in the new movie version. However, this new *Front Page,* with Walter Matthau as the glib, unscrupulous Walter Burns, the editor who will stop at nothing to prevent his star reporter, Hildy Johnson (Jack Lemmon), from leaving the paper, is a thick-necked, broad-beamed show. Opening with a ragtime tune, it comes riding in on *The Sting.* It's enjoyable, but, with about half of the dialogue rewritten for the worse

— uglified — it's enjoyable on a very low level. If one didn't know the play, or the previous film versions, one could never guess from the new production that it is based on a classic American play. In box-office terms, this probably represents a triumph for Wilder and Diamond — the movie has no style or distinction to scare people off. But something singular and marvelous has been diminished to the sloppy ordinary. It's quite possible that if the film had been done in a modern equivalent of the play's original style it wouldn't get the laughs it does. (Even so, *M*A*S*H,* which was close to a modern equivalent in style, was a big hit.) But it would have been worth Billy Wilder's attempting (though the producer, Paul Monash, and the executive producer, Jennings Lang, may not agree). This way, Wilder's got a box-office success; the other way, he might have come back in glory.

Hecht and MacArthur had intended to write a hardboiled exposé of the tabloid journalism of their youth, but, as Hecht said in his autobiography, *A Child of the Century,* "our friendship was founded on a mutual obsession." They went on into other fields, but "we remained newspaper reporters and continued to keep our hats on before the boss, drop ashes on the floor, and disdain all practical people." And so, as they admitted, *The Front Page* turned into a "valentine." But it's a hardboiled valentine: ribald, caustic, prankish — a celebration of a profession that once had its own wisecracking camaraderie. People became reporters because that's what they'd dreamed of being. The rewards certainly weren't financial; Sherman Reilly Duffy, another newspaperman of the period, noted, "Socially a journalist fits in somewhere between a whore and a bartender, but spiritually he stands beside Galileo. He knows the world is round." There are reporters from eight rival Chicago papers in the one-set play; it all takes place in the pressroom of the courthouse on the night before a timid, dazed anarchist is to be hanged for murder. The play lovingly satirizes the addiction to excitement that the newspapermen felt in the era when competitive papers, itching for scoops, tried to outreach each other in sensationalism; the reporters — razzing musketeers — play poker, bait the mayor and the sheriff, and run out after hot leads. Celebrating the lowdown talk of a cynical, male profession, Hecht and MacArthur achieved what American dramatists had long been trying to do: they demonstrated the expressive vitality of plain American speech. The rapid-fire dialogue that rips along can be so faultlessly rhythmed that the words snap into place. And when the phrasing is right *The Front Page* can give audiences the sharp pleasure that one gets from a perfectly orchestrated feat. It can be, and has often been, almost intoxicatingly skillful — a sustained high. That's what the new movie version isn't. It keeps you *up,* all right, but in the way that, say, TV's *Kojak* does — just because there's so much happening all the time. In Wilder's *Front Page,* the sound keeps blasting you. The engineer seems to have rammed the microphones into the performers' faces, as if to cover the noise of the slot machines at Vegas. The overlapping, hollering lines, which were funny in the past because they were so precise, are bellowed chaotically now and turned into sheer noise. I don't know whether the movie (which is still mostly set in one room) was actually post-synched, but it has that sour, dead post-synch tone, and with such extreme variations that in order to hear some of the actors at all you have to have Matthau's lines blistering your eardrums. Godard got sensitive live sound in the sixties on minuscule budgets, and Altman proved in *California Split* that audiences would respond to multiple-track "overheard" humor — why this barbaric, hog-callers' track? I won't deny that it works with many in the audience, but I imagine that it will also keep others away. The sound is insulting: it assumes that we're deaf to actors' verbal styles.

Suppose that instead of remaining a journalist a man like H. L. Mencken became a movie director. Would he stop warring with boob taste and try to satisfy it? And after a while would he be as divided as Billy Wilder, sometimes complaining that the public won't accept finesse anymore, and at other times deriding those who attempt it? Billy Wilder is a smart, sharp-toothed, sixty-eight-year-old venomous wit; he's too smart and too old not to know what he's doing here. He's debauching the Hecht-and-MacArthur play, exploiting a beautiful apparatus to produce a harsh, scrambling-for-laughs gag comedy. There are additions, such as having Walter Burns go to see Hildy's fiancée (Susan Sarandon), that are totally out of character: Burns wouldn't go to see the woman; she was no more than an obstacle to be brushed aside. And every once in a while Wilder slips into attitudes that pass beyond tough-guy cynicism into cretinous misanthropy. In one scene, the other reporters start pummelling Hildy, as if to beat him to death, and in the scene in which the streetwalker Mollie Malloy (Carol Burnett), whom the reporters have been jeering at, leaps out the pressroom window, the reporters' exclamations, which in the original express stupefied guilt mixed with the recognition that she's provided them with a story, have been altered to such unfeeling dumb cracks that the spirit of the play is violated. One can't deny Wilder his right to make a happy, high-spirited play more acrid, but this is Three Stooges acrid. Most of the performers seem badly in need of a director; you feel they've been told to shout, and not much else.

Walter Burns, the egomaniac who doesn't care about anything in the world but his newspaper, would seem to be a perfect Wilder hero — the Satan of the double-cross, the funny mean guy. And Burns, who knows that Hildy secretly wants to be saved from the boring respectability of marriage and a job in advertising, is an ideal role for Walter Matthau. It should be a cinch for him. One of the best hyperbolic comedians in movies since W. C. Fields, Matthau has the witty body of a caricaturist, and as Burns he should be able to uncoil to his full height and use the aplomb he's been storing up. Here's his opportunity to be suavely funny, and to develop in us the awe in which Walter Burns is held by newspapermen; Burns' maniacal spirit should itself be awe-inspiring. One would think that Matthau was already prepared for the role and that practically all he needed to do was to watch out for his squashed face, which can look waggish even when it isn't meant to, and be careful not to be droll and not to be facetious. He should be perfectly self-possessed for this character, who is a cartoon and yet mythic. How many great roles are there for Matthau? Walter Burns, maybe Saul Bellow's Tamkin — not very many. Yet, with this chance to play a really classy American character, he plays it like a rerun of other Matthau parts, with growling distortions. He mugs along cheerily, booming out the expletives and gags and jokes about flashers that Wilder and Diamond have contributed. What's funny about Walter Burns is his dapper confidence, his mad nonchalance. Matthau isn't the legendary *Herald Examiner* editor the play is written around; he's more like a whistle-stop Bear Bryant. Matthau doesn't even use his body for its line, for its design factor. He was infinitely better as Whiplash Willie, in the only performance that made Wilder's *The Fortune Cookie* worth sitting through. Is it possible that he's one of those performers who look great in crap and can't rise to real occasions? Or is it that he has got too lazy to work out a role the way he used to?

Matthau, however, still gets his laughs; Jack Lemmon doesn't. He's about fifteen years too paunchy for the role of Hildy, but maybe he could get by if he didn't look so logy and heartsick. Maybe he's played the tenderhearted fall guy so often that by now he takes one look at Matthau's dirty grin and figures that once again he's stuck playing the guy who doesn't have it and can't make it — the guy who lets himself be used. But that's not what Hildy Johnson is meant to be: Hildy isn't a schnooky victim — he's the top reporter in Chicago, he's cock of the walk. Anyone who saw the newspaper movies of the thirties knows the style in which Hildy Johnson is meant to be played. Lee Tracy, who created the part, never got to play it on the screen, but he brought Hildy to his performances in dozens of movies *(Blessed Event, Dinner at Eight, Bombshell),* and just about everyone else who played a newspaperman learned from Tracy's strutting style. Tracy could point up a line with a jabbing forefinger or a jiggle of the thumb, and you knew the raffish, cocksure pride that a reporter took in being a reporter. Hildy is conceived as an ace word-slinger who has a sense of showmanship about his profession. When he rants at Burns on the phone, he's proud of his invective, he gets a swingy rhythm to his insults; he's a virtuoso playing the violin — spiccato — when he tells off his boss. Lemmon's Hildy Johnson isn't big-time; Lemmon has been playing the patsy so long that even his most manic lines droop. There used to be a breezy, euphoric craziness in him; he had it when he played the drums in *Bell, Book and Candle,* and he certainly had it in Wilder's *Some Like It Hot.* Maybe it's not good for an actor to play so many defeatist roles; Lemmon carries them with him and plays Hildy Johnson like a mortuary assistant having a wild fling.

A great many fine performers are poorly used (like Carol Burnett) or not quite brought out (like Herbert Edelman and Doro Merande). And a little of Vincent Gardenia goes too far with me. (He looks strikingly like Mayor Daley here, but he plays the sheriff.) But if one needs a reason to see the movie, there is one freshly felt performance — Austin Pendleton's, as the nut-loner, the condemned man, Earl Williams. In this production, Earl is a fuddled court jester out of Woody Allen. Sniffling from a cold, speaking softly but hurriedly, the words tumbling together in a touching slight stammer, he has his own madman's sweetness and dignity. Pendleton provides the only touch of innocence in this loud production; he provides a luminous bit of nonsense — almost a pastoral touch. He's like a rabbit paralyzed by the noise of the locomotive coming at it. I wonder how Wilder let even this much innocence get through.

[January 27, 1975]

Don't Touch Me

SOMETIMES ASIDES REVEAL MORE about character than a full dramatic treatment does. In *Rafferty and the Gold Dust Twins,* two girls (Sally Kellerman and Mackenzie Phillips) kidnap a man (Alan Arkin) and force him, at gunpoint, to drive them from Los Angeles to Arizona. About halfway through, I was still wondering why the picture had been made. It was scrupulously crafted, and I was having a good time, but it seemed such a slender subject, and the ingredients were familiar from other road movies about the chance meeting of strays (such as *Slither*). After it was over, I was glad that Warners had taken a chance on such a marginal, small-scale idea. *Rafferty* doesn't pay off every few minutes; it sneaks up on you — you discover it, like a "sleeper." I found it a funny, velvety film, with the kind of tenderness that you can almost feel on your fingertips. The picture isn't directed for straightforward excitement; it's a sidewise vision. The director, Dick Richards, is a real southpaw. He's an attentive director, edging into the structure of relationships, and then, when the three principals, who have long since abandoned their kidnappers-and-victim relationship and become friends, are at a roadhouse called Sparky's, in Tucson, the whole thing comes together. Richards gives us a world in which everyone is alone, but the scruffy band of outsiders now accept that they care for each other; they've become so easy with each other that they even attract other rejects.

Sally Kellerman has been saying all along that what she really cares about is singing, and when she sings with the country-and-Western band at Sparky's, her emotion shows in her trembling face and throat. Her full aloneness is expressed in her plaintive country-music twang; it's as if we'd found out what was missing from Kellerman's character in *Slither.* Sally Kellerman's performance is softer and more flexible than any of her earlier ones; she seems to give herself over to the character in a way she hasn't done since *M*A*S*H.* And I think it may be the first time I've really been comfortable with Alan Arkin on the screen since his expansive impersonation of a muzhik in *The Russians Are Coming, The Russians Are Coming.* That wholesome fellow, with his enormous Slavic integrity, had a comic radiance that Arkin hasn't had since. I know that many people consider Arkin a great actor, and he's certainly highly skilled, but I don't think he's been a great movie actor. He doesn't project too much, as stage actors used to do onscreen, but his small modulations are just as tightly controlled as they would be on the stage, and what the camera picks up is taut, closed-in acting. There's no spontaneity; nothing shines forth. We never feel we're discovering something for ourselves in his face; we know he put every tiny mood in place. He plays too *small,* and I wondered that critics could admire his Yossarian, for example, when the character had so little life. In the current *Freebie and the Bean,* he's the same overcontrolled Arkin as before, deadfaced and relying on vocal tricks — hesitation humor, mostly — to do his acting, but as Rafferty he's beginning to move his facial muscles like a real person. His voice still lacks sensual appeal; it's a dry, flat voice that puts him among the comic losers. But if he could loosen it a little his whole personality might limber up. Probably he's more free as Rafferty because being free is absolutely essential for the role. The hard-shell character here is that of the teenager Frisbee (Mackenzie Phillips) — a balky, smart, foul-mouthed fifteen-year-old on the lam. Mackenzie Phillips was wonderfully spunky in *American Graffiti*; in this role her spunk is the outer form of misery — a self-protective crust. Frisbee is the grungy sleeping beauty of this schizo love comedy, and Rafferty must have the warmth and the fellow-feeling to melt her. If Rafferty didn't win Frisbee over in the car so that she finally climbs into the front seat to join the others, there wouldn't be any movie. The proof of Dick Richards's instinct is in the next scene. It's in the comic moment when Rafferty, having won, can parody Frisbee's earlier cry of "Don't touch me," and put his arm around her.

The script, an original by the young writer John Kaye, and his first to be produced, doesn't give Richards quite enough to work with. The movie doesn't make for a big evening, but, with a very few exceptions (I didn't like the line of dialogue that brings down an easy laugh on an old couple whose car is rammed), it sustains a half-fantasy, balloon-going-up mood. The way we learn about the background of each of the three may be a little too calculated, and the similarity of those backgrounds too predictably neat; the dénouement is almost comic-strip flip (a beginning as much as an end). Yet *Rafferty* has a fresh humor that is based not on desperation but on affection. Richards is a very companionable sort of director. A fashion photographer who became a whiz at TV commercials, he has made only one other film — *The Culpepper Cattle Co.*, a suicidally titled Western that came out in 1972, around the same time as another self-destructive Western, *The Great Northfield Minnesota Raid.* The title *Rafferty and the Gold Dust Twins* is hardly a come-on, either, and it's difficult to suggest any overwhelming reason the picture should be seen, but there are small, fringe reasons that add up. Richards has a fine responsiveness to faces (this may be what sent him into photography). The whole cast is effective — especially Alex Rocco, as the scrounger who attaches himself to the group in the Las Vegas episode, and Harry Dean Stanton, with his hollowed face (as if he'd worn away whatever life he had in him), as the man who shoots pool with Frisbee. Richards has a feeling for momentary encounters: what might be throwaways for another director are his most acutely realized moments. And maybe because he looks to see what's in people's faces he brought something out of Alan Arkin, instead of letting Arkin put it there. At the end, when Rafferty is playing dad to Frisbee and beaming, Arkin's relaxed face is a gift to us. He's got past his Second City shtick; the feeling in this charmingly inconsequential movie transforms him.

GAIL PARENT'S NOVEL *Sheila Levine Is Dead and Living in New York* — a top best-seller in paperback last year and still going strong — is in the form of a fat girl's jokey suicide note. It's all one-liners, and, reading it, you might almost be watching *Rhoda* on TV and hearing Rhoda's stocky sister Brenda getting laughs on the subject of how desperate she is for a date. (Mrs. Parent has, in fact, written for *Rhoda.*) In the book, Sheila's Jewish mother stuffed her with food, and when she's grown up, since she's fat and ugly and can't get a husband — which is her only mission in life — she stuffs herself. There wasn't much material for a movie in this extended TV skit, and as scriptwriters Mrs. Parent and her TV writing partner, Kenny Solms (they've written for Carol Burnett and done segments of *The Mary Tyler Moore Show,* among others), devised a different story. Now it's the Romance of Liberation. Sheila (Jeannie Berlin), no longer fat, comes to New York and meets a handsome doctor (Roy Scheider). But he's a "confirmed" bachelor, and it isn't until after she has made a jerk of herself trying to land him, and is deep in her work, producing records for children, that he extricates himself from an involvement with her aspiring-actress call-girl roommate, Kate (Rebecca Dianna Smith), and gets around to proposing. He loves Sheila, it turns out, for her openness — her willingness to humiliate herself — in contrast with his own self-protective bachelor reserve.

A confused, part-liberated rehash of old-Hollywood attitudes toward the young working girl in the big city, *Sheila Levine* isn't much of a movie. There are more star closeups of Jeannie Berlin than there were even of Joan Crawford or Susan Hayward in their working-girl days, or of Natalie Wood in *Love with the Proper Stranger,* and Jeannie Berlin's improvisatory manner is at odds with the worshipful camera. In most of the closeups, Sheila has nothing to express but bewilderment. Her extraordinarily passive doctor makes sheep's eyes at her while Kate leads him around by the nose. When he finally delivers his declaration of love to Sheila, a muscle in his face twitches, and you half expect the audience to burst into applause: at last, Scheider has *done* something besides point his virile nose, crinkle up his eyes, and grin like a dapper George C. Scott. The director, Sidney J. Furie, provides the disadvantages of the slick, impersonal style (every flutter of a false eyelash makes a point; nothing is believable) and none of the advantages, such as a coherent continuity. There are gaps in the plot and woozy lapses in time; at one point, when we think Sheila still lives in New York, she's suddenly teaching school in her hometown — Harrisburg, Pennsylvania.

The movie would seem to be a stupid fiasco; it barely escapes self-parody when it tries for romantic encounters. The doctor, his voice posh-full of emotion, greets Sheila with "How are you, Harrisburg?" Yet I have never before seen young women in an audience so riled up after a movie, and I've heard that at some showings they've booed. Clearly, it represents more than an ordinary piece of trash to them. A friend who had seen an advance screening told me not to bother going to it, because it was the worst movie she'd ever seen; a few days later she went to see it again. From what I can gather from talking with a few of the women, they're not angry because Sheila's whole drive in life is man-centered — they're angry because they feel that it's a lie that she'd win her doctor. I have heard several women say something like "The picture just isn't true," and each time it turned out that they weren't rejecting the whole slurpy vision but rejecting only Sheila's victory. Their idea seems to be that if you don't look like that L'Oreal blonde ("I don't mind spending more for L'Oreal, because I'm worth it"), you can't get a first-class husband. They don't take their attitudes from the TV commercials' message, which is that if you buy the products you, too, will be Waspy-lovely; they take them from the subliminal message, which is that if you're not Waspy-lovely you don't stand a chance. And since they know damned well that using L'Oreal won't turn them into that model they're bitterly defeatist about their chances for a model man.

Actually, Jeannie Berlin looks great; she needed to be lumpy-faced in *The Heartbreak Kid,* but here she has fine contours and her face is warm and appealing. Her performance almost does her in, however. Her big telephone scene should be her last telephone scene ever, and she ought never to appear in another movie with a Jewish wedding. Not only is this picture full of scenes that were clichés the first time they were done but Sidney Furie brings worse than nothing to them. Sheila is allowed to show vivacity only when she's clumsy or flustered or behaving idiotically; the more "mature" she becomes, the more slowed down she is. She has no normal range. Furie seems to think that she's being intelligent and reflective when she's openmouthed comatose. Jeannie Berlin has an expressive face, but her features are larger than those of most models, and in the subtext of this movie she might just as well be fat, because she's playing ugly duckling to skinny Kate. Though the picture takes the new homiletic view that she finds herself as a person and develops a career before winning her man, she feels she's a failure and behaves like one. And the women in the audience probably see her as a failure. They've got their own cynicism blended with women's-liberation ideas.

Sheila Levine gets to them in some prickly way, as if it were violating their hard-won knowledge of life. The movie has several primal scenes that relate to this knowledge. When Sheila first meets the doctor, she goes to bed with him and then fantasizes an enduring love, only to be painfully embarrassed when he explains to her that it was just casual sex. Later, she tries to lure him by being like the freakish Kate, since that seems to be what he goes for; rigged out in a dumb-tart dress and ankle-breaker shoes, and wearing layers of makeup, she's a gruesome parody. (She looks more like Helmut Berger than like Kate.) And at the end of this exhibition, when the doctor tells her that Kate is pregnant and he's marrying her, Sheila's humiliation is more devastating even than Bette Davis's in *Jezebel* when she knelt to Henry Fonda, only to be presented to his wife. And there's another degradation scene, also treated as primal soap opera: a girl who has just gone to bed with someone she met at a party makes a weepy speech about how disgusting these sex episodes always are but how she keeps getting into them, hoping for something wonderful to happen. These overwrought scenes may fool some of the women in the audience into thinking that the picture really is about their lives, and this may intensify their hostility toward the happy ending. There seems almost an anxiety to be liberated among young women now. Some of them in the audience may be so raw-nerved on these issues, and so eager to see them treated on the screen, that they become indignant when they perceive that *Sheila Levine* is no more than a sleazy con. But the wonder is that they don't see it from the start. It's perplexing, too, when they complain that the book was different. Is there anything in that facile joke book to preserve? Nothing but its sense of defeat.

What's disturbing about the movie is that it exploits the self-hatred of so many women in the audience, who identify with Sheila because they feel that they, too, are not top-quality love objects. (I think they may also transfer their self-hatred to an actress who plays this sort of role.) They experience the happy ending as a betrayal of their own sense of hopelessness. Maybe the movie plot was designed to give them hope, but it doesn't; it infuriates them. The advertising culture has set models of physical perfection and sexual expertise which have made a whole nation of plain or attractive — or even beautiful — young women feel that they are ugly ducklings. And here comes *Sheila Levine* to touch the sore spots and then fade out on a wish fulfillment.

There are genuine issues that are being corrupted in a number of recent popular women-as-sex-objects books. The rage that is in them is not about what created the author-heroine's fantasies and not about her own responsibility for forming them. The rage is about her fantasies' not being fulfilled. And that is what is being blamed on society. This picture piles a new fantasy on top of the others: you have to be an achiever. What Mrs. Parent and her partner have done goes further in exploitativeness than the earlier romances, because the new line here is that it is Sheila's development of independence and her "finding herself" that entitle her to a first-class man. The doctor sees through Kate and sees Sheila's worth. Achievement has made her more lovable. It's a pop conversion of women's liberation into: The libbers get the princes.

[February 3, 1975]

For Oscar's Sake

EVERY YEAR, there are a few ambitious performances so spectacularly bad that there are immediate cries for the performer to get an Oscar, and every year or two one of these performances does indeed get its Oscar. Who can deny that Shirley Jones earned hers in *Elmer Gantry,* Shelley Winters hers in *A Patch of Blue,* Red Buttons his in *Sayonara,* and Cliff Robertson his in *Charly*? In 1970 — a bumper year — there were two such awards: John Mills', for *Ryan's Daughter,* and Helen Hayes', for *Airport.* These are all classically bad performances, and it's only fitting that they should be acclaimed. I've never understood why it was that Susan Tyrrell, who was nominated for *Fat City,* didn't win; it's hard to see how a performance of that caliber could be ignored. (Perhaps it was because she was competing with Stacy Keach in the film, and his catatonic drabness soaked up her flamboyance.) And if Patrick Magee were an American his work in *A Clockwork Orange* might have received full recognition. Show-stopping bad acting isn't easy. Fabulous performances like these don't happen overnight; a lot of training, thought, and preparation go into them, plus a talent for shamelessness. There hasn't been a real beaut since Glenda Jackson sprang forth in *A Touch of Class,* so Michael Moriarty is bound to be discovered for his work in the new suspense film *Report to the Commissioner.*

Moriarty didn't do it without help from the role itself — that of a sensitive, innocent twenty-two-year-old undercover detective who breaks under stress. It gives him one of the opportunities that actors beg for: he can fall apart on camera. In this case, all the sympathy goes to his character, too, because he's the victim of a group of callous, blundering New York City Police officials. And, oh, how Moriarty falls apart. He can't wait for the climactic collapse: he's disoriented on his entrance, and he begins disintegrating before you've settled in your seat. Moriarty never quite looks at the person he's talking to; he's so dazed by his own sensitivity that his speech is slow and dissociated. He sweats, he twitches, he convulses; his deep breathing fills the sound track. (He breathes with the passionate conviction that Richard Cromwell used to bring to weeping.) Moriarty drains his cup of misery to the dregs and refills it from the pitcher. Unfortunately, *Report to the Commissioner* isn't a hypertense jewel like *The Bad and the Beautiful*, in which all the performers were jacked up to an Oscar frenzy, and Moriarty's style isn't entertaining in that splashy way. His physical movements are indefinite, his manner is bland — as if nothing had ever sunk into his consciousness. He signals wildly that he's in an artistic sphere of his own, but it's all very quiet. He's not much help to the picture, though he makes it a must for connoisseurs of egregious acting. (They are sometimes known as the Sandy Dennis Fan Club, but there has been some talk among the more historical-minded members of changing the name to the Charles Laughton Memorial Society.)

Moriarty's Beauregard (Bo) Lockley is a perfectly serious performance; the humor comes out of one's derangement while one watches him bucking for glory. Moriarty was a likable juvenile as the saintly, fair-haired, blue-eyed ballplayer in *Bang the Drum Slowly* — the role that Paul Newman had played on TV in 1956 — and he seemed destined to be a popular romantic lead. But he looks different now: his baby face is pale and formlessly soft; the blurry chin seems to melt into the neck. He's got the look of a sweet-voiced Irish tenor or a suety Hamlet — introspective and sexless. He seems too preoccupied with giving his facial muscles a workout to supply the young male sexuality that is essential to the motivation. Bo is meant to be a new kind of cop — a hippie cop with enlightened attitudes. It's his wanting to rescue a fresh-faced, blond young girl from a handsome black pusher that brings him to grief. But as Moriarty plays him Bo is a pathological case from the start, so the suspense element never really takes off.

As a novel, James Mills' *Report to the Commissioner* was transparently a screenplay. Mills, who used to be a crime reporter for *Life*, gave a journalistic veneer to a story that pretended to be a hard, inside look at a New York City Police foulup. It's almost a joke that Ernest Tidyman and Abby Mann were hired to adapt the book, since Mills structured the novel for the movies, provided the dialogue, and laid in the chase sequences. Mills doesn't have much talent for plotting, but he knows where he wants the story to get, and he barrels his way through. The gimmick is that Bo, a rookie detective who doesn't know the score about anything, is told to look for the young blonde — Chiclet (Susan Blakely) — and he is so confused by the Department's manipulations that he doesn't guess that she is an undercover narc. To tone up this plot, Chiclet's black lover, known as The Stick (Tony King), is not only a pusher but also a militant. However, things are carefully balanced out so that it won't seem as if all blacks were pushers and radicals; Bo is provided with a Kingfish black partner, an old-timer called Crunch (Yaphet Kotto), who beats up on blacks.

The novel was so much like a movie that probably a lot of readers imagined that it would be a real dilly on the screen, but sometimes when a novel reads like a screenplay it's because there's nothing under the material. And that can mean that there's not enough to draw upon and nothing to bring out. James Mills' characters are so flimsy that we need to be caught up in the suspense, but, as Milton Katselas has directed the film, we have plenty of time to notice how illogical each plot turn is. Katselas, whose previous movies were the transcribed stage plays *Butterflies Are Free* and *Forty Carats,* seems way out of his element here. The hints of lascivious repressed feelings dribble away aimlessly, and the scenes don't lead plausibly into the big action sequences. The first big chase, with a legless beggar, Joey (Robert Balaban), who has been befriended by Bo, giving a heroic demonstration of loyalty, assisting Bo by chasing a taxi through heavy traffic on his skateboard, is sickeningly gaudy. (Even in silent pictures, writers were embarrassed when they had to resort to a heart-wrencher this decrepit.) And it serves no plot function whatever: there's no urgency about chasing the taxi — Bo could have waited a couple of hours, until the people who went out in the taxi returned home. In the next big chase number — and it's so obviously a number that the audience titters — Bo pursues The Stick, who is dressed only in shorts. The two of them jump across rooftops, leap over cars, and wind up holding guns on each other in an elevator at Saks — where they opt for brotherhood, when it is too late. (Why Saks? The author has learned a thing or two from crisp, hardboiled fiction: after Bo, Chiclet, Crunch, and The Stick, it couldn't very well be Bloomingdale's or Bonwit Teller.) The standoff in the Saks elevator goes on so long, and we have so little involvement in the resolution, that it's just embarrassing, waiting while the two men pour sweat.

What is supposed to hold our attention? The movie follows the book very closely, but in the book the reader knows from the start that Bo killed Chiclet; the Report to the Commissioner is of a secret investigation within the Police Department to learn why. In the movie we're uncertain whether Bo did it; we suspect various higher-ups of being the killer, and anticipate plot developments that don't come. I kept wondering when someone was going to mention a ballistics test and tell us if Chiclet had been killed by a bullet from Bo's gun. The moviemakers apparently think that the material is more ironic if the facts can never be known, but since there's such an obvious way to solve the mystery, this is just a pain. They're not sure what sort of movie they're making — something indefinite between *The French Connection* and *The Defiant Ones* — and we don't know what to look for. At times, we're stuck at the rudimentary level of trying to figure out if Chiclet is more devious than she lets on or if it's just that Susan Blakely — she might have been called The Blank — is so shallow that we're assuming deviousness where none is intended. When the girl talks about why she's in police work — in a twittery little voice, like the early Gene Tierney — it could be a put-on for a screen test. Is she meant to be some sort of surreally dutiful bitch who takes pleasure in entrapping men, or is she meant to be no more than a riddle? To a viewer, it looks as if it were the movie that's fouling up, not the Police Department. The novelist was able to slick over what Katselas can't: that putting Bo on Chiclet's trail makes no sense — that it's just a gimmick to hang chases on.

The story is no more than an entry in the *French Connection* sweepstakes, smartened up with the newer *Serpico* theme (the hippie cop versus the old pros). However, this is not your ordinary rotten movie; you can tell by the way the Elmer Bernstein music, which percusses for the chase sequences, stops so that you can appreciate the dramatic passages in weighty silence. And Michael Moriarty's campaign to be the new big sensitivity star lifts the picture out of the failed-suspense category into the art-howler category. No actor before him had the delirious insight to play innocence as a tragic sickness, but perhaps the times weren't right until just this minute. By the end, Bo is innocence crucified, and it's the whole society that did it. Moriarty can hardly miss. American movies may have a new hysterical superstar.

[February 10, 1975]

Beverly Hills as a Big Bed

When George (Warren Beatty), the hairdresser hero of *Shampoo,* asks Jackie (Julie Christie), "Want me to do your hair?", it's his love lyric. George massages a neck and wields a blower as if he would rather be doing that than anything else in the world. When he gets his hands in a woman's hair, it's practically sex, and sensuous, tender sex — not what his Beverly Hills customers are used to. Their husbands and lovers don't have professionally caressing hands like the dedicated George's. Some ideas for films are promising, some are cocksure audacious, but a film about the movie colony featuring the lives of the rich, beautiful women who have a yen for their handsome hairdresser is such a yummy idea that it almost sounds like something a smart porno filmmaker would come up with. Exploited for gags, it might have been no more than a saucy romp, a modernized *Fanfan the Tulip,* and that may be what audiences expect — maybe even what some audiences want. But the way it has been done, the joke expands the more you think about it. *Shampoo* is light and impudent, yet, like the comedies that live on, it's a bigger picture in retrospect.

The attention George gives women is so exciting to him and to them that he's always on the go. He works in a fashionable salon, commutes to his assignations on a motorbike, and tells himself and his girl, Jill (Goldie Hawn), that they'll settle down as soon as he gets his own shop. The movie deals with his frantic bed-hopping during the forty-odd hours in which he tries to borrow the stake he needs from Lester (Jack Warden), the shyster tycoon who is married to Felicia (Lee Grant), a rapacious customer. Lester is also keeping Jackie, George's old girl friend, who is Jill's closest friend. *Shampoo* opens on Election Eve, November 4, 1968, when the hero's life has begun to boil over. The characters whirl in and out of bed with each other through Election Day and Night, watching the returns at a party at The Bistro, acknowledging Nixon and Agnew's victory by seeing in the dawn at another party, and preparing for the new era by shifting partners. The picture is a sex roundelay set in a period as clearly defined as the Jazz Age. (It's gone, all right, and we know that best when we catch echoes from it.) Maybe we've all been caught in a time warp, because the Beatles sixties of miniskirts and strobe lights, when people had not yet come down from their euphoria about the harmlessness of drugs, is already a period with its own bubbly potency. The time of *Shampoo* is so close to us that at moments we forget its pastness, and then we're stung by the consciousness of how much has changed.

Shampoo is set in the past for containment, for a formalized situation, just as Ingmar Bergman set his boudoir farce, *Smiles of a Summer Night,* in the operetta past of the *Merry Widow* period. What the turn-of-the-century metaphor did for Bergman the 1968 election, as the sum of an era, does for *Shampoo.* The balletic, patterned confusion of *Shampoo* is theatrical, and Los Angeles — more particularly, Beverly Hills, the swankest part of it, a city within a city — is, indisputably, a stylized, theatrical setting. But a bedroom-chase construction isn't stagey in Beverly Hills: *Shampoo* has a mathematically structured plot in an open society. Los Angeles itself, the sprawl-city, opens the movie up, and the L.A. sense of freedom makes its own comment on the scrambling characters. Besides, when you play musical chairs in the bedrooms of Beverly Hills, the distances you have to cover impose their own comic frenzy. As in a Feydeau play or some of the René Clair and Lubitsch films, the more complicated the interaction is, the more we look forward to the climactic muddle and the final sorting out of couples. The whirring pleasures of carnal farce require our awareness of the mechanics, and the director, Hal Ashby, has the deftness to keep us conscious of the structure and yet to give it free play. The plot isn't arbitrary; it's what George, who can never really get himself together, is caught in. The mixed pairs of lovers don't get snarled at the same parties by coincidence; they go knowing who else is going to be there, wanting the danger of collisions.

Shampoo expresses the emotional climate of the time and place. Los Angeles has become what it is because of the bright heat, which turns people into narcissists and sensuous provocateurs. The atmosphere seems to infantilize sex: sexual desire is despiritualized; it becomes a demand for immediate gratification. George's women have their status styles — money and sun produce tough babies — but George, the sexual courier, servicing a garden apartment as ardently as a terraced estate, is a true democrat. The characters are all linked by sex — and dissatisfaction. They're passionate people from minute to minute. They want to have something going for them all the time, and since they get it only part of the time, and it doesn't last long, they feel upset and frustrated. They're so foolish, self-absorbed, and driven that the film can easily seem a trifle — and at one level it is — but it's daringly faithful to the body-conscious style of life that is its subject, and it never falls into low farce by treating the characters as dumdums. They're attractively, humanly, greedily foolish, and some of their foolishness is shared by people much more complex. The movie gets at the kink and willfulness of the Beverly Hills way of life (which magnetizes the whole world), but it doesn't point any comic fingers. It's too balanced and Mozartean for that.

The scenarist, Robert Towne (Beatty, who shares the screenplay credit, contributed ideas and worked on the structuring with him), has brought something new to bedroom farce. The characters have more than one sex object in mind, and they're constantly regrouping in their heads. No one is romantically in love or devoted in the sense in which Bergman's characters are in *Smiles of a Summer Night. Shampoo* isn't about the bondage of romantic pursuit, it's about the bondage of the universal itch among a group primed to scratch. Ready and waiting, the characters keep all possibilities open. This variation on the usual love comedy is the trickiest, funniest, truest-to-its-freeway-love-environment ingredient of the movie. Except for George, who doesn't plan ahead, everyone is always considering alternatives. It's a small, rich, loose society, and its members know each other carnally in a casual way; it's in the nature of things that they take turns in the one big bed that is their world. Since the characters hold multiple goals, when they look depressed you're never sure who exactly is the object of their misery. The actors are much more free than in the confines of classic farce. They're free, too, of the stilted witticisms of classic farce: Towne writes such easy, unforced dialogue that they might be talking in their own voices.

Julie Christie's locked-in, libidinous face has never been harder, more petulant, or more magical than in her role as Lester's kept woman, who hates her position because she never gets to go anywhere with him. Jackie is coarse and high-strung (a true L.A. combo); she's a self-destructive winner, and Julie Christie plays her boldly, with a moody ruthlessness that I find uncanny. This is the first time Christie and Beatty have acted together since *McCabe & Mrs. Miller,* and each of them gains. Julie Christie is one of those screen actresses whose every half-buried thought smashes through; she's so delicate an actress that when she plays a coarse girl like Jackie there's friction in each nuance. On the stage last year in *Uncle Vanya* she was a vacuum; in *Shampoo* she's not only an actress, she is — in the high-class-hooker terms of her role — the sexiest woman in movies right now. She has the knack of turning off her spirituality totally; in this role she's a gorgeous, whory-lipped little beast, a dirty sprite.

Goldie Hawn, who began to come into her own as a screen actress in last year's *The Sugarland Express,* is probably going to be everything her admirers have hoped for. As the hysterical young Jill, she isn't allowed to be too hysterical; Hal Ashby doesn't let her go all frilly and wistful, either. She used to be her own best audience; now that she has stopped breaking up infectiously, we're free to judge her for ourselves. She has calm moments here — we see Jill's mind working without Goldie Hawn's goldfish eyes batting — and I think it's the first time I've noticed that she has a speaking voice. (She's always been a screamer.) She looks great in her baby dolls and minis, and it's a relief that her Jill doesn't have a mini baby-doll head. Lee Grant, who worked with Ashby in *The Landlord,* the film of his that *Shampoo* most resembles (though he was a beginner then, with nothing like the assurance he shows now), is such a cool-style comedienne that she's in danger of having people say that she's good, as usual. But she carries off the film's most sexually brutal scene: Felicia comes home late for an assignation with George and discovers that while he was waiting for her he has been occupied with her teenage daughter (Carrie Fisher), and she *still* wants to go to bed with him. She wants it more than ever. As her husband, Jack Warden is the biggest surprise in the cast. He's both a broad cartoon and an appealing character. Lester is triply cuckolded — George commutes between Lester's mistress and wife and daughter — and he's a heavy contributor to the Nixon-Agnew campaign, for business purposes. And yet he has more depth than anyone else in the movie. He's ready to investigate anything: invited to join a nymphs-and-satyrs bathing orgy, he considers getting into the water as he would a new investment, and thinks, Why not? Warden shows us Lester's pragmatic ruminations; we see that he's a business success because he's learned to make compromises in his own favor. While Nixon is on TV making his victory speech, Lester and George have it all out, in a final confrontation scene, and the astute Lester realizes that, despite the wear and tear on George's zipper, the hairdresser is no threat to him.

The central performance that makes it all work is Beatty's. George, who wears his hair blower like a Colt .45, isn't an easy role; I don't know anyone else who could have played it. Because of Beatty's offscreen reputation as a heterosexual dynamo, audiences may laugh extra hard at the scenes in which Lester assumes that a male hairdresser can't be straight, but that joke is integral to the conception anyway. Beatty makes George's impulsive warmth toward his customers believable. An uncomplicated Don Juan, George gets pleasure from giving pleasure. He doesn't smoke tobacco or dope; he doesn't pop pills; outside of soft drinks, the only beverage he takes in the whole film is a little white wine. George doesn't need to be raised high or brought down, and he has nothing to obliterate. Maybe when he's older, if he's still working in someone else's shop, he'll be embittered, and he'll be one of the garden-variety narcissists who must have attention from women (and secretly hate them). But at this point in his life, jumping happily to oblige any woman who wants him, he has the pagan purity of an adolescent. At the start of the film, George is in the middle of the whirligig, but by the end the game has moved on, and he's left behind, dreaming of a simpler life and longing for a sexual playmate from the past. "You're the only one I trust," he tells Jackie. The others are upward-mobile and moving fast, and they live as if upward mobility were a permanent condition. George wants something to hang on to, and he can't get it, because he's too generous. He lives in constant excitation, and so he's the closest to exhaustion. George is the only one of the characters who isn't completely selfish; he's the only one who doesn't function successfully in the society. The others know how to use people, but George, the compleat lover, does everything for fun. Making love to a beautiful woman is an aesthetic thing with him, and making her look beautiful is an act of love for him. He's almost a sexual saint.

Shampoo doesn't seem inspired the way Renoir's roundelay *Rules of the Game* does. It doesn't have the feeling that one gets from the Renoir film — that the whole beautiful, macabre chaos is bubbling up right this minute. And *Shampoo* is not as lyrical — or as elegantly moldy to the taste — as parts of Bergman's *Smiles.* It doesn't give the lunatic delight of *Bringing Up Baby,* which in its homegrown, screwball style also suggested an equivalent of Restoration comedy. But it's the most virtuoso example of sophisticated, kaleidoscopic farce that American moviemakers have ever come up with. And, as in *Rules of the Game,* the farce movement itself carries a sense of heedless activity, of a craze of dissatisfaction. In this game, George, who loves love too much to profit from it, has to be the loser. He's a fool (that's why Lester doesn't have him beaten up), but he's a pure fool (and Lester can appreciate that). George isn't a negligible dramatic creation. For the moviemakers, he's the foolish romanticism of youth incarnate, but some people may see him as a jerk and resent him. To them, possibly, the new romantic hero would be a cynical stud who gets it all and wins out. In its own way, *Shampoo* is a very uncompromising film, and it's going to cause dissension. People who are living the newer forms of the *Blow-Up* style, or want to, won't like this view of it. *Shampoo* may be put down as frivolous just because it really isn't; to lift a line from *The Earrings of Madame de . . . ,* it's "only superficially superficial." Was it Osbert Sitwell who said that life might be considered a comedy only if it were never to end? *Shampoo* tosses the fact of death into the midst of the beauty shop; we suddenly learn that Norman (Jay Robinson), the languid, pettish proprietor, whom we'd assumed to be strictly homosexual, has just lost his teenage son in a car crash. It's an artifice — reality intruding upon the clowns at their revels, death as an interruption to the babble and trivial bickering of the beauty-salon world. But it's needed, and it's the right death — the accidental death of someone young, the only event, maybe, that can't be converted into gossip.

There are minds at work in this film: three principal ones — Ashby, Beatty, who produced it (it is his second production; the first was *Bonnie and Clyde*), and Towne. Hal Ashby says that he had fifty or sixty jobs (starting when he was ten years old) before he landed as a Multilith operator at the old Republic Studios in L.A., and decided he wanted to become a director. As the first step, he went to work in the cutting room, where he spent the standard eight years as an apprentice before he was allowed (by feudal union regulation) to edit a film. Afterward, he edited Norman Jewison's *The Cincinnati Kid, The Russians Are Coming, The Russians Are Coming, In the Heat of the Night,* and *The Thomas Crown Affair,* and then, in 1968, Jewison, who was supposed to direct *The Landlord,* arranged with the moneymen to turn it over to Ashby. (*Shampoo* should cause *The Landlord* to get the attention it deserves.) His new film is only his fourth (*Harold and Maude* and *The Last Detail* came between), but he's developed quickly. Ashby's control keeps *Shampoo* from teetering over into burlesque. His work doesn't have the flash of an innovative, intuitive film artist, but for the script Towne has prepared, Ashby, the craftsman who serves the material, is probably the only kind of director.

Robert Towne didn't write a screenplay a director can take off from. *Shampoo* is conceived for the movies, and it's porous, yet the development of the themes is completely conceived. It isn't the basis for a director to work out his own conception; it *is* a conception. (Tall, his long face dark-bearded, Towne appears in one party shot in *Shampoo,* looking a little like Albrecht Dürer.) It's more apparent now why Towne collided with Polanski over his script (also an original) for *Chinatown.* He provided a script that culminated — logically — with the heroine's killing her lover-father in order to save her daughter. A Gothic-minded absurdist, Polanski didn't see why he shouldn't end it with the death of the heroine and the triumph of the father, who had raped the land, raped his daughter, and would now proceed to corrupt the child he'd had by her. Towne doesn't pull everything down like that. It has taken a while to get a fix on his talent, because he's not a published writer, and because he didn't receive credit for some of the films he worked on, and didn't take blame for others (*The New Centurions*). His earliest screen credits are for *Villa Rides* and *The Tomb of Ligeia,* but even before those, in 1964, he wrote an episode for TV's *Breaking Point,* called "So Many Pretty Girls, So Little Time," about a Don Juan. Beatty brought him in to do the rewriting on *Bonnie and Clyde* (he was listed as "Special Consultant"), and when Coppola accepted his Academy Award for the screenplay of *The Godfather* he acknowledged Towne's contribution (he wrote one scene and tinkered with a few others). Towne also did a major rewrite on *Cisco Pike* (the film has certain similarities to *Shampoo*) and on *The Yakuza,* which hasn't opened yet, and he wrote the script (an adaptation) of *The Last Detail.*

Towne's heroes, if we can take Gittes, of *Chinatown,* and George, here, as fair examples, are hip to conventional society, and they assume that they reject its dreams. But in some corner of their heads they think that maybe the old romantic dream can be made to work. Gittes is basically a very simple man. He wants the woman he loves to tell him the truth about herself; the truth is very important to him. And George is even simpler. Towne's heroes are like the heroes of hardboiled fiction: they don't ask much of life, but they are also romantic damn fools who ask just what they can't get. His characters are so effective on the screen because they have sides you don't expect and — a Towne idiosyncrasy — they tell anecdotes, mostly inane, backslapping ones (Jack Nicholson has several in *The Last Detail* and *Chinatown,* and Jack Warden gets off a real puzzler). With his ear for unaffected dialogue, and with a gift for never forcing a point, Towne may be a great new screenwriter in a structured tradition — a flaky classicist.

[February 17, 1975]

Male Revenge

IRA LEVIN'S NOVEL *The Stepford Wives* had a shrewd, potentially good movie idea — the same basic idea as that of the low-budget 1956 sci-fi horror film *Invasion of the Body Snatchers.* In the small-town setting of *Invasion,* everyone is turned into a vegetable. In the suburban community of Stepford, however, it's only the wives who are dehumanized; when they show the first stirrings of interest in consciousness-raising, their husbands turn them into domestic and sexual slave-robots. The plot of *The Stepford Wives* is *Invasion of the Body Snatchers* with a women's-lib theme. The idea of a quiet, undeclared all-out war of men against their wives has a perverse charm, and satirical possibilities leap to mind.

How could anyone with half a spark of humor resist showing us scenes of the husbands being irritated by the wives' new demands and then being blissfully, sneakily happy with the undemanding robots? But Levin's book was barely a novel at all; it was more like a solemn outline that he couldn't bother filling in. And the adapter, William Goldman, and the director, Bryan Forbes, probably had too much contempt for the book to think the film through. The dialogue is gummy, the situations dimly functional; the movie gives the impression of a patchwork script, and it's blah and becalmed.

The film of *Stepford* preys on women's fears (and men's guilt), as *Rosemary's Baby,* from an earlier novel of Ira Levin's, did, but not teasingly this time. The film *Rosemary's Baby,* keeping the spirit of the book, had a freaky-scary naughtiness, and a psychological dimension. Rosemary's terror was like a woman's worst masochistic pregnancy fantasies — that she was helplessly caught, involved with a husband who didn't care about her, and that she would give birth to a monstrosity. The audience identified with Mia Farrow's terrified, emaciated vulnerability, and the whole movie was told from her point of view. It was an honestly trashy thriller entertainment — skin-crawling but sophisticated and funny, and with a comic twist at the end: Rosemary cooing over her infant Satan. I don't like the queasy and the grisly mixed with entertainment, and I didn't really enjoy *Rosemary's Baby,* but it wasn't a boobish picture, like *The Stepford Wives.* The story of *Stepford,* too, is told from the threatened wife's point of view, but Katharine Ross, who plays the victim-heroine, Joanna, a wife who fears that the move from New York to Stepford will close her world in, doesn't have a very distinctive personality, and there isn't a hell of a lot of difference between her and the robot housewives right from the start.

It's a disastrous piece of casting. Katharine Ross is lovely-looking, and she's not a bad actress. It might be better if she were: a coarse performance might give us something to react to. But Katharine Ross is vacantly intelligent and somewhat reserved, almost blocked. Joanna goes through the motions of being a sympathetic mother to her two kids, as if she'd read about how to talk to children in a good, sound book. Ross is a peculiarly careful yet convictionless actress; she always looks tentative, as if she weren't quite sure that she wanted to come to life. Hardly the actress to make us feel the encroaching horror of suburban blandness. Levin's idea of making Joanna creative by having her be a gifted photographer is a lazy out — a substitute for writing a character with some life in her to lose. Even the worst cant of the women's movement has often been high-spirited — and the explosive charge told us more than the rhetoric — but Joanna is a low-spirited woman. And in the movie the photographs she takes of children at play are so wholesomely creative that they're practically the photographic equivalent of adding an egg to a packaged cake mix.

A suspense-horror film generally needs a certain amount of funkiness; even a little clumsiness and incompetence can help it along. But *Stepford* is tastefully tame; it has been made as if no one involved had any hope for it — it's literal in a way that seems a wasting disease. The super-household-appliance wives are Librium-slow. The reason is apparent, but robot people can be fun if they're quick and jerky, while these spacey robots are a drag. The pasty-faced automaton wives, with shiny, gluey eyes and bosoms tilted skyward, are like Raquel Welch or Ann-Margret without the lewdness. In other words — nothing. Instead of the developments one awaits, there are chunky scenes that don't come from the book and don't sound like Goldman's usual up-to-the-minute pseudo-hipness, either (Joanna reassuring one of her children, who's upset, by talking as if it were the child's Teddy bear who had the problem; Joanna and her friend Bobby, played by Paula Prentiss, visiting an old suitor of Joanna's named Raymond Chandler and having a pointless and horribly facetious chat about detective novels). Since the women haven't enough personality for us to get scared for them — where's the terror in robots' being turned into robots? — *Stepford* has nothing but its cautionary parable to go on. It's a depressing thought, but an awful lot of people may be willing to accept it on that humorless, cautionary level.

That is exactly the level on which, I think, it has no validity. As a statement — a text for our times — with the slave-wives parading somnambulistically in the aisles of the Stepford supermarket, stacking canned goods in their carts, it's really a crock. If women turn into replicas of the women in commercials, they do it to themselves. Even if the whole pop culture weighs on them — pushing them in that direction — if they go that way, they're the ones letting it happen. And as long as they can blame the barrenness of their lives on men, they don't need to change. They can play at being victims instead, and they can do it under the guise of liberation.

The Stepford Wives doesn't need to be a good movie in order to succeed, because it panders to the softheaded psychological commonplaces of the moment, just as *David and Lisa* did, and, on a somewhat more skillful level, *The Graduate,* or, in its own way, *Easy Rider.* It's a perfect movie for precisely those women for whom the tour of the supermarket is the high point of the day; *Stepford's* view of the relations of the sexes is just what those women are purchasing now from the magazine rack near the cash register. It's for women who have nothing in mind that they really want to do, except maybe fantasies of losing some weight and becoming an airline stewardess, women who feel trapped by the deadliness of their lives and are envious of their husbands' supposedly exciting time at work. These women can be turned on by *Stepford* because the ideas floating around in it confirm their fantasies. Joanna discovers that the automatons were active, creative, intelligent women before their husbands organized and, under the leadership of the sinister Dale Coba (Patrick O'Neal) — known as Diz, because he used to work at Disneyland — began systematically turning them into male ideals of femininity. The responsibility for suburban women's becoming overgroomed deadheads, obsessed with waxed, antiseptic households, is thus placed totally on the men. And one look at the men and you know that the women were their superiors in every way. The men (and this is a bit of shrewdness that's not in the book) are aging, courteous mice, nervously scuttling in and out of the woodwork. The only man in the movie meant to be even remotely attractive is the suave scientific mastermind Diz; he's unmarried — presumably his ego is bigger than his id.

As a guilt provoker for men, this picture may be peerless. It says to them, "You're a vacuous, inadequate excuse for a man; you've been demeaning a sensitive, intelligent woman, and now that she's trying to lift her head and get her consciousness raised, you'd rather kill her than let her find herself." It also says that these mousy men can be desired sexually only by women who are programmed to lie to them. *Stepford* hits men below the belt and tells them it's for their own good. Columbia Pictures may not know what it has got. The company seems to be selling *Stepford* as a sci-fi cheapo, but, given any halfway smart promotion, how can the picture not succeed?

The most salable part of the women's-liberation movement is the idea that women have been wronged by men — not "He done her wrong," as in the old he-robbed-her-of-her-virginity-and-wouldn't-marry-her sense, but, rather, "He done her wrong by marrying her for his comfort's sake, and that is all he cares about." It's a women's-lib continuation of soap opera: it all comes down to "He doesn't love me for myself," with the new addition of "How could he, when I've become a blank?" There's so much of this in the air now that men are probably beginning to accept the guilt, just as middle-aged parents accepted *The Graduate's* view of their materialistic dirtiness. *Stepford* is for wives with feelings of superiority mixed with feelings of hopeless inadequacy. If the movie had any wit or perspective, we'd see how the men, accepting their role as providers, strapped themselves into boring jobs and turned themselves into creeps, and maybe we'd even see some of the young wives' delicious relaxation in the pleasures of having snared men who were going to take care of them. It could be an entertaining parable only if we saw the women's dreams and the men's dreams go sour, and masochistic and sadistic fantasies build. *Stepford* provides nothing but drab masochism.

What is the danger represented by robotization but giving in to commercialism and letting the advertising society set the models for one's own behavior? Right now, there's a pop subculture peddling this gutted view of women's liberation. I dislike *The Stepford Wives* for reasons that go beyond its being a cruddy movie: I dislike it for the condescension implicit in its view that educated American women are not responsible for what they become. Women, the abused, are being treated like the innocent young potheads of the late sixties — as a suffering privileged class. This sentimentality is degrading.

[February 24, 1975

Coming: "Nashville"

IS THERE SUCH A THING AS AN ORGY for movie-lovers — but an orgy without excess? At Robert Altman's new, almost-three-hour film, *Nashville,* you don't get drunk on images, you're not overpowered — you get elated. I've never before seen a movie I loved in quite this way: I sat there smiling at the screen, in complete happiness. It's a pure emotional high, and you don't come down when the picture is over; you take it with you. In most cases, the studio heads can conjecture what a director's next picture will be like, and they feel safe that way — it's like an insurance policy. They can't with Altman, and after United Artists withdrew its backing from *Nashville,* the picture had to be produced independently, because none of the other major companies would take it on, U.A.'s decision will probably rack up as a classic boner, because this picture is going to take off into the stratosphere — though it has first got to open. (Paramount has picked up the distribution rights but hasn't yet announced an opening date.) *Nashville* is a radical, evolutionary leap.

Altman has prepared us for it. If this film had been made earlier, it might have been too strange and new, but in the five years since he broke through with *M*A*S*H* he's experimented in so many directions that now, when it all comes together for him, it's not really a shock. From the first, packed frames of a recording studio, with Haven Hamilton (Henry Gibson), in bespangled, embroidered white cowboy clothes, like a short, horseless Roy Rogers, singing, "We must be doing somethin' right to last two hundred years," the picture is unmistakably Altman — as identifiable as a paragraph by Mailer when he's really racing. *Nashville* is simply "the ultimate Altman movie" we've been waiting for. Fused, the different styles of prankishness of *M*A*S*H* and *Brewster McCloud* and *California Split* become Jovian adolescent humor. Altman has already accustomed us to actors who don't look as if they're acting; he's attuned us to the comic subtleties of a multiple-track sound system that makes the sound more live than it ever was before; and he's evolved an organic style of moviemaking that tells a story without the clanking of plot. Now he dissolves the frame, so that we feel the continuity between what's on the screen and life off-camera.

Nashville isn't organized according to patterns that you're familiar with, yet you don't question the logic. You get it from the rhythms of the scenes. The picture is at once a *Grand Hotel*-style narrative, with twenty-four linked characters; a country-and-Western musical; a documentary essay on Nashville and American life; a meditation on the love affair between performers and audiences; and an Altman party. In the opening sequences, when Altman's people — the performers we associate with him because he has used them in ways no one else would think of, and they've been filtered through his sensibility — start arriving, and pile up in a traffic jam on the way from the airport to the city, the movie suggests the circus procession at the non-ending of *8½*. But Altman's clowns are far more autonomous; they move and intermingle freely, and the whole movie is their procession. *Nashville* is, above all, a celebration of its own performers. Like Bertolucci, Altman (he includes a homage to *Last Tango in Paris*) gives the actors a chance to come out — to use more of themselves in their characters. The script is by Joan Tewkesbury, but the actors have been encouraged to work up material for their roles, and not only do they do their own singing but most of them wrote their own songs — and wrote them in character. The songs distill the singers' lives, as the mimes and theatrical performances did for the actors in *Children of Paradise.* The impulse behind all Altman's innovations has been to work on more levels than the conventional film does, and now — despite the temporary sound mix and the not-quite-final edit of the print he ran recently, informally, for a few dozen people in New York, before even the Paramount executives had seen the picture — it's apparent that he needed the technical innovations in order to achieve this union of ideas and feelings. *Nashville* coalesces lightly and easily, as if it had just been tossed off. We float while watching, because Altman never lets us see the sweat. Altman's art, like Fred Astaire's, is the great American art of making the impossible look easy.

Altman does for Nashville what he was trying to do for Houston in *Brewster McCloud,* but he wasn't ready to fly then, and the script didn't have enough layers — he needs ideas that mutate, and characters who turn corners. Joan Tewkesbury has provided him with a great subject. Could there be a city with wilder metaphoric overtones than Nashville, the Hollywood of the C. & W. recording industry, the center of fundamentalist music and pop success? The country sound is a twang with longing in it; the ballads are about poor people with no hope. It's the simplistic music of the conquered South; the songs tell you that although you've failed and you've lived a terrible, degrading life, there's a place to come home to, and that's where you belong. Even the saddest song is meant to be reassuring to its audience: the insights never go beyond common poverty, job troubles, and heartaches, and the music never rises to a level that would require the audience to reinterpret its experience. Country stars are symbolic ordinary figures. In this, they're more like political demagogues than artists. The singer bears the burden of what he has become, and he keeps saying, "I may be driving an expensive car, but that doesn't mean I'm happier than you are." Neither he nor the politician dares to come right out and confess to the audience that what he's got is what he set out for from the beginning. Instead, he says, "It's only an accident that puts me here and you there — don't we talk the same language?" Listening to him, people can easily feel that he owes them, and everybody who can sing a little or who has written a tune tries to move in close to the performers as a way of getting up there into the fame business.

Nashville is about the insanity of a fundamentalist culture in which practically the whole population has been turned into groupies. The story spans the five days during which a political manager, played by Michael Murphy, lines up the talent for a Nashville rally to be used as a TV show promoting the Presidential candidacy of Hal Phillip Walker. Walker's slogan is "New Roots for the Nation" — a great slogan for the South, since country music is about a longing for roots that don't exist. Because country singing isn't complex, either musically or lyrically, Altman has been able to create a whole constellation of country stars out of actors. Some of them had actually cut records, but they're not primarily country singers, and their songs are never just numbers. The songs are the story being told, and even the way the singers stand — fluffing out a prom-queen dress, like Karen Black, or coolly staring down the audience, like the almond-eyed, slightly withdrawn Cristina Raines — is part of it. During this movie, we begin to realize that all that the people are is what we see. Nothing is held back from us, nothing is hidden.

When Altman — who is the most atmospheric of directors — discusses what his movies are about, he makes them sound stupid, and he's immediately attacked in the press by people who take his statements literally. (If pinned to the wall by publicity men, how would Joyce have explained the "Nighttown" sequence of *Ulysses*?) The complex outline of *Nashville* gives him the space he needs to work in, and he tells the story by suggestions, echoes, recurrences. It may be he's making a joke about how literally his explanations have been taken when in this picture the phony sentiments that turn up in the lyrics recur in other forms, where they ring true. Haven Hamilton, the bantam king of Nashville, with a red toupee for a crown, sings a maudlin piece of doggerel, with a heavy, churchy beat, about a married man's breaking up with his girl friend ("For the sake of the children, we must say goodbye"). Later, it's almost a reprise when we see Lily Tomlin, as the gospel-singing wife of Haven's lawyer, Ned Beatty, leave Keith Carradine (the hot young singer in a trio) for exactly that reason. Throughout, there are valid observations made to seem fake by a slimy inflection. Geraldine Chaplin, as Opal, from the BBC, is doing a documentary on Nashville; she talks in flights of poetic gush, but nothing she says is as fatuous as she makes it sound. What's funny about Opal is that her affectations are all wasted, since the hillbillies she's trying to impress don't know what she's talking about. Opal is always on the fringe of the action; her opposite is the figure that the plot threads converge on — Barbara Jean (Ronee Blakley), whose ballads are her only means of expressing her yearnings. Barbara Jean is the one tragic character: her art comes from her belief in imaginary roots.

The movies often try to do portraits of artists, but their artistry must be asserted for them. When we see an actor playing a painter and then see the paintings, we don't feel the relation. And even when the portrait is of a performing artist, the story is almost always of how the artist achieves recognition rather than of what it is that has made him an artist. Here, with Ronee Blakley's Barbara Jean, we perceive what goes into the art, and we experience what the unbalance of life and art can do to a person. When she was a child, Barbara Jean memorized the words on a record and earned fifty cents as a prize, and she's been singing ever since; the artist has developed, but the woman hasn't. She has driven herself to the point of having no identity except as a performer. She's in and out of hospitals, and her manager husband (Allen Garfield) treats her as a child, yet she's a true folk artist; the Nashville audience knows she's the real thing and responds to the purity of her gift. She expresses the loneliness that is the central emotion in country music. But she isn't *using* the emotion, as the other singers do: it pours right out of her — softly. Arriving at the airport, coming home after a stretch of treatment — for burns, we're told — she's radiant, yet so breakable that it's hard to believe she has the strength to perform. A few days later, when she stands on the stage of the Opry Belle and sings "Dues," with the words "It hurts so bad, it gets me down," her fragility is so touching and her swaying movements are so seductively musical that, perhaps for the first time on the screen, one gets the sense of an artist's being consumed by her gift. This is Ronee Blakley's first movie, and she puts most movie hysteria to shame; she achieves her effects so simply that I wasn't surprised when someone near me started to cry during one of her songs. She has a long sequence on the stage of the Opry Belle when Barbara Jean's mind starts to wander and, instead of singing, she tells out-of-place, goofy stories about her childhood. They're the same sort of stories that have gone into her songs, but without the transformation they're just tatters that she clings to — and they're all she's got. Ronee Blakley, who wrote this scene, as well as the music and lyrics of all her songs, is a peachy, dimpled brunette, in the manner of the movie stars of an earlier era; as Barbara Jean, she's like the prettiest girl in high school, the one the people in town say is just perfect-looking, like Linda Darnell. But she's more delicate; she's willowy and regal, tipping to one side like the Japanese ladies carved in ivory. At one point, she sings with the mike in one hand, the other hand tracing the movements of the music in the air, and it's an absolutely ecstatic moment.

Nashville isn't in its final shape yet, and all I can hope to do is suggest something of its achievement. Altman could make a film of this magnitude for under two million dollars* because he works with actors whose range he understands. He sets them free to give their own pulse to their characters; inspired themselves, they inspire him. And so we get motifs that bounce off each other — tough-broad Barbara Baxley's drunken fix on the murdered Kennedys, Shelley Duvall's total absorption in celebrity, a high-school band of majorettes twirling rifles, and Robert Doqui's anger at a black singer for not being black enough. All the allusions tell the story of the great American popularity contest. Godard was trying to achieve a synthesis of documentary and fiction and personal essay in the early sixties, but Godard's Calvinist temperament was too cerebral. Altman, from a Catholic background, has what Joyce had: a love of the supreme juices of everyday life. He can put unhappy characters on the screen (Keenan Wynn plays a man who loses the wife he's devoted to) and you don't wish you didn't have to watch them; you accept their unhappiness as a piece of the day, as you do in *Ulysses.* You

*The final cost, after the prints were made, was about two million, two hundred thousand.

don't recoil from the moody narcissism of Keith Carradine's character: there he is in his bedroom, listening to his own tapes, with one bed partner after another — with Geraldine Chaplin, whom he'll barely remember the next day, and with Lily Tomlin, whom he'll remember forever. You don't recoil, as you do in movies like *Blow-Up* or *Petulia,* because Altman wants you to be part of the life he shows you and to feel the exhilaration of being alive. When you get caught up in his way of seeing, you no longer anticipate what's coming, because Altman doesn't deliver what years of moviegoing have led you to expect. You get something else. Even when you feel in your bones what has to happen — as you do toward the climax of *Nashville,* when the characters assemble for the rally at the Parthenon and Barbara Jean, on the stage, smiles ravishingly at her public — he delivers it in a way you didn't expect. Who watching the pious Haven Hamilton sing the evangelical "Keep A'Goin'," his eyes flashing with a paranoid gleam as he keeps the audience under surveillance, would guess that the song represented his true spirit, and that when injured he would think of the audience before himself? Who would expect that Barbara Harris, playing a runaway wife — a bombed-out groupie hovering around the action — would finally get her chance onstage, and that her sexy, sweetly shell-shocked look would, at last, fit in perfectly? For the viewer, *Nashville* is a constant discovery of overlapping connections. The picture says, This is what America is, and I'm part of it. *Nashville* arrives at a time when America is congratulating itself for having got rid of the bad guys who were pulling the wool over people's eyes. The movie says that it isn't only the politicians who live the big lie — the big lie is something we're all capable of trying for. The candidate, Hal Phillip Walker, never appears on the screen; he doesn't need to — the screen is full of candidates. The name of Walker's party doesn't have to stand for anything: that's why it's the Replacement Party.

Nashville isn't full of resolutions, because Altman doesn't set up conflicts; the conflicts, as in Lily Tomlin's character, are barely visible. Her deepest tensions play out in the quietest scenes in the movie; she's a counterbalance to the people squabbling about whatever comes into their heads. There's no single reason why anybody does anything in this movie, and most of the characters' concerns are mundane. Altman uses a *Grand Hotel* mingling of characters without giving false importance to their unions and collisions, and the rally itself is barely pivotal. A lot happens in the five days, but a lot happens in any five days. There are no real dénouements, but there are no loose ends, either: Altman doesn't need to wrap it all up, because the people here are too busy being alive to be locked in place. Frauds who are halfway honest, they're true to their own characters. Even the stupidest among them, the luscious bimbo Sueleen (Gwen Welles), a tone-deaf waitress in the airport coffee shop, who wiggles and teases as she sings to the customers, and even the most ridiculous — Geraldine Chaplin's Opal — are so completely what they are that they're irresistible. At an outdoor party at Haven Hamilton's log-cabin retreat, the chattering Opal remarks, "Pure, unadulterated Bergman," but then, looking around, she adds, "Of course, the people are all wrong for Bergman, aren't they?" *Nashville* is the funniest epic vision of America ever to reach the screen.

INSTEAD OF THE TRANSPARENCY CHARACTERISTIC of Vittorio De Sica at his greatest, his last film, *A Brief Vacation,* has an opaque dignity. It's split between magisterial, grim realism and swoony romanticism, with one no more convincing than the other. The scenarist Cesare Zavattini has set the story — of a love that was not to be — among working-class people; in the opening sequences, the put-upon heroine, Clara (Florinda Bolkan), is the sole breadwinner for a southern-Italian peasant family living in Milan. She's exhausted by her factory job and fed up with her narrow-minded, suspicious-of-everything relatives. She has become so depressed and ignorant that she's even forgotten how to read. Her Cro-Magnon husband (Renato Salvatori) uses her sexually as if she were a farm beast he owned, and she has sunk into a morose stupor, trudging to work, berating her husband and his mother and brother, sparing only her children. This section of the film is unrelieved: when Florinda Bolkan, with her strong shoulders and uniquely impersonal face, acts morose, it's as if the screen had gone blank. She's a handsome woman, in high-fashion terms, but her mask face doesn't take the light; she goes through the proper motions for her role, but her face says no to any curiosity we might have.

When Clara collapses and is sent to a sanatorium in northern Italy, to be cured of tuberculosis, the schizoid picture turns into a novelettish *Magic Mountain,* with the ideas left out. Clara makes friends among a group of suffering sophisticates, discovers a world of beauty and art which she has never known (and must soon relinquish — we can't forget that), and it's all much like a dressy fantasy starring Elizabeth Taylor. Clara's dewy-eyed newfound lover, Luigi (Daniel Quenaud), who has also been sent to the resort by the National Health, drips nobility as only a narcissistic bad actor can. Luigi, who looks like a frail cross between Montgomery Clift and Ian Holm, and acts like Richard Chamberlain, seems the aesthetic equivalent of impotence, but there's no doubt that we're meant to take the tragically doomed affair as Clara's awakening to the spirituality and tenderness — the full humanity — that has been missing from her life.

In silent pictures, and in the early years of talkies, it was very common for heroines to discover bliss in a vaporous love affair with a sickly Luigi, and sometimes even "ladies of the evening" were redeemed by contact with a little high art (Glara reads *Anna Karenina* and goes to a concert), but it seemed as if movies had grown beyond this sort of transformation through the power of the ethereal. And hadn't they grown beyond thirties-movies characters like the feverishly frisky La Scanziani (Adriana Asti), a dying music-hall entertainer who will do anything for attention? Asti plays it to the hilt, in the gallant-waif Piaf style (she even sings "Milord"), and with that same frightened-chicken look of desperate gaiety. It's one of those atrocious grand performances that you become grateful for in a heartfelt renunciation drama. *A Brief Vacation* joins a modern, somewhat ideological view of an oppressed, resentful working-class woman with a familiar, earlier fantasy of escaping from brute sex to angel sex. The reverse of Lady Chatterley, Clara becomes a starry-eyed ingénue walking with a tony, disembodied John-Boy, who will never have dirt under his fingernails. The picture has some of the same lumpish uplift as the American *Summer Wishes, Winter Dreams.* It gives one the sense that it is compromising between equally bad ideas.

[March 3, 1975]

New York Self-Hatred for Fun and Profit

Notes on "The Prisoner of Second Avenue"

ON the occasion of Jack Lemmon's birthday and the imminent arrival of his latest film, the movie version of Neil Simon's *The Prisoner of Second Avenue,* Pat Collins, the new WCBS arts critic, congratulated him on not having got a big head — on not believing that "he was the best thing to happen to light comedy since canned laughter." Was she involuntarily telling us that Lemmon's tiredness had got to her?

A Jack Lemmon picture has become something to dread. He's like Jack Paar. When Paar was a talk-show host, he imbued the show with soap opera; you couldn't feel any emotion about what went on, because he himself had so much that he filled everything up.

Lemmon, who isn't Jewish, plays Jews who aren't Jewish, either. He's cast as a Jew for the same reason Montgomery Clift was after the accident that disfigured him — because the look in his face passes for pain. It is pain, but it's the wrong kind — suggesting a mixture of dissipation, grogginess, gutlessness.

Mike Nichols, who directed *The Prisoner of Second Avenue* on Broadway, and also several other Neil Simon hits, is smart enough to avoid putting them on the screen. What works on the stage can be theatrical and empty at the same time. Melvin Frank has directed the film version in his usual sagging, fifties style, but I can't think of a filmmaker in the world who could substantially improve this movie except by throwing out the play altogether.

There is a stage convention that audiences accept as a necessary evil: the dead moment when an actor imparts background information to us by briefing another actor. It usually begins, "Remember when . . ." The mechanical sound of what follows is the sound of Neil Simon dialogue on the screen. You get the same sound in a TV sitcom like *All in the Family* — punchy, didactic, absolutely clear. There are no layers of meaning in *The Prisoner of Second Avenue*; it's a big-screen sitcom. Nobody can have a headache without the causes' being diagrammed, as in an Anacin commercial.

Neil Simon tells us exactly what each person is thinking, and each line cancels out the one before. This is bad enough on the stage, but on the screen it's intolerable. The camera isn't a participant in the story, and neither are we. *Prisoner* is gripe comedy; its hero, Mel, complains about accidents, trivia, temporary problems — the toilet that doesn't stop running until you jiggle the handle, the two noisy German airline stewardesses in the next-door apartment (Simon can't get enough of German jokes), a heat wave, a power failure. The movie is vaguely about urban despair, but Simon doesn't start with the environment; he starts with the payoff to a gag and then he finds a cubbyhole in which to stuff it. He works New York for nudges of recognition. Neil Simon is the Nelson Rockefeller of comedy — totally pragmatic.

But Simon isn't having a good time. The movie is extraordinarily self-centered; it's about Neil Simon grieving for himself, and he grieves like Jack Paar — self-protectively, warmly. He thinks he can get away with serious thoughts if he plays Hamlet as a kosher pickle. Mel loses his job as an advertising executive, and, feeling worthless, he cracks up. But he can't tell us that he feels he's disappearing without adding, "I don't need an analyst; I need Lost and Found." It's boomed out for us — another of those fabled Simon one-liners. We get a double load of fun from Simon — the bad jokes and the guilty misery. He fights being just a gag writer, instead of fighting being a rotten gag writer, and taking some pride in the craft.

The things that go wrong for Mel don't come out of anything fundamental. His wife, Edna (Anne Bancroft), a rock of sanity, looks great, and she loves him; his children are fine; he's had some bad luck because business was bad, but he really enjoys his work. Why, then, does he have a nervous breakdown? So that Neil Simon can get some gags in. It isn't a real breakdown; it's for our benefit. We're supposed to laugh at Mel's complaints, because he's overreacting to mostly petty inconveniences. When thieves take the TV and clean out his wardrobe, everything is kept at a cartoon level; there's no suggestion of the fear that many New Yorkers experience after a violation of their homes. The pressures that might have caused Mel's collapse are switched to jokes, as if they were irrational. Yet are they irrational for Simon himself, or is it that he can dare to deal with them only by pretending they are? He seems to be drawn to dealing with nightmarish anxieties but to treating them as slapstick.

The abrasiveness of New York is romanticized in movies now, the way movies used to romanticize French resistance to the Occupation. Implicit here, as in much of Simon's other work, is the familiar idea that New York is a battleground; either you put on your brass knuckles and become a power broker or a mugger, or you're buried. There are jokey news dispatches dropped in from time to time — by a narrator — as if from the front lines. And at the end, when Mel announces that he and Edna won't leave the city, it's like a wartime-movie speech about fighting on — and the audience responds with cheers. Is Simon saying that things are so awful in New York City that you're a hero if you live here and a coward if you escape? Or is it just that he can't resist the possibility of getting the audience on New York's side? There are two articles of faith for bellicose New Yorkers: that they have the toughness to survive here, and that they're in the place they want to be. (In the last shot, Mel, armed with a snow shovel, is prepared to do battle with his neighbors.) However, the subtext of this movie is that Mel is going to stay in New York so he can hate himself more.

When Mel pounds the wall to tell the stewardesses to be quiet, the plaster cracks. Simon's cheapness is in his reflexes, conditioned to give the public a good time in the easiest way. He wants to be a writer, but he has become a mechanic; he uses even Freudian family material mechanically, as if to prove that there's no revelation in it. He's hyperaware of how to get laughs out of exaggerated responses, and utterly blocked when it comes to creating a character who suffers from something more than irritation over a dribbling toilet. Yet Simon's persistence in setting up these boob heroes is almost a cry for help. Mel's despair is always a joke, and he's cured by a gag for an upbeat finish. It isn't really upbeat, though, because Lemmon just in himself projects a genuine despair; it takes the form of a coarsening of his talent. Typecast here, he gives a conscientious performance, but he gets clammy, mirthless laughs, and he looks humiliated. At the end of the picture, when Mel regains his self-respect, Lemmon can't convince us — or the muscles of his face — that anything has changed.

You don't have to be a New Yorker to recognize that this movie is lying to you: your instinct tells you that, deep down, Neil Simon was never a prisoner of Second Avenue and that it's all displacement. Can it be that Lemmon and Simon, both men of talent who give in to the tastes of a mass audience they can't fully respect, don't know how else to perform now, and mourn for themselves even as they go on giving in? Maybe the reason that the urban despair in *Prisoner* never makes much sense is that it's a disguise for an artist's despair, and for disappointments that a plumber and a plasterer can't fix.

Clark Gable, publicized as an outdoor type ("a man's man"), started to live up to the image and became a shooting-and-fishing enthusiast. Gregory Peck carries his sensible-man Lincolnesque image; Charlton Heston speaks in the weighted, sepulchral tones of Moses. Jack Lemmon's face says that the giddy comic spirit of his youth has left him and that he feels defeated — by success.

Neil Simon locks us in with a panicking nonentity who is a mask for a phenomenally successful purveyor of middle-class reassurance humor. Simon's grieving has the sickly odor of not calling attention to yourself. He makes himself small, as if to ward off danger. He cracks bad jokes as if he couldn't afford not to.

Simon says there's no escape for his hero. When Mel and Edna take a trip to the suburbs, Mel walks in poison ivy and stretches out on fresh fertilizer. It's degradation humor, and, in context, mercilessly unfunny. Simon's writing and Lemmon's acting are distress signals; maybe they both assume that we're all so insensitive that we can laugh at the pain they're showing us.

[March 10, 1975]

Talent Isn't Enough

"FUNNY LADY," the nine-and-a-half-million-dollar sequel to *Funny Girl,* crashes along for almost an hour and then it hits a failure point, from which it never recovers. Fanny Brice (Barbra Streisand) is starring in the show "Crazy Quilt," produced by Billy Rose (James Caan), a hot-shot young businessman and songwriter. He is so inexperienced that he has loaded the show down with cluttered routines and impossibly complicated scenery. On opening night in Atlantic City, it takes so long to get from one number to the next that most of the audience walks out and the show isn't yet over when the papers come out with the reviews of the first act. Fanny teaches Billy how to pare away the excess, and by the time they open in New York "Crazy Quilt" is a hit. But when Fanny's song ("There's gonna be a great day") stops the show in New York, it is ludicrously overproduced, with black bodies salaaming before the white goddess and gyrating on platforms among turgid Art Deco designs. This number violates our faith in what the movie has been saying; it's like something from a Streisand TV special. *Funny Lady* itself suggests a bigger version of "Crazy Quilt" in Atlantic City.

You can see that the moviemakers weren't just going to make a movie — they were going to kill us. That's the thinking that has all but destroyed the American musical, and it may destroy Barbra Streisand, too. There's a vast difference between an actress trying to do something new and an actress trying to wow the public by doing what got applause before. Streisand is in beautiful voice, and her singing is terrific — too terrific. It's no longer singing, it's something else — that strident over-dramatization that turns a song into a big number. The audience's attention is directed away from the music and onto the star's feat in charging it with false energy. Streisand is out to knock you cold, and you get cold, all right. The dialogue throughout is sharp and bitchy, and Streisand's inflections are beyond criticism — she doesn't deliver a wisecrack, she detonates it — but the cracks, too, are high-powered, designed to blitz us rather than to reveal character. This Fanny Brice isn't human. Streisand's performance is like the most spectacular, hard-edge female impersonator's imitation of Barbra Streisand. And her imitators have actually come so close that when she repeats herself she seems to be taking off from them, showing that she can outdo them. It's a performance calculated to make people yell without feeling a thing — except adoration.

People who make movie show-biz bios always seem to back away from their subject — the inner workings of the theater, and what life onstage does to people and what it brings out in them. In the first hour, *Funny Lady* gets into this subject; the approach is too brittle, but it has vitality. In these scenes, Fanny seems a knowledgeable, tough broad; it's surprising to see her in such a harsh light, but the pressure-cooker theatrical environment takes hold of the audience's imagination. This compelling, deliberately abrasive view is thrown away, however, in that "Great Day" number, and we're left with nothing but Fanny's arthritic torchbearing.

Fanny Brice herself, who summed up her marriage to the felonious candyman-gambler Nicky Arnstein and her subsequent marriage to the wizard-entrepreneur Billy Rose with "I never liked the man I loved, and I never loved the man I liked," was a profoundly straightforward woman. Surrounded by Ziegfeld glorification (she was a Ziegfeld star for a span of twenty-six years), she represented a woman without illusions about herself. The title of her 1930 movie — *Be Yourself!* — epitomized her appeal: her blond rival simpered and flirted, but Fanny had her head screwed on straight and she got the guy. If he left her, he came back — because he knew where he stood with her. Fanny Brice made earthiness sexy. Since she was urban and street-wise, hers was a very special earthiness — the maternal allure of a city woman who was on the level. Even her torch songs had a simple blues honesty that gave them depth; that's why you can still be moved by her records. Fanny Brice's comedy was a stylized form of honesty and a direct expression of her feelings about life. She didn't become an alcoholic, a suicide, or a narcissistic pain. She made big money, kept her footing, raised her children, remained loyal to her friends, and talked straight and dirty. How did she do it? Was humor her balance wheel? And how did she feel about her life? Did it hurt the dedicatedly elegant woman who had worked her way up from poverty and become part of the international aristocracy of the theater that as bratty Baby Snooks on radio she reached a wider audience than ever before? Was she bitter about becoming a caricature, or did she take that, too, in stride? *Funny Lady* concentrates on the heartbreak (which is the most ordinary thing about Fanny Brice), and not on what makes her legendary: she was a great sane comic — and there aren't many. She was an even greater ballad singer, and maybe the biggest mystery is how she managed to be accepted both as a comedienne and as a tragic-voiced popular artist.

Funny Lady (produced, like *Funny Girl,* by Ray Stark) opens temptingly with Streisand as Fanny Brice onstage at the "Ziegfeld Follies," wearing orange ruffles and a pink bonnet, and singing "Blind Date" in a wonky parody of a Jewish accent. When Fanny goes backstage, Bobby (Roddy McDowall), a chorus boy, hands her a blue envelope that has arrived with a bouquet — her divorce decree — and she goes into shock. It's an even worse blow to us — when we realize that she's been hoping for a reconciliation with that handsome heel (and audience depressant) Nicky Arnstein (Omar Sharif). Since in the first film she met Nicky before she became a Ziegfeld headliner, in 1910, and it's now the middle of the Depression, the moviemakers seem demented, asking her to drag that torch around for decades. (Actually, it was Fanny Brice who filed for divorce, not Arnstein, and that was back in 1927.) *Funny Girl* provided a satin cushion for Streisand; she nestled in the rich film craftsmanship while her fast, satirical lines expressed her disbelief — and delight. Parodying the romantic conventions, she was so poignant in her humor that she reactivated them, and the director, William Wyler, always kept us involved in her Cinderella-with-the-wrong-prince emotions. *Funny Girl* was true to its corrupt big-bio form; *Funny Lady,* directed by Herbert Ross, isn't true to anything. The zingers and the musical numbers are indebted to *Cabaret,* but the plot is right out of those terrible forties movies in which couples who break up spend a lifetime thinking about each other, with encounters every five or ten years. And we get a double load of it here, with two graying ex-husbands.

Every artist works on instinct, but when we talk about Barbra Streisand's working on instinct we mean something special: she's had so little experience in the theater she relies on instinct in a void. And her instinct has been playing her false lately. In her November, 1973, TV special, *Barbra Streisand . . . and Other Musical Instruments,* her voice was pure and she looked lovely, but the show was sterile. It was all externals — all satin cushion. The only time her singing warmed up was in "Cryin' Time," with Ray Charles, and during that song there was a moment when he was singing and she was harmonizing, listening to him too charmingly, her fingers busily toying on the piano — dear God, she was stealing scenes from a blind man. Her instinct played her false when she decided to do *For Pete's Sake,* a slapstick sitcom with exhausted jokes and no characterization. Her intuitive timing didn't work on the lines that were programmed to be pounded out, and she was a cartoon of her worst mannerisms. She was, in fact, what people who didn't like her had always said she was — shrill. And her instinct should have told her that it was lazy to imitate Liza Minnelli's success in Bob Fosse's *Cabaret. Funny Lady* has taken the screenwriter Jay Presson Allen and the songwriters John Kander and Fred Ebb from *Cabaret,* and among the Kander-and-Ebb numbers there are two that are done in the forced-emotion, fag-hag style of Big Broadway showstoppers. "How Lucky Can You Get?" is a gutsy-masochist Judy Garland-style number sung alone in a deserted theater after Fanny learns that Nicky has remarried; Streisand does some patented Minnelli tricks in it. "Let's Hear It for Me" is a self-assertive, slam-bang number to travel on — an embarrassing recap of "Don't Rain on My Parade," in *Funny Girl.* In that one, Streisand went from train to tugboat to ocean liner; here she goes from a silvery Rolls-Royce (valued at $85,000, according to the production notes) to a bi-plane, while the audience chuckles at the self-plagiarism. (It seemed to me that the audience didn't take the film even halfway seriously after this sequence.) When Streisand sang "My Man" at the close of the first film, gaining in force as she went along, her virtuosity told us that although Fanny had lost in love, she was strong enough to express her emotion in her singing, and that the end of the movie was barely the beginning of Fanny's career. The only dramatic function that these two new songs serve is exhibitionism. When you hear Streisand shout "Come on, kids, let's hear it, let's hear it for me!" you know damned well who the kids are: the song is destined to be a jukebox favorite in every gay bar in the world.*

There is a danger now for any woman musical-comedy star that she will begin to give her screaming fans what they want, not realizing how much malice and how much bad taste are mixed with their worship. (On the way out of the theater, the same young men who had shouted "Bravo!" after her musical assaults were exchanging spiteful remarks about how she looked.) Streisand was womanly in the midst of the circusy twenty-to-twenty-five-million-dollar *Hello, Dolly!* She didn't give it the drag-queen souping up that she gives *Funny Lady* and that is often now regarded as proof of a real star at work. The difference centers on how she carries herself: the Ray Aghayan and Bob Mackie clothes aren't becoming, because she wears them like a man and turns herself into a transvestite. The turbans and magenta fox are like a Halloween rig, and

*I guessed wrong. It wasn't "Let's Hear It for Me" that became the gay-bar smash; it was "How Lucky Can You Get?"

she swings into a room as if she were winding up for a shot put. Each scene is a fashion number, and for Fanny to spot Nicky in Los Angeles he has to be playing polo and she must arrive at the polo grounds in a Maybach Zeppelin touring car (valued at $250,000). Nothing happens in a casual setting, and that means finally that nothing happens except the changing sets and the new outfits (forty — count 'em).

The worst scene Herbert Ross has ever directed must be Nicky's telling Fanny that he can now afford to leave his millionaire wife and come back to her. Sharif takes so long to say his lines that you think maybe he's waiting for the daffodils, and Streisand is photographed so unflatteringly that all you can do is stare at her dainty, slenderizing dress and wonder why there's been so much care for her body and so little for her face — and her expression. When Sharif kisses her, we get the glitzy tenderness of throbbing Joan Crawford music on the track — only now it's the strains of "People who need people are the luckiest people in the world." The nostalgic glamour just barely squeaked by in *The Way We Were* (also produced by Ray Stark), but it doesn't get by here. When at last Fanny tells Nicky off, the audience's applause isn't for her awakening — it's because we're rid of his flumping in and out of the movie. On Fanny's and Billy's honeymoon train, Streisand sings Kander and Ebb's "Isn't This Better?" to the sleeping groom, cradling him and running her fingers through his hair, while a night-light gives her face a prima-donna blue glow — which is just what Joan Crawford would have wanted, if only she'd been able to sing.

The best scenes are the early ones with James Caan as Billy Rose, the short czar of mass-marketed live entertainment for world's fairs and centennials, and one of those rare individuals who become rich and world-famous without acquiring any class. Caan's Billy never stands up straight; he leans forward so he won't miss out on anything. He's a smart man who has never learned how to relax or play, a drone you'd be embarrassed to be seen with. In his awful greenish suits, and hats worn low, almost flat across the brow, he's essentially scrubby; he always needs a shave, and he's flushed and sweaty — his pores oozing anxiety and eagerness. Caan makes you care for this man's desperation. It's a shift from his recent roles, and his light, boyish voice — a disadvantage in some of them — is very effective, since, the way he uses it, Billy sounds uncultivated and unsure of himself. Billy's inability to accept what he is or to change provides the only believable tension. Roddy McDowall is wasted as the homosexual performer whom Fanny befriends and turns into a secretary-companion. It's an unenviable role: others get to make dirty cracks about Bobby, and McDowall doesn't get to answer. We never see what Fanny's relationship to Bobby is, so we can't judge whether the movie means to suggest that he fills a psychological need that a heterosexual would balk at. There's no attempt to show why so many women stars have homosexual attendants — often husbands — serving as idolatrous domestics, representatives of their audience in constant attendance. The crowded movie is remarkably empty except for Caan and McDowall. Ziegfeld and Billy Rose didn't go in for one-woman shows, and Streisand shouldn't be treated as a queen bee.

Herbert Ross used to be a choreographer, and he staged the musical sequences in *Funny Girl,* but the choreography here is garish and it's performed indifferently. When Ross tries to be Bob Fosse (an attempt that is blatant in the dance sequence "Clap Hands, Here Comes Charley," featuring Fosse's *Pippin* star, Ben Vereen), he's more like Jack Cole, the pre-Fosse master of steamy writhing. The Fosse mannerisms, which grew out of his own movements as a dancer and are organic with him (as one can see in his solo in *The Little Prince*), are hazardous without his choreography. The Fosse dynamism is compounded of speed and jerky movements; he uses stop motion for a more powerful immediate effect than one can obtain through fluid movement. Arresting the motion at its most distorted — the performers frequently turn their backs to the audience, hips wrenched out — Fosse has made a style by showing us the strain of Broadway's killer feats of movement. It's Broadway "excitement" converted into a choreographic conception, and round-bottomed Ben Vereen is a hypy practitioner of it. His number here brings down the house — predictably, since it's that kind of number — but it's a sloppy imitation of Fosse's spaz dancing.

Perhaps *Funny Lady* got into this mixture of styles out of fear that the optimism of Fanny Brice's period would appear old-fashioned now. One of the problems facing producers who want to do musicals is that if a musical is upbeat it seems square and if it isn't upbeat it seems to violate the musical-comedy form, which derives from the kinesthetic pleasures of song and dance. *Cabaret* found a solution to the happy-equals-square problem: it worked on electricity and wit, which made *us* happy. In the *Cabaret* finale, Liza Minnelli starts where her mother finished up: she works on our nerves. Good or bad, most of the musicals her mother was in had briskness and pace, and a sense of going somewhere; there's joy and hopefulness in the great Garland high-stepping "Get Happy." *Cabaret* is about living in the moment, Weimar being a metaphor for a futureless society. When Minnelli sings the title song, she's celebrating the fever of being alive. She does it with an energy that self-destructs: that's the Fosse style, and his jagged, quick camera angles intensify the performer's incandescence. But in Minnelli's TV appearances since *Cabaret* she doesn't seem to know how to do anything but finales, and at her worst she's so manic that when she does a number you think, What's she going to do for an encore — eat the audience? And *Funny Lady,* which tries for the Fosse electricity, loses its medium-sized effects (to say nothing of small ones) because of the hectic activity and the belted-out climaxes where no climax is called for. The best number in the movie, Streisand's wittily campy white-tie-and-tails version of "I Found a Million Dollar Baby in a Five and Ten Cent Store," is smothered in the frenzy. Something fundamental goes wrong: Streisand's acting has no normal range here; it's all set at extremes of vulnerability and domineering confidence. And the decadence integral to the *Cabaret* style confuses the whole meaning of Fanny Brice's life. She's famous for honesty, not for venom — or for venality. Billy says, "We've a mutual interest deep inside — money." This must be meant to make the picture seem acrid enough for the post-Watergate era. The script uses some of Fanny Brice's actual remarks, and variations of others, but without her congeniality.

When Fanny marries Billy Rose, a friend of hers asks "Why him?" and Fanny replies "I fell in like with him." The main problem I had with *Funny Lady* is that I fell out of like with Barbra Streisand. The soft focus of that *Instruments* TV special gave her a pale-blond Pre-Raphaelite radiance. It was too much like a perfume ad — celestially romantic — but it was awfully pretty. One wouldn't want that look extended throughout a movie, but when she's easy in scenes — as in parts of *Up the Sandbox* — she has that softness without looking like a gauzy ad. It's called sensitivity. She doesn't show any here. And her volatility is gone; something rigid and overbearing and heavy seems to be settling into her manner. She may have gone past the time when she could play a character; maybe that's why she turns Fanny Brice into a sacred monster. Has Streisand lost sight of the actress she could be?

[March 17, 1975]

The Rear Guard

WHILE MOST OF THE ARTISTS in Hollywood fight the constraints of genre pictures, some highly successful directors, who can do what they want, are so hipped on their own adolescent movie dreams — or the princely sums the studios offer them — that they try to recreate the magic of old Hollywood. Peter Bogdanovich's *At Long Last Love,* George Roy Hill's *The Great Waldo Pepper,* and Sydney Pollack's *The Yakuza* are all movie-spawned adolescent fantasies gone wrong.

At Long Last Love is the saddest — a stillborn picture, without a whisper of a chance to recoup its six-and-a-half-million-dollar cost. Using sixteen Cole Porter songs as a basis, Bogdanovich has written a pastiche of a thirties romantic-mixup script, and he has attempted to make a picture in the Art Deco Lubitsch-Paramount manner — not thirties musical-comedy style filtered through a seventies imagination but early musical comedy brought back just as it was. Of course, he can't, and we can't look at his bored millionaire playboy (Burt Reynolds) and spoiled heiress (Cybill Shepherd) the way we looked at the characters in the Paramount musicals. Theatrical forms and movie genres — such as the musical, the gallant-aviator film, the gangster picture — develop out of bargains struck between the past and the present, the artists and the audience. Each form has its set of conventions that audiences accept for a while; then the conventions, hollowed out, lose their zing, and the forms change. There's no way to retrieve the general frame of mind that the early musicals came out of. Bogdanovich may long for their "purity" and the innocence of the values enshrined in them; he may want to test himself against the revered directors of the past. But *At Long Last Love* is an infantile film, and the Cole Porter songs don't help it. At the time the songs were written, the people who sang them felt daringly naughty; when they're performed as they are here, with every last syllable of chat in place, their antique smartness sounds smug. Now that Cole Porter's once expurgated double-entendres can be heard in a G-rated picture, it should be a warning to the moviemakers that the concept of raciness and wicked charm has had its day. Burt Reynolds and Cybill Shepherd can't sing or dance, but probably the picture wouldn't be a success even if they could, because the roots of Bogdanovich's script atrophied during the Second World War. The Broadway songstress (Madeline Kahn), the debonair immigrant gambler (Duilio Del Prete), the unflappable valet (John Hillerman), and the comic Irish maid (Eileen Brennan) belong to a make-believe world cut adrift.

Bogdanovich has no point of view toward this upper-crust society in which the gentleman's gentleman is more formal than his master, in which the lady's maid is her mistress's confidante, in which the only pastimes are falling in love and spending the millions that relatives obligingly drop in one's lap. You wonder that Bogdanovich had the energy to push ahead with this relentless vapidity. Clearly, it represents fun to him, but since he never shows us why it does, it doesn't mean anything to us. The directors in the thirties knew why they were working in the form, and we knew why: it was light, romantic escapism — stylized happiness. But we no longer escape the same way, and we don't understand why Bogdanovich wants to. I'm not certain what it is that Bogdanovich wants from the movie past, but I don't think it's safety; I think he's genuinely pulled backward. His films show no interest in the present; they don't even allude to it. Bogdanovich's casting is erratic, and his actors don't fill their roles, but his star-creation, Cybill Shepherd, had something in *The Last Picture Show*: she was desirable in a mean, Gloria-Grahame-like way. She didn't have Grahame's marvellous trashiness (or her acting control, either), but she aroused the same vindictive masculinity. Men wanted to get at her to wipe the jeering smile off her face. Bogdanovich engendered these ambivalent feelings toward her: an overgrown baton twirler, she was a projection of men's resentment of the bitch-princesses they're drawn to. Within her limited role in *The Heartbreak Kid,* Cybill Shepherd was effective, but she's an object, not a star; people don't feel for her and don't identify with her. And this was a big problem in Bogdanovich's last film, *Daisy Miller;* we needed to empathize with Daisy's harmless gaucherie and respond to her naïve independence, but when Shepherd spoke she was hard and snippy and mechanical, rattling on so artificially that she sounded half mad. She got better as the picture went along; though her only way of showing emotion is through slightly blurred eyes and a stare, her opacity and her inexperience as an actress began to be affecting — they almost matched up with Daisy's unworldliness. The film was unevenly directed and too stilted to succeed, but it was a genuine attempt, and it was by no means a shameful failure. *At Long Last Love* is. It seems to be designed as a showcase for Cybill Shepherd's musical-comedy talents, and she's a hopeless amateur, flouncing around and mistaking sullenness for airiness. You can't ignore her, because she keeps trying, and yet you don't have the sympathy for her that you did in *Daisy Miller.* Not projecting onto her, not showing any emotion toward her, Bogdanovich reveals her as empty. Madeline Kahn is the real pastry here; she prisses the biggest bee-sting mouth you've ever seen, and she has lavish, teasing thighs in her "Find Me a Primitive Man" number. But all that the pros can do, actually, is make you miss them when the deadhead amateurs are on. Reynolds, attempting to turn his deadhead status to some advantage, tries for super-relaxation, adopting the sloshed-yet-still-ambulatory style of Dean Martin, but he looks incredulous, as if he couldn't figure out how he got turned into such a lunk.

Bogdanovich, despite his immersion in movies, directs scenes like the earlier directors trained in the theater. You're always aware of the scene's having been set up, of the actors as actors. He has a nice sense of how long a scene should run, but, like a man of the theater, he concentrates almost totally on story and feelings. He doesn't have the fluency that marks so many of the best young directors of his generation, here and abroad. An enjoyable movie of his, like *Paper Moon,* is thin; there's no real conviction under it, because in movies conviction comes partly from the atmosphere — the sense of life surrounding the action — and in Bogdanovich's movies there's hardly any. He probably didn't intend to distance the thirties period of *Paper Moon* but did it unconsciously: he gave us the desolate, empty thirties as modern romantics see them. People too young to have known the period might think his vision realistic — might think the past had been a time drained of color and life. Bogdanovich has the ability to communicate the emotions that his characters can't fully articulate. He has a feeling for hurt but little delicacy in expressing it; his approach to human emotion is rather blunt, yet he gets there. In moments — Cybill Shepherd's Daisy, unable to say what she feels as she looks at the man she wants to love her, or Timothy Bottoms's blocked face in *The Last Picture Show* as he reaches out to someone, part-way — Bogdanovich shows an understanding of loneliness. If he doesn't have enough film technique for his movies to have an illusion of life, these images nevertheless make direct contact with the audience. He has a real gift for simple, popular movies; he can tell basic stories that will satisfy a great many people, and this is not a common talent. But he's not developing it — he's not giving full emotional involvement to his own films. When he plays around with past forms without putting them into today's terms, there's no narrative pull to his plots. In *What's Up, Doc?* it was impossible to care whether Streisand would be on the plane with Ryan O'Neal at the end, and in *At Long Last Love* one has no interest in whether it is Reynolds or Del Prete who is meant to be in love with Shepherd — or with Kahn. The romance in *At*

Long Last Love must be between Bogdanovich and old movies, and the terrible thing is we don't feel that, either.

◈

CONSUMERS TODAY ARE BEING SOLD sweaters labeled "100% Virgin Acrylic," and George Roy Hill makes movies that are 100% pure plastic. *The Great Waldo Pepper* doesn't mar, and wipes clean with a damp cloth. It's a new version of the gallant-aviator movies, such as *The Lost Squadron,* of 1932, in which Richard Dix and Joel McCrea played aviators, unemployed after the First World War was over, who went out to Hollywood and became stunt men, recreating the air battles they'd been in. This one starts in 1926, with Waldo (Robert Redford) as a barnstorming pilot with a gift of gab; the William Goldman script is coldhearted and clever — scene after scene ends with a snapper. Hill brings back the Wasp world of old movies intact. After a day of taking up Nebraskans for five-dollar rides in his biplane, Waldo sits down to dinner with a farm family, and his flowing white shirt is so star-bright he seems to be saying "Fly me." You know how lovable Waldo is, because he has taken the farmer's little boy up for a ride, along with the kid's devoted dog. The boy is blond and old-movie freckled, and he's going to grow up to be just like Waldo, whom he idolizes; we know we're meant to think that the boy is Waldo as he once was. (The hero worship is a bit ingrown.) Little freckle-face isn't Redford's big romance, though. Waldo has a dream of battling it out in the skies with the No. 1 Imperial German ace, Ernst Kessler (Bo Brundin), whom he never got to fight during the war; when he reaches Hollywood, he meets Kessler, who's doing stunt work on the same picture he is. They adore each other, of course, and engage in philosophical conversations exquisitely calibrated for dim-witted ten-year-old males. Since they're both hooked on the glory of life in the clouds, and there's room for only one god up there, they turn a mock battle into a real one, and fight it out. It hardly seems necessary: Kessler is given to such maundering, ponderous thoughts he's practically the Eric Sevareid of the skies; he could bore his adversaries to death.

I can't tell if Americans will like this movie, but I think Hitler would have drunk a toast to it. It's a paean to purification through heroism, with the heroes fighting for the love of fighting and to determine who is the better man. Waldo and Kessler salute each other like lovers, and ram each other's plane. (George Roy Hill is such a straight, impersonal director that even this choice bit of homoeroticism has no kick. The picture might have been saved if Paul Newman had played the German — and had delivered the mystic poetry and paradoxes in a Sid Caesar dialect.) The offensive part of the fliers' adolescent-male-fantasy system is the contempt for the common folk down below. In one sequence, in the Nebraska days, Waldo's buddy Ezra (Edward Herrmann) crashes and is pinned under his plane. Waldo tries to pull him out, and then a spectator carelessly drops a cigarette and ignites the wreckage. Waldo appeals to the crowd of men who have gathered, begging for their help, but the thrill-seeking yokels just gape. He picks up a board and bludgeons his suffering friend on the head to spare him pain. This is only the most flamboyant of the incidents in which Hill and Goldman, both big-city boys, show their contempt for Midwesterners. Do they have to turn men who work on the ground into clods in order to push their five-and-a-half-million-dollar myth about the nobility in the sky which makes Waldo and Kessler spiritual brothers?

The picture actually celebrates the shortness of these aviators' lives: at the end, we're given the dates 1895–1931 for Waldo Pepper, the stunt flier, as if he had died a hero, *for us.* Hill seems to be enamored of the idea of the hollowness of tragedy, but at the point where this is being revealed (as at the end of *Butch Cassidy and the Sundance Kid*) he freezes it for an ambiguous comment. Maybe we're supposed to take it as a comment on heroism, but it's more like a comment on eternal stardom. (Waldo died with his youthful beauty untarnished.) There is also an attempt to latch on to the last-of-the-individualists glamour-gimmick by calling Waldo "the greatest natural flier around" and setting him down in the period when commercial aviation was coming in. The director is credited with the story on which Goldman based the screenplay, but the sources are obvious. This movie was made by men who have a big stake in movies' not growing up. Goldman wrote *Butch Cassidy,* which put Redford right over the top, and Hill and Redford did *The Sting* together. These movies, too, were by-products of old movies, and they weren't really much better than *The Great Waldo Pepper.* The film's understatement almost amounts to a style: total inauthenticity. In this uniquely modish universe, when anyone speaks his heart the pretty sentiments sit on his head like a dunce cap. When Waldo is told that he's going to need a license to fly, he cries out, "Are you going to license the clouds?" The passion Redford brings to the lines that should be thrown away is a key to what's going wrong with him as an actor. He suggests that there's no reason for him to try to know the character he plays; it's as if the character was complete as soon as Redford got fitted for his wardrobe.

Redford goes through some perfunctory sex scenes with Margot Kidder. She's normally a sexy actress, but Hill has turned her into a dishrag; she's there to prove that Waldo can — not that he wants to. In a Goldman script, the men are really pubescent boys, and the romance in their lives is fixated forever on boy games. Goldman's flip sense of humor, with its casual cruelty, enables the games to seem new. Early in the picture, carefree Waldo takes the landing wheels off another barnstorming flier's plane, so that it will crash, collects money from a crowd of onlookers for the pilot, and then, with a rakish smile, makes off with it. The only thing that distinguishes the hero from a rotten son of a bitch who enjoys mutilating people, and cheating them besides, is that captivating Redford grin. The heroes in *Butch Cassidy* were cuter than the Bolivian peasants they mowed down. Goldman writes in a make-believe world where heroes play boyish tricks on one another, and where they are masters of repartee one moment and strong, silent men the next. Hill's bland, dawdling direction of *The Great Waldo Pepper* — with music to match — obscures the real craziness of this world where the two heroes are kamikazes for the love of manly sport.

Is it unconscious adolescent fear that is behind the triggering device of the plot? It's a girl's hysteria that causes Waldo to be grounded just when he has the chance to be the first man to do "the outside loop" (a big thing in his life), and so she's also responsible for the death of his buddy Ezra, who flies in his place. As it turns out, Susan Sarandon, who plays the hysteric, and is killed because of her paralyzing fear in the air, is the only person in the movie who has an emotion the audience can recognize, and we care more about her falling to her death than about the dithering heroes. Probably her fall stays with us because the director provides no emotional release for the audience; Waldo and his air-circus friends, who talked her into risking her neck, don't shed a tear for her. *The Great Waldo Pepper* derives from movie fables, but Hill's fresh-painted, dry-eyed storytelling has none of the qualities of a fable. You come away feeling parched.

THE YAKUZA ARE the Japanese gangsters who in recent years have moved from gambling, drugs, and prostitution into shakedown rackets. Heads of Japanese corporations hire yakuza to police stockholders' meetings and intimidate any questioners — and sometimes the mobsters learn enough at the meetings to blackmail the corporations; and it was yakuza who maimed the photographer W. Eugene Smith when he was taking pictures of the victims of mercury poisoning at Minamata. Not the sort of men one would expect to see converted into movie heroes. But when the samurai pictures had run their bloody course Japanese action-film fans began to turn to modern-day gangster pictures, and the yakuza mores were molded into heroic patterns. Enter the Americans, who — recognizing that many people who saw *The Godfather* wanted to believe that the Mafiosi, living outside the law, had a better code of honor than law-abiding people — grasped the opportunity to import the fantasy and reap the profits. *The Yakuza* is an attempt to sell that phony, romantic view of gangsterism, in an exotic setting. The item in the yakuza "code" that appears to have had the greatest appeal for Paul Schrader, who sold his original script, based on his brother Leonard Schrader's story, to Warners, is the rite of showing penitence for an offense against the mob chieftain by slicing off one's little finger and presenting it to him. But Paul Schrader, who was a gifted, intense young movie critic for the Los Angeles *Free Press* a few years ago, must have seen a chance to create the kind of action-packed myth that he believes movies thrive on. Schrader is like John Milius plus philosophy; he wants to tear everyone's heart out, and his script whips up a mythic storm. The film offers a deliberate clash of genres: Harry Kilmer (Robert Mitchum), a professional loner and sometime private eye, goes to Japan to rescue a kidnapped American girl, the daughter of an old friend (Brian Keith). He enlists the aid of his Oriental counterpart, a "retired" yakuza (Takakura Ken), "the man who never smiles." (Yes, Schrader piled in a Japanese Clint Eastwood figure.) An ominously dignified master-teacher of swordsmanship, the man who never smiles comes back and fights next to Kilmer — the sword and the gun. Eventually, Kilmer, who has come to respect the yakuza code, realizes that he has offended the swordsman and commits his act of penitence. The idea is so swaggeringly meretricious an adolescent fairy tale about finger-chopping that it might have worked for the same action-film audiences that turned out for the Sergio Leone spaghetti Westerns. But the script is overloaded with exposition, and Robert Towne, who was called in for the rewrite, may have improved the dialogue (though it's hard to believe it could have been much worse), but he failed to simplify the plot. And Sydney Pollack, who signed to direct, came straight from *The Way We Were,* bringing much the same style to this discursive jumble. There's an aphoristic explanation of an ideogram one moment, a severed hand flying through the air the next.

Mitchum's massive head has grown, his face sunk — and he looks great. He doesn't look as if he regretted a wrinkle. He seems to be the only movie star who's becoming a more commanding figure as he ages. And Richard Jordan, who played the wily, baby-faced cop to Mitchum's tired hood in *The Friends of Eddie Coyle,* plays his bodyguard. Jordan's face shows the play of thought; he takes the camera in a deeper way than anyone else, and he gives the film fresh, unexpected moments. Takakura Ken, who has appeared in more than two hundred films (playing yakuza has made him the top box-office star in Japan), is the sort of actor who holds himself in; he dominates the space around him because his presence is an implicit threat. We can see that he's meant to be a smoldering hero, like Brando in *The Wild One,* but when Brando was docile we still knew why he was known as wild. The moviemakers here supply the packaging but not what's being contained, so we don't feel the excitement of Takakura Ken's threat, and since he speaks colloquial American English formally and with great difficulty, like Raf Vallone in his American films, he loses his potency.

The yakuza films have caught on in Japan, particularly with the political right (since many of the gangster federations are powerful right-wing forces) but also with students (they identify with the romantic individualism of the heroes, who go into a rage of killing at the ritual climax of the films). For American audiences, this film offers Oriental decadence, with emphasis on the extravagant tattooing popular among the yakuza, which seems much more erotic than American tattooing; for Japanese audiences, it offers a chance to see how Americans view their popular (though not culturally accepted) movie form. However, watching *The Yakuza* is work, and not only because it's confusing but because it's solemn when it means to be Orientally inscrutable. The script is humorless, and Pollack, despite his willingness to make action films, doesn't seem to understand how action-film mechanisms work. The picture is full of old-movie tricks, but there isn't the poetic insight — in the writing or the directing — to give them epic charge. *The Yakuza* might have been a disreputable, mad classic if the Sam Peckinpah of five years ago had made it. It might have been a sizzler of a reactionary, brutal fantasy if the Don Siegel of three years ago had done it — he'd have known how to crank it up so the violence hit you in the eye. If the Sam Fuller of twenty years ago had done it, it might have been a Grade B smash. Pollack isn't a violent director, and he has even lost his bearings on what he's usually good at. He doesn't seem to know where emotions stem from in a scene. In a dialogue between Harry Kilmer and the Japanese woman Eiko (Kishi Keiko), whom he has loved since he was part of the American Occupation in 1948, he once again proposes to her, and she, though she doesn't deny her love for him, refuses him, without an explanation. Her reason is the clue to what wiped the smile off the swordsman's face, yet Pollack doesn't give any emotional weight to the scene. This material connects with nothing in Pollack's experience — it's not *his* fantasy he's peddling — and maybe it's a tribute to some essential honesty in Pollack that he doesn't know how to fake it. Sydney Pollack wants to play corrupt big-money games, but his heart isn't in it. The finale, with the two last men of honor dispatching nineteen hoods, is designed as a homage to the Eastern and Western movie ways of killing. I'm sure the Japanese have a fine, graphically handsome ideogram for horse manure; it can also stand for *The Yakuza.* This film is designed to glorify the cheap mythology that Francis Ford Coppola countered in *The Godfather, Part II,* the first movie to say no in thunder.

[March 24, 1975]

The Darned

IF NATHANAEL WEST IS A SATIRIST at all, he's an unfunny satirist — showing his characters as grotesques but never releasing us to laugh at them. It's his sadomasochistic visionary tone, with the language pared down to essentials and each detail sharp, that makes *The Day of the Locust* such a distinctive and highly readable book. Readable and, in a certain sense, a literary achievement, but I don't find it likable. I feel a slight recoil from the hero Tod's attitudes and from West's assumptions, and the recoil prevents me from believing in the story as a valid metaphor for the American dream turned into a nightmare. To Nathanael West, the retired people who flock to Los Angeles for the sunshine and oranges are "savage and bitter," because they "haven't the mental equipment for leisure, the money nor the physical equipment for pleasure." To him, they are "all those poor devils who can only be stirred by the promise of miracles and then only to violence." His book ends with an orgasmic explosion — not a revolution but a vengeful mob scene at a movie première that becomes an apocalypse. West is more clever than convincing. Who can believe that Homer Simpson, the toadying mass-man from the Midwest, knows only one song — "Oh, say can you see"? Who can believe in that chaste blob Homer on any level? And what is Faye Greener, the seventeen-year-old sexpot who dreams of becoming a star, but an urban Tondelayo, a pre-Marilyn Monroe Marilyn Monroe— one of those James M. Cain dirty-animal women who destroy men? When West sees hatred in the faces of the elderly sitting on sidewalk benches, isn't it mostly a projection of his own fear of aging — a child's terror of deformity? Surely if you have to be poor and old it's better in a warm climate, better in a horizontal slum than a vertical one. West seems to have taken a medieval vision of the grave drawing him closer and converted it into a rambling series of journalistic impressions and symbolist speculations about a city that will be set on fire by its hollow-eyed gawkers and cripples — its walking dead.

The new John Schlesinger film version, from a screenplay by Waldo Salt, is generally faithful to the events of the novel. The leisureliness of the opening sections has a pleasing rhythm, allowing us to bask in the yellowy light and the fine thirties re-creation. The cinematographer, Conrad Hall, succeeds in achieving the painterly, calendar-art look of California Spanish, and the designer, Richard MacDonald, understands the lazy weight of it. The sunny slums, torpidly picturesque, like a giant piazza — that's what L.A. was like, all right, before it went proudly Pop and got its bright, wide-awake modern-city chic. The feel of the film is auspicious, and Schlesinger seems to be working at his peak, but we follow one character and then another, and each time we become engrossed we're yanked back from involvement. We expect the characters' separate dreams and problems to coalesce, and they don't. In the book, what holds the sketchy characters, the narrative chunks, and the ideas together is West's maggoty wit — positioning himself halfway between contempt and fear, clinging to literary sophistication as if it were the Mother Church. The film is a mosaic that never comes together.

Actually, these sleep-filled stucco cottages and the motionless atmosphere are so authentic that they work against West's conceits. If *The Day of the Locust* and the mauve, nightmarish *Chinatown* could exchange their atmospheres, they might both be better: the water-rights and real-estate swindles that formed the plot of *Chinatown* could have been clarified if the film had had a realistic base — if we had seen the dust in the air, as we do here — while *Locust,* to make any sense at all, should be a hysteric's view of L.A. Despite West's straightforward prose and his maplike accuracy about buildings and streets, his is a disjointed, fever vision, and his spangly scenes — a vicious cockfight, a party at which the lusting men circle around the lone woman Faye and fight over her, the ecstasy-seeking mob running wild at the première — might add up to something excitingly tumid if this movie were less literal. Schlesinger never finds a controlling mood or tone to suggest where he's heading, so the apocalyptic ending comes out of nowhere, and, since it's also the most inept part of the picture — hyperbolic yet dull — the movie disintegrates at the very point where it needs to fuse.

West sees people from the outside, and he deliberately makes his characters so limited that they're unreal; his device, like that of the painter Ensor (and, later, Francis Bacon), is to seize upon the excruciating, farfetched, everyday truth. The movie's mistake is to trust the book's sensibility, and to assume that the events of the book, when they are presented on film, will communicate what Schlesinger and many others believe to be the most important line in the novel: "Few things are sadder than the truly monstrous." But it was West's black-comedy whammy to see eccentrics and harmless nonconformists and old Angelenos — who may be brainwashed by the sun and the years — as monstrous, and to see L.A. as a place that attracts dreamers and then betrays their dreams, leaving them enraged. Without his rather forced prose explanations, almost none of this comes across, and if one hasn't read the book, the bit players, whores, extras, and hangers-on who live at the slummy San Bernardino Arms, and the pooped old people who stare blankly, like ambulatory statues, are just figures in disparate scenes from an L.A. Weimar.

Having no emotional center, the film leaves little impression — only a chill. There wouldn't be much to remember if it weren't for a few of the performers — especially Burgess Meredith. As Faye's father, Harry Greener, the washed-up old vaudevillian who sells "Miracle Solvent" door-to-door, Meredith does what is very likely his best acting in his forty-five years as a professional. Maybe you need forty-five years of experience to give this kind of performance. Meredith's Harry is a compulsive entertainer, a little, piggy-eyed, round-faced clown who failed on the stage but turns every place he's in — even his deathbed — into a theater. Harry Greener, boozy, his mind lost in a theater warp, doesn't know how *not* to put on an act. Life and show business are the same thing to him, and performing, wheedling, and conning have become indistinguishable. It's not a starring role, and it doesn't stand out and announce itself, yet Harry, the small-timer who has no world but the theater that never even knew he existed, is as fully lived-in a portrait as Olivier's Archie Rice. The conception is West's, but Meredith — strutting with a child's idea of raffishness, his face a frowzy high pink — makes you believe it. Meredith endows Harry with something of the frazzled indomitability of a Mickey Rooney, that giving-out even when one is faking giving-out. Like Rooney, Harry is manic by nature, and he never loses his awareness of the audience.

Billy Barty, who used to be Mickey Rooney's younger brother in the "Mickey McGuire" shorts, plays the dwarf gambler-tipster, Abe Kusich, and although his role is limited to a few scenes, he gives a major performance. In the novel, Abe, a macho dwarf, is an obscenely angry little man, but in realizing the character Billy Barty goes way beyond this. This Abe is dapper, with a hawk-eyed alertness to his rights and opportunities, and in the cockfight, when he tries to breathe life into his dying rooster, his whole soul is engaged in his side's putting up a fight, and there's tenderness in his handling of the wretched, mutilated bird. Many years ago, in *Gold Diggers of 1933*, when Barty popped up in the "Pettin' in the Park" sequence, winked at Dick Powell, and handed him a can opener to use on Ruby Keeler's shiny tin costume, he seemed to embody Busby Berkeley's most wayward flights of fancy; now, like Burgess Meredith, he moves right into the character he's playing, and lives there. He gives Abe Kusich a rambunctious fullness that exposes West's sadness-of-the-monstrous for the self-pitying, self-aggrandizing bull it is. These two — Harry and Abe — escape West's patronizing categories; they have an independent existence that Tod, who represents West's own consciousness, doesn't.

Tod, hired right out of Yale to work on set and costume designs, is meant to be a virile, gifted artist, at ease in society, and William Atherton (he was Goldie Hawn's husband in *The Sugarland Express*) is impressively sensitive in a difficult, bystander role. Schlesinger handles Tod well, and Atherton gives a fine Arrow-collar performance, but they can't cancel out the snobbish weakness in West's conception — that he wanted to see himself as a gentleman-artist, a courtly, impeccably dressed Yale Wasp, an outsider looking on at the grotesque world. Tod, who is putting the other characters into his giant painting "The Burning of Los Angeles," is redeeming his time in L.A. by making art of it — as West was doing in writing this book, which is essentially Tod's painting. But Tod is a thankless role, as authors' dream images of themselves so often are, and since he lacks a stake in the action and Faye doesn't respond to his advances, he seems sexless and unmagnetic — a gentleman, all right. Maybe *The Day of the Locust* wouldn't work however you adapted it, but if it wasn't to be stylized as Tod's phantasmagoria, Schlesinger and Waldo Salt might have done better to rethink the book radically and get rid of Tod. One possibility would have been to reconceive Homer the lump (Donald Sutherland), to take him out of his stupor and make him the central consciousness, because the theme doesn't need a Yalie-aesthete observer, it needs someone to draw us into the story — the person to whom the story is happening — so that we can see Los Angeles and the tinhorn show people through his duped, glamour-struck eyes. There's nothing specific the matter with Sutherland's performance as Homer, yet it's just awful. How is a screen actor supposed to express the collective yearnings of the inarticulate masses? The film begins to drag the moment Homer meets Faye, and it never fully recovers; we're there with Tod, watching Homer knead his big hands into his thighs, instead of feeling the rage building in him. As Faye, Karen Black is far from the teenager who occupied Tod's thoughts —the girl who looked "just born, everything moist and fresh, volatile and perfumed" — and his falling in love with her isn't convincing. Besides, Karen Black's lopsided caricature of a pretty face — her carnal squint and plush-pillow mouth — has been so overexploited that at the moment it's hard to see her as anything but Karen Black. She's so recognizable and so jangly that she kills illusion. She was perfectly cast in *Portnoy's Complaint,* but usually she can't disguise her acting. She's working seriously here; still, she spells out how she wants us to react, and she can't bring credibility to Faye (who is, in any case, one of those literary concepts whose day has passed — hallelujah).

All the way through, the biggest crowd sequences are the least effective; Schlesinger's direction generally seems to grow worse in direct ratio to the number of people on the screen. He frequently gets complex overtones going when he's dealing with a couple of characters, particularly if he likes them, but the ideas he's working on seem to become cheaper and more dubious as the crowd becomes larger. And when he goes into his gilded-irony numbers he loses the relations between people which he's built up. Schlesinger is usually at his dead worst when he's staging parties in the Sodoms of *Darling* and *Midnight Cowboy,* yet he's drawn to playing the bitchy moralist and exhibiting the damned damning themselves. This picture, which calls for a startling visionary, a sensualist like the young Buñuel, is exactly wrong for his talents, and the erratic Waldo Salt script gives him prize opportunities to be obvious: potshots at anti-Semites and racists, and a big tabernacle session, with Geraldine Page simulating Aimee Semple McPherson's erotic spiel, so that we'll recognize that when people have nothing to live for they turn to crank religions and are served a sexual experience as a religious experience. It's one thing for West to amuse himself by describing a costly blunder when an unfinished set collapses during the filming of a big battle for the film *Waterloo,* but, since this episode has no direct relationship to the story, when Schlesinger goes to all the trouble of staging the scene, West's whimsical diversion on the expensive insanity of picture-making becomes an example of it. Waldo Salt tries to make the sequence integral, but all he comes up with is a cosmetic trick — a peewee Watergate analogy — by using the blunder as evidence that the producer whom Tod works for is corrupt: the sort of demonstration which could be made just as graphically by having the fellow put a social lunch on an expense account. Some of Schlesinger's and Salt's decisions seem unfathomable. Why didn't they pull the action together by having the première that unleashes the furies be *Waterloo,* instead of a movie that has nothing to do with previous events? And what did they have in mind in the romantic framing device they provide? The picture opens with Tod's arrival at the San Bernardino Arms, and then at the end, after the big Inferno finale, Faye comes to his room looking for him after he is gone. Gone where, one wonders. Is he meant to have left that corrupt city? (West didn't.)

ONE CAN GO BACK to most writers one admired and re-experience what one admired them for, but with Nathanael West you're shocked by the élitist snobbery you once felt flattered to share. Cynical adolescents may accept *The Day of the Locust* as a brilliant Hollywood satire, on the order of *The Loved One.* What could be more attractive to them than West's view of the middle-aged and old as enraged grotesques, incapable of pleasure? He doesn't ask you to identify with his suffering grotesques — not even in *Miss Lonelyhearts.* He expects you to identify with his comic horror over their plight, and when you're young you're very vulnerable to West's highbrow-Christ attitude. But why is *The Day of the Locust* locked into so many people's minds as the definitive Los Angeles book? Maybe, in part, because of its thoroughgoing contempt for everything in Los Angeles. As a genre, Hollywood novels represent the screenwriters' revenge on the movies. In Hollywood, the writer is an underling whose work is trashed, or, at best, he's a respected collaborator without final control over how his work is used. Writing a Hollywood novel, he gets his own back: typically, he himself is the disillusioned hero, and the studio bosses, the producers, the flunkies are his boob targets — all those people who he feels have no right to make decisions about his work.

The writers romanticize the processes of corruption, seeing themselves as intellectual golden boys who go "out there" — as Edmund Wilson called it — and then turn their backs on that cheap glory, returning to write the fourth-rate book we've just plowed through. *The Day of the Locust* is far from fourth-rate, but it satisfies the loftiest expectations, since it deals with the victims of the movies — the poor in spirit who bought the commercial dreams. Edmund Wilson, one of the first to recognize West's literary worth, appreciated the book in the terms that generations of book reviewers have been using for Hollywood novels: "Mr. West has caught the emptiness of Hollywood; and he is, as far as I know, the first writer to make this emptiness horrible."

There's some truth in what Wilson said. The novel is about something, but it's not about as much as West wanted it to be — it's not about everything. West blew up his observations into a sweeping vision, and John Schlesinger takes the book seriously in all the wrong ways and compounds its overblown thesis — Faye becomes the bitch goddess, Homer is crucified, and masked figures, God help us, march toward the camera. Schlesinger's vice as a director has always been to score against his characters, crashing bricks on our skulls so we'll recognize how hideous they are. This picture is his primal scream: it says that women tease and humiliate men, that people are being driven mad by a lack of sex and love; it says that there's nothing to drink but poisoned milk and we're all dying. West created the clichés; Schlesinger falls over them, heavily, humorlessly.

[May 12, 1975]

Index